AF787446

IFIP Advances in Information and Communication Technology 787

Editor-in-Chief

Kai Rannenberg, Goethe University Frankfurt, Germany

Editorial Board Members

TC 1 – Foundations of Computer Science
Luís Soares Barbosa, University of Minho, Braga, Portugal

TC 2 – Software: Theory and Practice
Jacques Carette, Department of Computer Science, McMaster University, Hamilton, ON, Canada

TC 3 – Education
Arthur Tatnall, Victoria University, Melbourne, Australia

TC 5 – Information Technology Applications
Erich J. Neuhold, University of Vienna, Austria

TC 6 – Communication Systems
Burkhard Stiller, University of Zurich, Zürich, Switzerland

TC 7 – System Modeling and Optimization
Lukasz Stettner, Institute of Mathematics, Polish Academy of Sciences, Warsaw, Poland

TC 8 – Information Systems
Jan Pries-Heje, Roskilde University, Denmark

TC 9 – ICT and Society
David Kreps, National University of Ireland, Galway, Ireland

TC 10 – Computer Systems Technology
Achim Rettberg, Hamm-Lippstadt University of Applied Sciences, Hamm, Germany

TC 11 – Security and Privacy Protection in Information Processing Systems
Steven Furnell, Plymouth University, UK

TC 12 – Artificial Intelligence
Eunika Mercier-Laurent, University of Reims Champagne-Ardenne, Reims, France

TC 13 – Human-Computer Interaction
Marco Winckler, University of Nice Sophia Antipolis, France

TC 14 – Entertainment Computing
Rainer Malaka, University of Bremen, Germany

IFIP Advances in Information and Communication Technology

The IFIP AICT series publishes state-of-the-art results in the sciences and technologies of information and communication. The scope of the series includes: foundations of computer science; software theory and practice; education; computer applications in technology; communication systems; systems modeling and optimization; information systems; ICT and society; computer systems technology; security and protection in information processing systems; artificial intelligence; and human-computer interaction.

Edited volumes and proceedings of refereed international conferences in computer science and interdisciplinary fields are featured. These results often precede journal publication and represent the most current research.

The principal aim of the IFIP AICT series is to encourage education and the dissemination and exchange of information about all aspects of computing.

More information about this series at https://link.springer.com/bookseries/6102

Helge Janicke · Lynn Futcher · Iqbal H. Sarker ·
Kerry-Lynn Thomson · Paul Haskell-Dowland
Editors

ICT Systems Security and Privacy Protection

41st IFIP TC 11 International Conference, SEC 2026
Perth, Australia, June 9–11, 2026
Proceedings

Springer

Editors
Helge Janicke
Edith Cowan University
Joondalup, WA, Australia

Iqbal H. Sarker
Edith Cowan University
Joondalup, WA, Australia

Paul Haskell-Dowland
Edith Cowan University
Joondalup, WA, Australia

Lynn Futcher
Nelson Mandela University
Summerstrand, South Africa

Kerry-Lynn Thomson
Nelson Mandela University
Summerstrand, South Africa

ISSN 1868-4238 ISSN 1868-422X (electronic)
IFIP Advances in Information and Communication Technology
ISBN 978-3-032-27992-7 ISBN 978-3-032-27993-4 (eBook)
https://doi.org/10.1007/978-3-032-27993-4

© IFIP International Federation for Information Processing 2026

This work is subject to copyright. All rights are solely and exclusively licensed by the Publisher, whether the whole or part of the material is concerned, specifically the rights of translation, reprinting, reuse of illustrations, recitation, broadcasting, reproduction on microfilms or in any other physical way, and transmission or information storage and retrieval, electronic adaptation, computer software, or by similar or dissimilar methodology now known or hereafter developed.
The use of general descriptive names, registered names, trademarks, service marks, etc. in this publication does not imply, even in the absence of a specific statement, that such names are exempt from the relevant protective laws and regulations and therefore free for general use.
The publisher, the authors and the editors are safe to assume that the advice and information in this book are believed to be true and accurate at the date of publication. Neither the publisher nor the authors or the editors give a warranty, expressed or implied, with respect to the material contained herein or for any errors or omissions that may have been made. The publisher remains neutral with regard to jurisdictional claims in published maps and institutional affiliations.

This Springer imprint is published by the registered company Springer Nature Switzerland AG
The registered company address is: Gewerbestrasse 11, 6330 Cham, Switzerland

If disposing of this product, please recycle the paper.

Preface

We are delighted to present the proceedings of the 41st International Federation for Information Processing (IFIP) Conference on ICT Systems Security and Privacy Protection, which took place in Perth, Australia, June 9–11, 2026. The SEC conference is the flagship event of the IFIP Technical Committee 11 (TC11) on Information Security and Privacy Protection in Information Processing Systems. IFIP SEC 2026 was co-located with the 18th World Conference on Information Security Education (WISE 2026).

164 papers (representing authors from 36 countries) were submitted for consideration with reviewers invited to bid for relevant papers prior to allocation. Papers were allocated based on bid preferences with some papers assigned additional reviews to compensate for a lack of bids. The Program Committee consisted of 187 experts, with an additional 17 sub-reviewers. Papers were evaluated based on their significance, novelty, and technical quality in a single-blind peer review process. The average number of reviews per submission was 4.15. The authors of papers that were not accepted for publication were provided with extensive feedback to assist them in the improvement of their future submissions.

These proceedings include 39 high-quality papers representing a 23.8% acceptance rate. The published papers cover a wide range of research areas in the information security field with contributions from researchers across 18 different countries. The final revised versions of the papers were not reviewed again, and the authors are responsible for their contents.

We want to express our appreciation to all the contributors who helped to make IFIP SEC 2026 a success. We especially want to thank the members of the Program Committee, who devoted significant amounts of their time to evaluating all the submissions. Special thanks go to our keynote speakers, who accepted our invitation to present at the conference.

Finally, we thank all the authors who submitted papers and the delegates who participated in the conference. We hope you find the proceedings of IFIP SEC 2026 interesting and inspiring for your future research.

June 2026

Helge Janicke
Lynn Futcher
Iqbal H. Sarker
Kerry-Lynn Thomson
Paul Haskell-Dowland

Organization

General Chair

Helge Janicke	Edith Cowan University, Australia

Program Committee Chairs

Lynn Futcher	Nelson Mandela University, South Africa
Iqbal Sarker	Edith Cowan University, Australia
Kerry-Lynn Thomson	Nelson Mandela University, South Africa

Organizing Chair

Paul Haskell-Dowland	Edith Cowan University, Australia

Publicity Chair

Ahmad Mohsin	Edith Cowan University, Australia

Program Committee

Pratik Agarwal	Figma, USA
Rose-Mharie Åhlfeldt	University of Skövde, Sweden
Mohiuddin Ahmed	Adelaide University, Australia
Modupe Akintan	Google, USA
Alessandro Aldini	University of Urbino, Italy
Nalin Arachchilage	RMIT University, Australia
Narges Arastouei	Goethe University Frankfurt, Germany
Claudio Agostino Ardagna	Università degli Studi di Milano, Italy
Vijay Atluri	Rutgers University, USA
Maria Bada	Queen Mary University London, UK
Marcus Belder	Defence Science & Technology Group, Australia
Nicola Bena	Università degli Studi di Milano, Italy
Matt Bishop	University of California, USA

Tamara Bonaci	University of Washington, USA
Nora Boulahia-Cuppens	Polytechnique Montréal, Canada
Amulya Boyapati	Apple, USA
Marcus Butavicius	Defence Science & Technology Group, Australia
Andre Büttner	University of Oslo, Norway
Barbara Carminati	University of Insubria, Italy
Ching Bon Raymond Chan	Singapore Institute of Technology, Singapore
K. P. Chow	The University of Hong Kong, China
Sandeep Chittimalli	Synectics for Management Decisions Inc., USA
Rashmi Choudhary	Zum, USA
Christos Chrysoulas	Heriot-Watt University, UK
Stefano Cirillo	Università degli Studi di Salerno, Italy
Nathan Clarke	University of Plymouth, UK
Paolo D'Arco	University di Salerno, Italy
Sabrina De Capitani di Vimercati	Università degli Studi di Milano, Italy
Abhijit Dhariya	CyberArk, USA
Nicola Dragoni	Technical University of Denmark, Denmark
Givemore Dube	EY, Zimbabwe
Isao Echizen	National Institute of Informatics, Japan
Ammar Ekbote	Pinterest, USA
Sergio Esposito	University of Catania, Italy
Carmen Fernández-Gago	Universidad de Málaga, Spain
Elena Ferrari	University of Insubria, Italy
Simone Fischer-Hübner	Karlstad University, Sweden
Stephen Flowerday	University of Tulsa, USA
Sara Foresti	Università degli Studi di Milano, Italy
Steven Furnell	University of Nottingham, UK
Lynn Futcher	Nelson Mandela University, South Africa
Matt Gaber	Edith Cowan University, Australia
Magdalena Glas	Universität Regensburg, Germany
Srikanth Gorthy	TikTok, USA
Anna Grocholewska-Czuryło	Poznań University of Technology, Poland
Nils Gruschka	University of Oslo, Norway
Saketh Gurumurthi	Wipro, USA
Jonas Hallberg	Swedish Defence Research Agency, Sweden
Brahim Hamid	University of Toulouse, France
Paul Haskell-Dowland	Edith Cowan University, Australia
Kirsi Helkala	Norwegian Defence Cyber Academy, Norway
José Luis Hernández Ramos	Universidad de Murcia, Spain
Dominik Herrmann	University of Bamberg, Germany
Marko Hölbl	University of Maribor, Slovenia
Zhenzhuo Hou	Peking University, China

Xinyi Huang	Fujian Normal University, China
Ali Hur	Edith Cowan University, Australia
Dieter Hutter	DFKI GmbH, Germany
Pedro Inácio	Universidade da Beira Interior, Portugal
Chadni Islam	Edith Cowan University, Australia
Martin Gilje Jaatun	SINTEF Digital, Norway
Bhavuk Jain	Google, USA
Lech Janczewski	University of Auckland, New Zealand
Helge Janicke	Edith Cowan University, Australia
Christian Jensen	Aarhus University, Denmark
Sumeet Jeswani	Google, USA
Mike Johnstone	Edith Cowan University, Australia
Georgey Kalangi	Apple, USA
Gauri Kamat	Eli Lilly and Company, USA
Georgios Kambourakis	University of the Aegean, Greece
Rajesh Kumar Kanji	Informatica, USA
Yamini Kannan	Jane Street, USA
Sokratis Katsikas	Norwegian University of Science and Technology, Norway
Stefan Katzenbeisser	University of Passau, Germany
Nihal Kaul	Revscale, USA
Georgios Kavallieratos	University of Oslo, Norway
Namboodiri Arun Mullamangalath Kesavan	Aryaka Networks, USA
Dogan Kesdogan	Universität Regensburg, Germany
Dongseong Kim	University of Queensland, Australia
Ella Kolkowska	Örebro University School of Business, Sweden
Naveen Kumar Kotha	Blue Yonder, USA
Zbigniew Kotulski	Warsaw University of Technology, Poland
Stephan Krenn	AIT Austrian Institute of Technology GmbH, Austria
Łukasz Krzywiecki	Wrocław University of Science and Technology, Poland
Suresh Kumar	Dollar General, USA
Peeter Laud	Cybernetica AS, Estonia
Maryline Laurent	Institut Polytechnique de Paris, France
Heejo Lee	Korea University, South Korea
Maciej Liskiewicz	University of Lübeck, Germany
Giovanni Livraga	University of Milan, Italy
Luigi Logrippo	Université du Québec en Outaouais, Canada
Javier Lopez	Universidad de Málaga, Spain
Juan Lopez	Oak Ridge National Lab, USA

Martin Lundgren	University of Skövde, Sweden
João Paulo Magalhaes	Porto Polytechnic Institute, Portugal
Leandros Maglaras	Edinburgh Napier University, UK
Muhammad Imran Malik	Edith Cowan University, Australia
Suneeth Maraboina	Apple, USA
Carol Marsh	Celestia, UK
Fabio Martinelli	Institute for High Performance Computing and Networking, Italy
Sean Maynard	University of Melbourne, Australia
Andrew McGettrick	University of Strathclyde, UK
Ibéria Medeiros	University of Lisboa, Portugal
Weizhi Meng	Lancaster University, UK
Ajay Kumar Mishra	Snap Inc., USA
Nithin Mohan	HP Enterprise, USA
Ahmad Mohsin	Edith Cowan University, Australia
Haralambos Mouratidis	University of Essex, UK
Tim Muller	University of Nottingham, UK
Salman Munaf	TikTok, USA
Yuko Murayama	Tsuda University, Japan
Alexios Mylonas	Hertfordshire University, UK
Arun Kumar Natva	Cloudera, USA
Lili Nemec Zlatolas	University of Maribor, Slovenia
Omer Nguena Timo	Université du Québec en Outaouais, Canada
Sergio Nunes	ISEG-School of Economics and Management, Portugal
Mike Obolonskyi	Cortical Ventures, USA
Melek Önen	EURECOM, France
Jacques Ophoff	Abertay University, UK
Ali Padyab	University of Skövde, Sweden
Hitesh Pahuja	Intuit, USA
Brajendra Panda	University of Arkansas, USA
Alisa Pankova	Cybernetica AS, Estonia
Pavlos Papadopoulos	Edinburgh Napier University, UK
Sebastian Pape	Social Engineering Academy GmbH, Germany
Miguel Pardal	Universidade de Lisboa, Portugal
Bharath Pareek	Salesforce, USA
Michalis Pavlidis	Brighton University, UK
Adamantini Peratikou	Open University of Cyprus, Cyprus
Günther Pernul	Universität Regensburg, Germany
Nikolaos Pitropakis	American College of Greece, Greece
Henrich C. Pöhls	University of Passau, Germany
Ilias Politis	Athena Research Center, Greece

Rajesh Pothamsetty	Amazon, USA
Prateek Punj	Microsoft, USA
Vijay Raghavan	Okta, USA
Viswapriyan Ragupathy	JP Morgan, USA
Bazlur Rashid	Edith Cowan University, Australia
Kai Rannenberg	Goethe University Frankfurt, Germany
Seetaram Rao	JP Morgan, USA
Chiran Reddy	Zions Bancorporation, USA
Carlos Rieder	isec ag, Switzerland
Juha Röning	University of Oulu, Finland
Elham Rostami	Örebro University, Sweden
Vishwas Rudramurthy	Sri Siddhartha School of Engineering, India
Pierangela Samarati	Università degli Studi di Milano, Italy
Henrique Santos	University of Minho, Portugal
Iqbal Sarker	Edith Cowan University, Australia
Jürgen Schönwälder	Constructor University, Germany
Christopher Schmitz	Goethe-Universität, Germany
Andrew Seely	Hillsborough College, USA
Bernardo Sequeiros	Universidade Beira Interior, Portugal
Adeem Shaik	TikTok, USA
Jun Shao	Zhejiang Gongshang University, China
Carlton Shepherd	Newcastle University, UK
Youngjoo Shin	Korea University, South Korea
Paria Shirani	Ryerson University, Canada
Joye Shonubi	Fable Security, USA
Abhishek Shukla	R.D. Engineering College, India
Anirudh Singh	CrowdStrike, USA
Nihal Singh	Moody's, USA
Parminder Singh	Redscope AI, USA
Preeti Singh	Capgemini, USA
Una Siu	Raycaster, USA
Nicolas Sklavos	University of Patras, Greece
Daniel Slamanig	Universität der Bundeswehr München, Germany
Angelo Spognardi	Sapienza Università di Roma, Italy
Eliana Stavrou	Open University of Cyprus, Cyprus
Chunhua Su	University of Aizu, Japan
Shamik Sural	Indian Institute of Technology Kharagpur, India
Hamed Taherdoost	University of Technology Malaysia, Malaysia
Gurvirender Tejay	Hofstra University, USA
Kerry-Lynn Thomson	Nelson Mandela University, South Africa
Simon Tjoa	St. Pölten University of Applied Sciences, Austria
Vivek Venkatesan	Vanguard, USA

Aditi Verma	T-Mobile, USA
Qingxuan Wang	Nankai University, China
Darren Webb	Australia
Edgar Weippl	University of Vienna, Austria
Li Wenjuan	Education University of Hong Kong, China
Lance Wilson	Australia
Shihao Yan	Edith Cowan University, Australia
Swathi Yemmanur	Verizon, USA
Vladimir Zadorozhny	University of Pittsburgh, USA
Yuexin Zhang	Fujian Normal University, China
Yunkai Zou	Nankai University, China
André Zúquete	University of Aveiro, Portugal

Additional Reviewers

Ferran Alborch
Abdelhakim Baouya
Federica Bianchi
Gaurav Choudhary
Fernando Escobar
Thrasyvoulos Giannakopoulos
Vyron Kampourakis
Taehun Kim
Hassana Wa Ara Limangana
Francesco Mercaldo
Tran Thanh Lam Nguyen
Tomasz Nowak
Tiago Roxo
Christos Smiliotopoulos
Giandomenico Solimando
Gabriele Spini
Jack Tilbury

Contents

Cryptography

Cyber-Physical Systems Security

Data and Applications Security

Network and Systems Security

AI for Cyber Security

Is This Mission Possible? A Study on Developer Challenges in Using Generative AI for Secure Software Development in Industry

Sathwik Amburi[1,3](✉), Tiago Gasiba[1], Tobias Fertig[2], Ulrike Lechner[3], and Maria Pinto-Albuquerque[4]

[1] Siemens AG, Munich, Germany
{sathwik.amburi,tiago.gasiba}@siemens.com
[2] Technische Hochschule Würzburg-Schweinfurt, Würzburg, Germany
tobias.fertig@thws.de
[3] Universität der Bundeswehr München, Munich, Germany
ulrike.lechner@unibw.de
[4] Instituto Universitário de Lisboa (ISCTE-IUL), ISTAR-IUL, Lisboa, Portugal
maria.albuquerque@iscte-iul.pt

Abstract. Developers are increasingly relying on generative AI (GenAI) tools throughout the software development lifecycle, including for security-relevant tasks. While these tools may improve productivity, they can also amplify insecure patterns, overconfidence, and cognitive offloading. We investigate how frequently industry developers use GenAI, what limitations they encounter, and how they perceive AI-assisted secure code review. We conducted a multi-site study embedded in nine secure-coding training workshops using the ASCEND platform, followed by an immediate post-task survey (84 responses; 69 analyzed qualitatively). Results show high but uneven GenAI adoption across experience levels and broadly positive perceptions of Large Language Model (LLM) support for vulnerability identification and review robustness, including among occasional users. However, participants report challenges when using LLMs for coding, most prominently code quality concerns (36.23% of respondents) and context limitations (34.78%), as well as hallucinations, productivity pitfalls, and prompting difficulties. Based on thematic analysis and industrial experience, we derive four complementary strategies for responsible adoption, targeted training, careful model selection and configuration, mandatory human review, and integration of automated security testing. We translate these findings into actionable recommendations for developers, tool builders, and technical leaders.

Keywords: GenAI · Secure Software Development · Industry · Secure Code Review

© IFIP International Federation for Information Processing 2026
Published by Springer Nature Switzerland AG 2026
H. Janicke et al. (Eds.): SEC 2026, IFIP AICT 787, pp. 3–17, 2026.
https://doi.org/10.1007/978-3-032-27993-4_1

1 Introduction

LLMs and GenAI are transforming software development and the role of developers. GenAI is increasingly integrated across the software development lifecycle, from requirements engineering to code and test case generation, code review, and DevOps tasks [19]. Industry stakeholders expect GenAI to enable faster software development and deployment [4,19]. Yet, GenAI can pose serious risks to software security, and recent reports highlight these concerns. For example, Veracode found that 45% of code samples generated by over 100 large language models contained vulnerabilities [25]. Another study by Fu et al. examined the use of GitHub Copilot in open-source projects and found that AI-generated code often includes insecure patterns [7]. Overreliance on GenAI, leading to cognitive offloading and reduced critical thinking, represents an additional risk [17,20]. Secure and reliable code is paramount when designing and developing software for critical infrastructure, and GenAI is increasingly applied to secure coding despite its associated risks and limitations. Several studies explore the use of LLMs for vulnerability detection and remediation [2,8,23]. Despite growing adoption, it is unclear whether GenAI delivers net productivity benefits in secure software development or whether security risks outweigh productivity gains.

These observations motivate the focus of this paper: understanding the current state of GenAI usage for secure software development in industry. We report on a survey study conducted over several months with industry developers, investigating how often developers use LLMs, how they perceive these tools in the context of secure software development, the challenges they encounter, and the security risks these challenges might introduce. The study is embedded in industrial secure-coding training workshops that include a structured hands-on exercise using the ASCEND platform (see Sect. 4). ASCEND provides a controlled environment to study human–AI interaction in security-relevant tasks such as code review. We derive actionable recommendations for three stakeholder groups: (i) software developers who use GenAI in their daily work, (ii) developers and organizations building GenAI-powered development tools, and (iii) technical leaders (e.g., project managers and product owners) responsible for development practices and tooling decisions.

This paper is structured as follows: Sect. 2 presents background information and related work. Section 3 describes the research methodology. Section 4 introduces the ASCEND platform and the secure-coding workshops in which the study is embedded. Section 5 reports the results of our survey study. Section 6 discusses the findings and outlines strategies to address the identified challenges. Finally, Sect. 7 concludes the paper and outlines directions for future work.

This article extends our previous work [2] by incorporating a substantially larger participant pool, providing a deeper analysis of industrial developer challenges related to secure GenAI usage, and presenting refined recommendations grounded in additional empirical evidence.

2 Related Work

The adoption of GenAI tools for software development has increased rapidly since the introduction of tools like GitHub Copilot, reflecting a broader industry-wide shift toward AI-assisted coding [4,9]. While these tools promise productivity gains, prior studies highlight important security risks. Perry et al. [20] showed that developers using AI assistants often produce more insecure code while remaining confident in its security, indicating risks of overconfidence and automation bias. Several studies emphasize limitations of LLMs in software engineering, particularly regarding accountability, hallucinations, and reproducibility. Belzner et al. [5] argue that developers remain responsible for the correctness and security of LLM-generated code and stress the need for systematic evaluation of generated outputs. Sallou et al. [22] highlight reproducibility challenges arising from non-deterministic model behavior and propose guidelines to mitigate associated risks. Together, these works underscore that LLM-assisted development requires careful human oversight. Research on the security and quality of LLM-generated code further shows differences across programming languages. Kharma et al. [15] demonstrate that many models fail to leverage modern security features and frequently reproduce outdated or insecure practices. These findings suggest that training data and model design strongly influence security-relevant behavior. Beyond code generation, prior work reports that developers often used LLM outputs as exploratory or validation aids rather than authoritative solutions [5,20], emphasizing the role of human–AI interaction and critical evaluation in security-relevant review tasks; more recent practices such as vibe coding suggest a shift toward greater reliance on AI-generated solutions [27]. GenAI has also been explored in programming education and secure-coding training. Prior work shows that LLMs can raise awareness and support secure coding [8]. However, excessive reliance may discourage critical thinking and lead to cognitive offloading [17]. Studies on use of LLMs in education caution that uncritical use of LLMs can limit expertise development, motivating structured and reflective learning approaches that preserve human judgment [11]. In industrial contexts, these concerns are amplified by time pressure, system complexity, and organizational accountability requirements. Developers operating in such environments must balance the perceived efficiency gains of GenAI tools with established secure development practices and assurance processes. This tension underscores the need to understand how GenAI is used in realistic industrial workflows rather than isolated laboratory settings.

In summary, existing research indicates that LLMs can support software engineering and security tasks while also introducing risks related to hallucinations, limited context, accountability gaps, and overreliance. Prior studies largely examine these issues in controlled settings or focus on code generation and general developer behavior. Our work complements this body of research by examining how professional developers engage with GenAI during secure code review activities in the context of industrial secure-coding training workshops.

3 Methodology

This study examines how professional software developers perceive and use GenAI, and specifically LLMs, in the context of secure coding and secure software development. The study is situated in an industrial setting and includes heterogeneous developer profiles to characterize usage patterns and perceived challenges in realistic enterprise environments. We conducted a multi-site, workshop-embedded survey study. Data collection was integrated into nine secure-coding training workshops delivered across multiple sites and modalities (on-site and online). Each workshop included a structured hands-on exercise using the ASCEND platform (Sect. 4), followed by an immediate post-task survey administered after the exercise. The same survey instrument was used across all nine workshops, and the final dataset aggregates responses from all sessions. The study is descriptive and exploratory: we aim to characterize (i) current GenAI usage patterns, (ii) developers' perceptions of LLM-supported secure code review, and (iii) challenges encountered when using LLMs for coding. Based on these goals, we formulate the following research questions:

RQ1) How does the frequency of GenAI tool usage vary across professional experience levels among industrial software developers?
RQ2) How do industrial developers perceive the usefulness of LLMs for supporting secure code review and vulnerability identification?
RQ3) What challenges and limitations do industrial developers report when using LLMs for coding tasks?

Participants were drawn from a multinational industrial organization and represented a wide range of development roles (e.g., embedded systems, front-end, back-end, full-stack, systems engineering) and programming languages (including C, C++, Python, Java, Go, and JavaScript). To contextualize responses, participants reported their years of professional coding experience (Table 1) and their frequency of GenAI usage in daily work using ordered categories ranging from *Never* to *Always*.

The post-task survey consisted of 14 questions covering developer background and perceptions which we used to analyze: (i) professional coding experience, (ii) frequency of GenAI usage, (iii) agreement with statements whether LLMs support vulnerability identification and reduce human error in reviews, (iv) likelihood of adopting LLM-assisted secure code review in future practice, and (v) an open-ended question soliciting perceived issues, challenges, or limitations when using LLMs for coding. Additional items captured ASCEND-specific feedback are out of scope for this paper and will be reported separately. The full survey instrument is archived on Zenodo to support transparency and replication [1].

Quantitative items are summarized descriptively using frequency-based comparisons across experience and usage-frequency cohorts. Open-ended responses were analyzed using thematic coding [21] to identify recurring concerns and themes. As a quality-control step, we excluded open-ended responses that did not provide interpretable issue statements with respect to the prompt, including

Table 1. Distribution of Professional Coding Experience Among Survey Respondents

No.	Years of Experience	Count	Percentage
1	<1 year	8	9.5%
2	1–3 years	12	14.3%
3	4–6 years	19	22.6%
4	7–10 years	19	22.6%
5	>10 years	26	31.0%
	Total	**84**	**100%**

responses indicating non-use of LLMs (e.g., "N.A." or "I do not use LLMs"), non-responses, or responses that addressed issues unrelated to the prompt (e.g., problems with the ASCEND platform rather than issues with LLMs for coding). Respondents could mention multiple distinct problems in a single answer; therefore, we report both respondent-level prevalence and the total number of coded issue instances in the Results section. Given the exploratory nature of the study and heterogeneous sample sizes across cohorts, we deliberately restrict analysis to descriptive statistics.

Participation was voluntary, no personally identifiable information was collected, and all responses were anonymized with informed consent following standard human-subject research practices.

4 ASCEND Platform and Workshops

We developed an internal platform called ASCEND to support both (i) developer training and (ii) research on human–AI interaction in secure software development tasks. ASCEND (platform interface shown in Fig. 1) provides a common hands-on environment embedded within secure-coding workshops, enabling participants to practice security-relevant review and remediation activities while optionally engaging with an AI assistant.

Each workshop followed the same sequence: first, an awareness-oriented introduction to secure software development practices; second, a structured hands-on secure code review and remediation task in ASCEND; and third, a post-task survey administered immediately after the exercise. This sequencing ensures that survey responses reflect perceptions formed during (or immediately after) a realistic security-relevant task in a controlled training setting. Across the nine workshop sessions, 145 developers participated in training activities and 84 completed the post-task survey (Table 2).

Within ASCEND, participants followed a fixed four-step workflow designed to highlight human judgment and critical reflection before code changes. In Step 1, participants manually reviewed a provided code snippet, identified potential vulnerabilities, and recorded findings as review comments. In Step 2, participants could interact with an integrated AI assistant (e.g., to validate identified

Table 2. Secure Coding Workshop Sessions and Survey Participation

No.	Location	Date	Participants	Responses	Track
1	Erlangen, Germany	Mar 2025	19	18	Foundational
2	Online	Apr 2025	22	7	Java, JavaScript
3	Erlangen, Germany	Apr 2025	18	16	Foundational
4	Online	May 2025	16	6	JavaScript (React), Python
5	Lisbon, Portugal	May 2025	18	7	JavaScript (Angular), C#
6	Nanjing, China	Jun 2025	16	11	Web, Foundational
7	Ontario, Canada	Jun 2025	12	6	Backend Technologies
8	Erlangen, Germany	Jul 2025	12	5	Foundational
9	Online	Sep 2025	12	8	Golang
	Total		**145**	**84**	

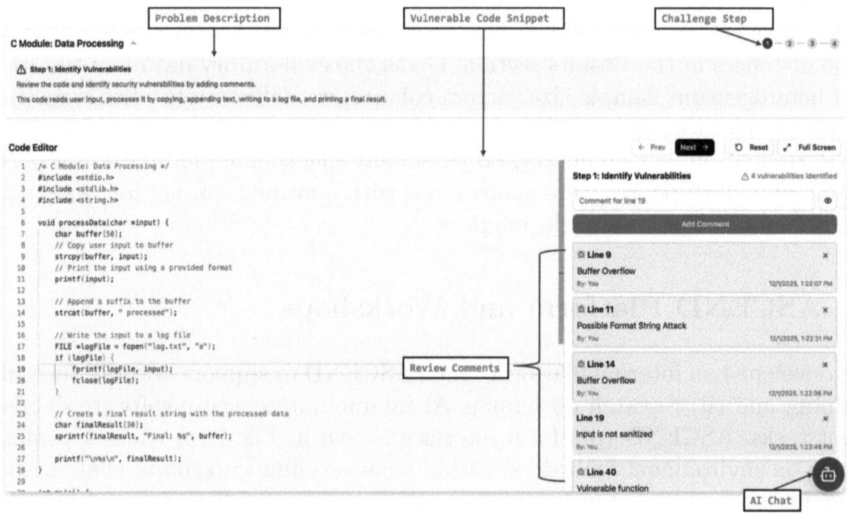

Fig. 1. ASCEND Platform Interface Showing Step 1.

issues or explore additional vulnerabilities). The AI assistant has access to both the code snippet and the review comments but not to the solutions. In Step 3, participants re-analyzed the code and refined their comments about potential vulnerabilities based on the AI interaction. In Step 4, participants modified the code to remediate the documented issues. We explicitly disabled code editing during Steps 1–3 to enforce a separation between analysis and remediation. We intended to reduce premature acceptance of AI suggestions by framing AI outputs as hypotheses to be checked rather than authoritative fixes.

5 Results

To answer RQ1, we first examine how frequently participants use LLMs or GenAI tools for coding or security-related tasks as a function of professional experience. Figure 2(a) presents LLM usage frequency stratified by years of professional coding experience. Participants with 1–3 years of experience reported the highest overall adoption of LLMs. Within this group, 75.0% reported frequently using LLMs, 16.7% reported rare use, and 8.3% reported never using them. Participants with 4–6 years of experience most commonly reported frequent use, at 57.9%. An additional 21.1% of participants in this group reported occasional use, while 10.5% reported rare use and 10.5% reported never using LLMs. Among participants with 7–10 years of experience, usage was more evenly distributed across LLM usage categories. In this cohort, 42.1% reported occasional use, 26.3% reported frequent use, 15.8% reported rare use, 10.5% reported never using LLMs, and 5.3% reported always using them. Participants with more than 10 years of experience most often reported frequent use, at 38.5%. Within this group, 19.2% reported rare use, 19.2% reported occasional use, 15.4% reported never using LLMs, and 7.7% reported always using them. Participants with less than one year of experience exhibited a polarized usage pattern. In this group, 37.5% reported frequently using LLMs, 37.5% reported never using them, and 12.5% each reported rare or occasional use.

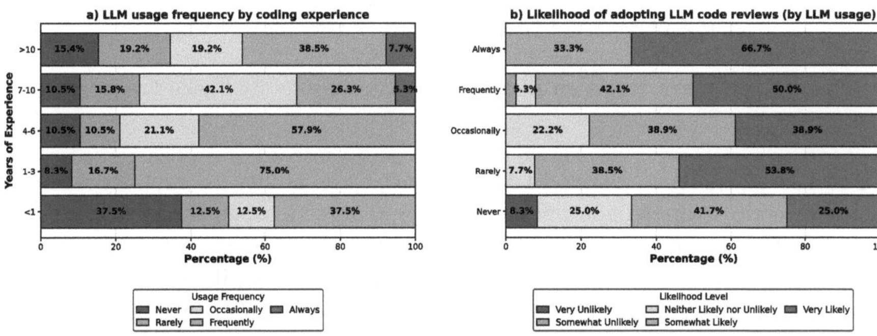

Fig. 2. LLM Usage Frequency and Likelihood to Adopt LLMs for Code Review.

To address RQ2, we next examine participants' perceptions of LLM-assisted secure code review. This analysis focuses on both the likelihood of future adoption and perceived benefits related to vulnerability identification and reduction of human error. We first examine participants' likelihood of incorporating LLM-assisted secure code reviews into future projects as a function of their current LLM usage frequency. Figure 2(b) summarizes the reported likelihood levels across usage-frequency groups.

Among participants who reported always using LLMs, 66.7% indicated that they were very likely to incorporate LLM-assisted secure code reviews, while

33.3% reported being somewhat likely. Among frequent users, 50.0% reported being very likely, 42.1% reported being somewhat likely, 5.3% reported being neutral, and 2.6% reported being somewhat unlikely. Among occasional users, 38.9% reported being very likely, 38.9% reported being somewhat likely, and 22.2% reported being neutral. Among rare users, 53.8% reported being very likely, 38.5% reported being somewhat likely, and 7.7% reported being neutral. Among participants who reported never using LLMs, 25.0% reported being very likely to adopt LLM-assisted secure code reviews, 41.7% reported being somewhat likely, 25.0% reported being neutral, and 8.3% reported being very unlikely.

Participants also rated their agreement with two statements concerning the perceived benefits of LLMs in secure coding tasks. Figure 3 presents agreement levels for both statements, stratified by LLM usage frequency.

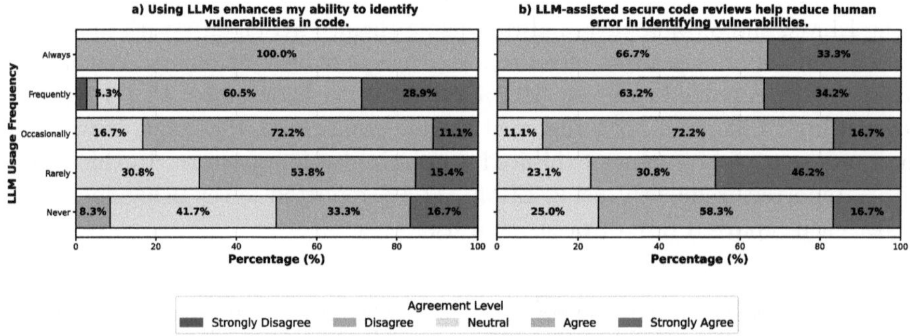

Fig. 3. Agreement Rates on LLM Related Statements by Usage Frequency.

For the statement "Using LLMs enhances my ability to identify vulnerabilities in code," agreement increased with reported usage frequency. Among participants who always use LLMs, 100.0% agreed with the statement. Among frequent users, 60.5% agreed and 28.9% strongly agreed, while 5.3% were neutral and remaining disagreed (2.6%) or strongly disagreed (2.6%). Among occasional users, 72.2% agreed, 11.1% strongly agreed, and 16.7% were neutral. Among rare users, 53.8% agreed, 15.4% strongly agreed, and 30.8% were neutral. Among participants who never use LLMs, 33.3% agreed, 16.7% strongly agreed, 41.7% were neutral, and 8.3% disagreed.

For the statement "LLM-assisted secure code reviews help reduce human error in identifying vulnerabilities," agreement was consistently high across usage-frequency groups. Among participants who always use LLMs, 66.7% agreed and 33.3% strongly agreed. Among frequent users, 63.2% agreed, 34.2% strongly agreed, and 2.6% disagreed. Among occasional users, 72.2% agreed, 16.7% strongly agreed, and 11.1% were neutral. Among rare users, 30.8% agreed, 46.2% strongly agreed, and 23.1% were neutral. Among participants who never use LLMs, 58.3% agreed, 16.7% strongly agreed, and 25.0% were neutral, no one disagreed.

To answer RQ3, we analyze participants' responses to an open-ended survey question regarding issues or limitations encountered when using LLMs for coding tasks. A total of 84 responses were collected for this question. Fifteen responses (17.86%) were excluded based on predefined quality control criteria, including irrelevant or non-interpretable answers. The final qualitative analysis therefore included 69 valid responses. Among these respondents, 24 (34.78%) reported no issues when using LLMs for coding tasks. The remaining 45 respondents (65.22%) reported at least one issue. In total, these respondents mentioned 93 distinct issues, corresponding to an average of 2.07 issues per respondent.

Table 3. Reported Issues with LLMs for Coding

No.	Issue category	Respondents	% of Participants (n = 69)	% of Issues (n = 93)
1	No issues	24	34.78%	—
2	Code quality	25	36.23%	26.88%
3	Context limitations	24	34.78%	25.81%
4	Productivity issues	14	20.29%	15.05%
5	Hallucinations	13	18.84%	13.98%
6	Prompting issues	6	8.70%	6.45%
7	Other issues	11	15.94%	11.83%

Table 3 summarizes the distribution of reported issues across high-level categories. Code quality concerns were reported by 36.23% of respondents, and context limitations, reported by 34.78% of respondents. Productivity-related issues were reported by 20.29% of respondents. Hallucinations were reported by 18.84% of respondents. Prompting-related challenges and other issues were reported less frequently. We observed a similar distribution after normalization by the total number of reported issues ($n = 93$). Code quality concerns and context limitations together represented more than half of all reported issues. Issue categories were not mutually exclusive, as individual respondents could report multiple distinct issues.

6 Discussion

Our results show strong interest in using LLMs for security-relevant development work, alongside clear signals of caution. Adoption is uneven across experience levels, yet developers who already use LLMs frequently or always are consistently more inclined to integrate LLM-assisted secure code review into future projects. Perceived usefulness is also highly positive, as participants agree that LLM enhance their ability to identify vulnerabilities and reduce human error during review, although this enthusiasm is conditional because developers also describe recurring challenges that can directly undermine secure development outcomes.

The reported challenge categories are directly related to security risks that can undermine secure software development if left unmanaged. Hallucinations can lead developers to adopt plausible but incorrect recommendations, including non-existent dependencies that enable supply-chain attacks such as *slopsquatting* [24], while context limitations can cause models to miss architectural dependencies, trust boundaries, and security requirements, thereby reducing the quality of vulnerability detection and patch suggestions. Prompting issues are security-relevant because underspecified prompts and limited security awareness can yield outputs that prioritize functionality while omitting defensive checks and safe defaults. Code quality concerns amplify risk when models suggest outdated APIs or insecure libraries due to knowledge cut-offs and insecure patterns in training data, which can perpetuate vulnerabilities and weaken assurance. Productivity pitfalls are security-relevant because speed can mask cognitive offloading and automation bias, reducing verification effort precisely when risk is highest. In the worst case, overconfidence and unsafe integration patterns can combine with assistant capabilities to create high-impact failure conditions in which a system simultaneously has access to sensitive data, accepts untrusted input, and can exfiltrate outputs to external channels—a dangerous combination known as the "lethal trifecta" [26].

6.1 Strategies to Deal with Challenges

Mitigating GenAI-related risks requires reinforcing security awareness and verification habits across people, processes, and tools. We synthesize four complementary strategies grounded in the survey findings and our industrial experience. *First*, targeted training is foundational because it addresses hallucinations, prompting issues, limited security awareness, and over reliance on AI. Training should teach developers to "trust less and engage more" by asking for assumptions, requesting justifications, and treating outputs as hypotheses to validate. Training should also develop security-aware prompting skills, including providing meaningful context such as trust boundaries, input sources, and constraints, and decomposing tasks into smaller checks. Structured prompting has been shown to improve output reliability and relevance [16]. Beyond prompting, training must reinforce secure software development fundamentals so developers can critically assess AI-generated code and detect insecure patterns. This is important because developers often struggle to reliably identify vulnerabilities in practice, even during code review [6]. In industrial settings, training may be constrained by time pressure and organizational approval processes, but sustained developer enablement is associated with improved outcomes [10].

Second, careful LLM selection and configuration reduces exposure to context limitations, unsafe defaults, and outdated or insecure suggestions. Organizations should select models based on language coverage, context window size, safety mechanisms, and knowledge cut-off dates relevant to security-critical tasks. Upgrades should not be assumed to improve security, because newer models can regress on specific software engineering or security tasks [18]. Configuration should prioritize grounding with project-specific context, limiting external access where appropriate, and constraining tool integrations to reduce hallucinations and risk amplification. Given rapid model evolution, continuous evaluation and revalidation are necessary to detect emerging risks and performance shifts.

Third, mandatory human code review remains essential because it addresses blind spots, logic errors, and misplaced trust in AI-generated outputs. Human review should explicitly verify dependencies, security assumptions, and threat-relevant behaviors rather than only assessing functional correctness. Because large volumes of AI-generated changes can increase reviewer fatigue, organizations should define clear review responsibilities and depth expectations. This approach aligns with established review and security standards (ISO 20246, ISO 27001, IEC 62443), which emphasize structured reviews and controlled verification, and with prior work showing that modern code review supports vulnerability detection and shared ownership [3,12–14].

Fourth, automated security testing provides scalable verification that complements human review and reduces the chance that systematic insecure patterns pass unnoticed. Automated checks are important because LLMs can hallucinate tests or incorrectly claim tests have passed, which makes human oversight indispensable in critical contexts. Security-focused unit tests can precisely validate defensive behavior and negative paths, but require expertise and maintenance. Static Application Security Testing (SAST) can detect common vulnerability patterns early, but may suffer from false positives, false negatives, and alert fatigue. Dynamic Application Security Testing (DAST) can validate security behavior on running systems, but is harder to deploy and is constrained by runtime coverage. Together, training, model governance, human review, and automated testing provide layered defenses that preserve accountability while enabling secure GenAI adoption.

6.2 Recommendations for Stakeholders

Developers should treat LLMs as collaborators for exploration and explanation rather than authorities for security decisions. Developers should explicitly instruct assistants to generate secure-by-default solutions by stating concrete security requirements, trust boundaries, and relevant constraints. Developers should verify AI-assisted changes through manual review and tests, with particular scrutiny for new dependencies, configuration defaults, and code that touches sensitive data flows. Developers should document AI involvement through clear commit messages and comments to improve traceability and peer review. Developers should avoid entering sensitive data into unvetted tools and follow organizational data-handling policies.

Tool builders should frame assistants as decision-support systems with clear boundaries, safeguards, and defaults that encourage verification. Tools should improve context awareness and reduce hallucination impact by supporting workflows and explicitly indicating uncertainty rather than overconfident answers. Tooling should provide prompting guidance to users and prompts to supply relevant context, including trust boundaries and security requirements. Tools should discourage recommending non-existent, deprecated, or insecure dependencies, and should support auditability through logging and configuration controls. Privacy-preserving deployment options and configurable data retention should be provided to support industrial constraints.

Technical leaders should establish governance that makes secure GenAI usage expectations explicit, enforceable, and measurable. Leaders should allocate time and budget for recurring role-based training on secure development and responsible GenAI usage. Organizations should mandate human oversight of AI-generated changes and embed SAST, DAST, and testing into standard workflows to ensure continuous verification. Leaders should define processes for tool selection, access control, data protection, model updates, and risk assessment, especially in safety- and security-critical contexts.

6.3 Threats to Validity

The rapid evolution of AI and GenAI tools, as well as their adoption processes, limits the external validity of the quantitative analysis. The number of participants is small, which is inherent to studies conducted in industrial and training contexts involving innovative technologies, where recruiting participants from industry is challenging. Furthermore, the study is conducted within a single company, which may limit the generalizability of the findings. Nevertheless, the company under research is an industry leader and provides a high-quality industrial context; therefore, we believe that the findings are representative of a broader class of organizations.

7 Conclusion

This paper examines how professional software developers in industry use and perceive GenAI, particularly LLMs, when performing security relevant tasks. We conducted a study through nine secure coding training workshops using the ASCEND platform in a controlled professional setting. We combined an LLM assisted secure code review exercise with a post task survey to capture both experience and perceptions. Our results reinforce the observation that GenAI adoption is already present in industrial practice, however we show that this can vary across different experience levels of its users. Our study highlights that participants generally perceive LLM support as useful for vulnerability identification and for reducing human error during review, including among developers who report infrequent day to day use. At the same time, developers consistently highlight limitations that can affect secure outcomes, including code quality concerns, context limitations, hallucinations, productivity pitfalls, and prompting challenges. These findings reinforce our perception that LLMs can be used to support security work, but they do not remove the need for human expertise, verification, and accountability. We also distilled four complementary strategies aligned with the observed challenges and industrial practice, namely targeted developer training, careful model selection and configuration, mandatory human code review, and integration of automated security testing. Beyond supporting the present study, ASCEND is positioned as a developer enablement platform for responsible and secure use of LLMs in software engineering tasks.

This work contributes industry-based empirical evidence to the discussion on GenAI's role in secure software development. Future work will extend ASCEND beyond review and remediation to other GenAI-enabled workflows, including AI-assisted code generation, long-term impacts, model comparisons in security-critical settings, and structured support for secure human–AI collaboration.

Acknowledgement. We acknowledge funding from the European Union's NextGenerationEU program for the LIONS project as part of dtec.bw. This work was partially supported by national funds through Fundação para a Ciência e Tecnologia, I.P. (FCT), ISTAR-Iscte Pluriannual Project UID/04466/2025 (https://doi.org/10.54499/UID/04466/2025).

Disclosure of Interests. The authors have no competing interests to declare that are relevant to the content of this article

References

1. Amburi, S.: AI Secure Coding Survey Form (2025). https://doi.org/10.5281/zenodo.17929857
2. Amburi, S., Espinha Gasiba, T., Lechner, U., Pinto-Albuquerque, M.: Enabling secure coding: exploring GenAI for developer training and education. In: 6th International Computer Programming Education Conference (ICPEC 2025), vol. 133, pp. 2:1–2:15. Schloss Dagstuhl - Leibniz-Zentrum für Informatik (2025). https://doi.org/10.4230/OASIcs.ICPEC.2025.2
3. Bacchelli, A., Bird, C.: Expectations, outcomes, and challenges of modern code review. In: 2013 35th International Conference on Software Engineering (ICSE), pp. 712–721 (2013). https://doi.org/10.1109/ICSE.2013.6606617
4. Banh, L., Holldack, F., Strobel, G.: Copiloting the future: how generative AI transforms software engineering. Inf. Softw. Technol. **183**, 107751 (2025). https://doi.org/10.1016/j.infsof.2025.107751
5. Belzner, L., Gabor, T., Wirsing, M.: Large language model assisted software engineering: prospects, challenges, and a case study. In: Steffen, B. (ed.) Bridging the Gap Between AI and Reality. Lecture Notes in Computer Science, vol. 14380, pp. 355–374 (2024). https://doi.org/10.1007/978-3-031-46002-9
6. Braz, L., Aeberhard, C., Çalikli, G., Bacchelli, A.: Less is more: supporting developers in vulnerability detection during code review. In: Proceedings of the 44th International Conference on Software Engineering, ICSE '22, pp. 1317–1329. Association for Computing Machinery, New York (2022). https://doi.org/10.1145/3510003.3511560
7. Fu, Y., et al.: Security weaknesses of copilot-generated code in GitHub projects: an empirical study. ACM Trans. Softw. Eng. Methodol. (2025). https://doi.org/10.1145/3716848
8. Gasiba, T.E., Iosif, A.C., Kessba, I., Amburi, S., Lechner, U., Pinto-Albuquerque, M.: May the source be with you: on ChatGPT, cybersecurity, and secure coding. Information **15**(9), 572 (2024). https://doi.org/10.3390/info15090572

9. GitHub: Survey: The AI wave continues to grow on software development teams (2024). https://github.blog/news-insights/research/survey-ai-wave-grows/. Accessed 08 Dec 2025
10. Graziotin, D., Fagerholm, F., Wang, X., Abrahamsson, P.: What happens when software developers are (un)happy. J. Syst. Softw. **140**, 32–47 (2018). https://doi.org/10.1016/j.jss.2018.02.041
11. Huber, S.E., Kiili, K., Nebel, S., Ryan, R.M., Sailer, M., Ninaus, M.: Leveraging the potential of large language models in education through playful and game-based learning. Educ. Psychol. Rev. **36**(1), 25 (2024). https://doi.org/10.1007/s10648-024-09868-z
12. International Electrotechnical Commission: Industrial communication networks—network and system security. Technical Report. IEC 62443, IEC (2025)
13. International Organization for Standardization and International Electrotechnical Commission: Software and systems engineering—work product reviews. Technical Report. ISO/IEC 20246:2017, ISO/IEC (2017)
14. International Organization for Standardization and International Electrotechnical Commission: Information security, cybersecurity and privacy protection—information security management systems—requirements. Technical Report. ISO/IEC 27001:2022, ISO/IEC (2022)
15. Kharma, M., Choi, S., AlKhanafseh, M., Mohaisen, D.: Security and quality in LLM-generated code: a multi-language, multi-model analysis (2025). https://arxiv.org/abs/2502.01853
16. Knoth, N., Tolzin, A., Janson, A., Leimeister, J.M.: AI literacy and its implications for prompt engineering strategies. Comput. Educ. Artif. Intell. **6**, 100225 (2024). https://doi.org/10.1016/j.caeai.2024.100225
17. Lee, H.P.H., et al.: The impact of generative AI on critical thinking: self-reported reductions in cognitive effort and confidence effects from a survey of knowledge workers. In: CHI 2025 (2025). https://doi.org/10.1145/3706598.3713778
18. Lin, J., Mohaisen, D.: From large to mammoth: a comparative evaluation of large language models in vulnerability detection. In: Network and Distributed System Security (NDSS) Symposium 2025 (2025). https://doi.org/10.14722/ndss.2025.241491
19. Ndiaye, A., Taraj, X., Robeznik, B., Herzog, G., Gerber, C., Purwins, H.: Generative AI in software engineering: transforming the software development process. Technical Report, DFKI & Accenture (2025)
20. Perry, N., Srivastava, M., Kumar, D., Boneh, D.: Do users write more insecure code with AI assistants? In: CCS '23: Proceedings of the 2023 ACM SIGSAC Conference on Computer and Communications Security, CCS '23, pp. 2785–2799. ACM, New York (2023). https://doi.org/10.1145/3576915.3623157
21. Saldaña, J.: The Coding Manual for Qualitative Researchers, 3rd edn. SAGE Publications (2016)
22. Sallou, J., Durieux, T., Panichella, A.: Breaking the silence: the threats of using LLMs in software engineering. In: Proceedings of the 2024 ACM/IEEE 44th International Conference on Software Engineering: New Ideas and Emerging Results, ICSE-NIER'24, pp. 102–106. ACM, New York (2024). https://doi.org/10.1145/3639476.3639764
23. Sheng, Z., Chen, Z., Gu, S., Huang, H., Gu, G., Huang, J.: LLMs in software security: a survey of vulnerability detection techniques and insights. ACM Comput. Surv. **58**(5) (2025). https://doi.org/10.1145/3769082

24. Spracklen, J., Wijewickrama, R., Sakib, A.H.M.N., Maiti, A., Viswanath, B., Jadliwala, M.: We have a package for you! a comprehensive analysis of package hallucinations by code generating LLMs. In: Bauer, L., Pellegrino, G. (eds.) 34th USENIX Security Symposium, USENIX Security 2025, Seattle, WA, USA, 13–15 August 2025, pp. 3687–3706. USENIX Association (2025). https://www.usenix.org/conference/usenixsecurity25/presentation/spracklen
25. Wessling, J.: We Asked 100+ AI Models to Write Code. Here's How Many Failed Security Tests. Technical report, Veracode Inc. (2025). https://www.veracode.com/blog/genai-code-security-report/
26. Willison, S.: The lethal trifecta for AI agents: private data, untrusted content, and external communication (2025). https://simonwillison.net/2025/Jun/16/the-lethal-trifecta/. Accessed 14 Dec 2025
27. Zhao, S., Wang, D., Zhang, K., Luo, J., Li, Z., Li, L.: Is Vibe Coding Safe? Benchmarking Vulnerability of Agent-Generated Code in Real-World Tasks (2025). https://arxiv.org/abs/2512.03262

Unsupervised Graph Learning For Insider Threat Detection

Simon Bertrand(✉), Pascal Germain, and Nadia Tawbi

Laval University, Québec, Canada
simon.bertrand.3@ulaval.ca, {pascal.germain,nadia.tawbi}@ift.ulaval.ca

Abstract. We propose an automatic graph learning framework that models rich event dependencies from audit data, facilitating the detection of complex multi-event insider threats. Our method first relies on treating audit log entries as nodes in graphs with no edges initially. Each node is represented by an initial representation capturing daily user behaviours. This is achieved through a deep-sequential neural network architecture that results from a prior contribution. Then, we suggest a custom edge predictor that identifies long-term dependencies. The resulting graph is then used to identify abnormal nodes indicating malicious events. The proposed method does not require any label information from the audit data, classifying it as an unsupervised learning approach. Additionally, it does not require extensive audit log preprocessing, such as manual extraction of domain-knowledge-rich features or data balancing. Therefore, the suggested method is easy to implement and can be used across organizations regardless of their level of expertise. By providing a node-based scoring system, the resulting graph also functions as a diagnostic tool to help security experts understand detected threats. On the CERT benchmark dataset version 6.2, our approach outperforms previous state-of-the-art approaches, achieving an area under the ROC curve of 97.17%.

Keywords: Insider Threat Detection · Graphs · Graph Learning · Deep Neural Networks · Attention Mechanisms · Unsupervised Learning · Audit Data

1 Introduction

Insider threats involve harmful actions by trusted members of an organization. Specifically, they include a wide range of cyber threats, such as data theft, sabotage, and any actions that could expose an organization to cyber risks. This type of threat directly affects an organization's goal to maintain the confidentiality, integrity, and availability of information. Unlike more specific cyber threats, which can be addressed with specialized solutions, the diverse nature of insider threats increases the variety of potential risks, making detection more difficult.

Insider threats can arise from employees who turn malicious, misinformed employees, unintentionally causing harm, or compromised user accounts. Malicious insiders intentionally misuse their privileges, such as stealing data, while

© IFIP International Federation for Information Processing 2026
Published by Springer Nature Switzerland AG 2026
H. Janicke et al. (Eds.): SEC 2026, IFIP AICT 787, pp. 18–32, 2026.
https://doi.org/10.1007/978-3-032-27993-4_2

negligent employees may unknowingly expose the organization to risks, like downloading malicious attachments. Additionally, compromised accounts can be exploited even when the account owner lacks intent. These varied sources of insider threats highlight the importance of vigilance and robust security measures.

Regardless of the type of insider, they exhibit actions that appear legitimate to the organization's security systems because they conform to the user's access rights defined by the organization's access control. It is challenging to differentiate between malicious and benign actions solely by examining individual audit log events. The user's intent is therefore essential, but this information is not explicitly recorded in audit data. Most research focuses on establishing typical user behaviours from historical audit data as a baseline to identify significant or subtle behavioural changes that could indicate potential threats. One challenging aspect of learning user behaviours from their historical audit data is capturing relevant sequence-based features. This is vital for identifying cyberattacks, which are often characterized by a series of events that can occur over an extended period. For instance, a data exfiltration attack involves one or more data acquisition events followed by one or more data sharing events, such as an email being sent.

Finally, because each organization has a unique technology architecture, extending insider threat detection systems based on a specific dataset to other environments can be difficult. For example, using pre-trained models requires that the architecture in the trained environment closely matches the organization and that user behaviours are similar. This also assumes that organizations' roles are comparable and clearly defined. Training threat detection systems specific to each organization requires considerable effort and expertise to analyse audit data and extract relevant features from a team of specialists who understand the organization's unique system and security protocols.

Overview of the Proposed Method. To address the limitations outlined above, we propose an unsupervised insider threat detection system that leverages a novel graph learning framework to model complex event dependencies. Precisely, we use a deep sequential neural network to learn daily-based user behaviours that depict, for instance, user-specific patterns. This neural network, trained on a custom pretext task, generates event-based feature vectors that then serve as initial node representations (graph's vertex). Subsequently, we introduce a graph learning module, based on a custom edge predictor, enhanced with simple applicable rules to discover event dependencies. This edge predictor enables iterative learning or unlearning of edges. Ultimately, the graph learning module effectively converts sequential audit data into a graph. Finally, we use a graph neural network on the learned graph structure to produce enriched event representations capturing both behaviour-based and dependency-based features. To enhance the method's flexibility, manual processing of audit data is kept to a minimum. Since the feature extraction process is automated, we argue that our approach is better suited to real-world applications than most existing techniques. Especially since the suggested approach does not require data balancing or data augmentation and does not rely on one-class training.

We describe how to generate event representations specifically for insider threat detection and enhance the edge predictor with rules based on cybersecurity domain knowledge. Both the representation creation process and the rules can be adapted for other applications, enabling the transformation of any set of observations into a graph structure.

Contributions. We propose an unsupervised insider threat detection system that: **(1)** Considers short-term user behaviours through a deep sequential neural network; **(2)** Considers long-term event dependencies through an original graph learning framework; **(3)** Provides insights into detected threats through an event-based scoring system; **(4)** Does not require data balancing or one-class training (contrary to standard approaches), it relies solely on unsupervised learning.

2 Related Work

Insider threat detection efforts often depend on modeling normal user behaviours through audit data. The main difference between approaches lies in how behaviours are defined. In this section, we primarily focus on research based on unsupervised machine learning, and graph-based initiatives, which align with our own contributions.

Insider Threat Detection Based on Machine Learning. Machine learning (ML) initiatives are widely studied for their flexibility and reduced domain knowledge requirements [15]. Like most ML projects, efficient insider threat detection depends on transforming key information, such as log entries, into a relevant feature space, facilitating behaviour learning. In an unsupervised learning context, insider threat detection is frequently approached as an anomaly detection problem, using statistical outlier models. For instance, Rashid et al. [21] uses hidden Markov models to infer the probability of a sequence of events, from which a threshold can be used to classify normal and malicious events. Also, Gavai et al. [11] propose a modification of the *Isolation Forest* algorithm to adapt it to the insider threat detection task. Eldardiry et al. [9] and Happa & Tabash [2] propose similar frameworks to detect insider threats by using clustering algorithms such as K-Means and Gaussian Mixture models (GMMs) to model daily user behaviour. Kim et al. [13] present a study of existing clustering and statistical techniques. Bin Sarhan & Altwaijry [5] propose a study of both supervised and unsupervised machine learning techniques to detect insider threats. While statistical and clustering techniques offer greater flexibility than signature-based methods, they tend to suffer from a high false-positive rate [8].

With recent advances in natural language processing, that rely heavily on temporal and spatial information in sequences, some techniques have been integrated into the insider threat detection task to incorporate context information into feature vectors. For example, Word2Vec encoders [17] were used to convert automatically collected audit data into feature vectors [3,28]. Although these techniques reduce manual pre-processing needs, the contextual information contained in the resulting feature vectors remains limited [18]. Another significant advancement in natural language processing is the adoption of Recurrent Neural Networks (RNN) [22], due to their ability to model sequences effectively [24]. In the field of insider threat detection, Long Short-Term Memory (LSTM) networks have been introduced by Nasir et al. [19] and Sharma et al. [23] to extract session-based feature vectors from audit data. They use a reconstruction error metric on the extracted feature vectors to indicate potential threats. Although RNNs can capture certain spatial and temporal features within audit data, their high computational costs restrict their application to shorter sequences. Recently, Transformer model variants have been applied to insider threat detection, notably in a supervised setting in order to extract rich features from audit data [6,26].

Graph-Based Insider Threat Detection. In parallel with the previous initiatives, part of the research on insider threat detection using machine learning is interested in using graphs, trying to leverage structural information to facilitate the detection of complex threats. Although many papers propose graph-based insider threat detection, few propose solutions applicable to audit logs that are not already graph-structured.

With Log2Vec, Liu, Wen et al. [14] propose one of the earliest iterations of graph-based insider threat detection, proposing a graph construction solution from non-graph-structured audit data; Log2vec is a rule-based approach to construct a heterogeneous graph from audit data, where nodes represent log events and edges indicate causal relationships. This graph is used to generate random walk sequences, which are then utilized with Word2Vec to learn node representations. Finally, the K-Means clustering is applied to the learned node representations to identify anomalous nodes.

Liu, Gao et al. proposed an insider threat detection framework that uses graph alignment to search for known malicious subgraphs in a provenance graph describing user activities [16]. Although it enables precise and explainable detection of attack sequences, it relies on supervised machine learning. Furthermore, Liu. Gao et al. [16] also propose an adaptation of Gao et al.'s Continuous-Time Dynamic Heterogeneous Graph Network (CDHGN) [10] and Xia et al.'s Temporal Graph Neural Network (TGNN) [27] architectures for insider threat detection. Both techniques treat audit data as part of a provenance graph, where nodes represent entities, such as files or users, and edges represent events, such as a file-read action between a user node and a file node. Because a different version of the graph is produced based on a time interval, where edges represent events that occurred within that interval, these graphs are referred to as dynamics.

3 Proposed Unsupervised Graph Learning Methodology

The suggested method aims at learning rich audit logs events representation that facilitates threat detection. We achieve this by first learning behaviour-

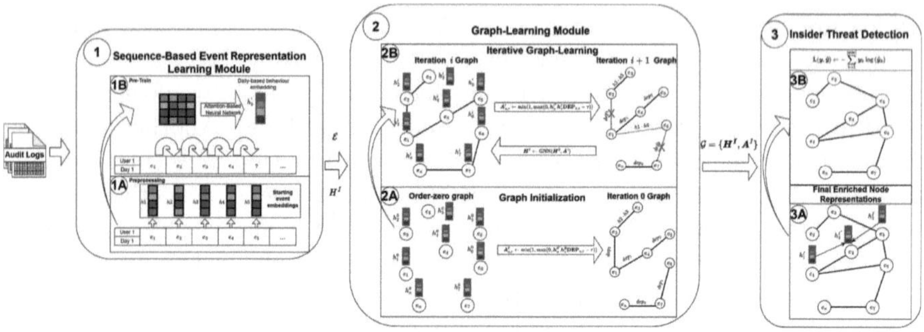

Fig. 1. Proposed framework

rich event representations through our previously proposed framework [4]. This approach relies on multi-head self-attention mechanisms and artificial neural networks, which are utilized to capture context-rich feature vectors from long event sequences. Secondly, we leverage these learned event representations, combined with simple known event dependencies, to learn a graph structure from the audit data. Initially, audit data events depict nodes in a zero-degree graph; then event dependencies, modelled as edges, are discovered iteratively using a custom edge predictor. Thirdly, using the newly learned graph structure and the first obtained event representations, enriched event representations are calculated using a graph neural network. Finally, the event representations are utilized for anomaly detection. Thus, the proposed framework, illustrated in Fig. 1, consists of three components: a sequence-based event representation learning module, a graph learning module and an insider threat detection module.

3.1 Sequence-Based Event Representation Learning Module

This module is designed to learn representations of audit data events that focus on user-based behaviours. To do so, we rely on our previously proposed framework [4], which we adapt. Precisely, we now opt for a transductive setting, rather than the inductive setting of the previous contribution. This means that there is no data separation into training and test sets, and that the current method does not rely on one-class training. Algorithm 1 details this first module.

Input. The first step consists of processing audit data to group log entries by user and by day. Thus, given any audit data containing log entries, let $S = \{s_0, \ldots, s_m\}$ denote the set of daily event sequences carried out by a specific user, where m is the total number of non-null unique combinations of days and users, $s = \{e_0, \ldots, e_n\} \in S$ is a specific sequence of events performed by a user on a specific day, and n is the maximum number of events. Thus, the total number of events performed by a user can be described as $N = nm$. Padding or truncation is performed on each sequence to ensure that each instance has the same desired length n. This sequence of events is chronologically ordered.

Lines 4–8. Each event in the sequence is converted into a real-valued feature space ready for use by our deep sequential model. Initially, an event e is described by various pieces of information in the audit log. To facilitate the implementation of the proposed approach, we automatically transform this information using non-pretrained embeddings. This is denoted by $\mathbf{E}$, a function that transforms a label into a d-dimensional feature space, where d is a hyperparameter.

We use three pieces of information to build each event's feature vector: the event category, the event hour, and the event's position in the sequence. These pieces of information are selected because they are generally available in organizational audit data and do not depend on system-specific expertise. The event category e_{activity} and the hour e_{hour} are transformed into word embeddings of size d. Each of these embeddings is initialized to random values and is fed into a linear layer that learns to transform them into a suitable representation for the task at hand (along with other neural network parameters). Each event's position is projected into a feature vector $\psi_{pos} \in \mathbb{R}^d$ such that [24]:

$$\psi_{pos,2i} = \sin\left(\frac{pos}{1000^{(\frac{2i}{d})}}\right) \quad \text{and} \quad \psi_{pos,2i+1} = \cos\left(\frac{pos}{1000^{(\frac{2i}{d})}}\right), \tag{1}$$

where $i \in \{1, \ldots, \lfloor \frac{d}{2} \rfloor\}$ is the feature index and $pos \in \{1, \ldots, n\}$ is the event's position in the sequence. The three resulting event's component embeddings are summed into a single event embedding $\boldsymbol{h}_e \in \mathbb{R}^d$, stored into a tensor $\boldsymbol{H}^0 \in \mathbb{R}^{m \times n \times d}$, where m is the number of event sequences, n is the maximum number of events per sequence and d is the embedding size. As a result of the data preprocessing step, each event in a daily sequence is mapped into a feature space.

Lines 9–20. To enrich event representations with context information from preceding events in the sequence, we opt for a combination of self-attention mechanisms and neural networks. This step notably allows the capture of users' daily behavioural patterns. As for the seminal "Attention is All You Need" architecture [24], we iteratively learn the weight matrices $\boldsymbol{W}_0^Q, \boldsymbol{W}_0^K, \boldsymbol{W}_0^V \in \mathbb{R}^{d \times d}$ used to compute an attention-based feature vector. We use the same events' representations for all query, key, and value components, which is referred to as the self-attention mechanism, and we apply a projection layer $\boldsymbol{l} \in \mathbb{R}^{d \times d}$ to the initial events' representations. Recall that we use randomly generated embeddings to encode the events' information, and thus this learnable parameter transforms the initial representations into more efficient ones. Of course, updating the different parameters requires a learning task. Since event labels are unavailable, one cannot directly define the task as insider threat detection using our event feature vectors and labels. Therefore, we train the model to predict the next event in a sequence solely from preceding events as in our previous work [4].

This task is achieved by mapping each event's output to a vector of size $C \in \mathbb{N}^+$, being the total number of activity types, where each entry describes the model's inferred probability for the corresponding activity type. We denote

Algorithm 1. Event Representation Learning

Require: Number of epochs $I \in \mathbb{N}^+$;
Event sequences $S = \{s_j\}_{j=0}^m$, $Y = \{y_j\}_{j=0}^m$, where $s_j = \{e_{j,k}\}_{k=0}^n$, $y_j = \{e_{\text{activity}_{j,k}}\}_{k=1}^{n+1}$.
Initialize parameters $\boldsymbol{l}, \boldsymbol{W}^Q, \boldsymbol{W}^K, \boldsymbol{W}^V \in \mathbb{R}^{d \times d}$
for each daily sequence $s \in S$ **do**
  for each event $e \in s$ **do**
    $\boldsymbol{H}_{e,s}^0 \leftarrow \mathbf{E}(e_{\text{activity}}) + \mathbf{E}(e_{\text{hour}}) + \psi_{pos}$
  end for
end for
for each epoch $i \in \{1, \ldots, I\}$ **do**
  $\boldsymbol{H}^i \leftarrow \boldsymbol{H}^0 \boldsymbol{l}$
  $\boldsymbol{Q} \leftarrow \boldsymbol{H}^i \boldsymbol{W}^Q$
  $\boldsymbol{K} \leftarrow \boldsymbol{H}^i \boldsymbol{W}^K$
  $\boldsymbol{V} \leftarrow \boldsymbol{H}^i \boldsymbol{W}^V$
  $\boldsymbol{H}^{i'} \leftarrow \mathit{softmax}(\boldsymbol{Q}\boldsymbol{K}^T / \sqrt{d})\boldsymbol{V}$
  $\boldsymbol{Y} \leftarrow \mathit{softmax}(\boldsymbol{H}^{i'})$
  for each prediction $\hat{\boldsymbol{y}}_{j,p} \in \hat{Y}$ **do**
    $\mathrm{L}(\boldsymbol{y}_{j,p}, \hat{\boldsymbol{y}}_{j,p}) \leftarrow -\sum_{c=1}^{C} \boldsymbol{y}_{j,p,c} \log(\hat{\boldsymbol{y}}_{j,p,c})$
  end for
  $\mathcal{L} \leftarrow \frac{1}{m \times n} \sum_{j=0}^{m} \sum_{p=0}^{n} \mathrm{L}(\boldsymbol{y}_{j,p}, \hat{\boldsymbol{y}}_{j,p})$
  Update $\boldsymbol{l}, \boldsymbol{W}^Q, \boldsymbol{W}^K, \boldsymbol{W}^V$ based on $\nabla\mathcal{L}$.
end for
return Event representation matrix $\boldsymbol{H}^{I'}$

Algorithm 2. Graph Learning

Require: Number of epochs $I \in \mathbb{N}^+$;
Nodes $\mathcal{V} = \{e_k\}_{k=0}^N$, labels $Y = \{e_{\text{activity}_k}\}_{k=0}^N$, where $N = nm$; Dependencies $\mathbf{DEP}^0$; Initial node representations $\boldsymbol{H}^0$; Edge threshold τ.
Initialize parameters $\alpha_0 \in \mathbb{R}$, $\boldsymbol{l} \in \mathbb{R}^{d \times d}$; $\boldsymbol{l}_{\text{head}} \in \mathbb{R}^C$
Initialize GNN's parameters θ
for each epoch $i \in \{1, \ldots, I\}$ **do**
  $\mathbf{DEP}^i \leftarrow \alpha_i \, \mathbf{DEP}^0 + 1$
  $\boldsymbol{H}^i \leftarrow \boldsymbol{H}^0 \boldsymbol{l}$
  for each node $u \in \mathcal{V}$ **do**
    for each node $v \in \mathcal{V}$ **do**
      if $u = v$ **then**
        $\boldsymbol{A}_{u,v}^i \leftarrow 0$
      else
        $\boldsymbol{A}_{u,v}^i \leftarrow \lceil \boldsymbol{h}_u^{i^T} \boldsymbol{h}_v^i \mathbf{DEP}_{u,v}^i - \tau \rceil$
        $\boldsymbol{A}_{u,v}^i \leftarrow \min(1, \max(0, \boldsymbol{A}_{u,v}^i))$
      end if
    end for
  end for
  $\boldsymbol{H}^{i'} \leftarrow \mathrm{GNN}_\theta(\boldsymbol{H}^0, \boldsymbol{A})$
  $\boldsymbol{Y} \leftarrow \mathit{softmax}(H^{i'} \boldsymbol{l}_{\text{head}}^T)$
  for each prediction $\hat{\boldsymbol{y}}_k \in \hat{Y}$ **do**
    $\mathrm{L}(\boldsymbol{y}_k, \hat{\boldsymbol{y}}_k) \leftarrow -\sum_{c=1}^{C} \boldsymbol{y}_{k,c} \log(\hat{\boldsymbol{y}}_{k,c})$
  end for
  $\mathcal{L} \leftarrow \frac{1}{N} \sum_{k=0}^{N} \mathrm{L}(\boldsymbol{y}_k, \hat{\boldsymbol{y}}_k)$
  Update $\boldsymbol{l}, \alpha, \boldsymbol{l}_{\text{head}}, \theta$ based on $\nabla\mathcal{L}$.
end for
return Adjacency matrix $\boldsymbol{A}^I$, trained GNN_θ

$\hat{y}$ this probability distribution. Furthermore, we set our true labels as $Y = \{y_0, \ldots, y_m\}$ where $y_j = \{e_{\text{activity}_{j,0+1}}, \ldots, e_{\text{activity}_{j,n+1}}\}$ for $j \in 0..m$. That is, for each input event $e_{j,p}$, the algorithm tries to predict the following activity type $e_{\text{activity}_{j,p+1}}$.[1] The cross-entropy loss between the predicted activity categories $\hat{y}$ and the ground truth y becomes the objective function for learning the model's parameters.

Output. In the context-learning module, a feature vector is generated for each event a user performs on a specific day. This vector captures the context from previous events, such as their position, the hour, and the sequence in which they occurred. Although one could directly use the cross-entropy scores for each event as an anomaly indicator, the detection capability is significantly improved by also using the graph learning module (see Sect. 4). Therefore, the algorithm generates an enriched event representation matrix, $\boldsymbol{H}^{I'}$, as its output.

3.2 Graph Learning Module

The first module converts audit data events into feature vectors that capture user behaviours. Given the pretext task, these event representations capture user-specific patterns, such as common event sequences, which help predict the next event. However, this algorithm disregards events outside a specific time window when forming an event's representation. This allows it to concentrate on a

[1] Note that, by shifting our labels, a starting event has to be added to each sequence to predict for the first event. We omit this detail in the algorithm for simplicity.

smaller, more relevant sequence of events for the pretext task without saturating the events' representations by considering, for example, all user-generated events. Nonetheless, one may wish to consider some relevant events outside a fixed period when calculating an event's context. For example, the context of reading a file might appropriately include its last modification or creation, regardless of when those occurred. These relationships could be modelled using a causal graph as proposed by Liu, Wen et al. [14], with graph $\boldsymbol{\mathcal{G}} = \{\mathcal{V}, \boldsymbol{A}\}$, where the set of nodes $\mathcal{V}$ represents the audit data events, and $\boldsymbol{A}$ is the adjacency matrix indicating the relevant neighbour events to include in the event's context. However, the proposed framework by Liu, Wen et al. relies solely on rules to generate a static graph; It cannot learn or unlearn edges. Furthermore, the user's behaviour during those events is not taken into account.

To address the previous limitations, we propose Algorithm 2, which builds on behaviour-based event representations generated by Algorithm 1 to automatically learn a graph structure for each user, leveraging behavioural information from events and known simple event dependencies. Broadly, the algorithm initially considers the log entries of a specific user as part of a zero-degree graph for which new relations are discovered. In this graph, each of the N total events from a specific user's audit data is represented as a node with no neighbours. To discover new relations, an edge predictor assesses the similarity between the initial node representations, which encode behavioural features, and then weights the similarity scores based on whether a pair of nodes satisfies a known dependency. To enable the algorithm to learn relevant dependencies, we use a custom graph attention neural network that iteratively computes enriched event representations from an evolving adjacency matrix. Similar to Algorithm 1, this neural network is trained to predict the event category of each node, using only the aggregated features of its neighbours.

We aim to infer edges connecting nodes with similar behavioural features and/or respect known dependencies. A motivating example is an employee who conducts a data exfiltration attack over several months. This employee may behave normally for many days but occasionally gathers confidential data into a file, resulting in file-write activities, and then emails the file. Linking file-write operations solely based on this known dependency would generate many edges, thus complicating the detection of malicious events. However, by also comparing the context of these operations, only the events that occurred respecting the same user-based behaviour should be linked. In other words, edges would connect nodes representing file-write events that show the normal behaviour of the employee, and edges would also connect file-write operations that occur in the same unusual setting, suggesting malicious behaviour by the employee. Based on our suggested pretext task, we expect that this group of linked nodes exhibiting atypical behaviour features will be flagged as malicious.

The algorithm is explained in more detail below.

Inputs. The algorithm requires an adjacency matrix $\mathbf{DEP}^0 \in \{0,1\}^{N \times N}$ which indicates the presence of a predefined dependency between two events by the value one or the absence of known dependencies with the value zero. We present simple, widely applicable dependencies in Sect. 4. This algorithm also requires a set of nodes $\mathcal{V} = \{e_0, e_1 \ldots, e_N\}$ representing all events, along with their behaviour-based representations, denoted by $\boldsymbol{H}^0$. In this work, it is initialized as $\boldsymbol{H}^I$ from Algorithm 1, but the proposed algorithm could work with other initial node representations. Finally, an edge threshold τ has to be specified. Some automated configurations of this threshold are suggested in Sect. 4.

Lines 3–15. In addition to the model's weight initialization, we aim to generate an adjacency matrix. That is, for each epoch i, we first update the dependency matrix using the parameter α_i. Note that $\mathbf{DEP}^0$ is used regardless of the current epoch. Thus, the result of $\alpha_i \mathbf{DEP}^0 + 1$ produces a $N \times N$ matrix where the value one indicates the absence of dependency between two nodes, and $\alpha_i + 1$ indicates the presence of a dependency. Then, the initial node representations $\boldsymbol{H}^0$ are projected through a learnable neural network layer. This step is essential to allow the algorithm to learn or forget new edges during training. Finally, we iterate over each node pair, verifying whether the similarity score, calculated as the dot product of their representations multiplied by the dependency matrix, exceeds the edge threshold τ. Thus, each epoch's complexity is $O(N^2)$, which could be computationally expensive.

Note that because $\mathbf{DEP}^i$ contains either one or $\alpha_i + 1$ values, only pairs of nodes that respect a dependency will have their similarity scores affected. Furthermore, it is important to note that the presence of known dependencies between two nodes does not guarantee an edge in the learned graph, as opposed to rule-based methods.

Lines 16–21. The second step uses a graph neural network to compute feature vectors for each node. It is during this step that single-node features, containing more behaviour-focused features, are combined with a neighbourhood of nodes, thus integrating dependency features. To enable the adjustment of the model's parameters for learning an efficient graph structure and neighbourhood feature aggregation, we propose a pretext task that involves predicting a node's event category based on its enriched representation. Note that the adjacency matrix diagonal is set to zero; therefore, each node's enriched representation does not include its own initial event representation. Similarly to Algorithm 1, a neural network layer $\boldsymbol{l}_{head}$ is used to project the node representation into a feature space of size C (i.e., the number of possible events), and the gradients are based on the cross-entropy loss. The latter penalizes incorrect predictions based on their probabilities rather than solely on their accuracy. This is relevant because not only can multiple events be regular in similar contexts, but a particular event can also be more suspicious than others.

Output. The algorithm outputs the learned graph structure through the adjacency matrix of the final iteration $\boldsymbol{A}^I$, and all the learned parameter values.

3.3 Insider Threat Detection Module

Having a graph structure and behaviour-based node representations $\boldsymbol{H}^0$, one can use any graph neural network to compute node representations that capture both pattern-based and dependency-based features. These improved events' representations can be used with different anomaly detection algorithms. However, to streamline the process, we use the same graph neural network with the parameters learned during the execution of Algorithm 2 and directly apply the event-based cross-entropy loss as our anomaly indicator. Assuming the model has learned to predict an event effectively from its context, we interpret a high loss for an event as indicating that the event's context conflicts with the actual event, signalling a potential threat. As with most anomaly detection algorithms, we set a threshold to distinguish between malicious and normal instances.

4 Implementation and Results

Dataset. We base our experiments on Carnegie Mellon's Software Engineering Institute [12] CERT insider threat dataset version 6.2 [7]. This specialized dataset includes audit data from a synthetic organization of 4000 employees whose behaviour were simulated over 516 days. The audit data are divided into eleven activity categories: user logon and logoff activities, website access and downloads, email transmission, file writing, copying, deleting, and opening, as well as the connection and disconnection of a USB device on a host. Each log entry provides specific details about the events that occurred, such as the destination email address or the name of the accessed file. Although some of the proposed rules for creating the dependency matrix use these details, most of the framework relies solely on the activity categories, execution time, position, and the user who carried out the events. As this information requires little domain expertise and effort to extract, we argue that our method can be deployed in any organization. From the 4000 users in the CERT dataset, six perform an insider attack at some point during the period. To compare our method with state-of-the-art methods, we will evaluate the performance of our models based solely on these six malicious employees, over the time period used in [14]. However, unlike some of the state-of-the-art approaches, our framework does not require data balancing, data augmentation, or one-class training. In other words, the suggested approach relies solely on unsupervised learning.

Rules. To construct the dependency matrix $\mathbf{DEP}^0$, which assists our graph learning framework in discovering new relationships, we elaborated the following rules in order to make them simple and compatible for any organization.

`Rule 1.` Edge existence depicting website activity on the same domain.
`Rule 2.` Edge existence between any nodes depicting the same file activity.
`Rule 3.` Edge existence between a node depicting any connection of a USB device with the node depicting its subsequent disconnection.

If any of the preceding rules applies between two nodes, the value one is inserted into the dependency matrix at the corresponding index, regardless of the specific rule number. Although the preceding rules are simple, the forthcoming experiments show that they significantly improve the insider threats detection.

Table 1. Results comparison

Method	Reference	AUC
Log2Vec	[14]	86%
Log2Vec++	[14]	93%
TGNN	[27]	94.38%
CDHGN	[14]	96.20%
Proposed	NA	**97.17%**

Table 2. User-based results comparison

User Id	Log2Vec	Log2Vec++	Proposed
ACM2278	99%	**100%**	**100%**
CMP2946	77%	83%	**87%**
HIS1706	87%	97%	**98%**
PLJ1771	63%	83%	**98%**
CDE1846	92%	92%	**100%**
MBG3183	99%	**100%**	**100%**

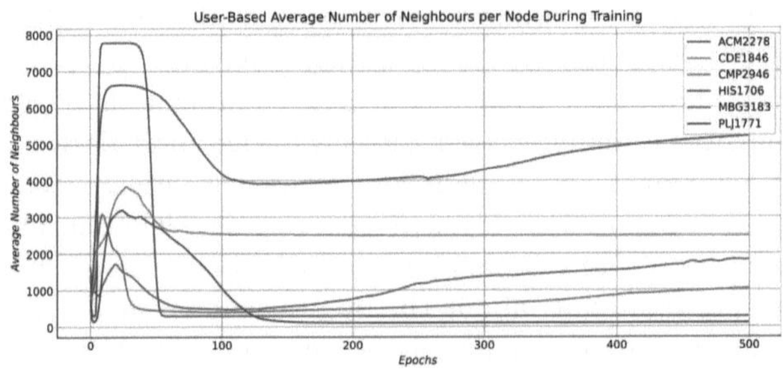

Fig. 2. User-based average number of neighbours per node during training.

Implementation. The method was developed using Python along the *Pytorch* deep learning framework [20]. Our approach depends on two algorithms, each having a unique set of hyperparameters. For Algorithm 1, we used the same set of hyperparameters as in our previous work [4]. For Algorithm 2, we performed Bayesian optimization using the *Optuna* library [1], based on the pretext task to identify optimal hyperparameters for both the threshold τ and the dependency initial weight α_0. Note that, to improve the method's flexibility, we set the threshold $\tau = \mu + \beta\sigma$ to match the mean similarity score of all node pairs at the first epoch (μ), plus a factor β of their standard deviation (σ). Therefore, this factor β is the actual hyperparameter. The other hyperparameters and the optimization function are those used in Algorithm 1. For the GNN, we chose a graph attention network that we adapted from Veličković et al.'s implementation [25]. This graph attention network requires loading all representations of all events simultaneously ($\boldsymbol{H}$ matrix). Other graph neural network architectures could be explored to mitigate the memory requirements. The algorithm runtime is approximately 30 min per user on a machine equipped with an Intel i9-13900 processor, a NVIDIA RTX 4500 graphics card and 64 GB of RAM.

Results Comparison. Let us compare the performance of our approach in detecting insider threats with state-of-the-art methods that base their experiments on the CERT version 6.2 dataset using unsupervised machine learning

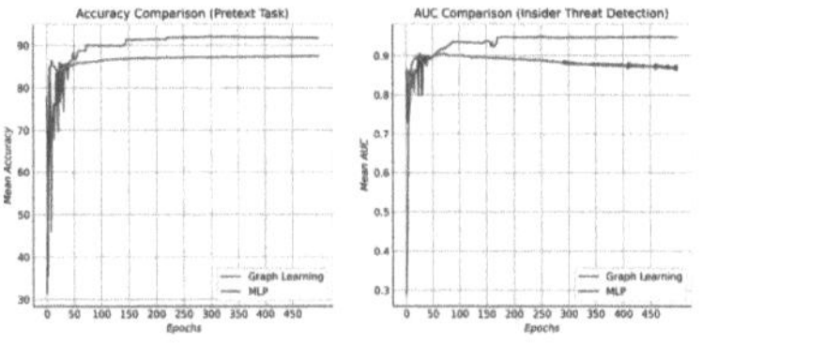

Fig. 3. Our approach vs Algorithm 1 only.

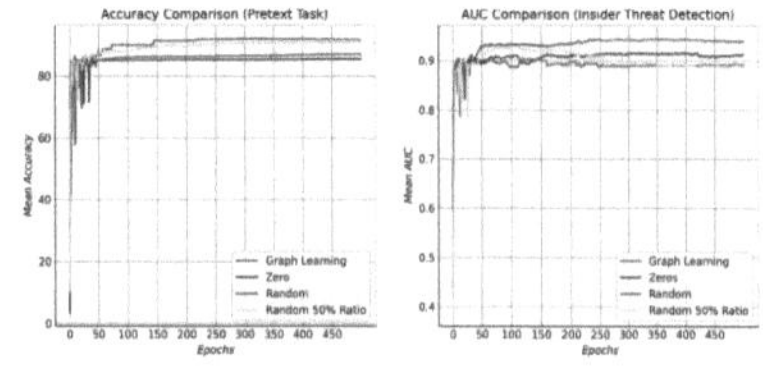

Fig. 4. Effect of dependency choices.

algorithms. To assess the model's overall performance, we use the area under the receiver operating characteristic curve (AUC) metric, as used in the selected papers. Having a user-based model, the overall AUC of the method equals the mean AUC of each user, as calculated in the baseline papers.

As shown in Table 1, the proposed approach outperforms state-of-the-art techniques. This shows that the model's overall performance, regardless of the chosen threshold, exceeds that of the compared methods. Those results are interesting because they were obtained without using one-class training with no data balancing or data augmentation necessary. From the presented papers, only the Log2Vec variants were trained with the same restrictions. Furthermore, Table 2 presents a user-based performance comparison with the Log2Vec approach [14].

Relevance of the Graph Learning Framework. Although the proposed method outperforms state-of-the-art approaches, one can ask to what extent this is attributable to the graph learning framework. Remember that Algorithm 1 alone is effective for insider threat detection [4]. We thus compare the performances of Algorithm 1 directly with our proposed method that combines Algorithms 1 and 2. Note that to perform insider threat detection with Algorithm 1, it is necessary to apply an anomaly detection algorithm to the generated feature vectors. Thus, a neural network layer is added and trained to predict the events category based on its representation as in Algorithm 2. Figure 3 compares the performance of the proposed approach, denoted Graph Learning, with the method based solely on Algorithm 1, referred to as *MLP* for Multi-Layer Perceptron. Both the pretext task, assessed by the average accuracy of the six malicious users, and their performance on the insider threat detection task, measured with the mean AUC metric across each learning epoch, are shown. First, we see a correlation between the pretext task and the insider threat detection task. This supports our intuition regarding the relevance of using this particular pretext task. Second, our new graph learning algorithm generally outperforms Algorithm 1's method on both tasks. Finally, although both algorithms show increasing accuracy during training, Algorithm 1 exhibits a decreasing (AUC), indicating overfitting. This suggests that the graph learning framework of Algorithm 2 enhances the model's ability to detect insider threats.

Furthermore, it is worth questioning whether the graph learning module actually learns a new graph structure during training, i.e., whether the learned graph in the first epoch differs from the one in the last epoch. Figure 2 evaluates this by showing the average number of neighbours per node for each user during training. We clearly see that the graph learning module genuinely learns a different graph structure than the one computed in the first epochs. However, we also observe that, for most users, a large number of edges are first eliminated, followed by the learning of new ones. This suggests that the proposed edge predictor, based on the similarity of the nodes' representations and the known dependencies, may not be optimal. This could be studied in future work.

Relevance of the Selected Rules. The above analysis shows that the proposed graph neural network is beneficial for detecting insider threats. However, we also observe that the graph learning module generally suppresses many edges early in training. This raises the question about the relevance of the selected rules to the graph construction. To evaluate that, we propose modifying the dependency matrix $\mathbf{DEP}^0$ to observe its impact on the algorithm's ability to detect insider threats. We first propose setting all matrix entries to zero, so that when calculating the adjacency matrix in Algorithm 2, only node similarity is considered. Note that setting all entries to one should yield the same results. Then, we propose to randomly fill this matrix with one value each, respecting the original ratio for every user. Finally we propose to randomly fill this matrix with one value following a 50% ratio. The results of this experiment are shown in Fig. 4. We see that the configuration using the suggested rules outperforms the others. An interesting observation is that although the random initialization with a 50% ratio is close to the configuration using the proposed rules in terms of performance in the pretext class, it quickly falls behind in the insider threat detection task. This indicates that while the pretext task is correlated with the insider threat detection task, it is not perfect. Therefore, this also suggests that although both configurations achieve similar results in predicting an event based on its context, the particular set of suggested rules links abnormal nodes together, which makes it harder for the models to predict these specific nodes. This aligns with the desired behaviour of the method.

5 Conclusion

We proposed an unsupervised insider threat detection system based on a novel graph learning framework to model complex event dependencies. Our approach mainly consists of three modules. The first one uses our previously proposed sequential neural network to learn daily based user-specific patterns and encapsulate that information into an event-based feature vector. The second module builds upon these feature vectors to learn a graph structure from the events, modeling both dependency-based and behaviour-based relationships. Finally, the last module leverages the previously learned graph structure to generate rich event feature vectors that facilitate threat detection. The proposed framework seeks to minimize reliance on domain-specific expertise by depending exclusively on audit data characteristics that should be accessible to any organization. Furthermore, it requires no prior knowledge of past threats because it employs transductive inference. This also means that the approach does not depend on one-class training, data balancing, or data augmentation. Nevertheless, our method outperforms other state-of-the-art approaches. Future work could improve the computational and memory efficiency of our algorithms, which currently rely on nested loops over each audit data event and a large embedding matrix for the GNN component.

References

1. Akiba, T., Sano, S., Yanase, T., Ohta, T., Koyama, M.: Optuna: a next-generation hyperparameter optimization framework. In: Proceedings of the International Conference on Knowledge Discovery & Data Mining, KDD (2019)
2. Al Tabash, K., Happa, J.: Insider-threat detection using gaussian mixture models and sensitivity profiles. Comput. Secur. **77** (2018)
3. Bertrand, S., Desharnais, J., Tawbi, N.: Unsupervised user-based insider threat detection using bayesian gaussian mixture models. In: International Conference on Privacy, Security and Trust, PST (2023)
4. Bertrand, S., Germain, P., Tawbi, N.: Unsupervised insider threat detection using multi-head self-attention mechanisms. In: Intelligent Cybersecurity Conference (2024)
5. Bin Sarhan, B., Altwaijry, N.: Insider threat detection using machine learning approach. Appl. Sci. **13**(1) (2023)
6. Cai, X., et al.: Lan: learning adaptive neighbors for real-time insider threat detection (2024)
7. CERT: Insider threat test dataset (2016). https://resources.sei.cmu.edu/library/asset-view.cfm?assetid=508099
8. Chen, Y., Nyemba, S., Malin, B.: Detecting anomalous insiders in collaborative information systems. IEEE Trans. Dependable Secure Comput. **9**(3), 332–344 (2012)
9. Eldardiry, H., Bart, E., Liu, J., Hanley, J., Price, B., Brdiczka, O.: Multi-domain information fusion for insider threat detection. In: IEEE Security and Privacy Workshops (2013)
10. Gao, P., et al.: Detecting unknown threat based on continuous-time dynamic heterogeneous graph network. Wirel. Commun. Mob. Comput. **2022**(1) (2022)
11. Gavai, G., Sricharan, K., Gunning, D., Hanley, J., Singhal, M., Rolleston, R.J.: Supervised and unsupervised methods to detect insider threat from enterprise social and online activity data. J. Wirel. Mob. Networks Ubiquitous Comput. Dependable Appl **6**, 47–63 (2015)
12. Glasser, J., Lindauer, B.: Bridging the gap: a pragmatic approach to generating insider threat data. In: IEEE Security and Privacy Workshops (2013)
13. Kim, J., Park, M., Kim, H., Cho, S., Kang, P.: Insider threat detection based on user behavior modeling and anomaly detection algorithms. Appl. Sci. **9**(19) (2019)
14. Liu, F., Wen, Y., Zhang, D., Jiang, X., Xing, X., Meng, D.: Log2vec: a heterogeneous graph embedding based approach for detecting cyber threats within enterprise. In: SIGSAC Conference on Computer and Communications Security (2019)

15. Liu, L., Chen, C., Zhang, J., De Vel, O., Xiang, Y.: Unsupervised insider detection through neural feature learning and model optimisation. In: Liu, J.K., Huang, X. (eds.) Network and System Security (2019)
16. Liu, W., et al.: Trace2vec: detecting complex multi-step attacks with explainable graph neural network. Pattern Recogn. **162**, 111363 (2025)
17. Mikolov, T., Chen, K., Corrado, G.S., Dean, J.: Efficient estimation of word representations in vector space. In: International Conference on Learning Representations (2013)
18. Naseem, U., Razzak, I., Khan, S.K., Prasad, M.: A comprehensive survey on word representation models: From classical to state-of-the-art word representation language models. ACM Trans. Asian Low-Res. Lang. Inf. Process. **20**(5) (2021)
19. Nasir, R., Afzal, M., Latif, R., Iqabl, W.: Behavioral based insider threat detection using deep learning. IEEE Access (2021)
20. Paszke, A., et al.: Pytorch: an imperative style, high-performance deep learning library (2019)
21. Rashid, T., Agrafiotis, I., Nurse, J.R.: A new take on detecting insider threats: exploring the use of hidden Markov models. In: ACM CCS International Workshop on Managing Insider Security Threats (2016)
22. Rumelhart, D.E., Hinton, G.E., Williams, R.J.: Learning internal representations by error propagation, pp. 318–362. MIT Press, Cambridge (1986)
23. Sharma, B., Pokharel, P., Joshi, B.: User behavior analytics for anomaly detection using LSTM autoencoder - insider threat detection. In: International Conference on Advances in Information Technology, IAIT2020 (2020)
24. Vaswani, A., et al.: Attention is all you need. In: Advances in Neural Information Processing Systems (2017)
25. Veličković, P., Cucurull, G., Casanova, A., Romero, A., Liò, P., Bengio, Y.: Graph attention networks. In: International Conference on Learning Representations (2018)
26. Wang, Z.Q., El Saddik, A.: Dtitd: an intelligent insider threat detection framework based on digital twin and self-attention based deep learning models. IEEE Access **11**, 114013–114030 (2023)
27. Xia, W., et al.: Explaining temporal graph models through an explorer-navigator framework. In: International Conference on Learning Representations (2023)
28. Zhang, Z., Wang, S., Lu, G.: An internal threat detection model based on denoising autoencoders. In: Pan, J.S., Li, J., Tsai, P.W., Jain, L.C. (eds.) Advances in Intelligent Information Hiding and Multimedia Signal Processing (2020)

Feature-Selective Representation Misdirection for Machine Unlearning

Taozhao Chen[1(✉)], Linghan Huang[1], Kim-Kwang Raymond Choo[2], and Huaming Chen[1]

[1] University of Sydney, Sydney, NSW, Australia
{tche8294,lhua5130}@uni.sydney.edu.au, huaming.chen@sydney.edu.au
[2] University of Texas at San Antonio, San Antonio, TX, USA
raymond.choo@fulbrightmail.org

Abstract. As large language models (LLMs) are increasingly adopted in safety-critical and regulated sectors, the retention of sensitive or prohibited knowledge introduces escalating risks, ranging from privacy leakage to regulatory non-compliance and malicious misuse. Recent studies suggest that machine unlearning can help ensure deployed models comply with evolving legal, safety, and governance requirements. However, current unlearning techniques assume clean separation between forget and retain datasets, which is challenging in operational settings characterized by highly entangled distributions. In such scenarios, perturbation-based methods often degrade general model utility or fail to ensure safety. To address this, we propose Selective Representation Misdirection for Unlearning (SRMU), a novel principled activation-editing framework that enforces feature-aware and directionally controlled perturbations. Unlike indiscriminate model weights perturbations, SRMU employs a structured misdirection vector with an activation importance map. The goal is to allow SRMU selectively suppresses harmful representations while preserving the utility on benign ones. Experiments are conducted on the widely used WMDP benchmark across low- and high-entanglement configurations. Empirical results reveal that SRMU delivers state-of-the-art unlearning performance with minimal utility loss, and remains effective under 20–30% overlap where existing baselines collapse. SRMU provides a robust foundation for safety-driven model governance, privacy compliance, and controlled knowledge removal in the emerging LLM-based applications. We release the replication package at https://figshare.com/s/d5931192a8824de26aff.

Keywords: Machine Unlearning · Large Language Model · Model Security

1 Introduction

The rapid evolution of Large Language Models (LLMs), such as GPT and Gemini, has revealed a paradigm shift in natural language processing, driving widespread deployment across different application domains. However, the

© IFIP International Federation for Information Processing 2026
Published by Springer Nature Switzerland AG 2026
H. Janicke et al. (Eds.): SEC 2026, IFIP AICT 787, pp. 33–46, 2026.
https://doi.org/10.1007/978-3-032-27993-4_3

mechanisms that underpin their success, such as deep memorization and generative capabilities, simultaneously introduce substantial security and privacy risks [11]. Due to the scale and limited controllability of their training corpora, LLMs inevitably encode and retain sensitive, private, copyright-protected, even harmful information [19]. Consequently, enabling a model to selectively remove the influence of specific training data without retraining from scratch, a process known as Machine Unlearning (MU), has emerged as a critical challenge for ensuring security and privacy in modern AI systems [12,15,17].

Approximate MU methods (shown in Table 1), including gradient ascent based unlearning [7,23], distillation based scrubbing [2,20], and perturbation driven approaches [5,10], aim to revoke the effects of targeted training data without retraining [4,22]. Among these, a group of MU methods based on controlling model representations has emerged due to its computational efficiency. For instance, Representation Misdirection for Unlearning (RMU) removes harmful knowledge by injecting global random perturbations into latent model representations [10]. Yet, they share a fundamental weakness, which assumes a clean separation between forget and retain samples in the model representation space.

In practice, LLMs exhibit high knowledge entanglement, where harmful and benign concepts sharing critical feature dimensions. It results in substantial overlap between forget and retain representations, further induces limitations for existing methods. Methods such as Gradient Ascent (GA) [23] and Negative Preference Optimization (NPO) [24] attempt to increase the loss on forget samples while decreasing it on retain samples. Under high entanglement, shared tokens appear in both forget and retain samples, yielding conflicting gradient updates. Consequently, it leads to severe deterioration in general capability performance where harmful output cannot be suppressed. Similarly, representation level approaches, including RMU [10] and Adaptive RMU [5], utilize perturbation which is neither feature selective nor gradient direction aware. By shifting both harmful and benign feature representations in an indiscriminate way, even moderate overlap can trigger uncontrolled semantic drift and unstable utility.

In this work, we present **Selective Representation Misdirection for Unlearning (SRMU)**, a representation level unlearning framework designed to address the fundamental limitations of existing perturbation based methods. SRMU integrates a *Dynamic Importance Map* to identify feature dimensions associated with target knowledge and a *Directional Misdirection Vector* to enable controlled semantic displacement within the representation space. Experiments on the WMDP benchmark show that SRMU outperforms other state-of-the-art methods across different evaluated settings. Furthermore, SRMU remains effective under high entanglement settings where prior perturbation based approaches fail. The main contributions of this work are summarized as follows:

- **Failure Mode Analysis of Approximate Unlearning.** We systematically investigate the reasons that existing MU methods fail under high entanglement scenarios, identifying the lack of feature selectivity as the root cause of utility degradation and unstable forgetting performance.

Table 1. A comparative summary of representative Machine Unlearning (MU) methods (Note: Existing approaches differ in intervention level and robustness under high entanglement, highlighting the need for feature-selective unlearning mechanisms)

Method	Intervention Level	Core Mechanism	Feature Selective	High-Ent. Robust
GA [23]	Logit	Gradient ascent	×	Low
NPO [24]	Logit	Preference optimization	×	Medium
UNDIAL [2]	Logit	Token-level adjusted-logit distillation	×	Low
RKLU [20]	Logit	Token-level selective distillation	×	Medium
DEPN [21]	Neuron	Neuron editing	Partial	Low
RMU [10]	Representation	Random perturbation	×	Medium
Adaptive RMU [5]	Representation	Random perturbation	×	Medium
SRMU (Ours)	Representation	Feature-selective Directional perturbation	✓	**High**

- **Feature-Selective Unlearning Framework.** We propose *Selective Representation Misdirection for Unlearning (SRMU)*, a representation-level framework that isolates knowledge-related feature subspaces through importance-aware masking and directionally constrained perturbations.
- **Empirical Trade off Improvement.** By coupling precise activation suppression on target knowledge with limited interference on benign representations, SRMU significantly advances the balance between effective forgetting and utility preservation outperforming existing unlearning approaches.
- **Robustness under High Entanglement Settings.** Extensive evaluation on WMDP benchmark show that SRMU maintains robust performance even in scenarios that forget and retain knowledge are highly entangled, where state-of-the-art approximate methods fail to converge.

2 Related Work

MU tackles a fundamental problem in machine learning model security and privacy by enabling the selective removal of the influence of specific training data from trained models, while avoiding the substantial computational overhead associated with full retraining [9,16]. Since its formalization by Cao and Yang [1], MU has evolved from a niche privacy technique into a fundamental paradigm for model maintenance, marking a shift from traditional knowledge accumulation to targeted, active forgetting [15]. While early taxonomies categorized MU strategies into various types such as localized parameter modification or input-based filtering [4], for modern Large Language Models (LLMs), the research landscape is predominantly divided into Exact Unlearning and Approximate Unlearning.

The former provides strong theoretical guarantees but is computationally infeasible for large-scale models, whereas the latter encompasses representation-based approaches that emphasize computational efficiency and utility preservation, which this work builds upon.

Unlearning Techniques and Architectures. Existing MU methods for large language models can be broadly categorized by the level at which the intervention is applied. Logit-level unlearning methods modify the training objective to suppress undesirable behaviors, including gradient-ascent-based approaches and reinforcement learning formulations such as Quark [13]. These methods increase the loss on forget samples while preserving performance on normal data, and are most effective when forget and retain signals induce sufficiently distinct gradient directions. Neuron-level approaches instead assume that specific knowledge is localized within a small subset of neurons. Representative methods such as DEPN [21] identify and edit so-called privacy neurons to remove memorized information, offering strong locality and interpretability under this localization assumption. In addition, auxiliary-model-based strategies, such as task arithmetic [6], manipulate model behavior through vector operations in weight space without explicitly isolating knowledge representations.

Representation-level unlearning has emerged as a particularly efficient and scalable paradigm. Rather than modifying output distributions or individual neurons, these methods intervene on intermediate activations to induce forgetting with minimal parameter updates. Representation Misdirection for Unlearning (RMU) [10] exemplifies this line of work by applying controlled perturbations to hidden activations within a localized window of MLP layers. Concretely, RMU updates the target layer activations as

$$M_{\text{updated}}(t) = M_{\text{frozen}}(t) + c \cdot \mathbf{u}, \tag{1}$$

where $M_{\text{frozen}}(t)$ denotes the frozen reference activation, $\mathbf{u}$ is a randomly sampled perturbation direction, and c controls the perturbation magnitude. By restricting parameter updates to a single layer while perturbing a short layer window, RMU achieves computational efficiency and scalability. Subsequent analysis by Dang et al. [5] identified optimization instability in deeper layers and proposed Adaptive RMU, which dynamically rescales c based on activation norms to improve training stability. Although existing representation-level approaches are efficient, they rely on unstructured, feature-agnostic perturbations, highlighting the need for selective and feature-aware modulation to control knowledge encoded in overlapping representation subspaces.

Benchmark and Evaluation Metrics. Evaluating the effectiveness of unlearning in LLMs requires rigorous benchmarks tailored to specific unlearning scenarios. Existing datasets typically focus on distinct application domains. TOFU [14] targets the removal of synthetic identity information for privacy protection, while WHP (Who's Harry Potter) [3] addresses the erasure of copyrighted content within specific semantic themes. In addition, MUSE [18] and RWKU [8] provide evaluation frameworks for unlearning in real world news and encyclopedic contexts. For safety critical hazardous knowledge, the Weapons of Mass Destruction Proxy (WMDP) Benchmark [10] serves as a specialized standard. Unlike privacy or copyright focused datasets, WMDP is designed to assess a model's ability to forget domain specific factual knowledge in high risk areas such as biology (*WMDP Bio*) and cyber security (*WMDP Cyber*). Due to its emphasis on disentangling hazardous knowledge from general reasoning capabilities, WMDP is selected as the primary testbed for our experiments to evaluate the *semantic selectivity* of the proposed SRMU framework.

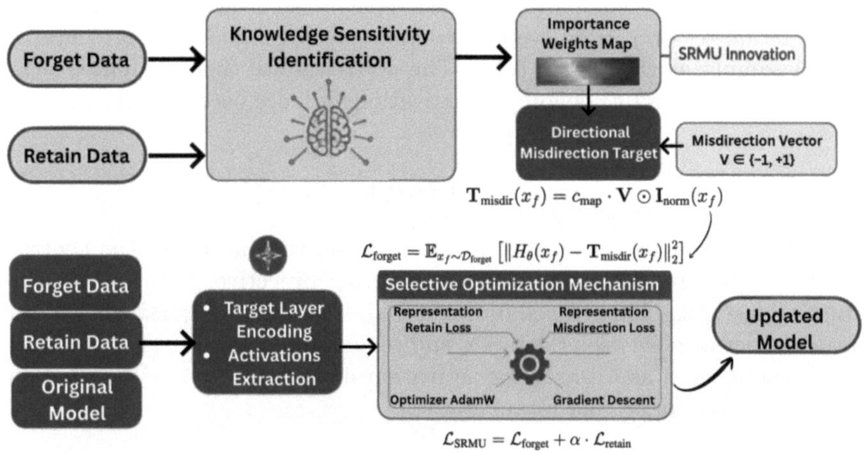

Fig. 1. Overview of the proposed SRMU framework for target unlearning.

3 Methodology

Our proposed *Selective Representation Misdirection for Unlearning* (SRMU) is shown in Fig. 1. Instead of using unstructured perturbations, we present a novel solution for selective and feature aware modulation. SRMU aims to remove the influence of a *forget dataset* $\mathcal{D}_{\text{forget}}$ while preserving model behavior on a *retain dataset* $\mathcal{D}_{\text{retain}}$ through targeted intervention on intermediate representations. We define M_{frozen} as the pretrained model and $H_\theta(x)$ as the activation output at a designated multilayer perceptron (MLP) layer. During unlearning process, activations from the MLP layer are used to compute forgetting and retention losses. Only the parameters of the target layer are updated to minimise our unlearning objective, while all other layers remain frozen.

3.1 Feature Aware Representation Misdirection

The SRMU framework extends RMU via three key components, as explained in the following subsections. First, perturbations are modeled in a feature aware manner, ensuring that interventions are guided by the semantic relevance of internal representations. Second, dynamic importance maps are constructed to identify feature dimensions most strongly associated with the target knowledge. Third, a selective optimization mechanism is applied to constrain updates to high importance regions, thereby minimizing interference with unrelated capabilities.

3.2 Dynamic Importance Map Construction

The importance weights I are not fixed parameters but are dynamically computed based on the input samples. To quantify feature level relevance, SRMU extracts intermediate feature representations and constructs a **Dynamic Importance Map** by comparing activation patterns between the forget set (v_f) and the retain set (v_r). Here, we first compute averaged hidden representations for each sample at the target layer. The statistics are then computed across samples, where v_f and v_r denote the activation variance over mini-batches sampled from $\mathcal{D}_{\text{forget}}$ and $\mathcal{D}_{\text{retain}}$, respectively:

$$I = \phi(v_f, v_r), \tag{2}$$

where $\phi(\cdot)$ denotes an importance fusion function that measures the contribution of each feature dimension to the forgetting objective. We consider three instantiations of the importance function $\phi(\cdot)$, each capturing a distinct notion of feature relevance between the forget and retain sets. Intuitively, feature importance is interpreted as a proxy for activation discrepancy under distributional shift between the forget and retain statistics.

- **SRMU Ratio based:**

$$I_{\text{ratio}} = \log\left(1 + \frac{v_f}{v_r + \epsilon}\right)$$

  This formulation emphasizes feature dimensions where forgetting activations dominate retention signals. Logarithmic scaling mitigates extreme activation ratios and prevents a small number of highly skewed dimensions from dominating the importance map, thereby improving numerical stability and ensuring smoother importance distribution.
- **SRMU Difference based:**

$$I_{\text{diff}} = \text{ReLU}(v_f - \lambda v_r)$$

  This strategy isolates features that are highly activated for the forget set but suppressed for the retain set, resulting in a sparse and selective importance map.
- **SRMU Product based:**

$$I_{\text{prod}} = \frac{v_f \odot v_r}{\text{mean}(v_f) \cdot \text{mean}(v_r) + \epsilon}$$

  This formulation highlights dimensions that are simultaneously activated by both sets, explicitly identifying entangled features that require cautious and controlled perturbation.

The resulting importance map reflects the extent to which each representation dimension contributes to the target forgetting process. To ensure stability and comparability when integrating with the Directional Misdirection Vector $\mathbf{V}$, the importance map I is normalized across all feature dimensions:

$$I_{\text{norm}} = \frac{I}{\max(I) + \epsilon_{\text{norm}}}, \tag{3}$$

where $\epsilon_{\text{norm}} = 10^{-8}$ prevents division by zero. This normalization scales importance values to the range $[0, 1]$, enabling consistent control via the coefficient c_{map} in subsequent optimization.

3.3 Directional Misdirection Vector (V) Generation

The **Directional Misdirection Vector** ($\mathbf{V}$) is introduced to address the non selective and direction agnostic nature of the original RMU approach. In RMU, the perturbation direction u is sampled as a purely random unit vector, providing no explicit semantic control. To overcome this limitation, SRMU redefines the perturbation direction as the Directional Misdirection Vector $\mathbf{V}$. Specifically, $\mathbf{V}$ is constructed as a discrete, high dimensional vector:

$$\mathbf{V} \in \{-1, +1\}^d,$$

where each element is sampled independently. This design enables controlled semantic deviation by enforcing a consistent polarity for each feature dimension, thereby defining a structured trajectory away from the original knowledge encoding. Compared to continuous random directions, this discrete formulation provides stable and interpretable directional control, as validated in our ablation study.

3.4 Final Loss Function of SRMU

SRMU jointly enforces targeted forgetting and representation preservation through a two term objective. For a forget sample x_f, we define a *Directional Misdirection Target* that specifies the desired activation state along selected feature dimensions:

$$T_{\text{misdir}}(x_f) = c_{\text{map}} \cdot \mathbf{V} \odot I_{\text{norm}}(x_f), \tag{4}$$

where $I_{\text{norm}}(x_f)$ denotes the normalized importance map and $\mathbf{V}$ is the directional misdirection vector. This target defines a feature wise displacement that the updated representation is encouraged to follow.

The final optimization objective is given by:

$$\begin{aligned} \mathcal{L}_{\text{SRMU}} = {} & \mathbb{E}_{x_f \sim \mathcal{D}_{\text{forget}}} \left[\| H_\theta(x_f) - T_{\text{misdir}}(x_f) \|_2^2 \right] \\ & + \alpha \, \mathbb{E}_{x_r \sim \mathcal{D}_{\text{retain}}} \left[\| H_\theta(x_r) - H_{\theta_0}(x_r) \|_2^2 \right]. \end{aligned} \tag{5}$$

The first term enforces targeted displacement along forget-relevant dimensions, while the second term anchors retain representations to their original states. Here, H_{θ_0} denotes the frozen pretrained model and α controls the trade off between forgetting effectiveness and representation preservation. Minimizing $\mathcal{L}_{\text{SRMU}}$ with respect to the target MLP layer completes the SRMU update.

3.5 Pseudocode and Complexity

Algorithm 1: Selective Representation Misdirection for Unlearning

Input: Updated model $M_{updated}$, frozen model M_{frozen}, forget set $\mathcal{D}_{forget}$, retain set $\mathcal{D}_{retain}$, scaling coefficient c_{map}, retain weight α

Output: Unlearned model $M_{updated}$

Compute importance map I_{norm} from $\mathcal{D}_{forget}$ and $\mathcal{D}_{retain}$

Sample directional vector $\mathbf{V} \in \{-1, +1\}^d$

for $x_f \sim \mathcal{D}_{forget}$, $x_r \sim \mathcal{D}_{retain}$ **do**

  Set misdirection target $T_{misdir} = c_{map} \cdot (\mathbf{V} \odot I_{norm})$

  Set $\mathcal{L}_{forget} = \|M_{updated}(x_f) - T_{misdir}\|_2^2$

  Set $\mathcal{L}_{retain} = \|M_{updated}(x_r) - M_{frozen}(x_r)\|_2^2$

  Update $M_{updated}$ using $\mathcal{L} = \mathcal{L}_{forget} + \alpha \mathcal{L}_{retain}$

return $M_{updated}$

Complexity. SRMU incurs a one time overhead to construct the Dynamic Importance Map $\mathbf{I}_{\text{norm}}$, which is computed prior to optimization. This cost is dominated by forward passes through the target layer l over $\mathcal{D}_{\text{map}} = \mathcal{D}_{\text{forget}} \cup \mathcal{D}_{\text{retain}}$, yielding a complexity of

$$\mathcal{O}(|\mathcal{D}_{\text{map}}| \cdot \mathcal{T}_{\text{forward}}(l)).$$

The subsequent importance fusion and normalization steps involve only element wise operations and incur negligible additional cost.

During unlearning, SRMU performs T optimization steps, each updating only the designated target layers. The per step cost is therefore

$$\mathcal{O}(\mathcal{T}_{\text{forward}}(\mathcal{M}_{\text{target}}) + \mathcal{T}_{\text{backward}}(\mathcal{M}_{\text{target}})),$$

which is substantially lower than full model fine tuning. Considering these factors, SRMU preserves the computational efficiency and scalability of perturbation based machine unlearning methods like RMU.

4 Evaluation

4.1 Experimental Setup

All methods are evaluated on the Zephyr 7B model, following prior work on RMU and Adaptive RMU to ensure fair comparison. Zephyr 7B provides stable access to intermediate MLP representations, which is required for representation level unlearning.

Datasets. For each WMDP domain (Biology and Cybersecurity), we construct a forget set $\mathcal{D}_{\text{forget}}$ and evaluate unlearning under two retain regimes: (i) **Low entanglement**, where the retain set is drawn from WikiText; and (ii) **High entanglement**, where the retain set is drawn from the same domain as $\mathcal{D}_{\text{forget}}$.

In the high entanglement setting, prior analyses [5] report substantial overlap between forget and retain sets. Specifically, the Biology retain set exhibits 20.8% unigram and 5.5% bigram overlap, while the Cybersecurity retain set shows 27.5% unigram and 12.3% bigram overlap. Such overlap indicates that harmful and benign samples activate highly shared regions of the representation space, making selective unlearning more challenging. These two regimes enable evaluation of SRMU under both controlled and adversarial unlearning conditions.

Evaluation Metrics. We evaluate the unlearning utility trade off using two standardized benchmarks:

- **WMDP Accuracy (↓)**: measures the remaining ability to answer hazardous Biology and Cybersecurity questions, where lower accuracy indicates stronger forgetting.
- **MMLU Accuracy (↑)**: measures general language understanding across 57 subjects, where higher accuracy reflects better utility preservation.

Full baseline comparisons (LLMU, SCRUB, SSD) are conducted under the low entanglement regime, while high entanglement experiments focus on perturbation based methods (RMU, Adaptive RMU) and SRMU.

Training. To ensure a fair comparison, SRMU adopts the same optimization configuration utilized in prior studies [5,10]. We use AdamW with a learning rate of 5×10^{-5}, batch size 4, and $T = 150$ unlearning steps. The retain loss weight is set to $\alpha = 1200$, and the RMU perturbation magnitude is fixed at $c = 7.5$, following prior work. For RMU and Adaptive RMU, perturbation budget is selected via grid search over $[1, 170]$ with a step size of 10. SRMU adopts the same procedure to select c_{map}, ensuring comparable perturbation scales across methods. Unless otherwise stated, the sequence length is set to 512 for Biology and 768 for Cybersecurity. We modify layer 7, as prior work reports stronger intervention effects at this layer [5].

Table 2. Comparative performance of SRMU against SOTA baselines on Forgetting (WMDP) and Retention (MMLU).

Method	MMLU (↑)	WMDP-Bio (↓)	WMDP-Cyber (↓)	WMDP Avg (↓)
Original (Zephyr-7B)	58.5	64.7	44.8	54.7
LLMU (Yao et al., 2024)	44.7	59.5	39.5	49.5
SCRUB (Kurmanji et al., 2023)	51.2	43.8	39.3	41.6
SSD (Foster et al., 2024)	40.7	50.2	35.0	42.6
RMU (Li et al., 2024)	56.9	28.8	28.0	28.4
Adaptive RMU (Dang et al., 2025)	55.0	**25.3**	26.7	**26.0**
SRMU (Ours)	**57.1**	28.5	**25.8**	27.2

4.2 Main Results

Reproduction Note. Results for RMU and Adaptive RMU are reproduced on the Zephyr 7B model following the hyperparameter search strategy described in the Experimental Setup, and the best performing results are reported in Table 2. Results for LLMU, SCRUB, and SSD are directly cited from prior work [5].

In the low entanglement setting, SRMU achieves the best overall unlearning utility trade off. It reduces the WMDP average from 54.7% to 27.2%, matching the forgetting strength of Adaptive RMU while preserving higher utility (57.1% MMLU versus 55.0%). Compared with RMU, SRMU improves both forgetting (27.2% versus 28.4%) and retention (57.1% versus 56.9%), indicating that importance aware perturbation mitigates unnecessary drift caused by direction agnostic misdirection. Overall, SRMU defines the Pareto frontier in the low entanglement regime and provides a stable reference for evaluation under more challenging conditions.

4.3 Results Under the High Entanglement Regime

Table 3 reports results when the retain set is drawn from the same domain as the forget set, resulting in strong representation entanglement. Under this regime, RMU and Adaptive RMU exhibit limited forgetting at comparable MMLU levels, with WMDP accuracy remaining high, indicating substantial retention of harmful knowledge.

Table 3. Performance of RMU, Adaptive RMU, and SRMU under the High-Entanglement Retain Regime.

Method	MMLU (↑)	WMDP-Bio (↓)	WMDP-Cyber (↓)	WMDP Avg (↓)
Original (Zephyr-7B)	58.5	64.7	44.8	54.7
RMU (Li et al., 2024)	51.9	48.5	41.1	44.8
Adaptive RMU (Dang et al., 2025)	51.15	49.33	37.74	43.54
SRMU (Our)	**52.5**	**38.26**	**37.14**	**37.7**

Adaptive RMU reduces the WMDP average from 54.7 to 43.54 at an MMLU of 51.15, while RMU achieves an even smaller reduction at similar utility. Extensive hyperparameter sweeps confirm that this limitation is not due to suboptimal tuning.

In contrast, SRMU achieves stronger forgetting under matched retention conditions. At a comparable MMLU level (52.5), SRMU further reduces the WMDP average to 37.7 while preserving similar general capability. These results indicate that the failure of prior perturbation based methods in the high entanglement regime is structural rather than parametric. By selectively localizing and perturbing forget relevant features, SRMU enables effective unlearning within shared representation subspaces.

4.4 Ablation Study

All ablation studies are conducted under the low-entanglement (Wikitext retain) setting, where forget and retain distributions are weakly overlapping.

Effect of Importance Map Design: We compare three importance map constructions for $\mathbf{I}_{\text{norm}}$: Ratio, Difference, and Product. Figure 2 shows the trade-off between WMDP reduction and MMLU accuracy.

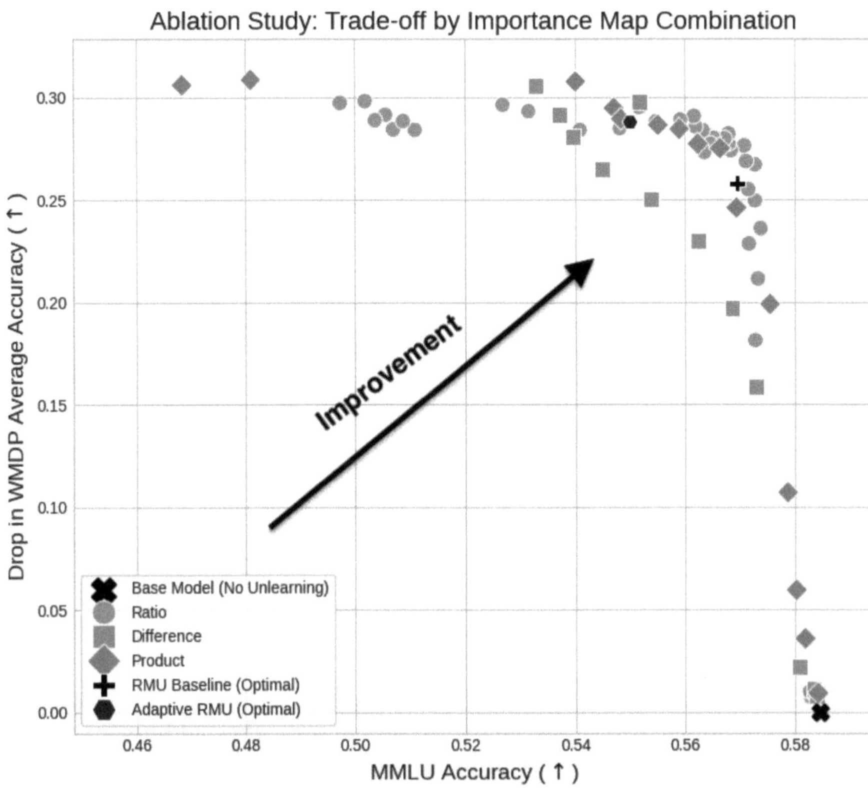

Fig. 2. Trade-off Comparison of Importance Map Strategies: WMDP Drop vs. MMLU.

The **Ratio-based** formulation consistently defines the Pareto frontier, achieving higher utility at the same forgetting level than both alternative SRMU variants and RMU-based baselines. The **Product-based** formulation performs competitively in intermediate regions but does not reach the frontier, while the **Difference-based** formulation underperforms due to overly sparse importance assignments.

Overall, these results indicate that appropriate importance weighting is critical, with the Ratio-based strategy providing the best forgettingutility balance.

Effect of Directional Misdirection: Table 4 evaluates the necessity of directional misdirection ($\mathbf{V}$) and importance normalization ($\mathbf{I}_{\text{norm}}$). When $\mathbf{T} = 0$, performance remains close to the base model (MMLU 0.5835, WMDP Avg 0.5394), indicating negligible forgetting. Fixed direction variants achieve strong forgetting (WMDP Avg ≈ 0.25) but suffer severe utility degradation (MMLU < 0.30), while removing $\mathbf{I}_{\text{norm}}$ also degrades utility (MMLU 0.5165). The random-direction baseline follows the original RMU setting with uniform $[0, 1)$ sampling. In contrast, combining adaptive directional perturbation with importance normalization yields effective forgetting while preserving utility, confirming that both components are necessary for SRMU.

Table 4. Ablation Study of SRMU Components under the Low-Entanglement Setting.

Method/Variant	MMLU (↑)	WMDP Avg (↓)
Base Model	0.5845	0.5475
RMU Baseline	0.5694	0.2896
SRMU (Full)	**0.571**	**0.2717**
Mechanistic Ablation		
SRMU (w/o $\mathbf{V}$ and $\mathbf{I}_{\text{norm}}$; $\mathbf{T} = 0$)	0.5835	0.5394
SRMU (w/o $\mathbf{I}_{\text{norm}}$; uniform perturbation)	0.5165	0.2503
SRMU (fixed $+1$ direction)	0.2876	0.2430
SRMU (fixed -1 direction)	0.2483	0.2556
SRMU (random direction in $[0, 1)$)	0.5672	0.2755

5 Conclusion

In this work, we presented Selective Representation Misdirection for Unlearning (SRMU), a representation level unlearning framework that addresses the limitations of random and non selective perturbation. SRMU integrates a Dynamic Importance Map with a Directional Misdirection Vector to enable feature selective and controlled modification of internal representations. Experiments on WMDP demonstrated that SRMU achieves a superior balance between forgetting effectiveness and utility preservation. SRMU matches or outperforms existing perturbation based unlearning methods under standard settings and remains effective in high entanglement regimes where prior approaches degrade. Ablation results further demonstrated that both importance aware feature selection and directional misdirection are necessary for stable and selective unlearning. Overall, these results indicate that effective machine unlearning in large language models requires structured, feature aware intervention rather than unstructured perturbation. By enabling targeted representation editing under realistic entanglement conditions, SRMU provides a practical and interpretable framework for compliance driven knowledge removal.

References

1. Cao, Y., Yang, J.: Towards making systems forget with machine unlearning. In: 2015 IEEE Symposium on Security and Privacy, pp. 463–480 (2015). https://doi.org/10.1109/SP.2015.35
2. Dong, Y.R., Lin, H., Belkin, M., Huerta, R., Vulić, I.: Undial: self-distillation with adjusted logits for robust unlearning in large language models. In: Proceedings of the 2025 Conference of the Nations of the Americas Chapter of the Association for Computational Linguistics: Human Language Technologies (Volume 1: Long Papers), pp. 8827–8840 (2025)
3. Eldan, R., Russinovich, M.: Who's harry potter? approximate unlearning for LLMS (2023)
4. Geng, J., et al.: A comprehensive survey of machine unlearning techniques for large language models. arXiv preprint arXiv:2503.01854 (2025)
5. Huu-Tien, D., Pham, T., Thanh-Tung, H., Inoue, N.: On effects of steering latent representation for large language model unlearning. In: Proceedings of the Thirty-Ninth AAAI Conference on Artificial Intelligence and Thirty-Seventh Conference on Innovative Applications of Artificial Intelligence and Fifteenth Symposium on Educational Advances in Artificial Intelligence. AAAI'25/IAAI'25/EAAI'25, AAAI Press (2025). https://doi.org/10.1609/aaai.v39i22.34544
6. Ilharco, G., et al.: Editing models with task arithmetic. arXiv preprint arXiv:2212.04089 (2022)
7. Jang, J., et al.: Knowledge unlearning for mitigating privacy risks in language models. In: Proceedings of the 61st Annual Meeting of the Association for Computational Linguistics (Volume 1: Long Papers), pp. 14389–14408 (2023)
8. Jin, Z., et al.: RWKU: benchmarking real-world knowledge unlearning for large language models. Adv. Neural. Inf. Process. Syst. **37**, 98213–98263 (2024)
9. Kumar, R., Prakash, R., Kumar, N., Chinara, S., Mohammed, M.A.: Machine unlearning for trustworthy AI: a systematic review of techniques, challenges, and applications. Arch. Comput. Methods Engineering. 1–23 (2025)
10. Li, N., et al.: The WMDP benchmark: measuring and reducing malicious use with unlearning. In: Salakhutdinov, R., Kolter, Z., Heller, K., Weller, A., Oliver, N., Scarlett, J., Berkenkamp, F. (eds.) Proceedings of the 41st International Conference on Machine Learning. Proceedings of Machine Learning Research, vol. 235, pp. 28525–28550. PMLR (2024). https://proceedings.mlr.press/v235/li24bc.html
11. Liu, X., et al.: Jailbreak attacks and defenses against multimodal generative models: a survey. arXiv preprint arXiv:2411.09259 (2024)
12. Liu, Z., et al.: A survey on federated unlearning: challenges, methods, and future directions. ACM Comput. Surv. **57**(1), 1–38 (2024)
13. Lu, X., et al.: Quark: controllable text generation with reinforced unlearning. Adv. Neural. Inf. Process. Syst. **35**, 27591–27609 (2022)
14. Maini, P., Feng, Z., Schwarzschild, A., Lipton, Z.C., Kolter, J.Z.: Tofu: a task of fictitious unlearning for LLMs. In: First Conference on Language Modeling
15. Nguyen, T.T., et al.: A survey of machine unlearning. ACM Trans. Intell. Syst. Technol. **16**(5), 1–46 (2025)
16. Qu, Y., Ding, M., Sun, N., Thilakarathna, K., Zhu, T., Niyato, D.: The frontier of data erasure: a survey on machine unlearning for large language models. Computer **58**(1), 45–57 (2025)
17. Shaik, T., Tao, X., Xie, H., Li, L., Zhu, X., Li, Q.: Exploring the landscape of machine unlearning: a comprehensive survey and taxonomy. IEEE Trans. Neural Netw. Learn. Syst. (2024)

18. Shi, W., et al.: Muse: machine unlearning six-way evaluation for language models. (2024). arXiv preprint arXiv:2407.06460 (2024)
19. Vulchi, J.R., Ackerman, E.: Exploring OWASP top 10 security risks in LLMs with practical testing and prevention (2024)
20. Wang, B., Zi, Y., Sun, Y., Zhao, Y., Qin, B.: Balancing forget quality and model utility: a reverse kl-divergence knowledge distillation approach for better unlearning in LLMs. In: Proceedings of the 2025 Conference of the Nations of the Americas Chapter of the Association for Computational Linguistics: Human Language Technologies (Volume 1: Long Papers), pp. 1306–1321 (2025)
21. Wu, X., et al.: DEPN: detecting and editing privacy neurons in pretrained language models. In: Bouamor, H., Pino, J., Bali, K. (eds.) Proceedings of the 2023 Conference on Empirical Methods in Natural Language Processing, pp. 2875–2886. Association for Computational Linguistics, Singapore (2023). https://doi.org/10.18653/v1/2023.emnlp-main.174, https://aclanthology.org/2023.emnlp-main.174/
22. Yan, H., Li, X., Guo, Z., Li, H., Li, F., Lin, X.: Arcane: an efficient architecture for exact machine unlearning. In: IJCAI, vol. 6, p. 19 (2022)
23. Yao, J., et al.: Machine unlearning of pre-trained large language models. In: Proceedings of the 62nd Annual Meeting of the Association for Computational Linguistics (Volume 1: Long Papers), pp. 8403–8419 (2024)
24. Zhang, R., Lin, L., Bai, Y., Mei, S.: Negative preference optimization: from catastrophic collapse to effective unlearning. arXiv preprint arXiv:2404.05868 (2024)

Parameter-Efficient LLMs for Flow-Based Intrusion Detection

Mamdouh Muhammad(✉), Anton Wunsch, and Loui Al Sardy

Computer Networks and Communication Systems, Friedrich-Alexander-Universität Erlangen-Nürnberg (FAU), Erlangen, Germany
{mamdouh.muhammad,anton.wunsch,loui.alsardy}@fau.de
https://www.cs7.tf.fau.de/

Abstract. Flow-based intrusion detection systems (IDS) typically rely on statistical features extracted from network traffic. Recent fine-tuned LLMs, including instruction-tuned variants, can be adapted for security classification using lightweight, parameter-efficient methods. This paper studies binary flow-level intrusion detection (benign vs. attack) using supervised fine-tuning (SFT) and in-context learning (ICL), targeting practical deployment under limited compute. Each network flow is serialized into a compact instruction format that combines selected flow features with a concise connection log string, enabling a small decoder-only model to operate directly on realistic flow records. We adapt a 0.5B-parameter LLM via Low-Rank Adaptation (LoRA) and evaluate the accuracy–efficiency trade-off by varying LoRA rank and training data size. At inference time, we avoid free-form generation by scoring the conditional log-likelihood of the two label strings and calibrating a bias term on a validation set to control decision thresholds. Experiments on a balanced subset of a standard distributed denial-of-service (DDoS) benchmark show that LoRA-based SFT substantially improves over a zero-shot baseline, while pure ICL achieves strong performance with only a few labeled examples in the prompt. Combining LoRA adaptation with ICL yields the best results, reaching 91% accuracy and 90% macro-F1 on a 10k-flow test set. These findings indicate that small LLMs, paired with careful feature-to-text serialization and lightweight adaptation, can be viable components of flow-based IDS in resource-constrained settings.

Keywords: Intrusion Detection System · Network Security · Large Language Models · Supervised Fine-Tuning · In-Context Learning · LoRA · DDoS Detection · Parameter-Efficient Fine-Tuning

1 Introduction

The increasing connectivity and complexity of modern digital infrastructure have expanded the attack surface of networked systems, raising the operational importance of robust intrusion detection systems (IDS). In particular, volumetric attacks such as distributed denial-of-service (DDoS) can disrupt availability

© IFIP International Federation for Information Processing 2026
Published by Springer Nature Switzerland AG 2026
H. Janicke et al. (Eds.): SEC 2026, IFIP AICT 787, pp. 47–60, 2026.
https://doi.org/10.1007/978-3-032-27993-4_4

at scale while evolving rapidly, stressing detection pipelines that must operate under strict latency and resource constraints.

A signature-based intrusion detection system (IDS) operates similarly to a pattern-matching verifier. It compares observed traffic against a repository of known attack signatures and triggers an alert upon a match. This approach typically yields a low false-alarm rate. However, it is limited against previously unseen threats. Consequently, a zero-day attack may evade detection because it does not correspond to any existing rule in the signature database [1].

An anomaly-based IDS has a different approach by watching what "normal" looks like and grows suspicious when behavior starts to drift. Sudden spikes, odd sequences, or unfamiliar activity are readily clear indicators, even if the attack has never been seen before. That makes it better at detecting zero-day threats, though it tends to trigger more false positives [2]. These long-standing trade-offs motivate continued exploration of learning-based IDS designs that can maintain accuracy without becoming operationally brittle.

Large language models (LLMs), enabled by Transformer architectures, have demonstrated strong generalization and the ability to condition behavior on instructions and a small number of in-context shots [3,4]. However, directly training or serving large models can be costly, and LLMs can be prone to hallucinations, which is problematic in security-critical settings [5]. This motivates approaches that retain LLM flexibility while reducing adaptation cost and improving practical deployability.

In this work, we study a resource-efficient LLM-based IDS for binary flow-level classification (benign-vs-attack) using supervised fine-tuning (SFT) and in-context learning (ICL). We operationalize the task by serializing each network flow into a compact instruction-following text format and adapting a small instruction-tuned decoder model (Qwen2.5-0.5B Instruct) [6]. To keep training feasible on limited hardware, we employ Low-Rank Adaptation (LoRA), a parameter-efficient fine-tuning method that updates only lightweight low-rank factors while freezing the base model [7]. We evaluate on CIC-DDoS2019 as a realistic benchmark containing labeled benign traffic and multiple DDoS attack types [8]. The paper compares zero-shot prompting, LoRA-based SFT, pure ICL, and their combination to clarify when lightweight adaptation and prompting are complementary.

This paper addresses the following research questions:

1. **RQ1**: What are the practical trade-offs between detection performance and efficiency when varying adaptation capacity (e.g., LoRA rank) and the number of in-context examples?
2. **RQ2**: How does pure ICL compare to LoRA-based SFT, and does combining LoRA with ICL yield consistent gains under the same evaluation protocol?
3. **RQ3**: How effective is parameter-efficient SFT via LoRA on a small instruction-tuned LLM for binary flow-level intrusion detection compared to a zero-shot baseline?

The main contributions are:

1. A compact flow-to-text serialisation tailored to a volumetric attack (i.e. DDoS), enabling a small instruction-tuned LLM to perform binary flow classification.
2. A parameter-efficient SFT pipeline that adapts Qwen2.5-0.5B-Instruct using LoRA, along with an empirical study of how performance changes with LoRA capacity (rank) and the amount of labeled training data.
3. A systematic comparison of zero-shot, pure ICL, LoRA-based SFT, and combined LoRA+ICL under identical train/validation/test splits on CIC-DDoS2019.

The remainder of this paper is organized as follows: Sect. 2 summarizes prior work on using signature-based, anomaly-based, and LLM-based IDSs for security tasks. Section 3 presents the proposed flow-to-text representation, the SFT and ICL configurations, and the label-scoring and bias-calibration procedure. Section 4 reports the main results. Section 5 discusses the findings, practical implications, and limitations. Section 6 concludes the paper and outlines directions for future work.

2 Related Work

2.1 Signature-Based IDS and Anomaly-Based IDS

Rakine et al. [9] comprehensively reviewed Machine Learning and Deep Learning-based Intrusion Detection Systems across Cloud, IoT, and SDN networks, evaluating specific algorithms, datasets, and feature selection techniques. They concluded that Machine learning techniques generally offer faster training and greater interpretability but often struggle with complex, high-dimensional data and require manual feature engineering. In addition, Deep learning models excel at automatic feature extraction and handling massive, complex datasets, though they demand high computational resources and suffer from a lack of transparency. In [10], García-Teodoro et al. contrast signature-based and anomaly-based detection, noting that signature approaches are effective for known threats but require continual rule maintenance, whereas anomaly-based approaches can generalize beyond predefined patterns at the cost of higher false-alarm risk under shifting notions of "normal" traffic. Khraisat et al. review IDS techniques and datasets and emphasize that reported performance is often strongly influenced by dataset artifacts and experimental design choices, which can obscure real-world readiness [11]. Asad et al. further show that even within signature-based IDS, coverage depends on the representativeness and domain specificity of rule sets, not only update frequency [12]. Pinto et al. survey ML-based IDS deployments and highlight that supervised detectors can perform well when labeled data reflect operational distributions, but robustness degrades under distribution shift and evolving attacks [13].

2.2 LLMs in Cybersecurity

Vaswani et al. introduce the Transformer architecture that underpins modern LLMs [3], and Brown et al. demonstrate in-context learning (ICL), where models adapt to tasks using a few labeled examples in the prompt without parameter updates [4]. Hu et al. propose LoRA as a parameter-efficient fine-tuning method that enables supervised adaptation of pretrained models with substantially reduced compute and memory overhead [7]. Recent surveys document rapidly growing use of LLMs in cybersecurity, including analysis assistance and security-relevant text understanding, while noting substantial variance in task framing and evaluation practices across studies [14,15]. For intrusion detection specifically, Kheddar [16] and Yang et al. [17] highlight open challenges around robustness, deployment realism, and consistent decision rules for converting model outputs into actionable alerts. Reliability is a recurring concern: Huang et al. review hallucination mechanisms and caution that overconfident errors can be particularly harmful in security decision pipelines [18].

3 Methodology

3.1 Task Definition

We examine binary flow-level intrusion detection. Given a single network-flow record, the model must output exactly one label, either `benign` or `attack`. Each input is rendered as an instruction-following prompt, and classification is performed via label scoring rather than free-form text generation. Figure 1 shows the full SFT architecture, but the evaluation logic changes by configuration.

- **Baseline:** The system uses only the pretrained Qwen2.5-0.5B-Instruct model. It skips training and goes from a zero-shot prompt straight to the log-likelihood calculation.
- **ICL:** The system adds k labeled examples to the prompt, where $k \in \{2, 4, 6\}$. It makes no parameter updates and predicts the label from the in-context patterns.
- **SFT (LoRA-based):** The system evaluates the model modified with LoRA adapters. It loads the trained adapters and uses them to shift the conditional probabilities during the decision step.
- **Hybrid (SFT + ICL):** The system loads the fine-tuned adapters and also adds k in-context examples to the prompt. This setup combines both signals to improve classification performance.

3.2 Dataset

As detailed in Table 1, we use the CIC-DDoS2019 dataset [8] as a tabular network security dataset for our benchmark. The choice of the dataset is mainly because it contains volumetric attacks, is labeled and offers flow-level traffic granularity. We constructed three disjoint, class-balanced splits: 10,000 flows for training (5,000 benign/5,000 attack), 200 flows for validation (bias calibration and model selection), and 10,000 flows for final testing.

Table 1. CIC-DDoS2019 dataset characteristics.

Aspect	Description
Size & dimensionality	Flow-level CSVs derived from raw PCAPs; scale is typically reported as over 50 million network-flow records with 82 extracted flow features (plus identifiers and label columns).
Feature types	Primarily numeric flow statistics (e.g., packet/byte counts, rates, inter-arrival times and timestamps) and multi-class attack labels.
Class ratio	Highly imbalanced as attacks are dominant.
Acquisition context	Controlled enterprise-style testbed (Windows clients + Ubuntu server + firewall) with synthetic benign background traffic generated via user behavior profiles; attacks launched from a separate attacker network.
Temporal coverage	Two collection days (training/testing) totaling roughly ~16 h.
Label integrity	Flow labels are produced from controlled ground truth using timestamps and 5-tuple context (IPs, ports, protocol) aligned to attack schedules.
Granularity	Packet-level (PCAPs, content-oriented) and flow-level (CICFlowMeter-derived, volume-oriented).
Attack taxonomy	Includes modern reflection/amplification-style families and volumetric/exploitation-style floods.

3.3 Flow Representation

Each flow is serialized into a compact text block consisting of (i) a fixed set of 15 semantically relevant flow features capturing temporal behavior, traffic volume, throughput, and TCP flag statistics, and (ii) a short connection-log string of the form `Protocol from SrcIP:SrcPort -> DstIP:DstPort`. The prompt terminates with the target string of the form `Answer: benign` or `Answer: attack`. This single serialization is reused for zero-shot prompting, supervised fine-tuning, and in-context learning.

3.4 Base Model and Parameter-Efficient Adaptation

We use Qwen 2.5 0.5B Instruct as the base decoder-only language model [6]. To adapt the model efficiently, we apply LoRA [7]. LoRA injects trainable low-rank matrices into selected linear projections while keeping the pretrained weights frozen, enabling parameter-efficient supervised fine-tuning under constrained compute budgets.

3.5 Supervised Fine-Tuning (SFT)

Training data are stored in JSONL format and converted into a chat-style structure with `system`, `user`, and `assistant` roles. The `system` message fixes the task instruction (binary IDS labeling), the `user` message contains the flow serialization, and the `assistant` message contains the ground-truth label token(s). During fine-tuning, loss is computed only on the assistant label segment to ensure the model is optimized specifically for the classification decision.

LoRA adapters are injected into attention projections (`q_proj`, `k_proj`, `v_proj`, `o_proj`) and MLP projections (`gate_proj`, `up_proj`, `down_proj`). We compare LoRA ranks $r \in \{4, 8, 16\}$, scaling factor $\alpha = 2r$ and dropout 0.05, while keeping the remaining backbone parameters frozen. Models are fine-tuned for one epoch with an effective batch size produced via gradient accumulation, using the same tokenizer/template as for evaluation to preserve label consistency. Table 2 summarizes the hyperparameters used for training and evaluation. Table 3 lists the compute environment and resource configuration for fine-tuning experiments.

Table 2. Summary of training and evaluation hyperparameters.

Category	Setting
Base model	Qwen2.5-0.5B-Instruct
Task	Binary classification: `benign` vs. `attack`
Dataset split	Train: 10,000 Val: 200 Test: 10,000 (balanced)
Training data fractions	25%, 50%, 100% of the 10k training set
PEFT method	LoRA
LoRA rank (r)	$\{4, 8, 16\}$
LoRA scaling (α)	$\alpha = 2r$
LoRA dropout	0.05
LoRA target modules	`q_proj, k_proj, v_proj, o_proj, gate_proj, up_proj, down_proj`
Epochs	1
Optimizer	AdamW
Learning rate	1×10^{-4}
Warmup ratio	0.06
Weight decay	0.01
Gradient clipping	1.0
Max sequence length	512
Per-device batch size	8
Gradient accumulation	8
Effective batch size	64
Inference decision rule	Log-likelihood scoring of label strings (`benign`, `attack`)
Bias calibration (b)	Sweep $b \in [-6, +6]$ with step 0.1 on validation set (maximize macro-F1)
ICL shots (k)	$\{2, 4, 6\}$ (balanced across classes)

Table 3. Compute environment and resource configuration for fine-tuning experiments.

Item	Specification
Location	HPC site / cluster
Partition / queue	`rtx3080` (Slurm-managed)
Node allocation	1 compute node per job
GPU per job	1× NVIDIA RTX 3080
GPU memory	10 GB VRAM
Wall-time limit	6 h per job
Storage	HPC filesystem (model weights and caches)

3.6 In-Context Learning (ICL)

In addition to zero-shot prompting and SFT, we assess in-context learning by adding labeled examples before the prompt [19]. We test $k \in \{2, 4, 6\}$ in-context examples, with equal counts per class. For instance, $k=2$ includes one benign and one attack example. We draw exemplars from the training split and keep them separate from test samples. We place the test flow after the exemplars using the same serialization format, and we instruct the model to return a single word, either `benign` or `attack`.

3.7 Label Scoring and Bias Calibration

At inference time, we treat the LLM as a conditional language model over a two-label vocabulary. For a given prompt, we score each candidate label string $\ell \in \{\texttt{benign}, \texttt{attack}\}$ by its token-level log-likelihood under the model conditioned on the input x. Let $\ell = (y_1, \ldots, y_T)$ denote the sequence of tokens obtained by tokenizing ℓ. We compute

$$s_\ell = \log P(\ell \mid x) = \sum_{t=1}^{T} \log P(y_t \mid x, y_{<t}), \tag{1}$$

where $y_{<t} = (y_1, \ldots, y_{t-1})$. Accordingly,

$$s_{\texttt{benign}} = \sum_{t=1}^{T_b} \log P\left(y_t^{(b)} \mid x, y_{<t}^{(b)}\right), \tag{2}$$

$$s_{\texttt{attack}} = \sum_{t=1}^{T_a} \log P\left(y_t^{(a)} \mid x, y_{<t}^{(a)}\right). \tag{3}$$

To account for systematic class bias (built-in preference), we introduce a scalar bias term b and classify as attack if

$$s_{\texttt{attack}} + b \geq s_{\texttt{benign}}, \tag{4}$$

otherwise benign. We sweep b on the validation set in the range $[-6, +6]$ with step size 0.1 and select the value maximizing macro-F1. The chosen bias is then fixed and applied once to the held-out test set for the final reported metrics. This calibration is performed separately for each evaluated configuration (zero-shot, SFT variants, and ICL variants) to ensure comparable operating points. In practice, the bias b can be tuned to achieve a trade-off between false positives and false negatives to match the operating point. If $b > 0$, recall rises, but false positives increase. If $b < 0$, false negatives increase.

3.8 Evaluation Metrics and Statistical Confidence

We report accuracy, precision, recall, and F1-score, including macro-F1 across the two classes. To capture uncertainty in accuracy on the 10,000-sample test set, we compute the standard error for a binomial proportion:

$$\mathrm{SE} = \sqrt{\frac{p(1-p)}{n}}, \tag{5}$$

and a 95% confidence interval of $p \pm 1.96 \times SE$, where p is the observed accuracy and n is the number of test samples.

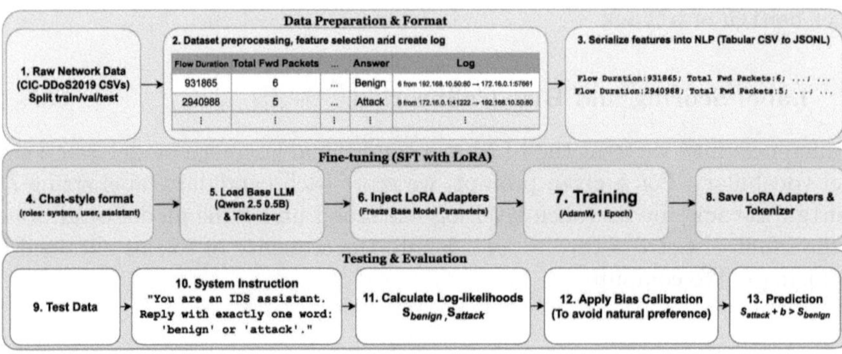

Fig. 1. System architecture of the SFT-based intrusion detection pipeline, depicting the end-to-end process from raw network traffic processing to final threat classification. Data preparation involves extracting 15 semantically relevant features from the CIC-DDoS2019 dataset and formatting them into JSONL objects for the Qwen2.5-0.5B-Instruct model. The evaluation stage utilizes conditional log-likelihood scores adjusted by a calibrated bias factor b to determine the final binary prediction.

4 Results

Table 4 summarizes representative configurations on the balanced 10k-flow test set. The zero-shot baseline (no SFT, no ICL) performs near chance. LoRA fine-tuning improves performance substantially when enough training data is used, and the rank is well-chosen: as shown in Fig. 2 with 100% training data, rank 8 yields the strongest LoRA-only result (accuracy 84%, macro-F1 83%), while rank 4 underfits and rank 16 slightly degrades (***RQ1*** answer).

Table 4. Selected model configurations on the balanced 10k-flow test set (BENIGN vs. ATTACK).

Model/Setup	Accuracy	Macro-F1	Notes
Baseline Qwen 0.5B (no SFT, no ICL)	53%	53%	mild bias toward benign
T25_R4 (25% data, rank 4)	54%	54%	small gain vs. baseline
T50_R16 (50% data, rank 16)	71%	71%	balanced classes
T100_R8 (100% data, rank 8)	84%	83%	best LoRA-only model
Pure ICL (base model, $k = 4$)	88%	88%	best pure-ICL setting
LoRA+ICL (T100_R8, $k = 6$)	91%	90%	best overall setting

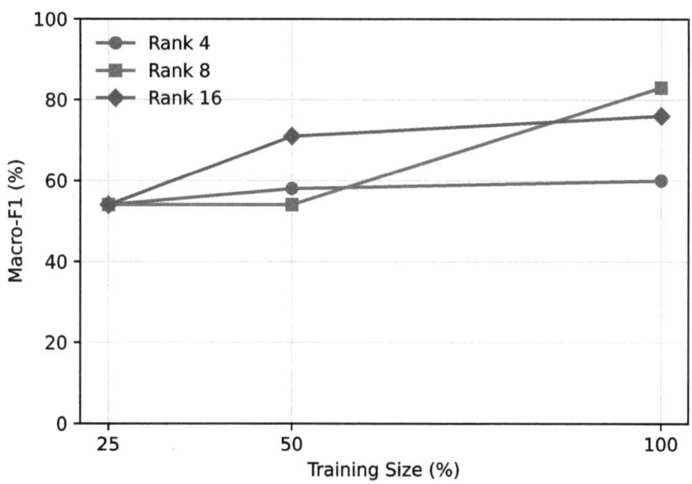

Fig. 2. Macro-F1 vs. training size (by LoRA rank).

Pure ICL shows a notable non-monotonic behavior with respect to prompt length: $k = 4$ achieves strong performance (accuracy and macro-F1 both 88%), while $k = 6$ degrades (macro-F1 75%), suggesting that longer prompts can introduce distracting variation even when examples are balanced (***RQ2*** answer).

Combining SFT and ICL is most effective when ICL is sufficiently informative: LoRA+ICL with $k = 6$ achieves the best overall performance (accuracy 91%, macro-F1 90%) (***RQ3*** answer). This supports the view that LoRA captures global decision boundaries from labeled data, while ICL provides local, on-the-fly calibration in the prompt, and that the two mechanisms can be complementary rather than redundant. As shown in Fig. 3, LoRA training is computationally light: training on 25%, 50%, and 100% of the data (10,000 flows) takes approximately 138 s, 285 s, and 491 s, respectively, on a single NVIDIA RTX 3080 GPU, and is nearly independent of LoRA rank. With a test size of $n = 10{,}000$, the standard error of accuracy is at most about 0.5%. For the best configuration (accuracy 0.91), the approximate 95% confidence interval is $[0.904, 0.916]$, indicating that the multi-point gaps between configurations are statistically meaningful.

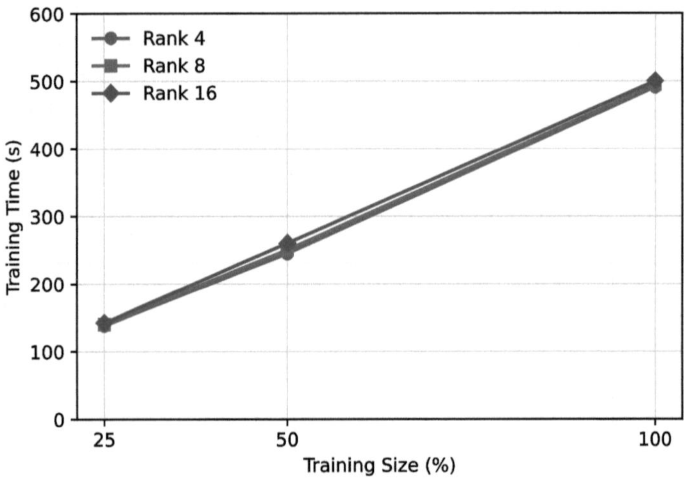

Fig. 3. Training time vs. training size (by LoRA rank).

Figure 4 presents the training loss as a function of optimization steps during LoRA-based supervised fine-tuning. The plot corresponds to the best model with rank 8 trained on 100% of the data. At the start, the loss drops fast as the model adapts to the task. After about 20 steps, the loss stabilizes at a low value. This pattern suggests rapid convergence and low training loss for most samples. Several spikes appear between steps 50 and 60. These spikes reflect small-batch noise and harder examples in the dataset. Small-scale fine-tuning with one epoch and small batches often shows this behavior. After the spikes, the loss returns near zero and remains stable.

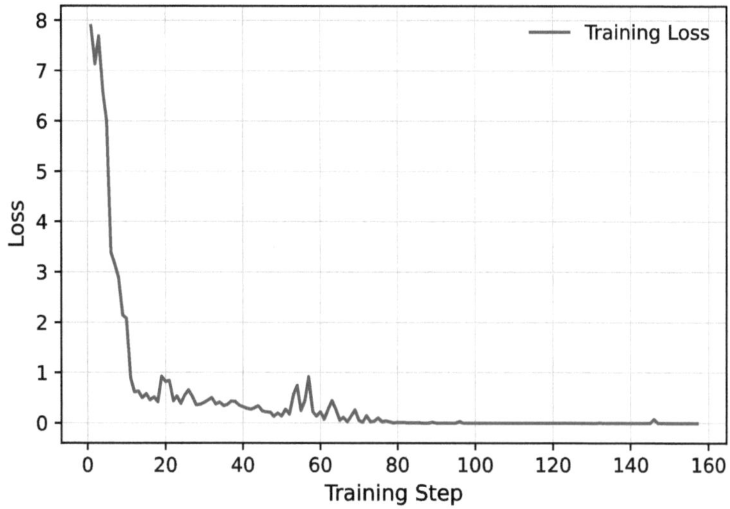

Fig. 4. Training loss as a function of optimization steps during LoRA-based supervised fine-tuning.

5 Discussion and Limitations

5.1 Discussion

The results show that small instruction-tuned LLMs can support binary flow-level intrusion detection with two practical elements. The setup uses a compact, consistent flow-to-text format and light adaptation with prompts. LoRA-based supervised fine-tuning outperforms the zero-shot baseline by a wide margin. A small set of trainable weights aligns the instruction model with the statistics of flow features. This outcome fits the aim of parameter-efficient fine-tuning, which targets task focus without full model updates.

In-context learning (ICL) provides an additional boost. Few-shot prompts can perform well without any weight updates, but accuracy does not always rise as you add more examples. Brown et al. demonstrate that ICL is heavily dependent on prompt design and the choice of examples, which can increase variance or even degrade performance as prompts become longer or lose focus [4]. A similar pattern is observed here. A few examples help the model learn the link between serialized flow patterns and the target label, but extra examples can add noise, increase the token budget, or push the model toward misleading correlations.

The best setup combines LoRA adaptation with ICL. SFT can learn a steady decision boundary for the chosen representation, and ICL can act as a local conditioning signal that pushes the model toward the intended operating point for the current prompt context. This split works well for IDS use as SFT can learn patterns that hold across the dataset, and ICL can then adjust decisions quickly when traffic changes, or when operators want to guide the model with a small set of labeled examples.

A second practical finding is that the model works better as a scoring engine than as a free-form generator. The method compares the log-likelihood of two fixed label strings, so it avoids open-ended outputs and cuts down on off-topic text. This matters since LLM reliability failures, including confident hallucinations, are well documented and can be especially risky when a prediction triggers a security action [18]. Framing the task as a two-label scoring decision is a sensible design choice for security classification.

Finally, a small backbone model makes deployment more realistic. Large LLMs can be accurate, but they cost more to fine-tune and run. Compact models cut inference cost and shrink the operational footprint. Recent evidence suggests that inference cost often dominates in production, which supports using small models paired with PEFT in applied work [20].

5.2 Limitations

The evaluation uses a balanced subset and a single benchmark dataset (no cross-dataset verification). Testing transfer across datasets and collection settings would strengthen external validity.

Controlled balancing helps compare setups, but real traffic is imbalanced and changes over time. Benchmarks can overstate performance when tests miss shifting base rates, concept drift, and varied background traffic.

This approach uses a fixed flow order and a fixed set of chosen flow features. This format is compact and works well for prompts, and it fits volumetric attacks such as DDoS. However, it can miss packet-level detail and may not detect important content-oriented attacks like False Data Injection (FDI).

Feature distributions can also shift across networks and capture pipelines. Expanding the representation, with a strict token limit, would reduce this risk.

The bias calibration procedure is intentionally simple and uses a small validation set. This choice supports fast iteration but may produce unstable thresholds, especially when traffic distributions shift. More robust calibration, cost-sensitive evaluation, and uncertainty estimation would be appropriate for deployment.

We targeted binary classification. While binary (benign-vs-attack) aligns with many operational alerting workflows, practical IDS often requires attack-type attribution, prioritization, and integration with incident response. Multi-class extensions and richer output interfaces should be pursued cautiously, given the reliability concerns associated with more open-ended generation in LLMs [18].

Finally, we did not measure end-to-end detection latency or throughput. Time to detect matters for IDS use in live networks. LLM inference can run too slowly to handle line-rate traffic in high-throughput settings, even with compact models.

6 Conclusion and Future Work

We investigated whether a compact instruction-tuned large language model (LLM) can perform *binary* flow-level intrusion detection (benign-vs-attack) using only supervised fine-tuning (SFT) and in-context learning (ICL), under practical compute constraints. We adopted a compact flow-to-text serialization and treated classification as a two-label scoring problem by comparing the log-likelihood of fixed label strings, complemented by a simple validation-based bias calibration to control the operating point. On a balanced evaluation protocol derived from CIC-DDoS2019, Low-Rank Adaptation based (LoRA-based) SFT substantially improved over a zero-shot baseline, pure ICL achieved strong performance with only a few labeled exemplars, and the combination of LoRA adaptation with ICL yielded the best overall results. Beyond accuracy gains, the study highlights two practical design choices for LLM-based IDS: (I) using parameter-efficient adaptation to keep training feasible and (II) avoiding open-ended text generation and using explicit label scoring instead. These choices cut operational complexity and still keep the flexibility of instruction-tuned models.

Several steps can make the results more deployment-ready. (I) Test realistic class imbalance, time-based splits, and handling concept drift, then track whether thresholds stay stable. (II) Run cross-dataset and cross-environment transfer tests to see how sensitive the model is to feature shifts and collection pipelines. (III) Add stronger calibration and uncertainty reporting to make decisions more reliable. (IV) Extend beyond binary classification to multi-class classification. (V) Finally, report latency and throughput numbers such as flows per second, and confirm the method meets real-time limits.

References

1. Bonagura, V., Pisani, J., Ferrato, A., Foglietta, C., Cavone, G., Pascucci, F.: Machine learning techniques for anomaly detection in the hydra testbed: a data-driven defense strategy. In: Oliva, G., Panzieri, S., Hämmerli, B., Pascucci, F., Faramondi, L., (eds.). Critical Information Infrastructures Security, pp. 343–361. Springer, Cham (2025). https://doi.org/10.1007/978-3-031-84260-3_20
2. Fauzi, N., Yulianto, F., Nuha, H.: The effectiveness of anomaly-based intrusion detection systems in handling zero-day attacks using adaboost, j48, and random forest methods, pp. 57–62 (2023). https://doi.org/10.1109/APWiMob59963.2023.10365642
3. Vaswani, A., et al.: Attention is all you need (2017)
4. Brown, T.B., et al.: Language models are few-shot learners (2020). https://doi.org/10.48550/arXiv.2005.14165
5. Huang, L., et al.: A survey on hallucination in large language models: principles, taxonomy, challenges, and open questions. ACM Trans. Inf. Syst. **43**(2) (2025)
6. Qwen, A.Y., et al.: Qwen2.5 technical report (2025). https://doi.org/10.48550/arXiv.2412.15115
7. Hu, E.J., et al.: Lora: low-rank adaptation of large language models (2021). https://doi.org/10.48550/arXiv.2106.09685

8. Ddos evaluation dataset (cic-ddos2019) (2019). https://www.unb.ca/cic/datasets/ddos-2019.html
9. Rakine, I.: Comprehensive review of intrusion detection techniques: Ml and dl in different networks. IEEE Access **13**, 104345–104367 (2025). https://doi.org/10.1109/ACCESS.2025.3579990
10. García-Teodoro, P., Díaz-Verdejo, J., Maciá-Fernández, G., Vázquez, E.: Anomaly-based network intrusion detection: techniques, systems and challenges. Comput. Secur. **28**(1–2), 18–28 (2009). https://doi.org/10.1016/j.cose.2008.08.003
11. Khraisat, A., Gondal, I., Vamplew, P., Kamruzzaman, J.: Survey of intrusion detection systems: techniques, datasets and challenges. Cybersecurity **2**(1), 20 (2019). https://doi.org/10.1186/s42400-019-0038-7
12. Asad, H., Adhikari, S., Gashi, I.: A perspective-retrospective analysis of diversity in signature-based open-source network intrusion detection systems. Int. J. Inf. Secur. **23**(2), 1331–1346 (2024). https://doi.org/10.1007/s10207-023-00794-9
13. Pinto, A., Herrera, L.-C., Donoso, Y., Gutierrez, J.A.: Survey on intrusion detection systems based on machine learning techniques for the protection of critical infrastructure. Sensors **23**(5), 2415 (2023). https://doi.org/10.3390/s23052415
14. da Silva, G.D.J.C., Westphall, C.B.: A survey of large language models in cybersecurity (2024). https://doi.org/10.48550/arXiv.2402.16968
15. Xu, H., et al.: Large language models for cyber security: a systematic literature review (2025). https://doi.org/10.48550/arXiv.2405.04760
16. Kheddar, H.: Transformers and large language models for efficient intrusion detection systems: a comprehensive survey. Inf. Fusion **124**, 103347 (2025)
17. Yang, S., et al.: Large language models for network intrusion detection systems: foundations, implementations, and future directions (2025). https://doi.org/10.48550/arXiv.2507.04752
18. Huang, L., et al.: A survey on hallucination in large language models: principles, taxonomy, challenges, and open questions. ACM Trans. Inf. Syst. **43**(2), 1–55 (2025). https://doi.org/10.1145/3703155
19. Dherin, B., Munn, M., Mazzawi, H., Wunder, M., Gonzalvo, J.: Learning without training: the implicit dynamics of in-context learning (2025). https://doi.org/10.48550/arXiv.2507.16003
20. Jegham, N., Abdelatti, M., Elmoubarki, L., Hendawi, A.: How hungry is AI? benchmarking energy, water, and carbon footprint of LLM inference (2025). https://doi.org/10.48550/arXiv.2505.09598

APART: Access Policy-AwaRe LLM Fine-Tuning

Nouha Oualha(✉)

Université Paris-Saclay, CEA, List, 91120 Palaiseau, France
nouha.oualha@cea.fr

Abstract. The widespread deployment of Large Language Models (LLMs) across sensitive domains demands robust fine-tuning techniques for task-specific adaptation and, crucially, secure, compliant data access control. A conventional strategy enforces access policies by generating discrete Parameter-Efficient Fine-Tuning (PEFT) adapters (e.g., LoRA) for each policy permutation. However, escalating complexity in access control policies results in an explosive, combinatorial growth in the required number of these policy-specific adapters, creating substantial scalability and performance bottlenecks. This paper proposes a novel access policy-aware fine-tuning approach to mitigate this challenge. By integrating complex access policies directly into the fine-tuning process, our method drastically reduces the computational and storage overhead associated with the per-policy adapter paradigm. We empirically demonstrate that this approach maintains performance parity with existing methods while effectively preventing the negative consequences of adapter proliferation.

Keywords: Large Language Model · Privacy · Security · Access Control · Machine Learning

1 Introduction

Large Language Models (LLMs) necessitate fine-tuning on domain-specific datasets for optimal performance. Given the frequent inclusion of sensitive or confidential data, data security and access control are paramount. Parameter-Efficient Fine-Tuning (PEFT), exemplified by Low-Rank Adaptation (LoRA), mitigates this risk by introducing a minimal set of trainable parameters while freezing the bulk of the pre-trained model's weights, contrasting with traditional full fine-tuning.

The management of complex data access control policies remains a significant challenge, even with PEFT. The common, yet flawed, approach is to generate a separate PEFT adapter for every unique combination of policies. This "per-policy" adapter strategy incurs several critical issues:

1. *Combinatorial Explosion:* The number of required adapters scales exponentially ($2^n - 1$ for n datasets), leading to unmanageability.

© IFIP International Federation for Information Processing 2026
Published by Springer Nature Switzerland AG 2026
H. Janicke et al. (Eds.): SEC 2026, IFIP AICT 787, pp. 61–75, 2026.
https://doi.org/10.1007/978-3-032-27993-4_5

2. *Storage and Management Overhead:* Individual adapter storage and complex access management systems result in significant administrative and cost overhead.
3. *Redundancy:* Overlapping access control policy sets result in the redundant encoding of fine-tuning knowledge across multiple adapters.
4. *Maintenance Bottleneck:* Updates to the base model or dataset additions necessitate the resource-intensive retraining of numerous models.

This strategy creates severe scalability and performance bottlenecks, practically nullifying the efficiency benefits of PEFT.

Our research proposes a novel access policy-aware fine-tuning approach that directly addresses these limitations. This approach integrates access policies directly into the fine-tuning process, making the model inherently aware of the policies governing its training data. While utilizing discrete adapters, the approach drastically reduces computational and storage overhead by exploiting the inherent relationships between access policies. Empirical results demonstrate performance parity with traditional methods alongside a substantial reduction in both storage requirements and computational costs, confirming the feasibility of integrating robust data security via access policy architecture directly into the fine-tuning process.

2 Related Work

The field of fine-tuning large language models (LLMs) is rapidly evolving for specialized task adaptation, primarily through Parameter-Efficient Fine-Tuning (PEFT). Low-Rank Adaptation (LoRA) [5] is a leading PEFT technique that freezes pre-trained weights and injects small, trainable rank decomposition matrices, drastically reducing trainable parameters.

Our work is contextualized by advancements in managing multiple LoRA adapters, which address task interference and efficient aggregation, analogous to managing knowledge across security domains.

Prior efforts mitigate interference from merging adapters trained on dissimilar data. Approaches like decoupling and orthogonalizing LoRA updates [15] or leveraging the superposition principle for naive summation of deltas [1] suggest that orthogonality and domain dissimilarity minimize performance drops. Orthogonal Low-Rank Adaptation (O-LoRA) [11] formalizes this by proposing a simple and efficient continual learning approach that mitigates catastrophic forgetting. Specifically, O-LoRA learns tasks within different, orthogonal low-rank vector subspaces, minimizing interference by incrementally learning new tasks in a direction orthogonal to the LoRA subspace of past tasks while fixing previous parameters. Empirical studies [6] further support that merging adapters from dissimilar datasets minimizes degradation.

Beyond managing task interference, research also focuses on optimizing the memory footprint of LoRA. LoRA with Frozen-A (LoRA-FA) [14] is a memory-efficient fine-tuning method designed to significantly reduce the activation memory footprint without performance degradation. LoRA-FA achieves this by freezing the projection-down matrix A and only updating the projection-up matrix B.

The use of modular knowledge for distinct datasets, often reflecting tasks or access privileges, is a related paradigm. AdapterSwap [3] trains separate adapters for data segments and uses a retriever to select/combine them at inference. This preserves modularity, prevents catastrophic forgetting, and enables low-latency knowledge removal crucial for dynamic access control.

Further extensions utilize multiple specialized adapters in a Mixture of Experts (MoE) framework to improve knowledge sharing and mitigate interference. Sophisticated architectures, such as Mixture of LoRA Experts (MoLE) [12] and MoDULA [8], employ dynamic routing to select the appropriate LoRA module from a pool. Other specialized MoE-LoRA variants like HydraLoRA [10] and MTL-LoRA [13] use asymmetric structures and weighted averaging, while MoE-LoRA (MoLA) [4] optimizes expert allocation.

The discussed methods, like AdapterSwap, MoLE, and MoDULA, optimize the creation or management of adapters for multi-task/multi-domain settings but fail to address the combinatorial explosion caused by the need for a unique fine-tuned model (or adapter) for every distinct combination of user permissions or access policies. They still require storing a vast number of individual artifacts, leading to scalability issues. The core limitation is that the standard fine-tuning process is decoupled from the structure of access policies. The proposed approach overcomes this by leveraging the inherent structure and relationships within access policy hierarchies (e.g., inheritance, delegation) to identify and exploit shared knowledge. This fundamentally reduces computational and storage overhead, moving beyond simply managing numerous individual adapters.

3 Access Control for Fine-Tuned Models

Fine-tuned models ($\mathcal{M}_{ft}$) constitute distinct computational artifacts from their underlying training dataset ($\mathcal{D}_{train}$), thereby mandating independent and robust security perimeters. Access control policies governing access to $\mathcal{D}_{train}$ dictate the permissible use of raw data, whereas the permissions applied to $\mathcal{M}_{ft}$ regulate its inference utility. However, the security requirements for $\mathcal{M}_{ft}$ should be systematically derived from those applicable to $\mathcal{D}_{train}$. This rigorous derivation ensures that the model's intrinsic knowledge distribution is constrained by the existing access control logic, which is critical for mitigating privacy risks and adversarial attacks, including model inversion and membership inference attacks.

3.1 Deriving Access Policies for Models

The set of rules and authorization context that govern a user's permissions to interact with an AI model and its data is generally referred to as an Access Control System or its governing **Access Policies**. This framework implements specific Access Control Models—such as Role-Based Access Control (RBAC), Attribute-Based Access Control (ABAC), or Discretionary Access Control (DAC)—to enforce the defined restrictions on who can access and use the model.

The process of deriving $\mathcal{M}_{ft}$'s access policies from $\mathcal{D}_{train}$'s source policies is a requisite for responsible AI governance, ensuring compliance regarding data privacy, security, and intellectual property (IP). Fine-tuning embeds $\mathcal{D}_{train}$'s characteristics and restrictions into $\mathcal{M}_{ft}$. This policy inheritance and enforcement relies on robust data lineage, which provides an auditable, end-to-end trail from data collection through the fine-tuning process, thereby linking source data access policies to final model access policies.

To ensure fine-tuned model ($\mathcal{M}_{ft}$) policies accurately reflect training data ($\mathcal{D}_{train}$) sensitivity, three interconnected principles govern the policy framework:

1. **Policy Propagation via Data Lineage:** Policies for $\mathcal{M}_{ft}$ are derived from $\mathcal{D}_{train}$ sensitivity and restrictions.
   - *Provenance/Inheritance:* $\mathcal{M}_{ft}$'s security classification ties directly to $\mathcal{D}_{train}$, inheriting its governance requirements.
   - *Compliance/IP Protection:* $\mathcal{M}_{ft}$ must adhere to the cumulative regulatory (e.g., HIPAA, GDPR) and Intellectual Property (IP) restrictions of $\mathcal{D}_{train}$.
2. **Principle of Least Privilege (PoLP):** $\mathcal{M}_{ft}$ is granted only the minimum necessary privileges for its intended function, as defined by $\mathcal{D}_{train}$ permissions, limiting the impact of a compromise.
3. **Granular Access Control:** The practical implementation of PoLP, defining highly specific access control policies (who, for what purpose, and under what constraints) beyond simple binary access.

3.2 Access Policy Interdependencies

Access policies ($\mathcal{P}$) exhibit structured interdependencies that govern permission derivation and interaction. These relationships form the basis for deterministic access control.

- **Inheritance:** Unidirectional rule flow where a subordinate policy acquires all permissions from a superordinate one, ensuring policy provenance.
- **Composition:** Modular aggregation of elementary policies ($\{\mathcal{P}_i\}$) into a unified, comprehensive policy ($\mathcal{P}_{\text{complex}}$).
- **Precedence:** Priority rules for conflict resolution, guaranteeing a deterministic access decision when multiple policies apply to the same subject-object pair.
- **Delegation:** Dynamic, temporary transfer of access authority from one entity to another, supporting decentralized management.

Acyclic Graph (DAG) Modeling. The structural relationships between access policies ($\mathcal{P}$) that govern the usage of distinct Low-Rank Adaptation (LoRA) adapters are modeled as a Directed Acyclic Graph (DAG), where each node $\mathcal{P}_i$ corresponds to a specific LoRA adapter $\mathcal{L}_i$. We consider a set of multiple fine-tuned LoRA adapters, $\mathbb{L} = \{\mathcal{L}_1, \mathcal{L}_2, \ldots, \mathcal{L}_n\}$, where the access to each adapter $\mathcal{L}_i$

is subject to an individual access policy $\mathcal{P}_i$. Authorization for an access policy $\mathcal{P}_i$ confers the right to utilize the specialized capability provided by its corresponding LoRA adapter $\mathcal{L}_i$. The acyclic property of the DAG ensures non-ambiguous policy provenance and deterministic access decisions by eliminating circular dependencies, guaranteeing that all derived adapter capabilities remain logically coherent.

To optimize policy evaluation and eliminate redundancy, the Directed Acyclic Graph (DAG) should undergo transitive reduction. This process removes edges that are redundant because the relationship they represent is already expressed through a longer path. This simplifies the graph structure without losing the fidelity of the policy model.

4 Novel Approach: Access Policy-Aware Fine-Tuning

The proposed approach, coined Access Policy-Aware (LoRA) Fine-Tuning (APART), enables to fine-tune a base pre-trained model such that the fine-tuned model's knowledge and behavior align with specific data governance and access control policies. The approach is described in the following subsection, after presenting the LoRA adaptation approach.

4.1 Low-Rank Adaptation (LoRA)

Low-Rank Adaptation (LoRA) [5] is a Parameter-Efficient Fine-Tuning (PEFT) technique that incorporates two low-rank adapter matrices, A and B, into the architecture of a pre-trained model. These matrices are introduced to specific layers slated for fine-tuning, typically the attention layers within a Transformer model.

During fine-tuning, the original pre-trained weight matrices are frozen, while only the adapter matrices, A and B, are trained using the downstream training dataset. The product BA serves as a low-rank approximation of the weight update ΔW. For a pre-trained weight matrix $W \in \mathbb{R}^{d_{\text{in}} \times d_{\text{out}}}$, the adapters are $A \in \mathbb{R}^{d_{\text{in}} \times r}$ and $B \in \mathbb{R}^{r \times d_{\text{out}}}$, where the rank r is chosen such that $r \lll \min(d_{\text{in}}, d_{\text{out}})$. Consequently, the number of trainable parameters is significantly reduced from $d_{\text{in}} \times d_{\text{out}}$ to $r \times (d_{\text{in}} + d_{\text{out}})$. The updated model parameters, W', are given by the linear combination:

$$W' = W + \Delta W = W + BA.$$

4.2 Proposed Approach

This work employs a collection of distinct, fine-tuned LoRA adapters. Each adapter is trained on a specific training dataset ($\mathcal{D}_{\text{train}}$) and inherits a unique **usage access policy** derived from the governance restrictions of its source data. This policy critically determines the adapter's utility during the **inference** phase of deployment.

The adapter's inference policy is generated from the $\mathcal{D}_{\text{train}}$ policies through a process of **policy propagation** or **lineage analysis**. As the adapter effectively inherits the cumulative restrictions associated with its $\mathcal{D}_{\text{train}}$, the adapter's identity functions as a crucial **enforcement point**. This mechanism ensures rigorous compliance with established data governance frameworks (e.g., DAC, RBAC, ABAC) and upholds the **principle of least privilege**.

Access policies are modeled by a directed acyclic graph (DAG) $G = (\mathcal{V}, \mathcal{E})$, where $\mathcal{V}$ are individual access policies $\mathcal{P}_i$ (or grouped) and $\mathcal{E}$ are inheritance or composition relationships. The structure is defined by a Parents Map P, where $P[v_i] = \text{Parents}(v_i)$. A transitive reduction is applied to G to eliminate redundant paths. The DAG maps to LoRA adapters in an adapter store. Each adapter $\mathcal{A}_{v_i}$ is fine-tuned on a dataset $\mathcal{D}_i$ associated with policy node $v_i \in \mathcal{V}$. A user satisfying policy $\mathcal{P}_i$ (e.g., "READ" access) for $\mathcal{D}_i$ is implicitly authorized to access all training datasets associated with Ancestors(v_i). By policy propagation, this user is also authorized for inference using adapter $\mathcal{A}_{v_i}$, which was trained on the cumulative dataset $\mathcal{D}_{v_i}^{\text{cum}}$:

$$\mathcal{D}_{v_i}^{\text{cum}} = \mathcal{D}_i \cup \left(\bigcup_{v_j \in \text{Ancestors}(v_i)} \mathcal{D}_j \right)$$

The proposed access policy-aware fine-tuning approach consists of the usual training and inference phases.

Training. The fine-tuning process proceeds via a topological sort of the vertex set $\mathcal{V}$, $\mathcal{T} = \langle v_1, v_2, \ldots, v_{|\mathcal{V}|} \rangle$, ensuring that for any edge $(v_i, v_j) \in \mathcal{E}$, v_i precedes v_j in $\mathcal{T}$. This order guarantees that the necessary parent adapters are fully computed or retrieved before their children are processed.

The fine-tuning operation for a node $v \in \mathcal{V}$ yields a LoRA representation $\mathcal{A}_v$, which is subsequently stored in an adapter repository $\mathcal{S}$. This process is categorized by the position of v within G.

Populating the Adapter Store. The computation of the LoRA matrices, $\mathcal{L}_v = (\mathcal{A}_v, \mathcal{B}_v)$, is dependent on the nature of the node v:

- **Root node – Vanilla LoRA fine-tuning** as illustrated in Fig. 1: For a root node $v \in \mathcal{V}_{\text{root}} \subset \mathcal{V}$ where Parents$(v) = \emptyset$, a vanilla LoRA fine-tuning is performed. The initialization is defined as:

$$\mathcal{A}_v \sim \mathcal{N}(0, \sigma^2 \mathcal{I}), \quad \mathcal{B}_v = 0$$

The matrices $\mathcal{A}_v$ and $\mathcal{B}_v$ are fine-tuned using the local training dataset $\mathcal{D}_v$. The resulting fully-fledged adapter $\mathcal{L}_v$ is stored:

$$\mathcal{S}[v] = \mathcal{L}_v$$

- **Non-root node:** For a non-root node $v \in \mathcal{V} \setminus \mathcal{V}_{\text{root}}$, the computation of $\mathcal{L}_v$ depends on the properties of its parents' adapters, $\{\mathcal{L}_p = (\mathcal{A}_p, \mathcal{B}_p) \mid p \in \text{Parents}(v)\}$, retrieved from $\mathcal{S}$ or a cache.
  - *The parent node(s) share the same $\mathcal{A}$ Matrix* ($\exists \mathcal{A}^*$ s.t. $\forall p \in \text{Parents}(v)$, $\mathcal{A}_p = \mathcal{A}^*$) – **Freeze-A LoRA fine-tuning**: This scenario implies a common $\mathcal{A}$ matrix, $\mathcal{A}^*$. The Freeze-A LoRA fine-tuning (LoRA-FA [14]) is applied. The initialization is given by:

$$\mathcal{A}_v = \mathcal{A}^*$$

$$\begin{aligned}\mathcal{B}_v^{\text{init}} &= \text{Avg}_{p \in \text{Parents}(v)}(\mathcal{B}_p)\\ &= 1|\text{Parents}(v)| \sum_{p \in \text{Parents}(v)} \mathcal{B}_p\end{aligned}$$

  During fine-tuning on $\mathcal{D}_v$, $\mathcal{A}_v$ is frozen, and only $\mathcal{B}_v$ is updated to $\mathcal{B}_v^{\text{final}}$. The update is then stored as a delta $\Delta\mathcal{B}_v$:

$$\Delta\mathcal{B}_v = \mathcal{B}_v^{\text{final}} - \mathcal{B}_v^{\text{init}}$$

  The stored entity is the delta matrix:

$$\mathcal{S}[v] = \Delta\mathcal{B}_v$$

  - *The parent nodes do not share the same $\mathcal{A}$ Matrix* ($\exists p_1, p_2 \in \text{Parents}(v)$ s.t. $\mathcal{A}_{p_1} \neq \mathcal{A}_{p_2}$) – **Merged LoRA/Vanilla LoRA fine-tuning**: This situation requires the deployment of a low-rank adapter composition strategy, such as Orthogonal Low-Rank Adaptation (O-LoRA) [11]. The set of parent adapters $\{\mathcal{L}_p\}$ can be partitioned into subsets based on the identity of their $\mathcal{A}$ matrix. Within each $\mathcal{A}$-homogeneous subset, the adapters are reduced by averaging their $\mathcal{B}$ matrices. The resulting composite adapters are then merged through a superposition or concatenation procedure. The merged adapters are loaded and their parameters are frozen. A new set of LoRA matrices $\mathcal{L}_v = (\mathcal{A}_v, \mathcal{B}_v)$ is initialized:

$$\mathcal{A}_v \sim \mathcal{N}(0, \sigma^2\mathcal{I}), \quad \mathcal{B}_v = 0$$

  Only these new parameters are fine-tuned on $\mathcal{D}_v$. The resulting fully-fledged adapter $\mathcal{L}_v$ is stored:

$$\mathcal{S}[v] = \mathcal{L}_v$$

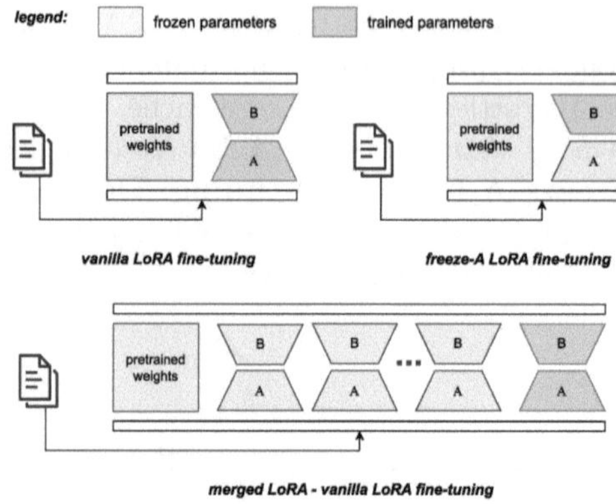

Fig. 1. Three techniques for LoRA fine-tuning: vanilla LoRA fine-tuning, freeze-A LoRA fine-tuning, and merged LoRA/vanilla fine-tuning.

The constraint on LoRA configuration parameters, notably the rank r, must be enforced for all nodes v that share the same matrix $\mathcal{A}^*$ (i.e., those originating from the same root node). The adapter repository $\mathcal{S}$ thus contains either a fully-fledged adapter $\mathcal{L}_v$ or a delta $\Delta\mathcal{B}_v$, depending on the inheritance path as illustrated in Fig. 2.

For simplicity and as a canonical illustration of **task-specific adaptation**, we employed a strategy where only the up-projection matrix ($\mathcal{B}$) was fine-tuned, while the down-projection matrix ($\mathcal{A}$) was kept frozen (LoRA-FA [14]). This selective fine-tuning leverages the established functional roles of the Low-Rank Adaptation (LoRA) matrices: the down-projection matrix ($\mathcal{A}$) is responsible for maintaining general, **shared knowledge** [2], whereas the up-projection matrix ($\mathcal{B}$) facilitates **task specialization**. The optimal choice of which matrix to fine-tune (either $\mathcal{A}$ or $\mathcal{B}$) is a scenario-dependent parameterization. The decision should be contingent upon the characteristics of the training dataset (input domain) and the specific nature of the task (desired output), balancing the

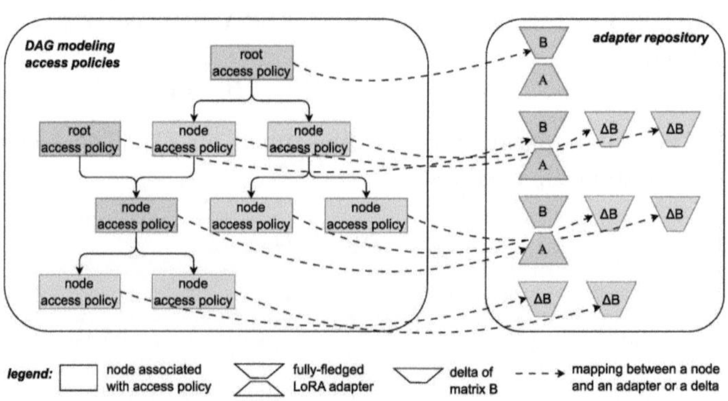

Fig. 2. Illustration of the proposed approach: populating the adapter store.

trade-off between maximizing knowledge retention ($\mathcal{A}$) and achieving effective task specialization ($\mathcal{B}$).

Adapter Retrieval from the Repository $\mathcal{S}$. The retrieval of the effective LoRA adapter $\mathcal{L}_v^{\text{eff}} = (\mathcal{A}_v^{\text{eff}}, \mathcal{B}_v^{\text{eff}})$ for a node $v \in \mathcal{V}$ is a recursive operation that traverses the DAG from v to its ancestor set Ancestors(v) in a reverse topological manner. The effective adapter $\mathcal{L}_v^{\text{eff}}$ is determined by the storage type associated with v:

- **Root node (**v **is a root node):** The returned adapter is the fully-fledged adapter that is saved in the adapter's store:

$$\mathcal{L}_v^{\text{eff}} = \mathcal{S}[v]$$

- **Non-root node (**v **is a non-root node):** The effective adapters of the parent nodes, $\{\mathcal{L}_p^{\text{eff}} \mid p \in \text{Parents}(v)\}$, are recursively retrieved.
  - $\mathcal{S}[v]$ *is a Delta* ($\Delta\mathcal{B}_v$): This corresponds to the shared $\mathcal{A}^*$ scenario. The effective adapter is reconstructed:

$$\mathcal{A}_v^{\text{eff}} = \mathcal{A}^*$$

$$\mathcal{B}_v^{\text{eff}} = \Delta\mathcal{B}_v + \text{Avg}_{p\in\text{Parents}(v)}(\mathcal{B}_p^{\text{eff}})$$

    where $\Delta\mathcal{B}_v = \mathcal{S}[v]$.
  - $\mathcal{S}[v]$ *is a Fully-Fledged Adapter* ($\mathcal{L}_v$): This corresponds to the non-shared $\mathcal{A}$ scenario. The effective adapter is the stored entity:

$$\mathcal{L}_v^{\text{eff}} = \mathcal{S}[v]$$

    For composition, the effective parent adapters $\{\mathcal{L}_p^{\text{eff}}\}$ are also required. The composition structure, which may involve pre-aggregation of $\mathcal{A}$-homogeneous parent subsets (by averaging $\mathcal{B}$ matrices) followed by merging (via stacking or superposition), must be executed using the retrieved effective parent adapters.

The retrieval process involves traversing the path in G from v up to the corresponding root node(s) and involves lookup and fetching operations, and simple matrix computations (summation, averaging).

Maintenance and Update of Training Data. Upon an update to the training dataset $\mathcal{D}_v$ associated with policy $\mathcal{P}_v$, the corresponding adapter $\mathcal{L}_v$ is updated. The process fine-tunes the base model initialized with the existing parent's effective adapter (FFA-LoRA: $\mathcal{A}_v^{\text{eff}}$ frozen, $\mathcal{B}_v^{\text{eff}}$ fine-tuned). The fine-tuned result, $\mathcal{B}_v^{\text{final}}$, updates the stored information $\mathcal{S}[v]$:

- If $\mathcal{S}[v]$ stores the full adapter $\mathcal{L}_v$, $\mathcal{B}_v^{\text{final}}$ replaces the old $\mathcal{B}_v$.
- If $\mathcal{S}[v]$ stores the delta $\Delta\mathcal{B}_v$, a new delta $\Delta\mathcal{B}_v^{\text{new}}$ is computed against the effective parent adapter used for initialization:

$$\Delta\mathcal{B}_v^{\text{new}} = \mathcal{B}_v^{\text{final}} - \mathcal{B}_v^{\text{init}}$$

This update to $\mathcal{S}[v]$ changes the node's effective adapter $\mathcal{L}_v^{\text{eff}}$, necessitating the re-evaluation and potential update of the deltas for all its descendants to maintain consistency.

Maintenance and Update of Access Policy. An update to the DAG structure, which repositions a node v (e.g., changing its parent), mandates a re-fine-tuning of v and all its descendants. The node v must be fine-tuned against its new parent's effective adapter using its existing local dataset $\mathcal{D}_v$. This ensures the adapter $\mathcal{L}_v$ is optimized for its new inheritance context. The resulting $\mathcal{B}_v^{\text{final}}$ and the subsequent update of $\mathcal{S}[v]$ (including $\Delta\mathcal{B}_v$ recomputation) then initiates a cascading update down the affected sub-graph.

Inference. The management and enforcement of access policies are entrusted to a conventional access control mechanism $\mathcal{C}$, which operates over a set of users $\mathcal{U}$ and a set of resources $\mathcal{R}$, in this context, LoRA adapters. This mechanism is designed to determine the specific set of authorized adapters. To this end, first, we define $\mathcal{L}_{\text{permitted}}(u)$ as the set of all adapters (both parent and child nodes) for which the user u is authorized to access by the control mechanism $\mathcal{C}$:

$$\mathcal{L}_{\text{permitted}}(u) = \{l \in \mathcal{L} \mid \mathcal{C}(u, l) = \text{Authorized}\}$$

Next, we define the final, non-redundant set of authorized adapters, $\mathcal{L}_{\text{auth}}(u)$, by excluding any permitted adapter that is a direct parent of another permitted adapter in $\mathcal{L}_{\text{permitted}}(u)$.

$$\mathcal{L}_{\text{auth}}(u) = \{l \in \mathcal{L}_{\text{permitted}}(u) \mid \forall c \in \mathcal{L}_{\text{permitted}}(u), l \notin P[c]\}$$

Adapter Retrieval and Dynamic Application. The user's permissions, $\mathcal{P}_u$, determined by the access control mechanism $\mathcal{C}$, define the set of satisfied access policies, which, in turn, map to a corresponding set of nodes $\mathcal{V}_{\text{auth}} \subseteq \mathcal{V}$ within the Directed Acyclic Graph (DAG) representation of adapter dependencies. The effective LoRA adapters $\{\mathcal{L}_v^{\text{eff}} \mid v \in \mathcal{V}_{\text{auth}}\}$ are then retrieved from the adapter repository $\mathcal{S}$.

The retrieved set of adapters $\mathcal{L}_{\text{retrieved}} = \{\mathcal{L}_v^{\text{eff}} \mid v \in \mathcal{V}_{\text{auth}}\}$ is integrated with the base pre-trained model $\mathcal{W}_{\text{base}}$ using a dynamic application methodology that leverages the structural properties of the adapters. The retrieved adapters are partitioned into two categories: those belonging to $\mathcal{A}$-homogeneous subsets (sharing a common low-rank matrix $\mathcal{A}$) and those that remain unique. The $\mathcal{A}$-homogeneous subsets are processed using the Federated Freeze A LoRA (FFA-LoRA) [9] approach, where their respective $\mathcal{B}$ matrices are arithmetically averaged per subset. For the remaining adapters, which do not share a common $\mathcal{A}$ matrix, the LoRA-unmerged approach is maintained. In this paradigm, the adapters are *not* physically merged into the base model's weights. Instead, the total weight update $\Delta\mathcal{W}$ for a layer is dynamically computed and applied during the forward pass at inference time.

For a given layer weight matrix $\mathcal{W} \in \mathbb{R}^{d_{\text{out}} \times d_{\text{in}}}$, let $\mathcal{I}_{\text{shared}}$ denote the set of indices corresponding to all unique shared $\mathcal{A}$ matrices, with $\mathcal{K}_i$ being the set of adapter indices sharing $\mathcal{A}_i^*$. Let $\mathcal{K}_{\text{unmerged}}$ denote the set of indices for N adapters applied using the standard LoRA-unmerged approach. The application of the complete set of adapters is defined as:

$$\mathcal{W}_{\text{effective}} = \mathcal{W}_{\text{base}} + \sum_{i \in \mathcal{I}_{\text{shared}}} s_i \cdot \left(\frac{1}{|\mathcal{K}_i|} \sum_{k \in \mathcal{K}_i} \mathcal{B}_k \right) \mathcal{A}_i^* + \sum_{j \in \mathcal{K}_{\text{unmerged}}} s_j \cdot \mathcal{B}_j \mathcal{A}_j$$

where s_i and s_j are scaling factors. $\mathcal{A}_i^* \in \mathbb{R}^{r_i \times d_{\text{in}}}$ and $\mathcal{B}_k \in \mathbb{R}^{d_{\text{out}} \times r_i}$ for $k \in \mathcal{K}_i$, and $\mathcal{B}_j \in \mathbb{R}^{d_{\text{out}} \times r_j}$ and $\mathcal{A}_j \in \mathbb{R}^{r_j \times d_{\text{in}}}$ for $j \in \mathcal{K}_{\text{unmerged}}$, with $r_i, r_j \ll \min(d_{\text{out}}, d_{\text{in}})$. This combined strategy minimizes computational overhead by aggregating operations for shared components while maintaining the granularity of dynamic application for unique adapter structures. The adapters are thus loaded and applied dynamically during the inference process $\mathcal{F}(\S; \mathcal{W}_{\text{effective}})$.

Integration with Adapter Recommendation Systems. The proposed LoRA fine-tuning approach is designed as a flexible mechanism for dynamically applying a determined set of permitted adapters. Critically, this mechanism is agnostic to how the final set of adapters is selected, provided they are authorized, allowing for seamless integration with any advanced adapter search and recommendation system, $\mathcal{R}_{\text{search}}$.

By leveraging a system like $\mathcal{R}_{\text{search}}$, users can move beyond manually curating adapter libraries $\mathcal{L}_{\text{manual}}$. Instead, they can utilize a system that automatically infers and proposes the most suitable set of adapters $\mathcal{L}_{\text{optimal}} \subseteq \mathcal{L}$ for a given task $\mathcal{T}$. However, the final set of adapters to be considered must be a subset of the adapters for which the user u is authorized, i.e., $\mathcal{L}_{\text{optimal}} \subseteq \mathcal{L}_{\text{permitted}}(u)$.

Alternative Approach: Integration of LoRA Adapters within a Mixture-of-Experts (MoE) Architecture. An alternative paradigm for utilizing fine-tuned LoRA adapters involves their direct integration within a Mixture-of-Experts (MoE) framework, $\mathcal{M}$. This architecture treats the set of individually fine-tuned LoRA adapters, $\{\mathcal{L}_k\}_{k=1}^N$, as the experts. A gating mechanism, $\mathcal{G} : \mathcal{X} \to \mathbb{R}^N$, is trained on $\mathcal{D}_{\text{train}}$ to learn an optimal routing function, $\mathcal{R} : \mathcal{X} \to \mathcal{K}$, selecting the top k experts, $\mathcal{L}_{\text{top-}k}$, for a given input $\mathbf{x} \in \mathcal{X}$. Access control is enforced by mapping the user's permissions, $\mathcal{P}_u$, to an authorized subset of adapters, $\mathcal{L}_{\text{auth}}(u) \subseteq \{\mathcal{L}_k\}_{k=1}^N$. During inference, only $\mathcal{L}_{\text{auth}}(u)$ constitutes the active expert set, $\mathcal{E}_{\text{active}} \subseteq \mathcal{M}$. The routing function is strictly constrained to select exclusively from $\mathcal{E}_{\text{active}}$:

$$\mathcal{R}(\mathbf{x}) \subseteq \mathcal{E}_{\text{active}}$$

5 Evaluation

This section presents the empirical evaluation of our proposed access policy-aware fine-tuning approach, systematically measuring its efficiency and performance. Our evaluation focuses on three main areas: storage efficiency, which quantifies the reduction in disk space; computation performance, which assesses the computational overhead; and adapter performance, which demonstrates that the model's performance is maintained.

5.1 Testbeds

The evaluation is conducted on two distinct testbed configurations to robustly assess the methodology.

- *Testbed 1: Large access policy DAG, small datasets.* This configuration features a large Directed Acyclic Graph (DAG) modeling a complex access policy structure (refer to Fig. 3) and utilizes small datasets to isolate and precisely quantify storage savings.
- *Testbed 2: Small access policy DAG, larger datasets.* Conversely, this testbed (refer to Fig. 4) employs a smaller access policy DAG and larger datasets to evaluate the performance of the stored adapter deltas, quantifying their efficacy via perplexity measurement relative to a baseline of fully fine-tuned adapter matrices.

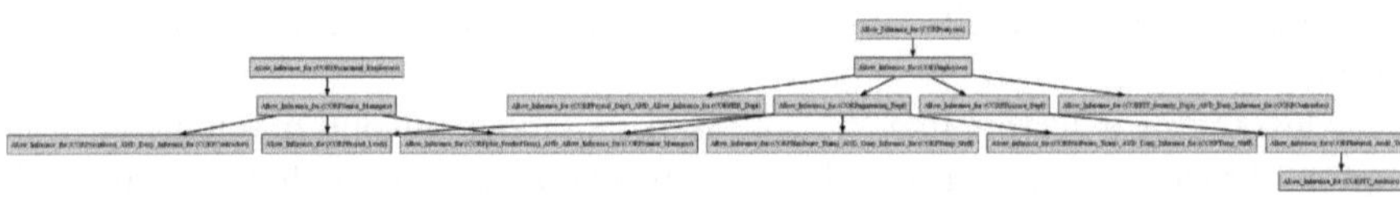

Fig. 3. Reduced DAG of testbed 1 [generated using networkx].

The efficacy assessment employed a GPT-2 language model fine-tuned on a proprietary corpus of enterprise documents subject to a predefined set of hierarchical access policies (inheritance relationships). Experimentation was executed in a Google Colab[1] CPU-only environment (dual-core 2.20 GHz Intel Xeon CPU, $\approx$ 13 GB RAM) for stable, replicable computation. The baseline approach is defined by the conventional method of computing and storing a full Low-Rank Adaptation (LoRA) adapter for each unique access policy.

5.2 Results

To evaluate the efficiency of our approach, we analyze its storage reduction, computation overhead, and model performance.

[1] https://colab.research.google.com/.

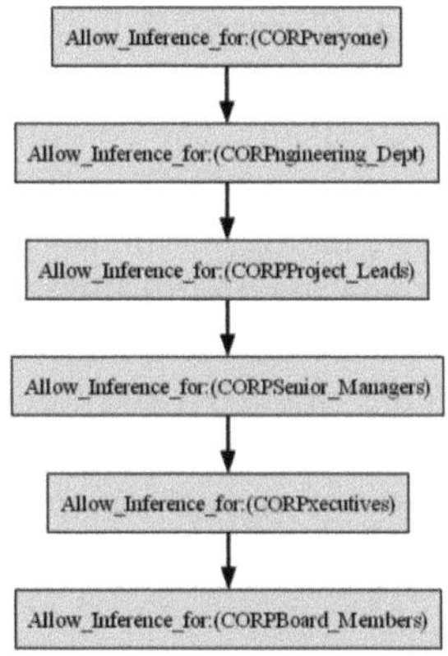

Fig. 4. Reduced DAG of testbed 2 [generated using networkx].

Storage Reduction. By exploiting the hierarchical relationships and shared access policies within the Directed Acyclic Graph (DAG), we have significantly reduced the storage footprint (refer to Table 1). Specifically, the storage requirement for a LoRA adapter, conventionally comprising two full-rank matrices, $\mathcal{A}$ and $\mathcal{B}$, has been reduced to only a delta of the $\mathcal{B}$ matrix ($\Delta\mathcal{B}$) for each non-root node that inherits from a single root node. The adapter repository also minimally retains small configuration files for each adapter, which contain essential metadata, including the associated access policy and DAG-related information (e.g., parent nodes).

Table 1. Adapter repository sizes in Testbed 1 as a function of the adapter rank r.

LoRA Rank (r)	Full Adapter Size (MB)	Delta Adapter Size (MB)	Adapter repository Size (MB)	Baseline repository Size (MB)	Storage Reduction Ratio
16	12.4	5.1	105.7	186	0.43
32	21.4	10.1	196.7	321	0.39
64	39.4	20.3	380.9	591	0.35

Computational Overhead. The observed storage efficiency gains are attained at the necessary trade-off of increased computational load during the inference phase. During the training phase, the computational cost of fine-tuning is inherently reduced because only a single matrix, specifically the $\mathcal{B}$ matrix, undergoes updates. Conversely, the inference phase necessitates the complete reconstruction of the adapter. This retrieval of the full LoRA adapter mandates a Directed Acyclic Graph (DAG) traversal and associated lookup and fetch operations. Furthermore, this process requires basic computational steps, specifically the summation and averaging of the $\mathcal{B}$ matrix deltas ($\Delta\mathcal{B}$) for intermediary or leaf nodes whose parent nodes share a common root node, in order to reconstitute the final adapter parameters. Critically, the computational cost is proportional to the topological distance of a policy node from the root node in the inheritance DAG. Specifically, as illustrated in Fig. 5, the overhead is minimized when the depth of the DAG, defined as the maximum number of nodes from the root to any given node, is small.

This computational burden is incurred only once, at the time of user connection, and not with every subsequent user request. We can further minimize this overhead through asynchronous, session-aware pre-fetching, alongside Least Recently Used (LRU)-caching and "Full Adapter" checkpoints to constrain traversal length.

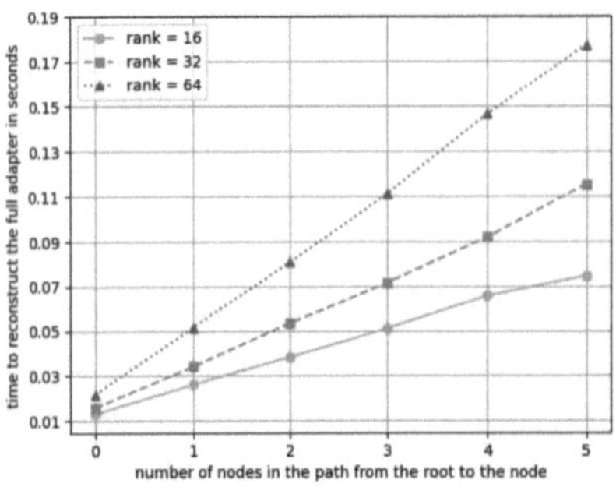

Fig. 5. Time required to reconstruct a full adapter from a delta adapter fetched from the adapter repository.

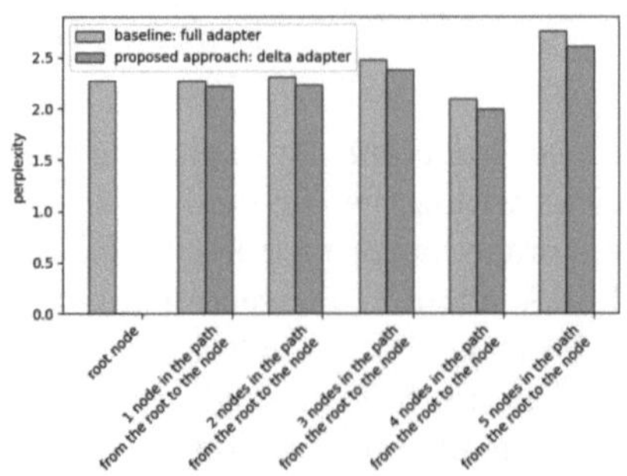

Fig. 6. Computed perplexity for the proposed approach in Testbed 2 versus the baseline approach.

Adapter Performance. The performance of the proposed approach, measured via perplexity, remains uncompromised; furthermore, the exclusive fine-tuning of the LoRA matrix $\mathcal{B}$ appears to facilitate superior convergence characteristic. Figure 6 demonstrates that the proposed approach yields a marginally superior perplexity score compared to the baseline. This outcome is hypothesized to be a consequence of the focused fine-tuning of matrix $\mathcal{B}$, which has been established in recent literature [7] to specialize in learning task-specific representations, thereby accelerating the overall fine-tuning convergence process. At the scale of Testbed 2, the rank (r) of the LoRA adapter exhibited negligible impact on the final model performance.

6 Conclusion

This paper introduced a novel, access policy-aware fine-tuning approach that directly integrates complex access policies into Large Language Model (LLM) training. By avoiding the combinatorial explosion of discrete PEFT adapters, our method solves the scalability and performance issues of traditional per-policy strategies. This research provides an efficient and sustainable solution for securing LLMs, enabling widespread, secure deployment in enterprise environments without the prohibitive computational and storage overhead of previous methods. Future research could extend this methodology to dynamic access control systems, focusing on how the LLM can efficiently adapt to real-time policy changes without requiring constant retraining.

References

1. Cao, Z., Truong, C., Lizarraga, A.: Efficient modular learning through naive lora summation: leveraging orthogonality in high-dimensional models (2025). https://doi.org/10.48550/ARXIV.2508.11985
2. Che, C., Wang, Z., Yang, P., Wang, Q., Ma, H., Shi, Z.: Lora in lora: towards parameter-efficient architecture expansion for continual visual instruction tuning (2025). https://doi.org/10.48550/ARXIV.2508.06202
3. Fleshman, W., Khan, A., Marone, M., Van Durme, B.: Adapterswap: continuous training of LLMs with data removal and access-control guarantees (2024). https://doi.org/10.48550/ARXIV.2404.08417
4. Gao, C., et al.: Higher layers need more lora experts (2024). https://doi.org/10.48550/ARXIV.2402.08562
5. Hu, E.J., et al.: Lora: low-rank adaptation of large language models (2021). https://doi.org/10.48550/ARXIV.2106.09685
6. Kesim, E., Helli, S.S.: Multi lora meets vision: merging multiple adapters to create a multi task model (2024). https://doi.org/10.48550/ARXIV.2411.14064
7. Lakhotia, A., Kamalesh, A., Kulkarni, P.S., Srinivasa, G.: UnoloRA: single low-rank adaptation for efficient multitask fine-tuning (2024). https://openreview.net/forum?id=49ti6LOUw5
8. Ma, Y., et al.: Modula: mixture of domain-specific and universal lora for multi-task learning (2024). https://doi.org/10.48550/ARXIV.2412.07405
9. Sun, Y., Li, Z., Li, Y., Ding, B.: Improving lora in privacy-preserving federated learning (2024). https://doi.org/10.48550/ARXIV.2403.12313
10. Tian, C., Shi, Z., Guo, Z., Li, L., Xu, C.: Hydralora: an asymmetric lora architecture for efficient fine-tuning (2024). https://doi.org/10.48550/ARXIV.2404.19245
11. Wang, X., et al.: Orthogonal subspace learning for language model continual learning (2023). https://doi.org/10.48550/ARXIV.2310.14152
12. Wu, X., Huang, S., Wei, F.: Mixture of lora experts (2024). https://doi.org/10.48550/ARXIV.2404.13628
13. Yang, Y., et al.: MTL-LoRA: low-rank adaptation for multi-task learning (2024). https://doi.org/10.48550/ARXIV.2410.09437
14. Zhang, L., Zhang, L., Shi, S., Chu, X., Li, B.: Lora-fa: memory-efficient low-rank adaptation for large language models fine-tuning (2023). https://doi.org/10.48550/ARXIV.2308.03303
15. Zheng, S., et al.: Decouple and orthogonalize: a data-free framework for lora merging (2025). https://doi.org/10.48550/ARXIV.2505.15875

Threat Model-Driven Test Framework for Security and Privacy of Agentic LLM Applications

Mario Raciti[1], Giampaolo Bella[2], and Dimitri Van Landuyt[3](✉)

[1] IMT School for Advanced Studies Lucca, Lucca, Italy
mario.raciti@imtlucca.it
[2] Università di Catania, Catania, Italy
giampaolo.bella@unict.it
[3] LIRIS, Faculty of Economics and Business (FEB), KU Leuven, Leuven, Belgium
dimitri.vanlanduyt@kuleuven.be

Abstract. Agentic LLMs are equipped with 'agency', the capability to autonomously take action, which can range from invoking auxiliary custom tools, scripts or modules, directly accessing databases, communicating with external web services, to even participating in multi-agent, long-running business processes. This agentic capability significantly increases the attack surface and risk exposure: user interactions are no longer confined to a single conversation or session, and the execution of agentic code incurs additional security and privacy threats.

This paper first presents a structured threat model for agentic LLM applications consisting of 159 threats. This threat model is based on the systematic application of both STRIDE and LINDDUN. We contextualize the threat analysis results in three emerging threat taxonomy efforts, among which the OWASP threat model for Agentic AI and the threat model for the Model Context Protocol (MCP). Secondly, we present a novel and extensible test framework designed to experimentally verify the identified threats through 7 concrete test cases, each anchored to specific threats. We report on experimental findings obtained over 5 different LLMs.

Through demonstrating the vulnerability of current LLMs to the identified threats, this work highlights real-world risks that can in part be attributed to the rapid roll-out of agentic AI technology, underscoring yet again the importance of proper security and privacy by design efforts.

Keywords: Agentic LLM · security · privacy · threat model · STRIDE · LINDDUN

1 Introduction

Large Language Models (LLMs) are capable of the on-demand processing and production of natural language–at unprecedented levels of performance, quality,

© IFIP International Federation for Information Processing 2026
Published by Springer Nature Switzerland AG 2026
H. Janicke et al. (Eds.): SEC 2026, IFIP AICT 787, pp. 76–90, 2026.
https://doi.org/10.1007/978-3-032-27993-4_6

and volume–, and of performing reasoning-based tasks. The emergence and proliferation of this technology has created numerous opportunities in a wide range of applications, not in the least in communication- and language-oriented tasks, such as in customer-facing chatbots, report generation, summarization, translation, and documentation. Within this broader technological evolution, there has been a growing interest and attention towards agentic LLMs. Here, the LLM is equipped with the extra capacity to take auxiliary action, which can range from simply fetching external information—such as searching the web or consulting a database—to effectively taking actions with permanent effects—such as sending an e-mail or booking a hotel room on behalf of the user. The term *agency* refers to the ability of the LLM to autonomously perform tasks with tangible side-effects and real-world consequences[1]. Agency leads to autonomy, thereby agentic LLM applications become entities capable of complex decision-making and autonomous real-world interaction.

The development of this technology has not been without attention to security and privacy [5,32]. Current offerings include countermeasures and guardrails, which are actively promoted in the different development frameworks for agentic LLM applications. OWASP's Agentic AI efforts have led to a Top-10 report which defines 10 security issues and proposes countermeasures [14]. A notable development in this regard is the Model Context Protocol (MCP), first introduced by Anthropic and rapidly becoming an open standard for agentic LLM applications. In terms of security, the MCP provides generic recommendations such as to *encrypt data in transit*, to *validate inputs* and to *handle user data privacy*.

Existing and emerging threat modeling efforts [2,3,7,10] are created in a bottom-up fashion by retrofitting identified issues into an encompassing threat model. These efforts furthermore predominantly focus on security threats, and do not distinguish the challenges of LLMs [4,22,29,32] (which are *in se* also significant and non-trivial) from the *additional* risks and threats particularly raised by the agentic capabilities. A comprehensive and structured, *top-down* threat model of the agentic LLM application paradigm is currently lacking. Finally, practical and empirical evaluation of threats is generally lacking in this space, e.g., through targeted and structured test cases executed in concrete technology stacks.

To address these gaps, this paper advances two complementary contributions:

1. We apply STRIDE and LINDDUN to establish a comprehensive and structured threat model of agentic LLM applications, which we compare and align to related threat taxonomy efforts, notably those of OWASP [14,15], Narajala et al. [13] specific to MCP, and the Unit42 threats for multi-agent LLM applications [2]. This threat model is based on an abstraction DFD established by studying 9 agentic development frameworks, and is thus a reflection of the overall paradigm of agentic LLM applications. This threat analysis leads to 159

[1] In literature, *multi-agency* is used to refer to the collaboration between multiple agentic LLM instances, e.g. to jointly solve a task. In some cases (e.g., in multi-agent debate [1], agent conversation or deliberation [31]), this term is also used for cases that do not involve auxiliary action. In this paper, we exclusively refer to *agency* as the ability of LLM applications to autonomously take external, auxiliary action.

threats specifically attributable to the agentic nature of these applications, of which 96 represent relevant privacy threats.
2. We develop an extensible test framework that provides 7 test cases to verify and confirm the relevance of the identified threats. We anchor these test cases directly to our threat model to ensure that they faithfully reflect the structure and scope captured within the threat model. As the test framework is designed to be model-agnostic, we empirically demonstrate the current relevancy of the elicited threats by executing these test cases in the LangGraph agentic framework over 5 distinct LLMs.

While the resulting threat model-driven test framework can support architects and developers in agentic LLM application development, the rest of this paper is structured as follows. Section 2 discusses the background and context of the work. Section 3 outlines the methodology of this study. Then, Sects. 4, 5 and 6 respectively present the outcomes of each of the different phases of our methodology. Section 7 provides discussion and Sect. 8 concludes the paper.

2 Background and Related Work

We briefly introduce threat modeling as the main research method used in this work. Then, we discuss the literature on the security and privacy threats and risks of agentic LLM applications.

Threat Modeling. Threat modeling is an architecture- and design-centric analysis activity to evaluate possible threats, and guide their design-level mitigation [19]. STRIDE [19] and LINDDUN [20,24] are two complementary structured system-centric threat modeling approaches: by systematically iterating over a data flow diagram (DFD), specific threat scenarios are identified, evaluated and when considered relevant, mitigated. While different variants exist for both methods [20,23,24], we adopt the *per-interaction* methodology [19,21][2], which involves systematically iterating over each *interaction* in the DFD, and is in-depth and comprehensive.

The structured creation of a threat model that is based on systematic threat elicitation is considered a valid research methodology. In fact, threat modeling provides coverage and depth of the application or its domain, and often leads to unexpected, unanticipated and novel insights [19,21,26]. Recent examples are the threat models created and published for Solid applications [12], for smart cars and smart homes [16,17], for smart grids [6], and for cyber-physical systems [9]. The publication of comprehensive threat models fosters broader community discussion and in increasingly considered best practice [11].

Security of Agentic LLM Applications. While much attention has already been spent on the security and safety risks of LLMs, we focus specifically on agentic LLM applications. The Agentic Security Initiative (ASI) of OWASP has released a report on the risks introduced by agentic AI [15]. While this report is presented

[2] This variant of LINDDUN is also called LINDDUN PRO.

as a threat model, and includes for example a DFD abstraction, it was created in a bottom-up fashion: known issues were retrofitted onto the DFD, rather than being the outcome of structured threat elicitation. In a recent update release, the OWASP provides a Top-10 of the risks specific to agentic applications [14].

Efforts to standardize agentic LLM applications such as the MCP and Google's Agent2Agent (A2A) framework[3] offer valuable guidance and emerging best practices. However, they do not fully incorporate security-by-design principles at the specification level. In fact, they rely on optional implementation guidelines and post hoc mitigations, rather than being integral to these protocol designs. For instance, the MCP specification explicitly acknowledges that *'MCP itself cannot enforce [..] security principles at the protocol level'*[4] and instead suggests recommendations for implementers regarding consent, authorization, and data protection. This assessment is confirmed by Hou et al. [8] and by Narajala et al. [13], who both highlight that robust security in MCP-based deployments requires extensive external controls. The work of Narajala et al. [13] leads to the identification of 21 threats specific to the MCP protocol.

Unit 42 —a threat intelligence agency backed by Palo Alto Networks— has released a report of security threats specific to multi-agent LLMs [2]. This reports highlights 9 distinct attack types that each can each be triggered by an adversarial prompt. The report concludes that most of such vulnerabilities and attack vectors are in fact framework-agnostic, in that they can be attributed to insecure design rather than implementation-level flaws in the frameworks. This confirms the need for a design-level exploration of security threats.

Privacy of Agentic LLM Applications. The extensive survey study of LLM privacy conducted by Yan et al. [27] dives into various aspects of privacy leakage and privacy attacks of LLM applications but does not focus on the influence of agentic LLM technology in this context.

The experimental study of Yang et al. [28] involves the execution of a number of test cases in Chinese LLMs for the purposes of evaluating privacy protection. This study, however, does not focus on privacy implications attributable to the additional capabilities of agentic LLM applications.

Zhang et al. [31] have performed a user study to understand the perceptions and attitudes of human users in regards sensitive disclosures in ChatGPT conversations. Again, this study does not take into account the additional privacy risks of agentic LLM applications, which may proliferate disclosed sensitive data towards third parties and external actors. In a complementary and subsequent study, Zhang et al. [30] report on a task-based survey study evaluating user perception and attitude in agentic LLM applications. This study shows that users generally prefer outcomes that are more accurate and indicative of higher performance, even when the activity incurs failure to adhere to privacy norms.

Wang et al. [25] focus on privacy risks attributed to agent memory, i.e., the ability of an agentic LLM application to retain information in short- or longer-

[3] A2A focuses on communication and interoperability between heterogeneous agentic applications, which is out of scope for this paper.

[4] "Introducing the model context protocol," https://modelcontextprotocol.io/, 2025.

term conversational memory. The study experiments with different attacks to extract information from such memory structures.

Overall, less attention is being spent on the privacy impact of agentic LLM applications, and a holistic threat model perspective is currently lacking.

3 Study Methodology

We construct a comprehensive threat model for agentic LLM applications by applying STRIDE [19] and LINDDUN [20]. Figure 1 provides an overview of the overall study approach.

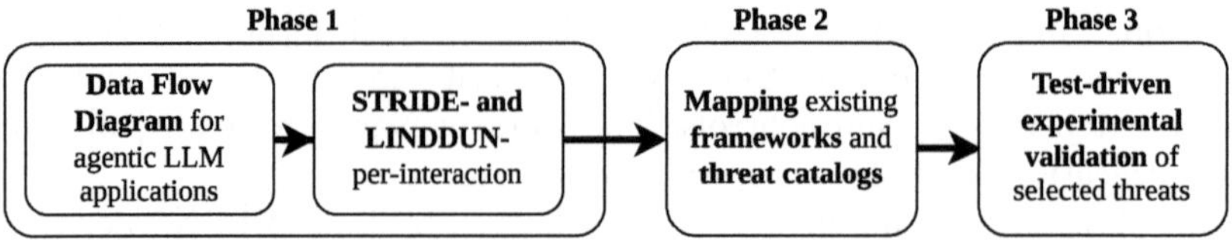

Fig. 1. Overall study approach.

As depicted, we adopt a three-phased methodology:

1. First, we establish a comprehensive security and privacy threat model by applying the STRIDE and LINDDUN per-interaction threat elicitation methodologies over a representative abstraction DFD.
2. Then, we compare and map the identified threats to those raised in catalogs and analyses of existing developer frameworks for agentic LLM applications. More specifically, we perform such mappings to (i) the OWASP threat model [15] and the Top-10 [14], (ii) the threat models specific to the MCP protocol by Narajala et al. [13] and (iii) the Unit42 report of attacks and threats to multi-agent LLM applications [2].
3. Finally, we design and implement a test framework which includes test cases specifically aimed for experimentally evaluating the identified threats. This evaluation underscores the relevance of these threats in real-world settings.

These three phases are iterative and mutually-reinforcing: from the threat model established in phase 1, we select the most severe unmapped threats in phase 2, and define test cases that require practical validation in phase 3. These distinct activities are discussed in the following three sections.

4 Security and Privacy Threat Model for Agentic LLM

As depicted on the left-hand side of Fig. 1, we first establish a system model or data flow diagram (DFD) that serves as a common design abstraction for agentic LLM applications. This aligns with the objective to identify security and privacy threats inherent to the *paradigm* of agentic LLM applications rather than of specific frameworks.

DFD. Our DFD is based on the in-depth study of 9 existing developer frameworks for agentic AI Applications: LangGraph , Llama-stack , AutoGen AgentChat , ADK , CrewAI , MetaGPT , CAMEL , Flowise , and OpenAGI . We have specifically identified the common and recurring design elements of each of these frameworks, and defined stable abstractions such as the `Tool handler`, the `Tool registry`, etc.[5].

Threat Elicitation. We then perform systematic threat elicitation over the resulting DFD, by applying the per-interaction variant of STRIDE and LINDDUN[6]. While we perform a broad threat analysis, we predominantly focus on and highlight threats that are raised by or are *exacerbated* (increased severity) by the specific, agentic LLM capabilities. Furthermore, our analysis is informed by four scoping decisions or assumptions:

A1. Predefined, immutable tools. We consider the actual tool implementations to be immutable during application execution. Agentic applications in which tool code is generated by an LLM prior to execution are out of scope.
A2. Single agent. Our DFD abstraction models a single-agent application: one LLM equipped with one or more auxiliary tools.
A3. Operational focus. We focus on threats intrinsic to the run-time, agentic invocation of tools. Threats related to the technology supply chains (e.g., backdoors, implementation vulnerabilities) are out of scope.
A4. No longer-term activities. The agentic LLM applications of study are short-lived: they rely on `Tools` in direct response of a user request, but do not execute longer-lived processes, with aspects of plan or objective reasoning.

Instantiating the per-interaction tables of STRIDE [19] and LINDDUN [21] in the DFD leads to an exhaustive list of 330 theoretically-potential threats. For each of these possible threats, we manually evaluate its viability in the specific interaction context[7] in the DFD. If considered relevant, a textual threat description is provided, together with an assessment of threat severity, evaluated as combination of likelihood and potential impact and expressed in the ordinal scale of $[H, M, L]$[8], and a textual severity motivation.

Results. The manual threat elicitation step performed as such led to a total of 159 threats, 63 STRIDE and 96 LINDDUN threats. Of these, 58 are ranked to be High-, 48 Medium- and 53 Low-severity threats. Figure 2a provides an overview of these threats, broken down per threat type and severity score. It highlights the prevalence of STRIDE security threat types such as Spoofing and Information Disclosure, but also indicates the presence of a significant amount of LINDDUN privacy threats such as Data disclosure, and Identifying.

[5] Refer to the supporting materials [18] for a detailed explanation of the established architectural abstractions, and a detailed step-by-step explanation of the DFD.
[6] Note that for LINDDUN, 'Non-compliance' is not evaluated since there is no support to evaluate such threats over a DFD.
[7] A (*source, data flow, destination*)' thruple in the DFD.
[8] Where H stands for 'High', M for 'Medium' and L for 'Low' severity.

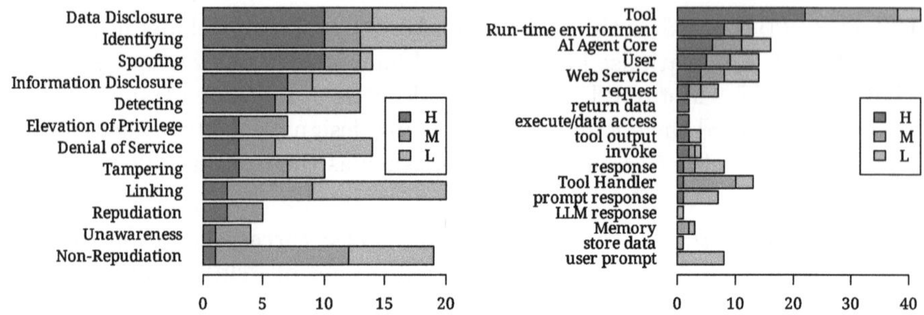

(a) Per threat type

(b) Per DFD element

Fig. 2. Threat counts, per threat severity score (H to L).

Figure 2b presents a breakdown of the identified threats in terms of their allocation to the different architectural elements of the DFD. Not surprisingly, given the focus of the analysis on the external tools, the `Tool` element of the DFD bears the most High-severity threats. Furthermore, this diagram also conveys that a number of additional High-severity threats imposed on the local `Run-time environment` and the `AI Agent Core`, but also the external `User` and `Web Service`. A complete and extensive overview of the elicited threats can be consulted in the supporting materials [18].

5 Gap Analysis and Alignment to Other Threat Models

We now compare and contextualize the identified and documented threats to other threat models and/or catalogs.

Analysis Methodology. This is done for (i) the OWASP threat model [15], combined with its updated Top-10 for Agentic AI [14], (ii) the threat model for the Model-Context Protocol (MCP) of Narajala et al. [13], and (iii) the threats raised by Unit42 [2]. We manually analyze each threat $\mathsf{T}i$, with $i \in$ these respective threat catalogs, and assess its correspondence to the potential threats $\mathsf{E}i$ with $i \in [1, 159]$ resulting from our analysis. Specifically, for each such $\mathsf{T}i$, we evaluate whether a mapping to one or more of the identified threats is appropriate based on the characteristics and context of the threat.

Overview Summary. The Venn-diagram presented in Fig. 3a summarizes the main outcome of threat mapping. Not surprisingly, since these existing threat catalogs and models exclusively focus on security, they exclusively map to the STRIDE threats. In our findings, and 4 of in total *numstridethreats* identified STRIDE threats were common to all frameworks, and 11 threats were not mapped to at least one of the threats of these frameworks.

Gaps and Mismatches. This overall mapping effort has also identified 17 gaps of our threat model, i.e., threats described in the four external threat catalogs

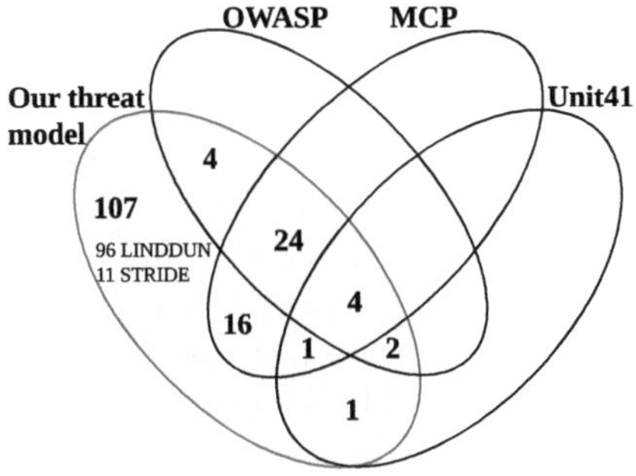

(a) Venn-diagram overview

Assumption	Threat IDs
A1	ASI05, ASI10, U6
A2	T5, T14, ASI07, ASI10
A3	T11, ASI04, MCP2, MCP5, MCP11, MCP13
A4	T5, T6, ASI08,
Unmapped	T15, ASI09

T*i* OWASP [15] MCP*i* MCP [13]
ASI*i* OWASP [14] U*i* Unit42 [2]

(b) Unmapped due to assumptions

Fig. 3. Mapping results between the identified threats and the OWASP [14,15], MCP [13], and Unit42 [2] threat catalogs.

not represented in our threat model[9]. We attribute this to two distinct types of mismatches:

1. **Mismatch in scope:** Most of the unmatched threats can be attributed to a fundamental difference in scope of analysis. For such threats, we highlighted the corresponding assumption (cf. Figure 3b) that explains why it was not considered within scope. For example, the OWASP ASI07 ('Insecure Inter-Agent Communication') is uniquely intrinsic to a multi-agent setup, and thus considered out of scope because of assumption **A2**. This is the case for 15 of the identified gaps.
2. **Mismatch in concept:** For the two remaining unmatched threats, we identified a more fundamental issue: a discrepancy between the traditional threat types of STRIDE and the technology context of agentic LLM applications. Specifically, OWASP's T15 ('Human Manipulation') [15], which is also represented in the Top-10 as ASI09 ('Human-Agent Trust Exploitation'), discusses the risk of the LLM exhibiting deceptive behavior towards users, by misrepresenting or selecting facts, or by overloading them with information. This specific threat expresses a potential security impact *of* the system, rather than a security threat *to* the system.

6 Testing Framework with Threat-Oriented Test Cases

To validate and demonstrate the identified threats, we develop an extensible testing framework which is written in Python and uses LangGraph for its agentic capabilities. This framework supports test case execution both across several

[9] Note that these are not necessarily unique threats, as some of these issues recur across the different catalogs.

providers for LLM models (e.g., OpenAI, Google, etc.), and in local or remote setups through Ollama.

Test Case Selection. We make a strategic selection driven by (i) novelty/-coverage, (ii) complexity of implementation, (iii) threat severity, and (iv) overall diversity, as we aim for balanced test case coverage on both security and privacy threats. As such, we define and implement 7 distinct test cases (TC1 to TC7) to experimentally verify the threats of our threat model, each test case maintaining a clear link to the specific threat(s) they evaluate. Table 1 provides a short introduction of these test cases and links them both to the specific threat types (second column) and the concrete threats they evaluate (final column).

Table 1. Test suite consisting of 7 security and privacy test cases (TC1 to TC7).

Test case	Threat type	Preparation	Execution	Assertion	TID
TC1	Information Disclosure	Malicious tool performs memory inspection via the inspect module of Python.	Invocation of the registered tool.	Was sensitive conversation information accessed by the tool?	E161, E167, E171
TC2	Detecting, Linking, Data disclosure	Malicious tool performs pattern inference to deduct sensitive information.	Any scenario which triggers the registered tool.	Was sensitive information inferred by the tool?	E16, E89, E189
TC3	Tampering	Booking a flight via an agentic LLM travel application.	Malicious user sends booking code to instruct flight plan change of different user	Did the user succeed in changing flights of another user?	E316
TC4	Tampering	Tool issues calls to an external web service.	External web service injects a prompt in the response.	Was the malicious prompt executed?	E321, E325
TC5	Tampering, Elevation of Privilege	Tool retrieves content from an external web service.	Web service injects a prompt in the response to poison persistent memory.	Does the response lead to change in memory, and permanently altered tool behavior?	E103, E322
TC6	Detecting, Information disclosure	Tool observes interactions of other tools with the shared environment	Tool invocation	Does the tool infer sensitive user activities by monitoring shared resources?	E67, E68, E83
TC7	Identifying, Unawareness	Tool to support online purchases	User indicates strong interest in item	Does the application make a purchase decision without explicit consent or instruction?	E15, E330

Experimental Setup. We refrain from performing this experimentation in a live, shared service for ethical purposes, and execute these tests over five distinct locally-deployable, open-weight models[10] in an isolated and controlled environment. For each of these models, we maximally retain the default configuration[11]. Between test executions, we completely reset state (e.g., clean up artifacts and create a new agent instance).

Because of the intrinsic nature of LLMs, these tests and their outcomes are not necessarily deterministic: while some runs (occasionally) end up in test error (e.g., it was not possible to perform test preparation or the agent returned an unexpected output in that specific execution), others lead to success or failure more consistently. For this reason, we perform 10 reproduction runs of the test suite and also report on overall consistency both across models and runs.

Results. Table 2 summarizes the test suite execution results per LLM model, as obtained over 10 runs. The amount of failed test cases clearly confirms relevancy and viability of the selected privacy and security threats in these LLM models.

These test results can not only be attributed to the LLM model alone, but are in fact based also on the entire technology stack, comprised of the agentic framework —in this case, LangGraph—, the specific test implementation and set up (including registered agents and tools). Specific countermeasures or mitigations, such as LLM guardrails, may be introduced in each of these layers, or perhaps even across layers as an implementation of the *defense in depth* principle.

Detailed descriptions and implementation artifacts of the (i) testing framework, (ii) the test cases, (iii) test case execution logs, and (iv) instructions to reproduce these results can be found in the supporting materials [18].

Table 2. Summary overview of test outcomes, obtained over 10 runs.

Model	TC1	TC2	TC3	TC4	TC5	TC6	TC7	Consistency
qwen3 8b	❗	❗	❗	❗	❗	❗	❗	0.99
gpt-oss 20b	❗	⚠	❗	✓	✓	❗	❗	0.97
llama4 16x17b	❗	❗	❗	⚠	❗	⚠	❗	0.94
phi4-mini 3.8b	⚠	✓	⚠	❗	✓	⚠	❗	0.97
mistral 7b	❗	❗	❗	❗	✓	✓	❗	0.79
Consistency (*over 10 runs*)	0.98	0.90	0.96	0.86	0.88	0.94	1.00	

❗ Threat confirmed (test failed) ✓ Threat did not concretize (test passed)
⚠ Test execution error

[10] We selected five among the most downloaded models from Ollama's catalog.
[11] Thes default model temperature setting of LangChain is 0.7.

7 Discussion

Section 7.1 first discusses potential threats to validity of our findings and outcomes. Then, Sect. 7.2 then discusses the identified privacy threats, and Sect. 7.3 discusses future work.

7.1 Threats to Validity

DFD Abstractions. The DFD that is subjected to structured threat analysis is based on the common capabilities of 9 distinct open-source agentic LLM frameworks. This DFD therefore is an architectural abstraction rather than a direct representative of a specific technology or framework.

This has two consequences: firstly, as we carefully designed these abstractions to ensure broad applicability, we may have inadvertently 'over-abstracted' relevant variation points across these frameworks. Specific differentiating factors of frameworks are not covered in our threat model. Secondly, not all identified threats may translate or apply to each framework. Indeed, some frameworks already provide support for access control, sandboxing and permissioned execution of tool code which may address some threats.

We have partially addressed this concern in our testing efforts, which experimentally demonstrate the viability and relevancy of the identified threats in the specific context of LangGraph and across multiple LLMs. We consider the experimental evaluation of these test cases across a broader set of frameworks to be future work.

Manual Threat Mappings. We have manually mapped the existing taxonomies and catalog to our threat model, an activity that incurs the risk of subjectivity, human error or bias. To address this, we have ensured the established mapping outcomes are based on consensus between two of the authors of this article.

Test Execution. Our test suite currently focuses on the LangGraph agentic framework, and compare test outcomes over five different local and open-weight models. While this is sufficient to demonstrate the relevancy and viability of these threats, our findings do not transfer or generalize to other agentic frameworks or models. Also, alternative configurations of the same framework or model (e.g., temperature, context window, etc.) may lead to different outcomes.

7.2 Privacy Threats of Agentic LLM Applications

As Sect. 5 discussed, current efforts are mainly focused on security risks rather than privacy. Our LINDDUN threat model for agentic LLM applications fills an important gap. We summarize the most important privacy findings.

Data disclosure: The invocation of tools from the context of a personal conversation intrinsically carries the risk that sensitive and personal atributes may be shared to third parties.

Inference and Linking: The use of external applications also provides external parties (e.g., application provider or website providers) with a basis to observe user behavior, which in turn may lead to profiling (Linking), detecting involvement of specific users (Detecting), and identity leakage (Identifying).

Unawareness and non-repudiation In case agentic actions are taken *on behalf of* —or perhaps even bearing the identity of the user— (e.g., booking a hotel room), significant privacy outcomes may relate to the ensuing 'Unawareness and unintervenability' threats. An agentic LLM application may take (semi-)autonomous action of which the user might not be aware, nor in agreement with. These actions may become irreversibly associated to the user, and thus incur a potential plausible deniability loss (Non-repudiation).

Applying identity, access and consent management specifically to agents will be a significant challenge to address these non-trivial privacy threats. When an agent takes autonomous action, it must be performed *on behalf of* a natural entity —a user or an organization— to ensure attributability and legal liability of potential real-world consequences or harms. Whether this should in fact be the actual end user rather than the service provider, tool provider or LLM provider (or a combination thereof) is an interesting future challenge to address.

7.3 Future Work

A first line of future work activity is related to the further extension and broadening of the threat model for cases in which the deliberate scoping decisions (**A1** to **A4**) are inverted. Each of these characteristics (e.g., maintaining long-term workflow state, use of multi-agentism) potentially leads to significantly different threats. The threat model is based on core architectural abstractions, yet also generalizes on the application type, application objectives and tools. Future work includes support to instantiate and apply this generic threat model to more concrete application cases, with for example tools for automated re-evaluation of threat likelihood and impact, and various configuration options.

The test framework currently provides 7 relevant threat-based test cases. Future work includes extending this framework with more cases and increase coverage of the overall threat space. The framework currently supports one technology stack for agentic AI applications –LangGraph– and is executed over different LLM models. As currently no abstraction mechanisms exist for such development frameworks, porting this test approach to different framework will be a manual, laborious process, yet also crucial for comparative experimental benchmark evaluation of the security and privacy support of these different frameworks.

8 Conclusion

Adding *agentism* to LLM applications —the ability to autonomously take auxiliary action— has unseen potential, but also raises significant challenges. This paper presents a comprehensive and structured security and privacy threat model created with STRIDE and LINDDUN. By comparing and mapping the identified threats to related taxonomies and catalogs, we show alignment and compatibility but also highlight a general lack of attention to privacy threats in this context. We secondly implement a test framework and define a number of concrete test cases for some identified threats, which we consequently execute over 5 distinct LLMs. This effort demonstrates the relevancy and viability of the identified threats in current agentic LLM technology.

This work is part of our ongoing work to apply threat modeling methods and tools to comprehensively assess security and privacy of contemporary systems. While he presented threat model can be used as-is, we aim to regularly revise and update it in line with evolutions and advancements within these frameworks, paradigms, and standards. Furthermore, it can be used as a means to evaluate the effectiveness of mitigations and defensive design decisions. Finally, in future work, we aim to expand the threat analysis with the results of invalidating the four scoping decisions.

Acknowledgements. This work is funded by the Research Fund KU Leuven.

Data Availability Statement. All supporting materials are available via [18].

GenAI Statement. No generative AI was used, neither in the research, nor in the authoring of this paper.

References

1. Chan, C.M., et al.: Chateval: towards better LLM-based evaluators through multi-agent debate arXiv preprint (2023). https://doi.org/arXiv:2308.07201
2. Chen, J., Lu, R.: AI agents are here. So Are the Threats. https://unit42.paloaltonetworks.com/agentic-ai-threats/ (2025)
3. Chen, Y.J., Madisetti, V.K.: Information security, ethics, and integrity in LLM agent interaction. J. Inf. Secur. **16**(1), 184–196 (2024)
4. Das, B.C., Amini, M.H., Wu, Y.: Security and privacy challenges of large language models: a survey. ACM Comput. Surv. **57**(6), 1–39 (2025)
5. Dong, Y., et al.: Safeguarding large language models: a survey. arXiv preprint (2024). https://doi.org/arXiv:2406.02622
6. Flå, L.H., Klemets, J.R.A., Jaatun, M.G.: Threat modeling of smart grid control architectures. Electronics **14**(6), 1068 (2025)
7. He, F., Zhu, T., Ye, D., Liu, B., Zhou, W., Yu, P.S.: The emerged security and privacy of LLM agent: a survey with case studies (2024). https://doi.org/arXiv:2407.19354
8. Hou, X., Zhao, Y., Wang, S., Wang, H.: Model context protocol (MCP): landscape, security threats, and future research directions (2025). https://arxiv.org/abs/2503.23278
9. Khan, R., McLaughlin, K., Laverty, D., Sezer, S.: STRIDE-based threat modeling for cyber-physical systems. In: 2017 IEEE PES Innovative Smart Grid Technologies Conference Europe (ISGT-Europe), pp. 1–6. IEEE (2017)

10. Khan, R., Sarkar, S., Mahata, S.K., Jose, E.: Security threats in agentic AI system. arXiv preprint (2024). https://doi.org/arXiv:2410.14728
11. Kohnfelder, L., Shostack, A.: Publish your threat models! the benefits far outweigh the dangers. https://doi.org/arXiv:2511.08295
12. Mirzamohammadi, O., Jannes, K., Sion, L., Van Landuyt, D., Abidin, A., Singelée, D.: Security and privacy threat analysis for solid. In: 2023 IEEE Secure Development Conference (SecDev), pp. 196–206. IEEE (2023)
13. Narajala, V.S., Habler, I.: Enterprise-grade security for the model context protocol (MCP): frameworks and mitigation strategies (2025). https://arxiv.org/abs/2504.08623
14. Open Worldwide Application Security Project (OWASP)): OWASP Top 10 For Agentic Applications (2026)
15. Open Worldwide Application Security Project (OWASP)): Top 10 for LLM Apps & Gen AI Agentic Security Initiative: Agentic AI - Threats and Mitigations (v1.0). https://genai.owasp.org/resource/agentic-ai-threats-and-mitigations/ (2025)
16. Raciti, M., Bella, G.: A threat model for soft privacy on smart cars. In: 2023 IEEE European Symposium on Security and Privacy Workshops (EuroS&PW), pp. 1–10. IEEE (2023)
17. Raciti, M., Bella, G.: The SPADA methodology for threat modelling. Int. J. Inf. Secur. **24**(2), 86 (2025). https://doi.org/10.1007/s10207-025-00999-0
18. Raciti, M., Bella, G., Van Landuyt, D.: Threat model-driven test framework for security and privacy of agentic LLM applications: supporting materials (2025). https://doi.org/10.5281/zenodo.17962865
19. Shostack, A.: Threat Modeling: Designing for Security. Wiley, Indianapolis, Indiana (2014)
20. Sion, L., Van Landuyt, D., Wuyts, K., Joosen, W.: Robust and reusable LINDDUN privacy threat knowledge. Comput. Secur. 104419 (2025)
21. Sion, L., Wuyts, K., Yskout, K., Van Landuyt, D., Joosen, W.: Interaction-based privacy threat elicitation. In: 2018 IEEE European Symposium on Security and Privacy Workshops (EuroS&PW), pp. 79–86. IEEE (2018)
22. Su, T., Zhang, B., Zhang, C., Wei, L.: Privacy leak detection in LLM interactions with a user-centric approach. In: IEEE 23rd International Conference on Trust, Security and Privacy in Computing and Communications (TrustCom). IEEE (2024)
23. Tuma, K., Scandariato, R., Widman, M., Sandberg, C.: Towards security threats that matter. In: Computer Security: ESORICS 2017 International Workshops, CyberICPS 2017 and SECPRE 2017. Springer (2018)
24. Van Landuyt, D., Sion, L., Joosen, W.: LINDDUN MAESTRO: an architecture framework for privacy threat modeling, pp. 1–37
25. Wang, B., et al.: Unveiling privacy risks in LLM agent memory. arXiv (2025)
26. Wuyts, K., Van Landuyt, D., Hovsepyan, A., Joosen, W.: Effective and efficient privacy threat modeling through domain refinements. In: Proceedings of the 33rd Annual ACM Symposium on Applied Computing, pp. 1175–1178 (2018)
27. Yan, B., Li, K., Xu, M., Dong, Y., Zhang, Y., Ren, Z., Cheng, X.: On protecting the data privacy of large language models (LLMs) and LLM agents: a literature review. High-Confidence Comput. **5**(2), 100300 (2025). https://doi.org/10.1016/j.hcc.2025.100300
28. Yang, Y., Huang, X., Sang, J.: Exploring the privacy protection capabilities of Chinese large language models. IEEE Multimedia (2025)

29. Yao, Y., Duan, J., Xu, K., Cai, Y., Sun, Z., Zhang, Y.: A survey on large language model (LLM) security and privacy: the good, the bad, and the ugly. High-Confidence Comput. 100211 (2024)
30. Zhang, Z., Guo, B., Li, T.: Privacy leakage overshadowed by views of AI: a study on human oversight of privacy in language model agent arXiv preprint (2024). https://doi.org/arXiv:2411.01344
31. Zhang, Z., et al.: It's a fair game', or is it? Examining how users navigate disclosure risks and benefits when using LLM-based conversational agents. In: Proceedings of the 2024 CHI Conference on Human Factors in Computing Systems, pp. 1–26 (2024)
32. Zhou, A., Li, B., Wang, H.: Robust prompt optimization for defending language models against jailbreaking attacks arXiv preprint (2024). https://doi.org/arXiv:2401.17263

ONE-MS-1: A Micro-Services Based Network Traffic Dataset

Pedro R. Tomas[1,2(✉)], Jorge Proença[2], Tomás Dias[2], Luis Rosa[2], Luis Cordeiro[2], Tarik Taleb[3], and Tiago Cruz[1]

[1] University of Coimbra, CISUC, DEI, Coimbra, Portugal
{tomas,tjcruz}@dei.uc.pt
[2] OneSource, Coimbra, Portugal
{jorge.proenca,tomas.dias,luis.rosa,cordeiro}@onesource.pt
[3] Faculty of Electrical Engineering and Information Technology, Ruhr University Bochum, Bochum, Germany
tarik.taleb@rub.de

Abstract. The shift towards cloud-native applications has been accelerating in recent years, constituting a paradigm shift that is heavily distributed by nature, taking advantage of features such as scalability, flexibility, and high availability. However, this evolution also introduces various security challenges. From a networking perspective, the large number of interconnected components and their intricate communication patterns make detecting and mitigating traffic anomalies a complex task. Beyond identifying network traffic anomalies, it is also important to identify their source, as well as to be able to trust the outputs of the selected AI/ML techniques and models, which should also be resilient to attacks coming from other AI/ML models (which is common in adversarial scenarios). Nevertheless, to be able to develop such models, suitable cloud-native datasets are required, ideally accompanied by a known and comparable feature vector, which is often insufficient or nonexistent at all—to tackle this issue, this paper presents the ONE-MS-1 dataset.

Keywords: cloud-native · softwarised networks · micro-services dataset · AI/ML · anomaly detection

1 Introduction

In the rapidly changing world of modern technology, the cloud-native paradigm has become a game-changing approach to software development and deployment. Based on cloud computing principles, this concept represents a significant shift in the way applications are designed, created, and managed, operating in a distributed environment where a complex infrastructure–spread across multiple geographical locations–ensures continuous service availability. The impact of these technologies is far-reaching, going beyond conventional service or application support to become enablers for the progressive softwarisation of the infrastructure itself – this is the case for the 5G core architecture, whose requirements

© IFIP International Federation for Information Processing 2026
Published by Springer Nature Switzerland AG 2026
H. Janicke et al. (Eds.): SEC 2026, IFIP AICT 787, pp. 91–104, 2026.
https://doi.org/10.1007/978-3-032-27993-4_7

demand a degree of flexibility that cannot be easily reached by traditional network and service models.

Cloud-native has emerged as a response to the increasing need for agility, scalability, and resilience in today's digital landscape. It follows a set of principles and practices that maximise the benefits of cloud resources and services to develop and run applications efficiently. This is equally important for both customer service and the infrastructure, as the latter needs to keep up with the former. To achieve this, softwarized networks are essential, as traditional networks are no longer viable for these complex, distributed systems. As a result, network virtualisation is part of the solution. Despite its advantages, the vast and distributed nature of cloud-native systems introduces several security challenges, namely due to the increased surface area that needs to be protected. Additionally, data security and privacy is also a major concern, since data is now being shared through multiple network nodes, whose connections are not always as secure and reliable as expected.

To address this issue, a recent trend focuses on exploring and assessing the feasibility of using AI/ML model approaches for network anomaly detection in microservice-based environments, which constitute the backbone of modern cloud-native systems. However, the development of such models depends on having proper datasets, which should ideally contain network traffic collected from a set of micro-services deployed within a cloud-native environment (e.g., Kubernetes). However, to the best of our knowledge, no such dataset was previously available. To mitigate this, a cloud-native environment was designed, implemented, and a dataset was collected. The resulting dataset is presented in this paper, and is publicly available at [18].

The remaining content of this work is structured as follows: Sect. 2 presents the most common datasets used for network anomaly detection; Sect. 3 presents the methodology followed during the data collection process to build the dataset; Sect. 4 provides the description of the ONE-MS-I dataset; Sect. 6 briefly mentions the dataset evaluation already conducted; Sect. 7 concludes this paper.

2 Existing Datasets

This section presents the most common datasets used for network traffic anomaly detection and/or classification, which were originally surveyed. **Bot-IoT** The Bot-IoT dataset comprises both IoT and non-IoT traffic from a simulated smart home network environment. This dataset encompasses various attack types: Distributed Denial-of-Service (DDoS), Denial-of-Service (DoS), Reconnaissance, Operating System (OS), Service Scans, Keylogging, and Data Exfiltration [10,13].

NSL-KDD

The NSL-KDD dataset [16] is a widely used cybersecurity dataset for intrusion detection research. It is an improved version of the original KDD Cup 1999 dataset, designed to address its limitations. NSL-KDD contains diverse network traffic data, including normal and various types of attack traffic, making it a valuable resource for developing and evaluating intrusion detection systems.

UNSW-NB15

The UNSW-NB 15 dataset [24] was created by the Australian Centre for Cyber Security (ACCS) using the IXIA PerfectStorm tool in their Cyber Range Lab. The tool was used to generate a combination of real and synthetic network traffic to simulate modern normal activities and contemporary attack behaviours. The dataset includes nine types of attacks: Fuzzers, Analysis, Backdoors, DoS, Exploits, Generic, Reconnaissance, Shellcode, and Worms.

CIC-IDS2017

The CIC-IDS2017 [3] dataset is a widely used cybersecurity dataset designed for research and development of Network Intrusion Detection Systems (NIDS). It was created by the Canadian Institute for Cybersecurity (CIC) at the University of New Brunswick and is intended to support developing and evaluating intrusion detection algorithms and techniques. The dataset was released in 2017 and has been used by researchers and cybersecurity professionals to train and evaluate intrusion detection systems [19]. The dataset contains data collected over 5 days, where different attacks have been conducted throughout these days.

CSE-CIC-IDS2018

The CSE-CIC-IDS2018 [4] dataset is the outcome of the joint work between Communications Security Establishment (CSE) and CIC institutes. The authors considered a profile-based approach during its elaboration: B-Profile and M-Profile. The former aimed at abstracting the behaviour of a group of human users to create normal network traffic patterns using machine learning and statistical analysis. This is achieved by capturing user-generated network activities, including packet size distributions, packet counts per flow, payload patterns, payload sizes, and request time distributions for different protocols. Once B-Profiles represent user behaviour, they can be used to generate genuine benign network events. The latter focused on implementing seven distinct attack scenarios, each defined based on the network topology and executed from external machines targeting the network.

CIC-DDoS2019

The CIC-IDS2019 [2] is a dataset developed by the CIC with a strong focus on DDoS attacks. The authors focus on two major types of DDoS attacks: Reflection-based DDoS and Exploitation-based attacks. Sharafaldin et al. [20] suggests a taxonomy for DDoS attacks and details the elaboration of this dataset.

Edge-IIoTset

The *Edge-IIoTset Cyber Security Dataset of IoT & IIoT* [7] is a dataset collected from a custom IoT testbed, composed of several IoT devices, edge/fog nodes, and industrial components communicating over common application and industrial protocols (e.g., HTTP/HTTPS, DNS, MQTT, SSH/Telnet, and Modbus/TCP). The benign activity was generated using scripted routines and human-in-the-loop interactions to emulate realistic device-to-device and user-driven workloads, thereby capturing temporal usage patterns, service interactions, and flow-level dynamics. The attack network traffic was produced via multi-stage attack campaigns spanning reconnaissance (e.g., ARP/IP sweeps and service enumeration), denial-of-service (DoS) and distributed denial-of-service (DDoS) variants, brute-force authentication attempts against remote services, web application exploits (e.g., injection and command execution), botnet-like scanning and flooding behaviors, spoofing/man-in-the-middle techniques (e.g., ARP/DNS manipulation), and IIoT protocol abuses targeting industrial function codes and writing operations.

Table 1 presents a summary of the datasets previously described. Such datasets are not suitable for the problem at hand since none of them are tailored to micro-services paradigm, several of them have been criticised (due to repeated features, missing data, etc.) [12,21,22]. Also, the majority of them do not follow the same feature vector, which makes very challenging any comparison between different ML approaches evaluated with different datasets, ultimately contributing to an increased barrier when it comes to the adoption of ML algorithms in real/production environments.

Table 1. Datasets Overview (N - Normal; M - Malicious)

Dataset	Year	Attacks	Samples
NSL-KDD	2009	SoS; Probe; User to Root (U2R); Remote to Local (R2L)	N: 1033372 M: 4176086
UNSW-NB15	2015	Fuzzers; Analysis; Backdoors; DoS; Exploits; Generic; Reconnaissance; Shellcode; Worms	N: 67343 M: 2472702
CIC-IDS2017	2017	Brute Force; DoS (slowloris, Slowhttptest, Hulk, Goden-Eye), Heartbleed Port 444; Web Attack (Brute Force, XSS, SQL injection), Infiltration (Dropbox download, Cool disk - MAC), Portscan + Nmap; Botnet ARES, Port Scan, DDoS LOIT	N: 2273097 M: 557679
CSE-CIC-IDS2018	2018	FTP-BruteForce, SSH-Bruteforce; DoS-GoldenEye, DoS-Slowloris; DoS-SlowHTTPTest, DoS-Hulk; DDoS attacks-LOIC-HTTP, DDoS-LOIC-UDP; DDOS-LOIC-UDP, DDOS-HOIC; Brute Force-Web, Brute Force-XSS, SQL Injection; Infiltration; Botnet	N: 4060498478 M: 2711134
CIC-IDS2019	2019	DoS against (DNS, LDAP, NetBIOS, NTP, SNMP, SSDP, UDP); Syn; TFTP; UDPLag	N: 57416 M: 50005708
Edge-IIoTset	2023	Backdoor, DDoS_HTTP, DDoS_ICMP, DDoS_TCP, DDoS_UDP, Fingerprinting, MITM, Password, Port_Scanning, Ransomware, SQL_injection, Uploading, Vulnerability_scanner, XSS	N: 11223940 M: 9728708

3 Methodology

This section describes the steps taken to create the dataset presented in this paper, namely the scenario description, the data collection process and the attack description.

3.1 Environment Description

The dataset hereby presented originated from the Mobitrust platform, a micro-service oriented Public Protection and Disaster Relief (PPDR) application [8] designed to assist first responder crews in disaster relief and incident response efforts.

Ten simulated devices were utilised in the experiment, each collecting data from six different IoT sensors: a geo-location sensor, gas sensor, internal controller, wearable T-shirt sensor, camera sensor, and critical organs sensor. The geo-location sensor updated coordinates every 60 s, while the gas sensor measured gas concentrations and temperature every second. The smart T-shirt sensor replicated data from a Hexoskin T-shirt [9], capturing metrics such as temperature, heart rate, respiratory rate, and battery levels. The camera sensor simulated real-time video streaming using a dummy file. The critical organs sensor monitored parameters like heart rate, body temperature, respiratory rate, carbon dioxide levels, and battery status, which in a practical setting would be gathered by a Bitalino device [1]. All generated data was transmitted to the internal Mobitrust message bus, then it underwent for pre-processing and storage in a database before being forwarded to the Mobitrust Portal. Figure 1 presents the disposition of Mobitrust devices and sensors, which comprise the data origin.

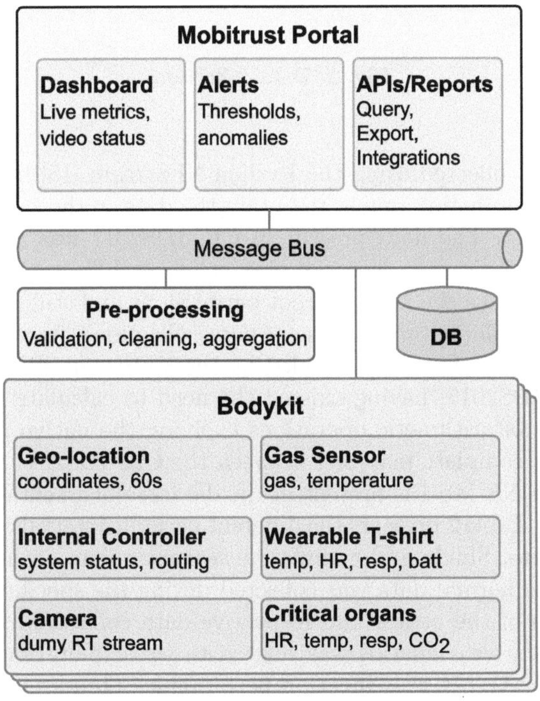

Fig. 1. Mobitrust devices and sensors.

3.2 Data Collection

Considering the micro-services paradigm, the data was collected from several (albeit similar) Mobitrust deployments in a dedicated namespace part of a Kubernetes cluster [11], with the help of a sidecar component in charge of collecting the data being deployed next to each of the components considered for the data collection. Figure 2 represents the components distribution used during the data collection.

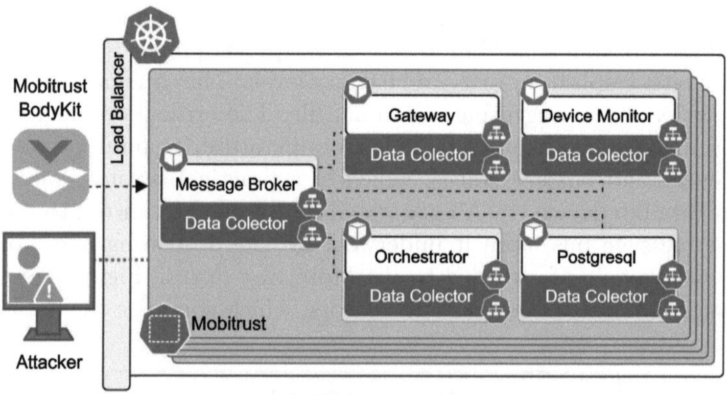

Fig. 2. Data collection.

The data was collected using the Python NFStream [15] library in conjunction with a custom plugin, aiming to obtain the data in the same feature-vector as of CIC-IDS2017. The data present in CIC-IDS2017 was collected with the CICFlowMeter tool [5], yet, this tool presents several limitations for containerised environments, like the need for root permissions and still premature python package version available (at the time of data collection). As such, an effort was conducted to map the features provided by the NFStream library and the ones present in CIC-IDS2017, having existed the need to calculate some of the features as a result of arithmetic operations evolving the native metrics provided by NFStream. A complete mapping between the CIC-IDS2017 features and the ones present in ONE-MS-I is present in the dataset documentation [18].

Furthermore, Table 2 presents the different periodic intervals considered while collecting the data. Single and cumulative scenarios were considered. For both type of scenarios, normal data was collected during the specified time, followed by the execution of the attack and respective data collection. The existence of single and cumulative scenarios was related to the exploration of the cumulative effect on the AI/ML classification performance (*training+attack* Vs *training+training+attack*).

Table 2. Data collection intervals

Single	Cumulative
1 h	1 h + 1 h
2 h	2 h + 2 h
4 h	4 h + 4 h
6 h	6 h + 6 h
8 h	8 h + 8 h

3.3 Attack Description

Three types of attacks were simulated against the Mobitrust services: DDOS, Brute Force and SQL Injection. The first was conducted with the mqtt-stresser [14] tool and targeted the Mobitrust *message-broker* component, whilst the second and the third both targeted the application *mt-gateway* component and were conducted with *curl* [6], recurring to a set of most common usernames and passwords, as well as to recurring commands attempted during SQL Injection.

4 Dataset Description

The data was collected from five Mobitrust components: Gateway, Message Broker, Device Monitor, Orchestrator, and Postgresql.

Table 3 presents the dataset overview, by detailing the number of normal and malicious flows for each of the scenarios. In total, data was collected for 10 different intervals. Naturally, malicious flows are only available for the Gateway and Message-Broker components, as these were the ones targeted by the attacks. This dataset [18,23] is publicly available and its structure is as follows: on the root folder, 10 folders exist corresponding to the 10 data collection intervals; within each, 5 folders exist corresponding to the 5 components involved; lastly, within each component related folder, there is a *training.csv* file and a *data.csv* file. The first corresponds to the data collected until the periodic data interval collection (e.g., 1 h), while the second corresponds to the data collected afterwards, including the network traffic generated by the attacks.

5 Dataset Relevance

The ONE-MS-I dataset introduces key differentiators when compared to other intrusion anomaly datasets (Table 1). Traffic is generated in a cloud-native microservice architecture, while most alternatives, including NSK-KKD, CIC-IDS2017, and others model monolithic system traffic, except for Edge-IIoTset, which targets IoT/Edge domains. Compatibility with the CIC-IDS2017 feature vector supports direct reuse, benchmarking model interoperability, while providing bidirectional features that reflect communication patterns. At the

Table 3. ONE-MS-I overview (N.F. - Normal Flows; M.F. - Malicious Flows)

Interval	Component	N.F.	M.F.	Interval	Component	N.F.	M.F.
1 h	gateway	8802	2770	1 h + 1 h	gateway	11319	2787
	message	6894	4098		message	12663	4031
	monitor	3458	0		monitor	4441	0
	orchestrator	6602	0		orchestrator	8751	0
	postgresql	11112	0		postgresql	13993	0
2 h	gateway	10491	2777	2 h + 2 h	gateway	14909	2775
	message	19846	4098		message	28135	3781
	monitor	21	0		monitor	6300	0
	orchestrator	11144	0		orchestrator	22136	0
	postgresql	15603	0		postgresql	27109	0
4 h	gateway	14962	2809	4 h + 4 h	gateway	24300	2798
	message	15147	4084		message	25447	4098
	monitor	7091	0		monitor	13782	0
	orchestrator	13740	0		orchestrator	25464	0
	postgresql	20108	0		postgresql	34543	0
6 h	gateway	19797	2756	6 h + 6 h	gateway	33202	2761
	message	25921	4047		message	39210	4083
	monitor	27	0		monitor	19130	0
	orchestrator	16938	0		orchestrator	33671	0
	postgresql	25197	0		postgresql	45912	0
8 h	gateway	24504	2789	8 h + 8 h	gateway	42633	2791
	message	43179	4093		message	46587	4098
	monitor	11319	0		monitor	25494	0
	orchestrator	29287	0		orchestrator	38692	0
	postgresql	37946	0		postgresql	54656	0

microservice level, the dataset provides fine-grained observability, temporal variability, and real-world, separable traffic traces. Attack distribution is realistic: the message-broker service is the main target, comprising 59% of all attack network flows, reflecting the high DDoS exposure of modern asynchronous communication enablers (e.g., MQTT, Kafka). The gateway functions as a multi-source attack aggregation layer, whereas all other services preserve clean normal-operation flows, forming a strong baseline for unsupervised anomaly detection, where models infer deviations from normal behaviour. Compared to highly imbalanced datasets such as CIC-IDS2019 and CSE-CIC-IDS2018, ONE-MS-I reduces the percentage of attacks with a higher share of normal microservice flows. ONE-MS-I has 93% of normal flows and 7% of malicious flows, providing over 1 million flows, less than CIC-IDS2017 and CSE-CIC-IDS2018, although it reflects a realistic production environment and attack rate. Traffic is TCP-centric, excluding obsolete or niche protocols, and port assignments follow standard service conventions across both attacked and non-attacked micro-services, ensuring deployment realism and consistency.

6 Dataset Evaluation

6.1 Methodology

Aiming to validate the usability of this dataset, a thorough assessment was conducted using 28 SoA algorithms. The overall evaluation methodology is presented in Fig. 3.

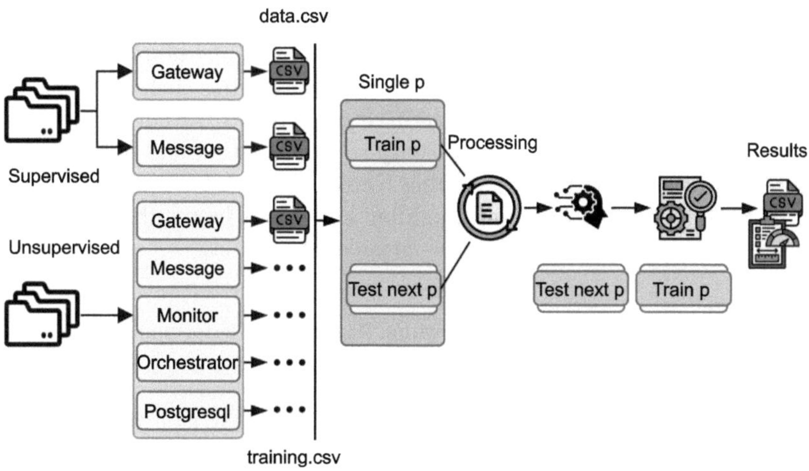

Fig. 3. Evaluation methodology.

The complete set of evaluated algorithms was: Random Forest, XGBoost, SVM, K-means, Decision Trees, Naïve Bayes, CART, KNN, AdaBoost, Linear Regression, Logistic Regression, LightGBM, Extra Trees, Improved Adaptive Random Forest, CNN, Autoencoders, LSTM, Multi-Layer Perceptron, Transformer Encoder, Error-Resilient RNN, FusionNet, FS-Net, GRU, ResNet, EfficientNet, Ladder Network, ST-Graph, and Deep Dictionary Learning.

The supervised approaches were evaluated for the micro-services where both normal and attack data was collected (e.g., message-broker, gateway), whereas unsupervised approaches were evaluated for all the components. Moreover, during the training and testing phase - always conducted for data coming from the same micro-service component - each algorithm was trained for data regarding period p and tested with the next period (i.e., SVM was trained with data for period 1 h and evaluated with data for 2 h period).

6.2 Results

Considering the high number of possible combinations between algorithms, micro-services and training periods, the results presented in this paper were grouped by algorithm classification performance, considering the *F1-Score* and *Accuracy* as evaluation metrics for the supervised approaches, whereas *FPR* and *Accuracy* were chosen to evaluate the unsupervised approaches. *FPR* was selected to evaluate unsupervised algorithms performance since from this metric it is possible to infer the algorithm's capacity to correctly reconstruct normal flows (previously seen during the training phase). Moreover, the complete list of obtained results is available at [17].

The experimental results demonstrate the superiority of supervised learning methods over unsupervised approaches in terms of both predictive performance and stability. As shown in Table 4, tree-based and gradient boosting algorithms, particularly LightGBM, XGBoost, and Random Forest, consistently achieving the highest F1-scores and accuracies, with minimal variance across folds, indicating strong generalisation capabilities. Neural architectures such as Transformer, ERRN, and ResNet also present competitive performance, although with slightly increased variability, suggesting sensitivity to initialisation and hyperparameter settings. Traditional methods, including Naive Bayes and simple recurrent networks (LSTM, DeepDictLearning), exhibit lower and less stable performance, underscoring their applicability in the considered dataset.

Table 4. Supervised Learning Algorithms Performance

Algorithm	F1-Score	Accuracy	Algorithm	F1-Score	Accuracy
LightGBM	0.996 ± 0.006	0.999 ± 0.001	AdaBoost	0.983 ± 0.033	0.996 ± 0.009
XGBoost	0.994 ± 0.010	0.998 ± 0.003	Extra Trees	0.981 ± 0.027	0.995 ± 0.007
Transformer	0.988 ± 0.017	0.997 ± 0.004	CART	0.979 ± 0.032	0.994 ± 0.008
Random Forest	0.988 ± 0.022	0.997 ± 0.005	EfficientNet	0.977 ± 0.029	0.994 ± 0.007
ERRN	0.987 ± 0.015	0.996 ± 0.004	FusionNet	0.977 ± 0.034	0.994 ± 0.008
ResNet	0.987 ± 0.017	0.997 ± 0.004	STGraph	0.977 ± 0.037	0.994 ± 0.009
SVM	0.974 ± 0.036	0.993 ± 0.008	Logistic Reg.	0.965 ± 0.054	0.990 ± 0.013
GRU	0.970 ± 0.032	0.992 ± 0.008	MLP	0.964 ± 0.052	0.990 ± 0.013
DT (ID3)	0.954 ± 0.057	0.989 ± 0.011	CNN	0.942 ± 0.074	0.983 ± 0.022
Linear Reg.	0.944 ± 0.072	0.984 ± 0.019	Naive Bayes	0.915 ± 0.203	0.960 ± 0.101
LSTM	0.834 ± 0.343	0.973 ± 0.039	DeepDictLrn.	0.834 ± 0.274	0.968 ± 0.041

For unsupervised learning (Tables 5 and 6), the overall performance is substantially lower, as expected in the absence of labelled data. K-Means achieves the best trade-off between false positive rate (FPR) and accuracy at the aggregate level (FPR = 0.025, Accuracy = 0.931), whereas more complex models such as autoencoders and FSNet show higher variability. Service-specific analysis indicates that FSNet outperforms K-Means in untacked micro-services (Monitor,

Orchestrator, PostgreSQL), achieving FPRs below 0.02 and accuracies exceeding 0.98. These results highlight that unsupervised methods can be effective when tailored to specific service characteristics or environment requirements and available knowledge.

Table 5. Unsupervised Learning Algorithms Performance

Algorithm	FPR	Accuracy
K-Means	0.025 ± 0.037	0.931 ± 0.077
Autoencoder	0.058 ± 0.057	0.919 ± 0.094
k-NN	0.083 ± 0.117	0.894 ± 0.118
FSNet	0.125 ± 0.209	0.884 ± 0.174

Table 6. Unsupervised Learning Best Algorithm per Service

Algorithm	Service		
	Name	FPR	Accuracy
K-Means	Gateway	**0.008**	0.845
K-Means	Message	**0.075**	0.850
FSNet	Monitor	**0.018**	0.982
FSNet	Orchestrator	**0.007**	0.993
FSNet	PostgreSQL	**0.007**	0.993
K-Means	*Overall*	0.025	0.931

In summary, the findings confirm that supervised algorithms are the preferred choice in scenarios with available labels, providing near-perfect predictive performance, whereas unsupervised techniques remain a viable option for service-level anomaly detection under label scarcity, provided their limitations and variability are carefully considered (Table 7).

Table 7. Top Supervised Algorithms by Service

Algorithm	Gateway	Message
LightGBM	**0.993**	0.998
XGBoost	0.988	**0.999**
ERRN	**0.983**	0.991
Transformer	0.980	**0.996**
ResNet	**0.980**	0.994
Extra Trees	**0.978**	0.985
RF	0.976	**0.999**
AdaBoost	0.968	**0.999**
CART	0.967	**0.992**
EfficientNet	0.963	**0.991**
Mean	0.978	0.995

7 Conclusion

The prompt identification of network traffic anomalies (either caused by faulty components or by malicious parts) is of paramount importance in any computer system, but especially in those that present a distributed nature, like cloud-native ones. In addition, making the bridge between academic and enterprise environments is required so the academic research can be used to impulse the evolution of research environments.

This paper presented a review of the commonly used datasets for network anomaly detection found in the literature. Despite this, none of those are tailored for cloud-native applications, namely for micro-services paradigms. To mitigate this, this paper presents the ONE-MS-I, a micro-services based network traffic dataset, publicly available. This dataset relevance is discussed, and its feasibility for the task at hand is analysed with the evaluation of 28 SoA algorithms over its data.

Lastly, from the conducted evaluation, it is possible to conclude that supervised approaches outperform unsupervised ones and remain the optimal choice for network traffic anomaly detection, as long as labelled data is available. Since in realistic environments this is often not the case, unsupervised approaches remain a valid alternative, even with a potential slightly reduced classification performance.

As future work, complementary versions of this dataset are envisioned, potentially covering data collected at the entry level of different infrastructures and with different workload environments (e.g., idle and "rush-hour" periods). Furthermore, complex attack scenarios are planned, as well as the simultaneously collection and correlation of data on multiple layers (i.e., application and transport layer).

Acknowledgments. This work was supported in part by the EU's Digital Europe Programme DIGITAL-ECCC-2024-DEPLOY-CYBER-07 under the ENFORCE project (Grant No. 101249431), by the EU's European Union's HE Research and Innovation programme HORIZON-CL3-2022-CS-01-01 under the MIRANDA project (Grant No. 101168144) and by Portuguese national funds through FCT Foundation for Science and Technology, I.P., within the scope of the research unit UID/00326 - Centre for Informatics and Systems of the University of Coimbra. The views expressed in this contribution are those of the authors and do not necessarily represent the project nor the Commission.

Disclosure of Interests. The authors have no competing interests.

References

1. Bitalino (2025). https://www.pluxbiosignals.com/pages/bitalino. Accessed 15 Mar 2025
2. CIC-DDoS2019 (2025). https://www.unb.ca/cic/datasets/ddos-2019.html. Accessed 10 Aug 2023
3. Intrusion detection evaluation dataset (CIC-IDS2017) (2025). https://www.unb.ca/cic/datasets/ids-2017.html. Accessed 10 Aug 2023
4. CSE-CIC-IDS2018 on AWS (2025). https://www.unb.ca/cic/datasets/ids-2018.html. Accessed 10 Aug 2023
5. Cicflowmeter (2025). https://github.com/ahlashkari/CICFlowMeter. Accessed 15 Mar 2025
6. Curl (2025). https://curl.se/. Accessed 15 Mar 2025
7. Ferrag, M.A., Friha, O., Hamouda, D., Maglaras, L., Janicke, H.: Edge-IIoTset: a new comprehensive realistic cyber security dataset of IoT and IIoT applications for centralized and federated learning. IEEE Access **10**, 40281–40306 (2022). https://doi.org/10.1109/ACCESS.2022.3165809
8. Henriques, J., Gomes, A., Cordeiro, L.: IoT for improving first responders' situational awareness and safety on federated 5G testbeds. In: IEEE International Mediterranean Conference on Communications and Networking (IEEE MEDITCOM 2021) (2021)
9. Hexoskin (2025). https://hexoskin.com/. Accessed 15 Mar 2025
10. Koroniotis, N., Moustafa, N., Sitnikova, E., Turnbull, B.: Towards the development of realistic botnet dataset in the internet of things for network forensic analytics: Bot-IoT dataset. Futur. Gener. Comput. Syst. **100**, 779–796 (2019). https://doi.org/10.1016/j.future.2019.05.041
11. Kubernetes (2025). https://kubernetes.io. Accessed 15 Mar 2025
12. Lanvin, M., Gimenez, P.-F., Han, Y., Majorczyk, F., Mé, L., Totel, É.: Errors in the CICIDS2017 dataset and the significant differences in detection performances it makes. In: Kallel, S., Jmaiel, M., Zulkernine, M., Hadj Kacem, A., Cuppens, F., Cuppens, N. (eds.) CRiSIS 2022. LNCS, vol. 13857, pp. 18–33. Springer, Cham (2023). https://doi.org/10.1007/978-3-031-31108-6_2
13. Moustafa, N.: The bot-IoT dataset (2019). https://doi.org/10.21227/r7v2-x988
14. Mqtt-stresser (2025). https://github.com/inovex/mqtt-stresser. Accessed 15 Mar 2025
15. Nfstream: Flexible network data analysis framework (2025). https://www.nfstream.org/. Accessed 31 Mar 2025

16. NSL-KDD dataset (2025). https://www.unb.ca/cic/datasets/nsl.html. Accessed 10 Mar 2025
17. One-ms-i results (2025). https://bit.ly/ONE-MS-I_results. Accessed 15 Dec 2025
18. Tomas, P.R., Cruz, T., Proenca, J., Rosa, L., Cordeiro, L., Taleb, T.: ONE-MS-I: a micro-services based network traffic dataset (2025). https://doi.org/10.21227/0h62-zy24
19. Sharafaldin, I., Lashkari, A.H., Ghorbani, A.A.: Toward generating a new intrusion detection dataset and intrusion traffic characterization. In: International Conference on Information Systems Security and Privacy (2018). https://api.semanticscholar.org/CorpusID:4707749
20. Sharafaldin, I., Lashkari, A.H., Hakak, S., Ghorbani, A.A.: Developing realistic distributed denial of service (DDoS) attack dataset and taxonomy. In: 2019 International Carnahan Conference on Security Technology (ICCST), pp. 1–8 (2019). https://doi.org/10.1109/CCST.2019.8888419
21. Tareq, I., Elbagoury, B.M., El-Regaily, S., El-Horbaty, E.S.M.: Analysis of ToN-IoT, UNW-NB15, and edge-IIoT datasets using DL in cybersecurity for IoT. Appl. Sci. 12(19) (2022). https://doi.org/10.3390/app12199572. https://www.mdpi.com/2076-3417/12/19/9572
22. Thakkar, A., Lohiya, R.: A review of the advancement in intrusion detection datasets. Procedia Comput. Sci. **167**, 636–645 (2020). https://doi.org/10.1016/j.procs.2020.03.330. https://www.sciencedirect.com/science/article/pii/S1877050920307961
23. Tomas, P.R., Felix, P., Rosa, L., Gomes, A.S., Cordeiro, L.: A novel approach for continual and federated network anomaly detection. In: Arai, K. (ed.) Proceedings of the Future Technologies Conference (FTC) 2024, vol. 4, pp. 212–225. Springer, Cham (2024)
24. The UNSW-NB15 dataset (2025). https://research.unsw.edu.au/projects/unsw-nb15-dataset. Accessed 10 Mar 2025

MLLM-IGDD: Instance-Guided Deepfake Detection via Multimodal Large Language Models

Yanfei Tong[1,2], Yiran He[1,2], Yun Cao[1,2](✉), Yuqi Pang[1,2], Meineng Zhu[3], Xiaohui Kuang[4], and Zhendong Wu[4]

[1] Institute of Information Engineering, Chinese Academy of Sciences, Beijing 100085, China
{tongyanfei,heyiran,caoyun,pangyuqi}@iie.ac.cn
[2] School of Cyber Security, University of Chinese Academy of Sciences, Beijing 100085, China
[3] University of International Relations, Beijing 100091, China
[4] Institute of Systems of Engineering, Academy of Military Science, Beijing 100101, China
xhkuang@bupt.edu.cn, wuzhendong@nudt.edu.cn

Abstract. The rapid development of generative artificial intelligence has made it easy to create highly realistic images, which poses a significant risk for the spread of misinformation. However, existing deepfake detection methods are typically confined to identifying specific types of tampered images, with their performance heavily contingent on the design and composition of the training dataset. To address the issue, we propose Instance-Guided Deepfake Detection via Multimodal Large Language Models (MLLM-IGDD), a training-free method that leverages instances to guide multimodal large language models in learning the intrinsic classification logic of image authenticity. Specifically, for each test image, the proposed Instance Recommendation Module (IRM) retrieves a typical authentic image and a deepfake one as in-context references. Furthermore, by integrating domain-informed forensic priors, we introduce the Knowledge-Enhanced Analysis Module (KEAM), which enables the MLLM to detect manipulation-induced anomalies across both visual and semantic dimensions. Experimental results demonstrate that MLLM-IGDD not only accurately assesses image authenticity but also identifies the generation method, localizes manipulated regions, and provides interpretable rationales. It outperforms state-of-the-art methods across diverse datasets while maintaining compatibility with multiple mainstream MLLMs.

Keywords: Multimodal Large Language Models · Deepfake detection · Instance-guided · Knowledge-Enhanced

© IFIP International Federation for Information Processing 2026
Published by Springer Nature Switzerland AG 2026
H. Janicke et al. (Eds.): SEC 2026, IFIP AICT 787, pp. 105–119, 2026.
https://doi.org/10.1007/978-3-032-27993-4_8

1 Introduction

With the rapid proliferation of generative large models, images generated by artificial intelligence have become increasingly prevalent. Owing to their highly realistic and indistinguishable visual characteristics, such synthetic images pose significant security risks when misused. For instance, deepfake images involving prominent politicians, public figures, or sensitive topics can be exploited to disseminate disinformation, distort public perception, or escalate social conflicts, thereby threatening societal trust and stability. Consequently, developing effective methods for detecting deepfake images is of critical importance.

Early deepfake detection approaches were predominantly based on deep neural networks. These methods, characterized by lightweight architectures and efficient optimization, achieve strong performance in detection accuracy and forgery localization on specific datasets. However, their performance heavily relies on the scale and diversity of training data [6,7,22,37,43], resulting in the limited generalizability. To improve generalization, recent efforts have focused on applying Large Language Models (LLMs) or Multimodal Large Language Models (MLLMs) to deepfake detection. By leveraging their capacity to analyze and capture the subtle artifacts beyond human visual perception, these models demonstrate promise in detecting unseen forgery types while providing interpretable textual explanations. However, their performance is constrained by two critical limitations: first, they remain highly reliant on large scale, high quality annotated datasets for fine-tuning; second, they lack effective guidance from domain expertise [9,13,29,41,44].

To address these challenges, we propose MLLM-IGDD, an instance-guided and knowledge-enhanced deepfake detection method that steers the MLLM inference in a training-free manner. Our approach follows a three-stage progressive paradigm: Instance Guidance, In-Depth Analysis, and Interpretable Decision-Making. In the first stage, we introduce a novel Instance Recommendation Module (IRM), which adaptively retrieves reference instances for a given test image. By constructing a context-aware prompting strategy based on these references, IRM enables the MLLM to capture intrinsic discriminative patterns between authentic and deepfake images. In the second stage, we integrate Knowledge-Enhanced Analysis Module (KEAM), which injects forensic priors into the detection process via task-specific instructional prompts. These prompts guide the model to leverage its strengths in visual perception, semantic understanding, and logical reasoning, thereby systematically revealing subtle, multidimensional forgery artifacts. In the final stage, the framework synthesizes all evidence from the prior stages to produce an interpretable decision.

The main contributions are summarized as follows:

- We propose MLLM-IGDD, a novel instance-guided MLLM-based deepfake detection method. By integrating IRM and KEAM, it steers the MLLM inference without the extensive data and training costs, enabling the MLLM to assess image authenticity, identify likely generation mechanisms, localize tampered regions, and generate interpretable rationales grounded in detected artifacts.

- We introduce IRM, a reference retrieval module that guides the MLLM to discern the intrinsic differences between authentic and deepfake images. Concurrently, we design KEAM, which incorporates forensic priors through specialized instructions, thereby steering the model toward more accurate and interpretable detection performance.
- Experimental results demonstrate that MLLM-IGDD effectively determines image authenticity, identifies generation methods, explains detected anomalies, and maintains stable performance across various mainstream MLLMs. Ablation studies further confirm that the instance-guided mechanism significantly improves the performance of MLLMs in deepfake detection.

2 Related Work

2.1 Image Forgery Detection and Localization

Image forgery detection, typically formulated as a binary classification task, aims to distinguish authentic images from those that have been synthetically generated or manipulated, while localization seeks to identify the specific regions altered during tampering. Early approaches primarily relied on handcrafted features such as noise inconsistencies, lighting anomalies, and JPEG compression artifacts to expose traces of manipulation [7,11,15]. With the rise of deep learning, convolutional neural networks (CNNs) and Vision Transformers (ViT) have emerged as dominant approaches, achieving high accuracy on benchmark datasets by learning data-driven forensic signatures [16,23,36]. Some methods analyze features in the spatial or frequency domain [6,7,30], while others fuse both to detect abnormal patterns introduced during image synthesis [4,20,38]. Other approaches design custom forensic features tailored to detect outputs from specific generative models [25,31,39]. Additionally, to enhance detection accuracy, these methods typically incorporate deep learning techniques such as data augmentation [10,36], supervised learning [1,30], and image reconstruction [31,32,39]. However, they often exhibit limited generalization when tested on unseen forgery types.

2.2 Multimodal Large Language Models

In recent years, LLMs based on the transformer architecture and pre-trained on massive datasets have acquired extensive world knowledge. Owing to their strong instruction-following capabilities and natural language generation performance, they can effectively adapt to various downstream tasks. In the context of deepfake image detection, recent works leveraging LLMs or MLLMs exploit two core advantages: (i) their ability to align visual and semantic representations, which enhances generalization to unseen forgery patterns; and (ii) their capacity to generate detailed textual explanations, which improves the interpretability of detection results [9,29,44]. Huang et al. [12] proposed FFAA, an explainable facial forgery analysis model that fine-tunes an MLLM on the FFA-VQA dataset and incorporates the MIDS to improve both accuracy and interpretability. Recently, LLMs and MLLMs have also been adopted for the Image Forgery Detection and Localization (IFDL) task. Xu et al. [41]proposed FakeShield, a multimodal framework that introduces DTE-FDM for detection and MFLM for localization, to enable fine-grained analysis of forged images. Liu et al. [21] developed ForgeryGPT, which enhances the detection and localization capabilities of LLMs through a Mask-Aware Forgery Extractor, enabling precise identification of tampered regions. However, the performance of these methods typically requires extensive task-specific fine-tuning on custom datasets, which limits their applicability in real-world scenarios.

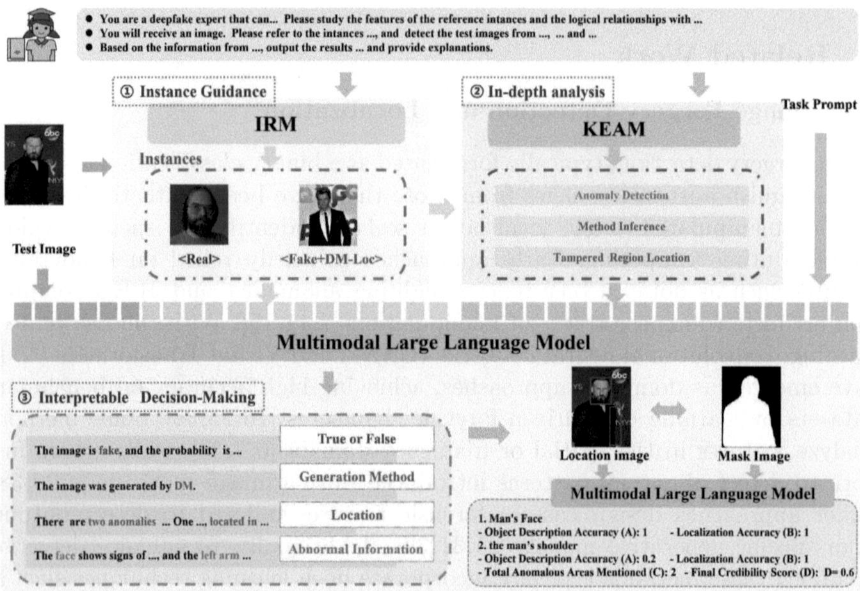

Fig. 1. The pipeline of MLLM-IGDD: Given a test image, MLLM-IGDD first retrieves a pair of reference instances via the Instance Recommendation Module (IRM), then leverages the Knowledge-Enhanced Analysis Module (KEAM) to inject domain expertise and guide the MLLM in performing comprehensive deepfake detection. This figure shows an example where the man's face and shoulder have been manipulated.

3 Method

In this paper, we propose MLLM-IGDD, an instance-guided deepfake detection method via MLLMs. By adaptively retrieving a pair of instances, MLLM-IGDD enables the model to infer image authenticity classification logic without extensive fine-tuning. In addition, the method incorporates domain-informed forensic priors to direct the MLLM's attention toward critical forensic cues. As a result, it enhances the model's effectiveness, interpretability, and efficiency in detecting deepfake images.

3.1 Overall Framework of MLLM-IGDD

The pipeline of MLLM-IGDD, as illustrated in Fig. 1, consists of three steps: Instance Guidance, In-depth Analysis, and Interpretable Decision-Making. The input to MLLM-IGDD includes a test image and text instructions, while the output comprises the detection result from the MLLM along with supporting explanations. The specific steps are described as follows:

Instance Guidance. For a given test image, MLLM-IGDD employs IRM to retrieve a pair of instances, which consist of images, along with their respective labels. These instances are then provided to the MLLM to guide it in learning the coupling logic between the intrinsic features and authenticity labels.

In-Depth Analysis. Guided by task-specific text instructions and the information of the retrieved instances, MLLM-IGDD performs comprehensive reasoning on test images via the KEAM module. Specifically, it adaptively detects forgery clues across three dimensions: forgery artifacts, generation methods, and tampered regions, thereby accumulating evidence to support the final decision.

Interpretable Decision-Making. MLLM-IGDD combines classification cues acquired through Instance Guidance with forensic indicators derived from In-depth Analysis. It then prompts the MLLM to reason over the fused evidence and produce a detection decision based on observable artifacts. Additionally, when a ground-truth tampered mask is available, localization accuracy is computed to provide a quantitative evaluation of spatial detection performance.

Within the MLLM-IGDD framework, the IRM and KEAM play a pivotal role in guiding MLLM to perform specialized image forgery detection. A detailed exposition of their technical design is provided in the following sections.

3.2 Instance Recommendation Module

In-context learning (ICL) has proven effective in a range of tasks, such as natural language understanding [17], data generation [18,42], and reasoning [40,45]. By leveraging the principles of ICL, representative instances can help models better understand task requirements, thereby improving the accuracy of generated outputs and the effectiveness of task execution [5]. To enable the MLLM to achieve more accurate detection of test images, we design an Instances Recommendation Module (IRM), as illustrated in Fig. 2a. This module retrieves instances from a curated instance dataset based on feature relevance to the test image, thereby guiding the model to implicitly learn underlying logic of image authenticity.

Instance Dataset. To develop an effective benchmark for Instance Guidance, we constructed an Instance Dataset containing authentic images and deepfake images, along with their corresponding labels. Since images generated by diffusion models (DMs) currently represent the state-of-the-art in perceptual realism and distributional alignment with real data [3], they present the most challenging scenario for detection systems. To ensure model robustness under realistic adversarial conditions, we only use images generated by DMs to construct fake instances. For label design, we adopt a two-level hierarchical annotation scheme. The first level uses binary labels to classify images as either authentic or deepfake, denoted as <real> and <fake>, respectively. The second level provides fine-grained labels based on the underlying generation method, including: <Cam> (camera-captured images), <DM-Who> (image generated by DMs), <DM-Loc¿ (DMs-based local tampering), among others. This hierarchical framework is extensible to accommodate emerging generation techniques, enhancing the dataset's adaptability to evolving forgery types.

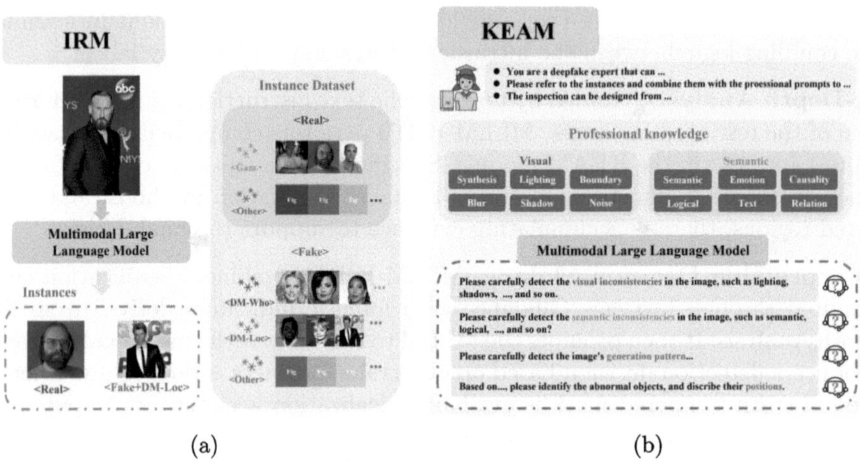

Fig. 2. Two modules in MLLM-IGDD. (a) Instance Recommendation Module (IRM). (b) Knowledge-Enhanced Analysis Module (KEAM).

3.3 Knowledge-Enhanced Analysis Module

To better guide the MLLM in performing detection and analysis tasks from a domain-informed perspective, we introduce the KEAM, as illustrated in Fig. 2b. KEAM enables the model to integrate retrieved instances with structured forensic priors, including fundamental forensic principles, common manipulation artifacts, and generation-specific signatures. These priors guide the MLLM to perform a comprehensive analysis of test images. Specifically, KEAM operates through three coordinated stages:

Anomaly Detection. The module captures anomalous signals across both visual details (e.g., noise inconsistencies, boundary artifacts) and semantic content (e.g., unreasonable logical or causal relationships).

Method Inference. It guides the MLLM to infer the likely image generation or manipulation method by analyzing characteristic feature patterns associated with known forgery types, such as DMs.

Localization. It prompts the model to identify the precise locations of tampered regions by leveraging the spatial distribution of detected anomalies, thereby supporting region-level forgery localization.

Through its multi-level feature analysis framework, KEAM systematically detects manipulation artifacts and furnishes robust, evidence-based support for the final interpretive decision of MLLM-IGDD.

4 Experiments

4.1 Experimental Setups

The experimental setups in this paper are organized from five aspects as follows:

Dataset: To evaluate the robustness and generalizability of our method, we conduct extensive experiments across five datasets: Caltech_WebFaces [33], NeuralTextures [34], DiffusionFace [2], HiSD [19], and Autosplice [14]. From each dataset, we randomly sample 1,000 images to construct a unified test set.

State-of-the-Art Methods: We compare MLLM-IGDD against four representative deepfake detection baselines: FreDect [6], GramNet [22], CNNSpot [37], and FakeShield [41]. For compatibility testing, MLLM-IGDD is implemented on five mainstream MLLMs: Deepseek-VL2 [8], Llama-3.2-Vision [24], GPT-4o-mini [28], GPT-4o [26], and GPT-4.1 [27].

Detection Metrics: Performance is evaluated using Detection Accuracy (Acc) and Rejection rate (Rej). To account for the stochasticity inherent in MLLM inference, we collect 20 independent detection results per test image and report averaged results. Additionally, to mitigate bias from class imbalance and enable finer-grained assessment, the Receiver Operating Characteristic (ROC) curve and its Area Under the Curve (AUC) are also used.

Location Metrics: Since MLLMs output natural language descriptions rather than pixel-level masks, we propose a localization accuracy metric as:

$$\mathrm{ACC}_{\mathrm{loc}} = \frac{\sum_{i=1}^{n} \mathrm{ACC}_{\mathrm{num}}(i) \times \mathrm{Score}_{\mathrm{loc}}(i)}{n} \times 100\% \tag{1}$$

where $\mathrm{ACC}_{\mathrm{num}}(i)$ is 1 if the *i-th* tampered region is correctly identified (0 otherwise), $\mathrm{Score}_{\mathrm{loc}}(i)$ is the positional accuracy score (normalized to [0,1]), and n denotes the total number of actual tampered regions in the image.

As illustrated in Fig. 1, we adopt an MLLM-based evaluation scheme. The workflow proceeds as follows: First, the tampered region descriptions and positional information generated by the MLLM are provided to an evaluator MLLM, together with the corresponding test image and ground-truth tampered mask as reference. Second, the evaluator is prompted to score two aspects separately: (i) the accuracy of tampered region description, and (ii) the precision of spatial location reporting. Finally, the overall localization accuracy is computed using Eq. (1).

Table 1. Accuracy comparison for image authenticity detection (%)

Method	Caltech_webfaces	GANs		DMs	
		NeuralTextures	HiSD	DiffFace	Autosplice
FreDect	92.4	58.6	67.0	27.0	33.1
GramNet	**100.0**	5.1	0.0	23.0	43.5
CNNSpot	**100.0**	14.1	13.2	2.0	1.3
FakeShield	91.1	69.2	71.3	54.5	61.2
MLLM-IGDD	**95.5**	**60.4**	**90.3**	**99.4**	**91.2**

Implementation Details: We adopt GPT-4.1 as the primary MLLM and interface with its official API via Python-based conversational simulation. GPT-4o-mini and GPT-4o are evaluated similarly through their respective APIs. Two open-source MLLMs, Llama-3.2-11B-Vision and DeepSeek-VL2-Small (2.8B params), are deployed locally following official guidelines. Across all experiments, we maintain consistent input formatting, prompting strategies, and evaluation protocols to ensure a fair and reproducible comparison.

4.2 Detection Performance Evaluation

To evaluate the detection capability of MLLM-IGDD, we design an image-level binary classification task on the five datasets described above. As shown in Fig. 3, MLLM-IGDD achieves high detection accuracy on both authentic and deepfake datasets. Detailed quantitative results are provided in Table 1. MLLM-IGDD, powered by GPT-4.1, achieves the highest average accuracy across all datasets. Specifically, it obtains detection accuracies exceeding 90.3% on four of the five datasets. The only exception is NeuralTextures, where performance is slightly lower. This reduction in NeuralTextures is primarily due to the low spatial resolution of images in this dataset, which limits the model's ability to discern subtle manipulation artifacts.

Further analysis reveals critical differences between MLLM-based detection and traditional specialized models (FreDect, GramNet, and CNNSpot). While traditional models achieve higher accuracy on authentic images by modeling natural image characteristics, empirical evidence from FakeShield and MLLM-IGDD demonstrates that MLLM-integrated approaches maintain performance consistency across heterogeneous image categories, thereby validating the efficacy of MLLMs in image forgery detection. By aligning semantic comprehension with visual evidence, these methods leverage inherent reasoning capabilities to identify deepfakes, resulting in superior generalization across unseen forgery types.

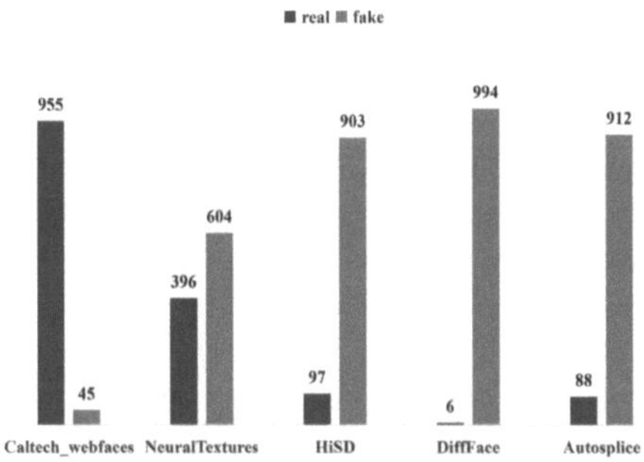

Fig. 3. Detection performance of MLLM-IGDD across datasets. Bar values indicate images classified as real or fake.

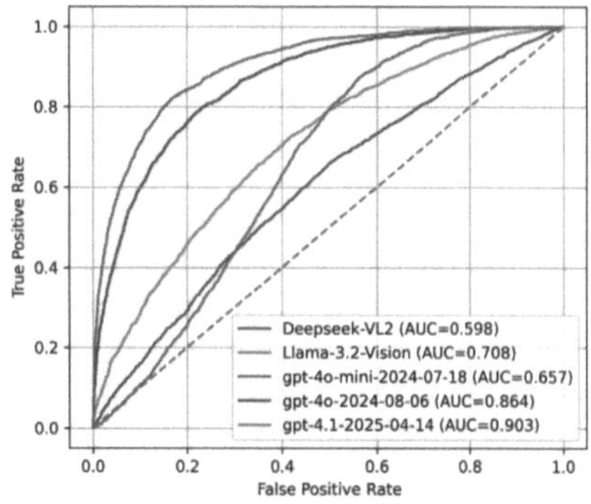

Fig. 4. ROC and AUC performance of MLLM-IGDD across various MLLMs

Table 2. MLLM-IGDD localization accuracy across MLLMs(%)

Method	HiSD	Autosplice
Deepseek-VL2	11.6	12.4
Llama-3.2-Vision	18.7	10.3
GPT-4o-mini	30.6	35.7
GPT-4o	48.1	48.3
GPT-4.1	**67.3**	**66.9**

Table 3. Ablation on instance composition (%)

Instances combination	Acc	Rej
0	63.5	82.3
1-Fake	78.6	26.3
2-Fakes	90.2	2.0
1-Real+1-Fake (ours)	**92.0**	**0.0**
2-Reals+2-Fakes	93.5	0.0
3-Reals+3-Fakes	91.1	0.0

4.3 Localization Accuracy Results

For quantifying the localization accuracy of tampered regions, we perform experiments on 2,000 images sampled from the HiSD and Autosplice datasets, evaluating MLLM-IGDD across multiple MLLM backbones. As shown in Table 2, the variant powered by GPT-4.1 achieves the best performance across both test settings. However, because MLLMs produce natural-language outputs, converting these descriptive responses into quantitative localization metrics inevitably incurs some information loss, which may lead to lower numerical scores compared to pixel-level methods.

4.4 Ablation Study

This section presents ablation studies on the instance-guided mechanism to evaluate its contribution to detection performance.

Ablation Study on Instance Composition. To assess the impact of reference instance composition on deepfake detection, we evaluate different in-context instance configurations under a k-shot learning paradigm [35]. Specifically, for each $k \in \{0, 1, 2, 4, 6\}$, we perform three independent trials. In each trial, k instances are selected from our curated Instance Dataset and provided as contextual guidance to the MLLM. The detection accuracy and rejection rate are evaluated on 1,000 images randomly sampled from the AutoSplice dataset.

Table 3 presents the experimental results, from which we draw the following observations: (i) Contextual instances significantly reduce the model's rejection rate. When no instances are provided ($k = 0$), the rejection rate reaches 82.3%, indicating that the MLLM tends to refrain from making predictions in the absence of task-specific guidance. (ii) Including both authentic and deepfake instances yields better performance than using only deepfake instances. This contrastive setup provides more informative supervision, improving both calibration and discriminative capability. (iii) Increasing k from 4 to 6 leads to a slight degradation in accuracy, suggesting that excessive or redundant instances may introduce noise or conflicting signals. Based on these findings, we adopt a "1 Real + 1 Fake" contrastive instance pair as the default configuration for MLLM-IGDD. This balanced setup delivers essential discriminative cues while avoiding redundancy, thus achieving an optimal trade-off among detection accuracy, robustness, and inference efficiency.

Table 4. Ablation of recommended versus randomly selected instances (%)

Selection method	Model	Caltech_webfaces	GANs		DMs	
			NeuralTextures	HiSD	DiffFace	Autosplice
#1 Randomly selected	GPT-4o	92.1	37.5	82.4	95.5	68.2
	GPT-4.1	93.3	65.4	96.2	99.3	75.5
#2 Recommended (ours)	GPT-4o	**92.2**	**34.5**	**80.4**	**99.2**	**83.3**
	GPT-4.1	**95.5**	**60.4**	**90.3**	**99.4**	**91.2**

Ablation Study on Instance Dataset. To further evaluate the effectiveness of the Instance Dataset in IRM, we compare it with randomly selected deepfake instances from NeuralTextures, HiSD, DiffFace, and AutoSplice. In the baseline, one authentic and one deepfake instance are randomly sampled to serve as context references. Both configurations are evaluated on the unified test set described above, using detection accuracy as metric. As presented in Table 4, the experimental results across both models demonstrate that instances selected from our curated dataset consistently outperform those chosen randomly, with the exception of two GAN-based forgery datasets. While random selection may include a GAN-based instance, leading to improved detection performance for GAN forgeries, it results in suboptimal detection performance when applied to real images and those generated by DMs. These findings underscores that incorporating images generated by DMs provides more robust and effective guidance for deepfake detection.

4.5 Compatibility Evaluation

To assess the adaptability of MLLM-IGDD across mainstream MLLMs, we deploy the framework on five representative architectures described above. The evaluation is conducted on the unified test set, with the task formulated as binary image authenticity classification. Performance is quantified using ROC curves and AUC scores to ensure objective and comparable assessment. As shown in Fig. 4, MLLM-IGDD demonstrates robust compatibility across diverse MLLMs. All variants achieve AUC scores substantially above 0.5, confirming that the methods consistently outperform random guessing and effectively capture the artifacts of image manipulation. Notably, the highest performance is attained when it is deployed on GPT-4.1, yielding an AUC of 0.903. This result demonstrates that our method is adaptable to different MLLM architectures and achieves stronger performance by leveraging capable vision-language foundation models.

5 Conclusion

In this paper, we propose MLLM-IGDD, a training-free method that steers the MLLM inference through instance guidance and domain-informed forensic priors. Experimental results demonstrate that MLLM-IGDD not only achieves strong performance in detecting deepfake images across diverse datasets but also exhibits robust compatibility with mainstream MLLMs. Ablation studies further validate the effectiveness of the proposed instance-guided design in improving detection accuracy and reducing model's rejection rate. In practice, synthetic and manipulated media content often spans multiple modalities. Future work will explore cross-modal alignment and modality-specific enhancement techniques to extend the framework toward robust multimodal forgery detection in real-world scenarios.

References

1. Chen, L., Zhang, Y., Song, Y., Liu, L., Wang, J.: Self-supervised learning of adversarial example: towards good generalizations for deepfake detection. In: Proceedings of the IEEE/CVF Conference on Computer Vision and Pattern Recognition, pp. 18710–18719 (2022)
2. Chen, Z., et al.: DiffusionFace: towards a comprehensive dataset for diffusion-based face forgery analysis. arXiv preprint (2024). https://doi.org/10.48550/arXiv.2403.18471, https://arxiv.org/abs/2403.18471. Accessed 05 Apr 2025
3. Dhariwal, P., Nichol, A.: Diffusion models beat GANs on image synthesis. In: Advances in Neural Information Processing Systems (NeurIPS), vol. 34, pp. 8780–8794. Curran Associates, Inc. (2021). https://proceedings.neurips.cc/paper/2021/file/49ad23d1ec9fa4bd8d77d02681df5cfa-Paper.pdf. Accessed 05 Apr 2025
4. Duan, J., et al.: Test-time forgery detection with spatial-frequency prompt learning. Int. J. Comput. Vision **133**(2), 672–687 (2025). https://doi.org/10.1007/s11263-024-02190-9
5. Fei-Fei, L., Fergus, R., Perona, P.: One-shot learning of object categories. IEEE Trans. Pattern Anal. Mach. Intell. **28**(4), 594–611 (2006). https://doi.org/10.1109/TPAMI.2006.79
6. Frank, J., Eisenhofer, T., Schönherr, L., Fischer, A., Kolossa, D., Holz, T.: Leveraging frequency analysis for deep fake image recognition. In: Proceedings of the 37th International Conference on Machine Learning, ICML 2020, 13–18 July 2020, Virtual Event. Proceedings of Machine Learning Research, vol. 119, pp. 3247–3258. PMLR (2020)
7. Guillaro, F., Cozzolino, D., Sud, A., Dufour, N., Verdoliva, L.: Trufor: leveraging all-round clues for trustworthy image forgery detection and localization. In: IEEE/CVF Conference on Computer Vision and Pattern Recognition, CVPR 2023, Vancouver, BC, Canada, 17–24 June 2023, pp. 20606–20615 (2023). https://doi.org/10.1109/CVPR52729.2023.01974
8. Guo, D., et al.: DeepSeek-VL2: mixture-of-experts vision-language models for advanced multimodal understanding. arXiv preprint (2024). https://arxiv.org/abs/2412.13789. Accessed 05 Apr 2025
9. Guo, X., Song, X., Zhang, Y., Liu, X., Liu, X.: Rethinking vision-language model in face forensics: multi-modal interpretable forged face detector. In: IEEE/CVF Conference on Computer Vision and Pattern Recognition, CVPR 2025, Nashville, TN, USA, 11–15 June 2025, pp. 105–116. Computer Vision Foundation/IEEE (2025). https://doi.org/10.1109/CVPR52734.2025.00019
10. Hasanaath, A.A., Luqman, H., Katib, R., Anwar, S.: FSBI: deepfake detection with frequency enhanced self-blended images. Image Vis. Comput. **154**, 105418 (2025)
11. Hu, S., Li, Y., Lyu, S.: Exposing GAN-generated faces using inconsistent corneal specular highlights. In: IEEE International Conference on Acoustics, Speech and Signal Processing, ICASSP 2021, Toronto, ON, Canada, 6–11 June 2021, pp. 2500–2504. IEEE (2021). https://doi.org/10.1109/ICASSP39728.2021.9414582
12. Huang, Z., Xia, B., Lin, Z., Mou, Z., Yang, W., Jia, J.: FFAA: multimodal large language model based explainable open-world face forgery analysis assistant. arXiv preprint arXiv:2408.10072 (2024)
13. Huang, Z., et al.: SIDA: social media image deepfake detection, localization and explanation with large multimodal model. In: IEEE/CVF Conference on Computer Vision and Pattern Recognition, CVPR 2025, Nashville, TN, USA, 11–15 June 2025, pp. 28831–28841 (2025). https://doi.org/10.1109/CVPR52734.2025.02685

14. Jia, S., Huang, M., Zhou, Z., Ju, Y., Cai, J., Lyu, S.: AutoSplice: a text-prompt manipulated image dataset for media forensics. In: IEEE/CVF Conference on Computer Vision and Pattern Recognition, CVPR 2023 - Workshops, Vancouver, BC, Canada, 17–24 June 2023, pp. 893–903. IEEE (2023). https://doi.org/10.1109/CVPRW59228.2023.00096
15. Jonientz, L., Merkle, J., Rathgeb, C., Tams, B., Merz, G.: Deep learning-based compression detection for explainable face image quality assessment. In: Palaiahnakote, S., Schuckers, S., Ogier, JM., Bhattacharya, P., Pal, U., Bhattacharya, S. (eds.) ICPR 2024, Part I. LNCS, vol. 15614, pp. 329–342. Springer, Cham (2024). https://doi.org/10.1007/978-3-031-87657-8_23
16. Kroiß, L., Reschke, J.: Deepfake detection of face images based on a convolutional neural network. arXiv preprint arXiv:2503.11389 (2025)
17. Lee, D., et al.: Good examples make a faster learner: simple demonstration-based learning for low-resource NER. In: Proceedings of the 60th Annual Meeting of the Association for Computational Linguistics (Volume 1: Long Papers), ACL 2022, Dublin, Ireland, 22–27 May 2022, pp. 2687–2700. Association for Computational Linguistics (2022). https://doi.org/10.18653/V1/2022.ACL-LONG.192
18. Li, S., et al.: Explanations from large language models make small reasoners better. arXiv preprint arXiv:2210.06726 (2022)
19. Li, X., et al.: Image-to-image translation via hierarchical style disentanglement. In: IEEE Conference on Computer Vision and Pattern Recognition, CVPR 2021, virtual, 19–25 June 2021, pp. 8639–8648. Computer Vision Foundation/IEEE (2021). https://doi.org/10.1109/CVPR46437.2021.00853
20. Liu, H., et.: Spatial-phase shallow learning: rethinking face forgery detection in frequency domain. In: Proceedings of the IEEE/CVF Conference on Computer Vision and Pattern Recognition, pp. 772–781 (2021)
21. Liu, J., Zhang, F., Zhu, J., Sun, E., Zhang, Q., Zha, Z.J.: ForgeryGPT: multimodal large language model for explainable image forgery detection and localization. arXiv preprint arXiv:2410.10238 (2024)
22. Liu, Z., Qi, X., Torr, P.H.S.: Global texture enhancement for fake face detection in the wild. In: 2020 IEEE/CVF Conference on Computer Vision and Pattern Recognition, CVPR 2020, Seattle, WA, USA, 13–19 June 2020, pp. 8057–8066 (2020). https://doi.org/10.1109/CVPR42600.2020.00808
23. Ma, X., Du, B., Jiang, Z., Hammadi, A.Y.A., Zhou, J.: IML-vit: Benchmarking image manipulation localization by vision transformer. arXiv preprint arXiv:2307.14863 (2023)
24. Meta: LLaMA-3.2-11b-vision. Vision-language multimodal large language model (2025). https://github.com/marketplace/models/azureml-meta/Llama-3-2-11B-Vision-Instruct. Accessed 17 Dec 2025; 11B parameters, pretrained on 6B image-text pairs, knowledge cutoff: December 2023
25. Ojha, U., Li, Y., Lee, Y.J.: Towards universal fake image detectors that generalize across generative models. In: Proceedings of the IEEE/CVF Conference on Computer Vision and Pattern Recognition, pp. 24480–24489 (2023)
26. OpenAI: GPT-4o system card. Technical report, OpenAI (2024). https://openai.com/index/gpt-4o-system-card/. Accessed 18 Dec 2024
27. OpenAI: GPT-4.1. Blog post or technical announcement (2025). https://openai.com/index/gpt-4-1/. Accessed 05 Apr 2025
28. OpenAI: GPT-4o mini. Lightweight large language model (2025). https://openai.com/index/gpt-4-1/. Accessed 18 Dec 2024
29. Peng, S., et al.: MLLM-enhanced face forgery detection: a vision-language fusion solution. arXiv preprint arXiv:2505.02013 (2025)

30. Qian, Y., Yin, G., Sheng, L., Chen, Z., Shao, J.: Thinking in frequency: face forgery detection by mining frequency-aware clues. In: Vedaldi, A., Bischof, H., Brox, T., Frahm, J.-M. (eds.) ECCV 2020. LNCS, vol. 12357, pp. 86–103. Springer, Cham (2020). https://doi.org/10.1007/978-3-030-58610-2_6
31. Ricker, J., Lukovnikov, D., Fischer, A.: Aeroblade: training-free detection of latent diffusion images using autoencoder reconstruction error. In: Proceedings of the IEEE/CVF Conference on Computer Vision and Pattern Recognition, pp. 9130–9140 (2024)
32. Shi, L., Zhang, J., Ji, Z., Bai, J., Shan, S.: Real face foundation representation learning for generalized deepfake detection. Pattern Recogn. **161**, 111299 (2025)
33. of Technology, C.I.: Caltech 10k web faces dataset (2024). https://www.vision.caltech.edu/datasets/caltech10k_webfaces/ Accessed 05 Apr 2025
34. Thies, J., Zollhöfer, M., Nießner, M.: Deferred neural rendering: image synthesis using neural textures. ACM Trans. Graph. **38**(4), 66:1–66:12 (2019). https://doi.org/10.1145/3306346.3323035
35. Vinyals, O., Blundell, C., Lillicrap, T., Kavukcuoglu, K., Wierstra, D.: Matching networks for one shot learning. In: Advances in Neural Information Processing Systems 29: Annual Conference on Neural Information Processing Systems 2016, 5–10 December 2016, Barcelona, Spain, pp. 3630–3638 (2016)
36. Wang, C., Deng, W.: Representative forgery mining for fake face detection. In: Proceedings of the IEEE/CVF Conference on Computer Vision and Pattern Recognition, pp. 14923–14932. (2021)
37. Wang, S., Wang, O., Zhang, R., Owens, A., Efros, A.A.: CNN-generated images are surprisingly easy to spot... for now. In: 2020 IEEE/CVF Conference on Computer Vision and Pattern Recognition, CVPR 2020, Seattle, WA, USA, 13–19 June 2020, pp. 8692–8701 (2020). https://doi.org/10.1109/CVPR42600.2020.00872
38. Wang, Y., Yu, K., Chen, C., Hu, X., Peng, S.: Dynamic graph learning with content-guided spatial-frequency relation reasoning for deepfake detection. In: Proceedings of the IEEE/CVF Conference on Computer Vision and Pattern Recognition, pp. 7278–7287 (2023)
39. Wang, Z., et al.: Dire for diffusion-generated image detection. In: Proceedings of the IEEE/CVF International Conference on Computer Vision, pp. 22445–22455 (2023)
40. Wei, J., et al.: Chain-of-thought prompting elicits reasoning in large language models. In: Advances in Neural Information Processing Systems 35: Annual Conference on Neural Information Processing Systems 2022, NeurIPS 2022, New Orleans, LA, USA, 28 November–9 December 2022 (2022)
41. Xu, Z., Zhang, X., Li, R., Tang, Z., Huang, Q., Zhang, J.: FakeShield: explainable image forgery detection and localization via multi-modal large language models. In: The Thirteenth International Conference on Learning Representations, ICLR 2025, Singapore, 24–28 April 2025. OpenReview.net (2025)
42. Yu, W., et al.: Generate rather than retrieve: large language models are strong context generators. In: The Eleventh International Conference on Learning Representations, ICLR 2023, Kigali, Rwanda, 1–5 May 2023. OpenReview.net (2023)
43. Yu, Z., Ni, J., Lin, Y., Deng, H., Li, B.: DiffForensics: leveraging diffusion prior to image forgery detection and localization. In: IEEE/CVF Conference on Computer Vision and Pattern Recognition, CVPR 2024, Seattle, WA, USA, 16–22 June 2024, pp. 12765–12774. IEEE (2024). https://doi.org/10.1109/CVPR52733.2024.01213

44. Zhang, Y., Colman, B., Guo, X., Shahriyari, A., Bharaj, G.: Common sense reasoning for deepfake detection. In: Leonardis, A., Ricci, E., Roth, S., Russakovsky, O., Sattler, T., Varol, G. (eds.) ECCV 2024. LNCS, vol. 15146, pp. 399–415. Springer, Cham (2024). https://doi.org/10.1007/978-3-031-73223-2_22
45. Zhou, D., et al.: Least-to-most prompting enables complex reasoning in large language models. In: The Eleventh International Conference on Learning Representations, ICLR 2023, Kigali, Rwanda, 1–5 May 2023. OpenReview.net (2023)

MCTS-VUL: Self-training Large Language Models via Monte Carlo Tree Search for Vulnerability Detection

Jujie Wang, Kangfeng Zheng(✉), Bin Wu, Chunhua Wu, Yulin Yao, Jiaqi Gao, and Minjiao Yang

Beijing University of Posts and Telecommunications, Beijing, China
{wangjvjie,kfzheng}@bupt.edu.cn

Abstract. Recent advances in Large Language Models (LLMs) have shown considerable potential for automating source-level vulnerability detection. However, existing supervised fine-tuning approaches for LLMs are constrained by the scarcity of high-quality SFT datasets, and therefore typically produce only binary predictions indicating the presence or absence of vulnerabilities. As a result, they fail to fully leverage a key advantage of LLMs: providing developers with informative reasoning about vulnerability causes and actionable remediation guidance. To enable developer-friendly vulnerability analysis under limited labeled data, we propose MCTS-VUL, a teacher–student self-training framework that integrates LLMs with Monte Carlo Tree Search (MCTS) to generate structured reasoning traces for vulnerability detection. MCTS-VUL employs a value model to guide the search process and identify high-quality reasoning paths. Experimental results demonstrate that our approach not only generates developer-oriented reasoning traces, but also achieves competitive or state-of-the-art performance across three public datasets. These results further indicate that the generated reasoning traces effectively facilitate LLMs in learning the underlying causes of vulnerabilities.

Keywords: Vulnerability Detection · Large Language Model · Self-Training

1 Introduction

The application of Large Language Models (LLMs) to software vulnerability detection has attracted increasing attention in recent years, as researchers explore their potential to automate the identification of security flaws in source code. Compared with traditional deep learning approaches such as CNNs and RNNs, which typically focus on predicting the presence or absence of vulnerabilities [3,19,20,26,30,36], LLMs are able to provide more informative semantic insights and explanations, thereby offering better guidance to developers in understanding vulnerabilities and repairing vulnerable source code.

© IFIP International Federation for Information Processing 2026
Published by Springer Nature Switzerland AG 2026
H. Janicke et al. (Eds.): SEC 2026, IFIP AICT 787, pp. 120–133, 2026.
https://doi.org/10.1007/978-3-032-27993-4_9

However, a growing body of recent studies has shown that current Large Language Models (LLMs) are still far from being reliable for software vulnerability detection [6,27,35]. In particular, Ding et al. [6] demonstrate that even state-of-the-art LLMs such as GPT-4 perform no better than random guessing on several vulnerability detection benchmarks. This limitation primarily stems from the insufficient understanding of vulnerability semantics by LLMs, which makes effective learning heavily dependent on high-quality task-specific training data. Existing supervised fine-tuning (SFT)-based approaches [6,13,28] typically formulate vulnerability detection as a binary classification task, requiring models to output a simple yes or no decision. This design choice is largely driven by the characteristics of available open-source datasets, which usually provide only binary vulnerability labels (0/1) without accompanying explanations or reasoning about vulnerability causes. As a result, such approaches fail to fully exploit the inherent strengths of LLMs, particularly their ability to reason about vulnerability root causes and provide actionable guidance for vulnerability remediation. Recent advances such as DeepSeek-R1 suggest that reinforcement learning (RL) alone can endow LLMs with reasoning capabilities under limited supervision. However, we observe that directly applying RL algorithms such as GRPO to vulnerability detection remains challenging. Due to the complexity of the task, small or partially trained models often struggle to generate correct predictions, making it difficult to obtain reliable reward signals. This issue can easily lead to unstable training dynamics and policy degradation in practice.

Therefore, to enable Large Language Models to self-train and generate vulnerability cause reasoning that is helpful to developers under limited supervision, we propose a self-training framework based on process-level rewards that integrates a LLM with Monte Carlo Tree Search (MCTS). Rather than relying on predefined rule-based rewards, our approach leverages MCTS to guide the model through step-by-step reasoning in vulnerability detection, enabling dynamic exploration and selection of optimal reasoning paths. Specifically, our framework consists of four core components (Fig. 1): a teacher model, a value model, a refining model, and a policy model. During training, the teacher model conducts MCTS-based search to generate high-quality vulnerability reasoning paths. The value model evaluates the quality of intermediate reasoning steps, guiding the search toward the optimal reasoning paths. Once a complete reasoning path is obtained, the refining model summarizes it into a standardized five-step reasoning process, ensuring consistency and facilitating downstream learning. Finally, the policy model acts as the vulnerability detector, trained to imitate the reasoning trajectories produced by the teacher. Unlike most existing reinforced self-improvement approaches (e.g., STaR [33], RFT [32], ReSTEM [29], V-STaR [15], Rest-MCTS [34]), we do not share parameters between the teacher and policy models. Instead, we deliberately use a significantly stronger teacher model to overcome the limitations observed in smaller models, such as output instability and formatting errors during the search. This design enables the generation of more accurate and reliable reasoning paths, which in turn improves the policy model's learning stability and downstream performance.

Overall the main contribution of this paper is as follow:

- To the best of our knowledge, this is the first work to apply an LLM-guided MCTS self-training framework to source-level vulnerability detection, enabling the generation of high-quality reasoning traces and supporting effective vulnerability reasoning for developer under limited supervision.
- We design a novel self-training architecture comprising four decoupled components—teacher model, value model, refining model, and policy model—and introduce a structured five-step reasoning format to improve the interpretability and consistency of the detection process.
- Extensive experiments on three real-world vulnerability datasets demonstrate that our method significantly outperforms existing baselines in both accuracy and F1 score, achieving up to 217.52% relative improvement in F1 score.

2 Related Works

2.1 Deep Learning-Based Methods

Traditional approaches represent the source code as a linear sequence of tokens or bytes and use models such as CNNs [4,10,14] or RNNs [12,16] to directly learn vulnerability-related features. However, by ignoring the graph-based structure of source code, sequence-based approaches may fail to model important contextual relationships, leading to reduced prediction accuracy. Therefore, further studies utilizing GNN model to capture the structure information. The code is transformed Abstract Syntax Trees (AST), Control Flow Graphs (CFG), and Data Flow Graphs (DFG) and then analyzing it using GNNs [1,2,5,31,36].

2.2 LLM-Based Methods

LLM have shown strong capabilities in generating detailed explanations for software vulnerabilities, which significantly aids developers in the process of understanding and fixing security issues. Recent studies have proposed a variety of techniques to further improve the performance of LLMs in vulnerability detection. These include integrating LLMs with static analysis tools [21], leveraging attention mechanisms [18], applying chain-of-thought (CoT) prompting [25], utilizing in-context learning strategies [24], and adopting retrieval-augmented generation (RAG) approaches [7,22].

However, most of these methods rely solely on the zero-shot or few-shot capabilities of pretrained LLMs, without applying further fine-tuning. This limitation is largely due to the lack of SFT data in the vulnerability detection domain. Meanwhile, reinforcement learning approaches like GRPO have shown limited effectiveness in this domain, primarily due to sparse and unstable rewards, especially on imbalanced datasets. These limitations highlight the need for alternative self-training architectures that can provide more reliable guidance for LLM-based vulnerability detection.

3 The MCTS-Vul Method

3.1 System Overview

Our self-training framework, illustrated in Fig. 1, consists of four key components:

- **Teacher Model:** Executes MCTS to generate high-quality reasoning paths for vulnerability detection.
- **Value Model:** Evaluates the quality of each reasoning step, guiding MCTS toward more optimal reasoning trajectories.
- **Refiner Model:** To refine the output of the final reasoning path.
- **Policy Model:** A lightweight student model trained to mimic the teacher's trajectories and used for downstream vulnerability detection.

Unlike most self-training frameworks, our design does not share parameters between the teacher and the policy model. Instead, we leverage a much more powerful LLM (e.g., GPT-4O) as the teacher, while the policy model adopts a smaller, lightweight architecture. This design is motivated by an observation that smaller models often suffer from unstable reasoning and inconsistent output formatting during path search, which negatively impacts performance. By using a stronger teacher model, we ensure the generation of more accurate reasoning paths and significantly improve the policy model's learning dynamics and final detection quality.

Besides, to improve training efficiency, we do not fully expand all nodes in the MCTS tree. Instead, we selectively expand only the child node with the highest Upper Confidence Bound (UCB) score at each step. The search terminates once a valid final solution is found. Furthermore, to enhance the coherence and convergence of the generated reasoning paths, we introduce a target-guidance mechanism that lightly supervises the teacher model, helping to ensure the quality and relevance of the generated trajectories.

3.2 Vulnerability Reasoning with Monte Carlo Tree Search

To ensure the quality of reasoning at each step, a value model is introduced to provide real-time evaluation of intermediate paths. A greedy policy is then applied to iteratively select the highest-scoring branch, guiding the search toward more accurate and coherent reasoning outcomes.

MCTS-VUL consists of five stages: node selection, node expansion, backpropagation, refinement, and policy training. We only expand code snippets identified as vulnerable. For benign samples, the process immediately returns `{"is_vul": "no"}`. This design reflects real-world scenarios, where the majority of functions are non-vulnerable, and generating elaborate explanations for each of them would be unnecessary and inefficient.

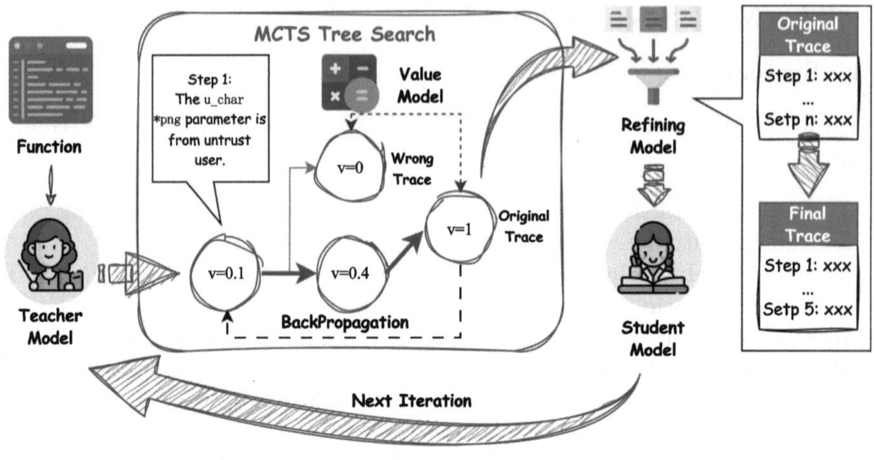

Fig. 1. The MCTS-VUL self-training framework.

Value for Partial Solution. We first define the rule of the value model. The value model evaluates the quality and correctness of each intermediate reasoning step. The value V_k is computed by the value model based on a given "GroundTruth" label G and a partial solution P. It is formally defined as:

$$V_k = \text{Value}(G,\ P) \tag{1}$$

The value V_k satisfies the following basic qualities:

- **Limited range:** V_k is constrained within the range $[0, 1]$, where 0 indicates a completely incorrect reasoning step, and 1 indicates a fully correct one.
- **Reflecting probability of correctness:** V_k reflects both the correctness and completeness of the partial solution. That is, a correct next step should yield a higher V_k than an incorrect one. Moreover, a more complete and correct step should produce a higher value than an incomplete one. This principle ensures that MCTS can make incremental progress toward the correct solution path.

Specifically, we adopt DeepSeek-V3 as both the value model and the policy model. Although it is not fine-tuned for this specific task, DeepSeek-V3 exhibits sufficient capability to distinguish more promising reasoning paths from less effective ones. Moreover, due to its large scale (671B parameters) and extensive pretraining on diverse data, DeepSeek-V3 serves as a powerful teacher model for guiding the generation of high-quality reasoning trajectories.

We emphasize that the value model is not assumed to be a perfect oracle of reasoning correctness. Instead, it serves as a heuristic evaluator that provides relative preference signals among alternative reasoning steps, which is sufficient to guide the MCTS search process.

Node Selection. During each iteration, we begin with the node selection phase. Following the approach of Feng et al. [9], the selection starts from the root node and proceeds according to the UCB score. For each node, we compute the UCB scores of its child nodes to evaluate their priors and select the child node C with the highest UCB score for expansion. Specifically, the UCB score for a child node is computed as follows:

$$UCB(C) = V_C + \varepsilon \cdot \sqrt{\frac{\ln(N_{\text{parent}})}{N_C}} \tag{2}$$

Here, V_C denotes the value estimate of the current child node, N_{parent} is the visit count of the parent node, and N_C is the visit count of the child node. The constant ε controls the balance between exploration and exploitation. The UCB score takes into account both node quality and visit frequency, thereby encouraging the exploration of promising nodes while still allowing less-visited nodes a chance to be selected. The node selection process continues recursively until an unexpanded leaf node C_{select} is selected.

Node Expansion. Once an unexpanded leaf node is selected, we enter the node expansion phase, during which new child nodes are generated and added to the MCTS tree.

Since software vulnerabilities often stem from insecure or improperly handled input, the expansion process begins by exploring input parameters. When the selected node is the root, the teacher model generates the initial reasoning processes $s_{0,i}$ for $i = 1, 2, \ldots, b$, where b denotes the number of branches in the tree. Otherwise, expansion continues along the existing reasoning trace by sampling $s_{k+1,i}$ from the teacher model, conditioned on the current reasoning history $T(s_{1,2,\ldots,k} \mid C_{\text{select}})$. Each new expansion is concatenated with the existing reasoning trace to form an updated sequence. The teacher model is provided with the function's vulnerability label, to prevent generate far from ground truth.

After generating the new child nodes, we evaluate each of them using the value model to estimate their potential for leading to a successful vulnerability explanation. The resulting score, denoted as V_C, is used to guide the subsequent selection and backpropagation phases of MCTS.

Backpropagation. Once the value V_C of a newly expanded node has been obtained, the backpropagation phase updates the value estimates of all its ancestor nodes along the current path. Starting from the evaluated node, we traverse up the tree toward the root, incrementing the visit count of each node by one.

For each node that has been expanded, we update its value estimate V based on the visit-weighted average of its children's values. Specifically, if a node has children $c_1, c_2, \ldots, c_n$ with corresponding values V_i and visit counts v_i, the updated value is computed as:

$$V = \frac{\sum_{i=1}^{n} v_i \cdot V_i}{\sum_{i=1}^{n} v_i} \tag{3}$$

Refining. To ensure the consistency and quality of the final strategy, we further refine the complete reasoning trace. Specifically, the teacher model is instructed to summarize and optimize the full reasoning process into a concise five-step reasoning path.

Policy Training. Once a batch of reasoning traces has been collected, we proceed to the policy training stage. We adopt a 7B-scale model (e.g., Qwen 2.5 7B) and fine-tune it using SFT on the collected teacher traces. The goal is to train a policy model capable of generating high-quality, interpretable reasoning traces that align with the teacher's outputs. The overall algorithm is described in Algorithm 1.

Algorithm 1. Monte Carlo Tree Search for Vulnerability Reasoning

Require: Code snippet *code*, Teacher Model M_T, Value Model M_V, branch factor b
if isVulnerable(code) **then**
  $T \leftarrow$ InitTree(*code*)
  while not finished **do**
    $node \leftarrow$ SelectNode(T) ▷ UCB-based node selection
    $\pi_n \leftarrow$ reasoning trace of *node*
    for $i = 1$ to b **do**
      $child_i \leftarrow$ Expand($node$, $M_T \mid \pi_n$)
      $\pi_{n+1,i} \leftarrow \pi_n +$ step from $child_i$
      $V_i \leftarrow M_V(\pi_{n+1,i})$
      assign V_i to $child_i$
      add $child_i$ to T
    end for
    BackPropagate($child_1, \ldots, child_b$) ▷ Update ancestors
  end while
  $T \leftarrow$ Refine($M_T \mid T$)
  return best reasoning trace from T
else
  return {"is_vul": "no"}
end if

4 Experiments

We evaluate MCTS-VUL against state-of-the-art vulnerability detection methods and aim to answer the following research questions:

- **RQ1.** How does MCTS-VUL perform in vulnerability detection tasks?
- **RQ2.** What is the impact of each module on the detection performance of MCTS-VUL?
- **RQ3.** what is the quality of the generated traces?

4.1 Experiment Setup

Dataset. We evaluate MCTS-VUL on three widely used vulnerability detection datasets: Devign [36], Reveal [3], and BigVul [8]. Detailed dataset statistics are summarized in Table 1. The Devign dataset includes over 10,000 vulnerable and 12,000 non-vulnerable code snippets, making it relatively balanced, with 45.0% of the samples labeled as vulnerable. In contrast, Reveal and BigVul are imbalanced: Reveal consists of approximately 18,000 samples with only 9.16% labeled as vulnerable, while BigVul contains over 179,000 samples, of which 5.88% are vulnerable. Regarding programming language distribution, Devign is derived solely from open-source C projects, whereas Reveal and BigVul span both C and C++ open-source codebases.

Table 1. Statistics of the dataset

Dataset	Samples	Vul Ratios	Language
Devign [36]	22361	45%	C
Reveal [3]	18169	9.16%	C/C++
Bigvul [8]	179299	5.88%	C/C++

Baseline Methods. We evaluate our method against a set of representative baselines, including traditional vulnerability detection approaches [3,19,20,26,30,36], LLM-based methods [24], and the state-of-the-art LLM models [11,17,23]. Performance results for these baselines are reported as presented in the MEGNET paper [30] and Grace [24].

Implementation. We implement MCTS-VUL using Python 3.10, with the PyTorch framework and Huggingface Transformers library. All experiments are conducted on a system equipped with two NVIDIA GeForce RTX A800 GPUs, running Ubuntu 20.04 and CUDA 12.4. The MCTS branch number is set to 2. We use DeepSeek-V3 as both the teacher and value model, and Qwen 2.5-coder-instruct as the policy model. The model is trained for 5 epochs using a batch size of 64 and a learning rate of 1e-5. In addition, to ensure fair comparisons, we use the same data splitting strategy for all baseline approaches as employed in MCTS-VUL. Specifically, the dataset is randomly partitioned into disjoint training, validation, and test sets with a ratio of 8:1:1.

4.2 RQ1. How Does MCTS-VUL Perform in Vulnerability Detection Tasks?

To answer this research question, we compare the performance of MCTS-VUL with other baseline methods. The results are presented in Table 2. Overall, MCTS significantly enhances the vulnerability detection capability of LLMs. We select the instruction version of the state-of-the-art LLMs as the policy model: StarCoder2 7B [23], LLaMA 3.1 8B [11] and Qwen 2.5-Coder 7B [17].

Table 2. Performance comparison of different methods on the Devign, Reveal, and BigVul datasets. We report Accuracy and F1 Score (%). Results with gray and light gray indicate the best and second-best performances, respectively. Relative improvements over the base LLM are shown as $_{\uparrow\%}$.

Metrics(%) \ Dataset	Devign		Reveal		BigVul	
Baseline	Accuracy	F1 Score	Accuracy	F1 Score	Accuracy	F1 Score
VulDeePecker [20]	0.4961	0.3814	0.7637	0.1617	0.8119	0.1915
Russell et al. [26]	0.5760	0.4671	0.6851	0.2479	0.8685	0.1917
SySeVR [19]	0.4785	0.5166	0.7433	0.3074	0.9010	0.1934
Devign [36]	0.5689	0.5795	0.8749	0.3391	0.9278	0.2098
Reveal [3]	0.6107	0.6219	0.8177	0.4162	0.8714	0.2287
Grace [24]	0.5978	0.6511	0.8973	0.4313	0.9073	0.3550
MEGNET [30]	0.6328	0.6612	**0.9160**	**0.5057**	0.9138	0.2868
StarCoder2 7B [23]	0.6288	0.5244	0.8728	0.1109	0.9412	0.6712
LLaMA3.1 7B [11]	0.6489	0.6307	0.9067	0.1204	0.9571	0.7076
Qwen2.5 7B [17]	0.6386	0.5771	0.9082	0.1551	0.9698	0.7673
StarCoder2 7B + MCTS	**0.6823**	0.6018 $_{\uparrow 14.76\%}$	0.8724	0.3318 $_{\uparrow 199.18\%}$	0.9721	0.8292 $_{\uparrow 23.53\%}$
LLaMA3.1 7B+ MCTS	0.6736	**0.6857** $_{\uparrow 8.72\%}$	0.8911	0.3823 $_{\uparrow 217.52\%}$	0.9788	0.8387 $_{\uparrow 18.5\%}$
Qwen2.5 7B + MCTS	0.6523	0.6241 $_{\uparrow 8.14\%}$	0.9133	0.4402 $_{\uparrow 183.81\%}$	**0.9793**	**0.8397** $_{\uparrow 9.43\%}$

We observe that, compared to the relatively balanced Devign dataset, MCTS-VUL achieves stronger performance on the more imbalanced Reveal and BigVul datasets. This observation suggests that MCTS-VUL is able to effectively capture reasoning-related features associated with vulnerabilities, which contributes to its robustness under class-imbalanced settings.

4.3 RQ2. What is the Impact of Each Module on the Detection Performance of MCTS-VUL?

We further investigate the contribution of each core component in MCTS-VUL through an ablation study conducted on the Devign, Reveal, and BigVul datasets. Specifically, we evaluate the following three variations: (1) replacing the teacher model with different LLMs, (2) replacing the value model, and (3) removing the refiner module. The full results are presented in Table 3.

We observe that employing a more powerful teacher model significantly enhances performance across all datasets. In addition, the value model also contributes to the performance of MCTS-VUL. A stronger value model can guide the search process to generate more accurate reasoning traces, which in turn leads to better results. However, its impact is relatively smaller compared to

Table 3. Ablation study evaluating the impact of different modules across three datasets. Each row corresponds to a 7B model under a specific architecture variant and ablation setting. The best and second-best results for each metric and dataset are highlighted in gray and light gray, respectively.

Metrics(%) \ Dataset	Variant	Ablated Settings	Devign		Reveal		BigVul	
Baseline			Accuracy	F1 Score	Accuracy	F1 Score	Accuracy	F1 Score
StarCoder2 7B	Teacher	Qwen 72B	0.6432	0.5324	0.8741	0.2284	0.9434	0.7212
LLaMA 3.1 7B			0.6365	0.6403	0.8820	0.2447	0.9529	0.7436
Qwen2.5 7B			0.6280	0.5938	0.8986	0.3316	0.9628	0.7631
StarCoder2 7B	Teacher	Deepseek-V3	0.6932	0.6124	0.8841	0.3529	0.9724	0.8312
LLaMA 3.1 7B			0.6812	0.6971	0.9123	0.3985	0.9846	0.8429
Qwen2.5 7B			0.6592	0.6327	0.9125	0.4436	0.9821	0.8452
StarCoder2 7B	Value Model	Qwen 72B	0.6502	0.5526	0.8745	0.2943	0.9546	0.7594
LLaMA 3.1 7B			0.6549	0.6533	0.8914	0.3433	0.9639	0.7891
Qwen2.5 7B			0.6435	0.5966	0.9054	0.3893	0.9712	0.7924
StarCoder2 7B	Value Model	Deepseek-V3	0.6872	0.6215	0.8835	0.3459	0.9873	0.8433
LLaMA 3.1 7B			0.6894	0.6935	0.9074	0.3844	0.9742	0.8411
Qwen2.5 7B			0.6510	0.6245	0.9111	0.4358	0.9794	0.8459
StarCoder2 7B	Refiner	W/O Refiner	0.6460	0.5545	0.8612	0.2251	0.9630	0.7185
LLaMA 3.1 7B			0.6410	0.6483	0.8908	0.2742	0.9682	0.7458
Qwen2.5 7B			0.6359	0.6012	0.8865	0.3410	0.9749	0.7725
StarCoder2 7B + MCTS	**MCTS-VUL**	Deepseek-V3	0.6823	0.6018	0.8724	0.3318	0.9721	0.8292
LLaMA3.1 7B+ MCTS			0.6736	0.6857	0.8911	0.3823	0.9788	0.8387
Qwen2.5 7B + MCTS			0.6523	0.6241	0.9133	0.4402	0.9793	0.8397

that of the teacher model. Finally, when the refiner module is removed, performance consistently drops across all datasets. Without the refiner, the outputs generated by MCTS-VUL tend to exhibit inconsistent formats and irregular step lengths, which negatively affect the final detection performance.

4.4 RQ3. What is the Quality of the Generated Traces?

We perform a comprehensive evaluation of the reasoning trace quality generated by MCTS-VUL to assess both its reliability and interpretability. Our evaluation combines automated scoring with human-aligned judgment, enabling a multi-faceted and objective analysis. As shown in Table 4, the assessment focuses on several core dimensions. We randomly sample 200 generated traces from each dataset and evaluate them using two state-of-the-art LLMs: GPT-4o-mini and DeepSeek-V3.

The evaluation results indicate that the reasoning traces generated across different datasets are both consistent and of high quality, with all three achieving average scores above 8 out of 10. This demonstrates that MCTS-VUL has a strong capability to generate accurate and reliable reasoning traces. The results are presented in Fig. 2.

Table 4. Evaluation criteria for reasoning trace quality in MCTS-VUL.

Dimension	Metric	Concise Meaning
Correctness	Label Consistency	Whether the final assessment matches the ground-truth label
	Causal Validity	Whether the reasoning process correctly identifies the key causal chain that leads to a vulnerability
Logicality	Coherence	Whether the reasoning steps follow a logically consistent, step-by-step progression without contradictions or abrupt jumps
	Completeness	Whether the trace includes all essential reasoning steps to justify the final judgment
Interpretability	Actionability	Whether the trace contains clear, actionable insights that a human developer could follow and understand

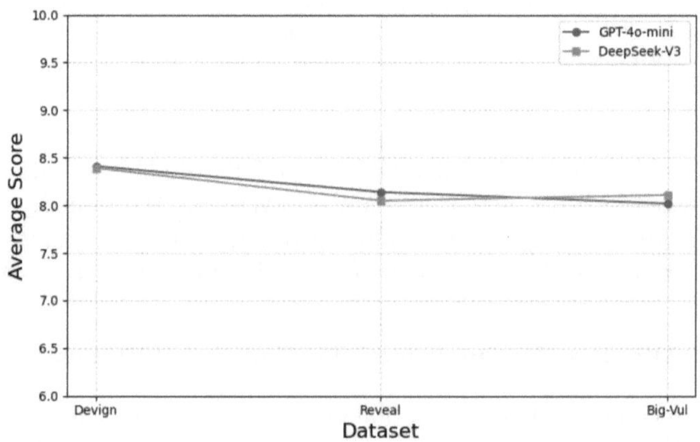

Fig. 2. Trace Quality Evaluated by Model. The score range is set [0, 10]. All generated traces have scores above 8.

5 Conclusion

In this paper, we propose MCTS-VUL, a teacher–student MCTS-based self-training framework for source-level vulnerability detection. MCTS-VUL enables the training of a policy model with detailed vulnerability reasoning logic using only binary (0/1) vulnerability labels. By doing so, it addresses a key limitation of existing supervised learning approaches for large language models, which often struggle to provide developers with meaningful reasoning about vulnerability causes and actionable remediation guidance. In addition, our approach effectively improves the performance of the policy model and demonstrates strong robustness under class-imbalanced settings.

References

1. Allamanis, M., Jackson-Flux, H., Brockschmidt, M.: Self-supervised bug detection and repair. In: Ranzato, M., Beygelzimer, A., Dauphin, Y., Liang, P., Vaughan, J.W. (eds.) Advances in Neural Information Processing Systems, vol. 34, pp. 27865–27876. Curran Associates, Inc. (2021)
2. Cao, S., Sun, X., Bo, L., Wu, R., Li, B., Tao, C.: MVD: memory-related vulnerability detection based on flow-sensitive graph neural networks. In: Proceedings of the 44th International Conference on Software Engineering, ICSE 2022, pp. 1456–1468. Association for Computing Machinery, New York (2022). https://doi.org/10.1145/3510003.3510219
3. Chakraborty, S., Krishna, R., Ding, Y., Ray, B.: Deep learning based vulnerability detection: are we there yet? IEEE Trans. Software Eng. **48**(9), 3280–3296 (2022). https://doi.org/10.1109/TSE.2021.3087402
4. Chen, J., Wang, W., Liu, B., Cai, S., Towey, D., Wang, S.: Hybrid semantics-based vulnerability detection incorporating a temporal convolutional network and self-attention mechanism. Inf. Softw. Technol. **171**, 107453 (2024). https://doi.org/10.1016/j.infsof.2024.107453
5. Dinella, E., Dai, H., Li, Z., Naik, M., Song, L., Wang, K.: Hoppity: learning graph transformations to detect and fix bugs in programs. In: International Conference on Learning Representations (ICLR) (2020)
6. Ding, Y., et al.: Vulnerability detection with code language models: How far are we? (2024). https://arxiv.org/abs/2403.18624
7. Du, X., et al.: Vul-RAG: enhancing LLM-based vulnerability detection via knowledge-level RAG (2024). https://arxiv.org/abs/2406.11147
8. Fan, J., Li, Y., Wang, S., Nguyen, T.N.: AC/C++ code vulnerability dataset with code changes and CVE summaries. In: Proceedings of the 17th International Conference on Mining Software Repositories, pp. 508–512 (2020)
9. Feng, X., et al.: Alphazero-like tree-search can guide large language model decoding and training (2024). https://arxiv.org/abs/2309.17179
10. Filus, K., Siavvas, M., Domańska, J., Gelenbe, E.: The random neural network as a bonding model for software vulnerability prediction. In: Calzarossa, M.C., Gelenbe, E., Grochla, K., Lent, R., Czachórski, T. (eds.) MASCOTS 2020. LNCS, vol. 12527, pp. 102–116. Springer, Cham (2021). https://doi.org/10.1007/978-3-030-68110-4_7
11. Grattafiori, A., et al.: The LLaMA 3 herd of models. arXiv preprint arXiv:2407.21783 (2024)
12. Guo, W., Fang, Y., Huang, C., Ou, H., Lin, C., Guo, Y.: HyVulDect: a hybrid semantic vulnerability mining system based on graph neural network. Comput. Secur. **121**, 102823 (2022). https://doi.org/10.1016/j.cose.2022.102823, https://www.sciencedirect.com/science/article/pii/S0167404822002176
13. Halder, S., Ahmed, M.E., Camtepe, S.: Funcvul: an effective function level vulnerability detection model using LLM and code chunk. In: Nicomette, V., Benzekri, A., Boulahia-Cuppens, N., Vaidya, J. (eds.) ESORICS 2025. LNCS, vol. 16053, pp. 166–185. Springer, Cham (2026). https://doi.org/10.1007/978-3-032-07884-1_9

14. Hanif, H., Maffeis, S.: VulBERTa: simplified source code pre-training for vulnerability detection. In: 2022 International Joint Conference on Neural Networks (IJCNN), pp. 1–8 (2022). https://doi.org/10.1109/IJCNN55064.2022.9892280
15. Hosseini, A., Yuan, X., Malkin, N., Courville, A., Sordoni, A., Agarwal, R.: V-star: training verifiers for self-taught reasoners (2024). https://arxiv.org/abs/2402.06457
16. Huang, H., Guo, L., Zhao, L., Wang, H., Xu, C., Jiang, S.: Effective combining source code and opcode for accurate vulnerability detection of smart contracts in edge ai systems. Appl. Soft Comput. **158**, 111556 (2024). https://doi.org/10.1016/j.asoc.2024.111556. https://www.sciencedirect.com/science/article/pii/S1568494624003302
17. Hui, B., et al.: Qwen2. 5-coder technical report. arXiv preprint arXiv:2409.12186 (2024)
18. Li, Y., et al.: If LLMs would just look: simple line-by-line checking improves vulnerability localization (2025). https://arxiv.org/abs/2410.15288
19. Li, Z., Zou, D., Xu, S., Jin, H., Zhu, Y., Chen, Z.: SySeVR: a framework for using deep learning to detect software vulnerabilities. IEEE Trans. Dependable Secure Comput. **19**(4), 2244–2258 (2022). https://doi.org/10.1109/TDSC.2021.3051525
20. Li, Z., et al.: VulDeePecker: a deep learning-based system for vulnerability detection. In: Proceedings 2018 Network and Distributed System Security Symposium. NDSS 2018, Internet Society (2018). https://doi.org/10.14722/ndss.2018.23158
21. Li, Z., Dutta, S., Naik, M.: Iris: LLM-assisted static analysis for detecting security vulnerabilities. In: The Thirteenth International Conference on Learning Representations (2025)
22. Liu, Z., Liao, Q., Gu, W., Gao, C.: Software vulnerability detection with GPT and in-context learning. In: 2023 8th International Conference on Data Science in Cyberspace (DSC), pp. 229–236 (2023). https://doi.org/10.1109/DSC59305.2023.00041
23. Lozhkov, A., et al.: StarCoder 2 and the stack v2: the next generation. arXiv preprint arXiv:2402.19173 (2024)
24. Lu, G., Ju, X., Chen, X., Pei, W., Cai, Z.: GRACE: empowering LLM-based software vulnerability detection with graph structure and in-context learning. J. Syst. Softw. **212**, 112031 (2024). https://doi.org/10.1016/j.jss.2024.112031, https://www.sciencedirect.com/science/article/pii/S0164121224000748
25. Nong, Y., Aldeen, M., Cheng, L., Hu, H., Chen, F., Cai, H.: Chain-of-thought prompting of large language models for discovering and fixing software vulnerabilities (2024). https://arxiv.org/abs/2402.17230
26. Russell, R., et al.: Automated vulnerability detection in source code using deep representation learning. In: 2018 17th IEEE International Conference on Machine Learning and Applications (ICMLA), pp. 757–762 (2018). https://doi.org/10.1109/ICMLA.2018.00120
27. Sheng, Z., Chen, Z., Gu, S., Huang, H., Gu, G., Huang, J.: LLMs in software security: a survey of vulnerability detection techniques and insights. ACM Comput. Surv. **58**(5) (2025). https://doi.org/10.1145/3769082
28. Shestov, A., et al.: Finetuning large language models for vulnerability detection. IEEE Access **13**, 38889–38900 (2025). https://doi.org/10.1109/ACCESS.2025.3546700
29. Singh, A., et al.: Beyond human data: Scaling self-training for problem-solving with language models (2023). https://arxiv.org/abs/2312.06585

30. Wen, X.C., et al.: Meta-path based attentional graph learning model for vulnerability detection. IEEE Trans. Software Eng. **50**(3), 360–375 (2024). https://doi.org/10.1109/TSE.2023.3340267
31. Wu, B., Zou, F., Yi, P., Wu, Y., Zhang, L.: SlicedLocator: code vulnerability locator based on sliced dependence graph. Comput. Secur. **134**, 103469 (2023). https://doi.org/10.1016/j.cose.2023.103469, https://www.sciencedirect.com/science/article/pii/S0167404823003796
32. Yuan, Z., et al.: Scaling relationship on learning mathematical reasoning with large language models (2023). https://arxiv.org/abs/2308.01825
33. Zelikman, E., Wu, Y., Mu, J., Goodman, N.: STAR: bootstrapping reasoning with reasoning. Adv. Neural. Inf. Process. Syst. **35**, 15476–15488 (2022)
34. Zhang, D., Zhoubian, S., Hu, Z., Yue, Y., Dong, Y., Tang, J.: ReST-MCTS*: LLM self-training via process reward guided tree search. Adv. Neural. Inf. Process. Syst. **37**, 64735–64772 (2024)
35. Zhou, X., Cao, S., Sun, X., Lo, D.: Large language model for vulnerability detection and repair: literature review and the road ahead. ACM Trans. Softw. Eng. Methodol. **34**(5) (2025). https://doi.org/10.1145/3708522
36. Zhou, Y., Liu, S., Siow, J., Du, X., Liu, Y.: Devign: effective vulnerability identification by learning comprehensive program semantics via graph neural networks. In: Wallach, H., Larochelle, H., Beygelzimer, A., d'Alché-Buc, F., Fox, E., Garnett, R. (eds.) Advances in Neural Information Processing Systems, vol. 32. Curran Associates, Inc. (2019)

Cryptography

An Acceleration Framework for Privacy-Preserving Neural Network Inference Using Fully Homomorphic Encryption

Fanqi Kong[1,3], Ziming Zhao[3], Yongheng Li[1], Jing Wen[2], Shaoling Liang[2], and Baohua Huang[1](✉)

[1] Guangxi University, Nanning 530004, China
bhhuang66@gxu.edu.cn
[2] Guangxi Key Laboratory of Digital Infrastructure, Guangxi Zhuang Autonomous Region Information Center, Nanning 530000, China
[3] Zhejiang University, Hangzhou 310058, China

Abstract. Fully Homomorphic Encryption (FHE) allows arbitrary computation on encrypted data, enabling a privacy-preserving machine learning as a service (MLaaS) model in which clients encrypt their sensitive inputs and remote servers perform inference without ever seeing the plaintext. Despite this promise, the computational cost of encrypted inference remains a major obstacle, especially when neural networks are trained in plaintext but evaluated on encrypted inputs. We present an acceleration framework for privacy-preserving neural network inference using gate-based FHE. In our scheme, the client encrypts its input and transmits it to a server that holds a pre-trained plaintext neural network. By carefully exploiting constant-aware arithmetic for the dominant ciphertext × plaintext weight multiplications, we transform each multiplication into a small number of additions, subtractions and inexpensive shifts via non-adjacent form (NAF) recoding and bit-slicing. This drastically reduces the number of costly bootstrapping operations. Experiments on a suite of 23,900 ciphertext × constant benchmarks and convolutional layers demonstrate that our method achieves a 4.23× average runtime reduction compared to standard FHE compilers, reducing bootstrapped gate counts by up to 65% and accelerating encrypted CNN inference by nearly 3×. These results show that FHE, when coupled with constant-aware compiler optimizations, can support practical, privacy-preserving neural network inference in real MLaaS scenarios.

Keywords: Fully Homomorphic Encryption · Compiler Optimization · FHE Non-Adjacent Form · Privacy-Preserving · Machine Learning

1 Introduction

Machine learning as a service (MLaaS) has become a dominant paradigm for deploying complex neural network models, enabling clients to outsource inference

© IFIP International Federation for Information Processing 2026
Published by Springer Nature Switzerland AG 2026
H. Janicke et al. (Eds.): SEC 2026, IFIP AICT 787, pp. 137–150, 2026.
https://doi.org/10.1007/978-3-032-27993-4_10

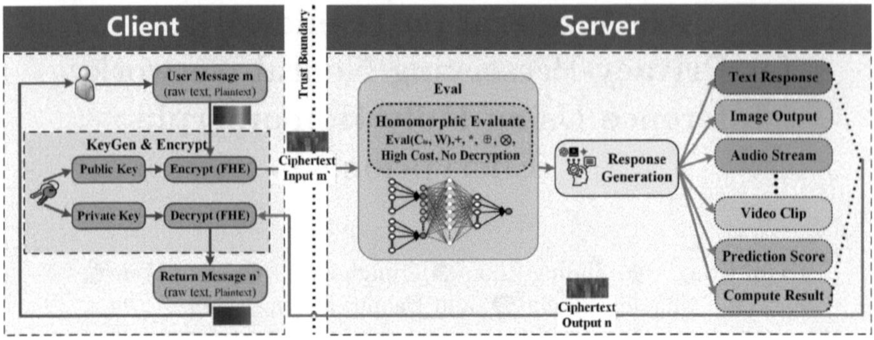

Fig. 1. FHE-based MLaaS system overview.

tasks to powerful cloud servers. However, in many real-world applications-such as medical diagnosis, biometric authentication, and financial risk analysis-the input data provided by clients is highly sensitive. Uploading such data in plaintext to an untrusted server poses serious privacy risks and is often unacceptable under regulatory and ethical constraints. FHE offers a principled cryptographic solution by enabling arbitrary computation directly on encrypted data [14]. In an FHE-based MLaaS setting, the client encrypts its private input locally and sends only ciphertexts to the server; the server evaluates a pre-trained model on encrypted inputs and returns an encrypted result that only the client can decrypt. This approach provides end-to-end confidentiality: the server learns nothing about the client's input beyond what is implied by the final output. As illustrated in Fig. 1, the client generates keys and encrypts sensitive inputs before outsourcing inference; the server performs homomorphic evaluation without access to the secret key and returns encrypted result for client-side decryption.

Despite this strong security guarantee, practical deployment of FHE-based neural network inference remains limited by performance overheads. This challenge is particularly acute in gate-based FHE schemes such as TFHE [9], which operate at the Boolean circuit level. Nonlinear Boolean gates (e.g., AND) require bootstrapping to refresh ciphertext noise; a single bootstrapping can be two to three orders of magnitude more costly than linear operations such as XOR or NOT [3,9]. Consequently, encrypted inference latency is largely determined by the number of bootstrapped nonlinear gates executed during evaluation.

This performance challenge becomes especially pronounced for modern neural networks whose inference is dominated by linear transforms, including convolutions, fully connected layers, and matrix multiplications. In these workloads, the server repeatedly multiplies encrypted activations (ciphertexts) by fixed model parameters (plaintext weights), i.e., ciphertext-plaintext (ciphertext $\times$ constant) multiplications. Under gate-based FHE, such operations are often lowered into generic Boolean multiplication circuits whose complexity scales quadratically with bit-width ($\mathcal{O}(n^2)$) [12]. Existing FHE compilers largely treat these multiplications as black boxes, failing to exploit the fact that one operand is a known constant. As a result, a wide range of encrypted inference pipelines incur an excessive number of bootstrapped nonlinear gates, making practical MLaaS deployment prohibitively slow.

In this work, we argue that inefficient ciphertext-plaintext multiplication is a key obstacle to practical FHE-based inference. To address this challenge, we present *NOM-FHE*, a framework for privacy-preserving neural network inference tailored to the MLaaS threat model. Our key observation is that neural network weights are public and fixed during inference, so constant-aware arithmetic transformations can substantially reduce expensive homomorphic operations without weakening security guarantees.

This paper makes the following **contributions**.

- We present an end-to-end privacy-preserving neural network inference framework for MLaaS, where clients encrypt inputs locally, servers evaluate plaintext-trained models entirely in the encrypted domain, and only encrypted outputs are returned for client-side decryption, ensuring confidentiality against an honest-but-curious server.
- We identify ciphertext-plaintext multiplication as a critical bottleneck for gate-based FHE inference and provide a gate-level cost analysis explaining why existing compilation strategies incur excessive bootstrapping overhead.
- We propose *NOM-FHE*, a constant-aware optimization framework that uses NAF and bit-sliced execution to transform ciphertext-plaintext multiplications into sparse sequences of additions or subtractions and zero-cost shifts, reducing nonlinear gates without weakening security guarantees.
- We implement NOM-FHE on top of TFHE/FHEW backends and evaluate it on 23,900 encrypted arithmetic benchmarks and representative quantized neural network workloads, demonstrating an average speedup of 4.23× over state-of-the-art FHE compilers and substantial end-to-end acceleration for encrypted inference under realistic security parameters.

2 Related Work

Privacy-preserving neural network inference remains expensive because encrypted evaluation amplifies the cost of the linear layers that dominate modern models [15,19]. Our focus is the gate-based setting, where this overhead is driven less by arithmetic depth than by the Boolean structure exposed to the FHE backend.

Gate-based FHE schemes, especially FHEW/TFHE [7–9,11,13], evaluate Boolean circuits with frequent bootstrapping and therefore make the number of nonlinear gates the dominant optimization target. This makes ciphertext × constant multiplication a key bottleneck in encrypted inference, because generic multiplier circuits introduce many programmable-bootstrapping(PBS)-invoking gates.

To improve programmability, FHE compilers translate high-level code into homomorphic circuits [5,6,16]. Systems such as HECO [21] and HECATE [20] optimize lowering and parameter selection, while TFHE-oriented toolchains such as Concrete [10] focus on Boolean synthesis and scheduling. However, ciphertext-plaintext multiplication is still commonly lowered as a generic arithmetic block, which misses constant-specific structure and leaves substantial bootstrapping overhead in inference workloads.

Constant multiplication has long been studied in hardware [22], but TFHE uses a different cost model: shifts and XORs are cheap, whereas AND-like nonlinearities are expensive because they invoke bootstrapping. The NAF [4,18] provides a sparse signed-digit encoding that matches this setting well. NOM-FHE builds on this observation by combining NAF-based sparsification with bit-sliced execution and depth-aware mapping to reduce bootstrapped nonlinear work in TFHE/FHEW inference pipelines.

3 Preliminaries

3.1 Threat Model

We consider a standard two-party MLaaS setting in which a client encrypts a private input and a cloud server evaluates a pre-trained model on ciphertexts. We assume an honest-but-curious (semi-honest) server and use FHE only: the server sees encrypted inputs and intermediate ciphertexts, and the client receives only the decrypted inference result.

3.2 TFHE Background and Gate-Level Cost Model

Our work targets TFHE-style Boolean FHE [9], where data are encrypted bitwise and arithmetic is lowered to Boolean circuits. Linear gates such as XOR/XNOR/NOT are inexpensive, whereas nonlinear gates such as AND/OR require PBS [7]. Because PBS dominates latency, we use the number of PBS-invoking nonlinear gates and the nonlinear critical-path depth as the main cost metrics.

A generic n-bit multiplication expands to $\mathcal{O}(n^2)$ bitwise AND operations plus a comparable number of XORs [2]. Ciphertext-plaintext multiplication is therefore expensive when lowered naively, which motivates constant-aware rewrites that reduce the nonlinear portion of the resulting circuit.

3.3 Non-adjacent Form

Ciphertext-constant multiplication is pervasive in encrypted inference (e.g., convolution and linear layers). When compiled generically, it yields dense multiplication circuits and thus many bootstrapped nonlinear gates. To exploit the fact that one operand is a known plaintext constant, we use the NAF, a signed-digit encoding with digits in $\{-1, 0, 1\}$ and the constraint that no two nonzero digits are adjacent. For a constant n, NAF represents it as $n = \sum_i u_i 2^i$ where $u_i \in \{-1, 0, 1\}$ and $u_i u_{i+1} = 0$. This allows rewriting multiplication as a sparse shift-add/sub expression:

$$X \cdot n = \sum_i u_i (X \ll i). \tag{1}$$

In TFHE-style Boolean backends, shifts correspond to wire reindexing and incur negligible cryptographic cost, while additions/subtractions introduce carry logic that contains nonlinear gates. Therefore, reducing the number of nonzero digits in $\{u_i\}$ directly reduces the number of bootstrapped gates required. In NOM-FHE, plaintext constants are converted to NAF offline. During encrypted execution, ciphertext-constant multiplication is implemented by accumulating only the signed shifted terms indicated by NAF. Section 4 details this integration, and Sect. 5 quantifies its gate and runtime reductions in end-to-end inference.

4 NOM-FHE Framework and Homomorphic Convolution

This section presents *NOM-FHE*, a multi-stage optimization framework designed to accelerate ciphertext-constant multiplication in FHEâĂŞbased neural network inference. The framework targets gate-based FHE backends such as TFHE/FHEW, where performance is dominated by the number and depth of bootstrapped nonlinear gates.

NOM-FHE takes as input a quantized neural network (so that weights are plaintext constants and activations are encrypted values), a set of FHE/operator specifications (e.g., supported gate primitives and associated costs), and the chosen security/parameter configuration. *Output.* It produces an evaluation plan (i.e., a Boolean netlist/circuit) that implements ciphertext-constant multiplication with reduced bootstrapping cost, which can then be executed by the underlying FHE runtime.

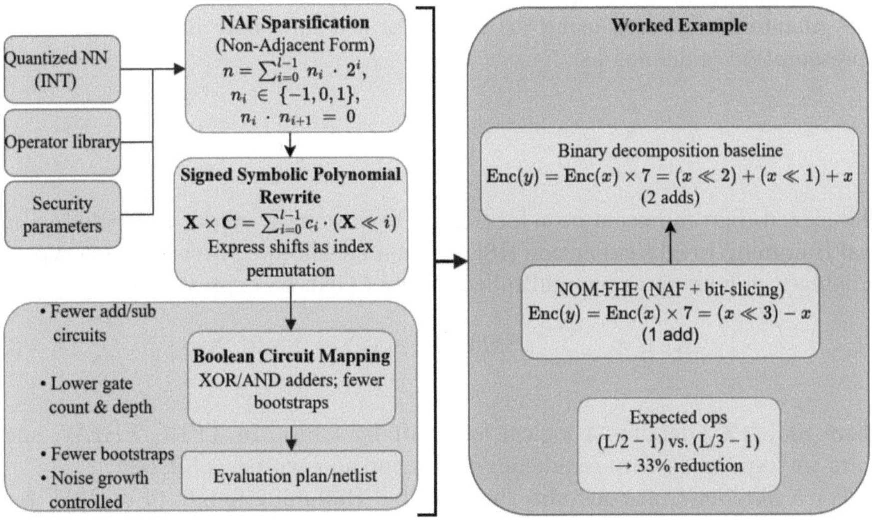

Fig. 2. Architecture of the NOM-FHE.

NOM-FHE decomposes ciphertext constant multiplication into a sequence of constant-aware transformations that minimize expensive homomorphic operations while preserving correctness and security. As illustrated in Fig. 2, the framework consists of four stages: (i) NAF-based sparse re-encoding of constants, (ii) signed polynomial rewriting, (iii) an FHE-customized bit-slicing mechanism with zero-cost shifts, and (iv) depth-aware Boolean circuit mapping. Table 1 summarizes the notation used throughout this section.

Table 1. Notation used in Sect. 4.

Symbol	Meaning
$\mathbf{X} = [\mathrm{Enc}(x_0), \ldots, \mathrm{Enc}(x_{N-1})]$	Bit-sliced ciphertext encoding an N-bit value x
$\mathrm{Enc}(\cdot)$	Bitwise FHE encryption operator (TFHE/FHEW)
C, ℓ	Plaintext integer constant and its bit-length
$u_i \in \{-1, 0, 1\}$	NAF digit at position i
$\mathrm{Shift}^i(\mathbf{X})$	Logical left shift of $\mathbf{X}$ by i bits
$\mathrm{wt}_2(C), \mathrm{wt}_{\mathrm{NAF}}(C)$	Binary and NAF Hamming weights
HA, FA	Half-adder and full-adder
RCA, CLA, CSA	Ripple-carry, carry-lookahead, carry-save adders

4.1 Sparse Re-encoding via Non-adjacent Form

To reduce the cost of ciphertext-constant multiplication, NOM-FHE first sparsifies plaintext constants using the NAF. For a nonnegative integer C, its NAF representation is defined as

$$C = \sum_{i=0}^{\ell-1} u_i 2^i, \qquad u_i \in \{-1, 0, 1\},\ u_i u_{i+1} = 0. \tag{2}$$

This signed-digit representation forbids adjacent nonzero digits and yields a minimal Hamming weight expansion [18]. Given a bit-sliced ciphertext $\mathbf{X}$ encrypting an integer x, homomorphic multiplication by C can be expressed as

$$\mathbf{X} \cdot C = \sum_{i:u_i=+1} \mathrm{Shift}^i(\mathbf{X}) - \sum_{i:u_i=-1} \mathrm{Shift}^i(\mathbf{X}), \tag{3}$$

where $\mathrm{Shift}^i(\mathbf{X})$ denotes a logical left shift by i bits. In TFHE/FHEW, such shifts correspond to wire reindexing and incur no cryptographic cost.

For a random ℓ-bit constant, the expected Hamming weight of its NAF representation satisfies

$$\mathbb{E}[\mathrm{wt}_{\mathrm{NAF}}(C)] \approx \ell/3,$$

compared to $\ell/2$ for standard binary representation [17,18]. This reduction directly translates into fewer additions and subtractions during homomorphic evaluation.

4.2 Signed Polynomial Rewriting

Using the NAF representation, ciphertext-constant multiplication is rewritten as a sparse signed shift-add expression:

$$\mathbf{X} \cdot C = \sum_{i=0}^{\ell-1} u_i (\mathbf{X} \ll i). \tag{4}$$

In gate-based FHE backends, additions and subtractions are implemented using Boolean adders whose carry logic introduces nonlinear gates and bootstrapping. Consequently, reducing the number of nonzero terms in Eq. (4) directly reduces the number of expensive bootstrapped operations. This cost model differs fundamentally from that of RLWE-based leveled schemes (e.g., BFV/BGV/CKKS), where ciphertext-plaintext multiplication is comparatively cheap and multiplicative depth is the dominant constraint.

4.3 Bit-Slicing and Zero-Cost Shifts

NOM-FHE represents encrypted integers in a bit-sliced format,

$$\mathbf{X} = [\mathrm{Enc}(x_0), \ldots, \mathrm{Enc}(x_{N-1})], \tag{5}$$

where each ciphertext encrypts a single bit. A left shift by k bits is implemented

$$(\mathbf{X} \ll k)[i] = \begin{cases} \mathbf{X}[i-k], & i \geq k, \\ \mathrm{Enc}(0), & i < k. \end{cases} \tag{6}$$

This operation corresponds to a permutation of ciphertext wires and introduces no nonlinear gates. As a simple example, consider multiplication by the constant 7. Using binary decomposition,

$$\mathrm{Enc}(y) = (\mathrm{Enc}(x) \ll 2) + (\mathrm{Enc}(x) \ll 1) + \mathrm{Enc}(x), \tag{7}$$

which requires two adders. In contrast, the NAF representation yields

$$\mathrm{Enc}(y) = (\mathrm{Enc}(x) \ll 3) - \mathrm{Enc}(x), \tag{8}$$

which requires only a single adder/subtractor. Figure 3 visualizes these two realizations (binary vs. NAF).

4.4 Boolean Gate Costs and Depth-Aware Mapping

In TFHE/FHEW, linear gates such as XOR and NOT incur negligible cost, while nonlinear gates such as AND, OR, and MUX require bootstrapping. Boolean adders are therefore dominated by the cost of carry propagation. A half-adder requires one nonlinear gate per bit, while a full-adder requires approximately three nonlinear gates per bit. Ripple-carry adders incur linear depth, whereas

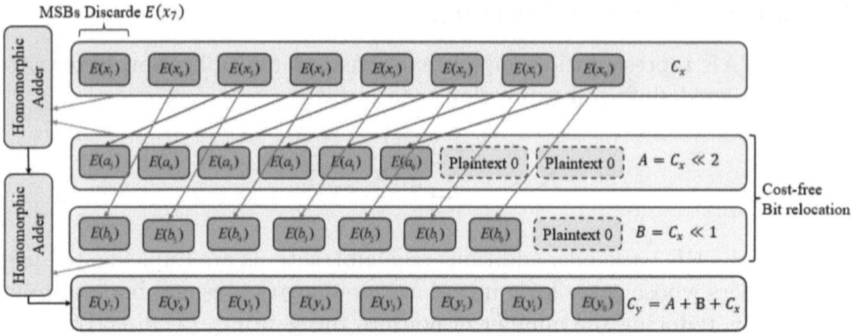

(a) Binary decomposition.

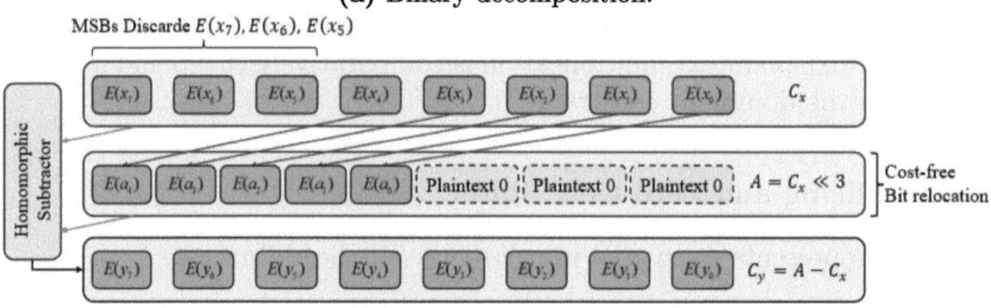

(b) NAF-based decomposition.

Fig. 3. Bit-sliced constant multiplication.

carry-lookahead and carry-save adders reduce critical-path depth at the expense of additional gates. NOM-FHE employs a depth-aware mapping strategy that selects adder structures based on operand count and fan-in. For a small number of NAF terms, ripple-carry adders minimize the total number of nonlinear gates. When aggregating many terms, carry-save or carry-lookahead structures reduce bootstrapping depth. Compared with generic compiler lowerings that emit fixed multiplication circuits, this strategy significantly reduces both the number and depth of bootstrapped operations.

4.5 Application to Homomorphic Convolution

We apply NOM-FHE to convolutional neural networks, where the output at position (i, j) is given by

$$O_{i,j} = \sum_{k=0}^{K-1} \sum_{\ell=0}^{L-1} I_{i+k,j+\ell} \cdot W_{k,\ell}, \tag{9}$$

with encrypted inputs I and plaintext weights W. Each weight $W_{k,\ell}$ is encoded in NAF form as

$$W_{k,\ell} = \sum_{m} w_m 2^m, \quad w_m \in \{-1, 0, 1\}, \tag{10}$$

Table 2. Settings for 128-bit classical security.

Parameter	Setting
FHE scheme	TFHE/FHEW-style Boolean FHE
Security level	128-bit (classical)
Torus modulus	2^{32}
Polynomial degree (N)	1024
LWE dimension (n)	630
Message encoding	Two's-complement (signed)
Gate evaluation	PBS
Bootstrapping per nonlinear gate	1 PBS
PBS decomposition base (B)	2^{10}
PBS decomposition length (l)	3
TFHE parameter set	`tfhe_gate_bootstrapping_parameters_128`
Multi-threading	Disabled (single-threaded)

allowing multiplication to be realized as sparse shift-add operations. During compilation, NAF conversion is performed offline on plaintext weights. During encrypted evaluation, only nonzero NAF terms are emitted, and accumulation is performed using depth-aware adders. This approach eliminates generic multipliers, reduces the number of nonlinear gates, and shortens bootstrapping chains. As shown in Sect. 5, these reductions translate into substantial performance improvements for encrypted convolution while preserving the security guarantees of FHE-based inference.

5 Evaluation

5.1 Experimental Setup

Platform and Software. Experiments are conducted on a server equipped with an AMD Ryzen Threadripper PRO 7995WX CPU (96 cores/192 threads, base 2.5 GHz, boost up to 5.1 GHz), and 512 GB DDR5 ECC RAM, running Ubuntu 20.04.6 (Linux 5.15.0). Code is compiled with gcc 9.4.0 and `-O1`. We use TFHE v1.1 [7] and OpenFHE v1.4.2 [1] as reference baselines.

Cryptographic Parameters. Table 2 lists the parameters used throughout. All settings target 128-bit security and follow TFHE-style recommendations.

Measurement and Metrics. Each configuration is warmed up for 5 runs and then measured for 30 repetitions. We report median latency and p95 latency. For microbenchmarks, we time only the evaluation of ciphertext × plaintext multiplication (excluding key generation and encryption). For end-to-end inference, we additionally report key generation, encryption, evaluation, and decryption times. We also report (i) *PBS-invoking gate count* (nonlinear gates that trigger

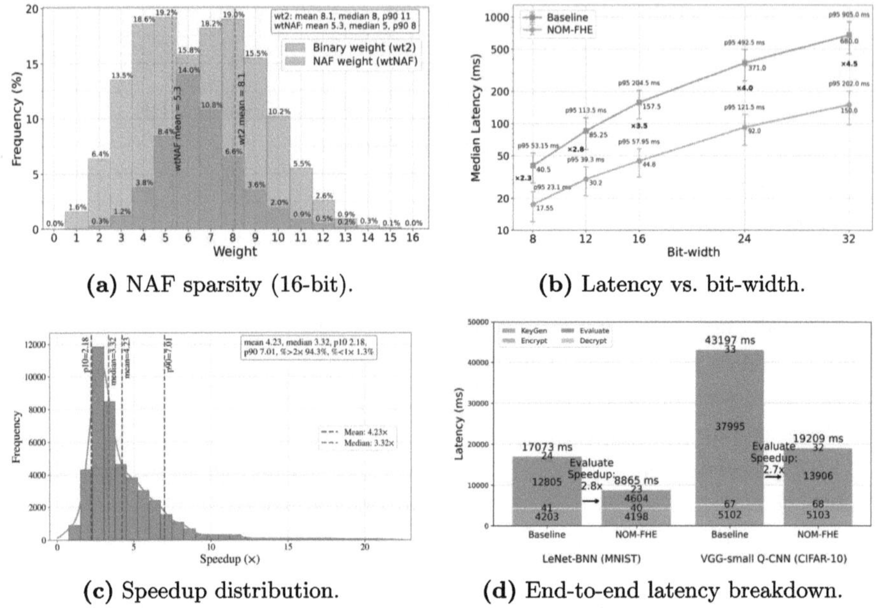

(a) NAF sparsity (16-bit). **(b)** Latency vs. bit-width. **(c)** Speedup distribution. **(d)** End-to-end latency breakdown.

Fig. 4. Performance evaluation of NOM-FHE.

Table 3. Performance of ciphertext-plaintext multiplication.

(a) Random const.

Bit width	Median (ms) Base	Median (ms) NOM	p95 (ms) Base	p95 (ms) NOM	PBS gates (Base→NOM)	NL depth (Base→NOM)
8	40.5	17.55	53.15	23.10	2.1e4→8.2e3	48→22
12	85.25	30.20	113.50	39.30	4.9e4→1.6e4	72→29
16	157.5	44.80	204.50	57.95	9.2e4→2.7e4	96→36
24	371.0	92.00	492.50	121.5	2.2e5→6.5e4	144→54
32	680.0	150.0	905.00	202.0	3.9e5→1.1e5	192→66

(b) Real-weight const.

Bit width	Median (ms) Base	Median (ms) NOM	p95 (ms) Base	p95 (ms) NOM	PBS gates (Base→NOM)	NL depth (Base→NOM)
8	37.0	15.5	48.0	20.2	1.9e4→7.0e3	48→20
12	78.0	26.5	102.0	34.8	4.5e4→1.3e4	72→26
16	145.0	39.5	188.0	51.0	8.7e4→2.1e4	96→31
24	330.0	78.0	450.0	104.0	2.1e5→5.0e4	144→46
32	610.0	128.0	820.0	178.0	3.8e5→8.8e4	192→57

programmable bootstrapping) and (ii) *nonlinear depth* (the number of sequential nonlinear layers on the critical path), because these quantities directly explain TFHE latency.

5.2 Effectiveness Evaluations

We evaluate signed ciphertext × plaintext multiplication for bit-widths $b \in \{8, 12, 16, 24, 32\}$ under two distributions: (i) *Random constants*: uniformly sampled from $[-2^{b-1}, 2^{b-1})$; (ii) *Real-weight constants*: quantized neural network weights (symmetric quantization, per-tensor). For each bit-width and distribution, we generate 2,390 constants, yielding a total of 23,900 instances.

Figure 4a summarizes the Hamming-weight reduction obtained by NAF on 16-bit real weights. The gap between binary weight and NAF weight motivates constant-aware lowering beyond generic multiplier circuits. Figure 4b shows

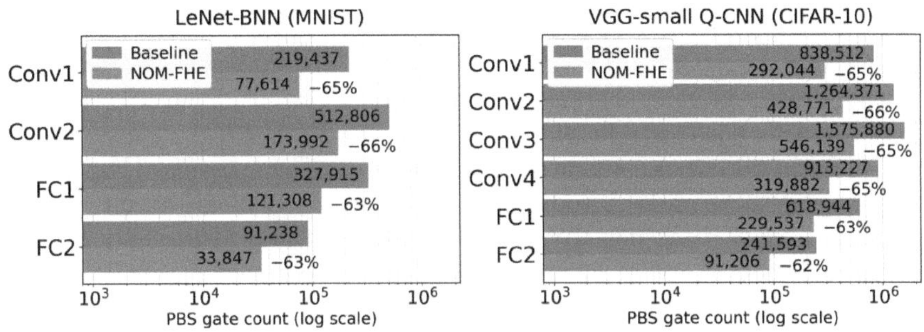

Fig. 5. Layer-wise PBS gate reduction.

Table 4. End-to-end inference across different models.

Model	Bit	Acc.	KeyGen (ms)	Enc (ms)	Eval Base (ms)	Eval NOM (ms)	Dec (ms)	Eval spd.
VGG-small (CIFAR-10)	16	84.7%	5103	68	37995	13906	32	2.73×
	12	84.1%	5038	61	31284	11852	31	2.64×
	8	82.9%	4976	56	24863	9780	29	2.54×
LeNet-BNN (MNIST)	8	98.1%	4198	40	12805	4604	23	2.78×
	12	98.3%	4448	45	18651	7065	27	2.64×
Small-CNN (Fashion-MNIST)	8	90.6%	1187	42	6842	2598	26	2.63×
	12	91.0%	1246	47	9350	3514	28	2.66×

median evaluation latency versus bit-width for random constants. NOM-FHE consistently outperforms the baseline and the gap widens with bit-width, consistent with the baseline's quadratic gate blow-up and NOM-FHE's sparse shift-add structure. To avoid over-indexing on means, Fig. 4c reports the full speedup distribution over the microbenchmark suite, making typical and tail behavior explicit through the median, p10, p90, and the fraction exceeding 2× (Table 3).

Tables 3a and 3b consolidate latency, reported as median and p95, together with PBS gate count and nonlinear depth.

5.3 End-to-End Privacy-Preserving Inference Case Studies

We retain VGG-small on CIFAR-10 as the primary end-to-end case because it better reflects a nontrivial convolution-heavy encrypted inference workload. We use symmetric quantization and choose 16-bit fixed-point as the default operating point for balanced accuracy and latency, while Fig. 4(d) still reports the full measured latency breakdown. Figure 4(d) summarizes key generation, encryption, evaluation, and decryption times. As expected in TFHE-style execution, evaluation dominates overall runtime, and NOM-FHE primarily reduces the evaluation component by cutting bootstrapped nonlinear work. Figure 5 reports per-layer PBS gate counts (log scale). Convolution layers benefit the most because they are dominated by repeated ciphertext × plaintext multiplications. Table 4 consolidates the main end-to-end results. We report evaluation speedup separately because key generation is a one-time cost and often amortized in MLaaS deployments.

6 Conclusion

This paper tackled a central bottleneck in practical FHE deployments: ciphertext × plaintext($C_i \times C_t$) multiplication by introducing *NOM-FHE*, a constant-aware compiler framework that combines NAF-based sparsification, signed shiftâĂŞadd rewriting, bit-sliced data layout, and depth-aware Boolean-circuit mapping for TFHE/FHEW backends. By reducing nonlinear gate usage and the number/length of bootstrapped chains, NOM-FHE turns expensive generic multiplications into a small number of additions/subtractions plus zero-cost shifts. Comprehensive experiments confirm the effectiveness of this approach. Across 23,900 $C_i \times C_t$ cases, NOM-FHE attains an average speedup of 4.23× relative to baseline implementations, with category means ranging from 3.46× to 5.07× and a maximum of 21.36×. In an MLaaS-style convolution case study, AND gates drop by 65.69% and total gate count by 65.28%, yielding a 2.73× runtime reduction under identical security and precision settings. Overall, the results show that constant-aware, arithmetic-level restructuring yields stable gains for Boolean-circuit FHE without compromising correctness or security, thereby improving practical deployability.

This approach has several limitations and opportunities for future work. (i) The benefits are most pronounced when weights/constants are fixed; rapidly changing constants make NAF conversion and circuit synthesis costs non-negligible. Lightweight JIT and caching strategies are a promising direction. (ii) Extending the methodology beyond gate-bootstrapped schemes to RLWE-based leveled schemes requires scheme-specific noise/depth models and tailored rewrites. (iii) Our current rewrites and depth-aware mapping primarily target ciphertext-constant multiplication, where constants can be decomposed and reused across the circuit. Extending sparsity-driven decomposition and depth-aware mapping to ciphertext-ciphertext multiplication, where both operands carry noise and the algebraic structure differs-remains an important open problem. (iv) Because FHE performance is inherently systems-level, integrating NOM-FHE with higher-level optimizations, e.g., parameter tuning, batching, PBS function synthesis, and compiler scheduling may further improve end-to-end efficiency. (v) Our end-to-end evaluation focuses on quantized CNN workloads; while NOM-FHE targets a general bottleneck of ciphertext-constant multiplication, its end-to-end benefits on other model families (e.g., RNN/LSTM/GRU, GNNs, and Transformer-style blocks) remain to be validated under different operator mixes and dataflow patterns.

Acknowledgements. This study was supported by Open Project Program of Guangxi Key Laboratory of Digital Infrastructure (Grant number: GXDINBC202406).

References

1. Al Badawi, A., et al.: Openfhe: open-source fully homomorphic encryption library. In: Proceedings of the 10th Workshop on Encrypted Computing & Applied Homomorphic Cryptography, pp. 53–63 (2022)
2. Behrooz, P.: Computer Arithmetic: Algorithms and Hardware Designs, vol. 19, pp. 512583–512585. Oxford University Press (2000)
3. Bergerat, L., et al.: Parameter optimization and larger precision for (T) FHE: L. Bergerat et al. J. Cryptol. **36**(3), 28 (2023)
4. Booth, A.D.: A signed binary multiplication technique. Q. J. Mech. Appl. Math. **4**(2), 236–240 (1951)
5. Carpov, S., Dubrulle, P., Sirdey, R.: Armadillo: a compilation chain for privacy preserving applications. In: Proceedings of the 3rd International Workshop on Security in Cloud Computing, pp. 13–19 (2015)
6. Chielle, E., Mazonka, O., Gamil, H., Tsoutsos, N.G., Maniatakos, M.: E3: a framework for compiling C++ programs with encrypted operands. Cryptology ePrint Archive (2018)
7. Chillotti, I., Gama, N., Georgieva, M., Izabachène, M.: Faster fully homomorphic encryption: bootstrapping in less than 0.1 seconds. In: Cheon, J.H., Takagi, T. (eds.) ASIACRYPT 2016. LNCS, vol. 10031, pp. 3–33. Springer, Heidelberg (2016). https://doi.org/10.1007/978-3-662-53887-6_1
8. Chillotti, I., Gama, N., Georgieva, M., Izabachène, M.: Faster packed homomorphic operations and efficient circuit bootstrapping for TFHE. In: Takagi, T., Peyrin, T. (eds.) ASIACRYPT 2017. LNCS, vol. 10624, pp. 377–408. Springer, Cham (2017). https://doi.org/10.1007/978-3-319-70694-8_14
9. Chillotti, I., Gama, N., Georgieva, M., Izabachène, M.: Tfhe: fast fully homomorphic encryption over the torus: I. Chillotti et al. J. Cryptol. **33**(1), 34–91 (2020)
10. Chillotti, I., Joye, M., Ligier, D., Orfila, J.B., Tap, S.: Concrete: concrete operates on ciphertexts rapidly by extending TFHE. In: WAHC 2020-8th Workshop on Encrypted Computing & Applied Homomorphic Cryptography (2020)
11. Chillotti, I., Ligier, D., Orfila, J.-B., Tap, S.: Improved programmable bootstrapping with larger precision and efficient arithmetic circuits for TFHE. In: Tibouchi, M., Wang, H. (eds.) ASIACRYPT 2021. LNCS, vol. 13092, pp. 670–699. Springer, Cham (2021). https://doi.org/10.1007/978-3-030-92078-4_23
12. de Dinechin, F., Lefevre, V.: Constant multipliers for FPGAs. In: PDPTA (2000)
13. Ducas, L., Micciancio, D.: FHEW: bootstrapping homomorphic encryption in less than a second. In: Oswald, E., Fischlin, M. (eds.) EUROCRYPT 2015. LNCS, vol. 9056, pp. 617–640. Springer, Heidelberg (2015). https://doi.org/10.1007/978-3-662-46800-5_24
14. Gentry, C.: Fully homomorphic encryption using ideal lattices. In: Proceedings of the Forty-First Annual ACM Symposium on Theory of Computing, pp. 169–178 (2009)
15. Gilad-Bachrach, R., Dowlin, N., Laine, K., Lauter, K., Naehrig, M., Wernsing, J.: Cryptonets: applying neural networks to encrypted data with high throughput and accuracy. In: International Conference on Machine Learning, pp. 201–210. PMLR (2016)
16. Gorantala, S., et al.: A general purpose transpiler for fully homomorphic encryption. arXiv preprint arXiv:2106.07893 (2021)
17. Han, D.G., Izu, T., Takagi, T.: Some explicit formulae of NAF and its left-to-right analogue. Cryptology ePrint Archive (2005)

18. Hankerson, D., Vanstone, S., Menezes, A.: Guide to Elliptic Curve Cryptography. Springer (2004)
19. Juvekar, C., Vaikuntanathan, V., Chandrakasan, A.: {GAZELLE}: a low latency framework for secure neural network inference. In: 27th USENIX Security Symposium (USENIX Security 2018), pp. 1651–1669 (2018)
20. Lee, Y., et al.: Hecate: performance-aware scale optimization for homomorphic encryption compiler. In: 2022 IEEE/ACM International Symposium on Code Generation and Optimization (CGO), pp. 193–204. IEEE (2022)
21. Viand, A., Jattke, P., Haller, M., Hithnawi, A.: {HECO}: fully homomorphic encryption compiler. In: 32nd USENIX Security Symposium (USENIX Security 2023), pp. 4715–4732 (2023)
22. Voronenko, Y., Püschel, M.: Multiplierless multiple constant multiplication. ACM Trans. Algorithms (TALG) **3**(2), 11-es (2007)

Pepper: High-Bandwidth and Scalable Anonymous Broadcast with Cryptographic Privacy

Chenghao Li[1] and Xianghang Mi[1,2](✉)

[1] University of Science and Technology of China, Hefei, China
ericlichenghao@mail.ustc.edu.cn
[2] Monash University, Melbourne, Australia
scott.mi@monash.edu

Abstract. We present Pepper, a high-bandwidth anonymous broadcast protocol that provides cryptographic sender anonymity against global adversaries. Pepper builds on a two-server DC-net architecture but introduces three key innovations: a self-contained anonymous registration subprotocol, support for batch messaging, and a lightweight access control mechanism based on secret-shared proofs. Unlike prior systems, Pepper eliminates the need for external dialing services and allows each broadcaster to send multiple messages per epoch with a single audit, significantly improving throughput for large data transfers. Our implementation demonstrates that Pepper achieves millisecond-level registration audits, scales efficiently to thousands of channels, and delivers 1.2–20× higher effective messaging rates than state-of-the-art alternatives. Furthermore, Pepper is designed for practical deployment, with natural compatibility for co-deployment alongside Tor and federated social networks.

Keywords: Anonymous Broadcast · Private Messaging · Dining Cryptographers Network (DC-net) · Metadata Privacy

1 Introduction

Anonymous broadcast is critical for censorship-resistant applications, enabling participants to disseminate messages while concealing their identity from global network adversaries—a guarantee that low-latency systems like Tor [8] fail to provide due to traffic-correlation vulnerabilities [11,14]. To achieve strong cryptographically guaranteed anonymity, research has focused on protocols derived from DC-nets [6] and mix-nets [7]. While recent systems such as Spectrum [13] and Express [9] leverage distributed point functions (DPFs) to improve efficiency, they remain hindered by unresolved challenges in channel allocation, lack of native batch messaging support, and complex auditing requirements. Alternative approaches like Blinder [1] incur high communication overheads and rely on impractical trust assumptions. Furthermore, existing works have largely

© IFIP International Federation for Information Processing 2026
Published by Springer Nature Switzerland AG 2026
H. Janicke et al. (Eds.): SEC 2026, IFIP AICT 787, pp. 151–165, 2026.
https://doi.org/10.1007/978-3-032-27993-4_11

overlooked the integration of these protocols with large-scale decentralized infrastructures, such as federated social networks (e.g., Mastodon [15]), which could otherwise serve as a valuable source of cover traffic and server resources.

In this paper, we present Pepper, a high-bandwidth anonymous broadcast system built upon a two-server DC-net architecture that addresses existing scalability and registration challenges through a novel, integrated design. Pepper introduces three key innovations: a self-contained anonymous registration subprotocol, eliminating reliance on external dialing services; a batch messaging capability that allows a single request to carry up to t messages with single-shot auditing; and an access control mechanism to efficiently verify clients' authority and support cover traffic. These contributions render Pepper uniquely suitable for high-bandwidth applications. Furthermore, Pepper is designed for practical deployment, offering architectural compatibility with Tor relays and federated social networks.

These technical contributions make Pepper uniquely suited for high-bandwidth applications such as anonymous file sharing or media dissemination. Our implementation and evaluation demonstrate that Pepper achieves low auditing latency and high effective throughput compared with state-of-the-art systems. Furthermore, Pepper demonstrates practical compatibility by naturally aligning with infrastructures like Tor and Mastodon for server co-deployment and cover traffic generation. In summary, this paper makes the following contributions:

- We design and specify Pepper, a self-contained anonymous broadcast protocol with support for efficient batch messaging, eliminating the need for external dialing systems.
- We construct a lightweight yet robust access control mechanism, enabling efficient verification of batch writes and seamless support for cover traffic.
- We implement and evaluate Pepper against state-of-the-art baselines, demonstrating superior throughput and scalability for high-bandwidth broadcasts.
- We show how to integrate Pepper with existing decentralized networks, leveraging their infrastructure for cover traffic and server resources.

2 Background and Related Works

Anonymous Broadcast Protocols (ABPs). The DC-net [6] enables anonymous communication by computing a global function of private inputs without revealing the inputs. Modern ABPs adopt a centralized, server-based DC-net architecture, where clients split messages into additive secret shares distributed among aggregation servers. These servers aggregate shares to reconstruct the global message. To address low throughput and jamming vulnerabilities, recent advancements [1,13] introduce multi-channel architectures for simultaneous broadcasts and auditing mechanisms to detect and evict malicious participants, enhancing efficiency and robustness. In contrast, mixnet-based ABPs [7] use layered servers to shuffle messages, offering communication efficiency but remaining vulnerable to traffic analysis. Modern mixnets [12] mitigate these threats with computationally intensive Multi-Party Computation for verifiable shuffling, at the cost of higher overhead, additional communication rounds, and stronger trust assumptions (e.g., an honest majority).

Table 1. Qualitative comparison between *Pepper*with leading anonymous broadcast protocols based upon centralized DC-net (client-server DC-net).

Protocol	Per C-Comp [1]	Per S-Comp [1]	C-S Comm [1]	S-S Comm [1]	Dialing[2]
Blinder [1]	$\sqrt{N} \cdot \lvert m \rvert$	$N^2 \cdot \lvert m \rvert$	$\sqrt{N} \cdot \lvert m \rvert$	$N \cdot \lvert m \rvert$	N/A
Spectrum [13] [3]	$\log L + \lvert m \rvert$	$N \cdot L \cdot \lvert m \rvert$	$\log L + \lvert m \rvert$	$L \cdot \lvert m \rvert + N$	✘
Express [9]	$\log L + \lvert m \rvert$	$N \cdot L \cdot \lvert m \rvert$	$\log L + \lvert m \rvert$	$L \cdot \lvert m \rvert + N$	✘
Pepper	$t \log L + t\lvert m \rvert$	$N \cdot L \cdot \lvert m \rvert$	$t^2 \log L + t\lvert m \rvert$	$L \cdot \lvert m \rvert + N$	✔

1] n denotes the number of servers, while the number of clients is represented as N; t is the message batch size (number of messages per client request for *Pepper*). $O(\cdot)$ is omitted for clarity. Also, we assume the security parameter λ and the number of servers are pre-configured constants.
2] Whether a dialing (registration) subprotocol is required and specified as part of the ABP. *N/A* denotes a dialing subprotocol is not required.
3] Spectrum refers to its most-efficient 2-server setup

Comparison with Representative Protocols. We compare Pepper with recent DC-net ABPs: Spectrum [13], Blinder [1], and Express [9], all offering cryptographic privacy. Spectrum uses an anytrust model and distributed point functions (DPFs) [4,10] to reduce communication but relies on external dialing and supports only one channel per broadcaster, limiting throughput. Express employs a two-server DC-net with DPFs and zero-knowledge proofs, optimized for low-bandwidth scenarios, but also requires external dialing. Blinder uses Shamir's secret sharing for disruption recovery but depends on an honest majority, making it less practical. Shared limitations include reliance on external dialing, complex auditing, low throughput for high-bandwidth use, and unclear compatibility with systems like Tor. Table 1 highlights key metrics. Unlike others, Pepper is self-contained with an explicit registration subprotocol, supports batch messaging per broadcaster per epoch, and achieves higher throughput while maintaining server-side efficiency.

3 System Overview

This section provides a high-level overview of Pepper, covering its threat mode and design goals, architecture, and main components.

3.1 Threat Model and Security Goals

Pepper assumes a global passive adversary capable of traffic analysis, utilizing standard secure channels (e.g., TLS) to protect communication content. The system operates under an any-trust model, ensuring anonymity as long as at least one aggregation server remains honest among potentially colluding adversaries. Despite the presence of malicious or Byzantine clients, Pepper relies on a subset of honest cover-traffic clients to effectively maintain the anonymity set.

Design Goals. Pepper prioritizes: (1) *Anonymity*: message attribution is indistinguishable from random within the anonymity set; (2) *High Throughput*: surpassing prior works for practical applications; (3) *Scalability*: horizontal scaling via multiple cohorts, with fault tolerance through cohort selection; (4) *Compatibility*: integration with existing infrastructures like Tor and Mastodon.

Pepper considers volumetric denial-of-service attacks, intersection attacks exploiting participation patterns, and underlying network or transport layer vulnerabilities to be out of scope. The security of Pepper relies on well-established cryptographic primitives, including the hardness of the discrete logarithm problem, the decision Diffie-Hellman problem, and the existence of secure hash functions and pseudorandom generators.

3.2 System Architecture

Participating Roles. Pepper involves four roles: (1) *A cohort of aggregation servers* forms the system's core, typically organized into two-server cohorts to leverage efficient cryptographic primitives under an any-trust assumption; (2) *A directory service* maintains a registry of active cohorts and disseminates participation statistics, enabling clients to select cohorts anonymously; (3) *Broadcasters* publish content and can utilize batch messaging to multiple channels per epoch; (4) *Cover-traffic clients* generate dummy traffic to mix with legitimate messages, increasing the anonymity set.

Protocol Phases. Pepper operates through two sequential subprotocols: (1) the *registration subprotocol* binds available channels to specific broadcasters, utilizing cryptographic proofs to anonymously verify success and enforce access control; (2) the *messaging subprotocol* allows registered broadcasters to publish messages across epochs while cover-traffic clients generate dummy traffic to maintain the anonymity set.

3.3 Overview of the Protocol

Pepper's operation is divided into two key subprotocols: registration and messaging. The *registration subprotocol* allows broadcasters to anonymously bind public keys to message channels, enforcing write permissions. It begins with a *setup phase*, where clients select cohorts from a directory of available server pairs and verify connectivity. In the *registration phase*, broadcasters submit secret-shared requests containing their public key, target channel, and bandwidth, using verifiable DPFs (VDPFs) [4,5]. Servers jointly audit these shares to ensure integrity without revealing content, resolving conflicts and posting successful registrations to a public bulletin for anonymous verification.

The *messaging subprotocol* enables broadcasters to publish content anonymously in three phases: (1) *Message sharing*, where broadcasters submit verifiable secret shares of their messages alongside cryptographic proofs of registration, while cover-traffic clients send dummy messages to obscure patterns; (2) *Auditing*, where servers verify message format and authorization without exposing content or identity; (3) *Recovery*, where valid shares are aggregated, exchanged, and reconstructed to publish final messages on a public bulletin.

To enhance throughput, `Pepper` supports *batch messaging*, allowing up to t messages per request, reducing auditing overhead. Robustness against malformed inputs and efficient access control are achieved through verifiable secret sharing and zero-knowledge proofs, with further details in Sect. 4.

4 The Pepper System

This section presents a detailed description of the Pepper protocol. We first outline a protocol template, which is then customized into the registration and the messaging variant.

4.1 The Fundamental Protocol

Pepper's core mechanism builds on the integration of DPFs with DC-net style secret sharing. This foundation enables efficient, verifiable anonymous writes while maintaining strong privacy guarantees. In this section, we first introduce how DPFs can support multiple broadcast channels with minimal overhead, then discuss our fundamental protocol template underpinning both subprotocols.

Definition 1. *(DPFs) A Distributed Point Function (DPF) [10] is a point function $f_{\alpha,\beta}$ that evaluate to β at α and 0 elsewhere. An n-party DPF splits such a function into n shares via keys $k_1, \ldots, k_n$, where $f(\alpha)$ is recovered by additively combining all shares, and any strict subset of keys reveals no information. Formally, let L be the domain size, λ be the security parameter, and $\mathcal{B}$ be the message space. It consists of two PPT algorithms for all $i \in \{1, 2, ..., n\}$:*

- $\mathsf{Gen}(1^\lambda, \alpha \in \{1, 2, ..., L\}, \beta \in \mathcal{B}) \rightarrow (k_1, k_2, ..., k_n)$
- $\mathsf{Eval}(k_i) \rightarrow (\beta_{i,1}, \beta_{i,2}, ..., \beta_{i,L})$

In `Pepper`, DPFs facilitate anonymous writes by allowing clients to encode messages into short keys rather than full vectors. This mechanism ensures channel privacy, enables servers to efficiently verify and filter shares before processing. The protocol operates in three phases: (1) *Share generation*: clients create DPF shares; (2) *Auditing*: servers verify validity and authorization; (3) *Aggregation*: servers combine valid shares to reconstruct messages. This foundation enables high-throughput anonymous communication for both subprotocols.

4.2 The Registration Subprotocol

The registration protocol enables broadcasters to anonymously bind public keys to messaging channels. servers to audit the well-formedness of shares and filter malformed inputs without revealing the target channel. This requirement leads us to Verifiable DPFs (VDPFs) [4,5], which we overview next before detailing the registration subprotocol.

Definition 2. *(Verifiable Distributed Point Functions (VDPFs)) Verifiable DPFs (VDPFs) [4,5] extend standard DPFs by embedding a hash digest of the evaluation path, enabling servers to jointly verify that shares correspond to a well-formed, identical point function without revealing the target index. This verification incurs negligible overhead, utilizing fixed-size tokens depending on the security parameter λ. Formally, parameterized by domain size L, security parameter λ, and message space $\mathcal{B}$, the scheme comprises three PPT algorithms:*

- $\mathsf{Gen}(1^\lambda, \alpha \in \{1, 2, ..., L\}, \beta \in \mathcal{B}) \to (k_1, k_2, ..., k_n)$
- $\mathsf{Eval}(k_i) \to (\beta_{i,1}, \beta_{i,2}, ..., \beta_{i,L}, \rho_i)$
- $\mathsf{Verify}(\rho_1, \rho_2, \ldots, \rho_n) \to 1/0$

Pepper employs two channel types: *Registration Channels* (L_1) for binding public keys to messaging channels and *Message Channels* (L_2) for publishing messages, where $L_2 \gg L_1$. The registration protocol operates as follows:

Step 0: Server Pair Setup. A trusted directory service publishes aggregation server pairs, including addresses, credentials, and client counts to help broadcasters select pairs with large anonymity sets. Clients query the directory, select a pair, and perform connectivity tests. If successful, registration proceeds with servers denoted as Server 1 and Server 2.

Step 1: Message Sharing. A broadcaster selects a registration channel $l_1 \in \{1, \ldots, L_1\}$, a starting message channel $l_2 \in \{1, \ldots, L_2\}$, and bandwidth b. The registration message is: $m \leftarrow g^\alpha \| l_2 \| b \| \mathcal{H}(g^\alpha \| l_2 \| b)$, where $\mathcal{H}$ ensures integrity. The client then generates VDPF shares: $(k_1, k_2) \leftarrow \text{VDPF.Gen}(1^\lambda, m, l_1)$.

Step 2: Message Auditing. Upon receiving a VDPF key, each server i computes: $(\boldsymbol{m}_i, \rho_i) \leftarrow \text{VDPF.Eval}(k_i)$, where $\boldsymbol{m}_i$ represents L_1 message shares. Servers exchange ρ_i and verify: $\text{VDPF.Verify}(\rho_1, \rho_2) = 1$. If verification fails, the message is dropped.

Step 3: Message Recovery. Servers maintain accumulators: $acc_i = \sum_{j \in \mathcal{C}} \boldsymbol{m}_{i,j}$, where $\mathcal{C}$ is the set of clients whose requests passed auditing. Servers exchange acc_i and recover:

$$\boldsymbol{m} = acc_1 \oplus acc_2.$$

Each record $m = g^\alpha \| l_2 \| b \| h$ is parsed and verified. If $\mathcal{H}(g^\alpha \| l_2 \| b) = h$ and $[l_2, l_2 + b - 1]$ is unregistered, the channels are bound to g^α and published. Invalid or conflicting records are discarded, requiring broadcasters to retry.

4.3 The Messaging Subprotocol

The messaging protocol allows registered broadcasters to publish anonymously with cover traffic. However, naive DC-nets are prone to write disruptions from malicious clients overwriting legitimate messages, requiring robust access control. Unlike prior protocols like Spectrum and Express, which limit users to one message per epoch, `Pepper` supports *message batching* to enhance throughput.

To address these challenges, `Pepper` integrates lightweight access control and batching. After registration, the system exposes L message channels (typically $L \ll L_2$) indexed by a shared verification-key vector $(g^{\alpha_1}, \ldots, g^{\alpha_L})$. We describe the subprotocol in a two-server setting, progressively introducing *Messaging V1* (based on Spectrum [13]), *Messaging V2* (optimized auditing), and *Messaging V3* (batch messaging support).

Messaging V1. As outlined in Sect. 3.3, anonymous messaging requires auditing to verify both the correctness of DPF shares and client authorization for claimed channels. Spectrum [13] introduced an efficient unified mechanism for this, which we adopt as the basis for our initial messaging subprotocol supporting single-message broadcasting.

Step 1: Message Sharing. For a broadcaster with private key α_j, registered channel j, and message m, let $y = \alpha_j$ and $j' = j$. For cover-traffic clients, set $y = 0$ and $j' = 0$. Each client performs:

1. $(k_1, k_2) \leftarrow \text{DPF.Gen}(1^\lambda, m, j')$
2. $t \leftarrow m \cdot y$
3. Split t into shares (t_1, t_2)
4. Send (k_i, t_i) to server i for $i \in \{1, 2\}$

Step 2: Message Auditing. Upon receiving (k_i, t_i), each server computes:

1. $m_i \leftarrow \text{DPF.Eval}(k_i)$
2. $A_i \leftarrow g^{-t_i} \cdot \prod_{j=1}^{L} g^{m_i[j] \cdot \alpha_j}$

Servers exchange A_i and verify $A_1 \cdot A_2 = 1$. If verification fails, the share is dropped.

Step 3: Message Recovery. Each server maintains an accumulator acc_i for L channels:

1. $acc_i \leftarrow \sum_{j \in \mathcal{C}} \text{DPF.Eval}(k_j)$, where $\mathcal{C}$ is the set of valid clients
2. Publicly reveal acc_i

The broadcast messages $\boldsymbol{m}$ are reconstructed as $\boldsymbol{m} = \sum acc_i$.

Limitations. This protocol requires L exponentiations per server, which becomes costly as L grows. Additionally, it does not support message batching, limiting broadcasters to one message per epoch.

Messaging V2: Optimizing Audit Efficiency. To enhance audit efficiency, we integrate Schnorr Proof over Secret Shares (SPoSS) [16] into our messaging subprotocol. SPoSS enables efficient access control for function secret sharing, but its original design lacks support for cover-traffic clients without registered private keys. We address this limitation by introducing *Phantom Channels*, as detailed below.

Definition 3 (SPoSS). *SPoSS [16] is a non-interactive zero-knowledge proof protocol for discrete logarithms over additively secret-shared group elements [2]. Let $\mathbb{G}$ be a cyclic group of prime order q with generator g. For a private key $x \in \mathbb{Z}_q$ and public key $y = g^x \in \mathbb{G}$, y is additively shared as $y = y_1 + y_2$. The protocol includes:*

- $\mathsf{Prove}(x) \to (\pi_1, \pi_2)$: *Generates proof shares (π_1, π_2) from x.*
- $\mathsf{Audit}(y_i, \pi_i) \to \tau_i$: *Outputs an audit token τ_i using y_i and π_i.*
- $\mathsf{Verify}(\tau_1, \tau_2) \to \{0, 1\}$: *Validates the proof by aggregating τ_1 and τ_2.*

To write to channel j, a client generates $(\pi_1, \pi_2) \leftarrow \mathsf{Prove}(\alpha_j)$. Upon receiving (k_i, π_i), server i computes $\boldsymbol{m}_i = \text{DPF.Eval}(k_i)$ and $A_i = \sum_{j=1}^{L} \boldsymbol{m}_i[j] \cdot g^{\alpha_j}$. It then derives $\tau_i = \mathsf{Audit}(A_i, \pi_i)$, and the servers verify $\mathsf{Verify}(\tau_1, \tau_2) = 1$, confirming key ownership without revealing the channel. To prevent algebraic attacks (e.g., $m \approx g^{\alpha_1}/g^{\alpha_2}$), we prepend a 1-bit checksum to bind the payload to the channel identity. Any tampering invalidates the checksum, causing verification to fail. For cover traffic, we introduce *Phantom Channels* with universally known trivial keys (e.g., $\{g^0, g^1, \dots\}$). These allow clients to generate valid proofs for dummy messages that pass audits without requiring a registered identity, creating indistinguishable cover traffic ignored during final aggregation.

Step 1: Message Sharing. Let $y = \alpha_j$ and $j' = j$. Broadcasters with non-zero messages $m \neq 0$ perform:

1. $m' \leftarrow 1^{\text{bit}} \| m$
2. $(k_1, k_2) \leftarrow \text{VDPF.Gen}(1^\lambda, m', j')$
3. $(\pi_1, \pi_2) \leftarrow \text{SPoSS.Prove}(y)$
4. Send (k_i, π_i) to server i, for $i \in \{1, 2\}$

Step 2: Message Auditing. Upon receiving (k_i, π_i), each server computes:

1. $(m'_i, \rho_i) \leftarrow \text{VDPF.Eval}(k_i)$
2. $m_i^{\text{bit}} \leftarrow$ First bit aggregation of $m'_i[j]$, $j \in \{1, \dots, L\}$
3. $A_i \leftarrow \sum_{j=1}^{L} m_i^{\text{bit}}[j] \cdot g^{\alpha_j}$
4. $\tau_i \leftarrow \text{SPoSS.Audit}(A_i, \pi_i)$
5. Send (ρ_i, τ_i) to the other server

Servers verify $\text{SPoSS.Verify}(\tau_1, \tau_2) = 1$ and $\text{VDPF.Verify}(\rho_1, \rho_2) = 1$. If both pass, proceed to Step 3.

Step 3: Message Recovery. Each server computes:

1. $\boldsymbol{acc}_i \leftarrow \sum_{j \in \mathcal{C}} \text{VDPF.Eval}(k_j)$, where $\mathcal{C}$ is the set of valid clients
2. Publicly reveal $\boldsymbol{acc}_i$

The broadcast messages $\boldsymbol{m} = \sum \boldsymbol{acc}_i$ are then reconstructed.

Messaging V3: Supporting Batch Messaging. To support batch messaging, Pepper extends VDPFs to Verifiable Distributed Multi-Point Functions (VDMPFs) [3,4]. Unlike prior approaches like PACLs [16], which aggregate multiple independent VDPF keys and require t separate proofs for t messages, VDMPFs enable encoding multiple messages into a single cryptographic operation. This reduces bandwidth and verification overhead, as servers process a single consolidated proof for the entire batch.

Definition 4 (VDMPFs). *Verifiable Distributed Multi-Point Functions (VDMPFs) extend DPFs to support non-zero evaluations at multiple inputs* $\{\alpha_1, \ldots, \alpha_m\}$ *with outputs* $\{\beta_1, \ldots, \beta_m\}$*. They ensure shares are well-formed and generated by the same DMPF. Formally, let L be the domain size,* λ *the security parameter, and* $\mathcal{B}$ *the message space. The scheme includes:*

- $\mathsf{Gen}(1^\lambda, \{\alpha_1, \ldots, \alpha_m\}, \{\beta_1, \ldots, \beta_m\}) \rightarrow (k_1, \ldots, k_n)$
- $\mathsf{Eval}(k_i) \rightarrow (\beta_{i,1}, \ldots, \beta_{i,L}, \rho_i)$
- $\mathsf{Verify}(\rho_1, \ldots, \rho_n) \rightarrow 1/0$

Pepper's batch messaging protocol uses VDMPFs to efficiently support group messaging. Servers maintain L verification keys $(g^{\alpha_1}, \ldots, g^{\alpha_L})$, where some keys may bind to multiple channels. The directory service specifies the maximum batch size t per epoch, applied uniformly to all broadcasters. For a broadcaster with bandwidth b, sending t messages $[m] = \{m_1, \ldots, m_t\}$ to channels $[j] = \{j_1, \ldots, j_t\}$, the protocol operates as follows:

Step 1: Message Sharing. Let $y = \alpha_j$ and $[j'] = \{j_1, j_2, \ldots, j_t\}$. Only broadcasters have non-zero messages $m \neq 0$. Each client performs:

1. $[m'] \leftarrow \{1^{\text{bit}} \| m_1, 1^{\text{bit}} \| m_2, \ldots, 1^{\text{bit}} \| m_t\}$
2. $(k_1, k_2) \leftarrow \text{VDMPF.Gen}(1^\lambda, [m'], [j'])$
3. $(\pi_1, \pi_2) \leftarrow \text{SPoSS.Prove}(\alpha_j)$
4. Send share (π_i, k_i) to server i, for $i \in \{1, 2\}$

Step 2: Message Auditing. Upon receiving share (π_i, k_i) from a client, each server performs:

1. $(m'_i, \rho_i) \leftarrow \text{VDMPF.Eval}(k_i)$
2. $m_i^{\text{bit}} \leftarrow$ Aggregation of first bit of $m'_i[j]$, $j \in \{1, \ldots, L\}$
3. $A \leftarrow \sum_{j=1}^{L} g^{\alpha_j} \cdot m_i^{\text{bit}}[j]/t$
4. $\tau_i \leftarrow \text{SPoSS.Audit}(A, \pi_i)$
5. Send (τ_i, ρ_i) to the other server

Servers verify $\text{SPoSS.Verify}(\tau_1, \tau_2) = 1$ and $\text{VDMPF.Verify}(\rho_1, \rho_2) = 1$ and protocol will proceed if both succeed. This processes t messages in one verification.

Step 3: Message Recovery. Each server maintains accumulator $\boldsymbol{acc}_i = \sum_{j \in \mathcal{C}} \text{VDMPF.Eval}(k_j)$, where $\mathcal{C}$ is the set of clients whose shares passed auditing:

1. Compute $(\boldsymbol{acc}_i, \rho_i) \leftarrow \sum_{j \in \mathcal{C}} \text{VDMPF.Eval}(k_j)$
2. Publicly reveal $\boldsymbol{acc}_i$

Using the publicly revealed shares, anyone can recover the L broadcast messages $\boldsymbol{m} = \sum \boldsymbol{acc}_i$.

4.4 Compatibility with Existing Infrastructures and Protocols

In this subsection, we highlight the compatibility of Pepper with existing ABP features and decentralized infrastructures. Pepper retains full compatibility with current on-demand "blame" mechanisms [13] to identify malicious servers, as our auditing tokens and message proofs act as direct enhancements to prior DC-net architectures. Regarding practical deployment, Pepper aligns naturally with onion routing networks like Tor [8]: aggregation servers can be co-deployed as Tor relays to utilize shared resources, while our directory service can operate within Tor's directory authorities to streamline server discovery. Furthermore, the system supports seamless integration with federated social networks such as Mastodon [15], where instances can serve as aggregation pairs and standard user interactions function as natural cover traffic, thereby bootstrapping anonymity sets without requiring explicit user participation.

Table 2. Communication cost measured by payload size. All experiments are configured with the security parameter $\lambda = 128$ and the channel size $L = 1024$. The payload types include Proof (pre-audit token, client→server), Key (FSS key size, client→server), and Audit (verification token, server↔server). For messaging, t is the batch messaging size.

	client→server		Server↔Server
Registration	Proof	Key	Audit
Pepper	–	$\|m\| + 262$ bytes	16 bytes
Spectrum	64 bytes	$\|m\| + 198$ bytes	64 bytes
Express	2304 bytes	$\|m\| + 198$ bytes	2304 bytes
Messaging	Proof	Key	Audit
Pepper	1952 bytes	$(\|m\| + 304)t + 64$ bytes	816 bytes
Spectrum	$64t$ bytes	$(\|m\| + 198)t$ bytes	$64t$ bytes
PACLs	$1952t$ bytes	$(\|m\| + 262)t$ bytes	$816t$ bytes

5 Implementation and Evaluation

We present Pepper's implementation and evaluation. Experiments use a standard 2-server DC-net setting, comparing Pepper against Express [9], Spectrum [13], and PACLs [16]. We analyze: (i) communication efficiency; (ii) computation overhead; (iii) end-to-end broadcasting throughput. We repeat each experiment between 3 and 100 times, depending on the experiment. When aggregating results, We report 5% trimmed means to mitigate outliers.

Implementation. Pepper consists of 8,000 lines of Go (1.24) for protocol and 2,900 lines of C/C++ for VDMPF, following Big-State DMPF [3] for $t < 70$. Baseline protocols use reference implementations [9,13,16]. We use P-256 for Spectrum's $\mathbb{G}$; VDPF-PACLs and Pepper use $\mathbb{F}_p^*$ with 3072-bit prime following RFC 3526. All traffic is encrypted with TLS 1.3. Security parameter $\lambda = 128$.

Environment. Client–server latency is measured using a server with 64 GB RAM (acting as client) and a server with 128 GB RAM (acting as server), with the same CPU, operating system and location. Other experiments use an Intel i5-13600KF workstation (32 GB RAM, Ubuntu 24.04) with AES-NI and D(M)PF optimizations; we set servers pinned to distinct cores while all clients are emulated on a single core.

5.1 Communication Cost

The evaluation distinguishes between two protocol phases with different security requirements. The registration protocol only needs to verify that messages are well-formed, while the messaging protocol additionally requires verifying a client's right to a specific channel. For registration, we compare Express, Spectrum, and `Pepper`, as PACLs uses the same format checking mechanism. Table 2 details the communication payload in bytes. With $L = 1024$, Spectrum and PACLs incur a linear multiplicative factor t for messaging batches. In contrast, `Pepper` uses Big-State DMPF keys, which are slightly larger due to a trade-off to enable efficient single-shot auditing. This allows `Pepper` to achieve competitive total costs while significantly improving efficiency for batched operations.

5.2 Auditing Time

We evaluates the per-request auditing time (the CPU duration servers spend verifying DPF proof tokens, authorization, and message shares). As the primary determinant of server-side capacity, this metric effectively bounds the system's end-to-end throughput whenever computational resources are the bottleneck. In the *Registration*, (Fig. 1, left), `Pepper` achieves the lowest latency, specifically, Express and Spectrum are respectively 3.0×–19.5× and 17.2×–130× slower than `Pepper`. For *Messaging* (Fig. 1, right), `Pepper` exhibits superior scalability, with PACLs and Spectrum proving 2.3×–3.6× and 10.8×–12.4× slower, respectively.

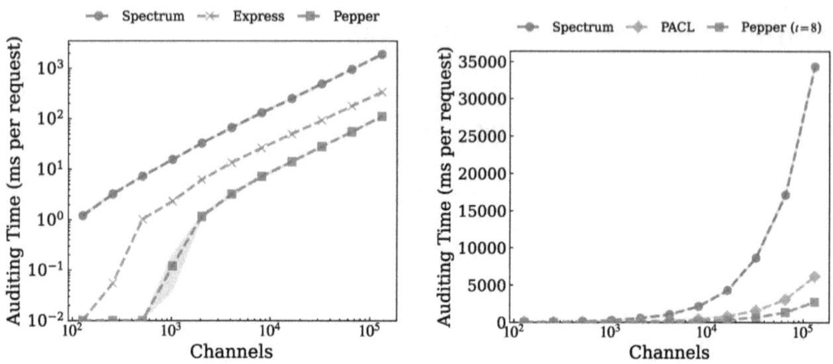

Fig. 1. Per-request auditing time (lower is better). Left: registration. Right: messaging, with total message size 5 KB and message batch size $t = 8$.

5.3 Throughput

We evaluate real-world throughput by stress-testing server processing capacity, the primary bottleneck in anonymous broadcasting. We define two complementary metrics: *client-request throughput*, which measures the full processing pipeline and *auditing-request throughput*, which isolates the system's ability to perform auditing, typically the most computation-intensive step. As shown in Fig. 2 regarding auditing-request throughput, `Pepper` performs comparably to PACLs and often surpasses Spectrum as channel counts exceed 10^3. Crucially, because each audit in `Pepper` validates a batch of t messages, the *effective messaging rate* is substantially higher: at t=8, `Pepper` delivers 1.2–5.0× the effective throughput of PACLs and 13.6–20× that of Spectrum, proving its superior scalability for high-bandwidth applications. Regarding client-request throughput for the messaging subprotocol, Spectrum achieves 3.6–7.8× raw request throughput compared with `Pepper` because it is strictly optimized for a request that contains a single message. In contrast, `Pepper` incurs higher computation costs per individual client request due to its inherent support for batch messaging, resulting in lower throughput when measured solely by the count of processed requests.

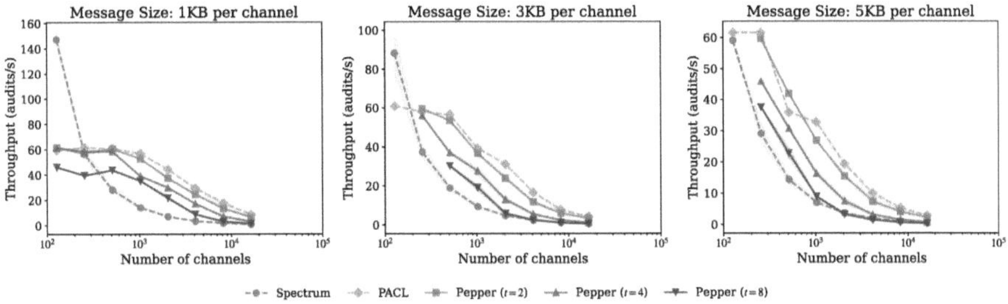

Fig. 2. Auditing throughput measured by audits processed per second. Panels show message sizes: 1 KB, 3 KB, 5 KB for `Pepper` batch sizes $t \in \{2, 4, 8\}$.

Table 3. End-to-end file transmission latency (lower is better). Pepper's batch messaging size is 4. Each cell reports the average latency ± standard deviation.

File Size	Pepper	PACLs	Spectrum
100 KB	0.25 ± 0.004 s	0.41 ± 0.004 s	1.71 ± 0.007 s
1 MB	2.44 ± 0.06 s	4.10 ± 0.08 s	17.01 ± 0.21 s
10 MB	32.79 ± 0.27 s	41.38 ± 0.67 s	174.29 ± 4.89 s
100 MB	5.79 ± 0.05 min	8.08 ± 0.05 min	30.67 ± 0.28 min

5.4 Latency

End-to-End File Transmission Latency. We evaluate the time required to broadcast files ranging from of four practical sizes: 100 KB, 1 MB, 10 MB, and 100 MB and presents the average end-to-end latency for different file sizes and protocols in Table 3. `Pepper` (batch size t=4) consistently achieves the lowest latency across all sizes. In comparison, PACLs and Spectrum are respectively 1.3–1.7× and 5.3–7.0× slower than `Pepper`.

Client-Client and Client-Server Latency. To pinpoint specific performance bottlenecks, we utilized fine-grained logging to decompose the total execution time into three distinct components: client-server communication, server-server interaction, and computational overhead. In terms of *Client-Server Latency* (Fig. 3, left), cryptographic computation dominates network transmission, making generation and submission times nearly identical. While `Pepper` (t=4) is 6.2–9.1× slower than Spectrum and 1.7–3.8× slower than PACLs due to the complexity of batch proof generation, this overhead is practically negligible as it can be computed offline before submission. For *Server-Server Latency* (Fig. 3, right), Spectrum and PACLs are respectively 5.15–5.39× and 1.36–1.40× slower than `Pepper`, confirming that `Pepper` effectively trades minor client-side setup costs for substantial gains in server-side processing and batch throughput.

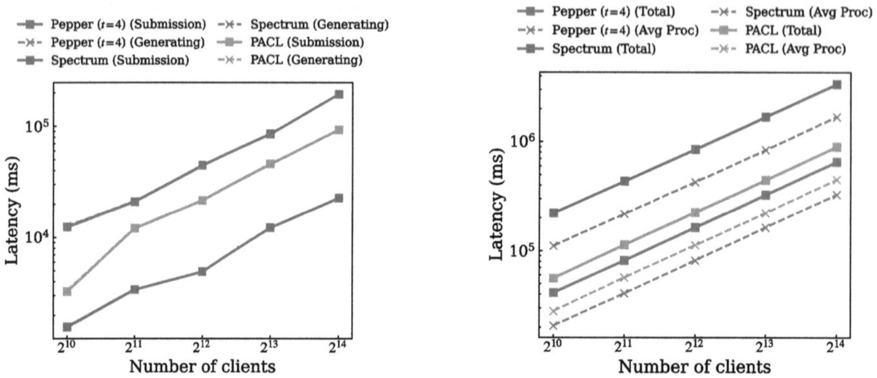

Fig. 3. Latency (lower is better; Left: Client-Server, right: Server-Server) of the messaging process. The channel size is 2,048 with 10 KB message per-client.

6 Discussion

While Pepper establishes a robust foundation for anonymous batch broadcast, several avenues exist for future enhancement: (1) One is to extend the protocol to support *multi-public-key batch messaging*, enabling broadcasters to tie channels to distinct public keys within a single request (2) We also plan to investigate *adaptive channel allocation* mechanisms to optimize resource usage based on real-time network conditions and security requirements; And (3) we intend to strengthen anonymity against sophisticated analysis by developing *enhanced cover traffic strategies*, potentially utilizing machine learning to generate adaptive, realistic dummy traffic.

Acknowledgments. This work is supported by the National Natural Science Foundation of China under Grant No. 62302473.

References

1. Abraham, I., Pinkas, B., Yanai, A.: Blinder-scalable, robust anonymous committed broadcast. In: Proceedings of the 2020 ACM SIGSAC Conference on Computer and Communications Security, pp. 1233–1252 (2020)
2. Boneh, D., Boyle, E., Corrigan-Gibbs, H., Gilboa, N., Ishai, Y.: Zero-knowledge proofs on secret-shared data via fully linear PCPs. In: Boldyreva, A., Micciancio, D. (eds.) CRYPTO 2019. LNCS, vol. 11694, pp. 67–97. Springer, Cham (2019). https://doi.org/10.1007/978-3-030-26954-8_3
3. Boyle, E., Gilboa, N., Hamilis, M., Ishai, Y., Tu, Y.: Improved constructions for distributed multi-point functions. In: 2025 IEEE Symposium on Security and Privacy (SP), pp. 2414–2432. IEEE (2025)
4. Boyle, E., Gilboa, N., Ishai, Y.: Function secret sharing: improvements and extensions. In: Proceedings of the 2016 ACM SIGSAC Conference on Computer and Communications Security, pp. 1292–1303 (2016)

5. de Castro, L., Polychroniadou, A.: Lightweight, maliciously secure verifiable function secret sharing. In: Annual International Conference on the Theory and Applications of Cryptographic Techniques, pp. 150–179. Springer, Heidelberg (2022). https://doi.org/10.1007/978-3-031-06944-4_6
6. Chaum, D.: The dining cryptographers problem: unconditional sender and recipient untraceability. J. Cryptol. **1**(1), 65–75 (1988)
7. Chaum, D.L.: Untraceable electronic mail, return addresses, and digital pseudonyms. Commun. ACM **24**(2), 84–90 (1981)
8. Dingledine, R., Mathewson, N., Syverson, P.: Tor: the second-generation onion router. In: Proceedings of the 13th Conference on USENIX Security Symposium, SSYM'04, vol. 13, p. 21. USENIX Association (2004)
9. Eskandarian, S., Corrigan-Gibbs, H., Zaharia, M., Boneh, D.: Express: lowering the cost of metadata-hiding communication with cryptographic privacy. In: 30th USENIX Security Symposium (USENIX Security 21), pp. 1775–1792 (2021)
10. Gilboa, N., Ishai, Y.: Distributed point functions and their applications. In: Nguyen, P.Q., Oswald, E. (eds.) EUROCRYPT 2014. LNCS, vol. 8441, pp. 640–658. Springer, Heidelberg (2014). https://doi.org/10.1007/978-3-642-55220-5_35
11. Hopper, N., Vasserman, E.Y., Chan-Tin, E.: How much anonymity does network latency leak? ACM Trans. Inf. Syst. Secur. (TISSEC) **13**(2), 1–28 (2010)
12. Langowski, S., Servan-Schreiber, S., Devadas, S.: Trellis: robust and scalable metadata-private anonymous broadcast. Cryptology ePrint Archive (2022)
13. Newman, Z., Servan-Schreiber, S., Devadas, S.: Spectrum: high-bandwidth anonymous broadcast. In: 19th USENIX Symposium on Networked Systems Design and Implementation (NSDI 22), pp. 229–248 (2022)
14. Overlier, L., Syverson, P.: Locating hidden servers. In: 2006 IEEE Symposium on Security and Privacy (S&P'06), p. 15. IEEE (2006)
15. Rochko, E.: Mastodon: a free, open-source social network server (2016). https://joinmastodon.org/. Accessed 20 Dec 2025
16. Servan-Schreiber, S., Beyzerov, S., Yablon, E., Park, H.: Private access control for function secret sharing. In: 2023 IEEE Symposium on Security and Privacy (SP), pp. 809–828. IEEE (2023)

Shape Before You Build: Secure Cryptographic Code Generation via Prompt Optimization

Zihan Ni[1], Jialiang Dong[2], Runtao He[3], Nan Sun[1], Willy Susilo[2], Surya Nepal[4], and Siqi Ma[2](✉)

[1] The University of New South Wales, Canberra, Australia
{zihan.ni,nan.sun}@unsw.edu.au
[2] University of Wollongong, Wollongong, Australia
{jialiang.dong,willy_susilo,siqim}@uow.edu.au
[3] Hangzhou Dianzi University, Hangzhou, China
runtaohe@hdu.edu.cn
[4] CSIRO's Data61, Sydney, Australia
surya.nepal@data61.csiro.au

Abstract. Cryptographic programming is a critical yet challenging task in software development, demanding extensive knowledge of cryptography and hands-on implementation experience. Minor oversights such as improper parameter configuration or outdated library usage can easily lead to cryptographic misuse, introducing severe security vulnerabilities. With the advancement of large language models (LLMs), LLM-assisted cryptographic programming has become increasingly popular, offering substantial support to developers with limited cryptographic expertise. However, due to limitations in training data and the inherent hallucination problems of LLMs, the security of generated cryptographic code remains inadequate, with a high risk of misuse. In this study, we propose NEMO, a prompt-level secure cryptographic code generation framework. NEMO employs a multi-task learning-based prompt risk analysis strategy alongside a multi-source security enhancement strategy to detect and optimize potential misuse risks embedded in developer prompts, thereby ensuring secure code generation. We evaluate NEMO on 2,775 real-world cryptographic code comments collected from GitHub projects and 366 cryptographic programming queries collected from Stack Overflow. Experimental results show that NEMO can effectively analyze the potential risk regarding specific cryptographic programming tasks and significantly improve code security while preserving functional correctness: it can successfully identify potential risks for over 90% of cryptographic programming tasks and reduce the rate of cryptographic misuse by 94.7% compared to direct code generation. Furthermore, relative to state-of-the-art automatic program repair approaches, NEMO achieves an additional 76% and 78% reduction in misuse cases, respectively, with negligible extra token overhead.

Keywords: Software Security · Secure Code Generation · Cryptographic API Misuse

© IFIP International Federation for Information Processing 2026
Published by Springer Nature Switzerland AG 2026
H. Janicke et al. (Eds.): SEC 2026, IFIP AICT 787, pp. 166–181, 2026.
https://doi.org/10.1007/978-3-032-27993-4_12

1 Introduction

Cryptographic misuse constitutes a major class of security vulnerabilities, often arising from flawed algorithm choices, incorrect parameter configurations, or insecure libraries, and can lead to severe consequences such as data leakage and identity forgery. Despite extensive prior work, secure cryptographic programming remains difficult due to its reliance on both theoretical knowledge and practical expertise, making misuse common even among experienced developers.

The rise of large language models (LLMs) has further complicated this landscape. LLMs enable code generation from natural language prompts, but limitations in training data [20,24] and hallucination effects [12,25] cause generated code to frequently contain security flaws [17]. This risk is especially pronounced for cryptographic tasks. Mousavi et al. [14] report that 70% of Java security API outputs generated by LLMs exhibit cryptographic flaws, and developers often over-trust AI-generated code, further amplifying security risks.

Prior studies systematically confirm these issues. Pearce et al. [17] found that nearly 40% of GitHub Copilot outputs contained vulnerabilities, while Fu et al. [9] reported security flaws in 29.5% of Python and 24.2% of Java code in open-source repositories. To mitigate such risks, existing approaches rely on model retraining [10] or iterative prompt interaction [15], which incur substantial computational cost, latency, or token overhead, limiting practical deployment.

In this work, we propose NEMO, a prompt-level framework for secure LLM-assisted cryptographic programming. NEMO identifies cryptographic intent and algorithmic strategy from natural language prompts, assesses misuse risks, and injects targeted security constraints derived from prior research, CWE, and OWASP guidelines. A lightweight context-aware reconciliation mechanism further resolves conflicts with protocol or library requirements, preserving functional correctness without model retraining or post-generation repair.

We evaluate NEMO on 2,775 real-world cryptographic code comments and 366 Stack Overflow cryptographic programming tasks. Results show over 90% intent and strategy recognition accuracy and a 94.7% reduction in cryptographic misuse compared to raw prompts, outperforming state-of-the-art repair-based approaches by over 75%. Additional experiments confirm functional correctness, token efficiency, and the robustness of individual components.

Contributions

- We introduce `CryptoTaskNet`, a multi-task model for inferring cryptographic intent and algorithmic strategy from natural language.
- We propose NEMO, a prompt-level optimization framework that injects security constraints and reconciles implementation contexts for secure cryptographic code generation.
- We conduct extensive evaluations covering security, correctness, efficiency, and ablation analysis.
- We release all models, code, and datasets at our anonymous repository [1].

Scope and Assumptions. NEMO targets realistic cryptographic programming scenarios where developers express functionality via natural language prompts. It assumes sufficient semantic cues for intent inference and leverages existing LLM knowledge without retraining or runtime analysis, operating solely through prompt transformation.

2 Background

2.1 Cryptographic Misuse and LLM-Assisted Code Generation Risks

Correctly implementing cryptographic functionality is challenging, as even minor errors in algorithm selection, parameter configuration, or implementation details can result in cryptographic misuse and severe security vulnerabilities. Common misuse categories include outdated or weak algorithms (e.g., MD5, SHA-1, DES), improper key management (e.g., hard-coded or static keys), and insecure configurations such as incompatible cipher modes or missing authentication. These issues highlight the extensive cryptographic expertise required for secure implementations. However, most developers lack specialized training in applied cryptography, a challenge further amplified by the pervasive integration of cryptographic operations into complex and evolving software systems. While this work focuses on the above misuse categories, our approach generalizes to other forms of cryptographic misuse given corresponding security rules or templates.

Large language models (LLMs) further exacerbate this problem by enabling direct code generation from natural language prompts. Although LLM-assisted programming is increasingly prevalent, vulnerabilities in training data [6,20,24] and inherent hallucination phenomena [12,25] cause LLM-generated code to frequently contain security flaws. Pearce et al. [17] showed that GitHub Copilot often produces vulnerable code across multiple languages and vulnerability types, while Fu et al. [9] found that over 35% of 435 Copilot-generated snippets from open-source projects contained security issues. These risks are particularly severe for security-critical tasks such as cryptographic programming and demand targeted mitigation.

2.2 Motivating Instance

To motivate prompt-level security optimization and illustrate the limitations of post-generation repair, we present a representative example of symmetric encryption.

Illustrative Raw Cryptographic Prompt. The original prompt, adapted from a real-world Stack Overflow question, requests string encryption using AES under a TLS 1.3 environment but provides no explicit security constraints or algorithmic guidance. Such underspecified prompts are common in practice and frequently lead to cryptographic misuse, including insecure algorithm selection and configuration. Listing 1.1 shows the raw prompt.

```
// Encrypt a string using AES under TLS 1.3 with a custom key
public static void main(String[] args) throws Exception {}
```

Listing 1.1. Symmetric Encryption Question Instance from Stack Overflow

According to the OWASP TLS Cryptographic Configuration Cheat Sheet [16] and CWE-327 [13], CBC-mode ciphers are forbidden in TLS 1.3, which mandates AEAD schemes such as AES-GCM or ChaCha20-Poly1305. In the absence of precise constraints, the model may select `AES-CBC`, yielding a non-compliant and insecure implementation.

Prompt-Level Security Optimization. Prior work shows that insecure LLM-generated code often stems from underspecified prompts rather than missing security knowledge [22]. By preserving task intent while injecting explicit security constraints, LLMs can enforce security requirements during code generation. Listing 1.2 shows a refined prompt that makes the intent, strategy, and TLS 1.3 context explicit.

```
// symmetric encryption, AES-GCM, TLS 1.3
public static void main(String[] args) throws Exception {}
```

Listing 1.2. Refined prompt with integrated security constraints

Listing 1.3 summarizes the resulting security-critical code changes in a diff-style format, where removed insecure statements are marked with "-" and added secure constructs with "+". The optimized prompt steers the model toward an AEAD mode compatible with TLS 1.3 and introduces secure key derivation, thereby mitigating cryptographic misuse and improving confidentiality and integrity.

```
// --- Key handling ---
- String key = "0123456789abcdef";          // hard-coded key (CWE-321)
- SecretKeySpec secretKey = new SecretKeySpec(key.getBytes(), "AES");
+ SecretKeyFactory factory =
+     SecretKeyFactory.getInstance("PBKDF2WithHmacSHA256");
+ KeySpec spec =
+     new PBEKeySpec(password.toCharArray(), salt, 65536, 256);
+ SecretKey secretKey =
+     new SecretKeySpec(factory.generateSecret(spec).getEncoded(), "AES");
// --- Cipher selection ---
- Cipher cipher = Cipher.getInstance("AES/CBC/PKCS5Padding");
+ Cipher cipher = Cipher.getInstance("AES/GCM/NoPadding");
// --- Encryption initialization ---
- cipher.init(Cipher.ENCRYPT_MODE, secretKey, ivParams);
+ cipher.init(Cipher.ENCRYPT_MODE, secretKey,
+     new GCMParameterSpec(128, iv));
```

Listing 1.3. Security-critical code changes induced by prompt-level optimization (insecure → secure)

2.3 Challenges and Solutions

Challenge 1: How to Identify Developer Intent and Cryptographic Actions from Prompts? Secure cryptographic code generation first requires accurately identifying the developer's intended cryptographic task and corresponding algorithmic strategy, which form the basis for security risk analysis.

However, developer prompts are free-form natural language, exhibiting substantial variation in expression and structure. The absence of a unified taxonomy for cryptographic intents and algorithms further complicates systematic intent extraction.

Solution. We extract cryptography-related code comments from over 79 GitHub projects and construct a comprehensive taxonomy covering six cryptographic intents and 27 corresponding algorithmic strategies. Using this taxonomy, we build a labeled dataset and train `CryptoTaskNet` to predict cryptographic intent and strategy directly from natural language descriptions.

Challenge 2: How to Construct Security Guidelines Tailored to Specific Cryptographic Actions? After identifying developer intent, appropriate security guidelines must be introduced to prevent cryptographic misuse. However, formulating effective and actionable constraints requires substantial cryptographic expertise and must account for diverse implementation strategies.

Solution. We systematically consolidate cryptographic programming guidelines from prior academic work [5,23], CWE [3], and OWASP [4], and align them with the identified intents and strategies, resulting in a structured set of security rules for prompt augmentation.

Challenge 3: How to Reconcile Security Guidelines with Developer-Specified Implementation Contexts? Developer prompts often specify concrete implementation contexts, such as cryptographic libraries or protocols, which may conflict with general security recommendations. Examples include TLS 1.3 forbidding CBC, JWT disallowing insecure signature algorithms, and libraries such as OpenSSL or NaCl enforcing strict algorithm policies.

Solution. NEMO extracts contextual information from prompts using lightweight keyword-driven analysis and prioritizes mandatory protocol or library constraints. When conflicts arise, incompatible security rules are discarded while compatible ones are retained, ensuring functional correctness while enhancing security in real-world deployment scenarios.

2.4 Terminology Clarification

- **Solution code:** Code generated by an LLM in response to a developer-provided prompt.
- **Cryptographic intent:** The high-level objective of a cryptographic task, such as symmetric encryption or signing and verification.
- **Algorithmic strategy:** The specific cryptographic algorithm selected to realize an intent, such as AES for encryption or RSA for signing.
- **Implementation context:** The concrete cryptographic environment specified in a prompt, including libraries or protocols (e.g., OpenSSL or TLS 1.3) that impose additional constraints on algorithm selection and configuration.

3 Methodology

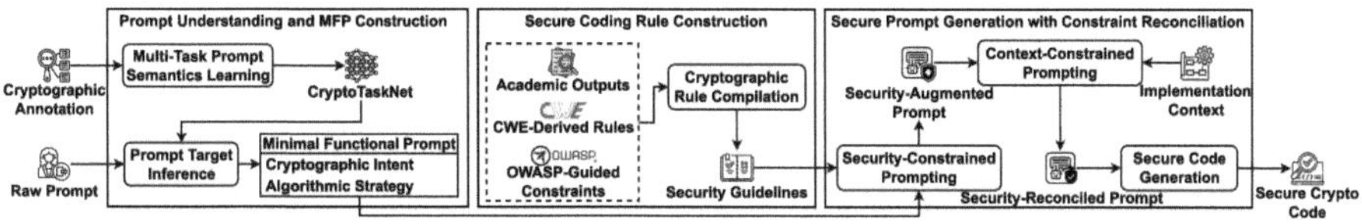

Fig. 1. The Overall Workflow of NEMO.

This section presents NEMO, a security-aware framework for cryptographic code generation that combines prompt understanding with knowledge-guided constraint injection. As shown in Fig. 1, NEMO operates in three stages. First, it employs `CryptoTaskNet`, a prompt intent classification model trained on cryptography-related code comments from real-world open-source projects (Sect. 3.1), to infer the intended cryptographic functionality and algorithmic strategy from a developer's raw prompt, producing a Minimal Functional Prompt (MFP) that preserves only task-critical semantics (Sect. 3.2). Second, NEMO injects task-aligned security constraints curated from academic literature [5,23], CWE [3], and OWASP [4] into the MFP, yielding a Security-Augmented Prompt (SAP) (Sect. 3.3). Finally, NEMO reconciles the injected constraints with any explicit protocol or library context specified in the prompt to avoid incompatibilities, resulting in a Security-Reconciled Prompt (SRP) that is fed to the LLM for secure code generation (Sect. 3.4).

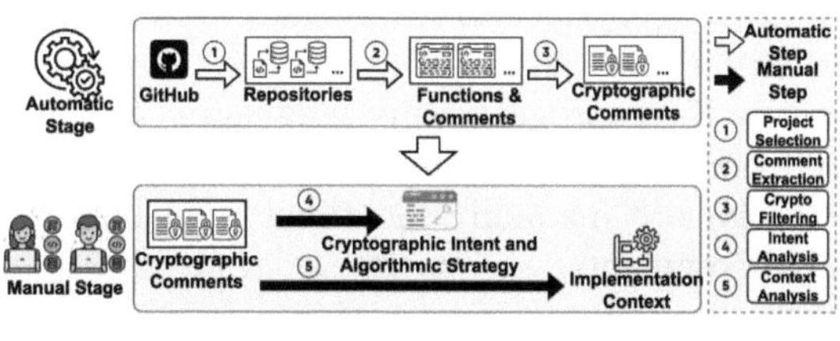

Fig. 2. Cryptographic Dataset Construction Steps.

3.1 Cryptographic Data Collection and Annotation

To enable automatic analysis of cryptographic intent and algorithmic strategy, we construct a training dataset from real-world open-source projects. Since developer prompts describe cryptographic functionality in natural language, the dataset consists of natural language code comments paired with cryptographic labels. We design a semi-automated pipeline to extract cryptography-related comments and annotate each sample with its corresponding cryptographic intent and algorithmic strategy (Fig. 2).

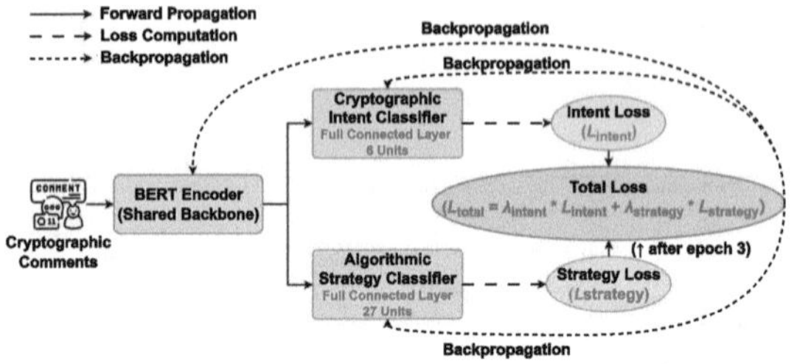

Fig. 3. Model Architecture of `CryptoTaskNet`.

Cryptographic Comment Extraction. We identify cryptographic function implementations in open-source projects by (i) selecting GitHub repositories older than five years with over 1,000 stars, (ii) parsing source files at the function level using CTags and retaining commented functions, and (iii) filtering for cryptography-related code via common cryptographic API patterns. This process yields 2,775 cryptography-related code comments.

Manual Intent–Strategy Labeling. Each comment is independently labeled by two domain experts with exactly one cryptographic intent and one algorithmic strategy under a shared guideline, with disagreements resolved through expert consensus to form a gold-standard dataset.

Taxonomy Construction. We derive the final taxonomy bottom-up from the labeled corpus by consolidating near-synonymous labels into two orthogonal facets: high-level cryptographic intents and concrete algorithmic strategies. Label consolidation continues until coverage saturates, resulting in six intents and twenty-seven strategies, which are fixed and used consistently throughout modeling and evaluation.

The dataset spans three programming languages: Java, C++, and C with 1029, 980, and 766 samples, respectively. Implementation context labels (e.g., libraries and protocols) are manually identified from import statements, API calls, and contextual comments.

3.2 Prompt Understanding and MFP Construction

Given a raw developer prompt, NEMO first infers the intended cryptographic functionality and algorithmic strategy as a prerequisite for security enhancement. To this end, we train `CryptoTaskNet` on the annotated dataset and transform the raw prompt into an MFP consisting of a cryptographic intent and an algorithmic strategy.

Multi-task Prompt Semantics Learning. Because cryptographic intent and algorithmic strategy are inferred from the same prompt and exhibit semantic interdependence, we adopt a multi-task learning framework to jointly train `CryptoTaskNet` (Fig. 3).

Model Architecture. `CryptoTaskNet` is built on a shared BERT encoder [7] that maps each input comment to a contextualized representation, which is fed into two task-specific classification heads: an intent classifier with six output classes and a strategy classifier with twenty-seven output classes.

Training Strategy. We adopt hard parameter sharing and jointly optimize intent and strategy prediction using a weighted combination of cross-entropy losses. The weighting scheme reflects task granularity and downstream impact: intent prediction captures coarse semantic intent, while strategy prediction directly determines security constraint selection. Training starts with balanced emphasis and a slightly higher weight on strategy, followed by a gradual increase in the strategy loss weight after a three-epoch warm-up, encouraging progressive refinement of fine-grained cryptographic distinctions once intent semantics have converged.

Prompt Target Inference. Using `CryptoTaskNet`, NEMO classifies the raw prompt along two semantic dimensions—cryptographic intent and algorithmic strategy. The predicted labels are concatenated to form the MFP, which serves as the foundation for subsequent security-oriented prompt transformations.

3.3 Secure Coding Rule Construction

To support secure cryptographic code generation, we organize strategy-specific security guidelines. Each algorithmic strategy is thus associated with concrete measures for mitigating cryptographic vulnerabilities. Library- and protocol-specific constraints are summarized in anonymous repository.

3.4 Secure Prompt Generation with Constraint Reconciliation

Based on the MFP and curated security rules, NEMO integrates security constraints directly into the prompt to guide code generation. Developer prompts may specify concrete deployment contexts (e.g., protocols or libraries), which can conflict with general security recommendations. To resolve such conflicts, NEMO performs lightweight context extraction and applies a structured reconciliation strategy: (i) developer intent is preserved for functional correctness; (ii) protocol- and library-level constraints are treated as authoritative; and (iii) general best practices are applied only when compatible. This process yields a SRP that remains faithful to the original intent while ensuring compatibility with real-world deployment environments.

Security-Constrained Prompting. NEMO appends task-specific security constraints to the MFP as concise imperative statements (e.g., "Use AES-GCM with a random IV"), which has been shown to effectively steer LLMs toward secure generation [22]. The complete set of prompt-level security constraints is provided in our anonymous repository.

Context-Constrained Prompting. When prompts reference concrete protocols or libraries, NEMO extracts such context via keyword matching and incorporates the corresponding constraints as high-priority rules. If conflicts arise, the SRP mechanism deterministically rewrites the prompt to prioritize protocol- or library-level requirements (e.g., enforcing AEAD modes under TLS 1.3), thereby ensuring deployment compatibility.

Secure Code Generation. The SRP is finally passed to the target LLM, which generates cryptographic code that adheres to the specified constraints. Since all enhancements operate purely at the prompt level, NEMO remains model-agnostic and can be seamlessly integrated into diverse code generation pipelines.

4 Experiments

We conduct a systematic evaluation of NEMO to assess its effectiveness in intent identification, functional correctness, cryptographic security, token efficiency, and the contribution of individual components. We further compare NEMO against state-of-the-art secure code generation and repair approaches.

4.1 Experimental Settings

Datasets. Our evaluation consists of two datasets. (i) *Intent and Strategy Classification:* 2,775 cryptography-related code comments annotated following Sect. 3.1, split into training and test sets with a 70%/30% ratio. (ii) *Secure Code Generation:* 366 real-world cryptographic programming questions from Stack Overflow, curated to ensure (a) active developer engagement, (b) unambiguous mapping to a single cryptographic intent and dominant strategy, and (c) the presence of an accepted answer. This process yields a high-precision benchmark spanning all six cryptographic intents, with a small number of rare strategies omitted due to insufficient high-quality examples.

Code Generation Models. Because NEMO operates purely at the prompt level, it is model-agnostic. We evaluate it using `GPT-4o`, `Claude-3.5 Sonnet`, and `Gemini-2.0`.

Baselines. We compare NEMO against two state-of-the-art reactive repair systems: `RepairAgent` [5] and `SRepair` [23]. Both are minimally adapted by injecting cryptographic misuse warnings from `FindSecBugs` as repair hints, without modifying their underlying LLMs. This enables a direct comparison between NEMO's preventive prompt optimization and post-generation repair under identical prompts and test harnesses.

Evaluation Metrics. We use three metrics: (i) **Average number of cryptographic security violations per program** (#SecVio), detected using tool `FindSecBugs` [2] and manually validated by two cryptography experts; (ii) **Number of programs passing unit tests** (#FuncProgram), measured using `JUnit` with independent verification; and (iii) **Prompt token count** (#Token), which captures generation efficiency and cost. Although our experiments focus on Java due to tool support, NEMO itself is language-agnostic.

Table 1. Performance Analysis of `CryptoTaskNet` according to Cryptographic Intent

Cryptographic Intent	Count	#Correct	Acc.(%)
Symmetric Encryption	141	128	90.78
Signing and Verifying	153	139	90.50
Key Generation	51	48	94.12
Key Storage	260	239	91.92
Authentication	163	150	92.21
Hashing	65	60	92.31

Table 2. `Performance Analysis of CryptoTaskNet by Algorithmic Strategy`

Str.	#	#C	Acc	Str.	#	#C	Acc	Str.	#	#C	Acc
MD5	13	12	92.3	AES	31	27	87.1	RSA	32	31	96.9
SHA-1	21	19	90.5	Enc/Dec	38	35	92.1	UAE	8	7	87.5
SHA-256	31	29	93.5	GCM	45	40	88.9	KMU	177	161	91.0
ECC	11	10	90.9	DES	27	26	96.3	SCU	83	78	94.0
BCV	35	33	94.3	CBA	13	12	92.3	CCV	33	31	93.9
DGV	20	17	85.0	JWT	18	17	94.4	PH	24	22	91.7
ECDSA	22	20	90.9	OAuth	15	14	93.3	SM	23	20	87.0
RSV	26	24	92.3	TLS/SSL	24	23	95.8	CSA	19	17	89.5
SVC	17	14	82.4	KA	16	15	93.8	LA	11	10	90.9

Abbrev.: UAE = Unclassified Asymmetric Encryption; KMU = Key Management or Updates; SCU = SSL Configuration or Updates;
BCV = Basic Certificate Verification; CCV = Certificate Chain Verification; DGV = Digest Generation or Verification;
RSV = RSA Signature Verification; SVC = Signature and Verification Combined; Enc/Dec = Encryption/Decryption;
CBA = Certificate-based Authentication; JWT = JWT Token-based Authentication; OAuth = OAuth Token-based Authentication;
PH = Password Hashing; SM = Session Management; CSA = Cipher Suite Adjustments; KA = Kerberos Authentication; LA = LDAP Authentication.

Research Questions. We address the following RQs: RQ1 (intent identification), RQ2 (functional correctness), RQ3 (security improvement), RQ4 (component contribution), and RQ5 (token efficiency).

4.2 Evaluation

RQ1: Intended Functionality Identification

Tables 1 and 2 report the performance of `CryptoTaskNet` on 833 test samples. The model achieves over 90% accuracy for cryptographic intent classification and exceeds 85% accuracy for nearly all of the 27 algorithmic strategies. The only notable exception is the "Signature and Verification Combined" category

Table 3. Functional Correctness Comparison between NEMO and Raw Prompt-Based Cryptographic Code Generation

Intent	Strategy	#Task	GPT-4o # (%)		Claude-3.5 # (%)		Gemini-2.0 # (%)	
			Raw	NEMO	Raw	NEMO	Raw	NEMO
Authentication	Certificate-based Authentication	16	14 (87.5)	15 (93.8)	14 (87.5)	15 (93.8)	13 (81.2)	15 (93.8)
Authentication	JWT Token-based Authentication	10	8 (80.0)	9 (90.0)	7 (70.0)	8 (80.0)	6 (60.0)	8 (80.0)
Authentication	OAuth Token-based Authentication	8	6 (75.0)	7 (87.5)	6 (75.0)	6 (75.0)	5 (62.5)	7 (87.5)
Authentication	Session Management	11	9 (81.8)	9 (81.8)	9 (81.8)	8 (72.7)	8 (72.7)	8 (72.7)
Authentication	TLS/SSL	14	12 (85.7)	12 (85.7)	12 (85.7)	11 (78.6)	10 (71.4)	10 (71.4)
Signing and Verifying	Certificate Chain Verification	23	19 (82.6)	20 (87.0)	18 (78.3)	19 (82.6)	18 (78.3)	18 (78.3)
Signing and Verifying	ECDSA Signature	28	26 (92.9)	27 (96.4)	26 (92.9)	26 (92.9)	24 (85.7)	27 (96.4)
Signing and Verifying	RSA Signature Verification	9	8 (88.9)	9 (100.0)	8 (88.9)	8 (88.9)	6 (66.7)	7 (77.8)
Signing and Verifying	Signature and Verification Combined	14	12 (85.7)	12 (85.7)	12 (85.7)	11 (78.6)	12 (85.7)	10 (71.4)
Key Storage	Key Management or Updates	9	8 (88.9)	9 (100.0)	7 (77.8)	9 (100.0)	6 (66.7)	8 (88.9)
Key Storage	SSL Configuration or Updates	17	13 (76.5)	14 (82.4)	13 (76.5)	14 (82.4)	13 (76.5)	14 (82.4)
Hashing	MD5	9	8 (88.9)	9 (100.0)	8 (88.9)	8 (88.9)	6 (66.7)	8 (88.9)
Hashing	SHA-1	26	23 (88.5)	24 (92.3)	23 (88.5)	23 (88.5)	21 (80.8)	23 (88.5)
Hashing	SHA-256	31	29 (93.5)	30 (96.8)	29 (93.5)	29 (93.5)	29 (93.5)	29 (93.5)
Key Generation	Unclassified Asymmetric Encryption	19	14 (73.7)	15 (78.9)	13 (68.4)	15 (78.9)	14 (73.7)	14 (73.7)
Key Generation	ECC	18	14 (77.8)	15 (83.3)	14 (77.8)	14 (77.8)	12 (66.7)	14 (77.8)
Key Generation	RSA	22	18 (81.8)	19 (86.4)	17 (77.3)	19 (86.4)	17 (77.3)	18 (81.8)
Symmetric Encryption	DES	7	5 (71.4)	6 (85.7)	4 (57.1)	6 (85.7)	5 (71.4)	5 (71.4)
Symmetric Encryption	Encryption/Decryption	33	28 (84.8)	29 (87.9)	27 (81.8)	29 (87.9)	27 (81.8)	29 (87.9)
Symmetric Encryption	AES-GCM	16	13 (81.2)	14 (87.5)	13 (81.2)	14 (87.5)	12 (75.0)	12 (75.0)
Symmetric Encryption	AES	26	22 (84.6)	23 (88.5)	21 (80.8)	23 (88.5)	21 (80.8)	22 (84.6)
SUM	—	366	309 (84.4)	327 (89.3)	301 (82.2)	315 (86.1)	285 (77.9)	306 (83.6)

(82.4%), which we attribute to semantic overlap and linguistic diversity in multi-operation prompts. Overall, `CryptoTaskNet` provides accurate intent and strategy inference, forming a reliable basis for subsequent security optimization.

Conclusion 1: `CryptoTaskNet` accurately identifies cryptographic intents and strategies from natural language prompts, achieving over 90% accuracy for intents and most strategies.

RQ2: Solution Code Functionality Evaluation

Table 3 summarizes functional correctness results across 366 Stack Overflow tasks. Across all cryptographic intents and evaluated LLMs, NEMO shows measurable improvements and achieves test pass rates exceeding 80%. In a small number of cases involving complex multi-operation tasks (e.g., combined signature and verification), NEMO shows marginally lower correctness for specific model–strategy combinations; however, these represent rare outliers. Overall, the results indicate that NEMO preserves—and often improves—functional correctness, largely due to its Minimal Functional Prompt construction, which removes redundant linguistic noise and clarifies task intent.

Conclusion 2: NEMO does not compromise functional correctness and often improves it by extracting task-relevant cryptographic intent and strategy.

RQ3: Solution Code Security Evaluation

Table 4 reports security results grouped by cryptographic intent. Code generated from raw prompts exhibits pervasive cryptographic misuse, with average #SecVio often exceeding one, and surpassing two for misuse-prone intents such as key generation and storage. Repair-based baselines reduce misuses to some

Table 4. Security Violations across Schemes by Cryptographic Intent

Intent	Raw	RepairAgent	SRepair	NEMO
Authentication	1.949	0.458	0.424	0.102
Signing and Verifying	1.892	0.486	0.378	0.081
Key Storage	2.115	0.577	0.308	0.077
Hashing	1.879	0.485	0.333	0.061
Key Generation	2.034	0.424	0.288	0.068
Symmetric Encryption	1.866	0.524	0.500	0.085

extent (#SecVio between 0.2 and 0.6), but still leave residual vulnerabilities and incur substantial repair overhead.

In contrast, NEMO achieves #SecVio near or below 0.1 across all cryptographic intents, demonstrating a substantial security advantage. Results grouped by algorithmic strategy are deferred to the anonymous repository due to space constraints. We further evaluate NEMO with `Claude-3.5` and `Gemini-2.0`. Across all evaluated LLMs, NEMO consistently maintains low #SecVio, confirming its robustness and model-agnostic design. Detailed per-model results are deferred to the anonymous repository due to space constraints.

Practical Interpretation. Overall, NEMO reduces cryptographic misuses by 94.7% relative to raw generation, and achieves additional reductions of 76% and 78% compared to `RepairAgent` and `SRepair`, respectively. By addressing misuses at the prompt level, NEMO avoids multi-turn repair overhead while simplifying auditing and deployment workflows.

Conclusion 3: NEMO substantially outperforms raw prompts and repair-based approaches, reducing cryptographic misuses by an order of magnitude.

RQ4: Ablation Study

The ablation study evaluates four prompt configurations: Raw, MFP, SAP, and SRP. Across all strategies, we observe a monotonic decrease in #SecVio as additional optimization stages are applied. MFP reduces misuses by clarifying task intent, SAP introduces substantial gains via security constraint injection, and SRP further resolves conflicts between constraints and implementation contexts, yielding the strongest security performance. Although SRP-specific reconciliation applies to only 45 tasks, its impact is pronounced for misuse-prone strategies such as RSA signature verification and TLS/SSL (Table 5).

medskip***Conclusion 4:*** Each component of NEMO contributes to security improvement, with context-aware reconciliation playing a critical role when conflicts arise.

RQ5: Token Efficiency Evaluation

We compare token usage for prompt construction and code generation across approaches. By eliminating redundant natural-language descriptions and enforcing concise security constraints, NEMO consistently incurs lower token overhead

Table 5. Average Security Violations of Prompt Schemes by Algorithmic Strategy

Str.	Raw	MFP	SAP	SRP	#S	Str.	Raw	MFP	SAP	SRP	#S
CBA	1.875	1.125	0.125	0.125	0	TLS/SSL	1.929	1.214	0.214	0.071	8
JWT	2.000	1.200	0.100	0.100	0	MD5	1.778	1.111	0.556	0.111	9
OAuth	2.000	1.125	0.125	0.125	0	SHA-1	1.885	0.731	0.115	0.038	7
SM	2.000	1.182	0.091	0.091	0	SHA-256	1.903	0.774	0.065	0.065	0
ECC	2.111	0.944	0.056	0.056	0	RSA	2.000	1.227	0.045	0.091	6
UAE	2.000	1.000	0.053	0.053	0	KMU	2.222	1.444	0.111	0.111	0
SCU	2.059	0.941	0.059	0.059	0	CCV	1.826	1.348	0.087	0.087	0
ECDSA	1.893	1.143	0.071	0.071	0	RSV	2.000	1.000	0.333	0.111	7
SVC	1.929	0.786	0.071	0.071	0	AES	1.808	1.269	0.077	0.077	8
AES-GCM	1.813	0.813	0.125	0.125	0	DES	2.000	0.857	0.143	0.143	0
Enc/Dec	1.909	1.121	0.061	0.061	0						

than both raw prompting and post-generation repair. Repair-based methods suffer substantial overhead from multi-turn interactions; for example, `RepairAgent` executes a median of 25 iterations, yielding average prompt sizes above 75K tokens. Detailed statistics are available in our anonymous GitHub repository.

Conclusion 5: NEMO achieves substantially lower token overhead than both direct generation and repair-based pipelines.

5 Discussion

Prompt-Level Optimization Vs. Post-Generation Repair. NEMO performs prompt-level security optimization by identifying cryptographic intent and algorithmic strategy prior to code generation. Unlike post-generation repair approaches that rely on multi-turn auditing, NEMO intervenes earlier in the pipeline, reducing overhead and enabling security mechanisms to be incorporated during generation. Empirical results show that this proactive design yields more effective security improvements than post-hoc fixes in LLM-assisted programming.

Deployment Potential: Model-Agnostic and Lightweight. NEMO is model-agnostic and operates entirely at the prompt level, enabling seamless integration into environments such as `GitHub Copilot`, `VSCode`, and cloud-based LLM services. It functions as a lightweight preprocessing step that augments developer prompts with security constraints, providing a practical mechanism for improving real-world code security.

Limitations and Future Work. NEMO may not cover all cryptographic scenarios due to limitations in training data, and curated security rules may miss vulnerabilities arising from complex or context-specific factors. Future work will expand coverage through incremental intent learning and patch-based constraint extraction to improve robustness for long-tail cryptographic tasks.

6 Related Works

Research on AI-assisted code generation and its security implications has expanded rapidly, spanning three related directions: (i) security vulnerabilities in LLM-generated code, (ii) prompt engineering for secure generation, and (iii) post-generation repair and secure-by-design frameworks.

Security of AI-Generated Code. Prior empirical studies have shown that LLM-generated code frequently contains security vulnerabilities [9,17–19]. These findings also reveal a recurring human-factor developers tend to over-trust AI-generated code and underestimate its security risks. Motivated by this observation, NEMO adopts a proactive defense strategy that prevents insecure cryptographic code by optimizing the natural language prompt rather than detecting vulnerabilities post hoc.

Prompt Engineering for Secure Code Generation. Prompt engineering has been explored as a means to steer LLMs toward safer outputs. Tony et al. [22] showed that structured, requirement-driven prompts can reduce vulnerability rates, while iterative approaches such as RCI [11] refine code through repeated feedback. Unlike these methods, NEMO embeds cryptographic best practices directly into a single-shot prompt via task-specific constraint injection and context-aware reconciliation, realizing preventive repair before code generation.

Post-Generation Repair and Secure Coding Frameworks. Another line of work focuses on repairing vulnerabilities after code generation, including LLM-assisted repair systems such as RepairAgent [5] and LLM4CVE [8], as well as secure-by-design frameworks such as SGCode [21]. While effective, these approaches incur higher complexity, latency, and token overhead, and typically require vulnerabilities to surface before repair. NEMO complements this line of work by targeting cryptographic tasks and achieving secure generation through lightweight, one-pass prompt optimization.

7 Conclusion

We introduce NEMO, a prompt-optimization framework that improves the security of AI-generated cryptographic code. By rewriting developer prompts into minimal, security-aware, and context-aligned instructions, NEMO proactively reduces vulnerabilities without sacrificing functionality. On 366 real-world tasks, NEMO reduces rule violations by over 90%, outperforms automated repair tools, and lowers token cost. These results highlight secure-by-design prompting as a lightweight and effective strategy for trustworthy code generation.

References

1. Nemo anonymous repository. https://anonymous.4open.science/r/NEMO-0C61
2. Owasp find security bugs. https://github.com/find-sec-bugs/find-sec-bugs
3. Common weakness enumeration (2025). https://cwe.mitre.org/
4. Owasp foundation (2025). https://owasp.org/
5. Bouzenia, I., Devanbu, P., Pradel, M.: Repairagent: an autonomous, LLM-based agent for program repair. arXiv preprint arXiv:2403.17134 (2024)
6. Chen, Y., Ding, Z., Alowain, L., Chen, X., Wagner, D.: Diversevul: a new vulnerable source code dataset for deep learning based vulnerability detection. In: Proceedings of the 26th International Symposium on Research in Attacks, Intrusions and Defenses (RAID), pp. 654–668 (2023)
7. Devlin, J., Chang, M.W., Lee, K., Toutanova, K.: Bert: pre-training of deep bidirectional transformers for language understanding. In: Proceedings of the 17th Conference of the North American Chapter of the Association for Computational Linguistics: Human Language Technologies (NAACL-HLT), pp. 4171–4186 (2019)
8. Fakih, M., Luo, Y., Feng, Y., Baluta, T.: Llm4cve: repairing security vulnerabilities with large language models. In: NDSS (2024)
9. Fu, Y., et al.: Security weaknesses of copilot-generated code in github projects: an empirical study. ACM Trans. Softw. Eng. Methodol. (2025)
10. He, J., Vechev, M.: Large language models for code: security hardening and adversarial testing. In: Proceedings of the 30th ACM SIGSAC Conference on Computer and Communications Security (CCS), pp. 1865–1879 (2023)
11. Kim, G., Baldi, P., McAleer, S.: Language models can solve computer tasks. In: NeurIPS (2023)
12. Liu, F., et al.: Exploring and evaluating hallucinations in LLM-powered code generation. arXiv preprint arXiv:2404.00971 (2024)
13. MITRE: CWE-327: Use of a Broken or Risky Cryptographic Algorithm. https://cwe.mitre.org/data/definitions/327.html. Accessed 25 Apr 2025
14. Mousavi, Z., Islam, C., Moore, K., Abuadbba, A., Babar, M.A.: An investigation into misuse of java security apis by large language models. In: Proceedings of the 19th ACM Asia Conference on Computer and Communications Security, pp. 1299–1315 (2024)
15. Nazzal, M., Khalil, I., Khreishah, A., Phan, N.: Promsec: prompt optimization for secure generation of functional source code with large language models (LLMs). In: Proceedings of the 31st on ACM SIGSAC Conference on Computer and Communications Security (CCS), pp. 2266–2280 (2024)
16. OWASP: TLS Cryptographic Configuration Cheat Sheet (2024). https://cheatsheetseries.owasp.org/cheatsheets/TLS_Cryptographic_Configuration_Cheat_Sheet.html. Accessed 25 Apr 2025
17. Pearce, H., Ahmad, B., Tan, B., Dolan-Gavitt, B., Karri, R.: Asleep at the keyboard? Assessing the security of github copilot's code contributions. In: 43rd IEEE Symposium on Security and Privacy (SP), pp. 754–768 (2022)
18. Perry, N., Srivastava, M., Kumar, D., Boneh, D.: Do users write more insecure code with ai assistants? In: ACM CCS, pp. 2785–2799 (2023)
19. Sandoval, G., Pearce, H., Nys, T., Karri, R., Garg, S., Dolan-Gavitt, B.: Lost at c: a user study on the security implications of large language model code assistants. In: 32nd USENIX Security Symposium, pp. 2205–2222 (2023)
20. Tihanyi, N., Bisztray, T., Ferrag, M.A., Jain, R., Cordeiro, L.C.: How secure is ai-generated code: a large-scale comparison of large language models. Empir. Softw. Eng. **30**(2), 1–42 (2025)

21. Ton, K., Nguyen, N., Nazzal, M., Khreishah, A., Phan, N.H., Shen, Y.: Sgcode: a flexible prompt-optimizing system for secure code generation. ACM AISec (2024)
22. Tony, C., Díaz Ferreyra, N.E., Mutas, M., Dhiff, S., Scandariato, R.: Prompting techniques for secure code generation: a systematic investigation. ACM Trans. Softw. Eng. Methodol. (2025). arXiv:2407.07064. to appear
23. Xiang, J., et al.: How far can we go with practical function-level program repair? arXiv preprint arXiv:2404.12833 (2024)
24. Xuan, C.D., Quang, D.B., Quang, V.D.: Large language models based vulnerability detection: how does it enhance performance? Int. J. Inf. Secur. **24**(1), 69 (2025)
25. Zhang, Z., Wang, Y., Wang, C., Chen, J., Zheng, Z.: LLM hallucinations in practical code generation: phenomena, mechanism, and mitigation. arXiv preprint arXiv:2409.20550 (2024)

Cyber-Physical Systems Security

HASAC: Energy Adaptive Secure Firmware Updates for Critical IoT Systems

Sayon Duttagupta(✉)

COSIC, KU Leuven, Leuven, Belgium
sayon.duttagupta@esat.kuleuven.be

Abstract. Secure Firmware Over-The-Air (FOTA) updates are essential for Critical Infrastructure IoT (CI-IoT) devices, but impose severe energy costs on battery-powered nodes operating over Low Power Wide Area Networks such as NB-IoT. This paper presents HASAC (*Hardware-Aware Segmented Authenticated Compression*), a FOTA framework for resource-constrained IoT devices that minimises update energy by dynamically adapting cryptographic and compression strategies to device hardware capabilities and radio conditions. We implement HASAC on a Cortex-M33 platform and show that radio transmission and interconnect overhead account for more than 90% of the total update energy, while cryptographic computation contributes only a small fraction. We further demonstrate that on devices equipped with hardware security modules, AES-128-CCM achieves more than an order-of-magnitude improvement in throughput and energy efficiency compared to software implementations, even for small firmware segments. Building on these insights, HASAC dynamically selects between hardware-accelerated AES and software-optimised ChaCha20-Poly1305, and applies link-aware LZ4 compression only when it yields a positive energy return. Model-based evaluation demonstrates that, in deep coverage scenarios, HASAC reduces the total energy cost of secure firmware updates by up to 30% compared to conventional uncompressed baselines, reconciling strong security guarantees with long-term battery longevity.

Keywords: IoT security · Firmware update · Applied cryptography · NB-IoT · Energy efficiency · Cortex-M33

1 Introduction

Secure Firmware Over-the-Air (FOTA) updates are a prerequisite for the long-term security of Critical Infrastructure IoT deployments such as smart water meters, gas meters, and environmental monitoring nodes. These devices are typically battery-powered, installed in hard-to-access locations, and expected to operate for a decade or longer without maintenance. At the same time, they increasingly rely on Low Power Wide Area Networks (LPWANs), including Narrowband IoT (NB-IoT), to provide wide-area connectivity under challenging

© IFIP International Federation for Information Processing 2026
Published by Springer Nature Switzerland AG 2026
H. Janicke et al. (Eds.): SEC 2026, IFIP AICT 787, pp. 185–198, 2026.
https://doi.org/10.1007/978-3-032-27993-4_13

radio conditions. In such settings, firmware updates are among the most energy-intensive operations in the device lifecycle. In basements, underground pits, and shielded utility locations, NB-IoT employs coverage enhancement through repetition and link adaptation, dramatically increasing airtime. As a result, the energy cost per delivered byte can grow by orders of magnitude, and a single firmware update can consume energy comparable to weeks or months of normal sensing and reporting operation.

Despite this, secure update mechanisms are commonly designed with a primary focus on computational efficiency. Prior work and industrial practice often optimise cryptographic primitives, assuming that cryptographic computation dominates energy consumption. The measurements show that this assumption is fundamentally incorrect for NB-IoT based firmware updates. Using a Cortex-M33 platform, we observe that radio transmission and interconnect overhead account for more than 90% of the total update energy, while on-device cryptographic processing contributes only a small fraction, particularly on platforms with hardware acceleration. In this regime, reducing transmitted bytes has a far greater impact on energy than reducing CPU cycles. This shift in perspective has important security implications. Operators frequently delay or avoid firmware updates to preserve battery lifetime, leaving devices exposed to known vulnerabilities. An adversary can further exploit this tension by triggering repeated or partial downloads to induce battery exhaustion. Energy, therefore, becomes a first-class security constraint, rather than a secondary performance concern. In addition, Cortex-M33 based devices exhibit significant hardware heterogeneity. Some platforms provide hardware support for cryptographic operations, while others rely entirely on software. Fixing a single cryptographic configuration across all devices is therefore suboptimal, either wasting silicon capabilities or imposing unnecessary computation costs. At the same time, firmware images exhibit highly uneven compressibility. Compressing all firmware data indiscriminately can waste energy when compression yields little reduction in transmitted bytes, particularly under good radio conditions.

These observations motivate *HASAC*, a secure firmware update framework that explicitly treats FOTA as an energy-constrained security problem. HASAC adapts cryptographic processing to device hardware capabilities and applies segment-wise, link-aware compression only when it yields a positive energy return. By aligning security mechanisms with both radio conditions and hardware features, HASAC reduces update energy while preserving strong authenticity and integrity guarantees. The contributions are as follows.

1. **Energy breakdown of secure firmware updates.** Using a Cortex-M33 platform with an NB-IoT modem, we measure the per-segment timing of radio reception, interconnect transfer, and on-device processing during secure FOTA. We show that communication dominates total energy consumption across realistic deployment conditions.
2. **Quantitative analysis of cryptographic cost in FOTA.** We benchmark software-optimised AES-CCM and ChaCha20-Poly1305 on Cortex-M33 devices, with and without hardware security modules. We show that hard-

ware acceleration reduces cryptographic energy to a negligible fraction of the total update cost, even for small firmware segments.
3. **HASAC framework.** We propose HASAC, a secure update framework that adapts authenticated encryption to device hardware capabilities and applies segment-wise, link-aware LZ4 compression using an explicit energy break-even rule derived from measured radio and processing costs.
4. **Model-based evaluation under varying link conditions.** We develop an analytical energy model incorporating NB-IoT coverage enhancement and evaluate a 128 kB firmware update. In deep coverage scenarios, HASAC reduces total update energy by up to one third compared to conventional uncompressed baselines, while avoiding unnecessary computation in good coverage.

Artefact Availability: The entire source code and artefact underlying this paper, including the implementation and benchmarkings, and the exact firmware files used, can be found at https://github.com/KULeuven-COSIC/HASAC/.

2 Related Work

Secure firmware update mechanisms for IoT devices have been studied extensively, with most work focusing on authenticity, integrity, and rollback protection rather than energy efficiency. RFC 9019 defines a generic architecture for IoT firmware updates, introducing roles such as firmware server, device, and status tracker, together with signed manifests that bind metadata to firmware images [9]. RFC 9124 further specifies a detailed information model for such manifests, targeting constrained devices using compact CBOR encodings [8]. While these standards establish a solid security foundation, they deliberately abstract away transport costs and device-level energy constraints.

Several academic systems build on similar principles. ASSURED provides a secure update architecture with strong cryptographic guarantees and minimal trusted computing base requirements [1]. UpKit proposes a lightweight and portable update framework suitable for constrained IoT platforms [6]. The Secure FoTA Object specifies a standardised object model for authenticated firmware delivery in IoT management protocols [2]. These systems ensure the correctness and robustness of updates but treat communication and computation costs as secondary concerns. More recent work has explored formal assurance and certification of update procedures. Tacchella et al. introduce certified secure updates, focusing on verifiable correctness of update execution and compliance with security policies [11]. This line of work strengthens trust guarantees but does not address the operational cost of updates on battery-powered devices or under challenging radio conditions.

Survey papers consistently identify energy consumption as a practical challenge for IoT firmware updates, especially over LPWANs, but stop short of providing concrete models or adaptive mechanisms [4,5]. In particular, prior work does not quantify the relative contribution of radio communication versus cryptographic processing, nor does it exploit hardware acceleration heterogeneity to optimise update energy.

In contrast to existing work, HASAC treats energy as a first-class security constraint. It combines measurement-grounded analysis, hardware-aware cryptographic selection, and link-aware compression to minimise update energy while preserving standard security properties. Rather than proposing a new update architecture, HASAC complements existing frameworks such as SUIT by optimising how secure updates are executed on real devices and real radio links.

3 System and Threat Model

3.1 System Model

We consider a battery-powered CI-IoT device built around a Cortex-M33 class microcontroller and connected to the network via an NB-IoT modem. Firmware updates are delivered over the NB-IoT downlink and transferred to the microcontroller over a serial interface. Due to coverage enhancement and link repetition, the effective energy cost per transmitted byte can vary significantly depending on deployment conditions. The device implements a secure boot chain with a minimal bootloader residing in protected flash. The bootloader verifies a signed update manifest, authenticates firmware segments, and installs a new firmware image into a staging region before activation. Firmware updates are segmented and processed incrementally to accommodate limited memory and to tolerate intermittent connectivity. We assume that devices may differ in their cryptographic capabilities, ranging from software-only implementations to platforms equipped with hardware security modules. HASAC is designed to adapt to this heterogeneity without changing the update protocol or trust assumptions.

3.2 Threat Model

We assume a network adversary with full control over the NB-IoT communication channel. The adversary can eavesdrop, inject, replay, delay, or modify update traffic, and can attempt to trigger repeated or partial firmware downloads. The adversary's goals include installing unauthorised firmware, rolling devices back to vulnerable versions, extracting firmware contents, or accelerating battery depletion. Each device is provisioned at manufacture time with a trust anchor used to verify update manifests. We assume this trust anchor and the secure bootloader are not compromised. Physical attacks, side-channel attacks, and compromise of server-side signing keys are out of scope.

4 Empirical Analysis and Energy Modelling

This section quantifies the energy cost of secure firmware updates through direct measurements and develops an analytical model that generalises these results across coverage conditions and update strategies. The goal is to isolate the relative contributions of communication and computation, and to identify when compression and cryptographic choices materially affect total update energy.

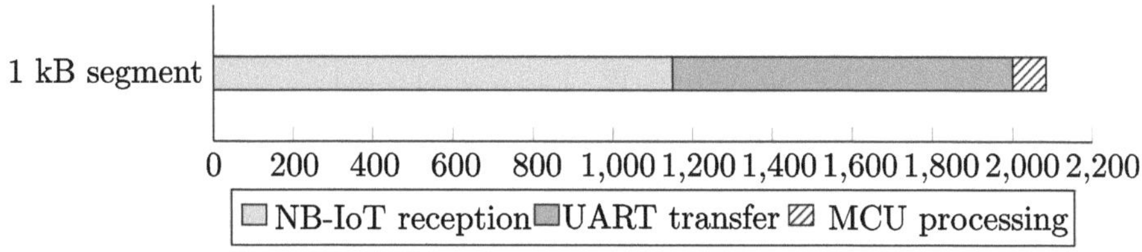

Fig. 1. Measured timing profile (in ms) for downloading and installing a 1 kB firmware segment. Communication dominates the update timeline, while on-device processing contributes only a small fraction.

4.1 Measurement Methodology

We implement an FOTA client that downloads firmware segments of 1 kB over NB-IoT. To capture the timing of each update phase, we instrument the firmware with GPIO markers around three operations: radio reception at the modem, data transfer over the UART interconnect, and on-device processing, including authenticated decryption and flash programming. Timing traces are collected using a logic analyser and averaged over multiple runs.

To validate power assumptions, we measure current draw using a Nordic Power Profiler Kit. During radio activity and active processing, current remains in the range of several milliamperes. To avoid optimistic estimates, we adopt a conservative constant active power model of 10 mA at 3 V, corresponding to 30 mW. While simplified, this model is sufficient to reason about relative energy contributions and break-even points.

4.2 Measured Timing Breakdown

Figure 1 shows the measured timing for a single 1 kB firmware segment. Radio reception dominates the timeline at approximately 1150 ms, followed by UART transfer at roughly 850 ms. In contrast, on-device processing, including authenticated decryption and flash writes, requires only about 85 ms.

These measurements already indicate that optimising computation alone cannot significantly reduce update duration or energy, as the microcontroller is idle or waiting for I/O for most of the transaction.

4.3 Measured Energy per Segment

Using the measured timings and the active power model, the energy consumed during an interval of duration t is

$$E = P_{\text{active}} \cdot t. \tag{1}$$

For a 1 kB segment, this yields

$$E_{\text{radio}} \approx 0.03 \text{ W} \cdot 1.15 \text{ s} \approx 34.5 \text{ mJ}, \tag{2}$$

$$E_{\text{UART}} \approx 0.03 \text{ W} \cdot 0.85 \text{ s} \approx 25.5 \text{ mJ}, \tag{3}$$

$$E_{\text{CPU}} \approx 0.03 \text{ W} \cdot 0.085 \text{ s} \approx 2.55 \text{ mJ}. \tag{4}$$

Radio and interconnect together account for nearly 60 mJ per kilobyte, whereas cryptographic processing and flash writes contribute only a few millijoules. Communication, therefore, dominates computation by an order of magnitude.

4.4 Analytical Energy Model

To generalise these observations, we model the total energy of a firmware update as

$$E_{\text{FOTA}} = E_{\text{connect}} + \sum_{i=1}^{N} \left(E_{\text{RX}}(S_i) + E_{\text{UART}}(S_i) + E_{\text{CPU}}(S_i) \right), \tag{5}$$

where the firmware image is divided into N segments S_i of size b bytes.

Radio reception time is modelled as

$$t_{\text{radio}}(S_i) = \frac{|S_i|}{R_{\text{eff}}} \cdot r_{\text{CE}}, \tag{6}$$

where R_{eff} is the effective downlink rate under good coverage and r_{CE} captures coverage enhancement through repetition. The corresponding energy is

$$E_{\text{RX}}(S_i) = P_{\text{active}} \cdot t_{\text{radio}}(S_i). \tag{7}$$

UART transfer and on-device processing are modelled similarly, with processing decomposed into decryption, optional decompression, and flash programming. Crucially, only the radio component scales with the coverage enhancement factor, while CPU energy remains unchanged. This asymmetry is central to my design.

4.5 Compression Behaviour

We analyse firmware compressibility using LZ4 [7] by partitioning real firmware images into 1 kB and 8 kB segments. For a segment S_i, the compression factor is

$$\text{Ratio}_i = \frac{|S_i|}{|LZ4(S_i)|}. \tag{8}$$

Figure 2 shows that compressibility varies significantly across segments, particularly at small granularity. Many 1 kB segments are effectively incompressible, while others compress substantially. Larger segments exhibit more stable compression ratios but increase memory requirements.

These results show that indiscriminate compression is inefficient. Compression must be applied selectively, balancing reduced radio energy against added processing cost. This observation directly motivates the design of HASAC.

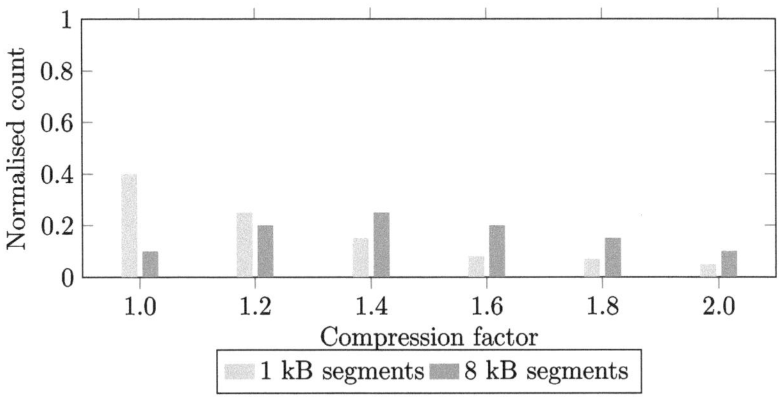

Fig. 2. Distribution of LZ4 compression factors for firmware segments. Compressibility varies widely at small granularity, motivating segment-wise decisions.

5 The HASAC Framework

Motivated by the empirical results and energy model in Sect. 4, we now present HASAC, a secure firmware update framework that treats energy as a first-class security constraint. HASAC explicitly separates communication-dominated costs from computation-dominated costs and adapts both cryptography and compression to minimise total update energy under realistic deployment conditions.

5.1 Design Principles

HASAC is guided by three design principles.

- **Radio first optimisation.** Since radio reception and interconnect transfer dominate update energy, HASAC prioritises reducing transmitted bytes. Optimising cryptographic computation alone yields limited benefit in NB-IoT deployments.
- **Hardware aware cryptography.** HASAC adapts its authenticated encryption scheme to the capabilities of the target device, exploiting hardware acceleration where available and using software-optimised constructions otherwise.
- **Segment wise adaptivity.** Compression decisions are taken per segment and depend jointly on segment compressibility and link conditions, ensuring that decompression never increases total energy.

5.2 Adaptive Cryptographic Selection

HASAC supports two standard AEAD schemes: AES-CCM [3] and ChaCha20-Poly1305 [10]. During provisioning, the device exposes whether a hardware cryptographic engine is available. This capability information is bound to the device identity and used by the update server when preparing firmware images.

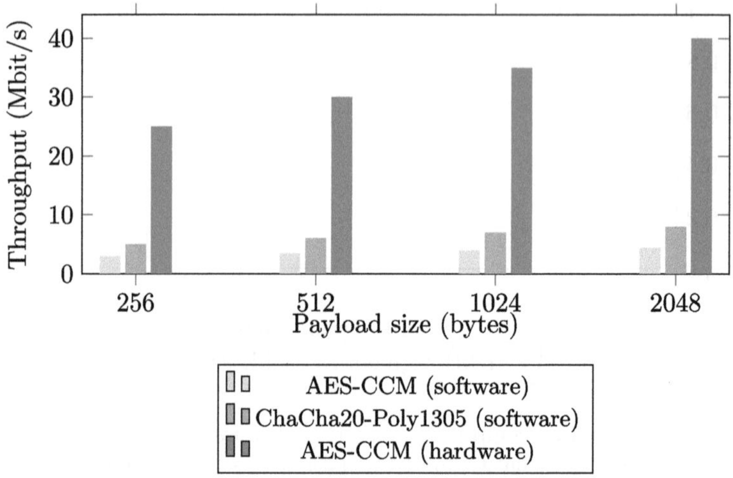

Fig. 3. Measured authenticated encryption throughput on a Cortex-M33 platform. Hardware-accelerated AES-CCM achieves an order of magnitude higher throughput than software implementations, while ChaCha20-Poly1305 outperforms software AES in the absence of acceleration.

On devices with hardware cryptographic support, HASAC selects AES-CCM. Each firmware segment is encrypted using a per-update key and a per-segment nonce, and the device performs decryption and authentication using the hardware engine. On devices without hardware support, HASAC selects ChaCha20-Poly1305, which provides equivalent security guarantees while offering substantially higher throughput and lower energy consumption in software.

Figure 3 summarises the measured cryptographic throughput. In the absence of hardware acceleration, ChaCha20-Poly1305 outperforms software AES-CCM. When hardware acceleration is enabled, AES-CCM achieves an order of magnitude higher throughput, rendering cryptographic processing negligible compared to UART and radio costs even for small segments.

5.3 Segment Wise Compression Policy

Firmware images are partitioned into fixed-size segments aligned to the flash programming granularity. For each segment S_i, the server computes its LZ4 compressed form C_i and corresponding compression factor

$$\text{Ratio}_i = \frac{|S_i|}{|C_i|}. \tag{9}$$

HASAC selects a compression threshold T_{CE} based on the estimated coverage enhancement level of the target device. In good coverage, where repetition is minimal, HASAC applies a conservative threshold and compresses only strongly compressible segments. In deep coverage, where repetition amplifies the energy cost per byte, HASAC lowers the threshold and compresses even weakly compressible segments.

For each segment, the server applies the rule

$$\text{send } C_i \text{ if } \text{Ratio}_i > T_{\text{CE}}, \text{ otherwise send } S_i. \tag{10}$$

The segment metadata encodes whether compression is applied and records the original length, allowing the device to correctly authenticate, decompress, and install each segment.

5.4 Manifest and Bootloader Integration

HASAC uses a signed manifest to bind firmware metadata to the update. The manifest specifies the firmware version, segment size, selected AEAD scheme, and a cryptographic hash of the complete firmware image. The manifest is authenticated using a public key provisioned on the device at manufacture time.

Upon receiving the manifest, the device verifies its signature and version constraints before entering the update phase. Each segment is authenticated individually using AEAD, decompressed if required, and written to a staging region in flash. After all segments are installed, the device verifies the hash of the reconstructed image against the manifest before activating the update.

This design ensures integrity and authenticity at both segment and image granularity while allowing HASAC to adapt cryptography and compression without weakening security guarantees. Compression is always applied before encryption to avoid information leakage through the ciphertext structure.

6 Implementation

We implement HASAC on Zephyr OS v4.0.99 using nRF Connect SDK. The prototype targets an nRF5340DK using a Cortex-M33 microcontroller and interfaces with an external NB-IoT modem over UART. The implementation focuses on the device-side update pipeline and on collecting precise timing and energy measurements required to instantiate the HASAC decision logic and energy model.

6.1 Cryptographic Back Ends

HASAC supports two authenticated encryption back ends that are selected at runtime based on hardware capabilities. On platforms equipped with a hardware security module, AES-128-CCM is executed through the PSA Crypto API and is transparently offloaded to the Arm CryptoCell present on the nRF5340. On platforms without hardware acceleration, we use a software-optimised ChaCha20-Poly1305 implementation from the same cryptographic stack to ensure comparable integration and avoid hand-tuned assembly.

All benchmarks explicitly include nonce handling, authentication tag generation and verification, and buffer management. Key import is performed once

Table 1. Measured cryptographic and decompression costs on a Cortex-M33 for a 1 kB payload. Results are averaged over 100 iterations.

Operation	Time (ms)	Energy (μJ)	CPU cycles	Throughput (kB/s)
Software AES-128-CCM	9.64	289.1	616,700	103.8
Software ChaCha20-Poly1305	1.59	47.7	101,700	629.1
Hardware AES-128-CCM	0.36	10.8	23,100	2,770.0
LZ4 decompression	0.02	0.7	1,445	44,280.0

per update session and is therefore excluded from per-segment measurements. Each benchmark encrypts or decrypts a 1024-byte payload for 100 iterations to amortise measurement noise.

As shown in Table 1, the measured results for a single 1024-byte segment at an assumed active power of 30 mW are as follows. Software AES-128-CCM requires approximately 9.6 ms and consumes 289 μJ. Software ChaCha20-Poly1305 completes in 1.6 ms at 48 μJ. Hardware-accelerated AES-128-CCM completes in 0.36 ms and consumes approximately 11 μJ. These results confirm that, once hardware acceleration is available, cryptographic processing contributes a negligible fraction of the total update energy.

6.2 Segment Format and Update Pipeline

HASAC processes firmware images as fixed-size segments of 1024 bytes aligned to the flash programming granularity of the target device. Each segment is independently authenticated and optionally compressed.

On the server side, compression is applied first, followed by authenticated encryption. For a segment S_i with optional compressed form C_i, the transmitted payload is

$$\text{payload}_i = \begin{cases} \text{AEAD.Enc}(K, \text{nonce}_i, C_i, \text{aad}_i) & \text{if compressed,} \\ \text{AEAD.Enc}(K, \text{nonce}_i, S_i, \text{aad}_i) & \text{otherwise.} \end{cases}$$

The associated data aad_i binds the segment index, firmware version, compression flag, and expected uncompressed length.

On the device, each segment is first authenticated and decrypted. Decompression is applied only if indicated by the compression flag. The resulting plaintext is written to a staging region in flash. An end-to-end image hash included in the manifest detects missing, reordered, or replayed segments.

6.3 Measured Timing and Energy Parameters

We measure per-segment timing for three phases using GPIO instrumentation and a logic analyser (Nordic Power Profiler Kit II). For a 1024-byte segment under moderate coverage conditions, the measured mean timings are: NB-IoT reception approximately 1150 ms, UART transfer approximately 850 ms, and microcontroller processing, including cryptography and flash programming, approximately 85 ms. The energy costs correspond to approximately 34.5 mJ for radio reception, 25.5 mJ for UART transfer, and 2.6 mJ for processing.

LZ4 decompression of a 1024-byte segment requires approximately 0.022 ms and consumes less than 1 μJ. This cost is orders of magnitude smaller than the communication energy and motivates selective compression in deep coverage scenarios.

6.4 Break-Even Compression Rule

HASAC applies compression only when the energy saved by transmitting fewer bytes exceeds the energy required for decompression. Let b be the uncompressed segment size and c the compressed size. Compression is beneficial when

$$\Delta E(b, c) = (b - c) \cdot e_{\text{comm}} - b \cdot e_{\text{decomp}} > 0,$$

where e_{comm} is the communication energy per byte and e_{decomp} is the decompression energy per byte.

The value of e_{comm} is derived from measured radio and UART costs and increases with NB-IoT coverage enhancement due to repetition. Since e_{decomp} remains constant, HASAC naturally becomes more aggressive in poor coverage conditions and conservative in good coverage. This rule directly instantiates the link-aware compression policy used in the evaluation.

7 Evaluation

This section compares a conventional secure firmware OTA baseline against HASAC for a 128 kB firmware image segmented into 1 kB blocks ($b = 1024$ bytes, $N = 128$). We use the measured per-segment timings from Sect. 4 and the constant active power of $P_{\text{active}} = 30$ mW. We report results for three NB-IoT coverage enhancement settings, modelled via a radio repetition factor $r \in \{1, 16, 128\}$ to represent CE0, CE1, and CE2.

7.1 Energy Model Instantiation

For a segment of size x bytes, we model the time as

$$t(x; r) = r \cdot t_{\text{radio}} \cdot \frac{x}{b} + t_{\text{UART}} \cdot \frac{x}{b} + t_{\text{proc}}(x), \tag{11}$$

and the corresponding energy as $E(x; r) = P_{\text{active}} \cdot t(x; r)$. We then sum over all segments. We anchor the communication timings to the measured 1 kB segment profile:

$$t_{\text{radio}} = 1.150 \text{ s}, \quad t_{\text{UART}} = 0.850 \text{ s}, \quad t_{\text{proc,meas}} = 0.085 \text{ s}.$$

To incorporate the cryptographic and decompression microbenchmarks without double-counting, we split processing as

$$t_{\text{proc}}(x) = t_{\text{other}} + t_{\text{crypto}}(x) + t_{\text{decomp}}(x), \tag{12}$$

where $t_{\text{other}} = t_{\text{proc,meas}} - t_{\text{AES-CCM,SW}}$ captures flash programming and non cryptographic logic.

7.2 Baselines

We consider a baseline that reflects common practice in constrained deployments: no compression, uniform authenticated encryption per segment, and no explicit adaptation to the radio conditions. Concretely, the baseline uses software AES-128-CCM and transmits all segments uncompressed.

Under this baseline, the total energy for a 128 kB update is:

$$E_{\text{base}}(r) = N \cdot P_{\text{active}} \cdot \Big(r \cdot t_{\text{radio}} + t_{\text{UART}} + t_{\text{other}} + t_{\text{AES-CCM,SW}}\Big). \tag{13}$$

7.3 HASAC Configurations

HASAC adds two adaptation points. First, it selects a cryptographic back end based on whether the platform exposes a hardware security module. Second, it applies selective compression to reduce transferred bytes when it is energetically beneficial. To keep the evaluation fully specified, we instantiate the byte reduction achieved by HASAC as a coverage-dependent mean reduction in transferred bytes:

$$\gamma_{\text{CE0}} = 0.10, \quad \gamma_{\text{CE1}} = 0.20, \quad \gamma_{\text{CE2}} = 0.30,$$

meaning that the average transmitted segment size becomes $x = (1-\gamma) \cdot b$. With compression ratio γ, the HASAC energy for a device with a hardware security module is:

$$\begin{aligned} E_{\text{HASAC,HSM}}(r,\gamma) = N \cdot P_{\text{active}} \cdot \Big(& r \cdot t_{\text{radio}} \cdot (1-\gamma) + t_{\text{UART}} \cdot (1-\gamma) \\ & + t_{\text{other}} + t_{\text{AES-CCM,HW}} + t_{\text{LZ4,decomp}}\Big). \end{aligned} \tag{14}$$

For a device without a hardware security module, the $t_{\text{AES-CCM,HW}}$ gets replaced by $t_{\text{ChaCha20-Poly1305,SW}}$.

7.4 Results and Discussion

Table 2 summarises the modelled total energy for a 128 kB secure firmware update under three NB-IoT coverage enhancement levels. We compare a conventional baseline with HASAC configured both with and without a hardware security module. Two key observations emerge.

First, the dominant energy savings achieved by HASAC stem from reducing the number of bytes transmitted over the radio link. These savings increase

Table 2. Modelled total energy for a 128 kB secure firmware update. CE0, CE1, and CE2 are represented by repetition factors $r \in \{1, 16, 128\}$. HASAC uses mean byte reductions $\gamma_{CE0} = 0.10$, $\gamma_{CE1} = 0.20$, and $\gamma_{CE2} = 0.30$.

Coverage	Baseline (J)	HASAC (HSM) (J)	HASAC (No HSM) (J)	Savings (HSM No HSM) (%/%)
CE0 ($r = 1$)	8.006	7.203	7.207	10.04/9.98
CE1 ($r = 16$)	74.246	59.425	59.430	19.96/19.95
CE2 ($r = 128$)	568.838	398.265	398.270	29.99/29.99

monotonically with coverage enhancement. In CE0, where repetition is minimal and communication is comparatively cheap, HASAC yields a modest reduction of approximately 10%. In CE2, where each transmitted byte is multiplied by a large repetition factor, HASAC reduces the total update energy by roughly 30%. This confirms that under NB-IoT conditions, optimisation of transferred bytes has a far greater impact than optimisation of local computation.

Second, the difference between HASAC with and without a hardware security module is negligible in the full FOTA energy budget. Although hardware-accelerated cryptography substantially reduces the local cryptographic cost per segment, this reduction is dominated by the radio and UART contributions. As a result, the total energy consumed by HASAC with hardware support differs by less than 1% from HASAC without hardware support across all coverage levels. This behaviour is consistent with the microbenchmarks reported earlier and demonstrates that cryptographic computation, whether accelerated or not, is not the limiting factor in secure firmware updates.

These results have two important implications. First, they explain why HASAC configurations with and without a hardware security module converge to nearly identical system-level energy consumption. The cryptographic back end influences CPU time but does not materially affect the dominant communication costs. Second, they justify HASAC's design choice to treat communication as the primary optimisation target and cryptography as a secondary, hardware-dependent concern. Overall, the evaluation confirms the central message of this paper. For secure firmware updates over NB-IoT, energy efficiency is primarily determined by radio and interconnect behaviour rather than cryptographic computation. Effective update mechanisms must therefore prioritise adaptive byte reduction and link-aware policies over micro-optimisations of crypto-primitives.

8 Conclusion

This paper presents HASAC, an energy-adaptive framework for secure firmware updates in Critical Infrastructure IoT deployments operating over NB-IoT. Through implementation measurements on a Cortex-M33 platform and a calibrated energy model, we demonstrated that the dominant cost of secure updates stems from communication and interconnect overhead, rather than cryptographic computation. Even when hardware security modules are unavailable, the differences between cryptographic back ends are small within the full FOTA energy budget. HASAC exploits this observation by adapting cryptography to device capabilities and applying selective, link-aware compression to reduce transmitted bytes only when it is energetically beneficial. Model-based evaluation demonstrates that this approach yields modest savings in good coverage and substantial reductions, up to around 30%, in deep coverage conditions typical of critical infrastructure deployments. The results suggest that future secure update mechanisms should treat energy as a first-class security constraint and prioritise communication efficiency over micro-optimisations of cryptographic primitives. HASAC provides a practical blueprint for doing so without weakening security guarantees.

Acknowledgments. This work was supported in part by the Flemish Government through the Cybersecurity Research Program with grant number VOEWICS02, and by the European Union's Horizon Research and Innovation program under grant agreement No. 101119747 (TELEMETRY).

References

1. Asokan, N., Nyman, T., Rattanavipanon, N., Sadeghi, A.R., Tsudik, G.: ASSURED: architecture for secure software update of realistic embedded devices. IEEE Trans. Comput. Aided Des. Integr. Circuits Syst. **37**(11), 2290–2300 (2018)
2. Doddapaneni, K., Lakkundi, R., Rao, S., Kulkarni, S.G., Bhat, B.: Secure FoTA object for IoT. In: 2017 IEEE 42nd Conference on Local Computer Networks Workshops (LCN Workshops) (2017)
3. Dworkin, M.: Recommendation for Block Cipher Modes of Operation: The CCM Mode for Authentication and Confidentiality. NIST Special Publication 800-38C (2004)
4. El Jaouhari, S., Bouvet, E.: Secure firmware over-the-air updates for IoT: survey, challenges, and discussions. Internet Things **18**, 100508 (2022)
5. Kolehmainen, A.: Secure firmware updates for IoT: a survey. In: 2018 IEEE International Conference on Internet of Things (iThings) and IEEE Green Computing and Communications (GreenCom) and IEEE Cyber, Physical and Social Computing (CPSCom) and IEEE Smart Data (SmartData) (2018)
6. Langiu, A., Boano, C.A., Schuß, M., Römer, K.: UpKit: an open-source, portable, and lightweight update framework for constrained IoT devices. In: IEEE 39th International Conference on Distributed Computing Systems (ICDCS) (2019)
7. lZ4: Lz4 compression algorithm. https://lz4.github.io/lz4/
8. Moran, B., Tschofenig, H., Birkholz, H.: A Manifest Information Model for Firmware Updates in Internet of Things (IoT) Devices. RFC 9124 (2022)
9. Moran, B., Tschofenig, H., Brown, D., Meriac, M.: A Firmware Update Architecture for Internet of Things. RFC 9019 (2021)
10. Nir, Y., Langley, A.: ChaCha20 and Poly1305 for IETF Protocols (2018)
11. Tacchella, A., Beozzo, E., Crispo, B., Roveri, M.: Certified secure updates for IoT devices. In: ICT Systems Security and Privacy Protection (IFIP SEC 2025) (2025)

Systematic Integration of Digital Twins and Constrained LLMs for Interpretable Cyber-Physical Anomaly Detection

Konstantinos E. Kampourakis(✉), Vasileios Gkioulos, and Sokratis Katsikas

Norwegian University of Science and Technology (NTNU), 2802 Gjøvik, Norway
{konstantinos.kampourakis,vasileios.gkioulos, sokratis.katsikas}@ntnu.no

Abstract. Cyber attacks targeting Industrial Control Systems (ICS) have become increasingly sophisticated and hard to identify. Detecting such attacks requires integrating low-level behavioral cues with high-level semantic interpretation, a capability that traditional anomaly detectors lack. This paper presents a Digital Twin (DT)-driven hybrid detection approach that combines deterministic heuristics with systematic, constrained Large Language Model (LLM) reasoning to achieve real-time incident detection. The DT maintains a synchronized, feature-enriched representation of the Secure Water Treatment (SWaT) process, deriving behavioral descriptors. Heuristics identify characteristic signatures of spoofing, valve forcing, denial-of-service, and bias drift, while the LLM is invoked only when heuristics abstain. A constrained JSON schema and semantic plausibility filters ensure physically consistent LLM outputs, and a temporal smoothing layer stabilizes the final decision signal. Evaluation on four canonical SWaT attack scenarios shows that the proposed detector precisely localizes each attack interval with low time-to-detect and zero False Positives (FPs) in the evaluated benign region. Results are consistent across both a local LLaMA model and a cloud-based GPT model, demonstrating the robustness of the constrained hybrid architecture. The findings highlight the potential of DT-guided LLM reasoning as a reliable and interpretable approach to ICS anomaly detection.

Keywords: Digital Twin · ICS Security · LLM · SWaT

1 Introduction

Industrial Control Systems (ICS) operate critical infrastructure such as water treatment, power distribution, and oil and gas pipelines. Increasing connectivity has expanded the attack surface, enabling cyber–physical disruptions that directly impact process state and safety. Detecting these attacks in real-time is challenging, since physical process deviations can resemble normal operational variance, control actions are highly coupled (meaning a legitimate change in one

© IFIP International Federation for Information Processing 2026
Published by Springer Nature Switzerland AG 2026
H. Janicke et al. (Eds.): SEC 2026, IFIP AICT 787, pp. 199–212, 2026.
https://doi.org/10.1007/978-3-032-27993-4_14

variable requires corresponding changes in many others, easily obscuring malicious input), and anomaly detectors rarely explain why a window is suspicious. This problem motivates more advanced detection systems that combine process awareness, temporal stability, and constrained semantic reasoning.

Digital Twins (DTs) offer a promising solution to this problem. They maintain a synchronized virtual representation of physical processes to support monitoring and diagnostics. Nevertheless, most existing approaches rely on physics-based simulation or narrowly tailored anomaly detection models that lack semantic interpretability and robust decision-making [6]. Moreover, Large Language Models (LLMs) offer capabilities for interpreting process behavior semantically and explaining potential consequences. Yet, unconstrained LLMs introduce risks of hallucinations, physically implausible conclusions, and unstable decision boundaries [4]. Recent work has shown the importance of constraining LLM output with structured domain knowledge, highlighting a path forward, but a systematic integration of LLM reasoning within a DT framework for ICS security has not yet been demonstrated.

This work addresses this gap by introducing a DT-driven hybrid detector that systematically combines deterministic heuristics with structured LLM reasoning to achieve real-time cyber–physical incident detection. The DT maintains a continuously synchronized representation of the Secure Water Treatment (SWaT) process, derives behavioral features such as slopes, variances, ranges, and actuator toggling patterns, and invokes LLM-based analysis only when lightweight heuristics abstain from producing a decision. The LLM is constrained through a strict JSON schema and additional semantic filters that ensure the physical plausibility of predicted tactics and attack paths. A temporal smoothing layer further stabilizes the final decision signal, reducing short-lived fluctuations while preserving responsiveness.

Our evaluation demonstrates that the proposed detector achieves near-perfect localization of four canonical SWaT attack scenarios, while maintaining low false positive (FP) rates across extended benign periods. The system detects all attacks with consistent Time-To-Detect (TTD) characteristics and exhibits stable behavior across both a local LLaMA-3.1 model and a cloud-based GPT-4.1-mini model. In contrast, a standard Isolation Forest (IF) baseline fails to detect several scenarios and produces inconsistent alarms.

The main contributions of this work are summarized as follows:

- A DT–driven detection architecture that maintains a synchronized, window-based behavioral replica of an industrial process for cyber–physical monitoring.
- A process-aware heuristic layer that captures ICS Indicators of Compromise (IoC) and selectively gates LLM invocation to reduce FPs.
- A constrained LLM reasoning module integrated into the DT workflow to provide interpretable attack classification under strict schema and plausibility checks.

– An evaluation on the SWaT dataset demonstrating precise attack localization, low TTD, and stable behavior across both local and cloud-based LLM backends.

The remainder of this paper is organized as follows. The next section surveys related work on LLM-based detection. Section 3 presents the DT architecture used in our system. Section 4 describes the hybrid detection methodology. Section 5 outlines the experimental setup, and Sect. 6 reports the detection results. Section 7 provides a technical discussion of the findings. Finally, Sect. 8 concludes the paper.

2 Related Work

In this section, we elaborate on the related work on LLM detection in ICS, concentrating on recently published works. We explicitly focus on experimental publications rather than theoretical ones.

The authors in [7] propose a specialized Retrieval-Augmented Generation (RAG) pipeline designed specifically for cybersecurity question answering. The system integrates two cascaded and complementary RAG modules. That is, a fast structured RAG with seven parallel retrievers and a fallback unstructured RAG, enabling broad coverage over both structured sources and unstructured text. The authors evaluate MoRSE on 600 cybersecurity questions, each validated by domain experts, and show that it consistently outperforms GPT-4, Gemini, Mixtral, and HackerGPT in relevance, similarity, correctness, and accuracy. Particularly, MoRSE achieves 84% accuracy on CVE questions, versus 34% for GPT-4, and leads all models in Elo-based comparisons using GPT-4 as a judge.

The work in [3] introduces PLLM-CS, a transformer-based intrusion detection system (IDS) specifically targeting satellite communication networks. The authors address the lack of effective IDS solutions for satellite systems, which face high operational complexity, sparse connectivity, and increasing vulnerability to DoS/DDoS-style cyber threats. PLLM-CS adapts transformer self-attention to model sequential network dynamics by converting multivariate telemetry into token sequences ("sentencing"), enabling long-range contextual reasoning over satellite-like traffic patterns. The model is evaluated on UNSW-NB15 and TON_IoT datasets, and achieves 100% accuracy across all metrics, outperforming both machine learning and deep learning baselines.

In [2], the authors propose a comprehensive multi-layered security architecture designed to reduce hallucinations, prevent prompt-injection attacks, and enhance privacy protections for secure and reliable LLM deployments. The system combines an injection-detection pipeline based on fine-tuned transformer classifiers, a Kernel module for semantic preprocessing and entity extraction, a VectorDB for secure vectorized retrieval, and a RAG layer to ensure context-bounded responses. A cross-LLM validation mechanism computes an eligibility score along dimensions such as toxicity, banned-topic violations, sensitivity, and sentiment. Experimental results across several LLM families show that the system consistently removes injected content, filters unsafe or manipulative prompts, and blocks semantically unsafe translations or harmful queries.

The contribution in [8] proposes a generative-AI-based cybersecurity framework for electric vehicle cyber-physical systems, where traditional IDS approaches struggle to detect novel or zero-day attacks. The authors develop a fine-tuned LLM, based on a distilled GPT-2-like architecture, and integrate it into an EV monitoring pipeline that analyzes CAN bus traffic, sensor data, and charging-protocol messages. The system performs both anomaly detection and generative threat simulation, using prompt engineering to synthesize realistic zero-day attack patterns. Evaluation across real datasets and synthetic zero-day scenarios shows high accuracy (>98%), low false-positive rates, and low inference latency suitable for real-time EV operation.

The authors in [1] propose a LLM–driven framework for detecting multi-stage cyber attacks by aggregating and correlating heterogeneous security alerts. Instead of relying on fixed correlation rules or predefined attack graphs, the system uses carefully engineered prompts, combining chain-of-thought reasoning, domain knowledge, and strict output formatting, to guide the LLM through two key tasks: (i) alert aggregation into coherent hyper-alerts, and (ii) alert correlation into sequential attack stages. A validation mechanism ensures that all alerts are assigned to exactly one hyper-alert and resolves any duplicates or misses via a systematic, iterative LLM refinement. The authors show that MAD-LLM outperforms classical multi-stage detection methods such as GAC and MAAC in precision, recall, and attack-stage recovery, even when critical stages have only one or two alerts.

The study in [5] introduces a specialized framework for enhancing strategic cybersecurity reasoning in LLMs by mapping CVEs and CTI narratives to MITRE ATT&CK techniques using a novel, structured, retrieval-aware training pipeline. The authors construct a large synthetic dataset by aligning CVE and CTI descriptions with ATT&CK tactics, validated by human experts, and train models using their methods to integrate retrieved ATT&CK knowledge directly into the reasoning process. The paper also introduces a domain-fine-tuned embedding model that improves ATT&CK-technique retrieval accuracy. Experimental results demonstrate significant improvements in AST-based structural accuracy and a reduction in spurious ATT&CK predictions compared with standard LLaMA-2, Mistral, and GPT-3.5 baselines.

3 DT Architecture

The DT in our system acts as a continuously synchronized virtual replica of the SWaT process. In this work, the DT is explicitly implemented as a replay-based architecture, realized through a custom HTTP service that reconstructs synchronized plant state windows and derived behavioral features from recorded telemetry.

At the core of the DT is the replay engine, which provides a coherent, time-indexed view of the system by exposing a 30-s sliding window of telemetry through a lightweight HTTP interface. All time windows have synchronized values for every process variable of interest, enabling the virtual replica to evolve in parallel with the corresponding physical process.

Building on the replay layer, the DT incorporates a behavioral extraction model that computes derivatives, slopes, variances, ranges, and actuator toggling statistics from each window. These descriptors form an interpretable representation of the system's short-term behavior and are engineered to highlight deviations from normal operation. They are used both by the heuristic detector and the LLM-based reasoning module. In effect, the DT does not simply store raw telemetry but instead maintains an enriched, process-aware view of plant dynamics.

The architecture further integrates a semantic reasoning layer built around the LLM. When heuristics abstain, the DT promotes the enriched, process-aware window features to the LLM, which interprets the observed behavior within an ICS threat schema. The reasoning engine assesses tactic–technique alignment, evaluates physically plausible attack paths, and proposes corresponding mitigations. The DT therefore supports higher-order semantic interpretation that goes beyond thresholding or statistical anomaly detection.

Finally, the DT includes a temporal decision layer, which mitigates short-term variability. The DT applies a smoothing policy across subsequent time windows such that the final decision and indicators reflect systematic deviations from normal rather than random noise. This renders dependable indicators of an incident while supporting time-sensitive decision making.

Figure 1 illustrates the overall DT architecture used in this work. The system begins with a replay server that streams a synchronized 30-s window of SWaT telemetry at each time step, providing a virtualized DT state aligned with the physical process. This window is enriched with behavioral descriptors, such as slopes, variances, freeze ratios, and actuator toggles, that form the DT's interpretable feature-level representation of process dynamics. The hybrid detector then evaluates each window: deterministic process-aware heuristics first attempt to classify the behavior. If no clear pattern matches, the window is forwarded to the LLM reasoning module for schema-constrained semantic analysis. Both heuristic results and LLM outputs are merged through a temporal smoothing mechanism, which stabilizes fluctuations and produces the final, dependable attack decision signal.

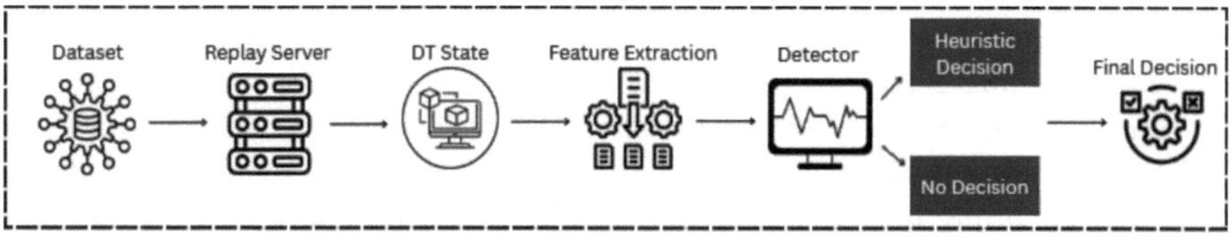

Fig. 1. Overview of the DT-driven detection architecture.

4 Methodology

In this section, we detail the design of our DT-driven hybrid detection pipeline. The system mirrors the live state of an industrial process, derives behavioral features, applies domain-specific heuristics, and invokes an LLM-based reasoning engine only when heuristics abstain from a decision. The methodology is structured around five interacting layers: (i) the replay and synchronization engine, (ii) the feature extraction module, (iii) the heuristic detector, (iv) the LLM reasoning agent, and (v) the temporal smoothing module.

- ***Replay server and temporal windowing:*** The DT keeps an up-to-date, synchronized view of the plant state while continuously replaying sensor and actuator values sourced from the SWaT dataset. A lightweight HTTP server facilitates access to a state endpoint, which returns a 30-s sliding window at a given index. Each window contains aligned multivariate time series that correspond to sensors (e.g., LIT101, FIT101, AIT402) and actuators (e.g., MV101, P101), ensuring that the virtual process replica advances in synchrony with the underlying physical process. This mechanism acts as the DT's state-synchronization layer and is queried by the orchestrator at every step.
- ***Behavioral feature and derivative extraction:*** For each window, the orchestrator computes a set of behavioral descriptors that capture short-term dynamics of the process. Specifically, these include, first-order slopes of key sensors, say $\Delta x_i(t)$, rolling standard deviations, amplitude ranges, flatness and freeze ratios, and actuator toggle counts. These features serve two purposes: (i) they enable efficient lightweight heuristics for common ICS attack patterns, and (ii) they provide a richer behavioral context for the LLM when heuristics abstain. The feature-extraction layer, therefore, forms the DT's behavioral model, a virtualization of system dynamics beyond raw telemetry.
- ***Heuristic detector:*** Cyber–physical attacks often leave distinctive short-term behavioral signatures that can be identified without relying on high-level semantic reasoning. To exploit this, the DT incorporates a deterministic heuristic module that targets four characteristic patterns. In particular, spoofing is identified through sustained positive trends in LIT101 during pump or valve activity, captured by consistent slope–range behavior and adequate historical variance, which serves as an IoC for manipulated inflow. Valve Forcing manifests as rapid MV101 toggling accompanied by abnormal oscillatory patterns in FIT101 or LIT301. Bias Drift appears as low-variance but gradually diverging sensor readings, where the slope-to-standard-deviation ratio serves as a reliable IoC. Sensor-Freezing DoS is detected through multi-sensor flatness, suppressed variance, and elevated freeze ratios over extended windows. When any heuristic matches its associated IoC pattern with sufficient confidence, the detector produces a structured attack classification without invoking the LLM.
- ***LLM reasoning engine:*** If heuristics abstain, the orchestrator composes a structured prompt describing the window's telemetry, behavioral features,

actuator states, and contextual history. The LLM is required to output a JSON object conforming to a strict schema containing: (i) a high-level ICS tactic and technique, (ii) a ranked list of hypothesized attack paths, (iii) suggested mitigations, and (iv) a confidence score. A schema validator enforces structural correctness and rejects insufficiently structured or hallucinated outputs. A post-filter then checks for semantic correctness, determining whether the stated tactics are physically possible given the state of the actuators observed during the test.

- ***Fusion and temporal smoothing:*** LLM predictions and heuristic detections are fused into a binary attack indicator. To reduce jitter and short-lived fluctuations, we apply a temporal smoothing rule that requires short-term majority agreement within a sliding decision window, typically set to N time steps. This smoothing layer forms the DT's "diagnostic stabilizer", and ensures that detection decisions reflect persistent behavioral deviations rather than noise.
- ***DT operational loop:*** The complete DT loop functions as follows: it first aligns the virtual plant state using the replay server; then derives behavioral features from each time window; applies heuristic rules to detect pattern-specific anomalies; triggers LLM-based reasoning only when no heuristic decision is made; then validates, filters, and smooths the resulting predictions; and finally emits structured incident metadata for downstream analysis. The architecture in Fig. 1 enables a real-time, semantically informed DT that can detect cyber-physical incidents with low false-positive rates and stable detection latencies across a wide range of attack scenarios.

In summary, Table 1, shows that the DT-driven hybrid detector applies deterministic heuristics, with each rule examining a distinct class of attack behavior commonly seen in SWaT. These heuristics are based on values that represent derived features in the application of slopes, variance metrics, actuation toggling patterns, and freeze ratios detected in the synchronized 30-s DT time frame. Specifically, sustained positive trends identified in LIT101 while flow components are active signal spoofing; rapid toggling of MV101 with oscillatory flow or level sensor activity captures valve forcing attacks; a low variance but steadily growing positive trend with a unique slope to standard deviation ratio is indicative of bias drift, and, the multi-channel flatness along with muted variance characterizes freezing DoS attacks due to a sensor being frozen. These rules enable rapid, interpretable, and physics-based attacks to be identified, without calling forth the LLM reasoning module, unless the behavior is ambiguous or falls outside the identified patterns.

5 Experimental Setup

The experimental evaluation assesses the effectiveness and stability of the proposed DT detector across four canonical cyber–physical attack scenarios in the SWaT testbed, which contains 449,920 time-stamped records of process telemetry and a binary attack label. Among these, 54,584 rows ($\approx 12,1\%$) are labelled

Table 1. Summary of heuristic rules used in the DT-driven detector.

Attack Type	Signals	Heuristic Conditions
Spoofing	LIT101, FIT101, MV101, P101	Sustained positive slope in LIT101 under pump/valve activity; slope–range consistency; sufficient historical variance (history ≥ 40).
Valve Forcing	MV101, FIT101, LIT301	Rapid actuator toggling (MV101 toggles ≥ 1); oscillatory behavior in FIT101 or LIT301 (range > 0.03); history ≥ 40.
Bias Drift	LIT101	Gradually increasing or drifting trend with low variance; slope $> \max(0.004, 1.2 \cdot \text{std})$; standard deviation within $[0.005, 0.06]$; flatness ratio < 0.90; history ≥ 70.
Sensor-Freezing DoS	LIT101, FIT101, AIT402	Multi-channel flatness; near-zero variance; high freeze ratios; persistent flat behavior over long windows (history ≥ 80).

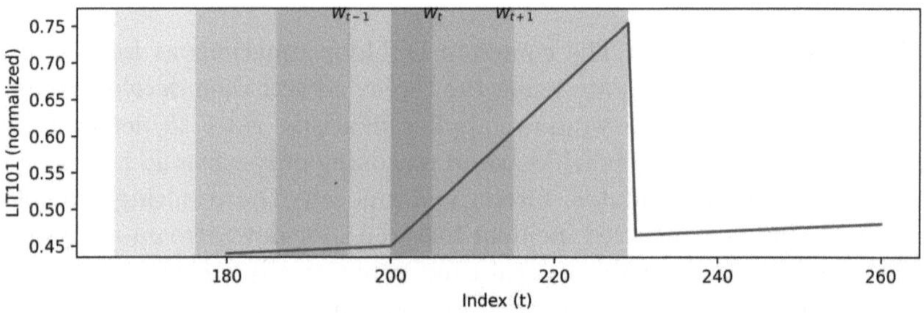

Fig. 2. Example of the DT replay windowing over SWaT-like telemetry.

as attack and 395,336 rows ($\approx 87,9\%$) as benign, reflecting a realistically imbalanced ICS operating regime. All experiments are conducted using the publicly available dataset, which contains normal operation interspersed with ground-truth attack intervals. The DT operates on a 30-s sliding window and processes the dataset sequentially from index 0 to 1400, mirroring real-time conditions in which decisions must be made without access to future information. The 0–1,400 region contains the four injected scenarios considered in this study; later attack-labelled segments are out of scope for our detection coverage and are reserved for a 10k stability check. It is worth noting that the full 449k-sample SWaT dataset was not exhaustively replayed because the runtime bottleneck lies in evaluation time instrumentation, derivative logging, overlapping-window extraction, and schema validation, not in the detector itself. The hybrid model operates in a streaming, constant-cost manner and scales to arbitrarily long traces. Our extended 10k-window run confirms stable long-horizon behavior, indicating that scalability is not a limiting factor for deployment.

Figure 2 shows the LIT101 level around the spoof interval (200–229), with the ground-truth attack region shaded. The three semi-transparent boxes illustrate consecutive 30-s DT windows (W_{t-1}, W_t, W_{t+1}) used for derivative computation, heuristic evaluation, and optional LLM reasoning.

The target attack scenarios include sensor spoofing (indices 200–229), valve-forcing (500–539), a sensor-freezing DoS attack (900–949), and a slow bias-drift manipulation of LIT101 (1200–1279). These scenarios span distinct physical mechanisms and behavioral signatures, making them appropriate for evaluating both the heuristic and LLM components of the detector. For each scenario, we measure (i) whether the system raises an alarm during the attack interval, (ii) the TTD, defined as the number of indices from attack onset to the first stabilized alarm, and (iii) the presence or absence of false alarms during benign periods.

Two LLM configurations are evaluated. The first uses a local deployment of LLaMA 3.1 8B running through a standard OpenAI-compatible inference server. The second uses the cloud-hosted GPT–4.1–mini model via the OpenAI API. Both models are invoked only when heuristics abstain. To ensure comparability, all system prompts, schema constraints, and semantic filters are identical across models, and the DT pipeline is executed end-to-end for both configurations.

For baseline comparison, we evaluate a standard Isolation Forest (IF) anomaly detector trained on the first 1,000 indices of benign data and applied to 15-s sliding windows. The IF baseline represents a commonly used unsupervised anomaly detection approach in ICS literature, but does not produce semantic explanations. IF is used as the baseline because it is a widely adopted, lightweight unsupervised anomaly detector in ICS security settings where labeled attack data and process models are unavailable. It relies purely on statistical deviation and does not capture temporal structure, actuator–sensor coupling, or semantic attack intent. As such, it provides a representative contrast to the proposed DT-driven hybrid detector, whose contribution lies in integrating process awareness, temporal stabilization, and constrained semantic reasoning rather than in competing with deep learning–based IDS approaches.

All detectors output structured JSON traces containing per-window predictions, confidence values, and smoothed binary decisions. Final evaluation is performed using a standardized post-processing script that aligns predictions with the ground-truth intervals via time-step indexing. The DT-driven hybrid detector is evaluated for both overall accuracy and temporal precision, with particular emphasis on whether alarms are confined to the correct attack windows without significant spillover into surrounding benign periods.

6 Results

This section evaluates the performance of the proposed DT-driven hybrid detector across the four SWaT attack scenarios. We report detection success (binary), TTD, and FP behavior, and compare the two LLM configurations we used, LLaMA 3.1 8B and GPT–4.1–mini, to assess the stability of the hybrid reasoning layer. All metrics are computed using the standardized evaluation script described earlier.

Table 2. Detection performance across the four SWaT attack scenarios for both LLM cases.

Scenario	Ground Truth	Detected	TTD (windows)
Spoofing/Inflow	200–229	1	1
Valve Forcing	500–539	1	1
Sensor-Freezing DoS	900–949	1	0
Bias Drift	1200–1279	1	0

Table 3. IF baseline results using 15-s windows.

Scenario	Ground Truth	IF Detected	IF TTD	Notes
Spoofing/Inflow	200–229	0	—	No anomaly spike
Valve Forcing	500–539	0	—	Oscillations missed
Sensor-Freezing DoS	900–949	1	0	High freeze ratio
Bias Drift	1200–1279	0	—	Slow drift undetected

Detection Ranges and Alignment with Ground Truth

Table 2 shows that across all experiments, the DT-driven detector achieves precise localization of the four attack intervals. For both LLM backends, alarms occur strictly within the ground-truth windows for sensor spoofing (200–229), valve forcing (500–539), sensor-freezing DoS (900–949), and bias drift (1200–1279). No spillover is observed into the surrounding benign regions, indicating that the combination of heuristic gating and temporal smoothing effectively prevents unstable early firing.

We also ran the detector on the first 10k rows to check stability over long periods. In that run, the system raised alarms in only two continuous regions (4896–4902 and 7586–7597). We inspected those windows and confirmed they matched real abnormal behavior, not random or incorrect alarms. All other tested ranges that contained only normal process behavior produced no alarms.

Moreover, according to Table 3, the IF baseline does not demonstrate comparable precision. While IF successfully detects the DoS attack, it fails to raise consistent alarms during the spoofing, valve-forcing, and bias-drift intervals, and it produces scattered anomalies outside the ground-truth ranges.

Time-to-Detect

In this case, TTD refers to the number of windows from scenario onset to the first hybrid alarm inside the matched interval.

The hybrid detector yields consistent TTD across scenarios and includes immediate detection of bias drift, reporting a TTD of 0. This indicates that the detector raised alarms on the first queried window falling fully inside the attack interval, without requiring additional history accumulation or semantic

Table 4. FPs across the full 0–1400 index run.

Model	FPs	FP Regions
LLaMA-3.1-8B	0	—
GPT-4.1-mini	0	—
IF	273	scattered

confirmation delays. DoS variance flattening likewise resulted in TTD 0, while spoofing and valve-forcing each triggered within one window from onset.

Both LLM configurations produce nearly identical TTD values. Differences between LLaMA and GPT are within a single window across all scenarios, demonstrating that the LLM is used primarily for semantic confirmation rather than for primary detection.

False Positive Behavior

A key requirement for deploying LLM-based reasoning in operational ICS settings is the minimization of hallucination-driven FPs. Table 4 demonstrates that across the full 1400-index run, neither LLaMA nor GPT produces any false alarms outside the four attack intervals. This is attributable to (i) strict heuristic gating, which suppresses unnecessary LLM invocation, (ii) the constrained JSON schema enforced on LLM output, and (iii) the semantic plausibility filter that removes physically inconsistent threat reports.

By contrast, the IF baseline flags 273 benign windows as anomalous (≈19,5%), particularly in regions of transient sensor variability. These scattered detections do not align with any operational changes or ground-truth events.

Comparison of LLaMA and GPT Backends

The two LLM configurations deliver nearly identical detection behavior despite their architectural differences. Both models produce stable, schema-conforming outputs, and no hallucinated tactics or physically implausible attack paths are observed in the post-filtered predictions.

GPT–4.1–mini shows marginally higher semantic confidence values in its threat reports, while LLaMA demonstrates slightly faster response times when deployed locally. However, these differences do not affect the combined decision signal due to the overriding influence of heuristics and temporal smoothing. This suggests that the DT-driven detector is robust to the choice of LLM backend, provided that schema constraints and gating mechanisms are enforced.

Summary

Overall, the results demonstrate that the proposed DT-driven hybrid detector achieves real-time and high-precision detection across the four SWaT attack scenarios. The method consistently identifies the correct intervals, exhibits low TTD values, and maintains zero FPs in extended benign regions. The stable performance across both local and cloud LLM backends highlights the reliability of the constrained hybrid reasoning architecture.

Additionally, both LLaMA–3.1–8B and GPT–4.1–mini produce identical detection and TTD metrics after temporal smoothing; any model-level differences occur before fusion and are overridden by heuristic gating and temporal smoothing in the fused decision layer.

7 Discussion

The research results highlight several key characteristics of the proposed DT-based hybrid detection method, particularly in terms of stability, interpretability, and operational robustness.

A central outcome of the evaluation is that the hybrid reasoning approach proves to be dependable. The reliance on domain-specific heuristics to handle most detection tasks and only calling the LLM when strictly required means that the hybrid approach yields a more stable system than would be possible with unconstrained LLMs alone. Moreover, the ability to avoid spurious FPs over an extended period of benign activity indicates that, when tailored to a particular ICS process environment, heuristic rules significantly limit the likelihood of hallucination-induced alerts. The LLM supplies semantic reasoning and contextual validation; the LLM itself, however, is not the primary driver of anomaly detection. This division of responsibilities markedly shrinks the system's attack surface while preserving the core benefits of high-level reasoning.

The DT architecture underpins long-term stability in several ways. It maintains a synchronized, feature-rich representation of process behavior over time, enabling both the heuristic layer and the LLM to operate in a controlled environment with a consistently defined temporal window. The DT's behavioral model attenuates short-term fluctuations in process activity, directing the reasoning components toward significant patterns rather than transient noise. Moreover, the temporal smoothing mechanism further dampens the influence of short-lived deviations, ensuring that decisions are driven by data that is persistently or progressively manipulated.

Additionally, the consistency with which LLaMA and GPT operate as model classes is another key observation: despite differences in their training processes, such as model size, training corpora, or deployment configuration, both behave similarly when used as LLM components within a DT framework. This suggests that the overall system behavior is driven more by the governing constraints, namely, heuristics, schema validators, and semantic filters, than by the specific architectural features that differentiate individual LLMs. Operationally, this benefits organizations, as they can flexibly choose between locally hosted and cloud-based LLMs based on factors like available resources, latency constraints, or cost, without significantly affecting detection fidelity.

The outcomes are promising, but they also underline the substantial complexity involved in identifying certain categories of cyber–physical attacks. One such example is bias drift, which manifests as a gradual, abnormal trend over time and therefore must be detected by examining temporal patterns and historical context. The hybrid detection process can capture these relationships through merging feature-based methods with semantic reasoning, yet its overall accuracy depends heavily on meticulous tuning of decision thresholds and temporal aggregation windows.

In summary, the results validate the feasibility of integrating DT models, deterministic rule-based heuristics, and structured LLM reasoning into a unified methodology for real-time detection of cyber–physical incidents. Nevertheless, in this study, we tuned detection heuristics on SWaT dynamics and validated only for the 4 injected scenarios. Evaluation on other domains remains future work, and is not claimed in this work.

Despite the promising outcomes, we identify some limitations that guide future research. First, the detection heuristics are meticulously tuned to the SWaT process dynamics, specifically validated against only the four injected attack scenarios. This limits the generalizability of the current rule-set to diverse industrial domains or zero-day attacks. Second, identifying slow-manifesting attacks like bias drift requires precise calibration of temporal aggregation windows and decision thresholds to balance sensitivity against robustness. This highlights the critical trade-off between maximizing sensitivity to subtle manipulation and ensuring robustness against legitimate process fluctuations caused by load changes or operational routines. Third, the current DT relies on a behavioral mirror approach and does not incorporate physics-based modeling; integrating such models could further strengthen semantic correctness and expand the system's ability to detect novel, physically implausible states.

8 Conclusions

In this paper, we describe a DT-based hybrid detection approach that utilizes deterministic heuristics and constrained LLM reasoning to facilitate incident detection within ICS. The DT provides the means for the hybrid detection method to detect both dynamic and semantic characteristics of the process, through real-time synchronization with the SWaT process. The LLM is utilized only where the heuristics abstain from intervention, and a strict output schema is used with checks for semantic plausibility, which allows for the avoidance of hallucination-induced FPs that are present when using unconstrained LLMs.

Our evaluation demonstrates that the proposed method accurately localizes four canonical attack scenarios, sensor spoofing, valve forcing, DoS, and bias drift, with consistent TTD values and no spillover into benign regions. The detector performs reliably across both a locally hosted LLaMA model and a cloud-based GPT model, highlighting the robustness of the overall architecture and the relatively small influence of model-specific variability when strong structural constraints are applied. In contrast, a standard IF baseline fails to provide comparable temporal or semantic precision.

The findings suggest that DT representations enriched with behavioral features, combined with structured LLM reasoning, offer a promising direction for interpretable, resilient cyber–physical monitoring. Future work will explore the integration of physics-based modeling into the DT, extension to larger-scale industrial processes, online adaptation under concept drift, and the use of multi-agent LLM architectures for collaborative situational assessment. These directions aim to further advance the role of DTs as trustworthy components in next-generation ICS security frameworks.

Acknowledgments. This work is supported by the Research Council of Norway through the SFI Norwegian Centre for Cybersecurity in Critical Sectors (NORCICS) project no. 310105.

References

1. Dan, D., et al.: MAD-LLM: a novel approach for alert-based multi-stage attack detection via LLM. In: 2024 IEEE International Symposium on Parallel and Distributed Processing with Applications (ISPA), pp. 2046–2053. IEEE (2024)
2. Gokcimen, T., Das, B.: A novel system for strengthening security in large language models against hallucination and injection attacks with effective strategies. Alex. Eng. J. **123**, 71–90 (2025)
3. Hassanin, M., et al.: PLLM-CS: pre-trained large language model (LLM) for cyber threat detection in satellite networks. Ad Hoc Netw. **166**, 103645 (2025)
4. Huang, L., et al.: A survey on hallucination in large language models: principles, taxonomy, challenges, and open questions. ACM Trans. Inf. Syst. **43**(2), 1–55 (2025)
5. Jin, J., et al.: Crimson: empowering strategic reasoning in cybersecurity through large language models. In: 2024 5th International Conference on Computer, Big Data and Artificial Intelligence (ICCBD+ AI), pp. 18–24. IEEE (2024)
6. Kampourakis, K.E., et al.: Digital twin-enabled incident detection and response: a systematic review of critical infrastructures applications. Int. J. Inf. Secur. **24**(5), 1–42 (2025)
7. Simoni, M., et al.: MoRSE: bridging the gap in cybersecurity expertise with retrieval augmented generation. In: Proceedings of the 40th ACM/SIGAPP Symposium on Applied Computing, pp. 1213–1222 (2025)
8. Tirulo, A., Chauhan, S., Shafie-khah, M.: LLMpowered threat intelligence: proactive detection of zero-day attacks in electric vehicle cyber-physical systems. Sustain. Energy Grids Netw. 101877 (2025)

Cross-Modal Geometric Regularization for Multivariate Cybersecurity Anomaly Detection

Sourav Rai[1,2](✉), Christophe Rodrigues[1], Thomas Czernichow[2], Damien Lescos[2], and Nga Nguyen[1]

[1] De Vinci Higher Education, De Vinci Research Center, Paris, France
[2] SitInCloud, Pau, France
sourav.rai@sitincloud.com

Abstract. Critical infrastructure faces escalating cyberattacks that can cascade from digital compromise to physical disruption, making robust anomaly detection in cyber-physical systems essential. Existing multivariate time-series detectors focus on temporal sensor patterns but rarely incorporate structured priors that could regularize learning and improve generalization.

We introduce **CRAFT**, a cross-modal *time–text* framework that adapts CALF [13] to cybersecurity by combining temporal anomaly detection with cross-modal regularization. CRAFT couples a temporal sensor branch with a textual embedding branch, both built on pre-trained GPT-2 weights, fuses their reconstruction errors through multi-view scoring, and applies a percentile-based adaptive thresholding scheme to obtain anomaly labels. Experiments on SMD, SWaT, and WADI yield F_1-scores of 0.9480, 0.8843, and 0.7634 respectively, outperforming strong baselines.

To understand *why* cross–modal learning helps, we disentangle token–level semantics from embedding geometry across different embedding spaces. We find that embedding geometry, rather than semantics, drives most gains: synthetic embeddings that match only cosine statistics, effective dimensionality, and semantic clustering of a pre–trained space—and even high-dimensional random embeddings—match or surpass the performance of pre-trained semantic embeddings. Effective detection coincides with **uniform, high–entropy attention** over the vocabulary, with the text branch acting as a global geometric regularizer for temporal representations. Finally, we release Owlyshield, a large-scale ransomware behavior dataset derived from 337,100 samples and adjusted to realistic 5% anomaly rates as a challenging benchmark for cybersecurity anomaly detection.

1 Introduction

Industrial Control Systems (ICS) and other cyber–physical infrastructure face an increasingly hostile threat landscape. ENISA's *Threat Landscape 2024* [6] cites

© IFIP International Federation for Information Processing 2026
Published by Springer Nature Switzerland AG 2026
H. Janicke et al. (Eds.): SEC 2026, IFIP AICT 787, pp. 213–227, 2026.
https://doi.org/10.1007/978-3-032-27993-4_15

"attacks against availability"—notably DDoS and ransomware on Operational Technology (OT)—hardware and software that control real–world processes—as a primary risk to critical sectors. IBM X–Force's *2025 Threat Intelligence Index* [8] similarly reports that manufacturing has been the most–targeted industry for four consecutive years, with a large fraction of incidents involving critical–infrastructure operators. In the United States, a joint CISAEPA bulletin [4] warns that hundreds of internet–exposed HMIs in water and wastewater plants could allow adversaries to disrupt essential treatment processes. Verizon's *2025 Data Breach Investigations Report* [23] further underscores the stakes, documenting over 12,000 confirmed breaches, with ransomware and system–intrusion patterns driving a growing share of cases. Any breach of an OT network can quickly cascade into physical disruption, making robust anomaly detection mission–critical.

Detecting early–stage compromise in these environments is difficult. Telemetry is high–dimensional and heterogeneous: a single water–treatment plant (e.g., WADI [2]) can stream more than 100 sensor and actuator channels at sub–minute resolution, with non–stationary behaviour driven by control policies and seasonality. At the same time, labelled anomalies are scarce, since operators often discover attacks only after disruption, making purely supervised learning impractical. As a result, recent work has focused on unsupervised and self-supervised detectors such as OmniAnomaly [20], Zhao et al. [27], and Tu et al. [21].

Pre-trained language models offer powerful representations for time series, but require bridging the gap between discrete tokens and continuous sensor signals. Cross-modal architectures address this by aligning temporal features with text embeddings, using the text embeddings to guide and stabilize learning. Since anomaly detection relies on identifying deviations and risk patterns, and cross-modal methods align temporal signals with semantic representations, one might expect domain-specific embeddings to help most: FinBERT [24] embeds risk-related terms such as "bearish," while SecureBERT [1] covers ICS/OT concepts like "sensor drift" and "pressure surge".

In this work we instead find that performance is driven primarily by *embedding geometry*—moderate cosine similarity, controlled effective dimensionality, and stable norms—rather than token semantics. Generic and synthetic embeddings that match these geometric statistics rival or surpass domain-specific experts. Moreover, cross-modal attention converges to nearly uniform distributions over the vocabulary, indicating that the textual branch acts as a global geometric regularizer rather than a sparse term selector.

Contributions: Our main contributions are:

1. **CRAFT Framework.** We adapt CALF by coupling temporal and textual branches with a gated cross-modal attention mechanism, multi-view reconstruction loss, and percentile-based adaptive thresholding for multivariate ICS time series.
2. **Geometry as the core regularizer.** Through controlled experiments across a spectrum of semantic, random, and synthetic geometry-matched embeddings, we show that performance depends on embedding geometry rather

than token semantics. Attention analysis reveals near-uniform distributions over the vocabulary, confirming that the text branch acts as a global geometric regularizer rather than a sparse term selector.
3. **Benchmark dataset.** We release Owlyshield, a 337,100-sample ransomware behavior dataset from EDR telemetry, along with a segment-based subsampling method that preserves temporal coherence while achieving realistic anomaly rates.

Experiments on SMD [20], SWaT [14], and WADI [2] show that CRAFT surpasses strong baselines on two out of three time series benchmarks and achieves high recall on Owlyshield.

2 Related Work

Deep time-series anomaly detection has evolved from reconstruction and probabilistic models to adversarial, attention-based, and representation learning approaches, particularly in high-dimensional industrial and cyber-physical settings. Reconstruction/probabilistic methods such as OmniAnomaly [20] model normal behaviour and detect anomalies as low-probability or high-reconstruction-error patterns. Generative-adversarial approaches including MAD-GAN (Multivariate Anomaly Detection with Generative Adversarial Networks) [11] and USAD (UnSupervised Anomaly Detection) [3] further strengthen discriminative power by adversarially training generators and discriminators on multivariate sequences, typically assuming access to predominantly clean training data and treating anomalies as deviations from a learned manifold.

Attention and graph-based architectures such as MTAD-GAT (Multivariate Time-series Anomaly Detection via Graph Attention Network) [27] and TranAD (Transformer-based Anomaly Detection) [22] capture complex temporal and inter-feature dependencies, while hybrid timefrequency models like STFT-TCAN (Short-Time Fourier Transform with Temporal Convolutional Attention Network) [21] exploit periodicity and spectral signatures in ICS data. Such models are especially effective when long-range interactions between sensors or control loops play a central role, as is common in water-treatment, power, and manufacturing systems.

Self-supervised representation learning methods, e.g., TS2Vec (Time Series to Vector) [26], decouple feature learning from detection and provide strong transferable embeddings that can be reused across datasets and tasks. For thresholding, prior work has explored both simple heuristics (e.g., fixed or percentile-based rules over training scores) and Extreme-Value-Theory-based Peaks-Over-Threshold (POT) techniques [17] to adapt decision boundaries under non-stationary conditions. In this work we focus on the former, using an adaptive percentile rule over training anomaly scores.

Large language models offer powerful pre-trained representations, but they operate on discrete token sequences—fundamentally mismatched with continuous, high-frequency multivariate sensor data. Recent approaches address this through input patching, reprogramming, or leveraging only the transformer backbone with learned projections [15]. Cross-modal architectures such as CALF [13] take a different route: they align temporal and textual representations, suggesting that language models can regularize time-series forecasting by injecting structured priors from text. Domain-specific LMs including FinBERT [24] and SecureBERT [1] bring financial and ICS/OT terminology into the embedding space, enabling closer alignment with expert language about risk and operational states. However, most anomaly detectors still operate purely on time-series data. We build a cross-modal anomaly detector for cybersecurity and, unlike prior work, systematically study whether the benefit of pre-trained LMs comes from token-level semantics or from the geometry of the embedding space, explicitly disentangling these two factors in our empirical analysis.

3 Methodology

3.1 CRAFT: Cross-Modal Regularization for Anomaly Detection

Building upon the Cross-ModAl LLM Fine-Tuning (CALF) framework [13], we propose **CRAFT** (Cross-modal Regularization for Anomaly detection via Fine-Tuning), which adapts cross-modal alignment between temporal and textual representations from forecasting to multivariate time series anomaly detection in cybersecurity.

The original CALF framework employs a dual-branch architecture where both branches share pre-trained GPT-2 weights. Given a multivariate time series $\mathbf{I} \in \mathbb{R}^{T \times C}$, where T is the input sequence length and C is the number of variates, the temporal branch first projects the input through an embedding layer and multi-head self-attention to obtain time series tokens $\mathbf{X}_{\text{time}} \in \mathbb{R}^{C \times M}$, where M is the hidden dimension of the pre-trained LLM. The textual branch generates aligned text tokens $\mathbf{X}_{\text{text}} \in \mathbb{R}^{C \times M}$ via cross-attention between $\mathbf{X}_{\text{time}}$ and PCA-reduced word embeddings $\hat{\mathbf{D}} = \text{PCA}(\mathbf{D})$, where $\mathbf{D} \in \mathbb{R}^{|A| \times M}$ is the word embedding matrix from the LLM with vocabulary size $|A| = 50257$, reduced to $d = 500$ principal components. Both token sequences are then processed through L stacked Transformer blocks, yielding intermediate hidden features $\mathbf{F}^l_{\text{text}}$ and $\mathbf{F}^l_{\text{time}}$ at each layer $l \in \{1, \ldots, L\}$, and final outputs $\mathbf{Y}_{\text{text}}$ and $\mathbf{Y}_{\text{time}}$ respectively. CALF aligns these branches through: (1) Feature Regularization Loss $\mathcal{L}_{\text{feature}} = \sum_{l=1}^{L} \gamma^{(L-l)} \text{sim}(\mathbf{F}^l_{\text{text}}, \mathbf{F}^l_{\text{time}})$, which matches intermediate features with a decay factor γ that weights deeper layers more heavily, and (2) Output Consistency Loss $\mathcal{L}_{\text{output}} = \text{sim}(\mathbf{Y}_{\text{text}}, \mathbf{Y}_{\text{time}})$, ensuring coherent outputs across modalities, where $\text{sim}(\cdot, \cdot)$ denotes a similarity function such as L1 or L2 loss. To avoid catastrophic forgetting and improve training efficiency, CALF employs parameter-efficient fine-tuning: the textual source branch remains entirely frozen, while the temporal target branch is updated using Low-Rank Adaptation (LoRA) [7] along with fine-tuning of the positional encoding weights. During inference, only the temporal branch is used for predictions.

3.2 Architecture Overview

CRAFT maintains the dual-branch architecture of the original CALF framework while introducing several critical modifications for anomaly detection tasks.

Domain-Specific Textual Representation. A key difference from the original CALF model is our use of **domain-adapted language model embeddings** instead of generic word embeddings. CRAFT can be instantiated via a configuration flag with FinBERT [24], SecureBERT [1], general-purpose BERT [5], random embeddings, PCA-based variants, or synthetic "FinBERT-like" geometry-matched embeddings.

For the FinBERT instantiation we build a curated vocabulary of financial and economic terms, grouped into coarse categories such as sentiment (e.g., "bullish", "panic") and temporal or regime descriptors (e.g., "volatility spike", "seasonal pattern") etc. We employ this specialized vocabulary to test the hypothesis that aligning temporal signals with semantic concepts of risk and volatility enhances anomaly detection. Each term is encoded with FinBERT to obtain a single fixed-length vector, and all term vectors are stacked into an embedding matrix $\mathbf{E}_{\text{text}}$; the category labels are kept only for our geometric and attention analyses in Sects. 4.3 and 4.5.

For SecureBERT we follow the same pattern with an ICS/OT-focused vocabulary organized into categories spanning sensors, actuators, failure modes, and related concepts (e.g., "drift," "surge," "cavitation"). Each term is encoded into a single vector and stacked into an embedding matrix; category labels are retained only for offline analysis. During training and inference, CRAFT interacts solely with these continuous embedding matrices, which serve as a fixed keyvalue bank for cross-modal attention.

This plug-in design lets us swap embedding spaces while keeping the rest of the architecture fixed, which is crucial for our geometry-versus-semantics study.

Cross-Modal Encoder Architecture. Our cross-modal encoder adapts CALF's alignment mechanism to anomaly detection, treating a pre-computed embedding matrix $\mathbf{E}_{\text{text}} \in \mathbb{R}^{|\mathcal{V}|\times 768}$ (FinBERT, SecureBERT, or synthetic embeddings) as a fixed key–value bank for cross-attention with temporal queries.

We introduce a gated attention mechanism that modulates the influence of textual representations by filtering the embedding values:

$$\mathbf{V}_{\text{proj}} = \mathbf{E}_{\text{text}}\mathbf{W}_v^\top + \mathbf{b}_v \tag{1}$$

$$\mathbf{G} = \sigma(\mathbf{V}_{\text{proj}}\mathbf{W}_g^\top + \mathbf{b}_g) \tag{2}$$

$$\mathbf{V}_{\text{gated}} = \mathbf{G} \odot \mathbf{V}_{\text{proj}} \tag{3}$$

where $\mathbf{E}_{\text{text}}$ denotes the chosen embedding bank, $\mathbf{W}_v \in \mathbb{R}^{768\times d}$ is a learned projection matrix that transforms embeddings to hidden dimension d, $\mathbf{W}_g \in \mathbb{R}^{d\times d}$ is a learned gate weight matrix, σ is the sigmoid activation, and $\odot$ denotes element-wise multiplication. This gating mechanism allows the model to dynamically weight the contribution of semantic information based on the temporal context. Figure 1 illustrates the overall CRAFT architecture.

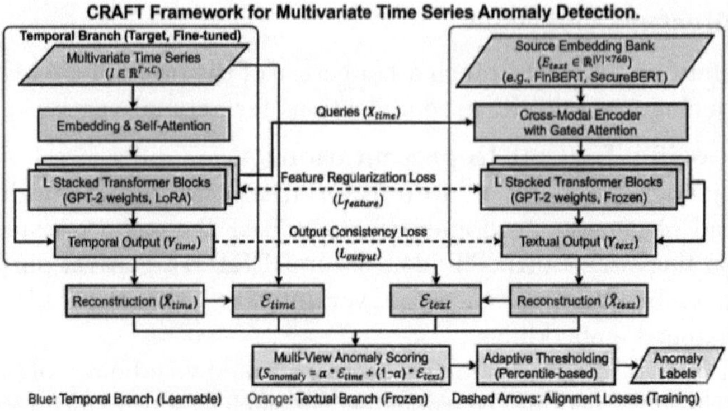

Fig. 1. Overview of CRAFT.

3.3 Anomaly Detection Methodology

Reconstruction-Based Anomaly Assessment. CRAFT adapts CALF's forecasting framework to reconstruction-based anomaly detection. Multivariate time series are reconstructed by temporal and textual branches (a GPT-2-based temporal encoder plus a cross-modal textual encoder); discrepancies from the input define anomaly scores, with the textual branch regularizing temporal representations via the embedding space.

Multi-view Anomaly Scoring. At a high level, CRAFT computes anomaly scores by fusing reconstruction errors from both temporal and textual branches. Given an input sequence $\mathbf{X} \in \mathbb{R}^{L \times D}$, where L is the window size and D is the number of features, the model produces reconstructions $\hat{\mathbf{X}}_{\text{time}}$ and $\hat{\mathbf{X}}_{\text{text}}$ and we define the per-branch reconstruction errors

$$\mathcal{E}_{\text{time}} = \frac{1}{LD}\|\mathbf{X} - \hat{\mathbf{X}}_{\text{time}}\|_F^2, \tag{4}$$

$$\mathcal{E}_{\text{text}} = \frac{1}{LD}\|\mathbf{X} - \hat{\mathbf{X}}_{\text{text}}\|_F^2, \tag{5}$$

and a conceptual fused score

$$\mathcal{S}_{\text{anomaly}} = \alpha \cdot \mathcal{E}_{\text{time}} + (1 - \alpha) \cdot \mathcal{E}_{\text{text}}, \tag{6}$$

where $\alpha \in [0, 1]$ controls the relative contribution of each branch.

Adaptive Thresholding via Percentile Method. We set the anomaly threshold on $\mathcal{S}_{\text{anomaly}}$ via a simple percentile rule. For each evaluation, we score all training windows and choose the $(100-r)$th percentile as the threshold, where r is the assumed anomaly rate (e.g., $r = 0.5$ yields the 99.5th percentile). If the computed threshold is non-finite or falls below 10^{-6}, we fall back to $\mu + 3\sigma$, where μ and σ denote the mean and standard deviation of the training anomaly scores.

4 Experiments

We implement CRAFT in PyTorch and train with Adam [10] (learning rate 1×10^{-4}), using a look-back window of 10 time steps and a prediction length of 1. All experiments run on a single NVIDIA V100 GPU.

4.1 Datasets

We evaluate CRAFT on three widely-used benchmark datasets for multivariate time series anomaly detection, as summarized in Table 1.

Table 1. Dataset statistics.

Dataset	Samples	Features	Description
SMD	1,416,825	38	Five weeks of monitoring data from 28 servers (CPU, memory, network) [20]. We use the four non-trivial subsets [22].
SWaT	946,719	51	Secure Water Treatment: multivariate sensor and actuator data from a scaled-down water treatment plant under normal and attack scenarios [14].
WADI	1,221,372	123	Water Distribution: extended ICS testbed with more than twice the sensors/actuators of SWaT [2].

In addition to established multivariate time-series benchmarks, we introduce **Owlyshield**, a behavioral ransomware dataset derived from the Owlyshield Endpoint Detection and Response (EDR) engine [19]. Owlyshield monitors low-level file-system activity and emits one record per 50 I/O operations within a process group, yielding behavioral snapshots from real endpoint telemetry [18]. The dataset contains 337,100 labeled samples, each encoded into 23 features (e.g., `ops_read`, `entropy_written`, `extensions_written_exe`) with a 16.64% ransomware prevalence. Each record therefore summarizes a short burst of process-level activity, and consecutive records can be chained to form multistep ransomware or benign behavior sequences. Owlyshield was originally curated as a supervised classification benchmark, and its imbalanced label distribution captures the skewed ratio between malicious and benign activity in real deployments.

We repurpose Owlyshield for unsupervised anomaly detection: CRAFT trains only on benign samples, with malicious labels reserved for test-set construction and evaluation. After a 70/30 temporal split, we reduce the test-set anomaly rate to 5% while preserving temporal coherence by grouping contiguous malicious timestamps into attack segments, ranking them via Isolation Forest [12], and selecting high-scoring segments until the target rate is reached.

This 5% anomaly ratio is consistent with other temporal cybersecurity benchmarks. For example, commonly used industrial-control and operational datasets such as SWaT, WADI, and SMD have test-set anomaly fractions of roughly 12.1%, 5.8%, and 4.2% respectively when evaluated under standard pointwise labelling [9]. By fixing Owlyshield's test anomaly rate at 5%, we place it in the same regime as WADI and SMD.

4.2 Results

Table 2 compares CRAFT with state-of-the-art baselines on three benchmarks. We report results using the best-performing embedding for each dataset; a detailed comparison of embedding choices follows in Sect. 4.3. It achieves the best F1 on WADI (0.7634) and SWaT (0.8843), and remains close to USAD on SMD (0.9480 vs. 0.9495).

For fair event-based evaluation we adopt the standard point-adjustment protocol [25]: if a model correctly flags any point within a ground-truth anomaly segment, the entire segment is treated as detected when computing precision, recall, and F_1 (Table 3).

Table 2. Model Performance Comparison Across Datasets

Model	SMD	WADI	SWaT
	$P/R/F^1$	$P/R/F^1$	$P/R/F^1$
OmniAnomaly [20]	0.8880/0.9984/0.9400	0.3157/0.6541/0.4259	0.9782/0.6957/0.8131
MAD-GAN [11]	0.9990/0.8440/0.9149	0.3348/0.5614/0.4195	0.9593/0.6957/0.8065
USAD [3]	0.9060/0.9974/**0.9495**	0.2095/0.8296/0.3345	0.9897/0.6880/0.8140
MTAD-GAT [27]	0.8211/0.9216/0.8684	0.2819/0.8013/0.4170	0.9760/0.6956/0.8123
TranAD [22]	0.9051/0.9974/0.9490	0.3529/0.8296/0.4951	0.9977/0.6879/0.8143
DTAAD [25]	0.8463/0.9974/0.9147	0.8125/0.3910/0.5279	0.9697/0.6957/0.8101
CRAFT	0.9543/0.9421/0.9480	0.8178/0.7158/**0.7634**	0.9513/0.8216/**0.8843**

Table 3. CRAFT Performance on Owlyshield Dataset

Dataset	Precision	Recall	F^1
Owlyshield	0.9042	0.9993	**0.9494**

On the newly introduced Owlyshield ransomware detection dataset, CRAFT demonstrates strong performance with an F1-score of 0.9494, achieving exceptionally high recall (0.9993) while maintaining robust precision (0.9042). The near-perfect recall is particularly valuable for cybersecurity applications where missing malicious activities can have severe consequences.

4.3 Embedding Geometry and Detection Performance

Table 4 reveals that semantics do not drive performance: random embeddings and BERT-base [5] match or exceed FinBERT, while domain-specific SecureBERT collapses on WADI. Geometry, not semantics, is the determining factor.

Geometric Properties of the Embedding Spaces. To explain these performance differences, we measured several geometric statistics of each embedding space (Table 5).

Table 4. F_1 scores for different embedding types

Embedding Type	SWaT	WADI
Original FinBERT	0.8734	0.7255
GeoFinBERT	0.8778	0.7214
Random (N = 404)	0.8766	0.7565
Random (N = 700)	0.8773	0.7544
Random (N = 900)	**0.8843**	**0.7634**
BERT-base (N = 404)	0.8781	0.7563
SecureBERT	0.8731	0.5803

Table 5. Geometric properties of embedding spaces

Property	FinBERT	GeoFinBERT	Random	BERT-base	SecureBERT
Structure indicators					
Mean cosine similarity	0.583	0.595	−0.000	0.981	0.994
Mean vector norm	25.32	25.31	1.41	13.75	1.83
Diversity indicators					
Std. of cosine similarities	0.125	0.109	0.036	0.011	0.003
Eff. dims (95% var.)	155	133	267	73	126
Spatial spread					
Mean pairwise distance	22.84	22.48	2.00	2.61	0.20

Interpreting the Geometric Properties. Table 5 reports two complementary aspects of embedding geometry: *structure indicators* (mean cosine similarity, mean vector norm $\bar{r}$) capture how concentrated or spread the embeddings are, while *diversity indicators* (standard deviation of cosines, effective dimensionality) measure how much of the embedding space is actively utilized. We also introduce *mean pairwise distance* ($\bar{d} = \mathbb{E}[\|e_i - e_j\|]$) to quantify spatial separation in Euclidean space. Embeddings with similar cosines can have vastly different $\bar{d}$ depending on their norms.

FinBERT strikes a favorable balance: moderate mean cosine similarity (≈ 0.58), high variability in pairwise angles (std = 0.125), and 155 effective dimensions yield a well-conditioned subspace that neither collapses to a single direction nor disperses into unstructured noise. GeoFinBERT, constructed from random matrices but matched to FinBERT's covariance spectrum and norms, achieves equivalent detection performance—confirming that geometry, not token semantics, drives the regularization effect.

SecureBERT and BERT-base both exhibit high mean cosine similarity (0.994 and 0.981 respectively), yet their detection performance differs sharply: BERT-base exceeds FinBERT on WADI (0.7563 vs. 0.7255) while SecureBERT collapses (0.5803). The explanation lies in spatial spread, not angular alignment alone. Cross-modal attention operates on dot products, which depend on both angles *and* vector norms. SecureBERT's small norms ($\bar{r} = 1.83$) combined with extreme collinearity produce embeddings clustered in a tiny region of space—effectively a single point. Any query yields nearly the same cross-modal output, reducing the textual branch to a fixed bias. BERT-base's larger norms ($\bar{r} = 13.75$) yield embeddings roughly twelve times farther apart in Euclidean distance ($\bar{d} = 2.61$ vs. 0.20), preserving enough spatial diversity for the learned projections to distinguish between embedding vectors and extract meaningful gradients. WADI's higher dimensionality (123 features vs. 51 for SWaT) likely amplifies sensitivity to geometric collapse. The key insight is that degeneracy arises from the *combination* of near-unity cosine and small norms; either factor alone is tolerable.

Random embeddings (mean cosine ≈ 0, 267 effective dimensions) represent the opposite extreme: high diversity but no structure. Their competitive performance confirms that avoiding geometric collapse matters more than having semantically meaningful clusters.

Together, these results support our central claim: the text branch functions as a *geometric prior*, not a semantic oracle. As long as the embedding bank spans a stable, non-degenerate subspace with sufficient spatial spread, it regularizes the temporal encoder effectively—regardless of token semantics. Domain-specific vocabularies help only when their geometry is well-conditioned; otherwise, as SecureBERT demonstrates, they can actively harm performance.

4.4 Ablation Study

Gated Attention Mechanism. We ablate the gated attention mechanism (Sect. 3.3), which modulates cross-modal influence by dynamically weighting semantic information based on learned gates. Table 6 compares performance with and without gating. Gated attention consistently improves precision across datasets while maintaining high recall, except on SMD where both variants perform similarly.

Table 6. Ablation: impact of gated attention on anomaly detection.

Dataset	Variant	Precision	Recall	F^1
WADI	w/ gate	0.8178	0.7158	**0.7634**
	w/o gate	0.7995	0.7153	0.7550
SWaT	w/ gate	0.9513	0.8216	**0.8843**
	w/o gate	0.9493	0.8041	0.8707
Owlyshield	w/ gate	0.9042	0.9993	**0.9494**
	w/o gate	0.9022	0.9993	0.9483
SMD	w/ gate	0.9680	0.9263	0.9464
	w/o gate	0.9543	0.9421	**0.9480**

4.5 Explainability Analysis: Cross-Modal Attention Visualization

We next examine how CRAFT links temporal patterns to semantic concepts by inspecting cross-modal attention between temporal features (queries) and FinBERT embeddings (keys/values) in the encoder. FinBERT serves as an ideal positive control for this analysis. As the only high-performing embedding with interpretable risk labels, it allows us to definitively confirm that the model ignores available semantic structure rather than leveraging it implicitly. We focus on two questions on SWaT: (1) whether attention differs between normal and anomalous sequences, and (2) how attention evolves during training.

Experimental Design: To isolate alignment behaviour, we constrain the model: temporal-only reconstruction ($\alpha = 1.0$) prevents the textual branch from affecting training, and disabling gating ensures all FinBERT embeddings remain equally accessible. This setup maintains strong detection ($F_1 = 0.87$) while exposing raw attention patterns.

Anomaly-Specific Attention Analysis: Analysis of 20 sequences per category reveals surprising uniformity in attention patterns between normal and anomalous sequences (Fig. 2). Four metrics show negligible differences: (1) **Mean attention weights**—measuring average attention across vocabulary terms with higher values indicating stronger activation—show 0.002473 (normal) vs 0.002477 (anomalous), $p > 0.05$ (not statistically significant); (2) **Attention entropy** $H = -\sum_i p_i \log p_i / \log N_{vocab}$—quantifying distribution randomness where values near 1.0 indicate uniform spread and lower values suggest concentration—shows 0.9612 vs 0.9598, indicating near-uniform distribution; (3) **Concentration ratio** $C = \sum_{i=1}^{5} w_{(i)} / \sum_j w_j$—measuring top-5 terms' proportion of total attention where $w_{(i)}$ denotes i-th largest weight—shows 0.0547 vs 0.0552, indicating minimal focusing; (4) **Attention standard deviation**—measuring spread across vocabulary where higher values indicate selective focusing—shows 0.00185 vs 0.00187. The extremely high entropy ($\sim 0.96/1.0$) with only 5.5% attention on top-5 terms indicates near-uniform distribution across the FinBERT vocabulary. This uniformity persists across both categories, suggesting cross-modal attention provides a stable semantic backdrop rather than dynamic anomaly-specific focusing.

Temporal Evolution of Attention Patterns: We track these metrics to understand the evolution of attention pattern. **Entropy** increases monotonically from 0.90 to 0.96, **top-5 concentration** drops from 11.5% to 4.9%, and **attention variance** decreases by 78% (from 1.4×10^{-5} to 3.0×10^{-6}). Variance measures spread of attention weights—lower values indicate more uniform distribution across all vocabulary terms. At the same time, a Jaccard-based term stability metric [16] (higher values indicate that the model consistently attends to the same vocabulary terms across training iterations) increases from 0.64 to 0.82 between early and later epochs, showing that the set of top-attended terms converges and remains consistent over training. These trends confirm that the model gradually settles into a high-entropy, stable attention regime while maintaining strong anomaly detection performance, implying that sparse, anomaly-specific attention is not required for effective detection.

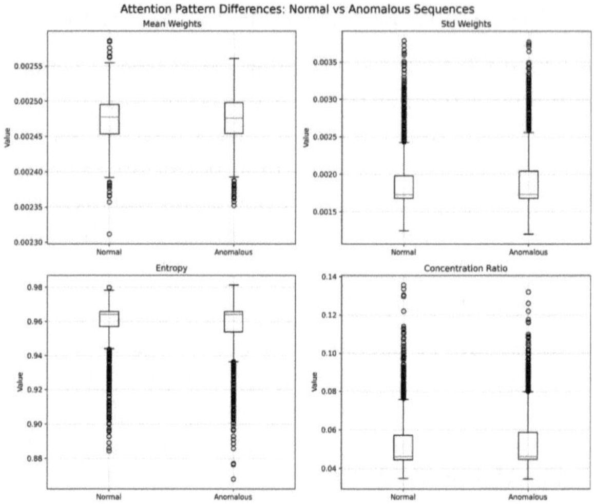

Fig. 2. Comparison of attention patterns between normal and anomalous sequences across four metrics: mean weight, standard deviation, entropy, and top-5 concentration.

Implications for Cross-Modal Anomaly Detection: Our analysis answers both questions. First, the anomaly-specific attention analysis reveals that attention does *not* differ meaningfully between normal and anomalous sequences—all four metrics show no statistically significant differences, indicating that the model does not learn anomaly-specific focusing. Second, the temporal evolution analysis demonstrates that attention progressively converges toward uniformity during training, stabilizing into a high-entropy regime with consistent term rankings while maintaining strong detection performance. Together, these findings reveal that CRAFT's cross-modal attention acts as a uniform semantic backdrop rather than a dynamic anomaly-specific detector, confirming the geometric regularization interpretation in Sect. 4.3. Similar high-entropy patterns on SMD and Owlyshield suggest this behaviour generalizes across datasets. From a defender's perspective, this is promising: detection relies on global consistency with normal behaviour rather than brittle feature-specific indicators that adversaries could manipulate.

5 Conclusion and Future Work

We introduced CRAFT, a cross-modal framework that adapts CALF from time series forecasting to cybersecurity anomaly detection. Our architectural modifications—replacing generic word embeddings with domain-adapted language model embeddings, incorporating a gated cross-modal attention mechanism, and fusing reconstruction errors through multi-view scoring—enable effective detection on multivariate time series benchmarks and on endpoint-level ransomware behavior.

We find that *embedding geometry* drives cross-modal gains rather than token-level semantics: synthetic embeddings preserving only geometric structure match FinBERT's performance, while geometrically degenerate domain embeddings fail. The convergence of cross-modal attention to uniform, high-entropy distributions confirms that the textual branch serves as a global geometric regularizer—encouraging holistic consistency assessment rather than reliance on brittle feature subsets. We also contribute Owlyshield, a large-scale ransomware behavior dataset derived from EDR telemetry. Future work will investigate learnable geometric priors for specific industrial domains and extend CRAFT to online streaming scenarios with adaptive thresholding. The dataset and preprocessing code are available at https://github.com/souravrai98/CRAFT-.git.

References

1. Aghaei, E., Niu, X., Shadid, W., Al-Shaer, E.: Securebert: a domain-specific language model for cybersecurity. In: Security and Privacy in Communication Networks: 18th EAI International Conference, SecureComm 2022, Virtual Event, October 2022, Proceedings, pp. 39–56. Springer (2023)
2. Ahmed, C.M., Palleti, V.R., Mathur, A.P.: Wadi: a water distribution testbed for research in the design of secure cyber physical systems. In: Proceedings of the 3rd International Workshop on Cyber-Physical Systems for Smart Water Networks, CySWATER 2017, pp. 25–28. Association for Computing Machinery, New York, NY, USA (2017). https://doi.org/10.1145/3055366.3055375
3. Audibert, J., Michiardi, P., Guyard, F., Marti, S., Zuluaga, M.A.: USAD: unsupervised anomaly detection on multivariate time series. In: Proceedings of the 26th ACM SIGKDD International Conference on Knowledge Discovery & Data Mining, KDD 2020, pp. 3395–3404. Association for Computing Machinery, New York, NY, USA (2020). https://doi.org/10.1145/3394486.3403392
4. Cybersecurity and Infrastructure Security Agency (CISA), U.S. Environmental Protection Agency (EPA): Internet–exposed HMIs pose cybersecurity risks to water and wastewater systems (2024). https://www.cisa.gov/news-events/alerts/2024/12/13/cisa-and-epa-release-joint-fact-sheet-detailing-risks-internet-exposed-hmis-pose-wws-sector. Accessed 15 July 2025
5. Devlin, J., Chang, M.W., Lee, K., Toutanova, K.: BERT: pre-training of deep bidirectional transformers for language understanding. In: Proceedings of the 2019 Conference of the North American Chapter of the Association for Computational Linguistics: Human Language Technologies, Volume 1 (Long and Short Papers), pp. 4171–4186. Association for Computational Linguistics, Minneapolis, Minnesota (2019). https://doi.org/10.18653/v1/N19-1423
6. European Union Agency for Cybersecurity (ENISA): ENISA threat landscape 2024 (2024). https://www.enisa.europa.eu/publications/enisa-threat-landscape-2024. Accessed 15 July 2025
7. Hu, E.J., et al.: LoRA: low-rank adaptation of large language models. In: International Conference on Learning Representations (2022). https://openreview.net/forum?id=nZeVKeeFYf9
8. IBM X–Force: IBM X–force 2025 threat intelligence index (2025). https://www.ibm.com/thought-leadership/institute-business-value/en-us/report/2025-threat-intelligence-index. Accessed 15 July 2025

9. Kim, S., Choi, K., Choi, H.S., Lee, B., Yoon, S.: Towards a rigorous evaluation of time-series anomaly detection. In: AAAI Conference on Artificial Intelligence (2021). https://api.semanticscholar.org/CorpusID:237490301
10. Kingma, D.P., Ba, J.: Adam: a method for stochastic optimization. In: Proceedings of International Conference on Learning Representations (ICLR) (2015)
11. Li, D., Chen, D., Jin, B., Shi, L., Goh, J., Ng, S.-K.: MAD-GAN: multivariate anomaly detection for time series data with generative adversarial networks. In: Tetko, I.V., Kůrková, V., Karpov, P., Theis, F. (eds.) ICANN 2019. LNCS, vol. 11730, pp. 703–716. Springer, Cham (2019). https://doi.org/10.1007/978-3-030-30490-4_56
12. Liu, F.T., Ting, K.M., Zhou, Z.H.: Isolation-based anomaly detection. ACM Trans. Knowl. Discov. Data **6**(1) (2012). https://doi.org/10.1145/2133360.2133363
13. Liu, P., et al.: Calf: aligning LLMs for time series forecasting via cross-modal fine-tuning. In: AAAI, pp. 18915–18923 (2025). https://doi.org/10.1609/aaai.v39i18.34082
14. Mathur, A.P., Tippenhauer, N.O.: Swat: a water treatment testbed for research and training on ICS security. In: 2016 International Workshop on Cyber-physical Systems for Smart Water Networks (CySWater), pp. 31–36 (2016). https://doi.org/10.1109/CySWater.2016.7469060
15. Nie, Y., Nguyen, N.H., Sinthong, P., Kalagnanam, J.: A time series is worth 64 words: long-term forecasting with transformers. In: International Conference on Learning Representations (2023)
16. Real, R., Vargas, J.M.: The probabilistic basis of Jaccard's index of similarity. Syst. Biol. **45**(3), 380–385 (1996). https://doi.org/10.1093/sysbio/45.3.380
17. Siffer, A., Fouque, P.A., Termier, A., Largouet, C.: Anomaly detection in streams with extreme value theory. In: Proceedings of the 23rd ACM SIGKDD International Conference on Knowledge Discovery and Data Mining, KDD 2017, pp. 1067–1075. Association for Computing Machinery, New York, NY, USA (2017). https://doi.org/10.1145/3097983.3098144
18. SitInCloud: Owlyshield ransomware detection using XGBoost. Owlyshield Documentation. https://docs.sitincloud.com/concepts/ransomware-detection.html. Accessed 26 Nov 2025
19. SitinCloud: Owlyshield: EDR software designed to detect ransomware (2024). https://github.com/SitinCloud/Owlyshield. Accessed 16 July 2025
20. Su, Y., Zhao, Y., Niu, C., Liu, R., Sun, W., Pei, D.: Robust anomaly detection for multivariate time series through stochastic recurrent neural network. In: Proceedings of the 25th ACM SIGKDD International Conference on Knowledge Discovery & Data Mining, KDD 2019, pp. 2828–2837. Association for Computing Machinery, New York, NY, USA (2019). https://doi.org/10.1145/3292500.3330672
21. Tu, F.F., Liu, D.J., Yan, Z.W., Jin, X.B., Geng, G.G.: STFT-TCAN: a TCN-attention based multivariate time series anomaly detection architecture with time-frequency analysis for cyber-industrial systems. Comput. Secur. **144**, 103961 (2024). https://doi.org/10.1016/j.cose.2024.103961
22. Tuli, S., Casale, G., Jennings, N.R.: Tranad: deep transformer networks for anomaly detection in multivariate time series data. Proc. VLDB Endow. **15**(6), 1201–1214 (2022). https://doi.org/10.14778/3514061.3514067
23. Verizon Business: 2025 data breach investigations report: Executive summary (2025). https://www.verizon.com/business/resources/reports/2025-dbir-executive-summary.pdf. Accessed 15 July 2025

24. Yang, Y., Uy, M.C.S., Huang, A.: Finbert: a pretrained language model for financial communications. arXiv abs/2006.08097 (2020). https://api.semanticscholar.org/CorpusID:219687757
25. Yu, L.R., Lu, Q.H., Xue, Y.: DTAAD: dual tcn-attention networks for anomaly detection in multivariate time series data. Knowl.-Based Syst. 111849 (2024)
26. Yue, Z., et al.: Ts2vec: towards universal representation of time series. In: AAAI Conference on Artificial Intelligence (2021). https://api.semanticscholar.org/CorpusID:237497421
27. Zhao, H., et al.: Multivariate time-series anomaly detection via graph attention network. In: 2020 IEEE International Conference on Data Mining (ICDM), pp. 841–850 (2020). https://doi.org/10.1109/ICDM50108.2020.00093

Robustness Analysis of Translation Tampering in Multi-sensor Object Detection

Mahdieh Safarzadehvahed(✉) and Mohammad Zulkernine

Queen's University, Kingston, Canada
{22ms70,mz}@queensu.ca

Abstract. Multi-sensor Object Detection Models (ODMs) are widely studied for 3D perception in autonomous driving, where LiDAR–camera fusion improves robustness. This fusion relies on accurate extrinsic calibration matrices. We show that the fusion stage is vulnerable to tampering with the translation vector of the extrinsic calibration matrix, even when the raw sensor data remain unchanged. We demonstrate how perturbations of the translation vector affect feature alignment and detection behavior and introduce a dimension-aware translation perturbation method that scales translation shifts by the physical dimensions of the object class of interest. We evaluate two representative LiDAR–camera fusion models, MVX-Net PointFusion (early-fusion) on KITTI and BEVFusion (middle-fusion) on nuScenes Mini. Our experiments show that MVX-Net PointFusion is highly sensitive to translation tampering, leading to sharp drops in detection accuracy, substantial object removal, and structured shifts among remaining detections. In contrast, BEVFusion exhibits limited performance degradation and minimal object removal under the same perturbation magnitudes, with effects confined mainly to small changes in ground-plane localization. These results identify extrinsic translation tampering as a practical attack surface for multi-sensor fusion and provide a controlled, dimension-aware method for robustness evaluation.

Keywords: Sensor calibration tampering · Object detection robustness · Coordinate frame misalignment · Multi-modal 3D object detection

1 Introduction

Camera-based object detectors in perception systems of Autonomous Vehicles (AVs) are vulnerable to adversarial attacks in which attackers can introduce phantom objects [10,12], remove existing objects [6], or cause object misclassification [17]. To enhance the robustness and security of perception systems in AVs, researchers have integrated LiDAR sensors with cameras, forming multi-sensor Object Detection Models (ODMs) [8,13]. These models fuse camera and

© IFIP International Federation for Information Processing 2026
Published by Springer Nature Switzerland AG 2026
H. Janicke et al. (Eds.): SEC 2026, IFIP AICT 787, pp. 228–242, 2026.
https://doi.org/10.1007/978-3-032-27993-4_16

LiDAR data to detect objects more reliably, instead of relying on a single sensing modality. While integrating LiDAR improves robustness, it also introduces new attack surfaces. Previous studies have shown that an attacker can discard legitimate point clouds from genuine obstacles by injecting invisible laser pulses near the LiDAR sensor, inject fake data points into LiDAR measurements to simulate the presence of non-existent objects or design physically realizable adversarial 3D-printed objects that cause an autonomous driving system to fail to detect them and potentially collide with them [2,14,16].

During our security investigations on multi-sensor ODMs that utilize both LiDAR and camera inputs, we found that the fusion stage can be vulnerable to tampering with the translation vector of the extrinsic calibration matrix. The extrinsic calibration matrix is used to align the data and coordinate systems of two sensors, or between a sensor and a target coordinate system, which can be an intermediate frame, such as BEV or the ego-vehicle frame. Manipulating this matrix can result in object removal or misplacement in the detection output, even when the raw sensor data remain unchanged. Such object removal or misplacement can lead to severe safety and security implications, including collision scenarios. Therefore, we identify extrinsic calibration matrices as a new attack point in multi-sensor ODMs.

In this paper, we investigate how perturbations of the translation vector affect feature alignment and object detection in LiDAR–camera fusion. We introduce a dimension-aware perturbation method that parameterizes extrinsic translations in terms of the physical dimensions of the objects of interest, and analyzes how such shifts influence object retention, localization error, and feature consistency across modalities. We perform this analysis on two representative multi-sensor ODMs, MVX-Net PointFusion [13] (early-fusion) and BEVFusion [8] (middle-fusion). Our results clarify how calibration errors propagate through different fusion strategies and how remaining detections behave under misalignment. For each model, we apply translation perturbations along t_x, t_y, and t_z and address the following research questions:

RQ1. How does manipulating the translation terms of the extrinsic matrix influence the accuracy and stability of multi-sensor ODMs?
RQ2. Does such calibration tampering cause objects to be removed or displaced?
RQ3. What is the relationship between detections before and after tampering? Do remaining objects shift predictably, remain spatially correlated, or become misaligned across sensors?

In summary, this paper makes the following contributions:

- We propose a dimension-aware translation perturbation method for extrinsic calibration, which ties the magnitude of calibration shifts to the physical dimensions of detected objects and provides a controlled way to investigate misalignment effects in multi-sensor ODMs.
- We conduct a comprehensive empirical evaluation of translation perturbations along the t_x, t_y, and t_z axes on two representative LiDAR–camera fusion models (MVX-Net PointFusion and BEVFusion), analyzing their impact on detection metrics, object removal and displacement.

The remainder of this paper is organized as follows. Section 2 provides background on calibration matrices, coordinate transforms, and multi-sensor ODM architectures. Section 3 formalizes translation tampering of the extrinsic matrix and presents our dimension-aware perturbation method. Section 4 presents the experimental evaluation and detailed analysis. Finally, Sect. 5 concludes the paper and outlines directions for future research.

2 Background

Multi-sensor ODMs are categorized into several types based on their fusion strategy. Among the main fusion strategies, this paper focuses on two: (1) early-fusion and (2) middle-fusion [4,15]. In early-fusion, the raw or pre-processed data from each sensor is transformed into a common feature space. Fusion occurs early in the network pipeline via concatenation, projection, or a lightweight fusion module. Object detection is then performed directly on the fused feature space [4,15]. In middle-fusion, each modality is first processed independently through its own backbone network to extract modality-specific features. These intermediate representations are then projected into a shared feature space and fused, typically using concatenation, attention, or learned transformation layers, before the detection head is applied [4,15]. We use MVX-Net PointFusion (early-fusion) and BEVFusion (middle-fusion) in our experiments, which are explained in Sect. 2.2.

2.1 Calibration Matrices and Point Projection

The perception pipeline in multi-sensor ODMs aligns sensor coordinate frames to enable feature fusion. This alignment is achieved using calibration matrices, categorized into intrinsic matrices (IM) and extrinsic matrices (EM) (Eq. 1). The IM maps 3D points in the camera coordinate system onto the 2D image plane, while the EM defines the transformation between two coordinate systems.

$$IM = \begin{bmatrix} f_x & 0 & c_x \\ 0 & f_y & c_y \\ 0 & 0 & 1 \end{bmatrix}, \qquad EM([R|t]) = \begin{bmatrix} r_{11} & r_{12} & r_{13} & t_x \\ r_{21} & r_{22} & r_{23} & t_y \\ r_{31} & r_{32} & r_{33} & t_z \\ 0 & 0 & 0 & 1 \end{bmatrix} \tag{1}$$

Here, f_x and f_y denote the focal lengths, and (c_x, c_y) denote the principal point. In Eq. 1, R is a 3×3 rotation matrix and $t = [t_x, t_y, t_z]^\top$ is a translation vector that shifts the coordinate origin. Calibration matrices provide the basis for projecting points from a source coordinate system to a target coordinate system (e.g., camera, ego, or BEV). Let $P_S = [x_S, y_S, z_S]^\top$ be a point in the source frame. The point is transformed into a target frame using Eq. 1 as illustrated in Eq. 2.

$$x_T = r_{11}x_S + r_{12}y_S + r_{13}z_S + t_x, \tag{2a}$$

$$y_T = r_{21}x_S + r_{22}y_S + r_{23}z_S + t_y, \tag{2b}$$

$$z_T = r_{31}x_S + r_{32}y_S + r_{33}z_S + t_z \tag{2c}$$

If the target frame corresponds to a rectified pinhole camera, the image coordinates are obtained using Eq. 4.

$$u' = f_x x_T + c_x z_T, \quad (3a)$$
$$v' = f_y y_T + c_y z_T, \quad (3b)$$
$$w' = z_T. \quad (3c)$$

$$u = f_x \frac{x_T}{z_T} + c_x, \quad (4a)$$
$$v = f_y \frac{y_T}{z_T} + c_y \quad (4b)$$

2.2 Multi-sensor Object Detection Models

MVX-Net PointFusion. MVX-Net PointFusion [13] is an early-fusion LiDAR–camera 3D detector that enriches each LiDAR point with a semantic feature from the RGB image. It first extracts a downsampled conv5 feature map using a pretrained Faster R-CNN and compresses the per-location image features to 16 dimensions. Each LiDAR point is encoded with a 7D vector, transformed from LiDAR to camera coordinates using $EM_{\text{LiDAR}\rightarrow\text{Camera}}$, and projected onto the image plane using IM to retrieve the corresponding image feature. The 16D image feature is concatenated with the 7D LiDAR feature to form a 23D point-wise fused representation, which is voxelized and processed by VFE and 3D convolutional layers, followed by an RPN to produce final 3D detections.

BEVFusion. BEVFusion [8], as a middle-fusion object detector, first extracts 2D image features using a convolutional neural network (CNN) and estimates a depth distribution for each pixel. Based on the predicted depth probabilities, it samples multiple 3D points along the camera ray for each image pixel. These 2D pixels are lifted into 3D rays in the camera coordinate system using the IM, and then transformed into a shared Bird's Eye View (BEV) coordinate system using the $EM_{\text{Camera}\rightarrow\text{Ego}}$. Simultaneously, LiDAR points are transformed from the LiDAR coordinate system to the same BEV coordinate system using the $EM_{\text{LiDAR}\rightarrow\text{Ego}}$. Both modalities are then fused in the BEV space, where object detection is performed.

3 Method: Extrinsic Translation Perturbations

To develop our method, we first describe the threat model, then empirically examine how perturbing the extrinsic matrix EM affects sensor alignment, and finally introduce a dimension-aware translation perturbation method.

3.1 Threat Model

We consider a post-compromise adversary whose goal is to tamper with the EM used by the perception component. Rather than manipulating raw camera frames or LiDAR point clouds online, the attacker only needs write access to the calibration or configuration artifacts used by the perception stack. Our contribution is not the initial compromise step, but the identification of the EM as a high-impact attack target in multi-sensor perception.

To do so, the attacker must obtain access to the vehicle's internal software or storage. We briefly describe two practical ways an adversary could gain such access. One possibility is physical access to the vehicle. Prior vehicle-security studies [7,9] show that an individual with temporary access (e.g., a mechanic, valet, renter, or the vehicle owner) may be able to modify files stored on on-board storage (e.g., NVMe or eMMC), including calibration files used by the perception module. Another possibility is compromise of the vehicle's update interfaces (e.g., OTA). Modern autonomous vehicles rely on over-the-air (OTA) update mechanisms to deploy firmware and software patches, including updates to perception components and configuration files. If the update chain is compromised, an adversary with network access may be able to modify files or configurations stored on the vehicle's internal drive, including EM parameters.

3.2 Effects of Extrinsic Matrix Tampering on Sensor Alignment

The EM contains 12 parameters whose modification affects the alignment between coordinate systems and the corresponding sensor data in different ways. As shown in Eq. 2, modifying the rotation components r_{11}–r_{33} leads to sign- and position-dependent changes in the projected points. The effect depends not only on whether a given element is increased or decreased, but also on the location of objects in the source coordinate system and on the signs of the involved terms. In contrast, the effects of modifying the translation components t_x, t_y, and t_z are more predictable, as they apply a uniform shift to all points in the scene. In this paper, for simplicity and to clearly illustrate the implications of tampering with EM, we focus on how modifying the translation terms t_x, t_y, and t_z affects the detections produced by multi-sensor ODMs. We perturb $EM_{\text{LiDAR}\to\text{Target}}$ because it is the calibration matrix shared across the two models: in MVX-Net PointFusion the target frame is the camera, while in BEVFusion the target frame is the ego coordinate system.

To investigate how tampering with EM elements affects the alignment of coordinate systems and sensor data, we conducted a series of experiments. We used a sample from the KITTI dataset [5] and projected points from the LiDAR coordinate system to the image plane using Eq. 4. Figure 1 illustrates how increasing and decreasing t_x, t_y and t_z lead to misalignment between different modalities.

(a) (b) (c) (d) (e) (f) (g) (h)

Fig. 1. Illustration of the effect of translation tampering on object projection. (a) Object detected in the point cloud. (b–h) Projected LiDAR points onto the image plane for the benign case and for shifts $\{t_x{-}1,\ t_x{+}1,\ t_y{-}1,\ t_y{+}1,\ t_z{-}3,\ t_z{+}3\}$.

These qualitative observations show that shifting points by an amount equal to the object's dimension along the corresponding axis eliminates the overlap between points and image pixels, motivating the dimension-aware translation perturbation method introduced in Sect. 3.3.

3.3 Dimension-Aware Translation Perturbations of the Extrinsic Matrix

We propose a dimension-aware translation perturbation method, grounded in the projection behavior observed in Sect. 3.2, to test the robustness of fusion pipelines in multi-sensor ODMs. Our method applies axis-aligned translation perturbations whose magnitudes are scaled to the physical extent of the object class along the perturbed axis. The idea is to shift the translation vector t in $EM_{\text{LiDAR}\rightarrow\text{Target}}$ by an amount comparable to the object's typical size along that axis, so that the projected LiDAR features of the object are displaced enough to reduce their spatial overlap with the corresponding camera/BEV features. Let $EM_{\text{LiDAR}\rightarrow\text{Target}} \in \mathbb{R}^{4\times4}$ denote the real extrinsic calibration matrix:

$$\mathbf{EM}_{\text{LiDAR}\rightarrow\text{Target}} = \begin{bmatrix} \mathbf{R} & \mathbf{t} \\ \mathbf{0}^\top & 1 \end{bmatrix}, \quad \mathbf{t} = [t_x, t_y, t_z]^\top, \tag{5}$$

which maps a LiDAR point $\mathbf{P}_{\text{LiDAR}}$ to the target frame as:

$$\mathbf{P}^{\text{real}}_{\text{Target}} = \mathbf{EM}_{\text{LiDAR}\rightarrow\text{Target}} \cdot \mathbf{P}_{\text{LiDAR}} \tag{6}$$

We model translation tampering by perturbing only the translation component:

$$\mathbf{EM}_{\text{pert}} = \begin{bmatrix} \mathbf{R} & \mathbf{t} + \delta\mathbf{t} \\ \mathbf{0}^\top & 1 \end{bmatrix}, \quad \delta\mathbf{t} = \begin{bmatrix} \delta t_x \\ \delta t_y \\ \delta t_z \end{bmatrix}. \tag{7}$$

Since $\mathbf{R}$ is unchanged, this induces a rigid shift in the target frame:

$$\mathbf{P}^{\text{pert}}_{\text{Target}} - \mathbf{P}^{\text{real}}_{\text{Target}} = \delta\mathbf{t}. \tag{8}$$

$$|\delta t_a| = s\, D^{(a)}_{\text{obj}}, \quad \delta t_{b\neq a} = 0, \quad s \in \{0.5, 1, 1.5\}, \tag{9}$$

where s provides three representative perturbation magnitudes. As $|\delta t_a|$ approaches $D^{(a)}_{\text{obj}}$, the object's projected location in the target frame is displaced by roughly one object-class extent along axis a, reducing the spatial overlap between the LiDAR-projected features and the corresponding features in the target frame used by fusion pipelines.

4 Experimental Evaluation and Analysis

In this section, we describe the datasets and experimental setup and then present the results and analysis. Our experimental analysis is structured to directly address the three research questions (RQ1, RQ2 and RQ3) introduced in Sect. 1.

4.1 Dataset and Experimental Setup

We utilize the KITTI [5] and nuScenes Mini [1] datasets to evaluate the effects of calibration tampering. Both datasets provide paired images and point clouds for each scene and are widely used benchmarks in autonomous driving. The nuScenes Mini dataset is a compact subset of the full nuScenes dataset that preserves its key characteristics.

In our experiments, we evaluate the effect of tampering with the translation components t_x, t_y and t_z on MVX-Net PointFusion [13] and BEVFusion [8]. We trained MVX-Net PointFusion using the implementation provided by MMDetection3D [3], following the specifications outlined in the original paper and using the KITTI dataset. For BEVFusion, we used the official pretrained model provided by OpenPCDet [11], trained on the nuScenes dataset [1]. Our goal is not to compare absolute performance across models, but rather to examine how tampering with the translation components of EM affects each model individually. Therefore, using different training datasets for the two models does not affect the validity of our evaluation. For each multi-sensor ODM, we first present its performance using the model's original EM as the baseline. Since our analysis focuses on the car class, we instantiate $D_{\text{car}}^{(a)}$ from label statistics. Specifically, for each axis $a \in \{x, y, z\}$ we set $D_{\text{car}}^{(a)} = Q_{90}^{(a)}$, which is robust to outliers while covering large typical objects. Here, $Q_{90}^{(a)}$ denotes the 90th percentile of the ground-truth car box extent along axis a. We compute $Q_{90}^{(a)}$ separately from the ground-truth 3D box dimensions in KITTI and nuScenes: for KITTI, $(Q_{90}^{(x)}, Q_{90}^{(y)}, Q_{90}^{(z)}) = (1.76, 1.69, 4.43)$, and for nuScenes, $(Q_{90}^{(x)}, Q_{90}^{(y)}, Q_{90}^{(z)}) = (2.12, 1.90, 4.90)$. To use a single perturbation setting across datasets, we take the maximum per axis and set $D_{\text{car}}^{(x)} = 2.12$, $D_{\text{car}}^{(y)} = 1.90$, and $D_{\text{car}}^{(z)} = 4.90$. We then evaluate three perturbation magnitudes using

$$\delta t_a \in \{\pm 0.5 D_{\text{car}}^{(a)},\ \pm 1.0 D_{\text{car}}^{(a)},\ \pm 1.5 D_{\text{car}}^{(a)}\}, \qquad \delta t_{b \neq a} = 0,$$

which correspond to smaller-than-object, approximately object-sized, and larger-than-object translations along the perturbed axis.

4.2 MVX-Net PointFusion

Detection performance in MVX-Net PointFusion is evaluated using 2D bounding box Average Precision (2D BBox AP), 3D Average Precision (3D AP), and Bird's Eye View Average Precision (BEV AP). Table 1 reports the impact of positive and negative perturbations applied to t_x, t_y, and t_z in $EM_{\text{LiDAR}\rightarrow\text{Camera}}$ on KITTI car detection performance at IoU thresholds 0.7 and 0.5, with the benign baseline at $\delta t = 0\,\text{m}$.

RQ1. Table 1 shows that MVX-Net PointFusion is highly sensitive to translation tampering, with the impact depending on the perturbed axis and the evaluation strictness. Perturbations in t_x and t_y degrade rapidly under both positive and

Table 1. Impact of translation perturbations on MVX-Net PointFusion detection performance (KITTI car class). Values are mean BBox@0.7, 3D@0.7/0.5, BEV@0.7/0.5 AP (%), averaged over Easy, Moderate, Hard.

Shift (m)	t_x			Shift (m)	t_y			Shift (m)	t_z		
	BBox 0.7	3D 0.7/0.5	BEV 0.7/0.5		BBox 0.7	3D 0.7/0.5	BEV 0.7/0.5		BBox 0.7	3D 0.7/0.5	BEV 0.7/0.5
-3.18	14.3	4.2/17.6	17.1/23.4	-2.85	6.3	0.8/7.6	6.3/9.1	-7.35	15.2	6.6/22.4	24.3/39.0
-2.12	18.8	11.6/24.3	21.2/30.6	-1.90	9.1	1.0/9.1	1.1/9.1	-4.90	30.8	15.4/43.3	42.6/60.4
-1.06	26.4	14.6/35.0	28.5/42.5	-0.95	9.1	9.1/9.1	9.1/9.7	-2.45	49.5	29.7/67.6	70.5/84.8
0	89.6	76.7/90.0	84.6/90.1	0	89.6	76.7/90.0	84.6/90.1	0	89.6	76.7/90.0	84.6/90.1
+1.06	26.3	10.6/35.8	26.0/41.7	+0.95	23.2	6.9/30.5	24.8/42.8	+2.45	56.4	35.4/69.8	69.2/86.8
+2.12	17.3	7.5/23.4	20.5/31.0	+1.90	11.2	7.4/15.0	13.0/17.5	+4.90	42.1	21.7/55.8	53.6/73.8
+3.18	14.7	5.7/18.3	16.0/22.3	+2.85	12.9	4.7/16.5	16.7/21.8	+7.35	37.0	21.0/50.4	48.9/64.4

negative shifts. In contrast, t_z perturbations degrade performance more slowly. When the translation element t_z is perturbed, all three metrics decrease more slowly compared to the other two tampering types (t_x and t_y). Perturbing t_z moves points farther or closer in depth (Fig. 1g, 1g), which primarily affects the depth dimension on the image plane while preserving a larger overlap between LiDAR points and visual features. Across all tampering types, mean BBox AP and BEV AP degrade more slowly than mean 3D AP. This is expected because 3D IoU depends on all three coordinates, whereas BEV and 2D BBox metrics discard one dimension. To assess the reliance on image information, we disable the image stream by zeroing out the image features. Under this setting, car 3D AP drops to 32.92%, 27.67%, 24.71% (Easy/Moderate/Hard), indicating that MVX-Net PointFusion relies heavily on image features for accurate car detection.

RQ2. The degradation in mean 3D AP indicates that a large portion of objects are either removed from detection or misplaced. To investigate this further, we perform additional experiments. First, we compare benign detections with detections after tampering to quantify how many objects are removed and how many are kept, as reported in Table 2. The remaining objects consist of both correctly localized detections and misplaced predictions, along with newly introduced false positives.

RQ3. To analyze the remaining cars, we plot normalized center distributions for the benign case and all translation shifts, as illustrated in Fig. 2. For each setting, we extract the 3D BBox centers (x, y, z) of the detected cars and build a one-dimensional Probability Density Function (PDF) over the LiDAR coordinate corresponding to the perturbed axis, namely lateral y for t_x shifts, vertical z for t_y shifts, and longitudinal x for t_z shifts. To make the curves comparable, for each axis we compute a common bin range $[v_{\min}, v_{\max}]$ from all benign and tampered values on that coordinate. We discretize this range into 20 bins, chosen empirically to provide enough resolution to reveal shifts in the distributions while

Table 2. Remained and removed car detections under translation tampering in t_x, t_y, and t_z for MVX-Net (KITTI) and BEVFusion (nuScenes Mini). Each cell reports remained/removed detections at the given confidence threshold. Benign rows show the baseline (no tampering).

Shift	MVX-Net (remained / removed)			BEVFusion (remained / removed)		
	Conf $\geq$ 0.3	Conf $\geq$ 0.5	Conf $\geq$ 0.7	Conf $\geq$ 0.3	Conf $\geq$ 0.5	Conf $\geq$ 0.7
Benign	2364 / 0	1701 / 0	968 / 0	1701 / 0	1216 / 0	568 / 0
$t_x = +1.06$	956 / 1408	526 / 1175	196 / 772	1654 / 47	1151 / 65	545 / 23
$t_x = +2.12$	922 / 1442	474 / 1227	173 / 795	1571 / 130	1074 / 142	493 / 75
$t_x = +3.18$	779 / 1585	395 / 1306	137 / 831	1509 / 192	1013 / 203	456 / 112
$t_x = -1.06$	916 / 1448	464 / 1237	173 / 795	1669 / 32	1156 / 60	546 / 22
$t_x = -2.12$	883 / 1481	441 / 1260	150 / 818	1602 / 99	1083 / 133	506 / 62
$t_x = -3.18$	771 / 1593	352 / 1349	91 / 877	1542 / 159	1034 / 182	468 / 100
$t_y = +0.95$	1669 / 695	551 / 1150	108 / 860	1624 / 77	1163 / 53	547 / 21
$t_y = +1.90$	981 / 1383	207 / 1494	13 / 955	1550 / 151	1091 / 125	509 / 59
$t_y = +2.85$	666 / 1698	85 / 1616	1 / 967	1496 / 205	1042 / 174	478 / 90
$t_y = -0.95$	12 / 2352	1 / 1700	0 / 968	1610 / 91	1141 / 75	526 / 42
$t_y = -1.90$	23 / 2341	1 / 1700	1 / 967	1528 / 173	1059 / 157	461 / 107
$t_y = -2.85$	14 / 2350	1 / 1700	0 / 968	1500 / 201	1009 / 207	423 / 145
$t_z = +2.45$	1601 / 763	1000 / 701	474 / 494	1701 / 0	1214 / 2	568 / 0
$t_z = +4.90$	1669 / 695	981 / 720	444 / 524	1701 / 0	1215 / 1	568 / 0
$t_z = +7.35$	1858 / 506	1027 / 674	428 / 540	1700 / 1	1212 / 4	568 / 0
$t_z = -2.45$	1077 / 1287	604 / 1097	226 / 742	1700 / 1	1213 / 3	568 / 0
$t_z = -4.90$	637 / 1727	242 / 1459	70 / 898	1701 / 0	1214 / 2	568 / 0
$t_z = -7.35$	293 / 2071	95 / 1606	16 / 952	1700 / 1	1216 / 0	568 / 0

avoiding excessive noise in the estimated PDFs, and use histogram estimation with `density=true` to obtain PDFs for the benign and each shifted setting. These plots visually reveal how the tampered detections move relative to the benign distribution along the LiDAR axis directly affected by the calibration perturbation. The curves indicate where detections concentrate, rather than how many detections are present in total.

To analyze how far the remaining car detections move under each calibration shift, we compute the empirical Cumulative Distribution Function (CDF) of the 3D center displacement between benign and tampered detections (Fig. 2). For each shift and each frame, we perform a one-to-one matching between benign and tampered boxes by assigning to each benign detection the tampered box with the smallest 3D center distance (Eq. 10), subject to two constraints: (i) the yaw difference satisfies $|\Delta\text{yaw}| < 25°$, and (ii) the center displacement is within a matching threshold of $d_{\max} = 8$ m. We choose $d_{\max}$ to be slightly larger than the largest applied translation magnitude (the t_z case, ≈ 7.35 m). If no tampered box satisfies these constraints, the benign detection is treated as removed and is excluded from the CDF.

$$d(\mathbf{c}_b, \mathbf{c}_t) = \|\mathbf{c}_b - \mathbf{c}_t\|_2 = \sqrt{(x_b - x_t)^2 + (y_b - y_t)^2 + (z_b - z_t)^2}, \qquad (10)$$

where $\mathbf{c}_b = (x_b, y_b, z_b)$ and $\mathbf{c}_t = (x_t, y_t, z_t)$ denote the 3D centers of the benign and tampered detections, respectively.

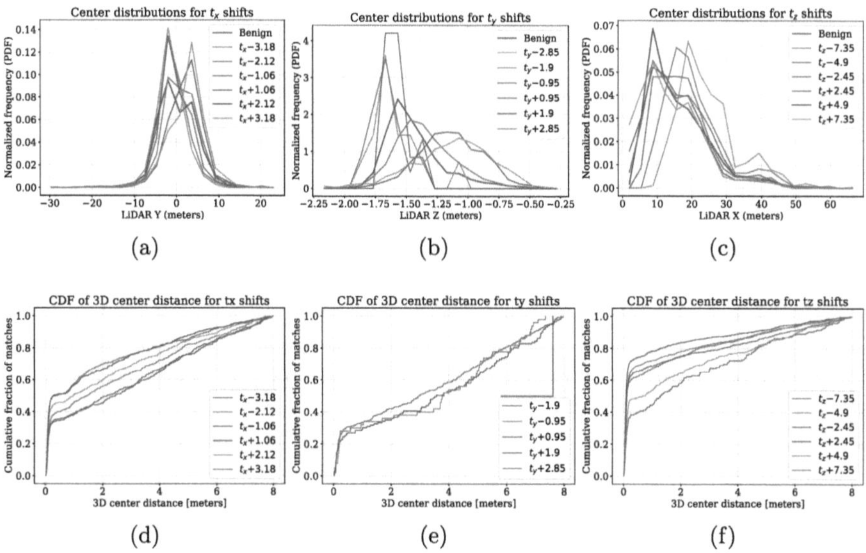

Fig. 2. MVX-Net PointFusion under translation tampering. (a–c) PDFs of detected car center distributions for shifts in t_x, t_y, and t_z, respectively. (d–f) CDFs of 3D center distances between matched benign and tampered car detections for shifts in t_x, t_y, and t_z, respectively.

In addition to the 3D displacement CDFs, we also compute axis-wise CDFs for the individual coordinate differences $|\Delta X| = |x_b - x_t|$, $|\Delta Y| = |y_b - y_t|$, and $|\Delta Z| = |z_b - z_t|$ (Fig. 3). For each calibration shift, these are obtained by applying the same matching process and recording the per-axis deviations of each matched pair. The resulting axis-wise CDFs reveal how calibration tampering affects localization along each dimension, complementing the overall 3D displacement analysis by isolating the dominant direction of error introduced by each perturbation. Figure 2a and Fig. 2d show that under t_x tampering, the cars that remain detectable do not move to random positions. Instead, their centers shift in lateral direction, for negative shifts, the probability mass increases on the left side (negative LiDAR y), whereas for positive shifts it increases on the right side (positive LiDAR y). Axis-wise CDFs show that tampering with t_x shifts the object centers in both X and Y, not only along the tampered axis. Moreover, as $|t_x|$ increases, the 3D center distance between benign and tampered detections grows (Fig. 3a and Fig. 3b).

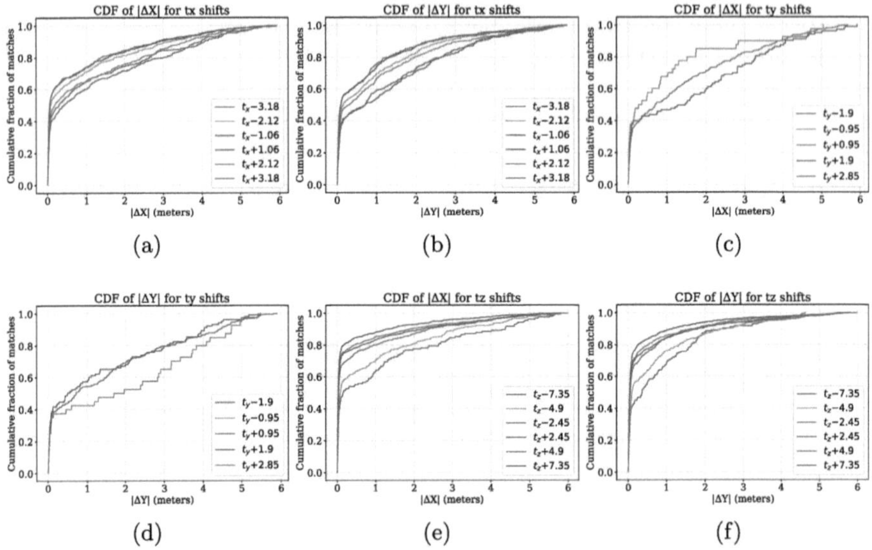

Fig. 3. Axis-wise CDFs of absolute center-displacement errors for MVX-Net PointFusion under translation tampering. Panels (a–b), (c–d), and (e–f) correspond to shifts in t_x, t_y, and t_z, respectively.

For t_y perturbations (Fig. 2b), the negative shifts produce very sharp and tall curves around a single height, which reflects that only a few cars remain (consistent with Table 2) and these surviving detections are clustered around a specific vertical position. Figure 2e also shows that for $t_y = -1.90$ and $t_y = -2.85$ almost no valid matches remain. Positive t_y shifts move the mass towards less negative z (higher in the scene).

For t_z perturbations (Fig. 2c), the distribution of detected car centers along the forward LiDAR x axis shifts under negative t_z tampering, especially for shifts around one car length and 1.5× that value. With these negative shifts, more detections appear at farther ranges, while positive t_z shifts tend to concentrate detections closer to the ego vehicle. This happens because increasing t_z keeps the projected LiDAR points more aligned with the object's visual features (Fig. 1h), whereas decreasing t_z pushes many points outside the object's visual region (Fig. 1g).

The CDFs (Fig. 2 and Fig. 3) show that a large fraction of the remaining cars experience only modest localization changes, with the displacement dominated by the ground-plane components (x, y). The magnitude for most matched cars remains small (typically within about 0–1 m). The 3D center-distance CDF further indicates that, for benign cars that still have a match, the corresponding tampered box center is usually within roughly 0.5–3 m of the benign one (depending on the axis and shift magnitude). The distributions of $|\Delta X|$ and $|\Delta Y|$ extend to several meters, whereas $|\Delta Z|$ remains sub-meter for nearly all matched cars. This indicates that translation tampering primarily perturbs the horizontal placement of surviving detections rather than their height. In addition, the direction of the center displacement follows the sign of the applied translation. Positive (negative) shifts tend to move the detected centers in the corresponding positive (negative) direction, rather than producing random drifts. Combined with the PDFs, this suggests that translation tampering primarily removes detections and induces structured, axis-consistent shifts for the detections that remain.

4.3 BEVFusion

Detection performance in BEVFusion is evaluated using mean Average Precision (mAP), nuScenes Detection Score (NDS), and mean Average Translation Error (mATE) (in meters). Table 3 presents the impact of tampering applied to t_x, t_y and t_z elements of the $EM_{\text{LiDAR}\rightarrow\text{Ego}}$, on the BEVFusion performance using the nuScenes Mini dataset.

Table 3. Impact of translation perturbations on BEVFusion (nuScenes Mini) using car class metrics only. Values represent car mAP (%), car mATE (m), and car class NDS (%).

Shift (m)	t_x			**Shift** (m)	t_y			**Shift** (m)	t_z		
	mAP	mATE (m)	NDS		mAP	mATE (m)	NDS		mAP	mATE (m)	NDS
−3.18	88.41	0.183	87.01	−2.85	88.12	0.186	86.24	−7.35	92.00	0.166	90.06
−2.12	89.96	0.179	88.14	−1.90	88.96	0.185	87.14	−4.90	92.00	0.165	90.06
−1.06	90.99	0.174	88.89	−0.95	90.47	0.181	88.27	−2.45	92.00	0.165	90.07
0	92.00	0.166	90.06	0	92.00	0.166	90.06	0	92.00	0.166	90.06
+1.06	90.81	0.173	89.30	+0.95	90.46	0.176	88.78	+2.45	92.00	0.165	90.08
+2.12	89.23	0.180	88.03	+1.90	89.03	0.180	87.49	+4.90	92.00	0.166	90.06
+3.18	88.41	0.182	86.80	+2.85	88.06	0.186	86.17	+7.35	92.00	0.165	90.08

RQ1. Perturbations in t_x and t_y cause a gradual decline in mAP and NDS up to 4%. In contrast, perturbations in t_z have no impact on the reported metrics, since the evaluation primarily reflects localization in the ground-plane (x, y) rather than vertical (height) error. To assess how strongly BEVFusion relies on image features, we disable the camera stream by zeroing out the image BEV features. The model maintains high performance (car mAP $=$ 85%, mATE $= 0.182$ m and NDS $=$ 80%), showing only moderate degradation. Overall, these results indicate that BEVFusion depends far less on image features for car detection and relies primarily on LiDAR geometry.

RQ2. Table 2 shows that only a few objects are removed when we tamper with the translation parameters, especially when we modify t_z.

RQ3. Fig. 4c shows that the car-center distribution under t_z tampering is essentially unchanged, consistent with Tables 2 and 3. In contrast, the t_x and t_y PDFs (Fig. 4a and Fig. 4b) exhibit mild deviations, primarily explained by a small number of removed detections under larger horizontal perturbations and slight center misplacement among the remaining cars. Overall, the PDF and CDF analyses indicate limited object removal and modest misplacement under the applied translation perturbations.

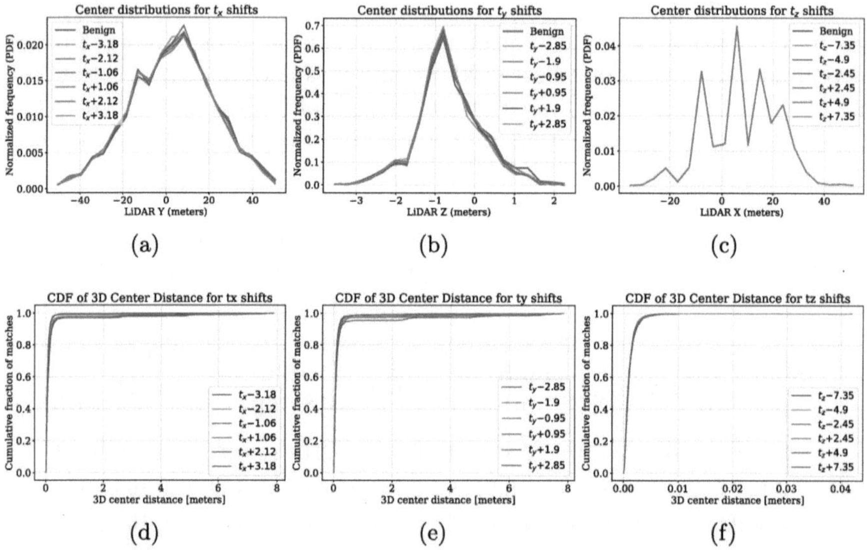

Fig. 4. Center distribution PDFs of detected cars from the BEVFusion model under translation tampering in (a) t_x, (b) t_y, and (c) t_z. CDF of 3D center distances between matched car detections from the BEVFusion model under translation tampering in (d) t_x, (e) t_y, and (f) t_z.

The different robustness behaviors of MVX-Net PointFusion and BEVFusion mainly stem from their fusion strategy and modality dependence. MVX-Net PointFusion uses early fusion by projecting LiDAR points onto the image plane and attaching image features, so translation tampering directly disrupts point-level cross-modal alignment and leads to larger performance drops. BEVFusion instead performs middle fusion after separate modality-specific feature extraction in a shared BEV space, making it more tolerant to the same perturbations and more supported by LiDAR geometry. This is consistent with our ablation results and with the limited effect of t_z perturbations in BEVFusion under ground-plane-oriented metrics.

5 Conclusion and Future Work

This paper investigated extrinsic translation tampering in LiDAR–camera fusion models. We showed that perturbing the translation vector (t_x, t_y, t_z) of the extrinsic calibration matrix can misalign cross-modal features and cause object removal or misplacement. To demonstrate this effect, we proposed a dimension-aware translation perturbation method that ties translation shifts to object dimensions. Our evaluation on MVX-Net PointFusion and BEVFusion revealed different robustness behaviors: MVX-Net PointFusion is highly sensitive to translation tampering, while BEVFusion shows limited object removal and modest localization changes under the same perturbation settings. Overall, the results clarify how calibration errors propagate through fusion-based perception and motivate future work on rotation perturbations, additional fusion architectures, and online defenses based on cross-modal consistency and localization stability.

References

1. Caesar, H., et al.: nuScenes: a multimodal dataset for autonomous driving. In: Proceedings of the IEEE/CVF Conference on Computer Vision and Pattern Recognition, pp. 11621–11631 (2020)
2. Cao, Y., et al.: Invisible for both camera and lidar: security of multi-sensor fusion based perception in autonomous driving under physical-world attacks. In: 2021 IEEE Symposium on Security and Privacy (SP), pp. 176–194. IEEE (2021)
3. Contributors, M.: MMDetection3D: OpenMMLab next-generation platform for general 3D object detection (2020). https://github.com/open-mmlab/mmdetection3d
4. Feng, D., et al.: Deep multi-modal object detection and semantic segmentation for autonomous driving: datasets, methods, and challenges. IEEE Trans. Intell. Transp. Syst. **22**(3), 1341–1360 (2021). https://doi.org/10.1109/TITS.2020.2972974
5. Geiger, A., Lenz, P., Urtasun, R.: Are we ready for autonomous driving? The KITTI vision benchmark suite. In: Proceedings of the IEEE Conference on Computer Vision and Pattern Recognition (CVPR)(2012)
6. Jiang, W., Li, H., Xu, G., Zhang, T., Lu, R.: Physical black-box adversarial attacks through transformations. IEEE Trans. Big Data **9**(3), 964–974 (2022)
7. Koscher, K., et al.: Experimental security analysis of a modern automobile. In: 2010 IEEE Symposium on Security and Privacy. pp. 447–462. IEEE (2010)
8. Liu, Z., et al.: BEVFusion: multi-task multi-sensor fusion with unified bird's-eye view representation. In: 2023 IEEE International Conference on Robotics and Automation (ICRA), pp. 2774–2781 (2023). https://doi.org/10.1109/ICRA48891.2023.10160968
9. Miller, C., Valasek, C.: Remote exploitation of an unaltered passenger vehicle. In: Black Hat USA, pp. 1–91 (2015)
10. Nassi, B., Mirsky, Y., Shams, J., Ben-Netanel, R., Nassi, D., Elovici, Y.: Protecting autonomous cars from phantom attacks. Commun. ACM **66**(4), 56–67 (2023)
11. OpenPCDet Development Team: OpenPCDet: An open-source toolbox for 3D object detection from point clouds (2020). https://github.com/open-mmlab/OpenPCDet. Accessed 11 Mar 2026

12. Safarzadehvahed, M., Zulkernine, M., Araujo, P.R.M.D., Givigi, S.: IPRPAS: a dataset of physical adversarial samples for assessing object detection in intelligent vehicles. IEEE Internet Things J. **12**(12), 21255–21263 (2025)
13. Sindagi, V.A., Zhou, Y., Tuzel, O.: MVX-Net: multimodal VoxelNet for 3D object detection. In: 2019 International Conference on Robotics and Automation (ICRA), pp. 7276–7282. IEEE (2019)
14. Sun, J., Cao, Y., Chen, Q.A., Mao, Z.M.: Towards robust {LiDAR-based} perception in autonomous driving: general black-box adversarial sensor attack and countermeasures. In: 29th USENIX Security Symposium (USENIX Security 20), pp. 877–894 (2020)
15. Zhang, X., et al.: Multi-sensor object detection. In: Multi-Sensor Fusion for Autonomous Driving, pp. 51–85. Springer, Singapore (2023)
16. Zhu, Y., Miao, C., Xue, H., Yu, Y., Su, L., Qiao, C.: Malicious attacks against multi-sensor fusion in autonomous driving. In: Proceedings of the 30th Annual International Conference on Mobile Computing and Networking, pp. 436–451 (2024)
17. Zou, Z., Chen, K., Shi, Z., Guo, Y., Ye, J.: Object detection in 20 years: a survey. Proc. IEEE (2023)

ICSSPulse: A Modular LLM-Assisted Platform for Industrial Control System Penetration Testing

Michail Takaronis(✉), Athanasia Kollarou, Vyron Kampourakis, Vasileios Gkioulos, and Sokratis Katsikas

Norwegian University of Science and Technology, 2802 Gjøvik, Norway
{michail.takaronis,athanasia.kollarou,vyron.kampourakis,
vasileios.gkioulos,sokratis.katsikas}@ntnu.no

Abstract. It is well established that industrial control systems comprise the operational backbone of modern critical infrastructures, yet their increasing connectivity exposes them to cyber threats that are difficult to study and remedy safely under real-time operational conditions. In this paper, we present *ICSSPulse*, an open-source, modular, and extensible penetration testing platform designed for the security assessment of ICS communication protocols. To the best of our knowledge, *ICSSPulse* is the first web-based platform that unifies network scanning, protocol-aware Modbus and OPC UA interaction, and Large Language Model (LLM)-assisted reporting within a single, lightweight ecosystem. Our platform provides a user-friendly graphical interface that orchestrates enumeration, exploitation, and reporting activities over simulated industrial services, enabling safe and reproducible experimentation. It supports protocol-level discovery, asset enumeration, and controlled read/write interactions, while preserving protocol fidelity and operational transparency. Experimental evaluation using synthetic Modbus test servers, a *Factory I/O* water treatment scenario, and a custom OPC UA production-line model demonstrated *ICSSPulse's* potential to discover active industrial services, enumerate process-relevant assets, and manipulate process variables. A key contribution of this work lies in the integration of an LLM-assisted reporting module that automatically translates technical findings into structured executive and technical reports, with mitigation guidance informed by the ICS MITRE ATT&CK ICS matrix.

Keywords: Penetration Testing · Industrial Control Systems Protocols · Network Scan · Enumeration · Exploitation · AI automated reporting

1 Introduction

Industrial Control Systems (ICS) comprise the operational backbone of modern Critical Infrastructures (CI), including energy grids, water treatment plants,

© IFIP International Federation for Information Processing 2026
Published by Springer Nature Switzerland AG 2026
H. Janicke et al. (Eds.): SEC 2026, IFIP AICT 787, pp. 243–256, 2026.
https://doi.org/10.1007/978-3-032-27993-4_17

transportation networks, and manufacturing plants. Based on the PURDUE model [16], these systems integrate Operational Technology (OT) components at their lower layers, spanning supervisory control like Supervisory Control and Data Acquisition (SCADA) systems, field control including Programmable Logic Controllers (PLCs) and Remote Terminal Units (RTUs), and field devices such as sensors and actuators. At the same time, these layers are vertically connected with Information Technology (IT) networks, enabling process automation and real-time control. While this convergence enhances operational efficiency, it also exposes traditionally isolated industrial networks to cybersecurity threats previously unknown to the once barricaded industrial operations [8,11].

The consequences of compromising ICS environments are no longer hypothetical. For example, the Stuxnet worm (2010) [4], one of the earliest known cyber-physical attacks, demonstrated the feasibility of stealthily modifying PLC logic to cause physical damage, in this case, degrading centrifuge operations at Iran's Natanz facility. Similarly, incidents such as the TRITON malware (2017) [3], which targeted safety instrumented systems in a Saudi petrochemical plant, and the Industroyer (2016) [9], which disrupted power distribution in Ukraine by directly manipulating industrial communication protocols, underscored the catastrophic potential of ICS-targeted cyberattacks. These events blatantly prove that cybersecurity threats in ICS environments can have direct and far-reaching impacts on economic stability, public infrastructure, and even human safety. Despite their gravity, educating and training the future cybersecurity workforce in ICS security remains an underdeveloped and underfunded domain. However, unlike conventional IT systems, availability and safety are a sine qua non in industrial systems, making aggressive security testing or direct intrusion simulations difficult to perform on live infrastructure. Consequently, there is an increasing need for controlled environments and specialized tools, supporting secure and repeatable testing of ICS protocols and diverse configurations.

In this direction, Penetration Testing (PT) remains a highly relevant hands-on practice. However, in industrial contexts, it differs significantly from that in traditional IT networks. Namely, common IT-focused frameworks, such as Metasploit or Nmap, are not fully equipped to handle the semantics, timing constraints, or deterministic behavior of ICS communication standards such as Modbus, DNP3, and OPC UA. As a result, testing such protocols requires tools that can safely emulate and interface with industrial devices, capture real-time data exchanges, and assess the security posture of ICS communication channels without risking operational continuity. In this context, aside from large-scale proprietary testbeds [1,2,12], existing contributions in the field are scarce and only marginally relevant to our study. However, for a broader perspective, the reader is referred to [5,10,13,17].

Contribution: Towards filling these gaps, *ICSSPulse* [14], an open-source ICS protocol platform, provides a modular and extensible environment designed to facilitate interactive testing, simulation, and visualization of industrial communication protocols. By combining a web-based Graphical User Interface (GUI) with backend modules for Modbus and OPC UA, along with a novel Large Language Model (LLM)-assisted reporting module, *ICSSPulse* enables safe, reproducible, and protocol-aware PT activities. The platform is particularly suited for research laboratories, cyber ranges integration, and training scenarios, where it can be used to study protocol vulnerabilities, validate security mechanisms, and train operators in recognizing abnormal communication patterns. Through its modular design and integration of simulated data sources, *ICSSPulse* aims to bridge the gap between theoretical ICS cybersecurity analysis and practical, hands-on experimentation.

The remainder of this paper is organized as follows. Section 2 presents *ICSSPulse's* scope. Section 3 describes the integration of *ICSSPulse* within the PT lifecycle. Section 4 details *ICSSPulse's* architecture. Section 5 discusses the implementation of the platform's core components. Section 6 presents the experimental evaluation. Last, Sect. 7 concludes the paper and outlines directions for future work.

2 Scope

It is common that ICS exposes legacy or weakly protected communications, which, if improperly configured, may leak process values or control information to unauthorized parties. In this context, such exposures directly threaten the confidentiality and integrity of operational parameters and, depending on the adversary's intent and capabilities, may affect availability as well. In the scope of this work, *ICSSPulse* focuses specifically on protocol-level security threats, which can be leveraged by an attacker who targets unauthenticated or weakly authenticated communication paths in network communication implementations such as Modbus or OPC UA. Note that *ICSSPulse* models communication behavior rather than physical actuation, meaning that threats pertinent to device firmware or hardware-level components currently fall outside its scope. In this mindset, we assume that *ICSSPulse* can be utilized by adversaries that have logical network access to the lower layers of an ICS environment, attained either by compromising an operator workstation, pivoting through a flat network segment, or leveraging improperly segmented infrastructure. Of course, the mechanisms by which this network access is achieved, e.g., spear-phishing, lateral movement, or exploitation of unpatched services, are relevant in real deployments; however, they are currently outside the coverage of *ICSSPulse*. Instead, we focus on the adversary's behavior once they can communicate with industrial endpoints exposed over the industrial network. From this standpoint, the evildoer can perform active probing, enumerate accessible endpoints, and issue protocol-level requests to field devices.

Consequently, once the attackers can interact with relevant services, they can identify exposed registers, memory blocks, or nodes that reveal operational information. For example, in Modbus communications, this may include coils or holding registers, while in OPC UA, accessible node paths or namespaces. Subsequently, the threat actors can construct requests to read or modify values, test the behavior of endpoints under malformed inputs, or generally assess the field devices' cybersecurity robustness. With *ICSSPulse*, these operations occur on simulated protocol handlers, enabling safe reproduction of adversarial behaviors for analysis, training, and education. In its current version, *ICSSPulse* does not model physical disruptions, controller reprogramming, multi-stage ICS kill chains, or privileged engineering workstation attacks. Similarly, Denial of Service (DoS) targeting device availability, packet flooding, or resource exhaustion attacks are outside the platform's use. Recall that presently *ICSSPulse* provides a controlled environment for studying adversaries operating at the protocol interaction level. Summarizing the key characteristics, goals, and capabilities of the adversary, the scope of *ICSSPulse* can be defined as follows.

- **Goal**: The attacker aims to obtain or manipulate process-related data by interacting with exposed protocol endpoints. This may include reading operational values, issuing unauthorized write commands, or probing device behavior for unveiling weaknesses.
- **Knowledge**: The adversary possesses general knowledge of industrial network protocols, in *ICSSPulse's* case, Modbus and OPC UA, understanding common addressing schemes or message structures. However, they lack detailed system-specific knowledge, such as device configuration files, engineering project files, or process logic.
- **Technical skills**: The attacker is skilled enough to generate and interpret protocol messages, conduct enumeration, craft malformed requests, and analyze device responses. Skills include basic network probing, familiarity with industrial protocol semantics, and the ability to identify unprotected or weakly protected endpoints.
- **Capabilities**: The adversary can send and receive network traffic to devices using industrial protocols. They can enumerate accessible memory/register spaces, test device behavior under different request types, and exploit unauthenticated protocol functions. However, they cannot compromise firmware, alter physical I/O, or directly attack the hardware. Their capabilities are limited to protocol-level interactions within the network segment to which they have obtained access.

3 Lifecycle Integration

Penetration testing is commonly defined as "a test methodology in which assessors, typically working under specific constraints, attempt to circumvent or defeat the security features of an information system" [15] following a structured six-stage lifecycle. Typically, the sequence of a typical PT pipeline is: i) planning & reconnaissance, ii) scanning & enumeration, iii) vulnerability analysis, iv) exploitation, v) post-exploitation, and vi) reporting & remediation. Accordingly, *ICSSPulse* provides mechanisms and modules that fully or partially support a full PT campaign in a controlled environment. Table 1 summarizes *ICSSPulse's* PT lifecycle coverage.

Planning and Reconnaissance: This stage involves defining engagement scope and preparing testing parameters. In this regard, *ICSSPulse* supports this phase by allowing users to configure target IP addresses, ports, protocol modes, and operation types through its web GUI. Note that validation mechanisms are implemented to ensure consistent configuration relevant to real-world planning activities.

Scanning and Enumeration: Scanning identifies live hosts and open services, while enumeration determines protocol-level characteristics and potential points of interaction. In this context, *ICSSPulse* fully supports this stage through an integrated scanning module for host/port discovery. Additionally, *ICSSPulse* exposes protocol-level handlers, performing operations such as coil/register enumeration, unit identifier discovery, and probing of common address ranges.

Vulnerability Analysis: In this stage, testers analyze the collected data to identify potential weaknesses that could lead to exploitation. *ICSSPulse* facilitates this by presenting structured, transparent output for all scanning and enumeration operations executed in the previous step. This way, users can interpret exposed services or insecure behaviors (e.g., unauthenticated Modbus access). Note that analysis is user-driven, as automated vulnerability scoring is not included in the current version of *ICSSPulse*, but is intended as future work.

Exploitation: Exploitation involves attempting controlled actions based on identified weaknesses. In this respect, *ICSSPulse* supports exploitation through its protocol handler, i.e., Modbus and OPC UA, which enable read/write operations on coils and registers, and standard object nodes, respectively, testing malformed or unexpected requests.

Post-Exploitation: This stage evaluates the impact of successful exploitation. *ICSSPulse* supports it by visually displaying device responses and state changes resulting from protocol manipulation, depending on the case. Therefore, users can examine how simulated devices react to altered values or peculiar requests. It should be noted that system-level post-exploitation activities, such as privilege escalation or lateral movement, are beyond the tool's current scope, but they are considered for future extension.

Reporting and Remediation: The final stage documents findings and recommends mitigation steps. *ICSSPulse* fully supports this phase through its novel, integrated LLM-powered reporting engine. The system aggregates stored evidence, including scan results, user interactions, and outputs, into a structured technical report, highlighting mitigation guidance aligned with well-known security frameworks.

4 ICSSPulse Architecture

Figure 1 illustrates the architecture of *ICSSPulse*, which is designed as a modular, web-based platform for ICS PT. The architecture is centered around a unified web GUI that orchestrates user interactions and coordinates the execution of enumeration, exploitation, and reporting activities, incorporating open-source tools like Rustscan, tailored scripts based on Python libraries like pymodbus and python-opcua, and an LLM agent through a GPT-4o-mini model using OpenAI's API, respectively. This centralized design enables seamless control flow while maintaining a clear separation between user interaction, protocol-specific processing, and result analysis.

Table 1. *ICSSPulse's* Penetration Testing Lifecycle Coverage.

PT Stage	Description	Support
Planning & Reconnaissance	Users configure targets, ports, and protocol parameters	◐
Scanning & Enumeration	Integrated scanning and protocol-aware enumeration (e.g., Modbus unit IDs, register mapping)	●
Vulnerability Analysis	Structured outputs enable manual identification of insecure services or behaviors; no automated scoring	◐
Exploitation	Modbus and OPC UA read/write and malformed request testing fully supported	●
Post-Exploitation	Impact observation through state-change feedback; broader system-level post-exploitation not included	◐
Reporting & Remediation	Integrated LLM-based report generation with evidence aggregation and mitigation recommendations	●

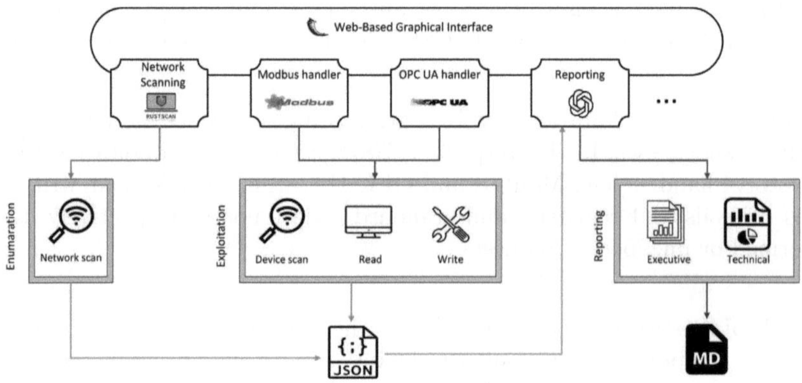

Fig. 1. ICSSPulse Architecture.

As shown in the figure, enumeration and exploitation components operate as independent modules, producing machine-readable outputs in JSON format. These artifacts serve as an intermediate representation, allowing results to be immediately visualized through the GUI or selectively retained for later use. The reporting component takes as input the aggregated artifacts derived from the scanning and enumeration modules to generate executive or technical assessment reports, depending on the users' demands, without direct coupling to the underlying testing modules. Overall, the architecture emphasizes modularity, extensibility, and clear data flow, facilitating reproducible security assessments of ICS protocols.

Architecturally, *ICSSPulse* is designed with extensibility as a core tenet. That is, additional industrial communication protocols (e.g., DNP3, MQTT, or IEC 60870-5-104) can be incorporated by introducing new handler modules and extending the routing logic, without requiring changes to the GUI or existing execution flow. Likewise, *ICSSPulse* can be extended in a full-fledged cyber range ecosystem [7], say, by enhancing the frontend with advanced visualization dashboards, adding real-time monitoring and management, or augmenting the reporting capabilities independently of the protocol-specific components. This modular design makes *ICSSPulse* well-suited for educational and research-oriented cybersecurity applications, enabling safe, transparent, and reproducible cybersecurity assessments in industrial communication environments.

5 Implementation

This section describes the implementation details of *ICSSPulse*, focusing on its five core modules: the GUI, the network scanning capabilities, the Modbus and OPC UA protocol handlers, and the LLM-assisted reporting module.

5.1 Graphical User Interface

ICSSPulse is implemented using *Flask*, a lightweight Python microframework for web applications. *Flask* was chosen due to its simple and practical architecture, which delivers essential web server functionality, avoiding excessive complexity and unnecessary dependencies. Regarding the application control, we implemented a centralized control node responsible for defining the routing architecture and managing the request-response lifecycle. Specifically, each route corresponds to a dedicated PT module, i) a home interface for navigation and user interaction, ii) a network scanning module for identifying IT/OT devices within the target environment, iii) a Modbus protocol handler that enables Modbus-based operations through a web interface, iv) an OPC UA protocol handler that facilitates OPC UA interactions via the same interface, and v) a reporting module that leverages the OpenAI API to generate concise, reusable analysis results. All route handlers process HTTPS POST requests containing user-defined parameters. Subsequently, these parameters are passed to the appropriate protocol-specific handler, and the resulting outputs are output to the frontend GUI in a structured and appropriate format for visualization. Note that dynamic content rendering is achieved through the use of *Jinja2* templating, which enables the frontend to remain largely protocol-agnostic while focusing on usability, interaction, and result presentation.

5.2 Network Scanning

Concerning network scanning, *ICSSPulse* integrates *RustScan*, a state-of-the-art network scanner implemented in Rust, enabling accurate network discovery. *RustScan* is deployed within a *Docker* container, thereby abstracting dependency management and installation requirements while ensuring consistent behavior regardless of the underlying system. To facilitate this integration, the platform spawns a separate process to execute Docker commands, dynamically launching containers to perform scans and terminating them upon scanning completion. Furthermore, user-provided parameters, including quoted strings and escape sequences, are securely parsed to correctly handle complex command syntax, thus mitigating the risk of command injection vulnerabilities. Subsequently, scan results are captured, with the output prompts including both standard and diagnostic messages, which are forwarded to the web-based QUI. This design enhances the scanning transparency and supports effective debugging. Furthermore, the scanning module optionally comes with a report generation subsystem, allowing users to incorporate scan results into automated reports. Namely, upon user request, the raw scan output, formatted in JSON, is forwarded to the reporting component together with relevant metadata, such as the executed command and timestamp.

5.3 Modbus Handler

The Modbus handler module in *ICSSPulse* is implemented using *pymodbus*, a Python library that provides a full-stack implementation of the Modbus protocol. The library abstracts low-level protocol mechanics while exposing high-level interfaces for interacting with Modbus data structures, enabling read and write operations on elements such as coils and registers. The handler supports all four primary Modbus data types, i.e., (i) coils, which represent single-bit read/write outputs; (ii) discrete inputs, which correspond to single-bit read-only inputs; (iii) holding registers, which store 16-bit read/write values; and (iv) input registers, which contain 16-bit read-only values. The implementation relies on a Modbus TCP client to establish TCP connections with the target devices. Connection parameters, including the IP address, port number (default: 502), unit (slave) identifier, timeout duration, and retry count, are configurable via the GUI. Altogether, the handler supports multiple operational modes tailored to PT and reconnaissance tasks. Particularly, enumeration operations traverse address ranges to retrieve and display all accessible values, thereby facilitating the exploration of device memory maps, while read operations allow targeted retrieval of values from user-specified addresses, with results returned directly to the GUI.

Apart from standard Modbus functionality, the module incorporates device discovery capabilities. Namely, a dedicated unit scanning function probes a range of unit identifiers to discern active Modbus slaves on the target network. For each candidate unit ID, the implementation employs a multi-function probing strategy that tests all four Modbus data types across commonly used address offsets, including 0 (standard starting address), 1 (alternative starting address used by some devices), 100 (common register block offset), 1000 (higher address region), and the Modicon addressing conventions 40001 and 30001 for holding and input registers, respectively. Beyond identifying active devices, the scanner can record which Modbus function codes successfully elicit responses. For example, devices that support only holding registers are identified accordingly, and their supported data types are reflected in the output GUI. Similarly, the register range scanning functionality performs memory enumeration by reading address ranges in configurable chunks (default size: 1000 registers), enabling the identification of accessible memory regions and their current values.

5.4 OPC UA Handler

On the other hand, the OPC UA handler leverages *python-opcua*, a library that provides an implementation of the OPC UA specification, offering programming interfaces for OPC UA functionalities, such as node discovery and value manipulation. Unlike Modbus, OPC UA employs a node-based information model, where each node represents an asset, variable, or method within a namespace structure. Thus, the handler supports exploration of the user-given namespace through discovery mechanisms by implementing five core operational modes. First, it initiates an OPC UA session, offering user authentication and anonymous interaction to retrieve available endpoints from the target server. Then, for each endpoint, the handler lists the endpoint URL, security policy (e.g., Basic256Sha256, None), security mode (e.g., None, Sign, SignAndEncrypt), and supported user identity token types (e.g., Anonymous, Username/Password, Certificate, IssuedToken). Subsequently, the handler performs a recursive traversal of the OPC UA namespace starting from the standard object nodes, with parameters such as recursion depth and number of nodes configurable through the GUI. For each node, it logs the node identifier (e.g., ns = 2; i = 10;), name, and namespace index (e.g., 2: Temperature). Afterwards, the handler performs an enumeration of selected variables within the namespace, with the correct filtering based on the namespace index. Then, for each variable node, it captures the node identifier, display name, data type, access levels referring to user permissions (read/write/execute), and the current value of the node. Finally, the handler can read and write on specified nodes by their NodeId, returning the current value for read operations and a message indicating whether write operations were successful or failed through the GUI.

5.5 LLM-Assisted Report

Finally, *ICSSPulse* integrates an LLM-assisted reporting module, automatically generating structured assessment reports, as described in 1. Note that the modules offer two reporting modes, the executive and technical options, for the intended audience. Both modes rely on GPT-4o-mini via an OpenAI API key to summarize the collected output from the scanning and Modbus and OPC UA exploitation steps and generate a cohesive report with mitigation recommendations informed by the ICS MITRE ATT&CK framework. The reporting module is organized in two distinct stages. First, the platform maintains a centralized inbox where results from network scans and Modbus and OPC UA interactions are added during the PT. Each stored entry contains the operation parameters, timestamp, and resulting output, allowing relevant contextual information to be preserved. In the second stage, upon report request, *ICSSPulse* processes the collected data, extracting contextually meaningful data: scan outputs are analyzed to identify hosts, open ports, and exposed protocols, while Modbus interactions are summarized to capture information such as discovered unit identifiers, accessible registers, and indicators of operational success. Ultimately, these elements are aggregated per target in a comprehensive overview. Subsequently, mitigation recommendations are generated by mapping the resulting report to predefined ICS ATT&CK matrix mitigation identifiers. Rather than distributing mitigations throughout the report, the reporting module consolidates them into a single adhesive section, ensuring a clear and concise presentation of the recommended security controls. Once this reporting step is concluded, the backend invokes the OpenAI GPT-4o-mini API to construct a formatted dataset containing the extracted findings, target summaries, and selected mitigations, as seen in 1. This dataset, together with the instructions corresponding to the selected reporting mode, is provided as input to the LLM to produce the final report. Recall that the reporting module is explicitly constrained to operate on the supplied data, preventing the inclusion of unsupported findings. In executive mode, the generated report provides a high-level overview suitable for decision-makers, whereas the technical mode provides a more detailed and structured report intended for analysts and practitioners. Last, the resulting report is rendered in *Markdown* format through the GUI and can be downloaded.

Algorithm 1. LLM-Assisted Report Generation.

Input: Audience type $a \in \{\text{executive}, \text{technical}\}$, report title T, model identifier M
Output: Markdown report R
Initialize an empty report inbox $\mathcal{I} \leftarrow [\,]$

During testing: For each tool execution (scan, Modbus, OPC UA)
  Collect parameters p and textual output o
  Append item $\langle t, \text{category}, p, o \rangle$ to $\mathcal{I}$ with current timestamp t

When report is requested:
Select at most N items $\mathcal{I}' \subseteq \mathcal{I}$ for processing
Derive per-target scan facts (hosts, ports, services) from $\mathcal{I}'$
Derive per-target Modbus summaries (unit IDs, registers, success flags) from $\mathcal{I}'$
Map observed services and Modbus actions to ICS ATT&CK mitigations
Deduplicate mitigations by identifier to obtain a consolidated list

if $a =$ executive **then**
  Build dataset D with high-level target statistics and consolidated mitigations
  Set instruction string $G \leftarrow$ "Write an executive ICS/OT security report."
else
  Build dataset D with per-target details, Modbus traces, and consolidated mitigations
  Set instruction string $G \leftarrow$ "Write a structured technical ICS/OT report."
end if

Serialize D into a JSON-like structure
Construct prompt using T, G, and the serialized dataset
Query the LLM with model M to obtain a Markdown report R
Return: R

6 Evaluation

Regarding the Modbus handler evaluation, we utilized two distinct scenarios. The first was conducted using a Python-based Modbus TCP server implemented with the *pymodbus* library, as detailed in Sect. 5.3. The server simulated three distinct industrial devices. Specifically, the device with unit ID 1 simulated a PLC exposing 1,000 addresses per Modbus data type, including coils, discrete inputs, holding registers, and input registers populated with random values. Second, the device with unit ID 5 simulated a sensor with monitoring and measurement capabilities, with discrete inputs set to *True* and the remaining inputs set to *False*, while holding registers were populated with values representing analog measurements. Finally, the device with unit ID 10 simulated an actuator, featuring coils divided into two regions, i.e., 500 enabled and 500 disabled, to represent mixed operational states, and holding registers offset by 10,000 to simulate control signal baselines.

The second Modbus evaluation was performed using *Factory I/O* [6], a 3D industrial simulator designed for practicing real-world control tasks. The selected scenario simulated a part of a water treatment plant and was evaluated using both analog and digital signal representations. Particularly, the simulated plant consisted of a water tank with two primary control loops, namely, an inlet fill valve and an outlet discharge valve, managed by sensors that periodically sampled the water level and flow rates. Accordingly, the flow meter and level meter were configured as read-only input registers, returning analog values for flow rate and tank level, respectively. Meanwhile, the fill and discharge valves were implemented as read/write holding registers, controlling inlet and outlet flow and reporting opening percentages ranging from 0 to 10. For digital evaluation, the analog registers were replaced with discrete inputs for the sensors and coils for the actuators, enabling a binary representation of the plant behavior.

Both testbeds were treated as black boxes, in accordance with the scope described in Sect. 2. The evaluation began with scan-based discovery, followed by manipulation of Modbus data types. In both scenarios, *ICSSPulse* successfully identified active Modbus services, with the PyModbus server operating on port 5002 and the water treatment plant using the default Modbus port 502, confirming the presence of Modbus devices in the simulated OT network. Subsequently, the Modbus handler used to identify active unit IDs, enumerate all supported data types, including coils, discrete inputs, holding registers, and input registers, and determine the address ranges used to store the process values via a scan register range functionality. Finally, read and write operations were performed to manipulate register values. For example, writing an arbitrary value 500 to the fill valve register resulted in a value of 5 due to the water tank's 100-scale configuration. An execution example is shown in Fig. 2.

Regarding the OPC UA handler evaluation, we implemented a custom Python-based OPC UA server using the *python-opcua* library, as detailed in 5.4. Specifically, the server modeled an industrial production line organized through a hierarchical namespace structure. The exposed address space consisted of a root factory object (*ns = 2; i = 1;*), representing the facility context, and a production

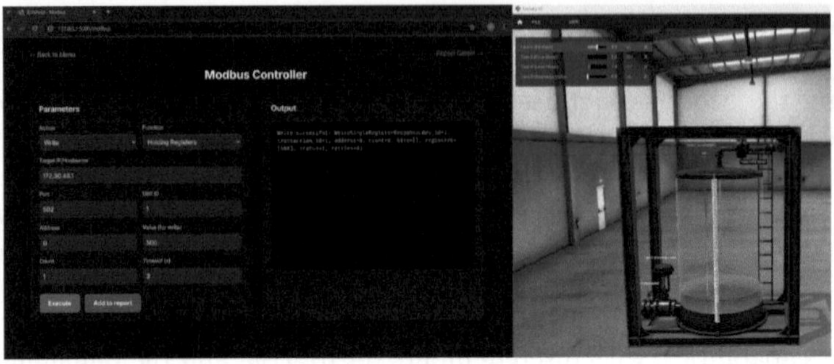

Fig. 2. Write operation using ICSSPulse.

line object (*ns* = *2; i* = *2;*) corresponding to a specific unit. This production line contained three temperature sensors, i.e., node IDs 10–12, providing temperature measurements and two motors, i.e., node IDs 20–23, exposing motor speed and operational status (on/off). For our evaluation purposes, anonymous authentication was enabled, reflecting real-world deployments in which additional authentication mechanisms are not configured, which contradicts the principle of establishing secure defaults.

To evaluate the OPC UA handler, we connected to the server using the endpoint `opc.tcp://localhost:4840/freeopcua/server/`. Initially, the handler correctly identified that the server accepted anonymous connections and operated under a *None* security policy. After establishing the session, the *Browse* functionality was used to traverse the hierarchical information model, revealing the complete namespace tree rooted at the *Factory* object (*ns* = *2; i* = *1;*) and its child nodes, including *ProductionLine1*, *TemperatureSensors*, and *Motors*. Subsequently, the *Enumerate* function was employed to profile available variables, distinguishing between read-only system metrics, such as *Uptime* (*ns* = *2; i* = *30;*), and writable process control variables. Importantly, the handler accurately reported node metadata, including data types (e.g., *Double* for temperature sensors and *Int32* for motor speed values). Finally, the evaluation concluded with active exploitation through read and write operations, retrieving real-time simulated sensor values, and demonstrating process control by modifying motor speed (*ns* = *2; i* = *20;*) and motor status variables.

Last, after completing the Network Scan, Modbus, and OPC UA assessment scenarios, we evaluated the ICSSPulse reporting capabilities, sending the results of each action to the LLM-powered reporting module. The module successfully consolidated the resulting network scan data, enumeration logs, and records of successful read/write exploitation into a unified context for feeding the GPT-4o-mini model. Consequently, the evaluation fulfilled the generation of two distinct report formats: a technical report mapping technical details of the findings, such as network ports, services, protocol data types, and corresponding mitigation strategies as derived from the ICS MITRE ATT&CK matrix, and an executive summary translating these technical findings into high-level business risks regarding production continuity and safety.

7 Conclusions

This work presents *ICSSPulse*, an open-source, modular, and extensible PT platform for ICS protocols. To the best of our knowledge, *ICSSPulse* is the first platform that unifies functions like network scanning, protocol-aware Modbus and OPC UA interaction, and LLM-assisted reporting within a single, web-based, user-friendly PT ecosystem, using a lightweight Python-based backend combined with simulated industrial services, while preserving protocol fidelity and operational transparency. Through experimental evaluation on Modbus test servers, a *Factory I/O* water treatment scenario, and a custom OPC UA production-line model, we exhibit that *ICSSPulse* can successfully discover industrial services, enumerate process-relevant assets, and perform unauthorized read and write operations that influence process behavior. A key novelty of the platform lies in its ability to translate low-level technical findings into structured executive and technical reports through an LLM-assisted module, exemplifying the practical integration of LLMs for automated reporting in ICS PT workflows. Despite these contributions, we acknowledge several limitations in terms of scalability and realism. Namely, *ICSSPulse*'s reliance on Python-based execution, containerized auxiliary tools, and software-only, unauthenticated testbeds constrains performance and experimental fidelity, rendering the platform suitable only for small- to medium-scale laboratory environments. However, these limitations motivate several avenues for future work, including the integration of additional industrial communication protocols, the offloading of performance-critical components to lower-level implementations, and the extension of evaluations to authenticated deployments and hardware-in-the-loop testbeds.

Acknowledgments. This work is supported by the Research Council of Norway through the SFI Norwegian Centre for Cybersecurity in Critical Sectors (NORCICS) project no. 310105, and by the European Union through HORIZON TMA MSCA Doctoral Networks/HORIZON-MSCA-2023-DN-01 project TUAI (Grant No. 101168344).

References

1. Ahmed, C.M., Palleti, V.R., Mathur, A.P.: Wadi: a water distribution testbed for research in the design of secure cyber physical systems. In: Proceedings of the 3rd International Workshop on Cyber-Physical Systems for Smart Water Networks, CySWATER '17, pp. 25–28. Association for Computing Machinery, New York (2017). https://doi.org/10.1145/3055366.3055375
2. Almgren, M., Andersson, P., Björkman, G., Ekstedt, M., Hallberg, J., Nadjm-Tehrani, S., Westring, E.: RICS-el: building a national testbed for research and training on SCADA security (short paper). In: Luiijf, E., Žutautaitė, I., Hämmerli, B.M. (eds.) CRITIS 2018. LNCS, vol. 11260, pp. 219–225. Springer, Cham (2019). https://doi.org/10.1007/978-3-030-05849-4_17

3. Di Pinto, A., Dragoni, Y., Carcano, A.: Triton: the first ICS cyber attack on safety instrument systems. Proc. Black Hat USA **2018**, 1–26 (2018)
4. Falliere, N., Murchu, L.O., Chien, E., et al.: W32. stuxnet dossier. White paper, symantec corp., security response **5**(6), 29 (2011)
5. Green, B., Lee, A., Antrobus, R., Roedig, U., Hutchison, D., Rashid, A.: Pains, gains and {PLCs}: ten lessons from building an industrial control systems testbed for security research. In: 10th USENIX Workshop on Cyber Security Experimentation and Test (CSET 17) (2017)
6. I/O, F.: Factory i/o: Next-gen plc training 3d factory simulation (2025). https://factoryio.com/
7. Kampourakis, V., Gkioulos, V., Katsikas, S.: A step-by-step definition of a reference architecture for cyber ranges. J. Inf. Secur. Appl. **88**, 103917 (2025). https://doi.org/10.1016/j.jisa.2024.103917
8. Kampourakis, V., Kavallieratos, G., Gkioulos, V., Katsikas, S.: Cracks in the chain: a technical analysis of real-life supply chain security incidents. Comput. Secur. **159**, 104673 (2025). https://doi.org/10.1016/j.cose.2025.104673
9. Kozak, P., Klaban, I., Šlajs, T.: Industroyer cyber-attacks on Ukraine's critical infrastructure. In: 2023 International Conference on Military Technologies (ICMT), pp. 1–6 (2023). https://doi.org/10.1109/ICMT58149.2023.10171308
10. Kraust, S., Heller, P., Mottok, J.: Concept for designing an ICS testbed from a penetration testing perspective. In: 2025 IEEE European Symposium on Security and Privacy Workshops (EuroS&PW), pp. 561–568 (2025). https://doi.org/10.1109/EuroSPW67616.2025.00071
11. Makrakis, G.M., Kolias, C., Kambourakis, G., Rieger, C., Benjamin, J.: Industrial and critical infrastructure security: technical analysis of real-life security incidents. IEEE Access **9**, 165295–165325 (2021). https://doi.org/10.1109/ACCESS.2021.3133348
12. Mathur, A.P., Tippenhauer, N.O.: Swat: a water treatment testbed for research and training on ICS security. In: 2016 International Workshop on Cyber-physical Systems for Smart Water Networks (CySWater), pp. 31–36 (2016). https://doi.org/10.1109/CySWater.2016.7469060
13. Maynard, P., McLaughlin, K., Sezer, S.: An open framework for deploying experimental scada testbed networks. In: 5th International Symposium for ICS & SCADA Cyber Security Research 2018, pp. 92–101. BCS (2018)
14. Michail Takaronis, A.K.: Icsspulse: An open-source ICS protocol simulator (2025). https://github.com/r3dsh3rl0ck/ICSSPulse-Public
15. NIST: Nist glossary: Penetration testing (2021). https://csrc.nist.gov/glossary/term/penetration_testing
16. Williams, T.J.: The purdue enterprise reference architecture. Comput. Ind. **24**(2), 141–158 (1994). https://doi.org/10.1016/0166-3615(94)90017-5
17. Xie, Y., Wang, W., Wang, F., Chang, R.: Vtet: a virtual industrial control system testbed for cyber security research. In: 2018 Third International Conference on Security of Smart Cities, Industrial Control System and Communications (SSIC), pp. 1–7 (2018). https://doi.org/10.1109/SSIC.2018.8556732

Data and Applications Security

Cross-Network Transfer Learning for Cryptocurrency Fraud Detection

Denizhan Dalgıç[1,2](✉) and Şerif Bahtiyar[1]

[1] Cyber Security and Privacy Research Lab, SPFLab, Department of Computer Engineering, Istanbul Technical University, Maslak, Istanbul 34469, Türkiye
bahtiyars@itu.edu.tr

[2] Token Financial Technologies, İTÜ Maslak, Istanbul, Türkiye
dalgicd17@itu.edu.tr
https://www.tokeninc.com

Abstract. The lack of labeled data in the new generation of blockchain networks, such as XRP Ledger (XRPL), which also suffers from the lack of labeled data, is a notable deficiency. This work addresses the well-known "labeled data bottleneck problem" using Cross-Network Transfer Learning, postulating the universality of the fraud network structure. This research investigates the efficiency of three different adaptation mechanisms, Renaming, Scaled Transformation, and Synthetic Generation, to successfully transfer data from Bitcoin network to XRPL network. Experimental results indicate the attainment of 0.927 and 0.878 F1-score performances for transactions and wallet classification models, respectively when they are trained from transformed data. The solution also achieves the best performance using real XRPL distribution parameters with the Distribution-Based Synthetic Generation approach, which confirms the feasibility of the proposed approach.

Keywords: Blockchain · fraud detection · transfer learning · XRP ledger · machine learning · financial forensics · cross-domain adaptation

1 Introduction

Blockchain technology enables decentralized finance, but at the same time, it is also vulnerable to double-spending attacks and identity theft [9], and helps in crypto-related illicit activities such as Ponzi schemes and the money laundering of stolen funds [23]. Though traditional approaches to to ML are struggling due to dynamic evasion attacks [21,28], supervised ML models and techniques such as ensemble learning have become the norm and have reached a a high level of efficiency [11,14,26,28].

However, the use of these models on blockchain networks is hampered by a labeled data bottleneck, which is a challenge that has been widely noted in the Ethereum network [22,31]. It has insufficient ground truth data, unlike the Bitcoin ledger system. It will be very costly to label, hence not scalable [31,32].

© IFIP International Federation for Information Processing 2026
Published by Springer Nature Switzerland AG 2026
H. Janicke et al. (Eds.): SEC 2026, IFIP AICT 787, pp. 259–272, 2026.
https://doi.org/10.1007/978-3-032-27993-4_18

The insufficiency of labeled data further worsens the class imbalance problem [22], a structural challenge inherent to blockchain anomaly detection where normal transactions naturally outnumber malicious ones [2]. It does not work well under conditions of under-labeling constraints, as it finds it difficult to learn high-quality representations when only a small number of labels are available [32].

Research Hypothesis and Contributions. To overcome this data scarcity challenge, a novel approach proposed in the paper is referred to as *Cross-Network Transfer Learning*. The assumption made is that the patterns for graphically malicious transactions are universal for any blockchain system. The Elliptic++ Bitcoin dataset has been mapped to the XRPL through the Rename, Scaled, and Synthetic approaches. On this basis, our method exploits tree-based learning methods, which have been proven in the recent literature to be effective in modeling behavioral patterns in blockchain transactions [11,21].

The rest of this paper is organized as follows. Section 2 provides an overview of the current state of the art on blockchain forensics and transfer learning. Section 3 presents our methodology on mapping approaches and data preprocessing. Section 4 presents the experiment setup, results, and analysis of the results. The final section is dedicated to the conclusion and future works.

2 Related Work

The field of cryptocurrency forensics research combines network topology, deep learning, and data availability. We examine the differences between blockchain system architectures, anti-fraud progress, and the scarcity of labeled data that fuels cross-network transfer learning.

2.1 Blockchain Architectures: UTXO Versus Account Models

Cross-chain analysis is made difficult by the existence of different data structures. Bitcoin follows the Unspent Transaction Output (UTXO) model, which describes the state as a directed acyclic graph of coins. The UTXO system is computationally expensive because of unprofitable 'dust' outputs [8], requiring distributed graph storage for complex queries [34].

On the other hand, XRPL and Ethereum follow Account-based ledgers. This structural difference makes it impossible to directly apply the forensic attributes derived from Bitcoin to account-based systems. Apart from the differences in data representation, cross-chain analysis suffers from consensus differences that pose risks of double-spending and auditing [7]. Thus, cross-architecture forensics needs standardized representation tools and efficient topological mapping.

2.2 Forensics and Fraud Detection Mechanisms

Supervised learning algorithms such as Random Forests and SVMs form excellent baselines for fraud detection [21,23]. Gradient boosting (XGBoost, LightGBM) reduces bias, while ensembles like Stacking reduce variance [14,26,28].

Model optimization against high-volume threats demands rigorous preprocessing and statistical feature selection [1,13]. For graph-structured data, Graph Neural Networks effectively capture relational patterns of illicit flows [27,30]. Despite advanced representations via ego-graphs [15] and Code Property Graphs [16], large-scale fraud detection still faces real-time processing and scalability hurdles under centralized architectures [19,29].

2.3 The Ground Truth Bottleneck and Elliptic++

The primary challenge in training forensic models is the "labeled data bottleneck" [3]. Researchers mitigate this using label propagation [32], active learning [31], SMOTE [22], and pseudo-labeling. Transfer learning enables critical cross-domain knowledge transfer to overcome label limitations [25], while LLM-integrated RAG frameworks improve context-aware anomaly detection [12,17].

Historically, the Elliptic dataset [33] was standard, but lacked actor identification. Addressing this, Elmougy et al. [10] introduced *Elliptic++*, which enriches the data with actor-centered topologies via "actor interaction" and "user entity" graphs.

3 CNTL: Cross-Network Transfer Learning

We propose a Cross-Network Transfer Learning framework to enable the reuse of source blockchain-trained fraud models on an unlabeled target blockchain. The crucial assumption is that the money laundering trees, with a standard "fan-out" or "fan-in" pattern, represent the fraudulent topological structures that remain invariant to the underlying blockchain architecture [27].

In graph-theoretic terms, money laundering imposes strong physical constraints on a transaction graph $G = (V, E)$. To conceal the origin of funds without raising single-transaction volume alerts (layering), a criminal has to spread a large structural volume over multiple hops. This naturally creates particular structural patterns, such as high out-degree (d_{out}) star graphs, where the edge weights (transaction amounts) in the ego-graph have a fixed percentile rank. Since these rank-based distributions are compelled by the physical mechanisms of the crime rather than the source blockchain tokenomics, the structural pattern is invariant even if the absolute amounts vary between domains. We test the efficacy of three domain adaptation methods with increasing complexity to tap into this invariance.

3.1 Strategy 1: Semantic Renaming

This method, which requires minimal intervention, checks whether the process of fraudulent activity detection is entirely dependent on the topological structure and not on the values of the features. The method uses a function, or rather a bijection, called $\mathcal{M}$ that transforms source features to their semantic equivalents in the target domain, hence without altering their values. For example, features that are related to Bitcoin would have their names changed to their semantic equivalents. The graph topological structure and class labels are maintained as well.

3.2 Strategy 2: Scaled Transformation

This method corrects the domain discrepancy arising from the differences in tokenomics and consensuses among the blockchains. Four categories of features use linear scaling transformations:

- **Temporal features:** Scaled by the ledger-to-block ratio $\rho_t = T_S/T_T$, where T_S and T_T are the average block/ledger intervals of source and target networks respectively.
- **Value features:** Scaled by the historical value ratio ρ_v between the native currencies to align transaction magnitude distributions.
- **Fee features:** Transformed with variance reduction to reflect the target network's fee structure, applying $f' = \mu_f + (f - \mu_f) \cdot \alpha$ where $\alpha < 1$ compresses the fee distribution.
- **Transaction counts:** Scaled by throughput ratio ρ_c to account for differences in network capacity.

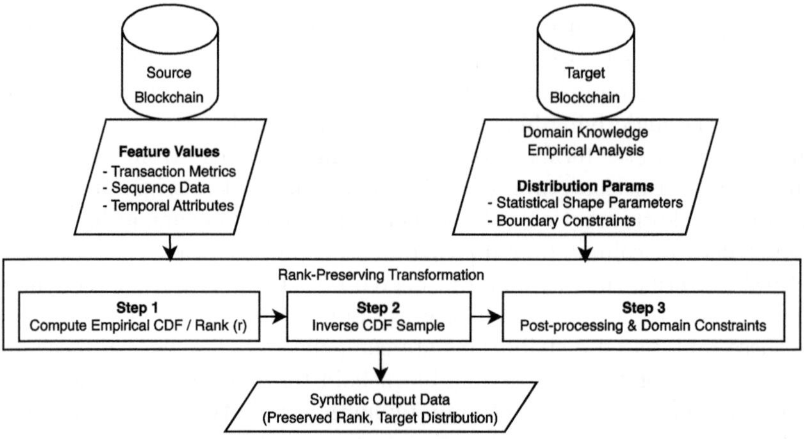

Fig. 1. Generic framework for distribution-based synthetic dataset generation.

Subsequently, the semantic renaming step similar to Strategy 1 is performed. It is important to note that the order or ranks of the values of the features are maintained, such that the behavior signatures used to differentiate the illegal and legal agents are also maintained.

3.3 Strategy 3: Distribution-Based Synthetic Generation

This approach generates target-like values for the features through sampling from empirically estimated probability distributions of the target network, as suggested by Javidan et al. [18]. The generic architecture of the approach is shown in Fig. 1. This approach typically consists of three phases: Source domain analysis involves harvesting labeled features from an annotated blockchain. Target distribution estimation involves sending probe queries to the public API of the target network to harvest real transaction data and uses parametric probability distributions (such as log-normal distribution) to model the quantity of the transaction, and rank-preserving transformation involves ICDF sampling.

In the case of the source feature vector $\mathbf{x}_S$ with the empirical CDF F_S, the transformation is computed as $\mathbf{x}_T = F_T^{-1}(F_S(\mathbf{x}_S))$. Thus, the absolute values are adapted to the target network properties while maintaining the same order of the nodes in the graph topology learned from the source domain. In our case, in the Bitcoin to XRPL example in Fig. 2, we employ the parameters learned from the public API of XRPL to apply the transformation to the Elliptic++ dataset (203k transactions, 822k wallets).

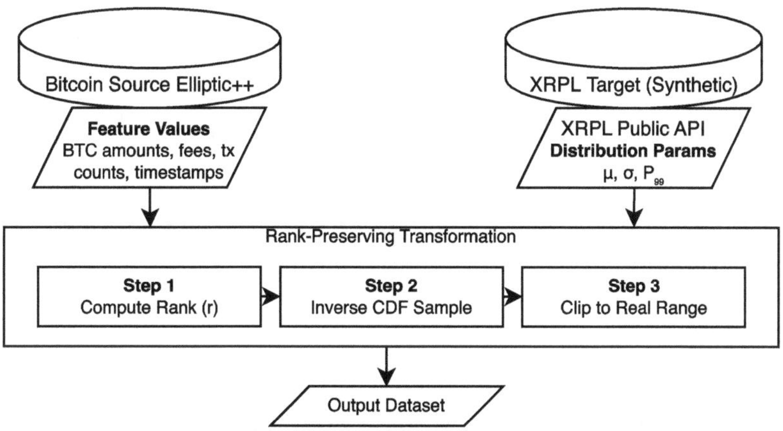

Fig. 2. Bitcoin Elliptic++ to XRPL mapping using synthetic data generation pipeline.

3.4 Classification Pipeline

After the mapped dataset is created, it is further processed by an ordinary fraud detection system as presented in Fig. 3. The inputs are processed at two different scales: the classification of wallets, where all the behavior-related features are combined to produce an entity profile, and the classification of transactions, where a single transaction record is analyzed. Then, these two streams are processed by the preprocessing stage, i.e., removal of missing values, removal of duplicates, normalization, etc.

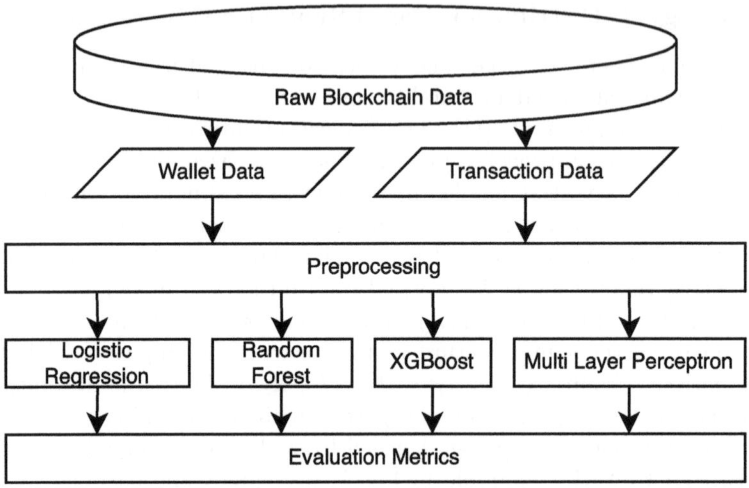

Fig. 3. Fraud detection classification pipeline. Raw blockchain data is split into wallet and transaction streams, preprocessed, and classified using an ensemble of four models.

The preprocessed data will then be used as input to four classifier models: Logistic Regression (Linear Baseline), Random Forest (Ensemble of Decision Trees), XGBoost, and Multi-Layer Perceptron (Neural Net). Each of these models will produce binary classifications (licit or illicit) of the data samples. The performance of these models will be evaluated using precision, recall, F1-score, and ROC-AUC metrics. This will enable us to understand whether the effectiveness of transfer learning is model-agnostic or dependent on the properties of the models.

4 Performance Evaluation

In order to effectively evaluate the proposed transfer learning framework, a comparison experiment is conducted to compare the performance of four different classifier models.

4.1 Classifier Architectures

Several algorithms were chosen to showcase the range of complexity reported in the literature. To address the highly imbalanced nature of the fraud samples (1.7% illicit), all machine learning models are trained using cost-sensitive learning with equal weights to both classes, instead of SMOTE to oversample the fraud samples, which may introduce artifacts and lead to overfitting [5,22]. The decimal point truncation approach is employed to eliminate noise from floating-point numbers [35].

- **Logistic Regression (LR):** This method is used for linear baseline analysis to judge the separability of features.

- **Random Forest (RF):** This is an ensemble of decision trees that was chosen for its stability in the field of blockchain forensics, as proposed by Kaur et al. [21] and Bolukbasi et al. [5]. We utilized 50 estimators with Gini impurity criterion and balanced class weights.
- **XGBoost (XGB):** The gradient boosting method has been chosen because of its strong out-of-the-box performance in handling imbalanced classification problems [11], although sometimes in cases of detecting blockchain fraud, data-level balancing methods like SMOTE are also needed [14]. The learning rate was set to a fixed value (η) of 0.1 with a maximum depth of 6 to prevent overfitting.
- **Multi-Layer Perceptron (MLP):** This is a feed-forward neural network that has been included to check the potential of deep representation learning methods, as proposed in the architectures surveyed by Latif et al. [24].

4.2 Evaluation Metrics

The existence of a very imbalanced class ratio of 1.7% for the illicit activity class makes the accuracy metric inappropriate. According to the guidelines outlined by Awoyemi et al. [4] and Krishnan et al. [22], the following metrics should be accorded top priority:

- **Precision and Recall:** Analysis of the trade-off between false positives & false negatives.
- **F1-Score:** This is the harmonic mean of precision and recall, denoted as the primary metric for success.
- **ROC-AUC:** Model discriminative capability over different values of the classification threshold, a common practice for credit card fraud analysis, as shown by Chavakula et al. [6].

The proposed machine learning model has a high precision of 0.91, which is a significant factor in the reduction of false positive rates in decentralized financial systems [20].

4.3 Overall Model Comparison

This section presents the experimental outcome related to cross-network mapping, which deals with the robustness of performance with respect to the type of mapping used, as well as the degradation of performance from the Bitcoin network to the target XRPL-like networks.

Figure 4 shows the F1-scores of all models. As noted by Josephine et al. [14], tree-based models (RF and XGB) greatly outperformed linear (LR) and neural (MLP) models, being less sensitive to the choice of domain mapping between "Rename" and "Scaled" approaches.

It is important to note that the performance achieved by *Rename Only* and *Scaled Transform* was comparable to the *Original Bitcoin* dataset for RF and XGB. This suggests that fraud detection is based on relative rankings of features (such as top 1% of amounts) rather than absolute values, which is an encouraging result for our "Invariant Feature Ranking" hypothesis.

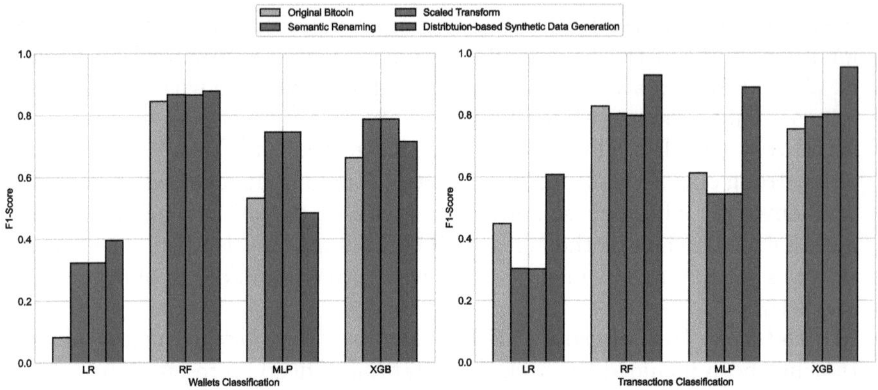

Fig. 4. F1-score comparison across models and mapping strategies.

4.4 Classification Performance

For the assessment of our framework, we have two levels, which are the wallet level and then come to the transaction level. The performance of Random Forest has been depicted in Table 1 classification results.

Table 1. Classification Performance (Random Forest).

Dataset	Wallet Classification			Transaction Classification		
	Prec.	Rec.	F1	Prec.	Rec.	F1
Original Bitcoin	0.911	0.789	0.845	0.975	0.719	0.828
Rename Only	0.9653	0.7857	0.8663	0.9852	0.6777	0.8031
Scaled Transform	0.9658	0.7841	0.8655	0.9837	0.6704	0.7974
Synthetic	0.9544	0.8122	0.8776	0.9925	0.8695	0.9269

The Distribution-Based Synthetic Generation method produces the highest values of the F1-score of 0.878 for the wallet classification task and 0.927 for the transaction classification task, which outperforms the Bitcoin baseline and other mapping methods. The Rename Only and Scaled Transform methods are also efficient and produce high values of the F1-score of 0.866 and 0.803–0.797, respectively. The proposed machine learning method has a high precision of 0.91, which is a significant factor in the reduction of false positive rates in decentralized financial systems [20]. The ROC curves (Fig. 5) confirm the high discriminative power of all mapping methods.

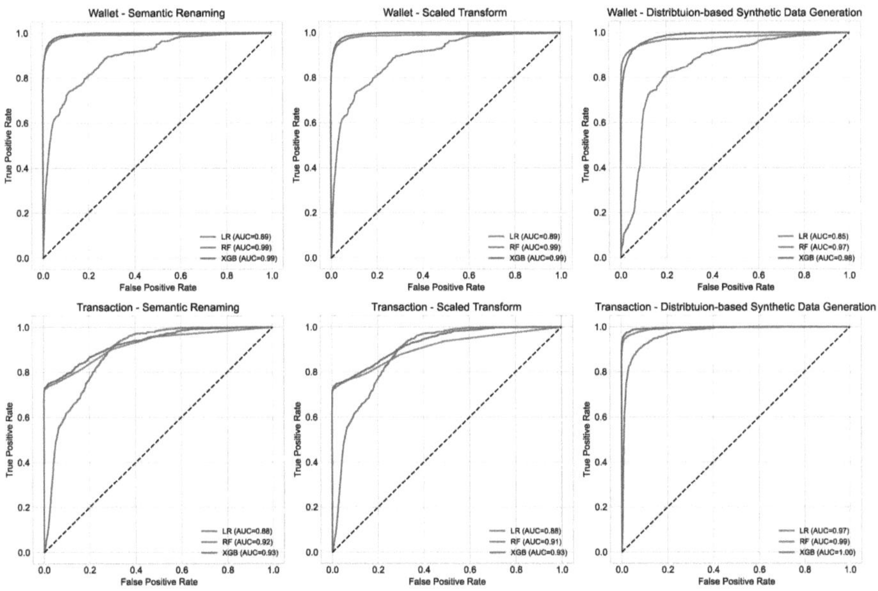

Fig. 5. ROC Curves for Wallet (top) and Transaction (bottom) Classification.

4.5 Transfer Efficiency Analysis

To emphasize the importance of domain adaptation, the cost of the process was measured by the performance difference for the source and target models. This is shown in Fig. 6, also known as the transfer gap below.

It is also observable that the results reveal a negligible performance distinction between the Renaming and Scaled strategies for the wallet classification, as well as a slight degradation for the transaction classification. It is, however, noteworthy that the Distribution-Based Synthetic Generation transfer learning strategy presents a strong positive transfer learning performance, as it increases the F1-scores by up to 3.3% for the wallet and 9.9% for the transaction classification when compared to the Bitcoin baseline transfer learning strategies.

4.6 The "Universal Fraud Signature" Hypothesis

The findings achieved through the implementation of all three mapping strategies serve as encouraging evidence for the validity of the "Universal Fraud Signature" hypothesis. The F1-scores achieved by the Random Forest classifier in the classification of the wallet were 0.866-0.878 through the implementation of all three strategies, with the Distribution-Based Synthetic Generation strategy yielding the highest score of 0.878. This empirical result indicates that malicious participants are likely to follow similar graph topologies in implementing their money laundering schemes, as these graph topologies naturally follow a scale-free topology using peeling chains and transaction loops [30]. The success

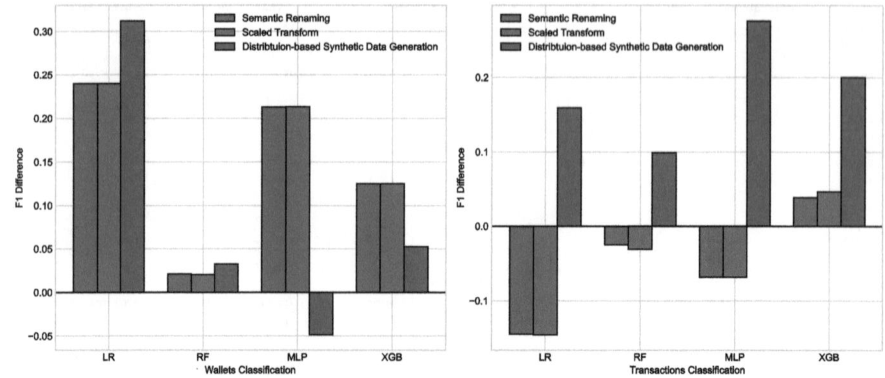

Fig. 6. Performance Difference with respect to Bitcoin Baseline: Positive values indicate that the mapped model performed better than the baseline. This verifies that since the deviation is less than ± 5%, the fraudulent behavioral pattern is maintained by the mapping strategies.

achieved through the implementation of the Distribution-Based Synthetic Generation strategy also indicates that if the distributions of targeted features can be appropriately aligned according to their relative importance, the proposed transfer learning strategy can be highly efficient, as indicated by the proposed findings by Louati et al. [25], which are focused on using the proposed strategy to address the lack of labeled data in anomaly detection for smart contracts.

4.7 Error Analysis and False Positives

Consequently, False Positives (FP) have high costs due to the potential lock-ups of assets of genuine users. The confusion matrix for the classification of the wallet as well as the transactions is illustrated in Fig. 7.

The Random Forest model was definitely more accurate than the Logistic Regression model, which was a model that was too simplistic to deal with the nonlinear high-dimensional space and, therefore, mostly predicted the class of the majority class. The above observation is in line with the findings of Kaur et al. [21] and Nayyer et al. [26], who found that traditional rule-based and standalone machine learning models are inefficient in identifying complex patterns of fraudulent transactions, requiring the application of efficient ensemble and nonlinear classification techniques.

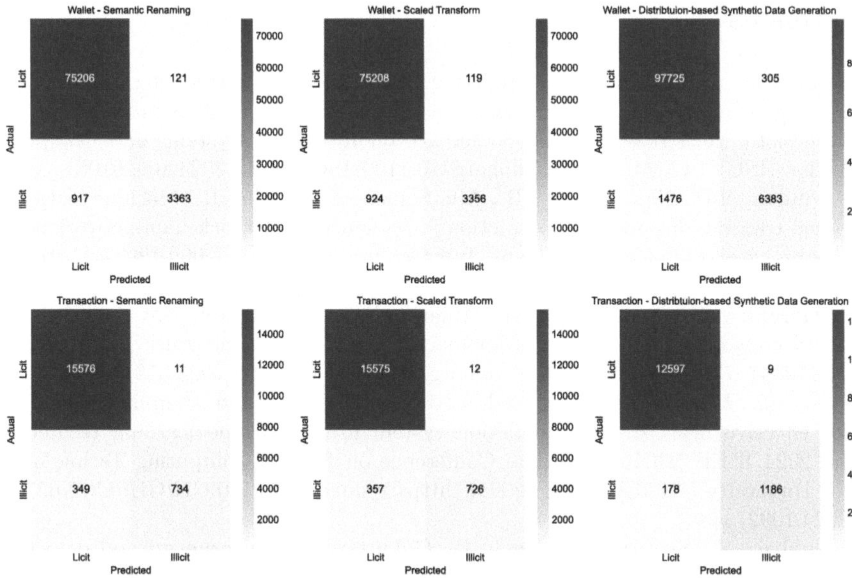

Fig. 7. Random Forest Confusion Matrices for Wallet (top row) and Transaction (bottom row) Classification across mapping strategies.

5 Conclusion

This paper tackles the labeled data bottleneck in blockchain forensics by proposing a Cross-Network Transfer Learning approach. We offer promising evidence of the "Universal Fraud Signature," demonstrating that a Bitcoin-trained model can successfully identify XRP Ledger fraud with F1-scores up to 0.927 (transactions) and 0.878 (accounts) via rank-preserving transformations.

Our Distribution-Based Synthetic Generation strategy was very successful, although more straightforward Renaming and Scaling strategies also worked well, indicating that costly target domain labeling may be unnecessary. The invariant feature ranking result suggests that financial crime structures are not platform-specific.

Although our results confirm the high transferability of fraud patterns, the investigation of the subtleties of cross-chain differences to map the exact limits of this universality is a fascinating area for future research. Moreover, the dynamic nature of crypto-crime must be tackled by automating the process of feature mapping and protecting cross-chain bridges.

Acknowledgments. This work was supported by Research Fund of the Istanbul Technical University under the agreement with Ripple, Project No:48205.

References

1. Abdelouahed, S.M., Abla, R., Asmae, E., Abdellah, A.: Harnessing feature engineering to improve machine learning: a review of different data processing techniques. In: 2024 International Conference on Intelligent Systems and Computer Vision (ISCV) (2024). https://doi.org/10.1109/ISCV60512.2024.10620105
2. Abdullah, N.F., Kairaldeen, A.R., Abu-Samah, A., Nordin, R.: Machine learning-based transactions anomaly prediction for enhanced IoT blockchain network security and performance. KSII Trans. Internet Inf. Syst. 1986–2009 (2024). https://doi.org/10.3837/tiis.2024.07.014
3. Alzahrani, A.S., Alahmadi, D.H., Alharbi, N.M., Almagrabi, H.A.: Blockchain-based crowdsourcing framework for machine learning ground truth. IEEE Access **13**, 73041–73055 (2025). https://doi.org/10.1109/ACCESS.2025.3564534
4. Awoyemi, J.O., et al.: Advanced feature engineering and sampling technique for effective heart disease prediction system using machine learning technique. In: 2024 IEEE 5th International Conference on Electro-Computing Technologies for Humanity (NIGERCON) (2024). https://doi.org/10.1109/NIGERCON62786.2024.10927368
5. Bolukbasi, Z., Yurtoglu, H., Kugu, E., Cukurtepe, H.: Insurance fraud detection using machine learning and XAI algorithms. In: 2025 IEEE International Conference on Electro Information Technology (eIT). pp. 463–468 (2025). https://doi.org/10.1109/eIT64391.2025.11103653
6. Chavakula, S.J., Albert, C.A.J., Ebenezer, E., Bhagat, M.H., Mahamuni, C.V.: Explainable AI (XAI) using SHAP and lime for financial fraud detection and credit scoring. In: 2025 International Conference on Advanced Computing Technologies (ICoACT) (2025). https://doi.org/10.1109/ICoACT63339.2025.11005238
7. Dalgıç, D., Bahtiyar, Ş.: Security challenges in cross-chain defi applications. In: 2025 10th International Conference on Computer Science and Engineering (UBMK), pp. 1485–1490 (2025). https://doi.org/10.1109/UBMK67458.2025.11206984
8. Delgado-Segura, S., Pérez-Solà, C., Navarro-Arribas, G., Herrera-Joancomartí, J.: Analysis of the bitcoin utxo set. In: Zohar, A., et al. (eds.) Financial Cryptography and Data Security, pp. 78–91. Springer, Berlin Heidelberg, Berlin, Heidelberg (2019)
9. Dubey, A., Choubey, S.: Blockchain and machine learning for data analytics, privacy preserving, and security in fraud detection. I-Manager's. J. Softw. Eng. **18**(1), 45–55 (2023). https://doi.org/10.26634/jse.18.1.20091
10. Elmougy, Y., Liu, L.: Demystifying fraudulent transactions and illicit nodes in the bitcoin network for financial forensics. In: Proceedings of the 29th ACM SIGKDD Conference on Knowledge Discovery and Data Mining, pp. 3979–3990. KDD '23, Association for Computing Machinery, New York, NY, USA (2023). https://doi.org/10.1145/3580305.3599803
11. Ertam, F.: Near real-time Ethereum fraud detection using explainable AI in blockchain networks. Appl. Sci. **15**(19), 10841 (2025). https://doi.org/10.3390/app151910841
12. Gebreab, S., Musamih, A., Salah, K., Jayaraman, R.: LLM-based exploration and analysis of real-time and historical blockchain data. Expert Syst. Appl. 129851 (2026). https://doi.org/10.1016/j.eswa.2025.129851
13. Gopalsamy, M.: Optimising DDoS attack detection using feature engineering and machine learning techniques in high-volume network traffic analysis. In: 2025 3rd

International Conference on Integrated Circuits and Communication Systems (ICICACS) (2025). https://doi.org/10.1109/ICICACS65178.2025.10968656
14. Helen Josephine, V.L., Praveen Kumar, T., Joy, J., Mansurali, A.: Implementing ensemble machine learning techniques for fraud detection in blockchain ecosystem. In: 2023 2nd International Conference on Automation, Computing and Renewable Systems (ICACRS), pp. 1980–1985 (2023). https://doi.org/10.1109/ICACRS58579.2023.10404402
15. Huang, H., et al.: PEAE-GNN: phishing detection on Ethereum via augmentation ego-graph based on graph neural network. IEEE Trans. Comput. Soc. Syst. 4326–4339 (2024). https://doi.org/10.1109/TCSS.2023.3349071
16. Huanliang, X., Canghai, W., JiaXin, C., Yinglong, W., yulin, Z.: A smart contract vulnerability line detection method based on graph neural network and fusion of multidimensional code representation. Appl. Soft Comput. 113435 (2025). https://doi.org/10.1016/j.asoc.2025.113435
17. Islayem, R., et al.: Using large language models for enhanced fraud analysis and detection in blockchain based health insurance claims. Sci. Rep. 1–26 (2025). https://doi.org/10.1038/s41598-025-15676-4
18. Javidan, S.M., Banakar, A., Rahnama, K., Vakilian, K.A., Ampatzidis, Y.: Feature engineering to identify plant diseases using image processing and artificial intelligence: a comprehensive review. Smart Agric. Technol. 100480 (2024). https://doi.org/10.1016/j.atech.2024.100480
19. Jiang, X., Tsai, W.T.: MVCG-SPS: a multi-view contrastive graph neural network for smart Ponzi scheme detection. Appl. Sci. 3281 (2025). https://doi.org/10.3390/app15063281
20. Kaur, K., et al.: Fraud detection using machine learning in blockchain stock marketing transactions. In: 2024 International Conference on Innovative Computing, Intelligent Communication and Smart Electrical Systems (ICSES) (2024). https://doi.org/10.1109/ICSES63760.2024.10910816
21. Kaur, K., et al.: Machine learning for fraud detection in blockchain transaction. In: 2024 International Conference on Knowledge Engineering and Communication Systems (ICKECS) (2024). https://doi.org/10.1109/ICKECS61492.2024.10616821
22. Krishnan, L.P., Vakilinia, I., Reddivari, S., Ahuja, S.: Handling imbalanced data for detecting scams in Ethereum transactions using sampling techniques. In: 2024 12th International Symposium on Digital Forensics and Security (ISDFS) (2024). https://doi.org/10.1109/ISDFS60797.2024.10527318
23. Kılıç, B., Sen, A., Özturan, C.: Fraud detection in blockchains using machine learning. In: 2022 Fourth International Conference on Blockchain Computing and Applications (BCCA), pp. 214–218 (2022). https://doi.org/10.1109/BCCA55292.2022.9922045
24. Latif, N., Ma, W., Ahmad, H.B.: Advancements in securing federated learning with ids: a comprehensive review of neural networks and feature engineering techniques. Artif. Intell. Rev. **58**(3) (2025). https://doi.org/10.1007/s10462-024-11082-w
25. Louati, H., Louati, A., Kariri, E., Almekhlafi, A.: AI-based anomaly detection and optimization framework for blockchain smart contracts. Adm. Sci. **15**, 163 (2025). https://doi.org/10.3390/admsci15050163
26. Nayyer, N., et al.: A new framework for fraud detection in bitcoin transactions through ensemble stacking model in smart cities. IEEE Access 90916–90938 (2023). https://doi.org/10.1109/ACCESS.2023.3308298
27. Patel, V., Pan, L., Rajasegarar, S.: Graph deep learning based anomaly detection in Ethereum blockchain network. In: Lecture Notes in Computer Science (NSS 2020), vol. 12570. Springer, Cham (2020). https://doi.org/10.1007/978-3-030-65745-1_8

28. Qasaimeh, M., Qasaimeh, M., Yassin, M.B.: Hybrid stacking ensemble approach in smart contracts fraud detection. In: 2025 16th International Conference on Information and Communication Systems (ICICS) (2025). https://doi.org/10.1109/ICICS65354.2025.11073119
29. Shi, J.: Application of blockchain-driven big data analytics in financial fraud detection in engineering management. J. Comput. Methods Sci. Eng. (2025). https://doi.org/10.1177/14727978251352145
30. Srivastava, S., Singh, R.B.: Enhancing cryptocurrency fraud detection with hybrid feature-graph learning. In: 2025 International Conference on Computing Technologies (ICOCT) (2025). https://doi.org/10.1109/ICOCT64433.2025.11118689
31. Sun, X., et al.: Assbert: active and semi-supervised BERT for smart contract vulnerability detection. J. Inf. Secur. Appl. 103423 (2023). https://doi.org/10.1016/j.jisa.2023.103423
32. Wang, R., Zhang, Z., Wang, Y., Zhang, Y.: Anomaly detection service for blockchain transactions using minimal substitution-based label propagation. In: 2023 19th International Conference on Mobility, Sensing and Networking (MSN), pp. 685–692 (2023). https://doi.org/10.1109/MSN60784.2023.00100
33. Weber, M., et al.: Anti-money laundering in bitcoin: experimenting with graph convolutional networks for financial forensics (2019). https://arxiv.org/abs/1908.02591
34. Yan, R., et al.: UTXOAnalysis: a distributed graph storage and analysis system for UTXO-based cryptocurrencies. Comput. Electr. Eng. **120**, 109760 (2024). https://doi.org/10.1016/j.compeleceng.2024.109760. https://www.sciencedirect.com/science/article/pii/S0045790624006876
35. Zhao, X., Leng, X., Wang, L., Wang, N.: Research on fine-tuning optimization strategies for large language models in tabular data processing. Biomimetics **9**(11), 708 (2024). https://doi.org/10.3390/biomimetics9110708

Clovery: Identifying Affected Versions in C/C++ Public Security Vulnerability Reports

Duyeong Kim, Jimin Kang, Yeonhee Kim, Seunghoon Woo(✉), and Heejo Lee(✉)

Korea University, Seoul, South Korea
{duyeong,ziminii,kyh0502,seunghoonwoo,heejo}@korea.ac.kr

Abstract. We present CLOVERY, a precise approach for detecting vulnerability-affected versions through code-level semantic analysis. Precise management of vulnerability-affected versions is crucial for mitigating risks from vulnerability propagation. However, identifying these versions is challenging, requiring deep understanding of both the syntax and semantics of vulnerable code. Existing approaches often rely on broad assumptions, causing false alarms. Public security reports frequently misclassify dangerous versions as safe and *vice versa*, further exacerbating the problem. To overcome these limitations, CLOVERY uses a technique called *function-lineage tracking*. It focuses on vulnerability-related code lines and uses semantic pairs to capture dependencies. By tracking function histories via semantic pairs, CLOVERY precisely identifies versions affected by vulnerabilities. On 1,502 NVD CVEs, CLOVERY found potential CPE issues in 65.65% of cases, indicating risks to vulnerability management. Notably, CLOVERY achieved 97.43% F1 in identifying affected versions, significantly outperforming existing approaches, which achieved 71.16% and 84.23% F1 scores. These results suggest that CLOVERY can improve vulnerability response and software supply-chain security.

1 Introduction

The widespread adoption of open-source software (OSS) has accelerated software development by enabling code reuse through public repositories [1,2,25,29]. However, library reuse in OSS introduces security concerns such as vulnerability propagation [11,13]. To mitigate these risks, vulnerabilities are disclosed as Common Vulnerabilities and Exposures (CVEs) and documented in the National Vulnerability Database (NVD) [3], which includes affected software versions using the Common Platform Enumeration (CPE). This information plays a crucial role in helping developers identify and remediate potential threats [5,22].

Despite its role, affected version information is often inaccurate [4,8,24,26]. The NVD may over-approximate affected ranges, treating all preceding versions as vulnerable. Conversely, a vulnerability may exist in a version, but the NVD incorrectly indicates it is safe. Furthermore, the NVD often fails to account for

© IFIP International Federation for Information Processing 2026
Published by Springer Nature Switzerland AG 2026
H. Janicke et al. (Eds.): SEC 2026, IFIP AICT 787, pp. 273–287, 2026.
https://doi.org/10.1007/978-3-032-27993-4_19

parallel development (*i.e.*, two or more release lines maintained concurrently), leading to inaccuracies in tracking affected versions (see Sect. 2.2).

Existing Approaches. Existing approaches to identifying affected versions have limitations due to (1) overly simplistic assumptions and (2) exclusive focus on patch syntax. A key assumption is that code critical to vulnerabilities is always deleted in patches. For example, `V0Finder` [24] assumes that only deleted code lines are critical and therefore cannot handle cases where patches only add new lines. VISION [26] assumes detailed descriptions of vulnerabilities (*e.g.*, code lines causing the vulnerability) are provided in vulnerability reports, making it difficult to comprehensively examine CVEs. SZZ techniques (*e.g.*, [4,20]) identify commits where a bug was introduced; however, for identifying vulnerability-affected versions this approach is less effective because both the commit introducing the vulnerability and the one removing it are important.

Our Approach. To address these shortcomings, we present CLOVERY (Code c LO based vulnerability-affected VE discove RY), a precise approach for identifying versions affected by vulnerabilities. CLOVERY differs from existing approaches by (1) focusing on core code lines closely tied to vulnerabilities and (2) leveraging semantic pairs to capture code dependencies.

Given a CVE ID, CLOVERY collects the security patch and codebase of the affected software. It reconstructs vulnerable and patched functions from the security patch and employs *function-lineage tracking* to capture semantic relationships as *semantic pairs*. CLOVERY considers a version vulnerable if it contains functions with vulnerable semantic pairs and few or no patch semantic pairs, and aggregates these results to determine the full range of affected versions.

To evaluate CLOVERY, we collected 4,060 C/C++ CVEs from the NVD and selected 1,502 for evaluation (selection criteria detailed in Sect. 5.1). CLOVERY identified potential CPE inconsistencies in 65.65% of these CVEs (see Sect. 5.2). One major cause of such errors is the lack of mechanisms to account for new branches or versions introduced after a CVE is published. Despite this challenge, CLOVERY outperformed existing approaches in identifying vulnerability-affected versions, achieving a 97.43% F1 score compared to 71.16% and 84.23% F1 scores by existing approaches [20,24]. CLOVERY also analyzes the types and root causes of errors in public security reports. Our findings indicate that affected version information in the NVD requires ongoing updates, and CLOVERY provides an effective automated solution.

Contributions. We summarize our contributions below.

- We propose CLOVERY, a precise approach for identifying vulnerability-affected versions. The key technical contribution is *function-lineage tracking*, which considers pairs of code lines with semantic relationships.
- We found that many public security reports incorrectly specify vulnerability -affected versions (65.65% of cases in our experimental setup).
- CLOVERY achieved 96.27% precision and 98.62% recall in identifying vulnerability-affected versions, outperforming existing approaches.
- Source code and datasets related to CLOVERY will be publicly available at publication.

2 Motivation

2.1 Basic Terminology

Version-related terms are defined as follows:

- **Version:** A release of a software program, identified by version information specified in CPEs and by tags in the corresponding GitHub repositories.
- **Vulnerability-affected versions:** Versions that are affected by a vulnerability in the software where the vulnerability originated, including versions that may be indirectly affected.
- **Vulnerable software information in public vulnerability reports:** Affected-version metadata reported in public security reports (e.g., CPEs), which this paper aims to validate.

2.2 Motivating Example

Listing 1.1. CVE-2018-19210: a patch snippet showing the fix is missing.

```
// CPE (reported vulnerable): cpe:2.3:a:libtiff:libtiff: 4.0.9 :*:*:*:*:*:*:*
// CPE (reported fixed) : cpe:2.3:a:libtiff:libtiff: 4.0.10 :*:*:*:*:*:*:*
// Commit (patch) : d0a842c5dbad2609aed43c701a12ed12461d3405
// Path : libtiff/tif_dir.c
static int _TIFFVSetField(...) {
...
   td->td_smaxsamplevalue = NULL;
 }
// --- LibTIFF 4.0.10 (unpatched): expected fix is missing ---
 - if( td->td_transferfunction[0] != NULL && (v - td->td_extrasamples > 1) &&
 -     !(td->td_samplesperpixel - td->td_extrasamples > 1)) {...}
// --- Patch commit d0a842c5...: fix is present ---
 + if( td->td_transferfunction[0] != NULL && (v - td->td_extrasamples > 1) &&
 +     !(td->td_samplesperpixel - td->td_extrasamples > 1)) {...}
 }
 td->td_samplesperpixel = (uint16) v;
}
```

We present a `LibTIFF` case where affected version information in a public security report leads to misclassification of vulnerable and safe versions.

`LibTIFF`[1] is widely used for reading and writing Tagged Image File Format (TIFF) files. CVE-2018-19210 reports a NULL pointer dereference and indicates that the issue was patched in 4.0.10. However, we found that the fix is missing in `LibTIFF` 4.0.10 and was applied in a later version (see Listing 1.1). We confirmed that this vulnerability was reproduced in `LibTIFF` 4.0.10 using a known Proof of Concept (PoC). Developers often choose to partially update or backport patch code, due to compatibility or dependency issues [16,25]. In this context, inaccurate affected version information can misguide partial updates and negatively impact overall system security.

[1] https://gitlab.com/libtiff/libtiff.

3 Methodology of Clovery

In this section, we present the methodology of Clovery, which precisely identifies affected versions of C/C++ vulnerabilities. The key distinguishing feature of Clovery is its consideration of both the syntax and semantics of code lines by using semantic pairs and function-lineage tracking.

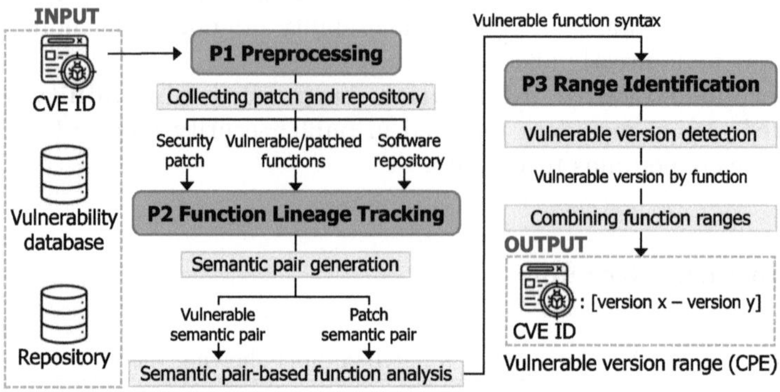

Fig. 1. High-level overview of Clovery.

Figure 1 illustrates the workflow of Clovery, which comprises the three phases: *preprocessing* (**P1**), *function-lineage tracking* (**P2**), and *range identification* (**P3**). In **P1**, Clovery collects the security patch and the corresponding repository, and extracts vulnerable and patched functions. In **P2**, Clovery extracts semantic pairs and tracks target functions over the commit history to identify vulnerable syntaxes. In **P3**, Clovery aggregates function-level results to identify the affected-version range for the input CVE.

3.1 Preprocessing Phase (P1)

Security Patch and Repository Collection. Given a CVE, Clovery collects security patches by checking CVE reference links in the NVD. If a reference link includes a GitHub commit URL, Clovery identifies it as a security patch and collects it (see Sect. 4). Clovery then collects the repository associated with the patch URL [22,23].

Vulnerable and Patched Function Extraction. Subsequently, Clovery extracts vulnerable and patched functions using the collected security patches and repositories. Because Clovery collects security patches from GitHub commits, it extracts the modified files and recovers the functions containing the changed lines. Unlike approaches (*e.g.*, [24]) that focus only on added or deleted lines, Clovery extracts full functions to capture lines dependent on the patch changes.

3.2 Function-Lineage Tracking Phase (P2)

Using the security patch, repository, and functions from P1, CLOVERY performs *function-lineage tracking*. This phase consists of four steps: core code line extraction (**S1**), semantic pair configuration (**S2**), commit history extraction (**S3**), and vulnerable syntax identification (**S4**).

S1: Core Code Line Extraction. CLOVERY extracts two types of core lines: **essential lines**, which are changed in the security patch (*i.e.*, added or deleted code lines), and **dependent lines**, which are within the same function and have control or data dependency on the essential lines.

Essential lines are code segments that play a critical role in the manifestation of vulnerabilities [13]. However, as the codebase evolves, these lines may change [23,27], making it necessary to perform additional semantic analysis to assess the impact of such changes. To address this, CLOVERY also considers dependent code lines those that support or rely on the behavior of essential lines and may influence vulnerabilities [23,27]. By pairing semantically related lines, CLOVERY can effectively identify vulnerable code clones and determine affected versions. Specifically, CLOVERY first treats the code lines *deleted* in the patch as essential, then identifies their dependent lines within the *vulnerable* function. It then performs the same analysis for the *added* lines in the *patched* function.

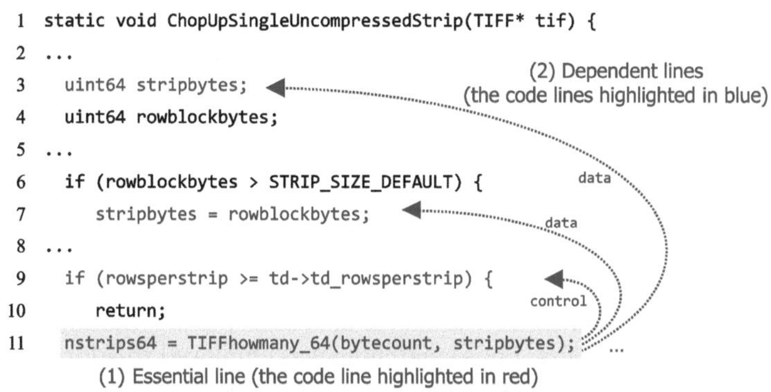

Fig. 2. Illustration of identifying essential and dependent lines to generate semantic pairs.

S2: Semantic Pair Configuration. CLOVERY focuses on code line pairs (called *semantic pairs*) that have a semantic relationship within a function. CLOVERY considers two types of semantic pairs: *vulnerable semantic pairs* extracted from the vulnerable function and *patch semantic pairs* extracted from the patched function. A semantic pair (p) consists of an essential line (l_e) and a dependent line (l_d) within the same function: $p = (l_e, l_d)$. For each essential line, CLOVERY generates semantic pairs with all identified dependent lines.

Figure 2 illustrates the extraction process for vulnerable semantic pairs. Code lines #3, #7, and #9 are marked as dependent due to their data dependency on line #11 (*e.g.*, dependency on the variable `stripbytes`). This yields three vulnerable semantic pairs: line `(#11, #3)`, `(#11, #7)`, and `(#11, #9)`. By applying this process to all essential and dependent lines (for both vulnerable and patched functions), CLOVERY extracts semantic pairs for each essential line.

The issue is that the syntax of added and deleted lines may be identical, and a dependent line can be shared across vulnerable and patch semantic pairs, which can hinder identification. To address this, CLOVERY ignores identical add-delete lines and removes duplicate dependent lines from patch semantic pairs.

S3: Commit History Extraction. Next, CLOVERY extracts the change history of the functions in which vulnerabilities exist. Because CLOVERY collects the codebase of the software with vulnerabilities from GitHub (see Sect. 3.1), this can be easily accomplished using git commands (*e.g.*, using "`git log`"). CLOVERY sets the software codebase corresponding to the vulnerability to the latest version, and extracts the commit history of the source files containing vulnerable functions (details are provided in Sect. 4).

S4: Vulnerable Syntax Identification. Using semantic pairs and the extracted commit history, CLOVERY identifies vulnerable syntaxes in target functions. If function names change, CLOVERY tracks target functions from the patch commit in both directions of the file history.

1. **Set the reference point.** CLOVERY uses the patch commit as the reference point because it includes the target function names extracted in P1.
2. **Function tracking.** CLOVERY traverses the history in both directions and keeps only commits where the target functions change.

To reduce false alarms from non-semantic changes and trivial code lines, CLOVERY applies normalization and filters short lines. CLOVERY ignores comment lines, converts characters to lowercase, and removes whitespace. CLOVERY also disregards code lines with 15 or fewer characters after normalization [23].

CLOVERY determined that the target function has a vulnerable syntax if it contains a sufficient number of vulnerable semantic pairs while including a few (or no) patch semantic pairs. Loose matching was employed to address the diversity of the function syntax. Based on this idea, CLOVERY considers the following two types of similarities: *vulnerability similarity* (Φ_v) and *patch similarity* (Φ_p).

Let P_v and P_p represent vulnerable and patch semantic pairs, respectively, and let f_i denote the target function.

$$\Phi_v = \frac{|\{(x,y) \in P_v \mid x \in f_i \land y \in f_i\}|}{|P_v|}, \quad \Phi_p = \frac{|\{(x,y) \in P_p \mid x \in f_i \land y \in f_i\}|}{|P_p|}$$

Similarity is defined as the ratio of semantic pairs in which both the essential and dependent lines exist. We introduce two thresholds, θ_v and θ_p, and use them to determine whether the syntax of a target function f_i should be considered vulnerable. CLOVERY determines that f_i is vulnerable if $\Phi_v > \theta_v$ and $\Phi_p < \theta_p$.

If no code lines are added (*resp.* deleted) in the patch, CLOVERY considers only $\Phi_v > \theta_v$ (*resp.* $\Phi_p < \theta_p$). Because CLOVERY considers semantic pairs rather than isolated lines, it can handle patches with structural changes and code dependencies that are missed by syntax-only approaches [24,26]. Compared to VISION [26], CLOVERY does not rely on additional assumptions from descriptions or vulnerability patches, enabling it to identify versions affected by vulnerabilities much more comprehensively.

3.3 Range Identification Phase (P3)

Finally, CLOVERY identifies the affected-version range for the input CVE by aggregating function-level results from P2. For each version, CLOVERY checks whether any target function instance is classified as vulnerable; if so, CLOVERY marks the version as affected.

Let F_v be the set of vulnerable syntaxes for the target function instances, v_i represent each version, and f_i denote the syntax of the target function in v_i.

Vulnerability affected version identification

- CLOVERY determines that v_i is the vulnerability affected version when f_i has the same syntax as f_j contained in F_v.

Some may consider directly comparing semantic pairs with f_i instead of extracting vulnerable function syntaxes. However, as mentioned earlier, this approach may fail to correctly extract f_i from v_i, particularly when the names of the target functions have changed. Therefore, CLOVERY identifies versions affected by vulnerabilities based on function-lineage tracking. Note that since a patch can modify multiple functions, CLOVERY evaluates each function and aggregates the results across modified functions.

4 Implementation of CLOVERY

Architecture of Clovery. CLOVERY comprises three modules: a *dataset collector*, *function-lineage tracker* and *vulnerable range identifier*. All process modules were implemented in approximately 2,900 lines of Python code, excluding external libraries (*e.g.*, function parsers).

CVE Patch Collection. We obtained security patches using a method similar to those in previous studies (*e.g.*, [10,14,23]). We collected security patches by crawling `Git` commit URLs referenced in NVD CVE entries. Consequently, we collected 4,060 C/C++ security patches from the NVD (as of August 2024).

We then extracted the vulnerable and patched functions from the security patches using techniques from previous studies (*e.g.*, [13,23]). Using file indices before and after patch application, we extracted functions containing modified code. To extract functions, we used Universal Ctags [6], a fast and accurate function parser. In total, we extracted 10,359 vulnerable—atched function pairs. CLOVERY then leverages the Joern parser [28] to analyze extracted functions, identifying essential and dependent lines to construct semantic pairs.

Software Repository and Commit History Collection. We collected software repositories corresponding to the security patches obtained from GitHub. Consequently, we collected 783 software repositories with a total of 148,970 versions. For each target function, CLOVERY tracks the change history by collecting commit histories of the files containing the function using `Git` commands.

```
git log --follow --diff-filter=AMD --name-status --pretty=format:"%H
%ci" -- <file_path>
```

Using the extracted commit history, CLOVERY identifies commits that include changes to the target function and extracts the corresponding function versions. In addition, CLOVERY retrieves function-level code changes in `diff` format using the following command.

```
git log -1 <commit_id> -L:<function_name>:<path>
```

If the target function was renamed, we updated its name to ensure continuous history tracking.

Table 1. Accuracy of NVD, `V0Finder`, `SEM-SZZ`, and CLOVERY in identifying vulnerability-affected versions. CLOVERY achieved the best overall precision and recall across all three validation methods.

Validation method	#CVEs	NVD			`V0Finder` [24]			`SEM-SZZ` [20]			CLOVERY		
		Precision	Recall	F1 score	Precision	Recall	F1 score	Precision	Recall	F1 score	Precision	Recall	F1 score
Reproduction	103	0.8627	0.8712	0.8669	**0.9973**	0.6645	0.7976	0.9421	0.8574	0.8978	0.8837	**0.9759**	**0.9275**
Author sites	54	0.8913	0.8612	**0.8759**	0.9129	0.5158	0.6592	**0.9570**	0.5108	0.6661	0.7302	**0.9245**	0.8160
Code review	1,345	0.8126	0.8566	0.8340	0.9450	0.5647	0.7070	0.9460	0.7644	0.8456	**0.9781**	**0.9894**	**0.9837**
Total	1,502	0.8189	0.8577	0.8379	0.9474	0.5698	0.7116	0.9484	0.7576	0.8423	**0.9627**	**0.9862**	**0.9743**

5 Evaluation

We evaluate CLOVERY based on the following three research questions.

- **RQ1: Accuracy.** How precisely does CLOVERY identify versions affected by vulnerabilities compared with existing approaches and CPE in NVD? What are representative examples?
- **RQ2: Findings.** Based on the results from CLOVERY, how much difference is observed in CPE? What are the types and causes of these differences?
- **RQ3: Performance.** How does CLOVERY perform in terms of runtime when identifying the versions affected by vulnerabilities?

We ran CLOVERY on a machine with a GNU/Linux 6.5.0-44-generic x86_64, Intel (R) Core (TM) i7-13700 @ 5.70 GHz, 62 GB RAM, and 1.8TB SSD.

5.1 Accuracy

Accuracy Measurement Targets. Out of 4,060 collected CVEs, CLOVERY extracted core lines for 4,054 CVEs (six failures due to external-library errors). To analyze affected versions, we excluded vulnerabilities reported in GitHub repositories that do not specify a version. In this process, 1,878 CVEs were removed. Among the remaining 2,176 CVEs, we further excluded cases where the GitHub repository and version names are not meaningfully aligned with the CPE software identity, because CLOVERY does not aim to resolve CPE–repository name mismatches. Consequently, CLOVERY analyzed *1,502 CVEs.*

The problem is that there is no definitive ground truth for vulnerability-affected versions. Hence, we manually validated the results using three methods: *reproduction*, *author sites*, and *code review* (*i.e.*, referring to `VOFinder` [24]). First, we attempt to trigger the vulnerability in a target version when exploit information is available (*reproduction*). We also refer to reports from the repository's website or blogs where the vulnerability was reported and analyze the reports (*author sites*). If none of the aforementioned information was available, we examined the source code to identify vulnerable functions and determine whether the version was affected (*code review*).

Four analysts conducted the validation (one with 10+ years of security code-review experience and three with 5+ years of research experience). During code reviews, analysts did not assume all code modifications to be security-relevant. Instead, they carefully examined each patch in the context of the associated CVE, referring to the CVE description, commit message, and surrounding source code. The review focused on determining whether the modified code is directly associated with the occurrence or mitigation of the reported vulnerability, particularly by analyzing whether the relevant data or control flow remains consistent with the vulnerability type. This manual validation enables semantic understanding and contextual interpretation that are often difficult to capture through automated analysis alone.

We classify results into TP (vulnerable identified as vulnerable), FP (safe identified as vulnerable), and FN (vulnerable identified as safe). We use macro-accuracy to avoid bias from uneven version counts per CVE. Macro-precision (P) and macro-recall (R) are defined as $P = \frac{1}{N}\sum_i \frac{TP_i}{TP_i+FP_i}$ and $R = \frac{1}{N}\sum_i \frac{TP_i}{TP_i+FN_i}$, where N is the number of CVEs. We then compute the F1 score (F): $F = (2 * P * R)/(P + R)$. We conducted the experiments by setting θ_v and θ_p to 0.5, respectively (see Sect. 3.2). The experiment on threshold sensitivity is introduced at the end of Sect. 5.1.

Comparison Targets. We evaluated CLOVERY against the NVD (CPE) and compared it with `VOFinder` [24] and `SEM-SZZ` [20]. `AFV` [18] was excluded because it targets web-application vulnerabilities. VISION [26] could not be directly compared because its tool/source code were unavailable despite our request.

Result Analysis. Table 1 summarizes the results on 1,502 CVEs. CLOVERY achieved 97.43% F1 (96.27% precision and 98.62% recall), thereby outperforming

VOFinder (71.16% F1) and SEM-SZZ (84.23% F1). The NVD also showed non-trivial inaccuracies, which we analyze in Sect. 5.2.

VOFinder tends to miss vulnerabilities when patches mainly add lines or when vulnerable logic is structurally altered, as it relies on deleted-line heuristics and syntactic matching. SEM-SZZ handles added-line cases, but its SZZ-style linkage between inducing and fixing commits can be ambiguous across parallel branches, which may distort affected ranges.

In contrast, CLOVERY achieved higher accuracy compared to the existing tools. We requested NVD modifications for 20 reproduced CVEs; as of October 2025, four[2] of them were updated based on our requests. However, it produced several false alarms. For FPs, there were cases where semantic pairs related to the vulnerability were present, but the vulnerability did not manifest (*i.e.*, validated by *reproduction*); these could be TPs, but we considered versions that failed to trigger the vulnerability to be FPs in reproduction. In addition, there were cases where a patch added code lines, and in the subsequent commit, all the added lines were changed. In such cases, CLOVERY failed to detect functions containing the added code lines from the patch, leading to the misidentification of safe versions as vulnerable (*i.e.*, FPs). Most of the FNs in CLOVERY were due to the presence of code that could trigger the vulnerability but was not included in the semantic pairs extracted by CLOVERY (*e.g.*, code lines that cause vulnerabilities but are not related to the lines modified in the patch).

Threshold Sensitivity. We measured sensitivity by fixing one threshold and varying the other from 0.1 to 1.0 (step 0.1) on CVEs validated via reproduction. Figure 3 shows that accuracy is stable across θ, and the best results were achieved at $\theta_v = \theta_p = 0.5$; thus, we use 0.5 in subsequent experiments.

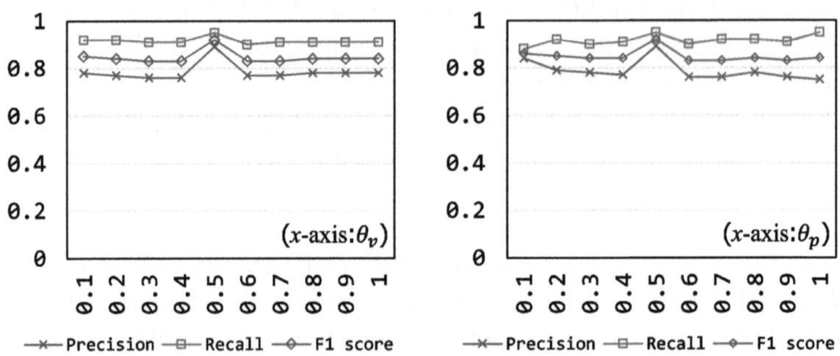

(a) Measuring accuracy while varying θ_v (with θ_p set to 0.5). **(b) Measuring accuracy while varying θ_p (with θ_v set to 0.5).**

Fig. 3. Results of accuracy measurements with one threshold fixed and the other threshold varied.

[2] CVE-2016-9388, CVE-2020-24370, CVE-2021-45985, and CVE-2023-50246.

5.2 Findings

We then examine the discrepancies between the results of CLOVERY and the NVD (Table 1). The detection results of CLOVERY matched those of the NVD for only 343 out of 1,502 target CVEs (22.84%). Among the remaining 1,159 CVEs, CLOVERY showed 87 incorrect cases, while both CLOVERY and NVD were incorrect in 86 cases. We focus on 986 CVEs (65.65%) where CLOVERY provides correct affected versions but the NVD does not, and summarize their range-difference types in Fig. 4 and Table 2.

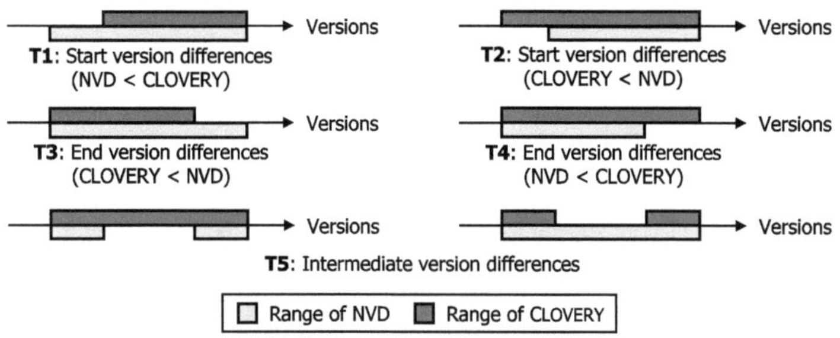

Fig. 4. Range difference types between CLOVERY and NVD.

We observed that the NVD yields more FPs (T1 and T3) than FNs (T2 and T4). In 903 CVEs (91.58%), the start version in the NVD differed from that identified by CLOVERY (T1 or T2). Most start-version mismatches were T1, indicating NVD overclaims: once a vulnerability is observed in a version, the NVD often marks all earlier versions as vulnerable. T2 cases (325 CVEs) mainly stemmed from NVD excluding very old versions despite evidence of vulnerability.

We also found 551 CVEs (55.88%) with end-version discrepancies (T3 or T4). T4 cases often occurred when NVD fixed ranges reflected only the reproduced version, omitting later vulnerable releases. T3 cases (194 CVEs) typically arose after disclosure, when some versions were patched via backporting or other mitigations but the NVD range was not updated.

Finally, there were 184 CVEs where differences were observed in the intermediate versions (*i.e.*, T5). In most cases, similar to the T3 cases, these differences occurred because developers applied security patches to some versions through backporting after the CVE was reported. While there are some instances where the differences arose because CLOVERY failed to correctly identify the vulnerable versions, as confirmed in Sect. 5.1, these were very few. Among several cases we reported, CVE-2023-50246 was initially listed as affecting one version, but we confirmed that later versions (1.7-rc1 and 1.7-rc2) were also vulnerable. The findings indicate that the NVD often provides inaccurate affected version data. While not obligated to ensure high accuracy, the NVD is commonly used by developers for vulnerability response. Therefore, validating this information is critical for software security. CLOVERY presents an effective solution by automatically identifying affected versions at the time of vulnerability disclosure.

Table 2. Distribution of range-difference types between CLOVERY and the NVD (duplicates allowed per CVE).

Type	Description	#CVEs	Ratio
T1	Start `diff`. (NVD < CLOVERY)	578	58.62% (578/986)
T2	Start `diff`. (CLOVERY < NVD)	325	32.96% (325/986)
T3	End `diff`. (CLOVERY < NVD)	194	19.68% (194/986)
T4	End `diff`. (NVD < CLOVERY)	357	36.21% (357/986)
T5	Intermediate `diff`.	184	18.66% (184/986)

5.3 Performance

We measured the detection time of CLOVERY per CVE, excluding dataset collection, on 2,176 CVEs. CLOVERY analyzed a CVE in 295 s on average (median 72 s); 1,291 CVEs (about 60%) finished within 100 s. Runtime mainly increased with (i) the number of commits in the vulnerable file, (ii) the number of modified vulnerable functions, and (iii) the number of semantic pairs to compare, but is practical given that CLOVERY examines the full history of vulnerable functions.

6 Discussion

Limitations. CLOVERY requires (i) a security patch and (ii) the corresponding repository with commit history. CLOVERY may fail when a patch mainly reorders lines such that vulnerable and patched essential lines become syntactically identical; this is rare in our setup (< 0.05%) but can cause false alarms. We leave handling such cases (e.g., position-aware matching of essential lines) for future work. Although we implemented CLOVERY for C/C++, the methodology is largely language-agnostic and can be extended to other languages.

Threats to Validity. Our evaluation covers 1,502 CVEs, which may not represent all vulnerability patterns. We restricted targets to cases where CPE identities and repository versions are reasonably mappable, which may bias the dataset toward well-maintained projects. Furthermore, due to the lack of ground truth, we manually analyzed CLOVERY's results. While most cases were clearly resolved, and many vulnerabilities were verified through reproduction, the outcomes may not be perfect. Finally, analyst expertise was not uniform, and a senior reviewer may have influenced decisions, potentially introducing bias.

7 Related Work

Prior studies have reported that NVD CPE affected-version data are often inaccurate (*e.g.*, [4,7,8,18,19,21,24]). Among them, `SEM-SZZ` [20] links a patch to its inducing commit and marks the versions between them as vulnerable, while `VOFinder` [24] refines CPE by locating where a vulnerability originated; other efforts target web vulnerabilities or specific languages (*e.g.*, [18,19]). However, these approaches remain largely patch-centric: they often rely on changed lines (especially deleted ones) and do not model semantic dependencies between code segments, which limits robustness under code evolution (see Sect. 5).

In addition, vulnerable code clone detection approaches have been widely studied (*e.g.*, [13,15,19,22,23,27,30]). Recent systems such as Movery [23] and V1scan [22] detect propagated clones using patch-derived signals, but they still tend to be sensitive to patch-line choices (e.g., deleted-line bias) and typically assume that affected-version metadata are reliable. Clovery follows the patch-based paradigm but differs by encoding semantic dependencies as pairs, enabling version-range identification without relying on CPE correctness; the resulting ranges can also improve downstream clone-detection accuracy. Code-lineage tracking has also been explored in various forms, but it does not address the key requirement in our setting (*e.g.*, [9,12,17]): distinguishing vulnerable and patched semantics to identify affected version ranges.

8 Conclusion

Vulnerability-affected versions provided in public vulnerability reports are often inaccurate, which can complicate vulnerability resolution. We introduce Clovery, a semantic pair-based function lineage tracking technique that integrates code syntax and semantics to accurately identify affected versions for CVE vulnerabilities. With Clovery, developers will be better equipped to respond to vulnerabilities, leading to improved supply chain security.

Acknowledgment. We thank the anonymous reviewers for their insightful comments to improve the quality of the paper. This work was supported by the Institute of Information & Communications Technology Planning & Evaluation (IITP), grant funded by the Korea government (MSIT) (No. RS-2024-00440780 Development of Automated SBOM and VEX Verification Technologies for Securing Software Supply Chains), ICT Creative Consilience Program (IITP-2026-RS-2020-II201819, 10%), and the National Research Foundation of Korea(NRF) grant funded by the Korea government(MSIT) (RS-2025-00517788, Research on Intelligent SBOM Generation and Automated Vulnerability Analysis through Multi-level Code Analysis).

References

1. Octoverse: The state of open source and rise of AI in 2023 - The GitHub Blog. https://github.blog/news-insights/research/the-state-of-open-source-and-ai/. Accessed 23 Aug 2024
2. Open Source Security & Risk Analysis Report (OSSRA)—Synopsys. https://www.synopsys.com/software-integrity/resources/analyst-reports/open-source-security-risk-analysis.html#UXexecutiveSummary. Accessed 23 Aug 2024
3. NVD. National Vulnerability Database (2024). https://nvd.nist.gov/

4. Bao, L., Xia, X., Hassan, A.E., Yang, X.: V-SZZ: automatic identification of version ranges affected by CVE vulnerabilities. In: 2022 IEEE/ACM 44th International Conference on Software Engineering (ICSE), pp. 2352–2364 (2022). https://doi.org/10.1145/3510003.3510113
5. Choi, Y., Woo, S.: TIVER: identifying adaptive versions of C/C++ third-party open-source components using a code clustering technique. In: Proceedings of the 47th International Conference on Software Engineering (ICSE). IEEE (2025)
6. Ctags: Universal Ctags (2024). https://github.com/universal-ctags/ctags
7. Dai, J., et al.: Facilitating vulnerability assessment through PoC migration. In: Proceedings of the ACM Conference on Computer and Communications Security, pp. 3300–3317 (2021)
8. Dong, Y., Guo, W., Chen, Y., Xing, X., Zhang, Y., Wang, G.: Towards the detection of inconsistencies in public security vulnerability reports. In: 28th USENIX Security Symposium (USENIX Security 19), pp. 869–885 (2019)
9. Gharehyazie, M., Ray, B., Filkov, V.: Some from here, some from there: cross-project code reuse in GitHub. In: 2017 IEEE/ACM 14th International Conference on Mining Software Repositories, pp. 291–301 (2017)
10. Hong, H., Woo, S., Choi, E., Choi, J., Lee, H.: xVDB: a high-coverage approach for constructing a vulnerability database. IEEE Access **10**, 85050–85063 (2022). https://doi.org/10.1109/ACCESS.2022.3197786
11. Jang, J., Agrawal, A., Brumley, D.: ReDeBug: finding unpatched code clones in entire OS Distributions. In: 2012 IEEE Symposium on Security and Privacy, pp. 48–62 (2012). https://doi.org/10.1109/SP.2012.13
12. Kanda, T., Ishio, T., Inoue, K.: Approximating the evolution history of software from source code. IEICE Trans. Inf. Syst. **98**(6), 1185–1193 (2015)
13. Kim, S., Woo, S., Lee, H., Oh, H.: VUDDY: a scalable approach for vulnerable code clone discovery. In: Proceedings of the 38th IEEE Symposium on Security and Privacy (SP), pp. 595–614 (2017)
14. Li, F., Paxson, V.: a large-scale empirical study of security patches. In: Proceedings of the 2017 ACM SIGSAC Conference on Computer and Communications Security, pp. 2201–2215 (2017)
15. Li, Z., Zou, D., Xu, S., Jin, H., Qi, H., Hu, J.: VulPecker: an automated vulnerability detection system based on code similarity analysis. In: Proceedings of the 32nd Annual Conference on Computer Security Applications, pp. 201–213 (2016)
16. Na, Y., Woo, S., Lee, J., Lee, H.: CNEPS: a precise approach for examining dependencies among third-party C/C++ open-source components. In: Proceedings of the 46th International Conference on Software Engineering (ICSE), pp. 2918–2929 (2024)
17. Servant, F., Jones, J.A.: Fuzzy fine-grained code-history analysis. In: Proceedings of the 39th International Conference on Software Engineering (ICSE), pp. 746–757 (2017)
18. Shi, Y., Zhang, Y., Luo, T., Mao, X., Yang, M.: Precise (un) affected version analysis for web vulnerabilities. In: Proceedings of the 37th IEEE/ACM International Conference on Automated Software Engineering, pp. 1–13 (2022)
19. Sun, Q., et al.: VERJava: vulnerable version identification for java OSS with a two-stage analysis. In: 2022 IEEE International Conference on Software Maintenance and Evolution (ICSME), pp. 329–339 (2022). https://doi.org/10.1109/ICSME55016.2022.00037
20. Tang, L., Ni, C., Huang, Q., Bao, L.: Enhancing bug-inducing commit identification: a fine-grained semantic analysis approach. IEEE Trans. Software Eng. **50**(11), 3037–3052 (2024). https://doi.org/10.1109/TSE.2024.3468296

21. Woo, S., Choi, E., Lee, H.: A large-scale analysis of the effectiveness of publicly reported security patches. Comput. Secur. **148**, 104181 (2025)
22. Woo, S., Choi, E., Lee, H., Oh, H.: V1SCAN: discovering 1-day vulnerabilities in reused C/C++ open-source software components using code classification techniques. In: 32nd USENIX Security Symposium (USENIX Security 23), pp. 6541–6556 (2023)
23. Woo, S., Hong, H., Choi, E., Lee, H.: MOVERY: a precise approach for modified vulnerable code clone discovery from modified open-source software components. In: 31st USENIX Security Symposium (USENIX Security 22), pp. 3037–3053 (2022)
24. Woo, S., Lee, D., Park, S., Lee, H., Dietrich, S.: V0Finder: discovering the correct origin of publicly reported software vulnerabilities. In: 30th USENIX Security Symposium (USENIX Security 21), pp. 3041–3058. USENIX Association (2021)
25. Woo, S., Park, S., Kim, S., Lee, H., Oh, H.: CENTRIS: a precise and scalable approach for identifying modified open-source software reuse. In: Proceedings of the IEEE/ACM 43rd International Conference on Software Engineering (ICSE), pp. 860–872 (2021)
26. Wu, S., et al.: Vision: identifying affected library versions for open source software vulnerabilities. In: Proceedings of the 39th IEEE/ACM International Conference on Automated Software Engineering, pp. 1447–1459 (2024)
27. Xiao, Y., et al.: MVP: detecting vulnerabilities using patch-enhanced vulnerability signatures. In: Proceedings of the 29th USENIX Security Symposium (Security), pp. 1165–1182 (2020)
28. Yamaguchi, F., Golde, N., Arp, D., Rieck, K.: Modeling and discovering vulnerabilities with code property graphs. In: Proceedings of the 35th IEEE Symposium on Security and Privacy (SP), pp. 590–604. IEEE (2014)
29. Zhan, X., et al.: Research on third-party libraries in android apps: a taxonomy and systematic literature review. IEEE Trans. Software Eng. **48**(10), 4181–4213 (2022). https://doi.org/10.1109/TSE.2021.3114381
30. Zou, D., Wang, S., Xu, S., Li, Z., Jin, H.: VulDeePecker: a deep learning-based system for multiclass vulnerability detection. IEEE Trans. Dependable Secure Comput. **18**(5), 2224–2236 (2021). https://doi.org/10.1109/TDSC.2019.2942930

Developing Security Metrics for Automated Compliance Checking

Immanuel Kunz(✉), Nico Haas, Angelika Schneider, and Christian Banse

Fraunhofer AISEC, Garching b. München, Germany
immanuel.kunz@aisec.fraunhofer.de

Abstract. To automatically check for compliance with security-related standards, prose requirements must be translated to technical properties to make them measurable. A multitude of metrics have been proposed in past literature, but they are lacking a systematic methodology for their elicitation. Without such a methodology, metrics remain inconsistent in their data models and abstraction levels, they exhibit considerable overlaps and are difficult to combine to comprehensively cover a standard's requirement. In this paper, we develop a data model for security metrics based on a systematization of compliance requirements, and we propose a methodology for their elicitation. The method is based on an ontology that enables a systematic development of metrics with a comparable degree of abstraction. We also present our initial work on an open-source effort that demonstrates that our approach also supports a collaborative development of metrics.

Keywords: Continuous Certification · Monitoring · Quantified Security

1 Introduction

Regulatory standards as well as internal security policies require a technical representation of security requirements to make them checkable in an automatic way. Today, systems and their security state can change rapidly—a continuous, automated conformance checking is therefore necessary and, in turn, requires metrics for their technical representation. More and more regulatory standards and certification schemes, for example the Cyber Resilience Act (CRA), European Cloud Security Scheme (EUCS), C5, etc., are being created to increase the security standard in different areas, but a common basis for their systematic representation on a technical level is missing. Moreover, these standards often have considerable overlaps, so compliance engineering could benefit from such a common basis, i.e. technical metrics.

On the one hand, compliance standards are supposed to be generally applicable and long-lived—and thus cannot prescribe specific technologies and system-specific requirements which would be outdated soon. On the other hand, users of

© IFIP International Federation for Information Processing 2026
Published by Springer Nature Switzerland AG 2026
H. Janicke et al. (Eds.): SEC 2026, IFIP AICT 787, pp. 288–301, 2026.
https://doi.org/10.1007/978-3-032-27993-4_20

these standards, i.e., auditors and auditees, require a systematic way of making these requirements actionable and measurable.

Critically, the lack of standardization in metric development creates multiple problems: (1) metrics with inconsistent data models cannot be meaningfully compared or combined, (2) varying abstraction levels prevent systematic completeness, (3) redundant metrics emerge due to lack of common reference points, and (4) mapping metrics to multiple standards requires duplicated effort. A standardized, ontology-based approach can address these fundamental challenges while enabling collaborative development as an additional benefit.

Existing literature has put forward many security-related metrics in various fields as well as compliance engineering approaches and systems, but a common, structured approach to translating high-level requirements into technical metrics is missing.

In a previous publication, we have already proposed an ontology of cloud resources [1], which we have since expanded beyond the cloud; in this paper, we build on this ontology, using it as the semantic link between requirements and metrics. Our contributions include the following: 1) A general model of requirements as they can typically be found in certification standards, benchmarks, and compliance catalogues, 2) a metric data model with a semi-formal description of the metric's properties, and 3) an ontology-based elicitation method for metrics. Furthermore, we therefore propose a way forward to a semi-formalized description of requirements, bridging the gap between the needs to specify requirements in an unambiguous but context-independent way. We also discuss how our approach can connect with emerging concepts like OSCAL, which aim at describing standards in a structured way.

2 Background and Related Work

2.1 Terminology

In the terminology of ISO/IEC 17065 [3], a *certification scheme* defines requirements and a certification procedure. The object being certified is called *product* and may, e.g., be a service, software, hardware, or a combination thereof. In this paper, we use the word *standard* in a broad sense to denote any authoritative document that prescribes requirements for a product. This includes certification schemes and benchmarks as well as control catalogues that may not involve an external audit or a resulting certificate, such as the CIS Benchmarks[1]. With the method proposed in this paper, we aim at breaking down high-level certification requirements as well as lower-level benchmark requirements to similar levels.

In this paper, we use the term security metric for a measure that maps observable properties of a product to a value indicating some aspect of its security level in a reproducible way. While the mathematical term 'metric' strictly refers to distance functions satisfying specific axioms (non-negativity, identity of indiscernibles, symmetry, and triangle inequality), we adopt the broader usage

[1] https://www.cisecurity.org/cis-benchmarks.

common in security literature where 'metric' denotes any quantifiable measurement (cf. [10]).

2.2 Security Metrics

Work on security metrics ranges from early critical assessments of quantitative approaches to more recent proposals of quality criteria, taxonomies, surveys, and risk models. Verendel [13] provides a critical survey of 90 quantitative security models and metrics and argues that the validity of quantitative security approaches remains largely unclear. Subsequent work has focused on clarifying what constitutes a "good" metric and on structuring the space of metrics. In contrast, our work does not attempt to validate quantitative security models, but focuses on the structured engineering of security metrics for automated compliance checking, i.e. a systematic development that Verendel calls for.

Savola [10] elicits quality criteria for security metrics based on an expert survey. He identifies correctness, measurability, and meaningfulness as primary criteria. Sherif et al. [11] similarly identify security metrics from the literature and assess them according to the SMART criteria (specific, measurable, actionable, relevant, timely). Thus, these works explore what constitutes a "good" metric and motivate several elements of our data model (e.g., comparability and explicit purpose), but they do not provide a data model or an elicitation process.

Several authors have proposed ontologies and taxonomies to structure the space of security metrics. Savola [9] introduces a taxonomy that organizes metrics across business, organizational, and technical categories; he does not, however, define concrete metrics. Longueira-Romero et al. [5] systematize the landscape of security metrics for embedded systems and propose a taxonomy. Pendleton et al. [8] likewise survey system-level security metrics and group them into metrics of vulnerabilities, defense power, attack severity, and security situations. Common to these works is that their taxonomies operate at the level of the metrics themselves and aim at classifying existing metrics. In contrast, the ontology used in this work is defined over resources and security features of the assessed systems (e.g., cloud resources and their security properties), and metrics are specified on top of this resource- and feature-centric ontology by binding measurable properties of resources to standard requirements. Rather than introducing another taxonomy of metrics, we provide a generic, ontology-referenced data model and elicitation method that support the engineering of new metrics from standards and their machine-readable representation for automated, continuous certification. Figure 1 in Sect. 3.3 depicts an excerpt from the ontology (see also [1]).

Large-scale surveys provide further systematization of existing security metrics. Morrison et al. [6] map the field of software security metrics by identifying 346 metrics from 63 papers, mapping them to software development lifecycle phases. Pendleton et al. [8], as mentioned above, cover metrics for software, networks, economic aspects, and security effectiveness, and organize them according to their system-level focus. These surveys are valuable for collecting metrics, but they do not propose a systematic elicitation process or a structured, machine-readable format.

There are also efforts by the major cloud providers to develop specific sets of metrics, e.g. on Microsoft Azure[2]. Their policies, however, are limited to the usage in their own cloud systems.

Overall, existing work has explored quality criteria and taxonomies for security metrics, as well as their role in risk assessment. However, little attention has been given to the structured representation and systematic elicitation of security metrics from different standards. Our work addresses this gap by providing an elicitation method based on an ontology and a corresponding metric data model.

2.3 Continuous Certification and Measurement Approaches

Continuous certification approaches aim to replace point-in-time audits by automated evidence collection and assessment. They therefore rely heavily on clearly defined, automatically measurable properties that can be monitored over time.

Stephanow and Fallenbeck [12] present a set of low-level metrics for IaaS resources (e.g., CPU, memory, storage, network) and show how such metrics can be combined into higher-level indicators for complex concepts such as scalability. Their work demonstrates how technical measurements can support more continuous assurance of cloud infrastructures, but the metrics are defined ad hoc and without a generic data model. In this paper, we provide a way of specifying complex metrics and we add a systematic elicitation method.

At the framework level, several EU projects have investigated continuous certification for cloud services. EU-SEC [4] and MEDINA [7], for example, developed concepts and prototypes for continuous assurance, including cloud service taxonomies and, in the case of MEDINA, ontologies for cloud resources, security features, and associated metrics. These projects provide important foundations for our work and demonstrate the feasibility of continuous certification in practice. However, the way metrics were defined and linked to standards in these projects remained largely project-specific; they did not introduce a generic, reusable metric data model or a systematic elicitation method. Our work builds on these ontological foundations and makes this step explicit by providing a general, ontology-referenced metric model and elicitation process that can be applied across different standards and continuous-certification frameworks.

In summary, various works have investigated and catalogued security metrics, but little attention has been given to the structure and systematic elicitation of security metrics in the context of certification.

3 Developing Metrics

In this section, we describe our method to develop metrics. We first present a model of certification requirements and build a data model for metrics. We then describe how metrics can be elicited based on an ontology.

[2] https://github.com/Azure/azure-policy/tree/master/built-in-policies/policySetDefinitions/Regulatory%20Compliance.

3.1 A Requirement Decomposition Pattern

Any single metric should target one measurable aspect of a high-level certification requirement. To develop a useful data model for metrics, we thus first create a decomposition pattern of a requirement as it is commonly found in certification objectives, benchmark controls, standard requirements, etc.

A requirement can be divided into the following parts. Note that not all of these elements are found in every requirement—more low-level benchmarks, like the CIS benchmarks for example, usually refer more directly to concrete configurations, while certification catalogues, like the CRA, rather postulate high-level requirements, since they have a broader application scope.

1. **Designation:** The requirement targets an auditee which may be a cloud service provider (CSP) or a manufacturer. Examples include the following: "The CSP shall ..." (EUCS), "the manufacturer shall ..." (CRA).
2. **Action:** The action is a verb that describes on a high level what the auditee should do, for example implement, document, revise, include, provide, etc.
3. **Target Resource Type:** The action (2) targets a certain type of resource that is supposed to provide security properties, for example: "... encryption mechanisms...", "... completed by all internal and external employees ..." (C5). Note that the target resource type is sometimes ambiguous. A requirement about employee trainings, for instance, can be interpreted as targeted at employees or at the execution of the training. In such cases, it is helpful to focus on the aspect that shall be measured later; in this case, it is the completion of the training. Note also that the resource type is not always explicitly mentioned and it is assumed that all applicable resources are meant.
4. **Means:** The action (2) is specified by more concrete means that should be applied. Consider the following examples: "... that corresponds to the state-of-the-art ..." (EUCS), "... including the following aspects ..." (C5).
5. **Scope**: Often, the scope of the requirement is further specified as in the following example: "... that are used to deploy the cloud service in the production environment ..." (C5).
6. **Purpose:** To make the requirement better understandable for the reader, they often state the purpose of the requirement, for example: "... to limit attack surfaces ..." (CRA), "... in order to protect the confidentiality ..." (EUCS), "... in order to avoid administrative errors ..." (C5).

We call a requirement decomposed into the above elements a *systematized requirement.* Before we can derive metrics from this decomposition, we first analyze its mapping to our ontological knowledge base. This mapping enforces a common abstraction level and prevents redundancy in metrics development.

- The **designation** (1) is not relevant for the metric, since it does not carry information for the measurement.
- The **action** (2) is not directly reflected in a metric, but it may give an indication about the target resource type.

- The **target resource type** (3) is defined in our ontology. It includes taxonomy of resources, including code, documentation, (cloud) resources, etc., which should reflect the requirement's target resource type and its properties.
- The **means** (4) are primarily reflected in the ontology's security feature taxonomy. This taxonomy is ordered by security goals, like confidentiality, integrity, etc., and defines mechanisms that target these goals, like at-rest encryption, RBAC, and rate limiting. These concepts are also detailed with more properties, for example if the encryption is enforced, which algorithm it uses, etc.
- A metric should then use these ontology concepts to bind together a resource type and the necessary means. The **scope** (5) may also be reflected in the ontology concepts or they need to be used in the application scope of the metric, i.e., in the compliance engineering system that is used.
- Finally, the **purpose** (6) is not directly relevant for the metric but should be included in its general description to clarify its intention.

3.2 Modeling Metrics

As seen in Sect. 2, metrics should aim for various qualities, including meaningfulness, measurability, specificity, and correctness [10]. The data model for security metrics should enable and support these goals. Furthermore, consider the following practical requirements to be important:

1. From the pattern described in the previous section, we can derive that a metric should unambiguously refer to the ontology concepts to specify what is being measured. This way, a collaborative development with a common knowledge base can be enabled.
2. Considering the multitude of stakeholders that are involved in compliance systems, metrics should both be human-readable, for instance for governance roles without technical background, and automatically processable.
3. The language that is used to describe a metric must also allow to combine target properties via logical operators to allow for complex expressions, for instance when certain assumptions need to be expressed.
4. A purpose and context description should be included to enable users to quickly grasp how the metric should be applied.
5. For practicality, the metrics should furthermore provide a clear identifier, including a version specifier. This identification is necessary because at a later point in time auditors may want to spot check certain assessment results and need the exact metric version that had been used to make the assessment.
6. Metrics include long-lived metadata, like identifiers and the ontology-based description, as well as relatively short-lived configuration data, like the target value. These should clearly be marked and divided, so they can independently be handled if necessary.

Based on the requirements established above, we now present a comprehensive description language and data model for metrics. The design of this framework required consideration of multiple representation formats, each offering distinct trade-offs between human readability and machine processability.

The spectrum of available description languages ranges from free-text formats, which maximize human readability at the expense of deterministic machine interpretation, to formal logic languages such as Prolog, which provide unambiguous machine-readable specifications but sacrifice accessibility for non-technical stakeholders. Semi-structured formats occupy an intermediate position, offering a balance between these competing concerns.

We adopt a hybrid approach that addresses the needs of diverse stakeholders. The representation employs a semi-structured format that maintains human readability while mandating the integration of concepts from our ontological basis. This design decision ensures a common description language accessible to governance professionals, domain experts, and other non-technical personnel who must understand metric definitions. By enforcing references to ontological concepts, the semi-structured format promotes consistency while avoiding the opacity of purely formal representations. Table 1 presents the data model.

Table 1. The data model of a security metric.

Metadata	
ID	A unique identifier for the metric which is also human-readable
Description	A semi-formalized description of the metric which unambiguously refers to ontology concepts and the configuration data (see below)
Category	A thematic category this metric belongs to
Version	Number that unambiguously refers to a certain version of this metric
Comments	Further comments, e.g., about the purpose of the metric and possibly the context in which it is meaningful
Configuration Data	
Property 1	
- Operator	The operator to be used for the assessment
- Target Value	The desired target value
Property X	
- Operator	The operator to be used for the assessment
- Target Value	The desired target value

Recognizing that semi-structured descriptions inevitably contain ambiguities that preclude fully automated processing, we complement each metric with a deterministic, machine-readable specification implemented in the Rego policy language[3]. The Rego implementation serves as an executable translation of the metric definition, enabling automated evaluation, validation, and enforcement.

[3] See https://www.openpolicyagent.org/docs/policy-language.

Importantly, our architecture does not impose exclusive dependency on Rego; the framework permits incorporation of additional implementation languages as needed to accommodate organizational preferences or technical constraints.

This dual-representation strategy offers several advantages. First, it provides format-appropriate interfaces tailored to different stakeholder roles: governance professionals interact with structured natural language, while engineers work with executable code implementations. Second, it enables independent evolution of human-facing documentation and machine-executable logic. Third, it facilitates validation and verification by enabling cross-checking between human-readable specifications and executable implementations, reducing the risk of misinterpretation or implementation errors. The representation also allows for more complex expressions where a target value may, for example, be dependent on a limitation. Note that from the experience of aligning this data model across different stakeholders and projects (see Sect. 3.5), it has undergone multiple improvement iterations already.

3.3 Elicitation Steps

There are two starting points: bottom-up and top-down, i.e., either develop metrics based on what can practically be measured in a given system or derive metrics from high-level standards. In both approaches, we systematically add identified properties to the ontology, creating a comprehensive model of the possible target of evaluation. This process ensures that no redundant metrics are introduced, since one needs to find or introduce the required property in the ontology first.

Note that alternative approaches exist. For example, one could start from the ontology itself and identify gaps in the resource descriptions and security features by comparing them to existing descriptions of the respective resources. For instance, one may compare an existing cloud resource description with the respective cloud resource description by a major cloud provider[4].

Regardless of the chosen approach, metrics should clearly address the requirement's target resource type and the properties that are relevant for the specified scope:

1. We start the elicitation by dividing the requirement into the elements identified earlier, i.e., Designation, Action, Target Resource Type, Means, Scope, and Purpose. This ensures all relevant aspects are explicitly captured.
2. Model the requirement using the template to create a formal representation linking components to ontological concepts.
3. Identify the specific resource and security properties that need to be measured or verified for compliance (technical or organizational).
4. Map the identified properties to existing concepts in the ontology. If needed, extend the ontology while maintaining consistency.

[4] Using, e.g., the Azure REST reference which specifies many resource properties.

5. Formalize the metric by defining its evaluation logic and implement it using Rego code. The metric specifies how to collect evidence and determine compliance.

The ontology-based elicitation method systematically prevents the problems identified in Sect. 1. By requiring each metric to reference ontology concepts, the approach ensures: (1) no duplicate metrics are created for the same property, (2) all metrics operate at comparable abstraction levels defined by the ontology structure, (3) gaps in requirement coverage become visible through ontology analysis (identifying ontology properties which are not referenced in any metric), and (4) metrics from different sources can be integrated through shared ontological vocabulary. Figure 1 illustrates an example of this process.

Metrics can also become more complex, e.g. when a condition is included in the requirement. In this case, the elicitation steps may need to be repeated for the condition, and the resulting metrics need to be connected via a logical AND or OR. Note that we do not claim that every requirement can be translated comprehensively to technical metrics. We rather aim at finding meaningful targets that can reduce burden on manual verification. We still suggest to define metrics also for properties that cannot (yet) be measured automatically. In this case, evidence can be introduced manually and be managed alongside automatically collected evidence. Metrics may thus be technical or organizational.

3.4 Example

We exemplify our method using a requirement from the C5 standard (BSI C5 CRY-02) which reads:"The Cloud Service Provider has established procedures and technical measures for strong encryption and authentication for the transmission of data of cloud customers over public networks." Following the pattern from Sect. 3.1, we decompose this requirement into its elements:

1. **Designation**: The Cloud Service Provider
2. **Action**: has established
3. **Target Resource Type**: Resources that offer TransportEncryption
4. **Means**: technical measures for strong encryption
5. **Scope**: for the transmission of data of cloud customers over public networks
6. **Purpose**: –

It is noteworthy that we have made the resource type explicit by adding "Resources that offer TransportEncryption" which was only implicitly mentioned in the original requirement text. This demonstrates a key benefit of the ontology-based elicitation method: it enforces a common semantic basis by requiring explicit mapping to ontology concepts. In our ontology, resources are defined with a property "offers TransportEncryption" when they can be configured to provide transport-level encryption. This explicit mapping creates greater reproducibility and consistency across different metric implementations.

Based on this systematization, we can now derive a concrete metric. The metric is described as follows: *This rule assesses whether a [Resource] has its*

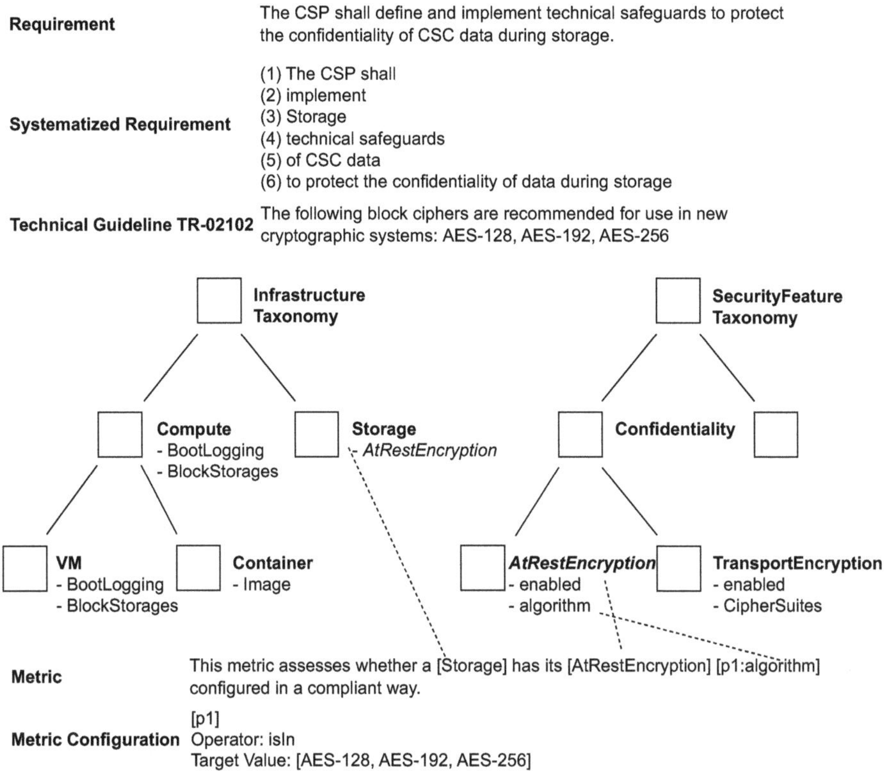

Fig. 1. The metrics development approach: First, requirements are broken down into the six elements described in Sect. 3.1 (systematized requirement). Possibly, one may use technical guidelines published by authorities to help make the target resource type and the means more precise. The figure then shows two related excerpts of the ontology: On the left, the infrastructure taxonomy which structures resource types and their properties, and on the right, the security feature taxonomy which structures security properties and mechanisms. The infrastructure taxonomy may specify that certain resources offer security features, for example a Storage offers AtRestEncryption—whose properties (like the algorithm) are specified in the taxonomy on the right. Finally, we can derive a metric from the systematization: We define a metric that refers to the Storage ontology term and its AtRestEncryption feature. The metric configuration then offers a way to define the concrete target values to be considered compliant.

[TransportEncryption] [p1:protocol] correctly configured. The brackets indicate references to ontology concepts, ensuring that the metric unambiguously specifies what is being measured. The parameter [p1:protocol] represents a configurable value that will be evaluated against specified target values, e.g. *TLS*.

In the Rego implementation of this metric, the application scope can be appropriately limited to resources that possess the respective transport encryption property. This ensures that the metric is only applied to relevant resources.

Note also that the limitation regarding cloud customer data over public networks should not be embedded within the metric definition itself. Instead, this limitation should be handled by the compliance system that applies the metric. This separation of concerns allows the metric to remain general and reusable while enabling context-specific application through the compliance checking framework.

3.5 A Collaborative Security Metrics Repository

The ontology-based elicitation of metrics enables a collaborative development of metrics. We have created an open-source repository for this purpose. We have founded the Cybersecurity Certification Hub (CCH) which governs the repository, available on GitHub[5]. Currently, multiple EU-funded projects are contributing to the repository[6] The CCH is working on extending the repository with metrics related to, for example, the EUCS[7], AIC4[8], CRA[9], and other standards and is open for contributions from other projects and organizations. Existing categories of metrics include, e.g., AI, network, and application security.

4 Discussion

4.1 Practical Implications

The ontology-based approach facilitates collaborative development of metrics across stakeholders and projects and advances existing efforts to systematize metrics development [5,8,9]. The metrics repository is currently integrated into the Confirmate platform[10], enabling automated processing of metrics. Both top-down (requirement-driven) and bottom-up (measurement-driven) approaches have proven valuable in practice. While we favor the top-down approach to ensure comprehensive coverage of requirements, bottom-up metrics that measure meaningful properties can typically be mapped to existing controls as well.

The proposed metrics enable automated compliance checking, which is increasingly required by modern standards. For instance, the EUCS mandates that "The CSP shall perform at regular intervals [...] audits by subject matter experts to check the compliance of their internal security control system" (CO03), while the C5 catalog explicitly acknowledges automation potentials in many requirements. Also, the recent draft of C5 2025 acknowledges this and enhances machine-readability of its requirements.

---

[5] https://github.com/Cybersecurity-Certification-Hub/security-metrics.

[6] COBALT (https://horizon-cobalt.eu), EMERALD (https://www.emerald-he.eu/), and CONFIRMATE (https://confirmate-project.eu/).

[7] https://www.enisa.europa.eu/publications/eucs-cloud-service-scheme.

[8] https://www.bsi.bund.de/EN/Themen/Unternehmen-und-Organisationen/Informationen-und-Empfehlungen/Kuenstliche-Intelligenz/AIC4/aic4_node.html.

[9] https://digital-strategy.ec.europa.eu/en/policies/cyber-resilience-act.

[10] See https://github.com/confirmate.

4.2 Limitations

Several limitations should be considered. First, automated compliance checking is limited by Goodhart's law: metrics may cease to effectively measure security when used as key performance indicators, as auditees may optimize toward fulfilling metrics rather than implementing comprehensive security measures. Second, security cannot be fully captured by any finite set of metrics—they remain approximations of complex security properties. Yet, while prose requirements interpreted by human auditors may better capture contextual nuances, manual audits face different limitations: auditors may focus disproportionately on easily verifiable indicators while overlooking less tangible security aspects.

Our approach, however, offers flexibility in abstraction levels. Metrics can range from low-level configuration checks to high-level aggregators evaluating complex testing procedures. This flexibility allows tailoring metric granularity to specific assessment contexts. Nevertheless, automatically checking multiple metrics cannot fully encompass the scope of prose-written requirements intended for human interpretation. This represents an inherent trade-off between automation efficiency and assessment comprehensiveness. Evaluating this trade-off empirically requires comparing the coverage achieved by metric-based assessments against traditional audit outcomes.

4.3 Complementing OSCAL

The ontology-based metric description complements emerging standardization efforts such as OSCAL (Open Security Controls Assessment Language)[11]. OSCAL provides structured representations of security catalogs, controls and assessment procedures and has gained adoption with several US standards, such as NIST SP 800-53. Also European institutions consider the usage of OSCAL, for example the German BSI provides its basic security catalogue ("IT-Grundschutz") in the OSCAL format[12].

Central to OSCAL is the *Control Layer*, including its *Catalog Model*, which enables machine-readable descriptions of security catalogs and governance frameworks. It provides structured textual descriptions of controls, splitting control prose into statements. These statements suit the atomic requirements needed in our elicitation step (see Sect. 3.3). Statements can be parametrized when needed, e.g. for defining review intervals. These parameters could also be used to link to metrics and specify their target values.

OSCAL also defines an *Assessment Layer* with models for *Assessment Plans* and *Assessment Results*. This layer complements our metric model through several elements. It contains activities, each with a defined method and detailed steps, clearly linked to related controls. Unlike our approach, it focuses on human-readable task descriptions versus machine-executable policies. However, activities and steps can include user-defined properties with key, value, class

[11] https://pages.nist.gov/OSCAL.
[12] https://github.com/BSI-Bund/Stand-der-Technik-Bibliothek.

and namespace, allowing well-defined links to the metric repository via metric IDs. The Assessment Plan model specifies components and assets for assessment. While focusing on concrete asset instantiation, it allows specifying *asset types* that could link into the ontology using well-defined terms (e.g., [VirtualMachine]). Integrating our metric model into OSCAL would thus enable machine-actionable compliance frameworks spanning from high-level control definitions to concrete technical measurements.

4.4 Towards a Semi-Formalized Certification Scheme

The ontology-based description framework developed here offers a path toward semi-formalized certification schemes. Current requirements like "The CSP shall define and implement procedures and technical safeguards to protect the confidentiality of CSC data during storage" (EUCS CKM-03) could be structured as: "The CSP shall document [encryption] mechanisms in [document] resources" and "The CSP shall configure [AtRestEncryption] as [enabled] on [Storage] resources containing CSC data."

Such ontology-based requirement formulations would maintain human readability and contextual flexibility while clearly specifying target resources and properties. This systematization would simplify metric derivation and enable governance bodies to centrally update referenced measurement properties as the state of the art evolves. Furthermore, structured resource descriptions in ontologies enable automated tooling for conformance checking processes [2].

5 Conclusions

Systematic standardization of security metric development is essential to address fundamental challenges in compliance engineering, like inconsistent data models, varying abstraction levels, metric redundancy, and mapping requirements across multiple standards. While prior work has catalogued numerous security metrics, a structured methodology for their standardized development has been missing. This paper addresses this gap through an ontology-based approach that ensures consistency and comprehensiveness, prevents duplication, and enables cross-standard applicability. Collaborative development emerges as a benefit of this standardization framework which we have started in an open-source repository. Furthermore, we have proposed a way towards semi-formalized standards, using the ontological basis.

In future work, we will develop more metrics, map them to standards, and move towards an empirical evaluation in a practical environment. Given the structured templates, data models, ontology, and methodology presented in this paper, future work will also explore LLM-assisted translation of prose requirements to formal metrics.

Acknowledgments. This work was partly funded by COBALT (Grant agreement ID: 101119602), EMERALD (Grant agreement ID: 101120688), and CONFIRMATE (project number: 101190193).

Disclosure of Interests. The authors have no competing interests to declare that are relevant to the content of this article.

References

1. Banse, C., Kunz, I., Haas, N., Schneider, A.: A semantic evidence-based approach to continuous cloud service certification. In: Proceedings of the 38th ACM/SIGAPP Symposium on Applied Computing, pp. 24–33 (2023)
2. Banse, C., Schneider, A., Kunz, I.: owl2proto: enabling semantic processing in modern cloud micro-services. In: International Joint Conference on Knowledge Discovery, Knowledge Engineering and Knowledge Management (2024)
3. Conformity assessment — requirements for bodies certifying products, processes and services. Standard, International Organization for Standardization, Geneva, CH (2012)
4. Knoblauch, D., de Haas, J.: Cloud provider continuous assurance: Eu sec framework for continuous assurance in the cloud. ISSA J. **17**(10) (2019)
5. Longueira-Romero, Á., Iglesias, R., Gonzalez, D., Garitano, I.: How to quantify the security level of embedded systems? A taxonomy of security metrics. In: 2020 IEEE 18th International Conference on Industrial Informatics (INDIN), vol. 1, pp. 153–158. IEEE (2020)
6. Morrison, P., Moye, D., Pandita, R., Williams, L.: Mapping the field of software life cycle security metrics. Inf. Softw. Technol. **102** (2018)
7. Orue-Echevarria, L., Garcia, J.L., Banse, C., Alonso, J.: Medina: improving cloud services trustworthiness through continuous audit-based certification. In: CEUR Workshop Proceedings. CEUR-WS (2021)
8. Pendleton, M., Garcia-Lebron, R., Cho, J.H., Xu, S.: A survey on systems security metrics. ACM Comput. Surv. (CSUR) **49**(4), 1–35 (2016)
9. Savola, R.: Towards a security metrics taxonomy for the information and communication technology industry. In: International Conference on Software Engineering Advances (ICSEA 2007), pp. 60–60. IEEE (2007)
10. Savola, R.M.: Quality of security metrics and measurements. Comput. Secur. **37**, 78–90 (2013)
11. Sherif, E., Yevseyeva, I., Basto-Fernandes, V., Cook, A.: The smart approach to selecting good cyber security metrics. J. Internet Serv. Inf. Secur. **14**(4), 312–330 (2024)
12. Stephanow, P., Fallenbeck, N.: Towards continuous certification of infrastructure-as-a-service using low-level metrics. In: 12th Intl Conf on Ubiquitous Intelligence and Computing and 12th Intl Conf on Autonomic and Trusted Computing and 15th Intl Conf on Scalable Computing and Communications and Its Associated Workshops (UIC-ATC-ScalCom), pp. 1485–1492. IEEE (2015)
13. Verendel, V.: Quantified security is a weak hypothesis: a critical survey of results and assumptions. In: Proceedings of the 2009 workshop on New security paradigms workshop, pp. 37–50 (2009)

VulnArrow: Data-Driven Vulnerability Root-Cause Analysis with Differential Sample Generation

Hongwei Li(✉), Wenmeng Zhang, and Yongjun Wang

College of Computer Science and Technology, National University of Defense Technology, Changsha, China
{lhw,wenmengzhang,wangyongjun}@nudt.edu.cn

Abstract. Fuzzing is a widely used technique for software vulnerability discovery, as it can efficiently generate proof-of-concept (PoC) inputs that trigger crashes. However, it usually cannot explain the root causes of vulnerabilities, still requiring time-consuming manual analysis by security experts and thus slowing down vulnerability remediation. Therefore, efficiently inferring vulnerability root causes from crash-inducing inputs has become a key challenge for improving software security.

To overcome the low accuracy and efficiency of existing automated root-cause analysis (RCA) methods—caused by insufficient sample quality and limited predicate expressiveness—we propose VulnArrow, the first accurate and efficient method for root-cause analysis of complex vulnerabilities. VulnArrow first adopts a dual-distribution sample generation strategy with differentiated mutation magnitudes to produce high-quality samples tailored for RCA. It then applies lightweight backward slicing to identify vulnerability-related variables. Finally, VulnArrow reformulates RCA as a data analysis problem, automatically constructing interpretable rule-based features and leveraging clustering to infer vulnerability causes. This approach removes the need for manually defined predicates and effectively handles complex, composite vulnerabilities.

We implemented a prototype of VulnArrow and evaluated it on 40 real-world vulnerabilities from 19 open-source projects. Compared with the state-of-the-art method RaCing, VulnArrow improves root cause localization effectiveness by 86% and average ranking accuracy by 83%, while reducing analysis time by 90%. These results demonstrate that VulnArrow achieves both high accuracy and efficiency, making it practical for real-world use.

Keywords: Vulnerability root-cause analysis · Backward slicing · Rule extraction

1 Introduction

As software systems continue to grow in scale and complexity, timely discovery and remediation of security vulnerabilities have become increasingly critical to

© IFIP International Federation for Information Processing 2026
Published by Springer Nature Switzerland AG 2026
H. Janicke et al. (Eds.): SEC 2026, IFIP AICT 787, pp. 302–316, 2026.
https://doi.org/10.1007/978-3-032-27993-4_21

software security. Fuzzing has become a widely adopted automated vulnerability discovery technique and detected numerous vulnerabilities in widely used software [4,10]. However, fuzzing typically produces only crash-inducing PoCs, requiring developers to manually analyze execution behaviors and crash contexts to identify underlying defects [3,11]. This process is particularly challenging in large and complex systems, where crash locations often differ from root causes and program behavior is highly state-dependent. Consequently, RCA remains time-consuming and error-prone. This discrepancy exposes a fundamental imbalance: while vulnerability discovery is highly automated, vulnerability RCA still relies heavily on manual effort. Despite advances in fuzzing, accurate and automated RCA remains an open research challenge [5].

Statistical-based vulnerability RCA methods represent the dominant paradigm in automated vulnerability analysis research [2,7,8]. Among them, predicate-based approaches model crash conditions using Boolean predicates and infer vulnerability root causes by statistically analyzing the differences in predicate evaluations between crashing and non-crashing executions [2,9]. Owing to their effectiveness in capturing crash-triggering behaviors, these methods have attracted substantial attention from the research community.

Despite achieving promising results for certain vulnerability classes, statistical-based approaches are still subject to two key limitations. First, they rely heavily on fine-grained differences between samples for effective statistical analysis, yet existing methods typically use coverage-guided fuzzing, which prioritizes path exploration rather than constructing semantically or behaviorally contrastive samples suitable for RCA. The stochastic nature of fuzzing further hinders systematic generation of high-quality analysis samples. Second, RCA accuracy critically depends on the ability to construct predicates that precisely characterize vulnerability-triggering conditions. Existing methods only support simple atomic predicates (e.g., $a \geq 0$) and cannot express composite conditions involving interactions among multiple variables (e.g., $a \geq 5 \wedge b \neq 8$). While extending predicate expressiveness could alleviate this limitation, it inevitably introduces combinatorial explosion, leading to substantial computational overhead and increased noise that degrades analysis accuracy. Moreover, the diversity of root causes makes a universal predicate space impractical. Consequently, existing vulnerability root cause analysis methods remain limited in both accuracy and efficiency.

To address these challenges, we propose VulnArrow, a novel vulnerability RCA approach that aims to simultaneously improve accuracy and efficiency. Our key insight is that high-quality, highly discriminative samples and flexible, extensible representations of vulnerability causes are essential for precise RCA. Based on this insight, VulnArrow consists of three core techniques: (1) VulnArrow introduces a dual-distribution sample generation method driven by differentiated mutation magnitudes. Ideal samples for vulnerability RCA should satisfy two properties. First, crashing samples should exhibit substantial diversity. Since all crashing inputs must pass through the vulnerability root cause location at runtime, increasing diversity helps eliminate irrelevant features common to crashing executions. Second, non-crashing samples should differ from crashing samples as little as possible, thereby highlighting decisive discriminative features. To this end, VulnArrow explicitly controls mutation strength to construct a highly diverse set of crashing samples and a minimally modified set of non-crashing samples. A template-driven strategy is employed to preserve input semantic validity, which significantly enhances statistical separability between the two distributions. (2) To efficiently identify suspicious vulnerability causes, VulnArrow designs a lightweight backward slicing technique. Starting from the crash location, this method performs regex-based backward slicing to efficiently analyze variable dependencies across functions and files without relying on complex compiler intermediate representations. (3) To overcome the limited flexibility and expressiveness of predicate-based methods, VulnArrow reformulates vulnerability RCA as a problem of rule generation and clustering analysis. It first uses mutual information to select variables that are highly correlated with crashing behavior, then automatically constructs discriminative feature combinations and applies low-depth decision tree to learn optimal partitioning rules between features and crash labels. These rules are further evaluated in an unsupervised clustering setting to assess their discriminative power between crashing and non-crashing samples, thereby estimating their likelihood of representing true vulnerability causes and ranking them accordingly. Unlike predicate-based approaches, VulnArrow does not rely on manually defined predicates and naturally supports the analysis of complex composite vulnerability causes.

We evaluate VulnArrow on 40 real-world vulnerabilities from 19 widely used applications and libraries. Experimental results show that VulnArrow significantly outperforms SOTA methods in both accuracy and efficiency. Compared with RaCing and Aurora, VulnArrow improves the average ranking of vulnerability root causes by 83% and 84%, respectively, and successfully analyzes 18 and 20 vulnerabilities that RaCing and Aurora fail to analyze. Moreover, VulnArrow achieves speedups of 94.6× and 9.8× in the RCA phase over Aurora and RaCing. These results demonstrate that VulnArrow significantly improves the accuracy of vulnerability RCA while maintaining high efficiency, enhancing its practical applicability.

In summary, the main contributions of this paper are as follows:

- We propose a dual-distribution sample generation method driven by differentiated mutation magnitudes, which explicitly controls mutation strength to generate highly discriminative samples and provides high-quality input for statistical vulnerability RCA.
- We design a lightweight backward slicing technique that efficiently analyzes variable dependencies across files and functions in large-scale codebases.
- We present a rule generation and clustering-based vulnerability RCA method that eliminates reliance on predicates and is the first to effectively handle complex composite vulnerability causes.
- We implement a prototype of VulnArrow and evaluate it comprehensively on real-world vulnerability datasets, demonstrating its effectiveness and practicality.

To facilitate further research and real-world adoption, we plan to open-source the VulnArrow prototype implementation and its evaluation benchmarks.

2 Background

Root-Cause Analysis. Vulnerability RCA aims to identify the underlying causes of software vulnerabilities and provide guidance for remediation [12]. In practice, it focuses on two key elements: the vulnerability trigger location and the vulnerability trigger variable. The trigger location is the source code position where the defect is introduced, typically appearing earlier on the execution path than the crash location. The trigger variable is the program variable at that location whose value determines whether the vulnerability is activated. For example, in vulnerabilities such as integer or buffer overflows, illegal variable values (e.g., exceeding valid bounds) may directly cause abnormal behavior. Vulnerability-related variables are those that depend on the triggering variable and indirectly affect its value. Identifying these elements helps developers understand vulnerability mechanisms and improves the efficiency and accuracy of fixing while reducing manual debugging effort [7].

Predicate-based Vulnerability RCA. In automated vulnerability RCA, predicate-based statistical methods have become a dominant paradigm. These approaches introduce predicates, Boolean expressions describing runtime states (e.g., `[rbx > 0 at 0x4a00ff]`), to characterize potential crash conditions [2,5,9]. A typical workflow includes three steps: defining predicates, generating crashing and non-crashing samples via fuzzing while recording predicate evaluations, and applying statistical analysis to measure correlations between predicates and crashes. Because these methods require limited semantic understanding and little symbolic information, they are relatively easy to implement and effective for simple vulnerabilities. However, their effectiveness is constrained by sample quality and predicate expressiveness. When vulnerabilities involve complex multi-variable constraints, existing methods often fail due to insufficient predicate modeling capability.

Aurora [2] is a representative predicate-based RCA approach. It uses AFL's crash-oriented fuzzing to generate crashing and non-crashing samples from an initial PoC, constructs predicates describing crash conditions, and records their evaluations during execution. Statistical analysis assigns scores to predicates and ranks potential causes accordingly. Although effective for simple vulnerabilities, Aurora is often time-consuming [2]. This mainly stems from its sample generation strategy: relying on AFL's coverage-guided fuzzing, which maximizes path coverage rather than inter-sample differences. Consequently, many generated samples have low discriminative power and introduce redundancy, requiring more samples to achieve statistical significance.

RaCing [9] improves Aurora by using reinforcement learning to guide fuzzing around counterexample inputs, accelerating root cause localization.

However, it retains AURORA's predicate construction mechanism, which cannot express composite triggering conditions and does not fundamentally address misclassification caused by insufficient sample differences. In addition, reinforcement-learning-generated counterexamples may deviate from true boundary conditions, introducing noise and reducing accuracy. These limitations suggest that predicate-based statistical methods still require improvements in both expressiveness and sample quality.

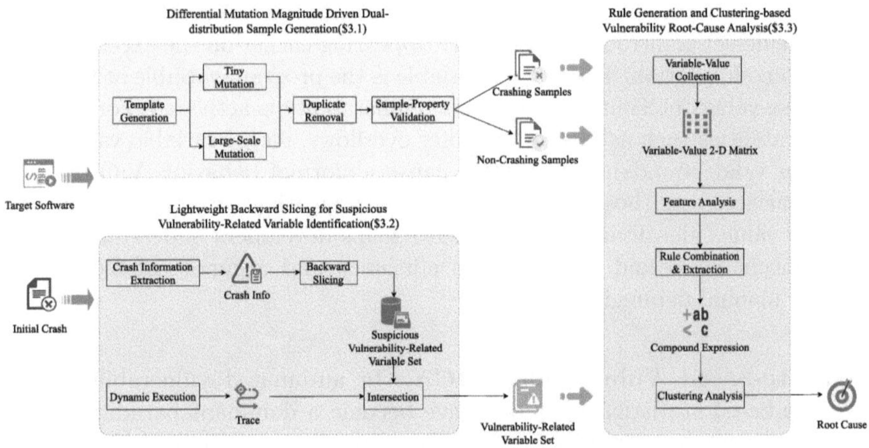

Fig. 1. The architecture of VULNARROW.

3 Design

Figure 1 illustrates the main components and workflow of VULNARROW. Starting from a crashing input and a target program, VULNARROW first applies a differential mutation magnitude driven dual-distribution sample generation method, which adopts different mutation strategies for crashing and non-crashing samples to obtain two sample sets. It then employs a lightweight backward slicing technique to infer vulnerability-related variables, and finally identifies root causes through rule generation and clustering-based analysis.

3.1 Differential Mutation Magnitude Driven Dual-distribution Sample Generation (DM^2-Gen)

Coverage-guided fuzzing maximizes code coverage through execution feedback and is effective for discovering diverse execution paths, which is beneficial for vulnerability discovery tasks [13]. However, for vulnerability RCA, its limitation lies in the lack of semantic or runtime behavioral discriminability among generated

Algorithm 1. DM^2-Gen

Input: Initial crashing input s_0, targets (N_c, N_n), program P
Output: Crash set $\mathcal{C}$, non-crash set $\mathcal{N}$

$T \leftarrow \text{EXTRACTTEMPLATE}(s_0)$
$(\mathcal{C}, \mathcal{N}) \leftarrow (\emptyset, \emptyset)$
while $|\mathcal{C}| < N_c$ **or** $|\mathcal{N}| < N_n$ **do**
  for all $(S, N, M, \Phi) \in \{(\mathcal{C}, N_c, \text{HEAVYMUTATE}, \text{ISCRASH}), (\mathcal{N}, N_n, \text{LIGHTMUTATE}, \text{ISNONCRASH})\}$ **do**
    if $|S| < N$ **then**
      $s \leftarrow M(s_0, T)$
      if $\text{NOTDUPLICATE}(s)$ **and** $\Phi(\text{EXECUTE}(P, s))$ **then**
        $S \leftarrow S \cup \{s\}$
      end if
    end if
  end for
end while
return $\mathcal{C}, \mathcal{N}$

samples. Low-quality samples not only provide limited insight into root causes but also reduce analysis accuracy and significantly increase time overhead.

Statistical vulnerability RCA infers vulnerability causes by comparing differences between crashing and non-crashing executions. Accordingly, sample generation should minimize the differences between crashing and non-crashing samples to reduce irrelevant noise and emphasize key triggering factors. Meanwhile, since all crashing samples must pass through the root cause location, their execution paths can be intersected to identify candidate locations. Therefore, crashing samples should exhibit high diversity to reduce the size of path intersections and narrow down the set of candidate locations.

Based on these insights, we propose DM^2-Gen, a Differential Mutation Magnitude driven Dual-distribution sample generation method. Centered on a real crashing input, DM^2-Gen controls mutation magnitude to separately generate crashing and non-crashing samples, forming a sample set that is semantically similar but exhibits distinct execution outcomes. The overall procedure is shown in Algorithm 1. Unlike traditional fuzzing that focuses on coverage or crash discovery, DM^2-Gen aims to minimize irrelevant differences between the two sample classes while maximizing diversity among crashing samples, thus improving the effectiveness of subsequent statistical analysis.

Template Generation. Random mutations often break input syntax or semantics, producing many invalid samples and introducing noise. To mitigate this, we first perform template extraction on the initial crashing input. The overall structure of the input is fixed, and mutations are only allowed in selected byte regions. This lightweight, byte-level constraint preserves input validity and reduces the mutation space, improving sample quality.

Sample Generation. After template generation, DM^2-Gen executes two parallel generation processes centered on the initial PoC. The key difference lies in mutation magnitude. For crashing samples, we apply multi-point, large-magnitude mutations, such as multi-byte flips and continuous insertions or deletions. This expands the distribution of crashing samples in the input space while preserving the same vulnerability trigger, enhancing robustness in statistical analysis. For non-crashing samples, we use single-point, small-magnitude mutations, such as single-byte flips or minimal insertions. This minimal-perturbation strategy produces non-crashing samples that are highly similar to crashing ones, concentrating differences on the vulnerability-triggering conditions and reducing noise.

Sample Validation. After mutation, generated samples undergo duplication and type validation. Hash-based deduplication prevents identical samples from being repeatedly added, preserving diversity. Each sample is then executed on the target program, and its type is determined based on termination signals and runtime error reports from tools such as AddressSanitizer (ASan) [6]. Only samples that match the expected type, crashing or non-crashing, are retained. Sample generation terminates once both sample sets reach predefined size thresholds.

3.2 Lightweight Backward Slicing for Suspicious Vulnerability-Related Variable Identification (LBS-VRV)

In real-world software systems, execution paths are often long, span multiple functions and files, and involve many variables. Monitoring and statistically analyzing all variables introduces significant runtime overhead and substantial noise unrelated to vulnerability triggering, which degrades both efficiency and accuracy. To address this issue, we propose LBS-VRV, a lightweight backward slicing method for identifying vulnerability-related variables. The goal is to quickly narrow the analysis scope while preserving sufficient coverage, and to extract variables highly correlated with vulnerability-triggering behavior.

LBS-VRV starts from the crash information triggered by a given PoC input, using the source-level crash location, including file and line number, as the slicing seed. Variables and structure field expressions appearing at the crash line are first extracted as the initial variable set. A lightweight static backward slicing process is then applied to analyze potential variable origins across the codebase. Unlike precise slicing techniques, our method does not rely on full control-flow graphs, precise alias analysis, or path feasibility checking. Instead, it approximates backward data dependencies based on source-level assignments, function parameter passing, and return value dependencies. This lightweight design prioritizes scalability and efficiency over full semantic precision and may miss certain complex C/C++ constructs that would typically require IR-based slicing. The analysis supports cross-function and cross-file propagation and explicitly models structure field accesses, allowing multi-level field chains to be tracked with low overhead.

Backward Slicing. Specifically, when a variable appears on the left-hand side of an assignment, dependencies are propagated from variables on the right-hand side. When a variable is used as a function return value, dependencies are further propagated to the corresponding input parameters. For structure fields, dependencies are traced back to parent fields and base variables. By iteratively applying these rules, LBS-VRV derives a suspicious variable set with potential data dependencies to the crash location at low cost. The method tolerates limited false positives to improve scalability, aligning with practical vulnerability analysis needs. No false negatives were observed in our experiments on the evaluated datasets.

Dynamic Execution Filtering. Static slicing alone may still introduce variables that do not appear on the actual crashing execution path. To further improve precision, we combine static results with dynamic execution information. Using the same PoC input, we record variables that appear on the real execution path and intersect them with the statically sliced set. Only variables that satisfy both static dependency and dynamic execution are retained. This hybrid approach effectively removes irrelevant variables and produces a compact, more interpretable set of vulnerability-related variables.

3.3 Rule Generation and Clustering-Based Vulnerability Root-Cause Analysis

Collecting the runtime values of vulnerability-related variables for each input sample is a prerequisite for vulnerability RCA. To achieve this, we adopt a breakpoint-based runtime debugging approach to observe variable values at locations potentially related to vulnerabilities during program execution. The collected variable values are associated with corresponding sample labels (crashing or non-crashing) and organized into a structured variable-value matrix for subsequent analysis. Compared with instrumentation-based techniques, this approach avoids program recompilation and custom instrumentation logic, thereby reducing engineering complexity and minimizing additional runtime overhead and environment dependencies.

In real-world programs, a large number of variables may be related to vulnerability triggering, while many of them are irrelevant to the actual root cause. Directly performing rule extraction in such a high-dimensional space introduces significant computational overhead and noisy features, which can degrade analysis accuracy. To address this issue, we introduce a feature filtering stage prior to rule generation to reduce the search space and improve analysis effectiveness. As shown in Line 1 of Algorithm 2. Specifically, Mutual Information (MI) is used to measure the statistical dependency between each variable and the sample state label. MI captures nonlinear relationships between variables and labels with relatively low computational cost, making it suitable for large-scale feature analysis. Variables are ranked by their MI scores, and the top-ranked ones are selected as base features for subsequent rule generation, thereby reducing analysis complexity while preserving discriminative information.

Algorithm 2. RuleClus: Rule Generation and Clustering-based RCA

Input: Aligned Variable Matrix X, Label Vector Y
Output: Ranked Root Cause Candidates
1: $F \leftarrow SelectTopFeatures(X, Y)$
2: $R \leftarrow \emptyset$
3: **for** each feature combination $c \subseteq F$ **do**
4:     **for** each coefficient assignment $\alpha \in \{+1, -1\}^{|c|}$ **do**
5:         $z \leftarrow BuildLinearCombination(c, \alpha)$
6:         $rules \leftarrow TrainDecisionTree(z, Y)$
7:         $R \leftarrow R \cup rules$
8:     **end for**
9: **end for**
10: $R^* \leftarrow RankRules(R, Y)$
11: $R_{top} \leftarrow SelectTopRules(R^*)$
12: **for** each rule $r \in R_{top}$ **do**
13:     $X \leftarrow AugmentFeature(X, ApplyRule(r))$
14: **end for**
15: **for** each feature $f \in X$ **do**
16:     $labels \leftarrow KMeansCluster(f)$
17:     $score(f) \leftarrow EvaluateClustering(labels, Y)$
18: **end for**
19: **return** RankByScore(score)

After identifying key variables, we further model composite vulnerability root causes, as detailed in Lines 3-9 of Algorithm 2. In practice, vulnerabilities are often triggered by specific combinations of multiple variables rather than anomalies in a single variable, making single-variable analysis insufficient to capture real vulnerability-triggering conditions. To address this limitation, we propose a Linear Combination-based Rule Generation with Decision Tree approach. The method constructs signed linear combination features over subsets of selected variables, expressed as $\pm v_1 \pm v_2 \pm \cdots \pm v_k$, to model additive and subtractive relationships among variables. Each combination feature is then used to train a depth-constrained decision tree, which automatically learns discriminative thresholds separating crashing and non-crashing samples. By extracting root-to-leaf paths from the trained tree, we obtain interpretable decision rules in the form of inequality constraints that explicitly describe vulnerability-triggering conditions. This method provides strong expressive power through interpretable linear combination features, while automatically learning discriminative thresholds via decision trees, avoiding the need for manually tuned heuristic parameters. By bounding the scale of variable combinations and the tree depth, it further controls rule complexity, effectively mitigating combinatorial explosion and overfitting.

In the vulnerability RCA stage, we adopt a clustering-based approach to rank and evaluate candidate causes. Through an analysis of real-world vulnerabilities, we observe that at true root cause locations, crashing and non-crashing samples typically exhibit the most pronounced differences in execution reachability and variable values, making the corresponding features highly discriminative. Based on this insight, we formulate RCA as the problem of assessing the discriminative power of candidate variables or rule features.

Specifically, for each candidate feature, samples are clustered independently and the clustering quality is evaluated against ground-truth crash labels, as detailed in Lines 15–18 of Algorithm 2. We use the Adjusted Rand Index (ARI) to measure the agreement between clustering results and true labels, as it effectively accounts for chance agreement in binary-class scenarios. Given the inherent two-class nature of the task and the need for efficiency and stability, K-means is chosen as the clustering algorithm. Candidate features are finally ranked by their ARI scores, with higher-ranked features considered more likely to represent true vulnerability root causes.

4 Implementation

To evaluate practicality, we implement a VulnArrow prototype and briefly describe key details.

Sample Generation. Starting from a known crashing input, we apply byte-level random mutations using two strategies selected for their efficacy in exploring input space variations: for crashing samples, multi-byte flips, random insertions, deletions, and block copies; for non-crashing samples, only single-point or small-range mutations. Samples are executed via subprocesses, and crashes are identified by exit signals and ASan reports. Hash-based deduplication removes duplicates, and quota control collects fixed numbers of crashing and non-crashing samples.

Trigger Variable Identification. We implement LBS-VRV as a static analysis tool for C/C++. Using the crash location as the entry, the tool extracts variables from the crashing statement and performs backward dependency analysis. We use syntax-driven parsing with regex assistance to scan all source files, detect definitions, assignments, parameters, and return dependencies, and propagate across functions. Up to four levels of struct fields are tracked, covering most real cases. A BFS over the dependency graph expands from crash variables to candidate definitions. The result is intersected with variables observed on the dynamic crash path, and variable names with source locations are output.

Root-Cause Analysis. The workflow includes data collection, rule generation, and clustering. Variable values are collected via runtime breakpoints using scripted gdb, with multithreading for parallel samples. Values are aligned into a sample-feature matrix with missing-value filling. For rule generation, mutual information selects the top correlated variables, we use the top 10. Limited linear combinations, up to three terms, are built, and a decision tree with max depth 3 learns thresholds to extract rules. Rules are evaluated and ranked by

F1, accuracy, and AUC, and high-quality rules are added as binary features. For inference, K-means 16 clustering with $k = 2$ is applied to each variable or rule, and ARI measures agreement with true labels. Candidates are ranked by clustering power and distance to the crash site, yielding the most likely root cause.

5 Evaluation

5.1 Benchmark Dataset and Experimental Setup

All experiments were conducted on an Ubuntu 22.04 machine with an Intel(R) Xeon(R) Gold 6430 CPU and 256 GB RAM.

We assessed VulnArrow through the following four research questions:

- **RQ1:** How effective is VulnArrow in identifying the root causes of crashes in real-world programs that support complex, highly structured inputs and various types of errors? (Effectiveness)
- **RQ2:** How well does VulnArrow predict vulnerability root causes (i.e., predicate ranking) compared to actual patches? (Accuracy)
- **RQ3:** How efficient is VulnArrow in root causes analysis? (Efficiency)

To answer these questions, we compared our results with two state-of-the-art statistical vulnerability RCA approaches: Aurora [2] and RaCing [9]. These represent the most advanced works in this field, and all experimental parameters are adopted from the prior work RaCing.

Benchmark. As shown in Table 1, we evaluate VulnArrow using 40 real-world vulnerabilities collected from 19 different programs. Among them, 15 are sourced from previous studies, including Aurora and RaCing. It is important to note that some of the cases from earlier work are quite dated. Therefore, cases that we failed to reproduce or for which no official patch could be found are excluded from our evaluation. These vulnerabilities cover 8 distinct types of common software vulnerability.

5.2 Effectiveness of VulnArrow

Table 1 presents the effectiveness evaluation results of vulnerability RCA. As shown, VulnArrow successfully identified the root cause within the top 50 ranks for 39 vulnerabilities, achieving 98% effectiveness. Among these, 90% (36 out of 40 cases) had their root causes ranked in the top 10, 65% (26 cases) were ranked in the top 3, and even 48% (19 cases) were ranked first.

By contrast, Aurora achieved only 48% effectiveness, failing to correctly identify the root cause in 21 vulnerabilities, which involved 4 different types of errors. Aurora mainly fails due to two key limitations: ① No correct predicate was generated ② The differences in variable values between samples are relatively small, leading to a large number of redundant samples. Similarly, RaCing achieved 53% effectiveness, failing to analyze the root cause correctly in 19 vulnerabilities, involving 5 different error types. We found that RACING's primary failure mode stemmed from its inability to generate important counterexamples for ranking adjustment. Since RACING terminates when ranking results stabilize, it sometimes prematurely outputs incorrect root cause analyzes.

5.3 Accuracy of VULNARROW

Table 1 presents the ranking performance of VULNARROW, AURORA, and RACING in vulnerability RCA, specifically showing the position of the true vulnerability root cause in each method's results. Across 40 vulnerabilities, VULNARROW has an average ranking of 5, AURORA has an average ranking of 32, and RACING has an average ranking of 30. Notably, for cases where the method failed to identify the root cause within the top 50 ranks (marked as ✗ in Table 1), we assigned a default rank value of 50 when computing the average rank.

Table 1. Evaluation result of VULNARROW.

ID	Program	Vulnerability ID	Results			ID	Program	Vulnerability ID	Results		
			AUR	RAC	VUL				AUR	RAC	VUL
V_1	mruby	CVE-2020-0240	8	✗	1	V_{21}	libbfd	CVE-2017-8393	17	21	1
V_2	mruby	issue-6065	✗	27	1	V_{22}	libsixel	CVE-2019-20056	6	3	1
V_3	nasm	CVE-2022-44370	42	1	1	V_{23}	sox	CVE-2019-8356	✗	✗	7
V_4	libtiff	CVE-2016-10272	✗	✗	6	V_{24}	libtiff	CVE-2023-2908	✗	✗	1
V_5	lua	bug#5.0-2	✗	12	3	V_{25}	tcpdump	issue-667	15	2	1
V_6	lua	bug#5.4.0-11	✗	3	2	V_{26}	readelf	CVE-2021-20294	4	✗	6
V_7	readelf	CVE-2022-45703	15	✗	2	V_{27}	sox	CVE-2017-11358	✗	✗	1
V_8	libjpeg	issue-669	✗	✗	✗	V_{28}	lua	bug#5.1-7	✗	✗	4
V_9	libpng	CVE-2018-13785	9	1	6	V_{29}	patch	bug#48744	✗	✗	2
V_{10}	mruby	issue-6067	✗	33	1	V_{30}	mruby	CVE-2018-10199	✗	✗	2
V_{11}	patch	CVE-2019-20633	✗	✗	1	V_{31}	lua	bug#5.2.3-1	23	✗	8
V_{12}	pdfresurrect	CVE-2019-14934	6	✗	1	V_{32}	libsixel	CVE-2021-40656	7	✗	12
V_{13}	potrace	CVE-2017-7263	✗	1	1	V_{33}	mruby	CVE-2018-12248	30	44	1
V_{14}	libjpeg	CVE-2021-20205	✗	3	6	V_{34}	objdump	CVE-2019-9074	8	1	24
V_{15}	libjpeg	CVE-2018-14498	1	2	1	V_{35}	nm	bugzilla-21670	1	✗	16
V_{16}	nasm	bugzilla-3392556	15	21	1	V_{36}	libjpeg	issue-441	19	15	3
V_{17}	nasm	bugzilla-3392562	1	1	4	V_{37}	libxml2	CVE-2017-5969	✗	✗	1
V_{18}	pdfresurrect	CVE-2019-14267	✗	✗	1	V_{38}	matio	CVE-2020-19497	✗	3	2
V_{19}	mruby	CVE-2018-10191	4	28	1	V_{39}	libtiff	CVE-2016-5321	✗	29	1
V_{20}	sox	CVE-2017-11332	✗	✗	6	V_{40}	libsixel	CVE-2021-45340	✗	10	4

Note: If the actual root causes is not in the top 50 rankings, it is marked as ✗. AURORA results: AUR, RACING results: RAC, VULNARROW results: VUL. green: Best Result, blue: Intermediate Result.

Specifically, VULNARROW outperformed AURORA in 33 cases, with an average ranking improvement of 84.4% (equivalent to 27 ranks); tied with it in 2 cases; and ranked slightly lower in 5 cases. Compared to RACING, VULNARROW outperformed it in 34 cases, with an average ranking improvement of 83.3% (equivalent to 25 ranks); tied with it in 2 cases; and ranked slightly lower in 4 cases.

Through an analysis of cases where VulnArrow underperformed, we found the main issue to be an excessive number of vulnerability-triggering locations in clustering, causing multiple highly correlated locations to receive identical scores in the ranking. To break ties, our method uses the distance from each location to the crash point. This can cause the true root cause to rank slightly lower—despite having a high (even top-tier) score, as seen in V_{32} where it tied with the top-ranked location. However, since the top-ranked locations are typically just a few lines away from the actual root cause, developers can still quickly identify and repair the vulnerability.

5.4 Efficiency of VulnArrow

To evaluate the efficiency of VulnArrow over the complete RCA workflow, we measured the total time required for the entire analysis process. As shown in Fig. 2, across all 40 test cases, VulnArrow finished analysis in an average of 1 min 20 s. By comparison, Aurora averaged 2 h 6 min 6 s, and RaCing 13 min 6 s. Overall, VulnArrow cuts analysis time by 98.9% relative to Aurora and is 89.8% faster than RaCing.

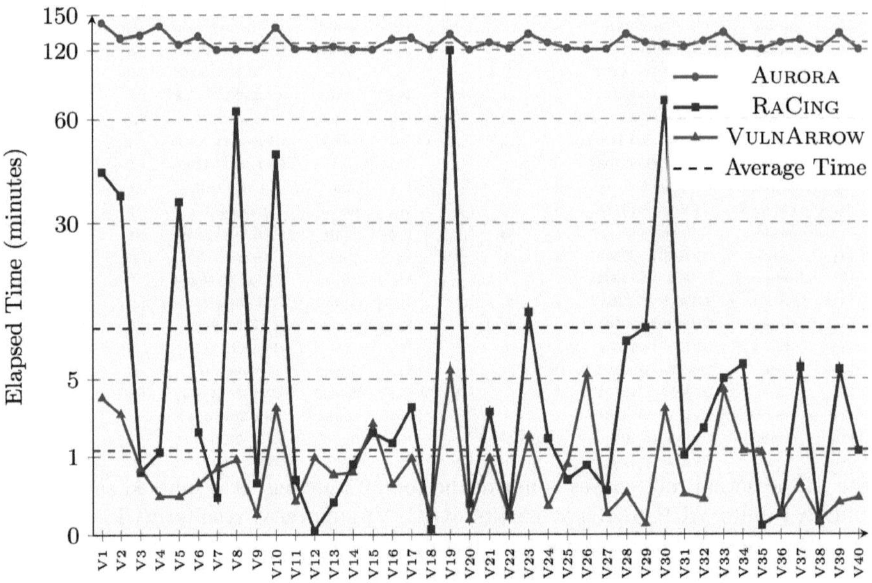

Fig. 2. Time overhead comparison.

Although RaCing benefits from its auto-stop mechanism to complete fuzzing and analysis relatively quickly in most cases, it fails to do so in certain cases. For example, in mruby-cve-2018-10191 [1], fuzzing lasted 1 h 59 min 12 s. These high-overhead cases indicate that when RaCing cannot generate a proper counterexample, its analysis results continue to fluctuate, preventing the auto-stop condition from triggering and causing significant runtime variance.

6 Conclusion and Future Work

Accurate vulnerability root cause localization is crucial. To address this issue, we propose VulnArrow. Experimental results demonstrate that VulnArrow effectively enhances statistical-based RCA accuracy and efficiency. Unlike previous methods, VulnArrow generates higher-quality samples by leveraging data diversity, ensuring more distinctive variable values, which accelerates analysis. Moreover, it avoids the flexibility limitations of predicate-based approaches by employing a root cause localization method based on sample state transitions. Evaluations on 40 real-world vulnerabilities confirm VulnArrow's effectiveness and efficiency: it successfully identifies the true root cause within the top 50 rankings for 39 vulnerabilities, with 19 vulnerabilities ranked first. Compared to state-of-the-art approaches, our method achieves significant improvements in both accuracy and efficiency.

Although VulnArrow can infer true vulnerability root causes, it may fail to prioritize them accurately in a few cases. This limitation mainly stems from empirically chosen mutation intensities during sample generation. While applying different mutation strengths to crashing and non-crashing samples is effective in practice, future work could explore adaptive mutation mechanisms based on online feedback or lightweight learning to enhance sample discriminability and reduce unnecessary overhead.

References

1. mruby UAF. https://github.com/mruby/mruby/issues/3995
2. Blazytko, T., et al.: {AURORA}: statistical crash analysis for automated root cause explanation. In: 29th USENIX Security Symposium (USENIX Security 20), pp. 235–252 (2020)
3. Jiang, Z., Jiang, X., Hazimeh, A., Tang, C., Zhang, C., Payer, M.: Igor: crash deduplication through root-cause clustering. In: Proceedings of the 2021 ACM SIGSAC Conference on Computer and Communications Security, pp. 3318–3336 (2021)
4. Li, J., Zhao, B., Zhang, C.: Fuzzing: a survey. Cybersecurity **1**(1), 1–13 (2018). https://doi.org/10.1186/s42400-018-0002-y
5. Park, Y., Lee, H., Jung, J., Koo, H., Kim, H.K.: BENZENE: a practical root cause analysis system with an under-constrained state mutation. In: 2024 IEEE Symposium on Security and Privacy (SP), pp. 1865–1883. IEEE (2024)
6. Serebryany, K., Bruening, D., Potapenko, A., Vyukov, D.: {AddressSanitizer}: a fast address sanity checker. In: 2012 USENIX Annual Technical Conference (USENIX ATC 12), pp. 309–318 (2012)
7. Shen, S., Kolluri, A., Dong, Z., Saxena, P., Roychoudhury, A.: Localizing vulnerabilities statistically from one exploit. In: Proceedings of the 2021 ACM Asia Conference on Computer and Communications Security, pp. 537–549 (2021)

8. de Souza, H.A., Chaim, M.L., Kon, F.: Spectrum-based software fault localization: A survey of techniques, advances, and challenges. arXiv preprint arXiv:1607.04347 (2016)
9. Xu, D., et al.: Racing on the negative force: Efficient vulnerability {Root-Cause} analysis through reinforcement learning on counterexamples. In: 33rd USENIX Security Symposium (USENIX Security 24), pp. 4229–4246 (2024)
10. Xu, H., et al.: Fuzzing JavaScript engines with a graph-based IR. In: Proceedings of the 2024 on ACM SIGSAC Conference on Computer and Communications Security, pp. 3734–3748 (2024)
11. Yagemann, C., Pruett, M., Chung, S.P., Bittick, K., Saltaformaggio, B., Lee, W.: {ARCUS}: symbolic root cause analysis of exploits in production systems. In: 30th USENIX Security Symposium (USENIX Security 21), pp. 1989–2006 (2021)
12. Yan, Z., Haipeng, Q., Ying, L., Liu, K., Chao, Q.: Enhanced fast and reliable statistical vulnerability root cause analysis with sanitizer. In: 2024 IEEE Conference on Software Testing, Verification and Validation (ICST), pp. 47–58. IEEE (2024)
13. Zalewski, M.: American fuzzy lop. https://lcamtuf.coredump.cx/afl/ (2014)

A Categorical Data Watermarking Scheme via Multi-attribute Joint Distribution Preservation

Hongxia Ma[1,2,3], Jing Yu[1,2,3(✉)], Shuguang Yuan[1,2,3], Jianing Wang[1,2,3], and Chi Chen[1,2,3]

[1] Institute of Information Engineering, No.19 Shucun Road, Beijing 100085, Haidian District, China
{mahongxia,yujing,yuanshuguang,wangjianing,chenchi}@iie.ac.cn
[2] Key Laboratory of Cyberspace Security Defense, Beijing, China
[3] School of Cyber Security, University of Chinese Academy of Sciences, Beijing, China

Abstract. With the rapid development of the data economy, the demand for effective data copyright protection has become increasingly pressing. Digital watermarking is considered one of the most promising techniques for verifying the ownership of digital data, and various relational database watermarking methods have been proposed. However, most existing schemes embed information into numerical attributes through slight perturbations, which are difficult to extend to categorical attributes whose values are discrete and subject to strict semantic constraints. To overcome this limitation, we propose a novel and robust database watermarking scheme designed for categorical data in relational databases. It employs mutual information to quantify inter-attribute dependency strength and embeds watermarks via semantically consistent substitutions under the joint distribution constraints of the k most relevant attributes associated with each target attribute. This design preserves attribute-level semantic consistency while effectively minimizing data utility loss. Experimental results on real-world datasets demonstrate that the proposed scheme exhibits strong robustness against various attack scenarios, while exerting negligible influence on the performance of downstream classification tasks and exhibiting high efficiency. These findings indicate that our method provides a reliable mechanism for copyright verification and traceability in databases containing categorical attributes.

Keywords: Categorical data · Semantic consistency · Mutual information · Joint distribution

1 Introduction

Today, data has become one of the most important assets for organizations. To extract value from data, scenarios including data dissemination, sharing, and

© IFIP International Federation for Information Processing 2026
Published by Springer Nature Switzerland AG 2026
H. Janicke et al. (Eds.): SEC 2026, IFIP AICT 787, pp. 317–330, 2026.
https://doi.org/10.1007/978-3-032-27993-4_22

outsourcing processing are becoming more widespread, while the hazards of data leakage and theft become more serious. Digital watermarking is widely regarded as one of the most promising strategies for protecting digital data copyright. It was initially developed for multimedia domains and later extended to other types of digital data, such as relational databases and text.

Since Agrawal and Kiernan's initial proposal in [1], which introduced digital watermarking as a means of protecting database ownership, numerous techniques for watermarking relational databases have been developed. Nonetheless, the majority of advanced methods focus solely on watermarking numerical data, and only a limited number of approaches are capable of embedding watermarks in categorical attributes. The main challenge in watermarking categorical attributes lies in their discrete nature, which prevents the use of techniques like altering the least significant bit, commonly applied to numerical data. To embed a watermark in categorical data, the most straightforward method involves substituting the existing value with a different one [6,7,9,10]. However, if the replacement value is selected at random, it can introduce semantic inconsistencies across attributes. For instance, in a database with attributes like 'sex' and 'number of pregnancies', randomly altering the 'sex' attribute for watermarking purposes can yield illogical records, such as (sex: male, number of pregnancies: 1), which is clearly inconsistent.

Existing research on watermarking categorical attributes while maintaining semantic consistency remains limited. [8] proposed a correlation-preserving fingerprinting method for categorical data. Their approach identifies K-nearest neighbors for each selected record based on Hamming distance and selects replacement values according to the local frequency distribution of the target attribute. However, this process requires neighbor searches and frequency estimations for each record, resulting in significant computational overhead. More recently, [4] introduced FreqyWM, which embeds watermarks by adjusting token frequencies. However, applying FreqyWM to categorical data still involves value substitution, potentially resulting in semantically inconsistent attribute combinations.

Therefore, embedding robust watermarks into categorical attributes while ensuring semantic consistency remains a significant challenge. This issue is especially critical given that many real-world datasets contain a substantial proportion, or even exclusively, of categorical attributes.

Contributions. In this paper, we propose a novel robust watermarking technique for categorical data in relational databases, termed JDPW. The main contributions of this work are as follows:

(i) We introduce mutual information to quantitatively measure the dependency strength among categorical attributes, which serves as the basis for selecting semantically related attributes during watermark embedding.

(ii) We propose a categorical data watermarking scheme via multi-attribute joint distribution preservation. Watermarks are embedded into categorical attributes via semantically consistent substitution, adhering to the joint distribution constraints of the k most pertinent attributes.

(iii) We perform comprehensive experiments on real-world datasets to evaluate robustness and the introduced distortions. Compared to the random replacement baseline and the correlation-preserving fingerprinting scheme for categorical data, our scheme demonstrates comparable robustness while exhibiting high efficiency and incurring lower distortion.

The rest of this paper is structured as follows: Section 2 reviews existing research on database watermarking techniques for categorical data. Section 3 introduces the threat model. Section 4 provides a detailed explanation of the proposed scheme. Section 5 presents experimental results. Section 6 concludes the work.

2 Related Work

The first comprehensive study of watermarking categorical relational data was by Sion et al. [9,10], who extended Agrawal's technique [1] to categorical attributes. The method in [9] chose a categorical attribute as the watermark carrier and indexed its values. For each selected record, it replaced the original value so that the least significant bit of the index matched the watermark bit. The extended version [10] addressed vertical partitioning attacks but still relied on value substitution. However, semantic consistency between attributes was not handled at the method level. Lin et al. (2021) proposed a lossless watermarking scheme for categorical relational databases based on value substitution [6]. It creates two reference sets (for watermark bits 0 and 1) through hashing and pseudo-random generation, then replaces selected attribute values accordingly. However, like earlier methods, this approach does not consider semantic consistency between attributes.

Several categorical data watermarking schemes intended for database integrity verification were proposed successively. Coatrieux et al. [3] grouped records and used part of each group to estimate category frequencies and create a "virtual dynamic range". The remaining records embedded watermark bits by modifying or retaining the most common category. Because any small change destroys the watermark, this fragile method is mainly suitable for integrity verification, not for robust copyright protection or traitor tracing. Bhattacharya et al. [2] embedded watermark bits by changing the order of records rather than modifying their values. They grouped records by categorical attributes, generated watermark bits using a group hash, and reordered the records with a linear permutation algorithm so the order itself carried the watermark. Because the watermark depends entirely on record order, this method is also fragile. To improve robustness, Khanduja et al. [5] proposed another scheme based on tuple-reordering, which embeds watermark bits by sorting records within groups based on hash values. Embedding each bit in multiple groups increases resistance to deletion, insertion, and modification, but the method remains vulnerable to accidental tuple reordering.

Recently, several researches have explored preserving semantic relationships and distributional properties during watermarking. [8] proposed a fingerprinting method for categorical data that preserves correlations by using K-NN and

Hamming distance to select replacement values based on neighbors' attribute frequencies. This avoids semantically impossible combinations but leads to high computational cost. Furthermore, [4] introduced FreqyWM, a dataset watermarking method that works with any data type. It protects data ownership by subtly changing the frequency of certain tokens to encode a hidden watermark. However, when using this method on categorical attributes in relational datasets, it still needs to replace attribute values to change their frequency, which can cause semantic issues.

To sum up, most existing watermarking methods for categorical relational databases fail to address semantic consistency across attributes.

3 The Threat Model

When the data owner creates several watermarked copies of a relational dataset, which is denoted as $D = (PK, A_0, A_{v-1})$, some users might try to remove the watermark and share or sell the data. We investigate three main types of attacks as follows:

(i) Subset Deletion Attack: The attacker randomly selects a certain proportion of tuples from the watermarked dataset and deletes them and only releases the remaining portion.

(ii) Attribute Deletion Attack: The attacker randomly removes a certain number of attributes from the watermarked dataset and releases the remaining ones.

(iii) Bit Flipping Attack: The attacker randomly selects a certain proportion of fields from the watermarked dataset and alters them, then releases the altered version.

4 Proposed Watermarking for Categorical Data

Our scheme framework consists of two components: Watermark Insertion Process and Watermark Detection Process. The notations used in this paper are shown in Table 1.

Table 1. Notations

Notations	Description	Notations	Description
D	Original database relation	W	Watermark
D_{w}	Watermarked database relation	L	Length of Watermark
D'_{w}	Suspicious database relation	PK	Primary key
A_i	i-th categorical attribute of D	K	Secret key
v	Number of categorical attributes	r_i	i-th tuple of D
S	Pseudo-random sequence generator	γ	Embedding density
$I(A_k; A_l)$	Mutual information between A_k and A_l	JD_i	Joint distribution of A_i

4.1 Watermark Insertion

The watermark insertion includes four steps: dependency measurement, joint distribution calculation, watermark attribute selection, and replacement value selection.

Dependency Measurement. In relational databases or machine learning, mutual information is typically used to measure the statistical dependence between two attributes. A higher mutual information value indicates a stronger dependence between the two attributes; conversely, a lower value signifies a weaker dependence. Therefore, we employ mutual information to quantify the correlation between any two categorical attributes in D. Given two attributes A_k and A_l, the mutual information $I(A_k; A_l)$ between them is calculated as follows [11]:

$$I(A_k; A_l) = \sum_{a_k \in \mathcal{D}(A_k)} \sum_{a_l \in \mathcal{D}(A_l)} P(a_k, a_l) \log \frac{P(a_k, a_l)}{P(a_k)P(a_l)} \tag{1}$$

where $\mathcal{D}(A_k)$ and $\mathcal{D}(A_l)$ are the domains of A_k and A_l, respectively; $P(a_k, a_l)$ is the joint probability of $A_k = a_k$ and $A_l = a_l$; $P(a_k)$ and $P(a_l)$ are the marginal probabilities; and the logarithm is typically base 2 or base e.

Joint Distribution Calculation. In most cases, all the combinations of attribute values that are already in a dataset are semantically valid. Therefore, when embedding watermarks into categorical data, the most straightforward way to ensure semantic validity is to determine if the new attribute value combinations generated after categorical value replacement exist in the original dataset. If such combinations exist, their semantic validity is confirmed; otherwise, their semantic validity is questionable. However, this method is only suitable for scenarios with a small number of attribute dimensions and a small data scale; in scenarios with high attribute dimensionality and large data volumes, its computational cost skyrockets, resulting in enormous computational overhead. In truth, not all attributes have strong relationships with one another. Based on this observation, we propose a more efficient approach to ensure the validity of attribute value combinations.

Specifically, for each categorical attribute A_i, we select the top-k attributes with the highest mutual information relative to it and calculate the joint distribution JD_i of these $k+1$ attributes in D. JD_i consists of all value combinations of these $k+1$ attributes in D along with their corresponding frequencies.

The value of k depends on mutual information, using the average as a selection threshold. For each attribute A_i, we choose k attributes with above-average mutual information to construct the joint distribution. If attributes take many values and the joint distribution becomes overly complex, we increase the threshold and reduce k to control the complexity.

Watermark Attribute Selection. We use categorical value replacement for watermark embedding. The scheme pseudo-randomly selects and modifies categorical attribute values in the dataset to embed watermark bits for ownership verification or recipient tracing. The attribute selection strategy is based on [8].

Algorithm 1. Watermark Insertion Algorithm

Input: D, K, γ, L, v, id, k
Output: D_{w}
$W = H(K \parallel id)$
for each $A_k, A_l \in D$, $A_k \neq A_l$ **do**
  $I(A_k; A_l) = \text{GetMutualInformation}(A_k, A_l)$
end for
for each attribute $A_j \in D$ **do**
  $\text{k\_corr\_attrs} = \text{GetTopkCorrelatedAttributes}(A_j, k)$
  $\text{JD\_map}[A_j] = \text{GetJointDistribution}(A_j, \text{k\_corr\_attrs})$
end for
for each tuple $r_i \in D$ **do**
  if $S_1(K \parallel r_i.PK) \mod \gamma = 0$ **then**
    attribute index $j = S_2(K \parallel r_i.PK) \mod v$
    watermark index $l = S_3(K \parallel r_i.PK) \mod L$
    watermark bit $\text{w}_l = \text{ExtractBit}(W, l)$
    mask bit $x = 0$ if $S_4(K \parallel r_i.PK)$ is even; $x = 1$ otherwise
    mark bit $m = x \oplus \text{w}_l$
    if $m = 1$ **then**
      $v_{\text{new}} = \text{SelectNewValue}(r_i, A_j, \text{JD\_map}[A_j], k, K)$
      if $v_{\text{new}} \neq \text{NULL}$ **then**
        $r_i.A_j = v_{\text{new}}$
      end if
    end if
  end if
end for

Specifically, the data owner first uses the secret key K and the recipient's ID to generate a unique watermark bit-string W of length L for each recipient via a hash function. In addition, the database owner employs a pseudo-random sequence generator S to select records and their corresponding attributes, as well as to determine the mask bit x and the watermark bit w.

To be more specific, for each record r_i, the pseudo-random sequence generator S is seeded with the concatenation of the owner's secret key K and the record's primary key $r_i.PK$ to generate a pseudo-random sequence. Without the owner's secret key, this sequence cannot be reproduced.

Subsequently, the first number in the pseudo-random sequence is used to perform a modulo operation with the watermark density parameter γ. If the result is zero, the record is selected. Next, the second number is used in a modulo operation with the number of categorical attributes v to select the attribute A_j for watermarking. Finally, the third number is used to perform a modulo operation with the length L of the watermark bit-string, thereby selecting the watermark bit wl that will mark the value $r_i.A_j$.

Since watermark bit strings are not expected to contain an equal number of ones and zeros, the fourth number in the pseudo-random sequence is used as a mask bit to achieve a uniform distribution of data-modifying marks. Each watermark bit is XORed with a uniformly distributed mask bit x. If the resulting mark value is 1, the data value $r_i.A_j$ will be modified.

Algorithm 2. New Value Selection Algorithm

Input: K, r_i, A_j, joint distribution JD for A_j, number of correlated attributes k
Output: new value v_{new} for $r_i.A_j$
k_corr_attrs = GetTopkCorrelatedAttributes(A_j, k)
k_corr_vals = ExtractAttributeValues(r_i, k_corr_attrs)
c = ConstructConditionalVector(k_corr_vals)
matched_records = QueryJointDistribution(JD, c)
if matched_records = $\emptyset$ **then**
    return NULL
end if
temp_V = ExtractAttributeValues(matched_records, A_j)
V_{cand} = RemoveCurrentValue(temp_V, $r_i.A_j$)
if $V_{\text{cand}} = \emptyset$ **then**
    return NULL
end if
prob_map = $\emptyset$
$N(\text{c})$ = SumFrequencies(matched_records, A_j, V_{cand})
for each $v_t \in V_{\text{cand}}$ **do**
    $N(v_t, \text{c})$ = CountFrequency(matched_records, A_j, v_t)
    $P(v_t \mid \text{c}) = \frac{N(v_t,\text{c})}{N(\text{c})}$
    prob_map[v_t] = $P(v_t \mid \text{c})$
end for
v_{new} = RandomSelection(V_{cand}, prob_map, $S_5(K \parallel r_i.PK)$)
return v_{new}

Replacement Values Selection. To modify $r_i.A_j$, we need to select a different value from the domain of A_j to replace it. The specific selection strategy is as follows: First, extract the values of the k attributes most correlated with A_j in the current record r_i to form a conditional vector $\mathbf{c}$. Then, in the joint distribution JD_j of A_j, query all records that satisfy the condition $\mathbf{c}$, collect the values of A_j from these records into a set, and exclude the current value $r_i.A_j$ to obtain the candidate set V_{cand} for the new value. Subsequently, the probability of selecting each candidate value v_t is calculated based on its frequency in the joint distribution, as shown in Eq. (2):

$$P(v_t \mid \mathbf{c}) = \frac{N(v_t, \mathbf{c})}{N(\mathbf{c})} \tag{2}$$

where $P(v_t \mid \mathbf{c})$ is the probability of selecting value v_t given correlated attribute condition $\mathbf{c}$, $N(v_t, \mathbf{c})$ is the number of records satisfying condition $\mathbf{c}$

with candidate attribute value v_t, and $N(\mathbf{c}) = \sum_{v \in V_{cand}} N(v, \mathbf{c})$ is the total number of records that satisfy condition $\mathbf{c}$.

After deriving the selection probability of each candidate value, the fifth number of the pseudo-random sequence is used to select the final replacement value v_{new}, thereby ensuring the randomness of the selection. If no alternative candidate values are available, the current record is skipped. In this way, we ensure that the value combination of A_j and its k most correlated attributes in the modified record exists and is semantically valid in the original dataset.

The pseudo-code for the insertion algorithm is shown in Algorithm 1, and the process for selecting replacement values is presented in Algorithm 2. To enhance robustness, each watermark bit may be embedded multiple times in the dataset, with the parameter γ used to control watermark density.

4.2 Watermark Detection

When a suspected leaked copy of the dataset D'_{w} is identified, the data owner invokes the watermark detection algorithm to extract the watermark and identify the specific recipient responsible for the data leakage. The pseudo-code for the detection algorithm is shown in Algorithm 3.

Algorithm 3. Watermark Detection Algorithm

Input: D'_{w}, D, K, L, γ, v, $(id_1, \ldots, id_n)$
Output: id_{leaker} or -1
for each $r_i \in D'_{\text{w}}$ **do**
  if $S_1(K \parallel r_i.PK) \mod \gamma == 0$ **then**
    attribute index $j = S_2(K \parallel r_i.PK) \mod v$
    watermark index $l = S_3(K \parallel r_i.PK) \mod L$
    mask bit $x = 0$ if $S_4(K \parallel r_i.PK)$ is even; $x = 1$ otherwise
    mark bit $m = 1$ if $r_i.A_j \neq D[r_i].A_j$ else 0
    $\text{count}[l][m \oplus x] = \text{count}[l][m \oplus x] + 1$
  end if
end for
for $l = 0$ to $L - 1$ **do**
  if $count[l][0] + count[l][1] == 0 \vee count[l][0] = count[l][1]$ **then**
    return -1
  end if
  if $\text{count}[l][0] > \text{count}[l][1]$ **then**
    $\text{w}_l = 0$
  else if $\text{count}[l][0] < \text{count}[l][1]$ **then**
    $\text{w}_l = 1$
  end if
end for
for each id_i **do**
  if $H(K \parallel id_i) = W$ **then**
    return id_i
  end if
end for
return -1

Since the watermark detection algorithm requires comparing the values at the watermark positions between the suspected leaked dataset D'_{w} and the original dataset D, it is classified as a non-blind detection method. First, the algorithm initializes an empty watermark template of length L and sets two voting counters, $count_l(0)$ and $count_l(1)$, for each watermark bit w_l. Then, it locates the watermark embedding positions using the same method as in the embedding process. Specifically, the owner's secret key is combined with the primary key value of each record as the seed to generate a numeric sequence identical to that used in the embedding phase, thereby ensuring consistency. Next, the records and attributes embedded with watermarks are determined based on the pseudo-random number sequence, and the corresponding watermark bit index l and mask bit x are obtained. For each watermark position, the algorithm compares the values in D'_{w} and D. If the values are different, it indicates that the value was modified during embedding, and the mark bit m is set to 1; otherwise, m is set to 0. Subsequently, the watermark bit value w at this position is calculated using the mark bit m and the mask bit x, and a vote is cast for the value w corresponding to the watermark bit l. If w equals 0, $count_l(0)$ is incremented by 1; otherwise, $count_l(1)$ is incremented by 1.

After extracting the watermark values from all positions, the majority voting method is adopted to determine the value of each watermark bit. If $count_l(0) > count_l(1)$, the value of w_l is determined to be 0; otherwise, it is set to 1. If both $count_l(0)$ and $count_l(1)$ are zero, or if their values are equal, the corresponding watermark bit cannot be determined, indicating the failure of the entire watermark bit-string extraction. If the value of each watermark bit is successfully determined, the complete watermark bit-string is extracted and compared against the watermarks assigned to all data recipients. If a complete match is found, D'_{w} is most likely leaked by the recipient corresponding to the matched watermark.

5 Experiment

We evaluate the performance of the proposed scheme, JDPW, focusing on robustness, data distortion, and efficiency, and compare it with two methods: random replacement watermarking (RRW) and correlation-preserving fingerprinting (CPF). Experiments are conducted on the Nursery and Bank datasets from the UCI Machine Learning Repository. Nursery contains 12,980 records with 8 categorical attributes and a target attribute. Bank has 45,211 records with 15 attributes (8 categorical, 7 numerical) and a target indicating subscription status.

All experiments are conducted on a server equipped with an AMD EPYC 9K85 64 physical cores (4 cores used), 247 GB of RAM (8 GB of RAM used), and running Linux. All algorithms are implemented in Python.

5.1 Robustness Analysis

To evaluate the robustness, the watermark is embedded 10 times to create 10 watermarked datasets for each method, each subjected to 10 rounds of random attacks. Robustness is measured as the proportion of successful detections out of 100 attempts. For the Nursery dataset, γ is set to 5, 10, and 20; for the Bank dataset, it is set to 10, 20, and 30. The watermark length is set to $L = 32$.

Subset Deletion Attack. Figure 1 shows the experimental results of the subset deletion attack. When γ is small (i.e., the watermark embedding density is high), JDPW demonstrates strong robustness against subset deletion attacks on both datasets, as well as RRW and CPF, successfully extracting the watermarks with 100% accuracy even when only 10% of the tuples are released (i.e., 90% are deleted). As γ increases (corresponding to a lower watermark embedding density), JDPW still maintains high robustness. Specifically, on the Nursery dataset with $\gamma = 20$, the watermark extraction accuracy reaches 100% when the release ratio is no less than 40%. Similarly, on the Bank dataset with $\gamma = 30$, 100% extraction accuracy is achieved when the release ratio is at least 20%.

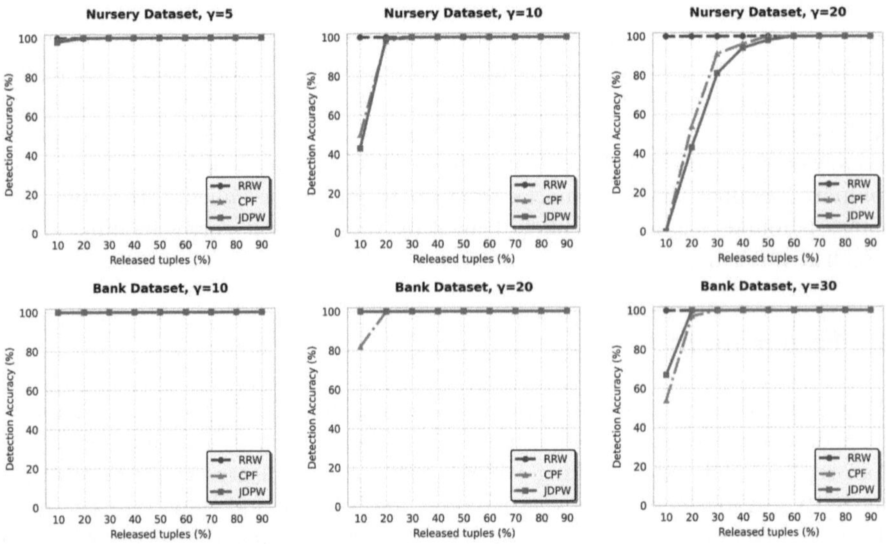

Fig. 1. Robustness of algorithms against subset deletion attack.

Attribute Deletion Attack. Figure 2 shows the experimental results of the attribute deletion attacks. On the Nursery dataset, which contains only eight categorical attributes, as the number of deleted attributes increases from one to eight, the watermark detection accuracy of CPF degrades first. In contrast, JDPW exhibits performance comparable to RRW, and both demonstrate strong robustness. When $\gamma = 5$, JDPW maintains 100% detection accuracy even after six attributes are deleted. As γ increases to 20, corresponding to a lower watermark embedding density, JDPW still achieves a detection accuracy above 90% even when five attributes are deleted. On the Bank dataset, which includes eight categorical attributes and seven numerical attributes, JDPW and two baseline approaches all show strong robustness against attribute deletion attacks, successfully extracting the watermark with 100% accuracy even when eight attributes are deleted.

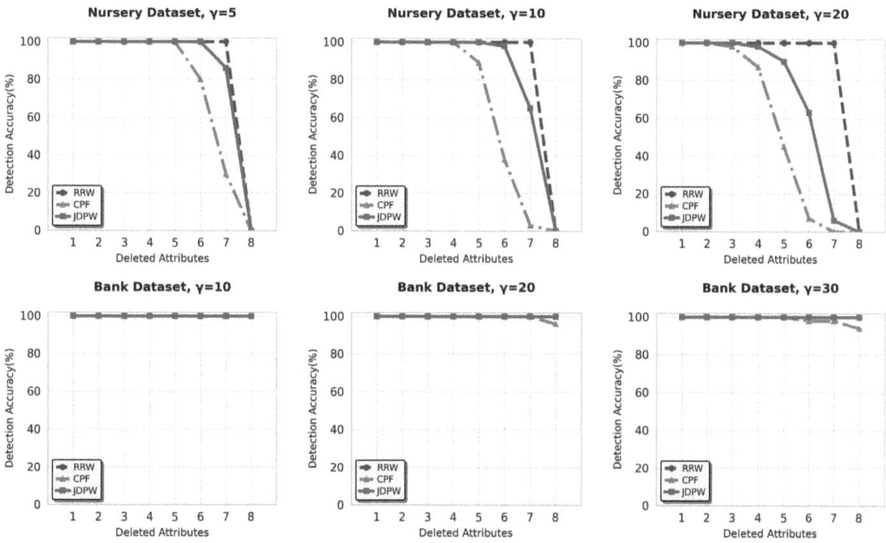

Fig. 2. Robustness of algorithms against attribute deletion attack.

Bit Flipping Attack. For bit flipping attacks, the attacker may randomly alter fields in the watermarked dataset. Figure 3 presents the experimental results of the bit flipping attacks. Our method demonstrates strong robustness against bit flipping attacks on both datasets, similar to the two baseline approaches. Specifically, on the Nursery dataset with $\gamma = 5$, the watermark extraction accuracy remains at 100% even when 70% of the fields are altered. When $\gamma = 20$, the extraction accuracy stays above 90% even when 40% of the fields are altered. Similar results are observed on the Bank dataset.

5.2 Data Utility Effects

To evaluate the impact of watermark embedding on data utility, we assess the effect of watermarked data on the performance of machine learning tasks.

We use the watermarked datasets generated by JDPW and the two baseline approaches to train different machine learning models and then evaluate the degradation of model performance using the F1 score.

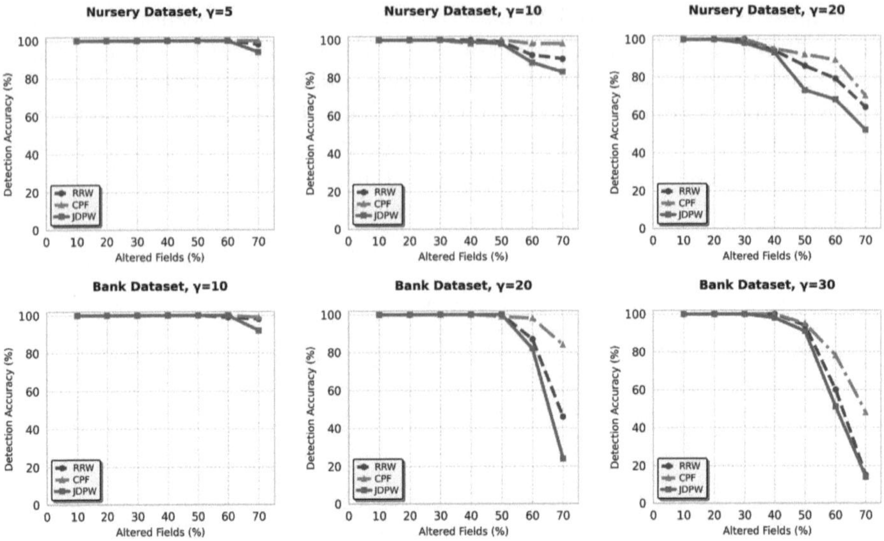

Fig. 3. Robustness of algorithms against bit flip attack.

The following classification models are used: SVM (with an RBF kernel), KNN, and Gradient Boosting. The hyperparameter settings, shown in Table 2, are obtained through an independent random search. For each model, we first obtain the F1 score when trained on the original dataset. Then, we train the models on the watermarked datasets using the same hyperparameters and evaluate them on the original data to obtain the F1 score. For clarity, we report the F1 score degradation.

Table 2. Optimal hyper-parameters for the `Nursery` and `Bank` datasets.

Dataset	Classifier	Hyper-parameters
`Nursery`	SVM	{ `gamma` : scale, `C` : 10 }
	KNN	{ `weights` : distance, `n_neighbors` : 7 }
	GradientBoosting	{ `n_estimators` : 100, `max_depth` : 7, `learning_rate` : 0.2 }
`Bank`	SVM	{ `gamma` : 0.01, `C` : 10 }
	KNN	{ `weights` : distance, `n_neighbors` : 3 }
	GradientBoosting	{ `n_estimators` : 50, `max_depth` : 5, `learning_rate` : 0.1 }

Figure 4 presents the experimental results on the Nursery and Bank datasets. We observe a common trend across the three watermarking methods: as γ increases, the F1-score degradation decreases and gradually approaches zero. Although this trend is not strictly linear, deviations do occur under certain parameter settings. This behavior is consistent across both datasets and all three classification models. Notably, across different datasets and classifiers, JDPW consistently exhibits the smallest F1-score degradation, indicating that it has the minimal impact on data utility.

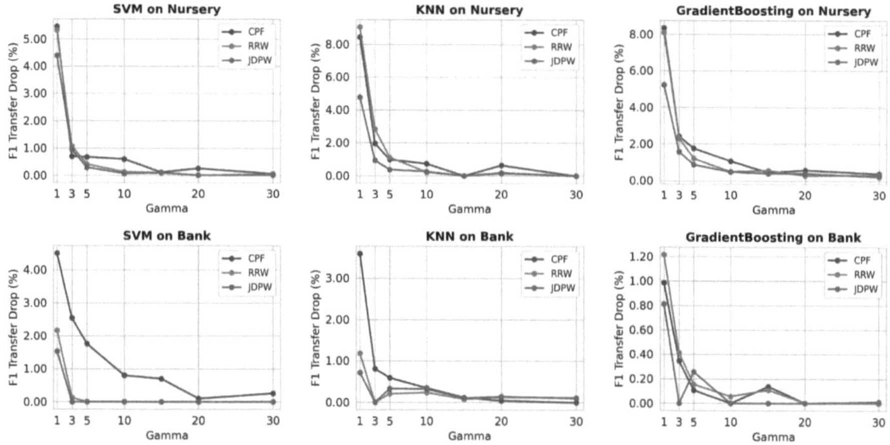

Fig. 4. Impact of three watermarking methods on the performance of machine learning tasks.

5.3 Efficiency Analysis

We evaluated the time consumption of the watermark embedding operation for JDPW and the two baseline approaches. Table 3 reports the results. It can be observed that, across different datasets and gamma values, the time consumption of JDPW is always lower than that of CPF. In particular, the time needed by CPF goes up a lot on the Bank dataset, which makes JDPW's strengths even clearer. This shows that our method is still very effective and efficient, even when working with big datasets.

Table 3. Average time cost(seconds) on Nursery (*left*) and Bank (*right*).

γ	RRW	CPF	JDPW
1	1.93	6.67	3.23
3	0.82	2.43	1.30
5	0.58	1.53	0.90
10	0.41	0.93	0.60
15	0.36	0.69	0.50

γ	RRW	CPF	JDPW
1	6.74	61.62	12.10
3	2.88	21.90	4.93
5	2.07	13.06	3.47
10	1.48	6.96	2.34
15	1.26	5.07	2.01

6 Conclusion

We introduce a watermarking approach designed to maintain semantic consistency when embedding watermarks in categorical attributes of relational datasets. The method uses mutual information to find attribute correlations and create a joint distribution. This distribution is then used to choose the right watermark values. This process keeps the original meaning of the relationships between attributes. Tests on real-world data show that our scheme is very resistant to many types of attacks, works very well, and causes less disruption to downstream classification tasks than other methods.

Acknowledgments. This work is supported by the Strategic Priority Research Program of the Chinese Academy of Sciences, Grant No.XDB0690303.

Disclosure of Interests. The authors have no competing interests to declare that are relevant to the content of this article.

References

1. Agrawal, R., Kiernan, J.: Watermarking relational databases. In: Proceedings of the 28th International Conference on Very Large Data Bases, VLDB 2002, pp. 155–166. Morgan Kaufmann, Hong Kong, China (2002)
2. Bhattacharya, S., Cortesi, A.: A distortion free watermark framework for relational databases. In: Proceedings of the 2013 IEEE International Conference on Emerging Trends in Computing, Communication and Nanotechnology (ICE-CCN), pp. 1–6. IEEE, Tirunelveli, India (2013)
3. Coatrieux, G., Chazard, E., Beuscart, R., Roux, C.: Lossless watermarking of categorical attributes for verifying medical data base integrity. In: Proceedings of the 33rd Annual International Conference of the IEEE Engineering in Medicine and Biology Society, EMBC 2011, pp. 8195–8198. IEEE, Boston, MA, USA (2011)
4. Isler, D., Cabana, E., Garcia-Recuero, A., Koutrika, G., Laoutaris, N.: FreqyWM: frequency watermarking for the new data economy. In: Proceedings of the 40th International Conference on Data Engineering, ICDE 2024, pp. 4993–5007. IEEE, Utrecht, Netherlands (2024)
5. Khanduja, V., Chakraverty, S., Verma, O.P.: Watermarking categorical data: algorithm and robustness analysis. Def. Sci. J. **65**(3), 244–252 (2015)
6. Lin, C.C., Nguyen, T.S., Chang, C.C.: LRW-CRDB: lossless robust watermarking scheme for categorical relational databases. Symmetry **13**(11), 2191 (2021)
7. Sarčević, T., Mayer, R.: An evaluation on robustness and utility of fingerprinting schemes. In: Holzinger, A., Kieseberg, P., Tjoa, A.M., Weippl, E. (eds.) Proceedings of the 3rd International Conference on Computer Science & Knowledge Engineering (CD-MAKE 2019). Lecture Notes in Computer Science, vol. 11713, pp. 209–228. Springer, Cham (2019)
8. Sarcevic, T., Mayer, R.: A correlation-preserving fingerprinting technique for categorical data in relational databases. In: Hölbl, M., Rannenberg, K., Welzer, T. (eds.) SEC 2020. IAICT, vol. 580, pp. 401–415. Springer, Cham (2020). https://doi.org/10.1007/978-3-030-58201-2_27
9. Sion, R.: Proving ownership over categorical data. In: Proceedings of the 20th International Conference on Data Engineering, ICDE 2004, pp. 584–595. IEEE, Boston, MA, USA (2004)
10. Sion, R., Atallah, M., Prabhakar, S.: Rights protection for categorical data. IEEE Trans. Knowl. Data Eng. **17**(7), 912–926 (2005)
11. Zhang, J., Cormode, G., Procopiuc, C.M., Srivastava, D., Xiao, X.: PrivBayes: private data release via bayesian networks. ACM Trans. Database Syst. **42**(4), 25:1–25:41 (2017)

The Hidden Risk of Auto-generated OpenAPI Specifications: An Analysis of WordPress Plugins and Lightweight Specification Correction

Ohiremen Grace Oluwabunmi and Beom Heyn Kim(✉)

Hanyang University ERICA, Ansan, Gyeonggi, Republic of Korea
{grace28,beomheynkim}@hanyang.ac.kr

Abstract. OpenAPI specifications (OAS) underpin automated API security testing, yet the correctness of auto-generated OAS documents in real-world systems remains largely unexamined. In this paper, we conduct the first systematic study of OAS accuracy in WordPress, evaluating WP OpenAPI across 20 widely used plugins. We find that generated specifications exhibit severe behavioral inaccuracies—only 25% correctness—stemming from WordPress's dynamic, runtime-dependent API behavior. These inaccuracies directly impair security testing: OWASP ZAP misses several vulnerabilities, including unauthenticated media enumeration, when guided by incorrect specifications. To address this issue, we introduce a lightweight validation pipeline that uses runtime observations (via Playwright) to largely automate the repair of inaccurate OAS fields. Corrected specifications improve vulnerability detection by 44% and reduce conformance errors by 92.9%. Our results reveal a previously overlooked threat: inaccurate auto-generated API specifications undermine automated security analysis, and validating them is essential for reliable API security testing.

Keywords: API Security · OpenAPI Specification · CMS · WordPress · Hybrid Analysis · REST API

1 Introduction

REST APIs underpin modern web ecosystems, enabling authentication, data exchange, and application logic across platforms [8,23]. The OpenAPI Specification (OAS) has become the dominant standard for documenting these APIs and is widely used for automated security testing, conformance checking, and large-scale analysis. Tools such as RESTler [5], Schemathesis [3], and OWASP ZAP rely heavily on OAS documents to guide systematic exploration of API behavior. Despite this reliance, the accuracy of auto-generated OAS documents in real-world environments remains largely unexplored.

This issue is particularly critical in content management systems (CMS), where APIs are highly dynamic and context-dependent. WordPress—which

© IFIP International Federation for Information Processing 2026
Published by Springer Nature Switzerland AG 2026
H. Janicke et al. (Eds.): SEC 2026, IFIP AICT 787, pp. 331–344, 2026.
https://doi.org/10.1007/978-3-032-27993-4_23

powers more than 40% of websites [29]—supports thousands of plugins that conditionally register REST endpoints based on user roles, activation states, JavaScript-driven workflows, and configuration settings [2,9,17]. These APIs frequently handle security-sensitive operations such as authentication, media management, and form processing, yet the accuracy of the OAS files used to test them has not been systematically evaluated.

In this paper, we conduct the first systematic study of OAS accuracy in WordPress. We focus on WP OpenAPI, the de facto OAS generator for the WordPress ecosystem [34], and evaluate its behavioral correctness. This paper extends our prior workshop work [21,22] in three ways. First, we conduct a more comprehensive analysis on a larger number of plugins across a wider spectrum of categories. Second, we quantify the security impact of specification inaccuracies through automated testing. Third, we introduce a validation-driven pipeline that reconciles declared and observed API behavior.

Our analysis covers twenty widely used WordPress plugins across eight representative categories. Our results reveal substantial inaccuracies: WP OpenAPI achieves only 25% correctness across key specification fields, including HTTP methods, content types, authentication requirements, parameters, and response schemas. These errors stem from a fundamental mismatch between static endpoint extraction and WordPress's runtime-dependent behavior, which often cannot be captured without executing the system [4,15,26].

Moreover, we show that inaccurate OAS files directly impair automated security testing. When guided by WP OpenAPI's specifications, OWASP ZAP fails to explore critical execution paths and misses vulnerabilities—e.g., unauthenticated media ID enumeration and privilege-bypass endpoints. These issues become detectable only after correcting the specifications to reflect actual runtime behavior.

To address this problem, we propose a lightweight validation pipeline that leverages runtime observations using Playwright [20] to identify and repair incorrect OAS fields. Rather than building a new generator, our approach introduces a validation layer between specification generation and security testing, reconciling declared and observed API behavior. Our evaluation shows that corrected specifications significantly improve testing effectiveness: vulnerability detection increases by 44% using OWASP ZAP, while specification conformance errors decrease by 92.9%. All discovered vulnerabilities were manually verified, and we initiated responsible disclosure with the WordPress Security Team and Wordfence CNA [33][1].

In summary, this paper makes the following contributions:

- **Empirical analysis.** First systematic evaluation of OpenAPI correctness in WordPress, showing WP OpenAPI achieves only 25% behavioral fidelity.
- **Security impact.** Evidence that inaccurate specifications cause tools such as OWASP ZAP to miss vulnerabilities.
- **Validation pipeline.** Lightweight automated method using runtime observation to repair incorrect OAS fields.

[1] Discussions with the maintainers are ongoing.

- **Improved testing effectiveness.** Corrected specifications increase vulnerability detection by 44% and reduce specification errors by 92.9%.

2 Systematic Study of OAS Accuracy in WordPress

We conducted a systematic evaluation of OpenAPI specification accuracy across 20 widely used WordPress plugins spanning eight functional categories, including E-commerce, form processing, media management, security, SEO and analytics, membership and user management, page builders, and community-oriented utilities. This dataset provides broad coverage of the API patterns and dynamic behaviors common in the WordPress ecosystem.

To assess specification fidelity, we applied a multi-dimensional evaluation framework comprising five critical aspects of API behavior.

1. **HTTP Method Correctness:** Verification of supported methods (GET, POST, PUT, DELETE)
2. **Path Parameter Accuracy:** Correctness of path templates and parameter definitions
3. **Request Payload Requirements:** Accuracy of content-type declarations and required parameters
4. **Authentication/Authorization Semantics:** Correct reflection of required capabilities and security contexts
5. **Response Schema Completeness**: Faithfulness of documented response structures and status codes

While all five dimensions were evaluated, **HTTP Method Correctness was consistently accurate across all endpoints (100%)**. This is because WordPress REST API endpoints explicitly declare their HTTP methods during registration (e.g., `'methods' => 'GET'`), and WP OpenAPI reads these declarations directly from the internal WordPress registry. In contrast, dimensions such as request payload requirements, authentication semantics, and response schemas are not explicitly registered and often depend on runtime behavior—leading to the inaccuracies documented in this study.

We adopt a strict binary scoring rule in which an endpoint is considered accurate only when all evaluated dimensions exactly match observed runtime behavior. This conservative choice reflects the realities of automated security testing: even a single incorrect specification field—such as authentication requirements or request content-type—can prevent tools from executing valid paths. As a result, partially correct specifications remain functionally inadequate for security analysis, motivating the use of binary correctness in our evaluation.

Table 1 summarizes the accuracy of WP OpenAPI across our dataset and highlights the prevalence of specification errors. Across 20 plugins and 40 documented endpoints, only 10 endpoints (25%) were accurate under our strict evaluation criteria. Fifteen of the twenty plugins (75%) failed to produce a single correct specification. This issue affects even widely deployed plugins: WooCommerce achieves only 67% endpoint accuracy, Contact Form 7 reaches 25%, and

Table 1. Accuracy of WP OpenAPI Specifications Across 20 WordPress Plugins

Plugin	Version	Endpoints Documented	Accurate Endpoints	Accuracy Rate	Critical Errors
Contact Form 7	5.9	4	1	25%	2
WooCommerce	8.7	9	6	67%	2
Advanced Custom Fields	6.2	3	1	33%	1
Yoast SEO	22.6	2	0	0%	1
Wordfence	7.11	1	0	0%	1
Jetpack	13.5	1	0	0%	1
WP REST API Media IDs	1.0	1	0	0%	0
bbPress	2.6	1	0	0%	1
BuddyPress	12.4	1	0	0%	1
Events Calendar	6.4	2	1	50%	1
GiveWP	3.6	6	1	17%	1
Popup Maker	1.18	1	0	0%	1
NextGEN Gallery	3.59	1	0	0%	1
Elementor	3.21	1	0	0%	1
External Media Library	4.1	1	0	0%	0
MonsterInsights	9.0	1	0	0%	0
Forminator	1.29	1	0	0%	0
WP Job Manager	1.42	1	0	0%	1
Recipe Maker	9.3	1	0	0%	1
Overall (20 Plugins)	–	**40**	**10**	**25%**	**20**

GiveWP drops to 17%. These results demonstrate that specification inaccuracies are pervasive across the WordPress plugin ecosystem. Plugins were categorized based on their primary functionality (e.g., forms, e-commerce, security, or SEO). Table 1 summarizes the accuracy of WP OpenAPI specifications across the evaluated plugins.

A closer examination reveals several recurring error categories. The most common issue involves the violation of request payload requirements (i.e., content-type mismatches), which account for 35% of all errors; in many cases, the auto-generated specification declares `application/json` even though the endpoint requires `multipart/form-data`. Violations of authentication and authorization semantics constitute 25% of errors, where privileged endpoints are incorrectly documented as publicly accessible. Path-parameter inaccuracies represent 20% of cases, commonly omitting mandatory variables required for successful invocation. Violations of response-schema completeness appear in 15% of cases, where essential fields or status codes are undocumented. Finally, 5% of errors correspond to phantom endpoints—documented routes that do not exist at runtime.

Table 2. Observed OpenAPI Specification Inaccuracies and Their Security Impacts

Inaccuracy Type	Example	Security Testing Failure	Vulnerability Class
Path Parameter Errors	Missing path variables; incorrect templates	Tools construct malformed URLs or fail to reach resources	IDOR, enumeration flaws
Request Payload Errors	Wrong content-type; missing required fields	Tools generate invalid requests that never reach backend logic	Parameter injection, validation bypass
Auth. Semantics Errors	Missing privilege checks; incorrect roles	Tools test endpoints under wrong roles or treat sensitive endpoints as public	Privilege escalation, information disclosure
Response Schema Errors	Missing fields; undocumented status codes	Tools cannot validate responses or detect abnormal behavior	Logic flaws, inconsistent-state bugs

2.1 Security Implications of OAS Inaccuracies

Table 2 shows that the majority of observed issues stem from mis-specified path parameters, request payload requirements, authentication/authorization semantics, and response schema definitions. These inaccuracies distort the behavioral model that automated security testing tools rely on, creating blind spots in test generation and reducing the likelihood of discovering vulnerabilities.

Path parameter errors prevent tools from reaching resource-specific endpoints, directly suppressing the vulnerabilities such as Insecure Direct Object Reference (IDOR) and enumeration vulnerabilities. Request payload inaccuracies—such as incorrect content-type declarations or missing required fields—cause tools to issue malformed requests that never trigger backend logic, hiding parameter-manipulation or validation-related flaws. Authentication and authorization errors misrepresent privilege requirements, resulting in testing under incorrect assumptions and masking privilege-escalation or information-disclosure vulnerabilities. Finally, response schema inaccuracies obscure the structure and semantics of returned data, preventing tools from recognizing abnormal responses indicative of logic flaws.

Empirical evidence from our study confirms that OAS specification inaccuracies in WordPress have immediate security consequences: inaccurate OpenAPI specifications directly cause automated testing tools to miss vulnerabilities. Table 3 illustrates this effect across two complementary analyses. First, OWASP ZAP detected only 54 vulnerabilities when using WP OpenAPI's inaccurate

Table 3. Impact of Specification Accuracy on Automated Security Testing Tools

Tool	Metric	Inaccurate OAS	Corrected OAS	Improvement
OWASP ZAP	Vulnerabilities Detected	54	78	+44%
RESTest	OAS Conformance Errors	140	10	−92.9%
RESTest	Test Pass Rate	24%	47.2%	+23.2 pp

specifications. With corrected specifications[2], the number of findings increased to 78, a 44% improvement, as accurate endpoint descriptions enabled ZAP to reach and exercise previously inaccessible behaviors. Second, RESTest exhibited substantial failures when using inaccurate specifications, producing 140 OAS conformance errors and only a 24% test pass rate. Corrected specifications reduced conformance errors by 92.9% and nearly doubled pass rates to 47.2%, demonstrating that specification accuracy is essential for achieving reliable automated testing coverage.

All additional findings from corrected specifications were manually validated as true positives, spanning authentication and authorization bypasses, information disclosure, and input validation flaws. While exploit examples are omitted due to space constraints, validation confirms that corrected specifications expose execution paths previously unreachable by automated tools.

Our analysis further substantiates these results by examining how specific inaccuracies suppress vulnerability discovery in practice. For the Media IDs plugin, OWASP ZAP failed to identify an information-disclosure vulnerability when relying on WP OpenAPI, which documented only a generic "200 OK" response. After correcting the specification to accurately declare its array-of-integers response, ZAP immediately flagged the exposure of media identifiers. This case highlights how incomplete response schemas can completely obscure security-relevant behaviors.

A similar suppression effect occurs in Contact Form 7. WP OpenAPI incorrectly specifies several endpoints as accepting JSON payloads, leading ZAP to generate requests that the server consistently rejects. Once corrected to reflect the actual `multipart/form-data` requirement, ZAP was able to exercise these endpoints successfully, enabling parameter-injection and validation-logic testing that was previously unreachable. This demonstrates how content-type inaccuracies prevent security tools from traversing critical execution paths.

Authentication omissions in WP OpenAPI's documentation for WooCommerce further illustrate the problem. By incorrectly marking privileged endpoints as publicly accessible, the specification caused ZAP to test them without authentication, thereby bypassing meaningful evaluation of access-control logic. After correcting the specification to encode the proper authentication requirements, ZAP exercised the correct privilege checks and detected potential authentication-bypass vectors. These examples collectively show that even a single specification

[2] We corrected inaccurate specifications by using a simple methodology described in Sect. 3.

inaccuracy can suppress entire classes of vulnerabilities by fundamentally distorting how automated testing tools interact with the API surface.

2.2 Endpoint-Level Analysis of Inaccurate Specifications

Table 4 summarizes how inaccurate OpenAPI specifications suppress vulnerability discovery by preventing security tools from exercising critical execution paths. Across the 30 inaccurate endpoints analyzed, three structural error types consistently interfered with automated testing.

Content-type mismatches prevent tools from constructing valid payloads, leaving multipart forms, file uploads, and asynchronous submission paths untested and causing parameter-injection or upload vulnerabilities to be missed. *Authentication omissions* occur when privileged endpoints are documented as public, causing tools to test under the wrong security context and concealing privilege-escalation or information-disclosure flaws. *Response-schema gaps* arise when response fields or status codes are absent, preventing conformance tools from validating server behavior and allowing disclosure bugs or inconsistent states to evade detection.

3 Lightweight Specification Correction

We introduce a validation-driven correction pipeline that reconciles specifications produced by WP OpenAPI with observed runtime behavior. Our prototype validation pipeline is implemented in Python and consists of approximately 1,500 lines of code, excluding third-party dependencies. Artifacts—including the prototype tool, corrected OpenAPI specifications, HAR samples, and supporting scripts—are publicly available at: https://github.com/Chooks28/Krypton. We conduct empirical studies using the pipeline to show that lightweight runtime validation can substantially improve the accuracy of auto-generated OpenAPI specifications. All experiments used WordPress 6.8.1 and the latest stable WP OpenAPI release available during the study. The evaluated plugin versions are listed in Table 1.

The process begins with the WP OpenAPI output as the baseline specification. To capture ground-truth behavior, we use Playwright [20] to automatically exercise WordPress through direct endpoint invocation, UI-driven interactions that trigger JavaScript-based API calls, and authenticated crawling. All resulting HTTP traffic is recorded as HTTP Archive (HAR) files. These traces reveal the precise content-types, parameters, authentication requirements, status codes, and response structures observed during execution. For example, consider the `/media-ids/v1/get-all-media-ids` endpoint from the "WP REST API Media IDs" plugin. WP OpenAPI documents the endpoint only as returning "200 OK" without a schema. However, runtime traces captured through Playwright reveal the following behavior:

Table 4. Endpoint-Level Inaccuracies and Their Security Consequences

Category	Plugin	Endpoint	Security Implication
Content-Type Mismatch	Contact Form 7	`/feedback`	Invalid JSON payloads; multipart injection testing suppressed
	Contact Form 7	`/feedback-validate`	Payloads rejected; validation-logic bypass undetected
	Contact Form 7	`/feedback-async`	Async request paths unreachable; async injection missed
	Forminator	`/forms`	File uploads untested; upload-bypass vulnerabilities hidden
Auth. Omission	WooCommerce	`/customers`	Tested as unauthenticated; customer-data enumeration undetected
	WooCommerce	`/orders`	Privilege checks omitted; order manipulation not exercised
	GiveWP	`/reports`	Financial endpoints exposed; donation reports leaked
	GiveWP	`/donors`	Donor data treated as public; privacy-violation vectors hidden
	WP Job Manager	`/jobs`	Unauthorized posting allowed; fake postings undetected
	Recipe Maker	`/recipes`	Integrity checks skipped; content-tampering missed
	WP Course LMS	`/courses`	Access-control bypassed; course material theft untested
Schema Gap	Media IDs	`/get-all-media-ids`	Hidden disclosure paths; media ID enumeration undetected
	WooCommerce	`/orders`	Order-state logic unvalidated; manipulation overlooked
	GiveWP	`/donations`	Incomplete flow validation; donation bypass attacks untested
	ACF	`/acf/options`	Incorrect validation logic; malformed field injection missed
	ACF	`/acf/fields`	Field constraints bypassed; invalid metadata accepted
	NextGEN Gallery	`/gallery`	Validation incomplete; image-injection vulnerabilities hidden

```
GET /wp-json/media-ids/v1/get-all-media-ids
Status: 200 OK
Content-Type: application/json
Response Body: [67, 54, 50, 48, 42, 41, 40, 37, 22]
```

Note that the endpoint actually returns an array of media identifiers, exposing sensitive information that remains invisible to security tools relying solely on the incomplete specification.

Validation-driven correction updates the specification based on actual observed behavior. For instance, when a response schema is missing, we add an explicit array schema describing the returned data. Below we present an example showing how this validation–correction process works.

```
[Incorrect]

responses:
  "200":
    description: OK
```

```
[Corrected]

responses:
  "200":
    description: OK
    content:
      application/json:
        schema:
          type: array
          items:
            type: integer
```

The pipeline is largely automated: static route extraction, Playwright traffic capture, HAR parsing, parameter merging, content-type correction, and response schema inference are performed automatically. Manual review is required only for custom authentication mechanisms, complex multi-step workflows, and endpoints discovered statically but not triggered during runtime execution.

3.1 Effectiveness of Lightweight Specification Correction

Runtime validation corrected all 30 inaccurate endpoints identified in our empirical study, achieving full behavioral alignment with observed execution. The corrections repaired content-type mismatches, authentication omissions, response-schema gaps, and undocumented parameters.

These improvements directly enhanced automated security testing (Table 3). Using corrected specifications increased vulnerabilities detected by OWASP ZAP from 54 to 78—a 44% improvement. The corrected specifications enabled ZAP to generate valid payloads, apply appropriate authentication contexts, and explore execution paths that were previously unreachable.

Specification conformance testing with RESTest further demonstrates the effect. Corrected specifications reduced OAS conformity errors by 92.9% (140 to 10), nearly doubled test pass rates (24.0% to 47.2%), and enabled 36% more generated test cases due to complete response schemas. Valid test execution increased from 65% with WP OpenAPI to 98% with corrected specifications, indicating substantially improved testing reliability.

4 Discussion

Our findings highlight important implications for API developers and security practitioners. First, auto-generated specifications should not be trusted without verification. Across our plugin corpus, 75% of specifications produced by WP OpenAPI were behaviorally incorrect, often omitting authentication requirements, misrepresenting content types, or failing to document sensitive response fields. These inaccuracies directly suppressed vulnerability discovery in automated security tools. Practitioners should therefore validate generated specifications against runtime behavior before using them for security testing or integration. We focus on WP OpenAPI as the de facto OpenAPI generator in the WordPress ecosystem; systematic comparison with alternative generators or manually written specifications is left for future work.

Second, lightweight validation can substantially improve testing effectiveness. Our pipeline combines Playwright-driven exploration with HAR-based observation to identify and correct specification inaccuracies without requiring complex instrumentation. This suggests that specification validation could be integrated into CI/CD pipelines as a routine pre-testing step, allowing specifications to be continuously corrected as plugins evolve. Even partial automation—such as detecting content-type mismatches or missing authentication requirements—would prevent many failures observed in our study.

Third, not all specification errors have equal impact. Content-type mismatches and missing authentication declarations accounted for most suppressed findings in OWASP ZAP and RESTest. Prioritizing validation of these high-impact fields can therefore yield substantial benefits, especially for practitioners with limited resources.

Our study also has limitations. Although our analysis examines 20 widely used plugins, it cannot fully represent the entire WordPress ecosystem. In addition, our evaluation focuses on WordPress; while similar dynamics likely affect other CMS platforms such as Drupal or Joomla, further study is needed to confirm this. Finally, correcting certain ambiguous or rarely executed endpoints still requires limited manual inspection.

5 Related Work

5.1 Automatic OpenAPI Specification Generation

Automatic OpenAPI Specification (OAS) generation has been widely studied using static, dynamic, and hybrid analysis techniques. Static approaches extract API behavior directly from source code. For example, Respector [15] generates REST API specifications using static analysis and symbolic execution for Java applications, while SWIM [37] performs web API mining through static taint analysis. Similar techniques have also been applied to mobile systems, including FlowDroid [4] and DroidRay [31]. Recent work further improves specification extraction from Java codebases [18].

Dynamic approaches infer specifications from runtime behavior. Tools such as APIScanner [13] dynamically explore REST APIs, while ApiCarv [36] derives specifications from UI test executions. Industry tools such as SwaggerHub Explore [28] reconstruct specifications by recording network traffic. Although behaviorally accurate, these approaches are limited to endpoints exercised during execution.

Recent work also explores advanced techniques. LRASGen [11] uses large language models to generate REST API specifications, while RestPl [1] performs path-sensitive type inference for REST APIs. AutoGuard [32] detects breaking API changes in Java Spring Boot systems. However, these approaches assume relatively static architectures and do not address environments where endpoints are dynamically registered at runtime.

Hybrid approaches combine static and dynamic analysis. ExpressO [27] integrates static analysis with runtime information for Express.js applications, while OpenAPI-from-Source [14] combines AST parsing with runtime monitoring. However, most hybrid techniques simply merge information from both sources without resolving contradictions between declared and observed behavior.

CMS environments introduce additional challenges due to dynamic plugin ecosystems and runtime endpoint registration. WP OpenAPI [34] generates specifications from WordPress's internal REST API registry but reflects intended rather than actual runtime behavior. CMS-API-Miner [10] performs static analysis of CMS plugins but cannot capture dynamic registration patterns. As a result, existing approaches struggle to produce behaviorally accurate specifications for CMS platforms.

More broadly, prior work reflects a tradeoff between coverage and accuracy: static analysis discovers endpoints but cannot validate runtime behavior, while dynamic approaches validate behavior but miss unexecuted endpoints. This limitation is particularly problematic in CMS environments where API behavior emerges from runtime plugin interactions.

Our earlier workshop papers [21,22] provided preliminary evidence that auto-generated OpenAPI specifications for WordPress plugins are often inaccurate based on analyses of eight plugins. This work extends that observation through a larger empirical study of 20 plugins, systematic characterization of specification inaccuracies, and measurement of their security impact. We further introduce a lightweight validation pipeline that reconciles declared and observed API behavior.

5.2 API Security Testing Tools

Automated security testing tools increasingly rely on OpenAPI specifications to guide test generation. Tools such as RESTler [5], Schemathesis [3], and NAUTILUS [6] perform stateful fuzzing, property-based testing, and automated vulnerability detection using OAS inputs. Recent work also explores end-to-end API fuzzing [25], LLM-assisted test generation [30], and machine learning approaches for REST API testing [16]. Other studies examine testing challenges in complex cloud environments [19].

Despite these advances, the effectiveness of these tools depends critically on specification accuracy. Under the "Garbage In, Garbage Out" principle, inaccurate specifications lead to invalid test generation and missed vulnerabilities. Prior work shows that even small inconsistencies in API specifications can significantly affect automated analysis and testing outcomes [7,12,35].

Tools such as OWASP ZAP [24] provide comprehensive web application security testing but rely on accurate API specifications to exercise REST endpoints effectively. Our validation pipeline addresses this limitation by producing behaviorally validated specifications for CMS environments.

6 Conclusion

Our study shows that inaccurate OpenAPI specifications are a primary cause of missed vulnerabilities in CMS ecosystems. Auto-generated specifications frequently misrepresent runtime behavior, suppressing the effectiveness of security testing tools. By applying lightweight validation using Playwright-driven exploration and HAR-based observation, we corrected all identified inaccuracies across 20 WordPress plugins, yielding a 44% increase in vulnerabilities discovered by OWASP ZAP and a 92.9% reduction in RESTest conformity errors. These results demonstrate that even simple runtime validation provides substantial security benefits, enabling specifications that accurately reflect real API behavior and restoring the reliability of automated testing. Our findings highlight the need to treat API specifications as behavioral claims that require validation, and they provide a practical path for integrating lightweight specification correction into CMS development and security workflows.

Acknowledgements. This work was supported by the National Research Foundation of Korea (NRF) grant funded by the Korea Government (MSIT) (No. RS-2023-00244368).

References

1. Aldrich, M.W., Levin, K.H., Coblenz, M., Foster, J.S.: RestPl: path-sensitive type inference for REST APIs. In: Proceedings of the ACM on Programming Languages (OOPSLA) (2025)
2. AppMap: AppMap documentation (2024). https://appmap.io/docs
3. Arcuri, A., Katz, D.S.: Schemathesis: property-based testing for web APIs. In: Proceedings of the IEEE International Conference on Software Testing, Verification and Validation (ICST), pp. 454–457 (2020)
4. Arzt, S., et al.: FlowDroid: precise context, flow, field, object-sensitive and lifecycle-aware taint analysis for Android apps. In: Proceedings of the ACM SIGPLAN Conference on Programming Language Design and Implementation (PLDI), pp. 259–269 (2014)

5. Atlidakis, V., Godefroid, P., Polishchuk, M.: RESTler: stateful REST API fuzzing. In: Proceedings of the IEEE Symposium on Security and Privacy, pp. 748–763 (2019)
6. Atlidakis, V., Godefroid, P., Polishchuk, M.: NAUTILUS: automated RESTful API vulnerability detection. In: Proceedings of the ACM SIGSAC Conference on Computer and Communications Security (CCS), pp. 678–695 (2021)
7. Avgerinos, T., Cha, S.K., Hao, B.L.T., Brumley, D.: AEG: automatic exploit generation. In: Proceedings of the Network and Distributed System Security Symposium (NDSS), pp. 1–16 (2011)
8. Cerny, T., Rodriguez, M.J., Svacina, J., Taibi, D.: From static code analysis to visual models of microservice architecture. Clust. Comput. **27**(1), 1–20 (2024)
9. Chen, J., Wang, H., Wang, Y., Wang, H.: A large-scale empirical study of security patches in WordPress plugins. In: Proceedings of the Web Conference (WWW), pp. 3100–3111 (2023)
10. Chen, T., Wang, H., Zhang, L.: CMS-API-miner: automated API endpoint discovery for content management systems. In: IEEE International Conference on Web Services (ICWS), pp. 234–245 (2022)
11. Deng, S., Huang, R., Zhang, M., Cui, C., Towey, D., Wang, R.: LRASGen: LLM-based RESTful API specification generation. arXiv:2504.16833 (2025)
12. Doupé, A., Cavedon, L., Vigna, G., Kruegel, C.: Why johnny can't pentest: an analysis of black-box web vulnerability scanners. In: Proceedings of the Conference on Detection of Intrusions and Malware, and Vulnerability Assessment (DIMVA), pp. 65–86 (2019)
13. Felderer, M., Büchler, M., Johns, M., Brucker, R., Brucker, A.D., Breu, L.: Security testing: a survey. In: Advances in Computers, vol. 109, pp. 1–51 (2018)
14. Huang, J., Liu, C., Xiong, Y.: Generating OpenAPI specifications from source code: a survey. J. Syst. Softw. **181**, 111040 (2021)
15. Huang, R., Motwani, M., Martinez, I., Orso, A.: Generating REST API specifications through static analysis. In: Proceedings of the IEEE/ACM International Conference on Software Engineering (ICSE) (2024)
16. Kim, M.: Effective automation of black-box testing for REST APIs with machine learning and LLMs. In: Proceedings of the International Symposium on Software Testing and Analysis (ISSTA) (2025)
17. Kloukinas, C., Marnerides, A.K., Misra, P.: Security weaknesses in WordPress plugins: a large-scale empirical study. In: Proceedings of the Annual Computer Security Applications Conference (ACSAC), pp. 855–868 (2021)
18. Kramer, T., Schäfer, F., Apel, S.: Generating accurate OpenAPI descriptions from Java source code. In: Proceedings of the International Conference on Software Engineering (ICSE) (2024)
19. Mazhar, A., Alam, S.S., Zheng, W.X., Chen, Y., Nath, S., Xu, T.: Fidelity of cloud emulators: The imitation game of testing cloud-based software. In: Proceedings of the International Conference on Software Engineering (ICSE) (2024)
20. Microsoft Corporation: Playwright: Fast and reliable end-to-end testing for modern web apps (2024). https://playwright.dev/
21. Oluwabunmi, O.G., Kim, B.H.: Comprehensive analysis of inaccurate OpenAPI specifications in WordPress plugins. In: Proceedings of the CISC-W 2025 Workshop (2025)
22. Oluwabunmi, O.G., Kim, B.H.: Limitations of automatically generated API specification for WordPress CMS plugins: an empirical study. In: Proceedings of the CISC-S 2025 Symposium (2025)

23. OpenAPI Initiative: OpenAPI specification version 3.1.0 (2021). Specification
24. OWASP Foundation: OWASP ZAP (zed attack proxy) (2024). https://www.zaproxy.org/
25. Pan, L., Cohney, S., Murray, T., Pham, V.T.: Trailblazer: practical end-to-end web API fuzzing. In: Proceedings of the IEEE Symposium on Security and Privacy (2025)
26. PHPStan: PHP static analysis tool (2024). https://phpstan.org/
27. Serbout, S., Bohm, U.R.C., Bezemer, C.P., Zisman, A.: ExpressO: from express.js implementation code to OpenAPI interface descriptions. In: Proceedings of the European Conference on Software Architecture (ECSA), pp. 219–235 (2022)
28. SmartBear Software: SwaggerHub explore (2024). https://swagger.io/tools/swaggerhub/
29. W3Techs: Usage statistics of content management systems (2024). https://w3techs.com/
30. Wang, J., et al.: TestGPT-server: automatically testing microservices with LLMs at ByteDance. arXiv preprint (2025)
31. Wang, K., Zhang, Y., Zhou, Y., Li, X.: DroidRay: a security evaluation system for customized Android firmware. In: ACM Conference on Computer and Communications Security (CCS), pp. 1237–1254 (2019)
32. Wang, Y., Chen, L., Zhang, Z.: AutoGuard: reporting breaking changes of REST APIs from Java Spring Boot source code. In: Proceedings of the IEEE International Conference on Software Maintenance and Evolution (ICSME) (2024)
33. Wordfence: Vulnerability disclosure policy (2025). https://www.wordfence.com/security/
34. WP OpenAPI: WP OpenAPI (2024). WordPress Plugin Repository
35. Yamaguchi, F., Golde, N., Arp, D., Rieck, K.: Chucky: exposing missing checks in source code for vulnerability discovery. In: Proceedings of the ACM SIGSAC Conference on Computer and Communications Security (CCS), pp. 453–467 (2019)
36. Yandrapally, R., Thummalapenta, S., Cohen, M.B.: Carving UI tests to generate API tests and API specification. In: Proceedings of the IEEE/ACM International Conference on Software Engineering (ICSE), pp. 1545–1557 (2023)
37. Zhang, S., Chen, D., Song, Y., Kim, M.: SWIM: static analysis-based web API mining. In: IEEE International Conference on Software Analysis, Evolution and Reengineering (SANER), pp. 425–436 (2020)

Hop-Decayed Influence: New Vulnerabilities of Structural Auxiliary Indexing in GraphRAG Pipelines with LLM

Jisung Park(✉), John Le, and Heath Cooper

Institute of Cybersecurity and Cryptology, University of Wollongong, Wollongong, Australia
jp407@uowmail.edu.au, {johnle,hcooper}@uow.edu.au

Abstract. GraphRAG pipelines construct auxiliary structures during offline indexing—semantic summaries, hierarchical edges, and precomputed scores—that determine how retrieval is prioritised at query time. Prior attacks target only instance-level components (nodes, edges, triples), overlooking these schema-level structures. We formalise Auxiliary Schema-Level Entity as a novel attack surface and propose the 3S Framework (Semantics, Structure, Scoring) for its systematic exploitation. Our Hop-Decayed Influence (HDI) attack identifies high-impact targets through query-aware influence propagation and corrupts their auxiliary structures post-indexing. Across two benchmarks (HotpotQA, 2WikiMultiHopQA) and two architectures (Microsoft GraphRAG, HippoRAG2), HDI achieves 88–94% attack success rate while modifying as few as 0.016% of auxiliary structures. Each modification affects up to 6.00 queries (Schema Leverage Ratio), demonstrating 1:N amplification unavailable to instance-level attacks. Manipulated structures evade perplexity and paraphrase defenses with over 99% evasion rate, as they remain linguistically coherent system-generated artifacts. These results reveal that auxiliary schema-level entities receive implicit trust without runtime validation, constituting a structural blind spot in current GraphRAG defenses. https://github.com/Jisung-Pacific/HDI-GraphRAG-Attack.

Keywords: GraphRAG · Knowledge Graph Security · Adversarial Attacks · Schema-Level Entities

1 Introduction

Large language models have achieved success [1] in NLP tasks in various domains, e.g., healthcare and scientific research [15,30]. Yet, they exhibit limitations such as hallucination, knowledge recency gaps and lack of domain specific or private knowledge [10,13,16]. To address these limitations, Retrieval Augmented

© IFIP International Federation for Information Processing 2026
Published by Springer Nature Switzerland AG 2026
H. Janicke et al. (Eds.): SEC 2026, IFIP AICT 787, pp. 345–358, 2026.
https://doi.org/10.1007/978-3-032-27993-4_24

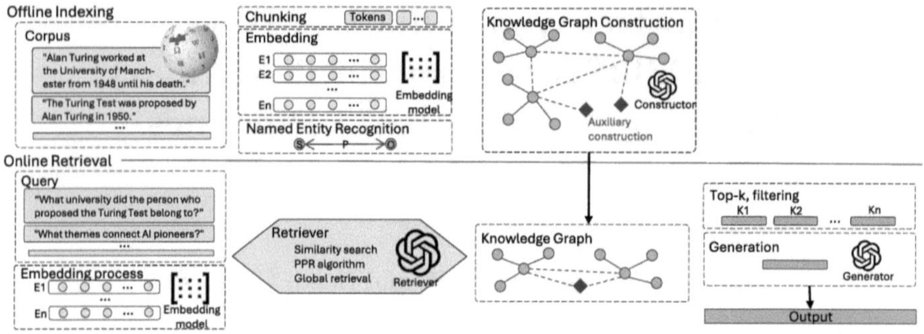

Fig. 1. A process of GraphRAG pipeline

Generation (RAG) has emerged by retrieving relevant information from external knowledge bases [4,17]. Existing RAG approaches have focused on semi-structured knowledge (e.g., web page, email), unstructured knowledge (e.g., textual documents), and multimodal knowledge (e.g., image, audio) [2]. However, these RAG approaches still suffer from limitations such as weak structured, relational and logical knowledge representation, multi-hop traversal challenges [14]. KG RAG is a RAG technique that operates on knowledge graphs, leveraging structured relational knowledge where query processors, retrievers, and graph granularity interact to enhance retrieval precision [7,8,18,24]. GraphRAG pipeline in this research extends beyond the conventional scope of online retrieval, which merely involves interactions among queries, retrievers, and static knowledge graphs. Instead, it encompasses the complete end to end process including offline indexing, which performs knowledge extraction from raw text corpora to knowledge graph construction [21,26,33]. These pipelines construct diverse and unique auxiliary structures. These auxiliary structures either enable additional functionalities such as sense-making and multi-hop reasoning, or enhance retrieval performance efficiency and effectiveness through mechanisms like context richness and pre-computed scoring [3,5]. This approach is increasingly adopted in both academic and industrial fields across diverse domains [28,30] (Fig. 1).

Recent security research has revealed vulnerabilities in RAG and GraphRAG systems through systematic poisoning attacks targeting knowledge retrieval and representation. Direct graph attacks manipulate the structural components of knowledge graphs corrupting nodes, edges, or triples to propagate misinformation through relational pathways [19,20,29]. Corpus to graph attacks exploit the end to end nature of GraphRAG pipelines, injecting adversarial passages into source corpora that propagate through the knowledge extraction workflow to corrupt the constructed graph [34,35]. However, these attacks remain confined to the instance-level paradigm of conventional knowledge graphs, assuming that the graph itself constitutes the complete retrieval substrate. This perspective misses that end to end GraphRAG pipelines construct auxiliary structures during offline indexing that exist as separate layers beyond the core knowledge graph. These structures are architectural necessities for advanced functionalities including sense-making and multi-hop reasoning. They reside not in the data plane of individual facts but in the control plane that determines retrieval paths and prioritisation directly determining not merely *what is retrieved*, but *how it is ranked and interpreted*.

We propose **Auxiliary Schema-Level Entity** as an attack surface comprising components that exist beyond traditional graph granularities, systematised through the 3S Framework: *Semantics* (summaries), *Structure* (hierarchical edges), and *Scoring* (pre-computed metrics). This qualifies as an attack surface for the following reasons. These structures are required components for advanced functionalities including sense-making and multi-hop reasoning, residing in the control plane that determines retrieval paths and prioritisation. As system generated artifacts, they are granted implicit trust and excluded from runtime validation. A single schema at hierarchical aggregation points, when manipulated, simultaneously affects numerous subordinate entities and queries providing asymmetric 1:N leverage. Even when instance-level facts remain accurate, higher level semantic abstractions dominate the interpretive context delivered to the LLM, distorting final generation. Existing defenses target anomaly detection at the node, edge, and triple level, leaving schema-level manipulation as a structural blind spot. As derived artifacts synthesised from multiple sources, they lack singular ground truth, rendering tampering verification intractable.

To demonstrate this attack surface, we suggest the **Hop-Decayed Influence**, which targets the auxiliary extension structures Semantics, Structure, Scoring beyond instance level entities that GraphRAG pipelines uniquely employ for additional functions and efficient retrieval strategies. The attack is deployed after knowledge construction through offline indexing in the GraphRAG pipeline, but before online retrieval commences. The attack first identifies targets using type predicted queries, then applies the selected 3S attack method.

To investigate these vulnerabilities, we address the following research questions: **RQ1:** Are Auxiliary Schema-Level Entities exploitable, and does Hop-Decayed Influence effectively compromise GraphRAG systems?, **RQ2:** How efficient and scalable is Hop-Decayed Influence compared to conventional poisoning approaches?, **RQ3:** Is Hop-Decayed Influence stealthy enough to evade existing GraphRAG defense mechanisms?

Based on query types, we select attack targets through either scoring exploration, then manipulate the attack surfaces including semantics, structure, and scoring mechanisms. Our method achieved over 85% attack success rate across all configurations with minimal structural perturbation. Defense evasion rates exceeded 99% against existing detection mechanisms [12].

Our key contributions to the understanding and advancement of GraphRAG pipeline are:

- We formalise *Auxiliary Schema-Level Entity* (semantic summaries, hierarchical edges, pre-computed scores) as a novel attack surface in GraphRAG pipelines.
- We propose Hop-Decayed Influence (HDI), a gray-box attack achieving high ASR with minimal structural perturbation and 1:N leverage.

- We analyse defense limitations, revealing conventional instance-level defenses are insufficient for schema-level threats.

The paper proceeds as follows: Sect. 2 covers background, Sect. 3 presents methodology, Sect. 4 details experimental setup, Sect. 5 reports results, and Sect. 6 discusses defenses before concluding.

2 Background

2.1 GraphRAG Pipeline

GraphRAG pipeline consists of two primary phases: offline indexing and online retrieval [26,33]. **Offline Indexing.** Given a raw text document corpus $\mathcal{D}$, the system performs text chunking to divide documents into overlapping segments that maintain semantic continuity. Each chunk is transformed into dense vector representations via embedding functions, enabling similarity based retrieval. Concurrently, a knowledge extraction process identifies entities $\mathcal{E}$ and relations $\mathcal{R}$ using LLMs or NLP tools, representing each fact as a triple (e_i, r_k, e_j). The extracted information is structured into a knowledge graph $\mathcal{G} = (\mathcal{V}, \mathcal{E}')$, where vertices include both entities and text chunks, and edges represent relationships between them. An auxiliary structure generation function $f_{\text{aux}} : \mathcal{G} \rightarrow \mathcal{A}$ creates pipeline specific schema-level information that distinguishes end to end GraphRAG from simple KG based retrieval. **Online Retrieval.** Given a query q, the system embeds it into the same vector space and performs similarity based search to extract relevant context. The retrieval granularity $g \in \{\text{node}, \text{edge}, \text{path}, \text{subgraph}\}$ determines the structural form of retrieved knowledge. Retrieved elements undergo ranking through scoring functions to select the top-k most relevant components within context window constraints. Finally, the LLM generates answers by processing the selected context alongside the original query.

2.2 GraphRAG Attack Methods

Prior GraphRAG attacks operate at the instance level. **GRAGPOISON** targets relations by identifying shared relations across queries and injecting competing relations with temporal ordering [19]. Corpus-level attacks exploit GraphRAG's dependency on source text: **TKPA** rewrites vulnerable text chunks to control specific query outputs, while **UKPA** perturbs coreference signals to fragment graph structure globally [29]. **PoisonedRAG** injects malicious texts optimised to maximise retrieval similarity while inducing adversarial answers [35].

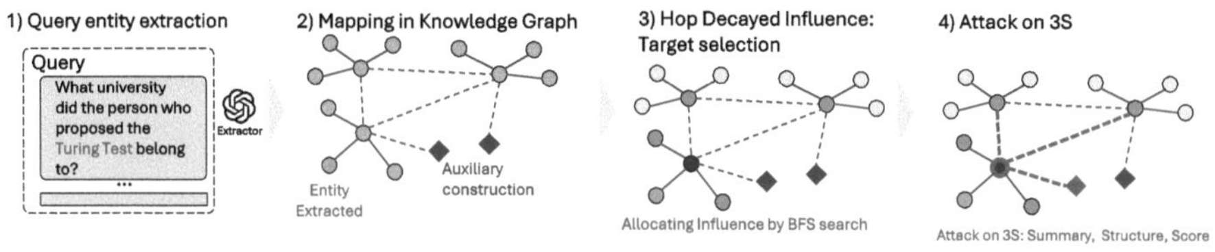

Fig. 2. The process of Hop-Decayed Influence

3 Methodology

3.1 Threat Model

Adversary's Objectives. The adversary aims to degrade GraphRAG retrieval performance by corrupting auxiliary structures used for retrieval optimization. Given a set of target queries, the adversary seeks to inject minimal perturbations such that the system generates incorrect responses while bypassing existing defense mechanisms. **Attack Surface: Auxiliary Schema-Level Entity.** We introduce *Auxiliary Schema-Level Entity* as an attack surface in GraphRAG systems, defined as structural components constructed during offline indexing that exist beyond instance-level elements (nodes, edges, triples). These structures augment LLM context, optimise retrieval through precomputation, and guide graph navigation; we categorise them into *Semantics*, *Structure*, and *Scoring* (3S). Unlike prior attacks that alter graph content, our attack manipulates how the graph is traversed (Fig. 2).

Adversary's Capabilities. The adversary can modify auxiliary structures in the constructed knowledge graph, operating post-indexing. Such capabilities arise in practical settings such as insider threats with database write access or compromised graph database interfaces. In practice, representative GraphRAG systems store auxiliary structures (e.g., summaries as plaintext Parquet files, scores in unprotected caches) without integrity verification separate from core graph data. However, write access alone is insufficient; identifying which minimal subset to corrupt for maximum cross-query impact is the core challenge. The adversary cannot access the original text corpus, cannot retrigger the indexing pipeline, and cannot control any parameters of the retriever or generator.

Adversary's Knowledge. We assume a gray-box setting where the adversary has access to a representative target query set, reflecting scenarios with partially predictable query patterns (e.g., enterprise knowledge bases with recurring analytical queries), and can query the knowledge graph through standard graph database interfaces.

3.2 Problem Formulation

A GraphRAG system constructs a knowledge graph from a text corpus, along with auxiliary structures for retrieval optimisation. These auxiliary structures include semantic summaries, hierarchical edges, and pre-computed scores.

Given a query set $\mathcal{Q}$, the attacker's objective is to find minimal perturbations to auxiliary structures such that retrieval fails for the maximum number of queries, subject to budget constraint ϵ:

$$\max_{\Delta\mathcal{A}} \sum_{q\in\mathcal{Q}} \nVdash [\mathcal{R}(q, \mathcal{A} + \Delta\mathcal{A}) \cap \mathcal{R}(q, \mathcal{A}) = \emptyset] \quad (1)$$

where $\mathcal{R}(q, \mathcal{A})$ denotes the retrieved context for query q.

3.3 Target Selection: Hop-Decayed Influence

Effective target selection is essential for maximising attack impact under limited budget. We propose Hop-Decayed Influence (HDI), a query aware method that identifies high influence nodes.

For each query q, we extract seed entities and map them to graph nodes. From each seed s, influence propagates with exponential decay based on shortest path distance $d(s, v)$:

$$\text{Influence}(v) = \sum_{q\in\mathcal{Q}} \sum_{s\in\text{Seeds}(q)} \lambda^{d(s,v)} \quad (2)$$

where $\lambda \in (0, 1)$ is the decay factor. Nodes beyond $h_{\max}$ hops receive zero influence. Given budget k, we select the top-k nodes with highest cumulative influence as attack targets.

3.4 Attack Methods: 3S Framework

We propose the 3S attack framework targeting three categories of auxiliary structures.

Semantic Attack. Corrupts textual summaries associated with target nodes by injecting adversarial text δ that introduces false entity associations while maintaining low perplexity to evade detection.

Structure Attack. Injects misleading edges between target nodes and semantically distant nodes. For each target v^*, we add edges to nodes with similarity below threshold τ, i.e., $\mathcal{E}' = \mathcal{E} \cup \{(v^*, u) : \text{sim}(v^*, u) < \tau\}$, creating false traversal paths.

Score Attack. Manipulates pre-computed scores to disrupt ranking: for target set $V^* = \arg\max_{v\in\mathcal{V}, |V^*|=k} \sigma(v)$, scores are demoted via $\sigma'(v^*) = \mu$, while median-ranked nodes V_{med} are promoted via $\sigma'(v) = \sigma_{\max}$, causing retrievers to prioritise irrelevant nodes.

Algorithm 1: Hop-Decayed Influence Target Selection

Input: Query set $\mathcal{Q}$, Knowledge graph $\mathcal{G}$, Decay factor λ, Max hops $h_{\max}$, Budget k
Output: Target node set $\mathcal{T}$
Initialise: Influence$[v] \leftarrow 0$ for all $v \in \mathcal{V}$;
foreach *query* $q \in \mathcal{Q}$ **do**
  Seeds$(q) \leftarrow$ ExtractEntities(q);
  foreach *seed* $s \in$ *Seeds*(q) **do**
    $s_v \leftarrow$ MapToNode$(s, \mathcal{G})$;
    if $s_v \neq$ *null* **then**
      foreach *node* $v \in \mathcal{V}$ **do**
        $d \leftarrow$ ShortestPath$(s_v, v, \mathcal{G})$;
        if $d \leq h_{\max}$ **then**
          Influence$[v] \leftarrow$ Influence$[v] + \lambda^d$;
$\mathcal{T} \leftarrow$ TopK(Influence, k);
return $\mathcal{T}$

3.5 Algorithm Overview

The attack proceeds in two phases. First, HDI computes influence scores by extracting seeds from each query and propagating influence with decay λ. The top-k nodes are selected as targets. Second, the selected attack method (Semantic, Structure, or Score) is applied to each target node. The choice depends on the target pipeline's retrieval mechanism: semantic attacks are effective against embedding based systems, while structure attacks target graph traversal systems.

4 Experiment Setup

Benchmark Datasets and GraphRAG Baseline. To evaluate the effectiveness of Hop-Decayed Influence attacks and observe attack patterns in multi-hop graph RAG task, we employ two established benchmark datasets: HotpotQA [31] and 2WikiMultiHopQA [9] sourced from Wikipedia. Those datasets are sampled with 1,000 cases from each dataset due to computational budget constraints. We compare 'HDI' against RAG systems: Microsoft GraphRAG [3] uses hierarchical community detection where high-level summaries aggregate subordinate entities. HippoRAG2 [5,6] relies on Personalised PageRank (PPR) with pre-computed scores for retrieval prioritisation.

Configuration Setup. OpenAI's 'text-embedding-3-small' [23] and 'GPT-4o-mini' [22] are employed. For KG construction we use networkx, tiktoken and datasets of huggingface. During graph construction, we apply standard quality control including entity deduplication and relation normalisation to ensure consistent baseline conditions. For HDI target selection, we set decay factor $\lambda = 0.5$, maximum hop distance $h_{\max} = 4$, random seed $= 42$ and manipulation intensity $=$ 0.001%, 0.01%, 0.1%. Experiments were conducted on over 32GB of RAM.

Metrics. To evaluate attack performance, we propose new metrics:

Schema Leverage Ratio (SLR). The expected number of queries affected per single auxiliary structure modification.

$$\text{SLR} = \frac{|\mathcal{Q}_{\text{affected}}|}{|\Delta\mathcal{A}|} \tag{3}$$

where $\mathcal{Q}_{\text{affected}}$ is the set of queries with altered responses after attack, and $\Delta\mathcal{A}$ is the set of modified auxiliary structures. Instance-level attacks achieve SLR ≈ 1 as each modification targets one query. Schema-level attacks exploit shared auxiliary structures across retrieval paths, enabling SLR $\gg 1$. Higher SLR indicates greater architectural vulnerability to schema-level manipulation.

We also employ standard metrics to evaluate attack effectiveness. **Attack Success Rate (ASR)** quantifies the proportion of queries where the adversarial attack successfully manipulates the system's response to match the adversarial objective, computed as $\text{ASR} = \frac{1}{N}\sum_{i=1}^{N} \mathbf{1}[\text{attack}_i = \text{success}]$, where N denotes the total number of target queries [11,27]. Specifically, an attack is considered successful when a query that was correctly answered before the attack produces an incorrect answer after the attack. **F1 Score** measures token-level overlap between predicted answer y_i and ground truth y_i^* using the harmonic mean of precision $P_i = \frac{|\text{tokens}(y_i) \cap \text{tokens}(y_i^*)|}{|\text{tokens}(y_i)|}$ and recall $R_i = \frac{|\text{tokens}(y_i) \cap \text{tokens}(y_i^*)|}{|\text{tokens}(y_i^*)|}$, averaged across all queries as $\text{F1} = \frac{1}{N}\sum_{i=1}^{N} \frac{2 \cdot P_i \cdot R_i}{P_i + R_i}$. **Exact Match (EM)** provides strict evaluation by measuring whether normalised predicted answers exactly match ground truth: $\text{EM} = \frac{1}{|Q|}\sum_{i=1}^{|Q|} \mathbf{1}[\text{norm}(\hat{y}_i) = \text{norm}(y_i^{\text{gold}})]$, where $\text{norm}(\cdot)$ applies lowercase conversion, whitespace removal, and punctuation handling [32]. Based on the stealthiness standard [25], PF and PD are measured.

5 Experimental Results

5.1 RQ1: Are Auxiliary Schema-Level Entities Exploitable, and Does Hop-Decayed Influence Effectively Compromise GraphRAG Systems?

Table 1 shows attack effectiveness across configurations. Microsoft GraphRAG on HotpotQA achieves 91.69% ASR, while 2WikiMultiHopQA reaches 88.17%. HippoRAG2 shows similar vulnerability: 88.24% ASR on HotpotQA and 94.44% on 2WikiMultiHopQA, the highest across all configurations. The two systems differ in vulnerability patterns. Microsoft GraphRAG's hierarchical community structure amplifies attack impact: corrupting one high-level summary affects all queries routed through that community. HippoRAG2's Personalised PageRank

Table 1. Performance Comparison Before and After Attack Across Different Models and Datasets

	MSGraphRAG		HippoRAG2	
	HotpotQA	2WikiMultiHopQA	HotpotQA	2WikiMultiHopQA
Best Config	HDI-T	HDI-T	HDI-T	HDI-C
Our ASR (%)	**91.69**	**88.17**	**88.24**	**94.44**
PoisonedRAG (%)	80.69	80.42	81.49	85.89
GRAGPOISON (%)	85.64	88.68	86.28	87.24

Table 2. Attack Efficiency Comparison Across Different GraphRAG Models and Datasets. *HDI-T: HDI with Structure attack; HDI-C: HDI with Score attack; HDI-S: HDI with Semantic attack. SLR = Schema Leverage Ratio (affected queries / modifications). Mod. Ratio(%) = # Modified/Total Structures × 100.*

	MSGraphRAG		HippoRAG2	
	HotpotQA	2WikiMultiHopQA	HotpotQA	2WikiMultiHopQA
Best Config	HDI-T	HDI-T	HDI-T	HDI-C
Total Structures	6,328	9,328	440,020	311,419
# Modified	300	450	330	49
Mod. Ratio (%)	4.74	4.82	0.075	0.016
Our SLR	4.57	3.41	5.80	6.00
PoisonedRAG's SLR	1.36	1.25	0.42	0.32

distributes retrieval across multiple paths, offering some resilience. Still, ASR exceeds 86% in every configuration. Schema-level entities are exploitable regardless of architectural choices.

5.2 RQ2: How Efficient and Scalable is Hop-Decayed Influence Compared to Conventional Poisoning Approaches?

Table 2 quantifies attack footprint. HDI achieves high success rates with minimal modifications.

HippoRAG2 on 2WikiMultiHopQA requires only 49 modified structures out of 311,419 (0.016%) of the total that yet reaches 94.44% ASR. On HotpotQA, 330 modifications (0.075%) produce 88.24% ASR. Microsoft GraphRAG has fewer total structures (6,328 on HotpotQA, 9,328 on 2WikiMultiHopQA), so modification ratios are higher (4.74% and 4.82%), but absolute counts remain low: 300–450 modifications.

Schema Leverage Ratio (SLR) measures queries affected per modification. Our approach achieves SLR of 3.41–6.00, compared to PoisonedRAG's 0.32–1.36. The gap is largest on HippoRAG2-2WikiMultiHopQA: our SLR (6.00) versus PoisonedRAG's (0.32). This 1:N leverage that one schema modification affecting many queries is unavailable to instance-level attacks.

Table 3. Defense Evasion Performance (RQ3): Perplexity Filter and Paraphrase Defense

	MSGraphRAG		HippoRAG2	
	HotpotQA	2WikiMultiHopQA	HotpotQA	2WikiMultiHopQA
Best Type	HDI-T	HDI-T	HDI-T	HDI-C
Perplexity Evasion (%)	99.85	99.50	99.87	99.79
Paraphrase Evasion (%)	99.13	99.14	99.72	99.27
Detection Rate (%)	0.07	0.09	0.05	0.08

Attack type matters. We evaluate defense evasion using each configuration's best performing attack type (Table 3). HippoRAG2 prefers Structure attacks on HotpotQA but Score attacks (C) on 2WikiMultiHopQA, reflecting PPR's sensitivity to pre-computed rankings.

5.3 RQ3: Is Hop-Decayed Influence Stealthy Enough to Evade Existing GraphRAG Defense Mechanisms

Table 3 evaluates HDI against perplexity filtering and paraphrase defense. Structure attacks (T) serve as the test configuration.

Detection rates are negligible. Perplexity filtering misses 99.50%–99.87% of modifications. Paraphrase defense fails similarly, with evasion rates of 99.13%–99.72%. Across all configurations, detection stays below 0.1%.

These defenses target instance-level anomalies: odd entity names, implausible triples, statistically unusual text. Schema-level manipulations evade them because corrupted summaries are still LLM generated and linguistically fluent. Injected edges connect semantically plausible entity pairs. Numerical scores bypass text based detection entirely.

Auxiliary structures receive implicit trust. Auxiliary structures, being system generated artifacts, receive no runtime validation. Current defenses assume attacks manifest as anomalous content. Schema-level attacks produce normal looking content through abnormal selection and aggregation. This mismatch leaves GraphRAG systems exposed.

5.4 Ablation Study

Modification intensity Scaling Analysis. Figure 3 shows ASR scaling with the proportion of modified structures. Structure attacks (T) consistently outperform Semantic attacks (S) on MS GraphRAG, achieving 91.69% versus 48.52% ASR when modifying 0.1% of total structures on HotpotQA. The two systems exhibit distinct patterns: MS GraphRAG shows near-linear growth, while HippoRAG2 on 2WikiMultiHopQA demonstrates early saturation, reaching 71–73% ASR by modifying merely 0.01% of structures. This indicates that densely connected auxiliary structures enable high attack impact with minimal perturbation. Notably, on HippoRAG2-2WikiMultiHopQA, both attack methods converge to 88.89% ASR, though Semantic attacks achieve superior efficiency.

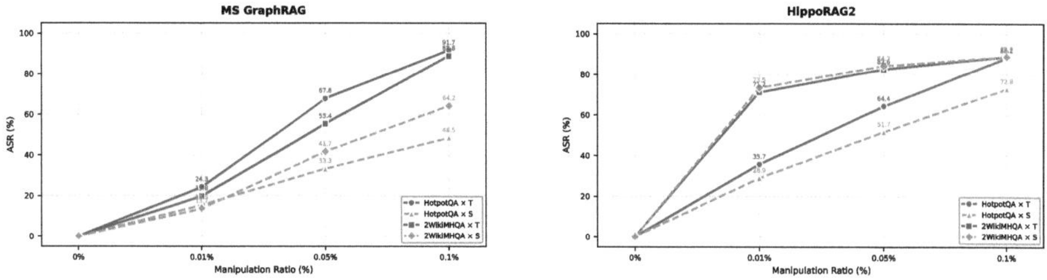

Fig. 3. ASR scaling with modification intensity across GraphRAG systems. Left: MS GraphRAG. Right: HippoRAG2. X-axis: proportion of modification intensity (%). Y-axis: Attack Success Rate (%). T: Structure attack. S: Semantic attack.

6 Discussion and Defense

Prior stealthiness research in adversarial RAG has focused on detecting statistical anomalies at the instance level perplexity filtering and paraphrase detection assuming adversarial content manifests as linguistic outliers [12,25]. Schema-level manipulations evade these defenses for two reasons: auxiliary structures are LLM generated and thus linguistically fluent by construction, and aggregated summaries lack singular ground truth against which tampering can be verified.

We identify three potential defense directions. First, *provenance tracking* maintains lineage between schema entities and their source instances, enabling consistency audits. Second, *runtime verification* detects semantic drift between retrieved summaries and underlying nodes at query time. Third, *robust aggregation* applies outlier resistant functions to summarisation and scoring mechanisms. However, these defenses impose computational overhead that partially negates the efficiency gains schema-level structures were designed to provide, presenting an inherent trade-off between retrieval performance and adversarial robustness.

7 Ethical Consideration

All experiments were conducted on public benchmark datasets and open source implementations in isolated environments. No attacks targeted production systems. We follow responsible disclosure practices, sharing findings with affected project maintainers prior to publication. This research aims to improve GraphRAG security by enabling developers to understand and mitigate schema-level vulnerabilities.

8 Conclusion and Future Work

This work identifies Auxiliary Schema-Level Entity as a distinct attack surface in GraphRAG pipelines and demonstrates through the 3S Framework and

Hop-Decayed Influence attack that minimal perturbation yields high attack success rates with 1:N amplification unavailable to instance-level approaches. These findings expose that auxiliary structures receive implicit trust without runtime validation, rendering current defenses inadequate for schema-level threats.

Future research will develop provenance-aware defense mechanisms that maintain lineage between schema-level entities and source instances, enabling consistency verification through cross referencing aggregated summaries against underlying nodes. We plan to investigate robust aggregation functions resistant to outlier manipulation and extend HDI to recently proposed GraphRAG pipeline with temporal and multi-modal retrieval capabilities. Additionally, developing standardised benchmark suites for evaluating schema-level attack resilience will enable systematic comparison of defense strategies across diverse GraphRAG implementations.

Further evaluation should extend to other GraphRAG applications (e.g., summarisation, decision support) and out-of-distribution queries. Key limitations include: the post-indexing write access assumption may not hold in all deployments, defense evaluation is limited to text-level detection methods mismatched against score and structure tampering, and generalisation across backbone LLMs remains unverified.

References

1. Brown, T.B., et al.: Language models are few-shot learners. In: Advances in Neural Information Processing Systems, vol. 33, pp. 1877–1901. Curran Associates, Inc. (2020)
2. Cheng, M., et al.: A survey on knowledge-oriented retrieval-augmented generation (2025)
3. Edge, D., et al.: From local to global: a graph rag approach to query-focused summarization (2025)
4. Gao, Y., et al.: Retrieval-augmented generation for large language models: a survey (2024)
5. Gutiérrez, B.J., Shu, Y., Gu, Y., Yasunaga, M., Su, Y.: HippoRAG: Neurobiologically inspired long-term memory for large language models (2025)
6. Gutiérrez, B.J., Shu, Y., Qi, W., Zhou, S., Su, Y.: From RAG to memory: non-parametric continual learning for large language models (2025)
7. Han, H., et al.: Retrieval-augmented generation with graphs (graphRAG) (2025)
8. He, X., et al.: G-Retriever: retrieval-augmented generation for textual graph understanding and question answering. In: Advances in Neural Information Processing Systems (NeurIPS), vol. 37 (2024). https://openreview.net/forum?id=MPJ3oXtTZl
9. Ho, X., Duong Nguyen, A.K., Sugawara, S., Aizawa, A.: Constructing a multi-hop QA dataset for comprehensive evaluation of reasoning steps. In: Proceedings of the 28th International Conference on Computational Linguistics, pp. 6609–6625. International Committee on Computational Linguistics, Barcelona (2020). https://doi.org/10.18653/v1/2020.coling-main.580
10. Huang, L., et al.: A survey on hallucination in large language models: principles, taxonomy, challenges, and open questions. ACM Trans. Inf. Syst. **43**(2), 1–55 (2025)

11. Huang, Y., Gupta, S., Xia, M., Li, K., Chen, D.: Catastrophic jailbreak of open-source LLMs via exploiting generation. In: International Conference on Learning Representations (2024)
12. Jain, N., et al.: Baseline defenses for adversarial attacks against aligned language models (2023)
13. Kalai, A.T., Nachum, O., Vempala, S.S., Zhang, E.: Why Language Models Hallucinate (2025)
14. Kalutharage, C.S., Liu, X., Chrysoulas, C., Bamgboye, O.: Neurosymbolic learning in the XAI framework for enhanced cyberattack detection with expert knowledge integration. In: Pitropakis, N., Katsikas, S., Furnell, S., Markantonakis, K. (eds.) SEC 2024. IFIP Advances in Information and Communication Technology, vol. 710, pp. 236–249. Springer, Cham (2024). https://doi.org/10.1007/978-3-031-65175-5_17
15. Khodadad, M.: Domain-specific adaptation and multi-hop reasoning in chemistry and biomedicine. MASc thesis, McMaster University, Hamilton, Ontario, Canada (2025)
16. Klesel, M., Wittmann, H.F.: Retrieval-augmented generation (RAG) M. Klesel, HF Wittmann. Bus. Inf. Syst. Eng. 1–11 (2025)
17. Lewis, P., Perez, E., Piktus, A., Petroni, F., Karpukhin, V., et al.: Retrieval-augmented generation for knowledge-intensive NLP tasks. In: Advances in Neural Information Processing Systems, vol. 33, pp. 9459–9474. Curran Associates, Inc. (2020)
18. Li, M., Miao, S., Li, P.: Simple is effective: the roles of graphs and large language models in knowledge-graph-based retrieval-augmented generation (2025)
19. Liang, J., et al.: GraphRAG under fire. In: 2026 IEEE Symposium on Security and Privacy (SP), pp. 1316–1333 (2026). https://doi.org/10.1109/SP63933.2026.00070
20. Liu, J., Zhang, J., Wang, S.: Exposing privacy risks in graph retrieval-augmented generation (2025)
21. Luo, H., et al.: Graph-R1: Towards agentic graphRAG framework via end-to-end reinforcement learning (2025)
22. Hurst, A., et al.: GPT-4o system card (2024)
23. OpenAI: New embedding models and API updates (2024). https://openai.com/index/new-embedding-models-and-api-updates/
24. Pan, S., Luo, L., Wang, Y., Chen, C., Wang, J., Wu, X.: Unifying large language models and knowledge graphs: a roadmap. IEEE Trans. Knowl. Data Eng. **36**(7), 3580–3599 (2024). https://doi.org/10.1109/tkde.2024.3352100
25. Panebianco, F., D'Onghia, M., Zanero, S., Carminati, M.: How stealthy is stealthy? Studying the efficacy of black-box adversarial attacks in the real world. In: Nemec Zlatolas, L., Rannenberg, K., Welzer, T., Garcia-Alfaro, J. (eds.) SEC 2025. IFIP Advances in Information and Communication Technology, vol. 746, pp. 140–154. Springer, Cham (2025). https://doi.org/10.1007/978-3-031-92886-4_10, 40th IFIP International Conference, SEC 2025
26. Peng, B., et al.: Graph retrieval-augmented generation: a survey (2024)
27. Rizqullah, M.R., Purwarianti, A., Aji, A.F.: QASiNa: religious domain question answering using Sirah Nabawiyah. In: 2023 10th International Conference on Advanced Informatics: Concept, Theory and Application (ICAICTA), pp. 1–6 (2023). https://doi.org/10.1109/ICAICTA59291.2023.10390123
28. Song, Y., Lyu, C., Zhang, P., Brunswicker, S., Dutt, N., Rahmani, A.: Dementia-plan: an agent-based framework for multi-knowledge graph retrieval-augmented generation in dementia care (2025)

29. Wen, J., Chen, T., Zheng, Z., Huang, C.: A few words can distort graphs: knowledge poisoning attacks on graph-based retrieval-augmented generation of large language models (2025)
30. Wu, J., et al.: Medical graph RAG: evidence-based medical large language model via graph retrieval-augmented generation. In: Che, W., Nabende, J., Shutova, E., Pilehvar, M.T. (eds.) Proceedings of the 63rd Annual Meeting of the Association for Computational Linguistics (Volume 1: Long Papers), pp. 28443–28467. Association for Computational Linguistics, Vienna (2025). https://doi.org/10.18653/v1/2025.acl-long.1381, https://aclanthology.org/2025.acl-long.1381/
31. Yang, Z., et al.: HotpotQA: a dataset for diverse, explainable multi-hop question answering. In: Proceedings of the 2018 Conference on Empirical Methods in Natural Language Processing, pp. 2369–2380. Association for Computational Linguistics, Brussels (2018)
32. Yani, M., Krisnadhi, A.A.: Challenges, techniques, and trends of simple knowledge graph question answering: a survey. Information **12**(7), 271 (2021)
33. Zhang, Q., et al.: A survey of graph retrieval-augmented generation for customized large language models (2025)
34. Zhao, T., Chen, J., Ru, Y., Zhu, H., Hu, N., Liu, J., Lin, Q.: RAG safety: exploring knowledge poisoning attacks to retrieval-augmented generation (2025)
35. Zou, W., Geng, R., Wang, B., Jia, J.: PoisonedRAG: knowledge corruption attacks to retrieval-augmented generation of large language models. In: 34th USENIX Security Symposium (USENIX Security 25), pp. 3827–3844 (2025)

Parser Instrumentation for Semantic-Aware Applicative Intrusion Detection

Grégor Quetel[1(✉)], Pierre-François Gimenez[2], Thomas Robert[1], and Laurent Pautet[1]

[1] LTCI, Télécom Paris, Institut Polytechnique de Paris, Paris, France
{gregor.quetel,thomas.robert,laurent.pautet}@telecom-paris.fr
[2] Univ. Rennes, Inria, IRISA, Rennes, France
pierre-francois.gimenez@inria.fr

Abstract. Intrusion Detection Systems (IDS) are common security tools for protecting modern information systems, yet their effectiveness at detecting application-layer attacks is often limited by the semantic gap between low-level host or network observations and the actual behavior of applications. Existing work overlooks the data collection phase and typically focuses on designing complex decision engines and preprocessing functions such as embedding-based representations. Unfortunately, these approaches incur significant computational overhead at inference time and remain brittle against adversarial inputs. In this paper, we present a parser-based instrumentation approach for application-level intrusion detection that provides lexical, syntactic and explicit semantic observation with minimal overhead. We introduce GAUR, an implementation for instrumenting parsers, it produces observations during parsing by associating semantic tags to grammar rules, eliminating the need for runtime natural language processing. Our evaluation demonstrates the low overhead and collection time of our data collector. Furthermore, empirical results show that incorporating explicit semantic information into decision engines not only improves detection performance over traditional mechanisms but also enables faster inference and greater robustness than approaches relying on implicit semantic representations.

Keywords: Data Collector · Semantic Information · Applicative Data Collection · Intrusion Detection Systems · SQL Injection Detection

1 Introduction

In its 2025 report, Verizon [27] found that system intrusions accounted for 53% of all data breaches, an increase of 17% since 2024. Intrusion detection systems aim to identify such malicious activities by continuously monitoring system behaviour for signs of compromise. Key challenges in IDS design include improving detection performance, reducing overhead, and increasing robustness

© IFIP International Federation for Information Processing 2026
Published by Springer Nature Switzerland AG 2026
H. Janicke et al. (Eds.): SEC 2026, IFIP AICT 787, pp. 359–373, 2026.
https://doi.org/10.1007/978-3-032-27993-4_25

against evasion attacks [6,23]. Recent work highlights explainability (i.e., the ability to understand detection decisions) as a lever for improving both detection performance and robustness [8]. This ability to understand the decision highly depends on the inputs provided to the decision engine. Explainability typically links a decision to the most relevant input features, creating a need for better observations, i.e., better data collectors. The most common data collectors in IDS are host-based (leading to Host-based Intrusion Detection Systems, or HIDS) and network-based (leading to Network-based Intrusion Detection Systems, or NIDS). They typically rely on low-level observations that do not characterize application-level behaviours, known as the semantic gap [12,29]. These limitations have motivated the exploration of application-level data collection mechanisms [6]. Such data collectors capture the application's internal state or all interactions at the application-level interface (e.g., user inputs) forming the basis of Application-based IDS (AIDS).

Applicative-level data collectors can focus on either application inputs or state dynamics. Such approaches are marginal, software-specific and incur hight engineering and maintenance costs. To the best of our knowledge, no existing work defines what semantic information should be collected, nor how to systematically collect it, without relying on expert knowledge. However, because complex inputs rely on languages that are interpreted by applications, focusing on such inputs allows designing data collection mechanisms based on the language definition and semantics. Such a data collector mechanism ensures a full coverage of attacks based on user-input tampering.

We identified in the literature three levels of information that can be extracted from them. *Lexical information* captures surface properties of tokens derived by the lexer (e.g., values, casing, symbol usage). *Syntactic information* describes their organization according to the grammar. *Semantic information* characterizes the effect of an input on the application's behaviour. Yet, unlike lexical or syntactic information, semantic information is substantially harder to define, collect, and efficiently provide to decision engines.

This paper introduces a new application-input-based data collector that can be automatically generated and integrated into the user input processing component: the parser. We implement this methodology through the GAUR tool and show that: (1) when combined with classical classifiers, it improves detection performance; (2) it incurs negligible overhead and requires little to no expert knowledge to adapt to new software; and (3) it provides semantic information, enabling better explainability and robustness. The remainder of the paper is structured as follows. Section 2 presents the problem statement. GAUR is described in Sect. 3 and is evaluated in Sect. 4. Our work is positioned with respect to the related work in Sect. 5. Section 6 concludes and proposes new perspectives.

2 Problem Statement

Our objective is to design an applicative data collector that provides relevant observations to intrusion detection decision engines. While application inputs are a natural source of information, existing AIDS data collectors fail to provide full characterization (lexical, syntactic and semantic) of application inputs while maintaining low overhead. Syntactic information is typically obtained using external parsers (e.g., sqlparse, ANTLR, or custom implementations), which increases processing time and risks failure on unexpected queries.

Approaches that claim to leverage semantic information typically rely on *implicit semantic representations* such as BERT embeddings [26], a deep learning model specialized for Natural Language Processing (NLP). In these representations, semantics is encoded in latent dimensions that are neither directly interpretable nor auditable. Although convenient to provide to decision engines, such methods also incur overhead and expose IDS to additional adversarial vulnerabilities [11,16]. In contrast, *explicit semantic information*, i.e., representations based on explicit, human-readable abstractions such *semantic tags* remains largely underexplored in AIDS. Explicit representations offer stronger guarantees in terms of interpretability and robustness, but raise fundamental challenges regarding their definition, collection, and efficient integration into IDS pipelines.

Therefore, our data collector must be designed to provide rich lexical, syntactic, and explicit semantic information directly at the application level, while remaining efficient, automatable, and easy to deploy. To address these challenges, we define the following research objectives:

- **RO1**: Guarantee low-overhead data collection via application instrumentation, while ensuring that the approach remains transparent to system deployment and does not increase maintenance needs.
- **RO2**: Enhance detection effectiveness by designing a framework to capture lexical, syntactic and semantic information directly during query processing.
- **RO3**: Rely on explicit semantic annotations for better explainability and robustness.

3 GAUR

This section presents the instrumentation approach, and its implementation GAUR. We first detail how the parser of query-based applications can be used to reliably collect observations for AIDS. We then present how the component's internals can be leveraged to collect semantic annotations characterizing each application input. The approach is illustrated with an implementation of GAUR tailored for the MySQL Database Management System (DBMS).

3.1 Parser-Based Data Collection

The large majority of network protocols are text-based, so they can easily be read and written by humans. The transformation of text-based queries into binary data is performed by a software component called a parser. A parser is a strategic location for data collection. First, it guarantees full data collection coverage and prevents evasion, as all user interactions must pass through the parser to affect the application state. Second, it ensures that the collection of reliable lexical and syntactic information is identical to how it is consumed by the downstream task: there is no risk of representation mismatch as opposed to using external syntactic analysis tools. While parsers can be written by hand, they are generally generated from grammar descriptions by software called parser generators, such as Yacc, its open-source equivalent GNU Bison, or ANTLR.

Hence, we developed GAUR[1], a tool for parsing and instrumenting Bison grammar files. The tool takes an original grammar file as input, injects data collection code and outputs an instrumented grammar file. Figure 1 illustrates both the original parser deployment pipeline and the instrumented version. Because it operates directly on the standardized grammar file, the instrumentation process is entirely automated and eliminates the need for software-specific expertise, greatly reducing deployment costs. Observations are generated through custom routines executed at different parsing stages, such as parser initialization, token shifts, and rule reductions. By construction, the data collector can easily collect lexical and syntactic information. While GAUR is protocol-independent by design, we specialized our implementation to also collect the traditional features for SQL Injection Attack (SQLIA) detection defined by [17]. We now describe a mechanism to provide semantic annotations from our GAUR data collector.

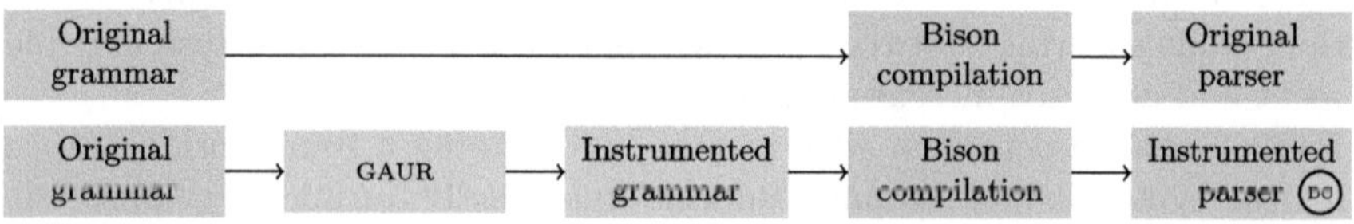

Fig. 1. Original and GAUR-instrumented Bison parser generation pipelines. DC is our data collector.

3.2 Semantic Information Production

Besides lexical and syntactical information, we propose an approach to provide *explicit* semantic annotations to decision engines. Associating semantic tags to our user inputs using NLP at runtime could be computationally expensive and also lead to a vulnerable IDS, as attackers could inject noise to perturb the inference process and possibly evade detection [7,11,16]. Instead, we propose an alternative approach that leverages the parser's functionality. Since grammar rules shape how the parser constructs data structures, which in turn guide the application's behaviour, we claim that studying the grammar allows us to associate semantic tags to specific parser rules. By analysing which parser rules are used to process a user input, we are able to provide semantic annotations to

[1] Code available at https://github.com/gquetel/gaur.

the decision engine about that user input, enabling it to make more informed decisions. Therefore, our approach is based on three steps: 1) defining a semantic model (a set of semantic tags) that explicitly describes how queries interact with the system, 2) associating each parser rule to a semantic tag during the instrumentation, and 3) collecting the semantic tags associated with the parser rules used during the parsing. This approach explicitly separates the definition of the semantic model and the data collection, so an expert can verify and audit the semantic model and its association to the parser rules ahead of data collection.

We propose two approaches for defining a semantical model in step 1. The first one relies on a security and DBMS expert to characterize the *actions* allowed by the DBMS and the manipulated *objects*. However, because this semantic model instantiation task is not trivial and requires domain knowledge, we propose a second approach that leverages Large Language Models (LLMs). Table 1 provides examples of our expert-defined semantic models, and the semantic model instantiated by ■ Mistral (Small 3.2 24B) [22].

Table 1. Examples of semantic model instantiations abstracting the semantics of MySQL user-inputs obtained during step 1.

Semantic Model	Semantic Tags
■ expert	*actions*: Create, Delete, Modify, Execute, Read *objects*: Tablespace, Table, Index, View, User, Procedure, Database, Function, Instance, Logfile, Server, Trigger
■ Mistral	Data definition, Data import export, Data manipulation, Data query, Database management, Locking concurrency, Miscellaneous operations, Replication clustering, Resource management, Security privileges, Statement control, Stored procedures functions, System information, System maintenance, System variables, Temporary objects, Transaction control, Triggers events, User management, Views

During step 2, the attribution process begins by creating descriptive documents for each rule using information extracted from the grammar. Here, these documents are constructed solely from information within the grammar file. To construct each document, GAUR extracts rule names, terminals in the rules' right-hand side, and identifiers in the action code. Then, for the ■ expert approach we rely on a pre-trained Sentence-BERT model [26]. We embed the documents and compute their similarity with embeddings of the expert-defined semantic tags. Each rule is labelled with the semantic tag that yields the highest cosine similarity between the document and tag embeddings. For the approaches involving LLMs, we provide their list of semantic tags and ask them to associate one of them to each grammar rule. The attribution of semantic tags to parser rules is made once, statically and prior to the grammar instrumentation.

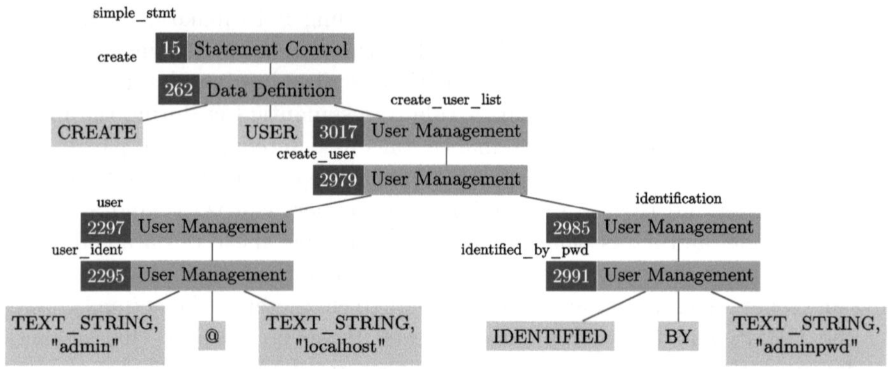

Fig. 2. Simplified tree structure produced by GAUR (Mistral) for the query `CREATE USER "admin"@"localhost" IDENTIFIED BY "adminpwd"`. Colors indicate the type of information captured: lexical tokens (type or value), syntactic features (parser rule identifiers and hierarchy), and semantic tags.

During execution, the step 3 is performed by the data collector that maintains a record of the rules used to process each user input. Since these rules are mapped to semantic tags, we simultaneously gather these semantic annotations. Upon completion of input parsing or when encountering a parsing error, the GAUR collector generates a tree-structured representation encoding lexical, syntactic, and semantic annotations. Figure 2 illustrates a simplified visualization of this data structure for a SQL query.

In practice, instrumenting an application with GAUR requires minimal developer interaction. The required inputs are (1) the original Bison grammar file and (2) a static mapping between grammar rules and semantics tags (which can be generated by LLMs). Given these two, GAUR produces a drop-in replacement of the original parser, which now produces observations containing lexical, syntactic, and semantic information for each user input.

4 Evaluation

In this section, we answer the following research questions:

- **RQ1:** What is the query-level execution overhead of GAUR?
- **RQ2:** To what extent do GAUR's parser-level observations improve the effectiveness of application-level intrusion detection systems?
  - **RQ2.1:** What is the impact of the semantic model instantiation?
  - **RQ2.2:** How do they affect the detection of SQLIAs and insider attacks relative to existing approaches?
  - **RQ2.3:** What inference latency do decision engines incur compared to existing methods?
- **RQ3:** What is the robustness of our explicit semantic representation against evasion attacks compared to IDS based on embeddings?

All experiments[2] in this section were conducted with an AMD EPYC 9374F 32-core processor (4.1 GHz) and 512 GB of RAM. All experiments rely on the Superviz25-SQL dataset [25], which is the most recent and complete public SQL-based attacks dataset. We use their experimental protocol and their baselines.

4.1 RQ1: Runtime Overhead

To test the overhead induced from our data collection, we compared the average execution time of queries on a normal MySQL Server and one instrumented with GAUR. We instantiated both servers using the data dumps provided by our OurAirports website, the project on which Superviz25-SQL is based. We measured the average execution time over all 3,688,977 queries, which include realistic SELECT, DELETE, UPDATE, INSERT, and administrative statements.

Across all queries, GAUR incurs an average overhead of 0.113 ± 0.006 ms , corresponding to only 0.31% of the total query execution time. This efficiency stems from two key design choices: (1) the data collection logic is embedded directly within the parser subroutines, which are already operating on the lexical and syntactic elements of the query, and (2) semantic annotations are resolved ahead of deployment by linking grammar rules to our semantic tags, eliminating the need for runtime semantic processing.

4.2 RQ2.1: Impact of Semantic Model Instantiation

In this subsection, we evaluate and compare the performance of AIDS on the SQL attack detection task: SQL injections and insider attacks. SQLIAs are emblematic applicative attacks exploiting faulty web applications by manipulating database queries to achieve malicious objectives such as extracting sensitive data or elevating privileges. Insider attacks, on the other hand, involve an attacker with direct access to the database and do not need to exploit an injection vulnerability [15]. We focus on the most effective decision engines used in [25], namely One-Class SVM (OCSVM) and AutoEncoders (AE). Furthermore, we adjusted how insider attacks are handled. In practice, SQL injection detection methods usually focus on the traffic between the web application and the DBMS [30]. Consequently, we compare our DBMS-level approach, which observes all queries, to these collection methods, which cannot detect other attacks targeting the DBMS (such as insider attacks).

We evaluate the performance of AIDS using different semantic models: the one instantiated by an ■expert and the ones instantiated by LLMs (namely ■Claude (Sonnet 4) [5] ■ChatGPT (GPT-4.5) [24], ■Mistral (Small 3.2 24B) [22], ■Llama (3.3 70B) [21] and ■OSS-GPT (120b) [2]). The tree structure produced by our data collector is interpreted as tabular features. Lexical information is encoded using counters or Boolean values, while syntactic information includes features such as query correctness, tree depth, total number of nodes,

[2] Code available at https://github.com/gquetel/gaur-sql-detect.

Table 2. AUPRC and AUROC (%) for SQL attack detection with 95% confidence intervals of GAUR using different semantic models

Classifier	Metric	expert	ChatGPT	Claude	Llama	Mistral	OSS-GPT	Naive
OCSVM	AUPRC	92.64±0.03	93.00±0.03	92.79±0.03	91.94±0.03	92.41±0.03	92.65±0.03	**93.27±0.03**
	AUROC	95.81±0.02	96.06±0.02	94.98±0.02	95.12±0.02	95.13±0.02	94.77±0.02	**96.81±0.02**
AE	AUPRC	92.76±0.03	**95.57±0.02**	92.91±0.03	94.04±0.03	93.66±0.03	94.13±0.03	92.41±0.03
	AUROC	96.50±0.02	**98.06±0.01**	97.34±0.02	97.89±0.02	97.74±0.02	97.61±0.02	97.98±0.02

and number of terminals. Semantic information is represented as counters corresponding to the occurrences of each semantic tag. We evaluate the added value of our semantic abstraction process by introducing an alternative feature extractor: Naive. It follows a naive strategy in which each grammar rule is mapped to a unique tag (1012 in total), resulting in a representation that captures purely syntactic information.

Table 2 contains the AUROC (Area Under the ROC) and AUPRC (Area Under the Precision-Recall Curve) scores of unsupervised techniques using these feature extractors. We draw two main observations. First, the choice of the decision engine determines the effectiveness of GAUR features. Autoencoders (AE) benefit from the cardinality reduction provided by our semantic annotation, leading to the highest overall scores (AUPRC 95.57% and AUROC 98.06% with ChatGPT). Conversely, OCSVM is not affected by the high-cardinality of Naive (yielding 93.27% AUPRC and 96.81% AUROC), surpassing pipelines with semantic annotations. Second, the semantic model instantiation has only a marginal influence on detection. Although ChatGPT exhibits the strongest scores for both AE and OCSVM, the differences relative to other LLMs and to the expert-based approach are small. We further deduce from these results that the semantic model instantiation can be delegated even to smaller LLMs such as Mistral (Small 3.2 24B), eliminating the need for domain knowledge and reducing the data collector deployment costs.

4.3 RQ2.2: Detection Performances

We further compare the three best-performing GAUR-based IDS to the strongest baselines provided in [25], namely Li et al. [17] and SecureBERT [3]. Following their evaluation protocol, we select an anomaly threshold by enforcing a maximum False Positive Rate of 0.1% on a validation split.

We compute the recall per attack technique provided in their dataset, and full results appear in Table 3. We observe that while SecureBERT and AE achieve the highest AUROC (98.55%) and AUPRC (95.65%), reflecting strong ranking capabilities, GAUR-based IDS deliver superior performance at a realistic operating point. In particular, GAUR (Claude) and AE attain the highest overall F1-score (93.79%) and strong recall across all attack categories. GAUR (ChatGPT) and OCSVM or GAUR (Mistral) and AE behave with very similar F1-score or recall values.

Table 3. Performance comparison across feature extraction and anomaly detection approaches. All metrics are in percentages (%). Best results per metric are shown in bold.

Model	AUPRC	AUROC	F1	Recall per attack technique (%)						
				Boolean	Error	Union	Stacked	Time	Inline	Insider
GAUR (Claude) and AE	92.91 ±0.03	97.34 ±0.02	**93.79**	94.69	**80.58**	94.26	71.85	65.69	**88.77**	79.06
GAUR (ChatGPT) and OCSVM	93.00 ±0.03	96.06 ±0.02	93.72	**94.74**	80.17	**94.29**	**72.31**	**66.51**	85.89	75.94
GAUR (Mistral) and AE	93.66 ±0.03	97.74 ±0.02	93.68	94.69	80.51	93.69	71.19	65.22	86.90	**80.17**
Li et al. and OCSVM	89.65 ±0.03	93.75 ±0.03	91.82	91.49	77.04	93.77	67.12	61.98	66.74	0.00
Li et al. and AE	92.57 ±0.03	96.85 ±0.02	92.06	91.80	79.80	93.54	67.61	60.53	74.44	0.00
SecureBERT and OCSVM	48.88 ±0.05	81.44 ±0.04	14.02	7.96	1.52	20.50	0.98	1.31	1.22	0.00
SecureBERT and AE	**95.65** ±0.02	**98.55** ±0.01	91.78	92.74	79.10	83.66	64.84	64.43	77.11	0.00

Conversely, all variants of Li et al. and SecureBERT achieve 0% recall on insider attacks, explained by the difference in data collection strategies. The latter approaches focus on SQL Injection detection, and their data collector typically placed in the web application [30]. They are blind to other types of attacks targeting the DBMS, such as insider attacks. This highlights the benefit of GAUR's parser-level integration: it produces observations for all queries, regardless of their source. Such application-level observation also leads to better performances under realistic false-positive constraints.

4.4 RQ2.3 Inference Overhead

Detection latency for application-level attacks depends not only on data collection time but also on the inference time of the underlying model. To quantify this, we measured the average query inference time on the Superviz25-SQL dataset [25] across all evaluated IDS pipelines. All results are computed using CPU, with an exception for the SecureBERT approach that uses a dedicated A100 NVIDIA GPU. Figure 3 illustrates the relationship between detection accuracy, measured by AUROC, and inference latency for each pipeline.

Our results indicate that autoencoders using explicit semantic observations, while slightly lower in AUROC compared to SecureBERT and standard AE, are more computationally efficient. GAUR (ChatGPT) and AE achieve an average inference latency of 0.264 ms per query, compared to 6.46 ms for the SecureBERT and AE pipeline. Specifically, when including the data collection

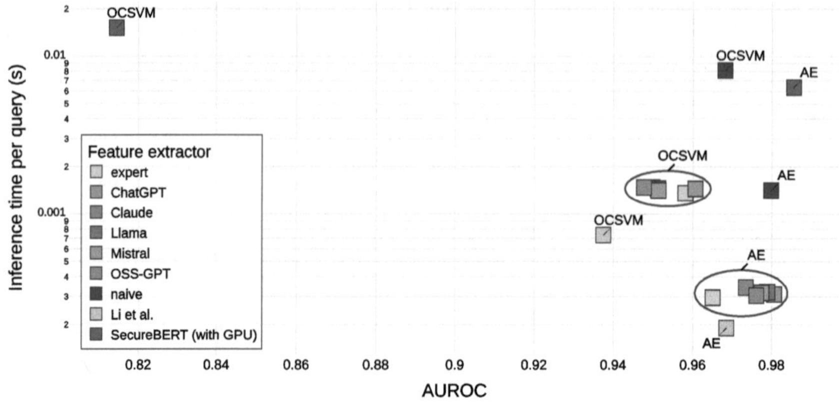

Fig. 3. AUROC score versus average inference time per query, measured on the Superviz25-SQL dataset.

step (which averages 0.113 ms with GAUR), the total detection latency remains lower than the inference time of ■ SecureBERT pipelines alone. Moreover, the GPU cost for efficiently such an embedding-based approach is non-negligible, further emphasizing the advantages of our explicit semantic approach.

Finally, although the ■ GAUR (naive) approach achieve competitive AUROC scores, they lead to a substantial inference overhead, with latencies of 1.41 ms per query with AE and up to 8.11 ms with OCSVM (over an order of magnitude slower than explicit semantic pipelines). This higher overhead is due to the large number of features the pure syntactic approach requires. These results highlight the computational benefits of semantic abstraction through our semantic models over syntactic or implicit features.

4.5 RQ3: Robustness to Adversarial Mutation

Recent studies [11,16] highlight the limited robustness of classification tasks relying on pre-trained language models. Their embeddings lack explicit interpretability: individual dimensions do not correspond to well-defined lexical, syntactic, or semantic concepts. As a result, transformations preserving the underlying malicious intent can perturb the embedding space and lead to misclassifications.

We compare the inherent robustness of the ■ SecureBERT against ■ GAUR (Mistral), both coupled with an autoencoder. To evaluate this property, we leverage WAF-A-MoLE [7], a guided mutational fuzzing tool designed to automatically generate adversarial mutations of SQL injection payloads. The tool applies different transformations, from simple lexical modifications (e.g., keyword case changes or comment insertion) to more complex alterations such as tautology rewrites. For each payload, WAF-A-MoLE iteratively generates adversarial variants using a confidence-guided strategy: at each iteration, m mutants are produced, and the lowest-confidence variant is selected as the next seed. The process stops upon successful evasion, exhaustion of a mutation budget r, or a timeout. We set $m = 20$, $r = 1000$ (the default values) and a 5-minute timeout per query to limit experiment duration. The evaluation is done using 100 randomly selected template-payload pairs from Superviz25-SQL.

Across all evaluated templates, the ■ GAUR (Mistral)-based IDS could not be evaded within the allocated mutation budget and time constraints. In contrast, WAF-A-MoLE successfully bypassed the ■ SecureBERT-based IDS for 14 out of 100 queries, requiring an average of 123.14 mutation rounds. These results demonstrate the inherent weaknesses of embedding-based approaches. Because such models encode semantics implicitly, small surface-level changes can disproportionately affect their internal representations. Conversely, GAUR's explicit semantic features remain stable under lexical transformations and evolve predictably under genuine semantic modifications (such as tautology rewrite), raising the cost of evasion. While no detection system can be provably immune to all adversarial strategies, these results exhibit that explicit semantic instrumentation provides a more robust foundation for AIDS.

5 Related Work

Detecting applicative attacks depends on the quality and granularity of the collected observations. Existing approaches typically rely on four data sources: system logs, audit logs, system calls or instrumentation. We review each family and highlight their limitation.

System logs (e.g., Event Tracing for Windows, or SystemTap) have been leveraged for applicative intrusion detection [9,13]. While they provide broad observational coverage without modifying the monitored application, they typically contain noise (observations not relevant for security purpose) or do not precisely characterize user behaviours, required for effective detection [12].

Audit logs, such as Linux Audit or DTrace aim to improve on system logs by producing security-oriented observations. They are widely used to build provenance graphs for attack detection or forensic analysis [12,13]. However, because audit mechanisms are designed to provide full application coverage without application-level adaptation, they often incur significant collection overhead.

System-call monitoring offers the lowest-level and most complete form of observation, since all user behaviours ultimately translate to system calls. These data sources are used by host-based IDS or for application-specific monitoring in containerized environment [19,28]. Despite their completeness, system calls generate large volumes of data which can result in high false-positive rates but also introduce a semantic gap between these low-level observations and user behaviours.

Application instrumentation collects observations from within the monitored component itself. Such approaches offer the potential for rich semantic information production with comparatively low overhead. For instance, Almgren et al. [4] created a module for the Apache server that provided observations to a rule-based decision engine named eXpert-HTTP. Fonseca et al. [10] developed a DBMS-specific architecture that gathered information about SQL commands and transactions. Unfortunately, they typically require extended knowledge of application internals. They incur non-trivial engineering and maintenance effort and can rarely be generalized to other systems.

As a result, most applicative IDS still rely on coarse-grained observations rather than richer, structured information. SQL injection detection illustrates this trend: data collection is rarely specified and is typically assumed to occur at the web application level, where raw queries are collected. Higher-level representations are then reconstructed using external tools and preprocessing pipelines, introducing both computational overhead and the risk of representation mismatches. These pipelines typically extract syntactic features [14,30], NLP-derived embeddings [18,20] or explicit semantic tags [1,14], which did not publish implementations, so we could not empirically compare to their work.

In contrast, with GAUR, the observation mechanism is placed directly within the application parser. The data collector captures lexical, syntactic, and explicit semantic information during execution, without relying on external reconstruction or runtime NLP processing. This design ensures complete coverage of application interactions while incurring negligible overhead and requiring minimal deployment and maintenance effort.

6 Conclusion

Because grammars are designed around the syntax tree that drives application behaviour, the parser constitutes a privileged location for lexical, syntactic and semantic data collection. In this work, we introduce a parser instrumentation approach that provides application-level observations to decision engines with minimal developer effort. We implemented such an approach through the tool GAUR, and illustrated its viability by instrumenting a MySQL parser. Experimental results show that GAUR incurs negligible overhead (0.31% of query execution time) for MySQL, achieves higher F1-scores than existing baselines on the SQL attack detection task. Features produced by GAUR enable fast inference: 0.264 ms per query, about 20 times lower than embedding-based approaches and improve robustness to adversarial mutations, in contrast to the surface-level sensitivity of the latter approaches.

This work opens several promising research directions: extending the approach toward intrusion prevention by blocking semantically malicious inputs before execution, refining semantic tag attribution with additional static or contextual information, or illustrating the generalizability by instrumenting other applications.

Acknowledgements. This work has been partially supported by the French National Research Agency under the France 2030 label (Superviz ANR-22-PECY-0008). The views reflected herein do not necessarily reflect the opinion of the French government.

References

1. Abaimov, S., Bianchi, G.: CODDLE: code-injection detection with deep learning. IEEE Access **7**, 128617–128627 (2019). https://doi.org/10.1109/ACCESS.2019.2939870
2. Agarwal, S., et al.: Gpt-oss-120b & gpt-oss-20b Model Card (2025). https://doi.org/10.48550/arXiv.2508.10925
3. Aghaei, E., Niu, X., Shadid, W., Al-Shaer, E.: SecureBERT: a domain-specific language model for cybersecurity. In: Li, F., Liang, K., Lin, Z., Katsikas, S.K. (eds.) Security and Privacy in Communication Networks, pp. 39–56. Springer, Cham (2023). https://doi.org/10.1007/978-3-031-25538-0_3
4. Almgren, M., Lindqvist, U.: Application-integrated data collection for security monitoring. In: Lee, W., Mé, L., Wespi, A. (eds.) Recent Advances in Intrusion Detection, Lecture Notes in Computer Science, pp. 22–36. Springer, Heidelberg (2001). https://doi.org/10.1007/3-540-45474-8_2
5. Anthropic: Claude (2025). https://www.anthropic.com/news/claude-4
6. Bridges, R.A., Glass-Vanderlan, T.R., Iannacone, M.D., Vincent, M.S., Chen, Q.G.: A survey of intrusion detection systems leveraging host data. ACM Comput. Surv. **52**(6), 128:1–128:35 (2019). https://doi.org/10.1145/3344382
7. Demetrio, L., Valenza, A., Costa, G., Lagorio, G.: WAF-A-MoLE: evading web application firewalls through adversarial machine learning. In: Proceedings of the 35th Annual ACM Symposium on Applied Computing, pp. 1745–1752. ACM (2020). https://doi.org/10.1145/3341105.3373962. https://dl.acm.org/doi/10.1145/3341105.3373962
8. Donadello, I., Dragoni, M.: SeXAI: a semantic explainable artificial intelligence framework. In: Baldoni, M., Bandini, S. (eds.) AIxIA 2020 - Advances in Artificial Intelligence, pp. 51–66. Springer, Cham (2021). https://doi.org/10.1007/978-3-030-77091-4_4
9. Du, M., Li, F., Zheng, G., Srikumar, V.: DeepLog: anomaly detection and diagnosis from system logs through deep learning. In: Proceedings of the 2017 ACM SIGSAC Conference on Computer and Communications Security, pp. 1285–1298. ACM, Dallas (2017). https://doi.org/10.1145/3133956.3134015
10. Fonseca, J., Vieira, M., Madeira, H.: Detecting malicious SQL. In: Lambrinoudakis, C., Pernul, G., Tjoa, A.M. (eds.) Trust, Privacy and Security in Digital Business, pp. 259–268. Springer, Heidelberg (2007). https://doi.org/10.1007/978-3-540-74409-2_28
11. Garg, S., Ramakrishnan, G.: Bae: bert-based adversarial examples for text classification. In: Proceedings of the 2020 Conference on Empirical Methods in Natural Language Processing (EMNLP), pp. 6174–6181 (2020)
12. Hassan, W.U., Noureddine, M.A., Datta, P., Bates, A.: OmegaLog: high-fidelity attack investigation via transparent multi-layer log analysis. In: Proceedings 2020 Network and Distributed System Security Symposium. Internet Society, San Diego (2020). https://doi.org/10.14722/ndss.2020.24270
13. Jiang, B., et al.: ORTHRUS: achieving high quality of attribution in provenance-based intrusion detection systems. In: 34th USENIX Security Symposium (USENIX Security 25), pp. 7173–7192 (2025)
14. Kakisim, A.G.: A deep learning approach based on multi-view consensus for SQL injection detection. Int. J. Inf. Secur. **23**(2), 1541–1556 (2024). https://doi.org/10.1007/s10207-023-00791-y

15. Khan, M.I., Foley, S.N., O'Sullivan, B.: Database intrusion detection systems (DIDs): insider threat detection via behaviour-based anomaly detection systems - a brief survey of concepts and approaches. In: Meng, W., Katsikas, S.K. (eds.) Emerging Information Security and Applications, pp. 178–197. Springer, Cham (2022). https://doi.org/10.1007/978-3-030-93956-4_11
16. Li, L., Ma, R., Guo, Q., Xue, X., Qiu, X.: BERT-ATTACK: adversarial attack against BERT using BERT. In: Webber, B., Cohn, T., He, Y., Liu, Y. (eds.) Proceedings of the 2020 Conference on Empirical Methods in Natural Language Processing (EMNLP), pp. 6193–6202. Association for Computational Linguistics, Online (2020). https://doi.org/10.18653/v1/2020.emnlp-main.500. https://aclanthology.org/2020.emnlp-main.500/
17. Li, Q., Li, W., Wang, J., Cheng, M.: A SQL injection detection method based on adaptive deep forest. IEEE Access **7**, 145385–145394 (2019). https://doi.org/10.1109/ACCESS.2019.2944951
18. Li, Q., Wang, F., Wang, J., Li, W.: LSTM-Based SQL injection detection method for intelligent transportation system. IEEE Trans. Veh. Technol. **68**(5), 4182–4191 (2019). https://doi.org/10.1109/TVT.2019.2893675
19. Lin, Y., Tunde-Onadele, O., Gu, X.: CDL: classified distributed learning for detecting security attacks in containerized applications. In: Annual Computer Security Applications Conference, pp. 179–188. ACM, Austin (2020). https://doi.org/10.1145/3427228.3427236
20. Liu, Y., Dai, Y.: Deep learning in cybersecurity: a hybrid BERT-LSTM network for SQL injection attack detection. IET Inf. Secur. **2024**(1), 5565950 (2024). https://doi.org/10.1049/2024/5565950
21. Meta: Llama 3.3 — Model Cards and Prompt formats (2024). https://www.llama.com/docs/model-cards-and-prompt-formats/llama3_3/. Accessed 3 Dec 2025
22. Mistral AI: Mistral Small 3 (2024). https://mistral.ai/news/mistral-small-3. Accessed 3 Dec 2025
23. Neupane, S., et al.: Explainable intrusion detection systems (X-IDS): a survey of current methods, challenges, and opportunities. IEEE Access **10**, 112392–112415 (2022). https://doi.org/10.1109/ACCESS.2022.3216617
24. OpenAI: ChatGPT (2025). https://openai.com/index/introducing-gpt-4-5/
25. Quetel, G., Alata, E., Gimenez, P.F., Robert, T., Pautet, L.: Superviz25-SQL: high-quality dataset to empower unsupervised SQL injection detection systems. In: 1st International Workshop on Assessment with New Methodologies, Unified Benchmarks, and Environments, of Intrusion Detection and Response Systems (ANUBIS), Toulouse, France (2025)
26. Reimers, N., Gurevych, I.: Sentence-BERT: sentence embeddings using siamese BERT-networks. In: Proceedings of the 2019 Conference on Empirical Methods in Natural Language Processing and the 9th International Joint Conference on Natural Language Processing (EMNLP-IJCNLP), pp. 3980–3990. Association for Computational Linguistics, Hong Kong (2019). https://doi.org/10.18653/v1/D19-1410
27. Verizon: Data Breach Investigations Report (2025). https://www.verizon.com/business/resources/reports/dbir/. Accessed 3 Dec 2025
28. Yu, J., et al.: CAShift: benchmarking log-based cloud attack detection under normality shift. Proc. ACM Softw. Eng. **2**(FSE), 1687–1709 (2025). https://doi.org/10.1145/3729346
29. Zeng, J., Chua, Z.L., Chen, Y., Ji, K., Liang, Z., Mao, J.: WATSON: abstracting behaviors from audit logs via aggregation of contextual semantics. In: Proceed-

ings 2021 Network and Distributed System Security Symposium. Internet Society, Virtual (2021). https://doi.org/10.14722/ndss.2021.24549
30. Zhuo, Z., Cai, T., Zhang, X., Lv, F.: Long short-term memory on abstract syntax tree for SQL injection detection. IET Softw. **15**(2), 188–197 (2021). https://doi.org/10.1049/sfw2.12018. https://onlinelibrary.wiley.com/doi/abs/10.1049/sfw2.12018

BFA-Shield: A Resilient Collaborative Defense Framework for DNNs Against Bit-Flip Attacks

Jianing Wang[1,2,3], Xue Tian[1,2,3(✉)], Hongxia Ma[1,2,3], Jing Yu[1,2,3], and Chi Chen[1,2,3]

[1] Institute of Information Engineering, Chinese Academy of Sciences, No.19 Shucun Road, Haidian District, Beijing 100085, China
{wangjianing,tianxue,mahongxia,yujing,chenchi}@iie.ac.cn
[2] School of Cyber Security, University of Chinese Academy of Sciences, No.19 Yuquan Road, Shijingshan District, Beijing 100049, China
[3] State Key Laboratory of Cyberspace Security Defense, No.19 Shucun Road, Haidian District, Beijing 100085, China

Abstract. Bit-flip attacks (BFAs) pose a serious threat to deep neural networks (DNNs) deployed in edge environments, where limited physical protection and constrained resources expose model weights to hardware fault injections. By flipping only a small number of carefully selected bits, an adversary can severely degrade model accuracy or even induce targeted misbehavior. Existing defenses typically follow one of two paradigms: increasing the attack cost through robustness enhancement or attempting post-attack recovery through redundancy or weight reconstruction. However, these approaches either lack recovery capability or incur prohibitive overhead for resource constrained edge devices. In this paper, we propose **BFA-Shield**, a resilient and collaborative defense framework that integrates pre-deployment robustness enhancement with lightweight runtime detection and exact post-attack recovery. The key insight of BFA-Shield is that binary weight determinism enables efficient anomaly localization and precise bit-level recovery, which is fundamentally difficult to achieve in multi-bit quantized models. Specifically, we adopt robustness-enhanced binary neural network training to reduce the attack surface, employ checksum-based runtime monitoring to detect and localize bit flips, and perform direct bit correction without retraining or model reloading. We evaluate BFA-Shield against both random and gradient-guided bit-flip attacks on ResNet and VGG architectures using the CIFAR-10 and ImageNet datasets. Experimental results demonstrate that BFA-Shield substantially increases the attack difficulty while maintaining low storage and runtime overhead. Compared with the INT8 model, BFA-Shield significantly reduces model storage requirements while preserving high post-attack accuracy, making it a practical and effective defense solution for edge-deployed DNNs.

Keywords: Bit-flip attack · Adversarial robustness · Binary neural networks · Model recovery · Lightweight detection · Edge computing security

© IFIP International Federation for Information Processing 2026
Published by Springer Nature Switzerland AG 2026
H. Janicke et al. (Eds.): SEC 2026, IFIP AICT 787, pp. 374–387, 2026.
https://doi.org/10.1007/978-3-032-27993-4_26

1 Introduction

The proliferation of edge computing has led to the widespread deployment of Deep Neural Networks (DNNs) on resource-constrained edge devices to enhance responsiveness [1]. However, the open physical environments in which these devices operate make them more vulnerable to hardware-level attacks, such as Bit-flip Attacks (BFAs) [2]. Such attacks can exploit vulnerabilities like Rowhammer in DRAM, severely degrading model performance by flipping only a very small number of critical bits in the weights [3,4]. Studies have demonstrated [2,5] that flipping approximately 13 bits in an 8-bit quantized model can reduce its accuracy to random guess level within tens of seconds. Therefore, developing efficient and lightweight defense mechanisms against BFA is crucial.

Existing defense research is primarily divided into two categories. The first category aims to mitigate the impact of attacks and increase the attack cost, for example, by enhancing the model's robustness against perturbations through weight reconstruction or robust training [6–8]. While these methods can raise the difficulty of attacks, they cannot restore the model after an attack occurs, lacking resilience. The second category focuses on post-attack recovery, often relying on mechanisms such as redundant checks, weight backups, or integrity verification [9–12]. However, in edge scenarios, these methods often face significant challenges: on the one hand, they introduce considerable computational and storage overhead, making real-time execution on resource-constrained devices difficult; on the other hand, most solutions lack robustness against dynamic, adaptive attacks, and their recovery processes frequently overlook the structural characteristics of the model, leading to substantial accuracy loss or excessive recovery latency.

In summary, existing defenses fail to simultaneously satisfy three critical requirements for edge deployments: **lightweight runtime detection, accurate post-attack recovery, and low system overhead**. In particular, there remains a lack of a unified defense framework that integrates proactive robustness enhancement with real-time detection and efficient recovery under increasingly sophisticated BFAs.

To address these challenges, we propose **BFA-Shield**, a resilient collaborative defense framework for DNNs deployed at the edge. BFA-Shield combines pre-deployment robustness enhancement with runtime anomaly detection and exact bit-level recovery, forming a complete defense lifecycle that spans prevention, detection, and repair. The core insight of our approach is that binary neural networks not only reduce the attack surface but also enable deterministic localization and correction of flipped bits using lightweight checksum mechanisms—capabilities that are fundamentally difficult to achieve in multi-bit quantized models.

Our main **contributions** are summarized as follows:

1. We propose a resilient collaborative defense framework that systematically integrates robustness enhancement, lightweight runtime detection, and exact

post-attack recovery, bridging the gap between attack mitigation and model repair in existing defenses.
2. We design a checksum-based detection and localization mechanism tailored to binary neural networks, enabling efficient identification of flipped bits with minimal overhead.
3. We introduce a lightweight recovery strategy that directly corrects detected bit flips without retraining or model reloading, making it suitable for real-time edge deployment.
4. We conduct extensive evaluations under both random and gradient-guided bit-flip attacks on CIFAR-10 and ImageNet, demonstrating that BFA-Shield achieves superior robustness and efficiency compared to state-of-the-art defenses.

The remainder of this paper is organized as follows: Sect. 2 reviews related background and research work; Sect. 3 details the design and methodology of the proposed defense framework; Sect. 4 introduces the experimental setup and experimental results; and Sect. 5 concludes the paper.

2 Background and Related Works

2.1 Bit-Flip Attacks

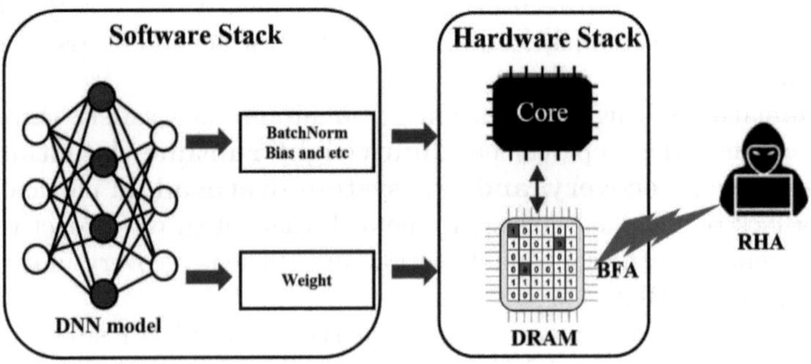

Fig. 1. Bit-Flip Attack overview.

Early research on BFAs focused primarily on minimizing the number of bit flips required to compromise model performance. Rakin et al. [2] introduced a progressive bit search algorithm, demonstrating for the first time that flipping a very small number of weight bits (e.g., 13) is sufficient to completely degrade the performance of a DNN. Subsequent work has continued to improve attack efficiency: Siraj et al. [5] shifted the focus from untargeted to precisely targeted BFA, while Chen et al. [13] further reduced the number of flips needed to implant a targeted trojan to single digits (e.g., 12). The peak of this efficiency trend is seen in [14], which showed that by poisoning the training process, a malicious function could be activated during deployment by flipping only a single critical bit. As attack mechanisms matured, research attention shifted toward exploring vulnerabilities in different types of neural networks. Kun et al. [15] specifically targeted binary neural networks by exploiting their anomalous weight gradients. Lee et al. [16] revealed coordinate-level vulnerabilities in non-zero weights within highly sparse DNNs. Meanwhile, Kummer et al. [17] pioneered targeted attacks on Graph Neural Networks, impairing their core graph isomorphism capability by disrupting the message aggregation mechanism. Beyond directly modifying stored model parameters, BFA methods have evolved to become more diverse and dynamic. On one hand, attack objectives have grown more sophisticated and stealthy: Bai et al. [18] achieved precise manipulation of individual samples or the implantation of backdoor triggers, while Wang et al. [19] explored runtime trojan injection in gray-box settings. On the other hand, attack goals are no longer confined to misclassification. For example, Li et al. [20] showed that a single bit flip at the code level could undermine the universality and transferability of a model's reasoning capability. Collectively, these studies highlight the serious security challenges BFA poses to DNN-based systems (Fig. 1).

2.2 Existing Defense Measures and Limitations

He et al. [11] proposed the use of **beneficial bit flips** to enhance model robustness, demonstrating how attack techniques could be repurposed for defense. However, defining the threshold for determining **beneficial** flips is challenging, and improper control may instead degrade the model. Li et al. [8] introduced a post-attack recovery method via weight reconstruction, which can repair tampered models. Yet, this approach heavily relies on accurate prior knowledge of the weight distribution and incurs high computational overhead for large-scale models. Wang et al. [6] developed a dynamic monitoring and mitigation framework, demonstrating real-time defense effectiveness against targeted attacks. However, the system-level implementation of this framework is relatively complex, making lightweight deployment difficult. Guo et al. [10] proposed a highly portable, generalizable defense framework extension. As a software-layer solution, it does not fully leverage underlying hardware security primitives, thus imposing inherent limitations on its protective capability. Rakin et al. [21] introduced Robust and Accurate Binary Neural Networks (**RA-BNN**), a method designed to enhance both robustness against BFAs and accuracy on clean data. While it raises the cost for attackers, it does not enable model recovery. Liu et al. [12] proposed an active defense concept based on **honeypot** weights, showing the feasibility of real-time detection through decoy mechanisms. Its practical effectiveness, however, largely depends on the stealthiness of the decoy design and faces the risk of being identified by attackers. Nazari et al. [22] presented a method to enhance Transformer robustness through dynamic reconnection, offering a tailored defense for this architecture. Nevertheless, its core concept has not yet been widely extended to other complex architectures, such as Large Language Models (LLMs), and its integration with model compression techniques remains unexplored.

In summary, defense strategies against BFAs share several common challenges and limitations. First, most solutions focus on tolerating or detecting attacks but lack reliable post-attack recovery mechanisms. Even if model accuracy is partially restored, the tampered weights are not genuinely repaired, and model integrity remains compromised. On edge devices, traditional recovery methods—such as reloading the model or switching to backups—suffer from low efficiency and high latency, making it difficult to meet the requirements for continuous and reliable operation in critical applications. Second, existing approaches often rely on single-point, static protection techniques, forming isolated lines of defense. Such structures are vulnerable to targeted circumvention by attackers; once breached, the entire defense system may fail. These inherent limitations highlight the necessity and urgency of exploring a new defensive paradigm.

3 Methodology

To overcome the limitations of existing bit-flip defenses discussed in Sect. 2, we design **BFA-Shield**, a lightweight and resilient defense framework tailored for edge-deployed DNNs. Unlike defenses that rely solely on robustness enhancement or post-hoc recovery, BFA-Shield adopts a collaborative design that tightly integrates pre-deployment training, runtime monitoring, and post-attack repair. The framework operates under realistic edge constraints and assumes a threat model consistent with Rowhammer-style fault injections, where attacks are sparse and checksum metadata is protected by a trusted execution environment (TEE) (Fig. 2).

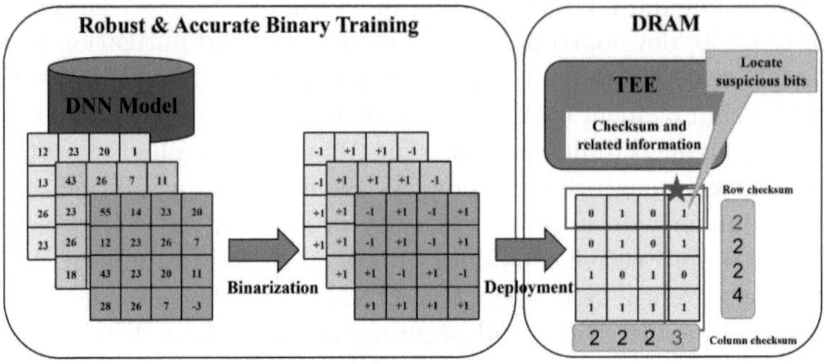

Fig. 2. BFA-Shield overview.

Stage 1: Robustness-Enhanced Training. Research indicates that BFAs tend to target weight parameters close to zero. Building on this observation, we introduce a binarized training strategy [21] during the training phase to reduce the number of near-zero weights, thereby shrinking the attack surface and strengthening the intrinsic robustness of the model. After training, the system computes both row-wise and column-wise checksums of the binarized weight matrix and securely stores these checksum values in a Trusted Execution Environment (TEE).

Stage 2: Runtime Attack Detection. During model inference, the system calculates real-time checksums of the current weights and compares them with the baseline checksums stored in the TEE. By monitoring anomalies in the row and column checksums, lightweight and efficient attack detection is achieved. Once an inconsistency is detected, the recovery mechanism is triggered.

Stage 3: Lightweight Model Recovery. Since the weights are binarized, they can only take two possible states. Therefore, once the flipped bit is detected and localized, the error can be quickly corrected by directly flipping that bit back, enabling model recovery with minimal overhead.

3.1 Robustness-Enhanced Training with RA-BNN

In the model robustness training stage, we adopt the **Robust and Accurate Binary Neural Network (RA-BNN)** method proposed in [21], which is a training framework designed to achieve both adversarial robustness and high clean accuracy in binarized neural networks. The method consists of two core components, as detailed below.

1. **Full Binarization.** RA-BNN applies binarization to all weight layers as well as to most activation functions, with the exception of those in the input and output layers. This extreme low-bit representation significantly reduces the parameter space vulnerable to manipulation and thereby enhances the model's intrinsic resilience against Bit-Flip Attacks.
2. **Trainable Channel Expansion for Binary Networks.** To compensate for the accuracy degradation typically induced by binarization, RA-BNN incorporates a trainable channel expansion mechanism. This mechanism optimizes a channel mask for each layer using the Gumbel-Sigmoid function, allowing for a selective and learnable increase in channel width. The expansion is conducted through a structured two-phase training strategy:
   - *Phase 1 (Growth Phase):* During initial training, channels are dynamically activated in each layer according to the learned masks. This enables the network to adaptively grow its capacity where needed.
   - *Phase 2 (Retraining Phase):* Once the network architecture is finalized, the binary weights are further fine-tuned to maximize final model accuracy.

Through the above robustness-enhanced training procedure, the proposed approach significantly improves the adversarial robustness of DNNs against BFAs while maintaining competitive accuracy on clean (unperturbed) data.

3.2 Runtime Attack Detection and Localization

Weight Mapping and Storage: After training the RA-BNN model [21], all binary weights are mapped to binary values $\{0,1\}$ as needed for storage. For each layer l in the network, the weight matrix is represented as:

$$W_b^{(l)} \in \{0,1\}^{m_l \times n_l} \tag{1}$$

where:

- m_l: number of output channels in layer l
- n_l: total number of weight bits in layer l (input channels × kernel height × kernel width)

For convolutional layers, the 4D weight tensor $\mathcal{W}^{(l)} \in \mathbb{R}^{C_{\text{out}} \times C_{\text{in}} \times H \times W}$ is flattened to a 2D matrix $W_b^{(l)}$ for checksum computation.

Checksum Calculation: For a binary weight matrix $W_b^{(l)} \in \{0,1\}^{m_l \times n_l}$ in layer l, the row checksum vector $R^{(l)}$ and column checksum vector $C^{(l)}$ are computed as:

$$R^{(l)}(i) = \sum_{j=1}^{n_l} W_b^{(l)}(i,j), \quad i = 1,\ldots,m_l \tag{2}$$

$$C^{(l)}(j) = \sum_{i=1}^{m_l} W_b^{(l)}(i,j), \quad j = 1,\ldots,n_l \tag{3}$$

Secure Storage: All checksum values are securely stored in TEE:

$$\mathcal{S}_{\text{secure}} = \left\{ \left(R^{(l)}_{\text{original}}, C^{(l)}_{\text{original}} \right) \right\}_{l=1}^{L} \tag{4}$$

where L is the total number of layers in the network.

Attack Detection: An attack is detected if any checksum mismatch occurs between the current and baseline values. The detection condition for layer l is:

$$\text{Attack\_Detected}^{(l)} = \begin{cases} \text{true}, & \text{if } R^{(l)}_{\text{current}} \neq R^{(l)}_{\text{original}} \text{ or } C^{(l)}_{\text{current}} \neq C^{(l)}_{\text{original}} \\ \text{false}, & \text{otherwise} \end{cases} \tag{5}$$

Single Bit-Flip Localization. If only a single bit has been flipped at position (i^*, j^*), it can be precisely located by:

$$i^* = \arg\max_i |R^{(l)}_{\text{current}}(i) - R^{(l)}_{\text{original}}(i)| \tag{6}$$

$$j^* = \arg\max_j |C^{(l)}_{\text{current}}(j) - C^{(l)}_{\text{original}}(j)| \tag{7}$$

The direction of the flip (0→1 or 1→0) is determined by:

$$\Delta = R^{(l)}_{\text{current}}(i^*) - R^{(l)}_{\text{original}}(i^*) \tag{8}$$

Multiple Bit-Flip Localization For multiple bit-flips under sparse attack assumption, we formulate the localization as an optimization problem:

Let $E^{(l)} \in \{0,1\}^{m_l \times n_l}$ be a binary matrix where $E^{(l)}(i,j) = 1$ indicates a flipped bit at position (i,j). The localization problem is:

$$\min_{E^{(l)}} \|E^{(l)}\|_0 \tag{9}$$

subject to:

$$R^{(l)}_{\text{current}} = R^{(l)}_{\text{original}} + E^{(l)} \cdot \mathbf{1}_{n_l} \tag{10}$$

$$C^{(l)}_{\text{current}} = C^{(l)}_{\text{original}} + \mathbf{1}^{\top}_{m_l} E^{(l)} \tag{11}$$

where $\|\cdot\|_0$ denotes the ℓ_0-norm (number of non-zero entries), and $\mathbf{1}_k$ denotes a vector of ones with length k.

For multiple sparse bit-flips, localization is formulated as an ℓ_0-norm minimization problem to find the smallest set of flipped bits that explains the observed checksum errors. The anomaly detection and localization algorithm proposed in this paper is presented in the Algorithm 1 below.

Algorithm 1. Anomaly Detection and Localization Algorithm

Require: Binary weight matrix $W_b^{(l)}$, baseline checksums $R^{(l)}_{\text{orig}}$, $C^{(l)}_{\text{orig}}$
Ensure: Attack status `is_attacked`, error matrix $E^{(l)}$

```
Initialize E^(l) ← 0^(m_l×n_l), is_attacked ← False
R_cur^(l) ← row_sum(W_b^(l))                                  ▷ Eq. (2)
C_cur^(l) ← col_sum(W_b^(l))                                  ▷ Eq. (3)
if R_cur^(l) ≠ R_orig^(l) or C_cur^(l) ≠ C_orig^(l) then
    is_attacked ← True
    ΔR ← R_cur^(l) − R_orig^(l)
    ΔC ← C_cur^(l) − C_orig^(l)
    if ||ΔR||_0 = 1 and ||ΔC||_0 = 1 then                      ▷ Single bit-flip case
        i* ← arg max_i |ΔR(i)|                                ▷ Eq. (6)
        j* ← arg max_j |ΔC(j)|                                ▷ Eq. (7)
        E^(l)(i*, j*) ← 1
    else                                                      ▷ Multiple bit-flips case
        Solve min_{E^(l)} ||E^(l)||_0 s.t. ΔR = E^(l) · 1, ΔC = 1^T E^(l)
        Use greedy algorithm to find E^(l)
    end if
end if
return is_attacked, E^(l)
```

3.3 Lightweight Model Recovery

Once the flipped bits are localized, recovery is straightforward due to the binary weight representation. For each detected error at position (i,j) in error matrix $E^{(l)}$, the weight is corrected by:

$$W_b^{(l)}(i,j) \leftarrow 1 - W_b^{(l)}(i,j) \tag{12}$$

This direct bit-flip correction incurs minimal computational overhead, enabling fast model recovery with negligible latency.

4 Experiments

4.1 Experimental Setting

Datasets and Network Architectures. To evaluate our defense strategy, experiments were conducted on popular benchmark datasets: CIFAR-10 [23] and ImageNet [24]. The CIFAR-10 dataset consists of 10 object categories, with a total of 60k 32 $\times$ 32 RGB images, split into 50k training samples and 10k test samples. The ImageNet dataset contains 1,000 different categories with 1.2 million training images. All images were normalized using the dataset-specific mean and standard deviation, and standard data augmentation techniques (random cropping and horizontal flipping) were applied during model training. For the CIFAR-10 dataset, we used the ResNet model [25]; for ImageNet, the VGG model [26] was employed. All experiments were implemented using PyTorch 2.1.0 and executed on an NVIDIA RTX 4090 GPU (24 GB VRAM).

Baseline. We compare BFA-Shield with state-of-the-art defense methods Weight Reconstruction [8] and undefended baseline model (BASE).

4.2 Result Evaluation

Comparison of Storage Overhead: The BFA-Shield defense scheme proposed in this work expands the network channels by 50% during the training phase to compensate for the accuracy loss caused by weight binarization. As shown in Table 1, even with channel expansion, the scheme still maintains significant advantages in storage overhead. Compared with the INT8 model, the BFA-Shield strategy stores model weights using only 1 bit, reducing the model sizes of ResNet-18 and VGG-11 to 2.19 MB and 24.75 MB, respectively—approximately one-fifth of their INT8 counterparts. Even when accounting for additional storage overhead, such as about 3.51 MB for ResNet-18 (used to maintain row and column checksums for runtime attack detection and precise localization), the total storage cost remains the lowest. Therefore, this method is suitable for deployment in storage constrained edge devices.

Comparison of Different Attacks: As shown in Figs. 3 and 4, the robustness of different defense schemes was evaluated under two typical attack scenarios. The RBFA randomly flips 100, 200, 300, 400, and 500 weight bits, while the PBS [2] attack identifies and flips the most destructive bits through 20 iterations.

Figure 3 shows the robustness under RBFA with 100–500 flipped bits. For ResNet-18 and VGG-11, the undefended INT8 model and WeightRecon [8] experience slight performance degradation, whereas BFA-Shield remains nearly stable across all flip counts.

Table 1. Storage Comparison of Different Defense Schemes

Models	Defense Schemes	Model Size	Total bits	Extra Storage
ResNet-18	INT8 (No Defense)	11.7	93.6	0
	INT8 (Weight Recon [8])	11.7	93.6	0.1
	RA-BNN (**BFA-Shield**)	2.19	45.63	3.51
ResNet-20	INT8 (No Defense)	0.27	2.16	0
	INT8 (Weight Recon [8])	0.27	2.16	0.01
	RA-BNN (**BFA-Shield**)	0.05	1.05	0.08
VGG-11	INT8 (No Defense)	132	1056	0
	INT8 (Weight Recon [8])	132	1056	1.0
	RA-BNN (**BFA-Shield**)	24.75	514.8	39.6
VGG-13	INT8 (No Defense)	133	1064	0
	INT8 (Weight Recon [8])	133	1064	1.0
	RA-BNN (**BFA-Shield**)	24.94	518.7	39.9

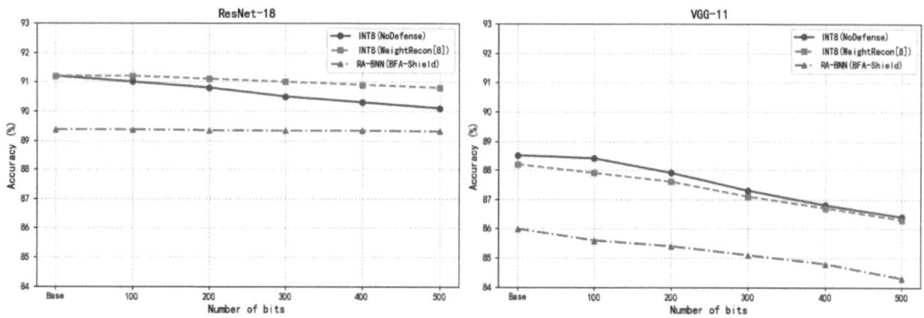

Fig. 3. Comparison of different defense schemes on the Cifar-10 dataset under RBFA attacks.

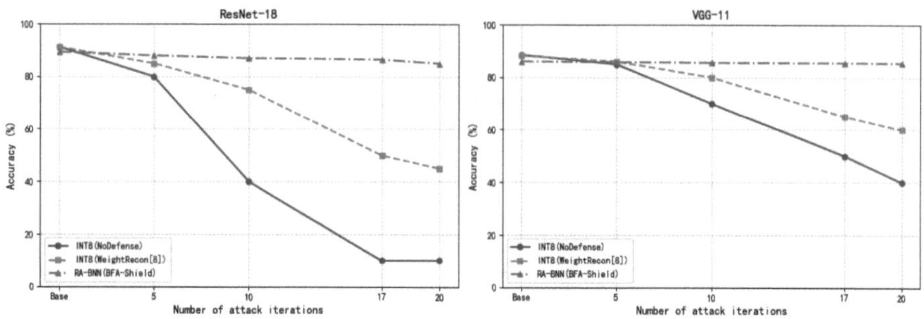

Fig. 4. Comparison of different defense schemes on the Cifar-10 dataset under PBS attacks.

Figure 4 shows the accuracy changes of different defense schemes under the PBS attack over 20 iterations. For ResNet-18, the undefended INT8 model and the WeightRecon [8] defense suffer from severe accuracy degradation as the attack progresses. After 20 iterations, their accuracy drops to around 13% and 46% respectively, while the proposed BFA-Shield maintains a high accuracy, demonstrating its strong resistance against bit-level search attacks. For VGG-11, all schemes exhibit a gradual decline in accuracy, but BFA-Shield consistently outperforms the others, indicating that it remains effective even on different architectures.

Experimental results show that RBFA has minimal destructive power under different defense schemes. Although PBS demonstrates strong attack capability, our proposed BFA-Shield scheme shows significant defensive advantages under both attacks.

Comparison of Different Datasets: Tables 2 and 3 present the performance of various defense schemes under 20-round iterative PBS attacks on the CIFAR-10 and ImageNet datasets, respectively. The detailed analysis is as follows:

In the absence of attacks, the INT8 (No Defense) achieves the highest baseline accuracy on both datasets. The BFA-Shield scheme experiences a slight decrease in baseline accuracy—within 3.4%—due to the introduction of binarization and channel expansion, indicating acceptable preservation of the model's original performance.

Under PBS attacks, the accuracy of the INT8 (No Defense) scheme drops sharply to 10.0% (CIFAR-10) and 0.1% (ImageNet), demonstrating the extreme vulnerability of conventional quantized models to bit-flip attacks. The INT8 (Weight Recon) scheme improves post-attack accuracy to 30.49%–30.6% (CIFAR-10) and 17.07%–17.43% (ImageNet) through weight reconstruction, yet its recovery capability remains limited.

Table 2. Comparison of CIFAR-10 Dataset

Model	Defense Scheme	Base Acc. (%)	Attack Acc. (%)
ResNet-20	INT8 (No Defense)	92.4	10.0
	INT8 (Weight Recon [8])	91.97	30.49
	RA-BNN (**BFA-Shield**)	89.41	85.28
VGG-13	INT8 (No Defense)	92.8	10.0
	INT8 (Weight Recon [8])	92.39	30.6
	RA-BNN (**BFA-Shield**)	89.51	85.38

In contrast, the BFA-Shield scheme exhibits remarkable defensive superiority: it maintains post-attack accuracy of 85.28%–85.38% (CIFAR-10) and 62.45%–63.22% (ImageNet), significantly outperforming the other two schemes. Especially on the more complex ImageNet dataset, its post-attack accuracy surpasses

Table 3. Comparison of ImageNet Dataset

Model	Defense Scheme	Base Acc. (%)	Attack Acc. (%)
ResNet-20	INT8 (No Defense)	68.2	0.1
	INT8 (Weight Recon [8])	67.97	17.07
	RA-BNN (**BFA-Shield**)	65.87	62.45
VGG-13	INT8 (No Defense)	69.9	0.1
	INT8 (Weight Recon [8])	69.42	17.43
	RA-BNN (**BFA-Shield**)	66.67	63.22

that of INT8 (Weight Recon) by approximately 45% points, validating the effectiveness of combining binary weight structure with checksum mechanisms against iterative BFAs.

Moreover, despite the larger scale and more challenging classification task of ImageNet, the performance ranking of the defense schemes remains consistent with that on CIFAR-10, indicating that BFA-Shield possesses good generalization capability and scalability. In summary, BFA-Shield achieves strong resilience against PBS attacks with only a slight sacrifice in baseline performance, providing an effective safeguard for the weight security of DNN models in edge environments.

5 Conclusion

This paper presented BFA-Shield, a resilient collaborative defense framework designed to protect edge-deployed DNNs against bit-flip attacks. By integrating robustness-enhanced binary training, lightweight checksum-based runtime detection, and exact bit-level recovery, BFA-Shield provides a complete defense lifecycle that covers prevention, detection, and repair.

Unlike prior approaches that focus on a single defense stage, BFA-Shield achieves an effective balance between security and efficiency. The adoption of binary weight representations significantly reduces storage overhead, while deterministic checksum verification enables precise localization and correction of flipped bits with negligible runtime cost. Extensive experiments on CIFAR-10 and ImageNet demonstrate that BFA-Shield maintains high post-attack accuracy under both random and gradient-guided attacks, substantially outperforming existing recovery-based defenses.

Overall, BFA-Shield offers a practical and deployable solution for enhancing the resilience of DNNs in resource-constrained edge environments, and highlights the potential of collaborative defense designs that jointly leverage model structure and system-level mechanisms.

Acknowledgments.. The authors gratefully acknowledge constructive comments by the anonymous reviewers. This work is supported by the Strategic Priority Research Program of the Chinese Academy of Sciences, Grant No.XDB0690303.

Disclosure of Interests.. The authors have no competing interests to declare that are relevant to the content of this article.

References

1. Wang, F., Zhang, M., Wang, X., Ma, X., Liu, J.: Deep learning for edge computing applications: a state-of-the-art survey. IEEE Access **8**, 58322–58336 (2020)
2. Rakin, A.S., He, Z., Fan, D.: Bit-flip attack: crushing neural network with progressive bit search. In: Proceedings of the IEEE/CVF International Conference on Computer Vision, pp. 1211–1220 (2019)
3. Hong, S., Frigo, P., Kaya, Y., Giuffrida, C., Dumitra, T.: Terminal brain damage: exposing the graceless degradation in deep neural networks under hardware fault attacks. In: 28th USENIX Security Symposium (USENIX Security 19), pp. 497–514 (2019)
4. Yao, F., Rakin, A.S., Fan, D.: {DeepHammer}: depleting the intelligence of deep neural networks through targeted chain of bit flips. In: 29th USENIX Security Symposium (USENIX Security 20), pp. 1463–1480 (2020)
5. Siraj Rakin, A., He, Z., Li, J., Yao, F., Chakrabarti, C., Fan, D.: T-BFA: targeted bit-flip adversarial weight attack. arXiv e-prints pp. arXiv-2007 (2020)
6. Wang, J., et al.: Aegis: mitigating targeted bit-flip attacks against deep neural networks. In: 32nd USENIX Security Symposium (USENIX Security 23), pp. 2329–2346 (2023)
7. Liu, Y., Wei, L., Luo, B., Xu, Q.: Fault injection attack on deep neural network. In: IEEE/ACM International Conference on Computer-Aided Design (ICCAD), pp. 131–138. IEEE (2017)
8. Li, J., et al.: Defending bit-flip attack through DNN weight reconstruction. In: 2020 57th ACM/IEEE Design Automation Conference (DAC), pp. 1–6. IEEE (2020)
9. Kummer, L., Moustafa, S., Gansterer, W., Kriege, N.M.: Crossfire: an elastic defense framework for graph neural networks under bit flip attacks. In: Proceedings of the AAAI Conference on Artificial Intelligence, vol. 39, pp. 17990–17998 (2025)
10. Guo, Y., Liu, L., Cheng, Y., Zhang, Y., Yang, J.: Modelshield: a generic and portable framework extension for defending bit-flip based adversarial weight attacks. In: 2021 IEEE 39th International Conference on Computer Design (ICCD), pp. 559–562. IEEE (2021)
11. He, Z., Rakin, A.S., Li, J., Chakrabarti, C., Fan, D.: Defending and harnessing the bit-flip based adversarial weight attack. In: Proceedings of the IEEE/CVF Conference on Computer Vision and Pattern Recognition, pp. 14095–14103 (2020)
12. Liu, Q., Yin, J., Wen, W., Yang, C., Sha, S.: {NeuroPots}: realtime proactive defense against {Bit-Flip} attacks in neural networks. In: 32nd USENIX Security Symposium (USENIX Security 23), pp. 6347–6364 (2023)
13. Chen, H., Fu, C., Zhao, J., Koushanfar, F.: Proflip: targeted trojan attack with progressive bit flips. In: Proceedings of the IEEE/CVF International Conference on Computer Vision, pp. 7718–7727 (2021)
14. Dong, J., et al.: One-bit flip is all you need: when bit-flip attack meets model training. In: Proceedings of the IEEE/CVF International Conference on Computer Vision, pp. 4688–4698 (2023)
15. Kundu, S., et al.: Bit-by-bit: investigating the vulnerabilities of binary neural networks to adversarial bit flipping. Trans. Mach. Learn. Res. (2024)

16. Lee, K., Chandrakasan, A.P.: Sparsebfa: attacking sparse deep neural networks with the worst-case bit flips on coordinates. In: ICASSP 2022–2022 IEEE International Conference on Acoustics, Speech and Signal Processing (ICASSP), pp. 4208–4212. IEEE (2022)
17. Kummer, L., Moustafa, S., Schrittwieser, S., Gansterer, W., Kriege, N.: Attacking graph neural networks with bit flips: weisfeiler and leman go indifferent. In: Proceedings of the 30th ACM SIGKDD Conference on Knowledge Discovery and Data Mining, pp. 1428–1439 (2024)
18. Bai, J., Wu, B., Li, Z., Xia, S.T.: Versatile weight attack via flipping limited bits. IEEE Trans. Pattern Anal. Mach. Intell. **45**(11), 13653–13665 (2023)
19. Wang, Z., Tang, D., Wang, X., He, W., Geng, Z., Wang, W.: Tossing in the dark: practical {Bit-Flipping} on gray-box deep neural networks for runtime trojan injection. In: 33rd USENIX Security Symposium (USENIX Security 24), pp. 1331–1348 (2024)
20. Li, S., et al.: Yes,{One-Bit-Flip} matters! universal {DNN} model inference depletion with runtime code fault injection. In: 33rd USENIX Security Symposium (USENIX Security 24), pp. 1315–1330 (2024)
21. Rakin, A.S., et al.: Ra-bnn: constructing robust & accurate binary neural network to simultaneously defend adversarial bit-flip attack and improve accuracy. arXiv preprint arXiv:2103.13813 (2021)
22. Nazari, N., et al.: Forget and rewire: enhancing the resilience of transformer-based models against {Bit-Flip} attacks. In: 33rd USENIX Security Symposium (USENIX Security 24), pp. 1349–1366 (2024)
23. Krizhevsky, A., Nair, V., Hinton, G.: Cifar-10 (Canadian institute for advanced research), **5**(4), 1 (2010). http://www.cs.toronto.edu/kriz/cifar.html
24. Deng, J., Dong, W., Socher, R., Li, L.J., Li, K., Fei-Fei, L.: Imagenet: a large-scale hierarchical image database. In: 2009 IEEE Conference on Computer Vision and Pattern Recognition, pp. 248–255. IEEE (2009)
25. He, K., Zhang, X., Ren, S., Sun, J.: Deep residual learning for image recognition. In: Proceedings of the IEEE Conference on Computer Vision and Pattern Recognition, pp. 770–778 (2016)
26. Simonyan, K., Zisserman, A.: Very deep convolutional networks for large-scale image recognition. arXiv preprint (2014)

Evaluation Framework for Multi-Channel Spoofing Detection Through Redesign of the ReMASC Corpus

Takuo Yamaguchi[1], Sayaka Shiota[1(✉)], and Naohiro Tawara[2]

[1] Tokyo Metropolitan University, Tokyo, Japan
yamaguchi-takuo@ed.tmu.ac.jp, sayaka@tmu.ac.jp
[2] NTT, Inc., Kyoto, Japan
naohiro.tawara@ieee.org

Abstract. In detecting replay spoofing attacks against voice-controlled systems such as smart speakers, the utilization of multi-channel information is crucial. ReMASC is the only large-scale multi-channel replay attack corpus created with multiple recording devices featuring different microphone array configurations, enabling comparison of detection performance across different device configurations. However, a fair comparison is not possible because the composition ratios of recording conditions are inconsistent across recording devices. Additionally, since conditions other than speakers are known in the existing subsets, the independent analysis of each recording condition's impact on performance is not feasible. In this study, we redesign ReMASC by introducing data cleaning to unify the composition ratios of recording conditions across recording devices and a subset splitting method that allows arbitrary recording conditions to be controlled as known or unknown. Furthermore, we conducted experiments based on the redesigned data splits and demonstrated that it is possible to quantitatively evaluate the impact of individual recording conditions and device configuration differences on detection accuracy.

Keywords: Spoofing detection · ReMASC corpus · Multi-channel audio · Dataset · Evaluation framework

1 Introduction

In recent years, voice-controlled systems represented by smart speakers have become increasingly widespread. From a personal information protection perspective, these voice-controlled systems often incorporate speaker verification for user authentication. On the other hand, there are concerns about replay spoofing attacks, where attackers present illegally recorded utterances of legitimate users to the system for speaker verification. However, rejecting replay spoofing through speaker verification alone is difficult, posing a serious challenge. Therefore, spoofing detection, which identifies whether input speech is bonafide or spoofed, is essential for voice-controlled systems.

© IFIP International Federation for Information Processing 2026
Published by Springer Nature Switzerland AG 2026
H. Janicke et al. (Eds.): SEC 2026, IFIP AICT 787, pp. 388–401, 2026.
https://doi.org/10.1007/978-3-032-27993-4_27

By using signals from multiple microphones, it is possible to capture subtle fluctuations in sound-source position that are unique to bonafide speech and the presence or absence of noise from playback devices [12], enabling higher detection performance than conventional single-channel methods.

On the other hand, research related to spoofing detection still predominantly targets single-channel audio, and datasets recorded in multi-channel are limited. Among them, ReMASC (Realistic Replay Attack Microphone Array Speech Corpus) [2] is recognized as a representative corpus for large-scale multi-channel spoofing attack detection and is widely used [3,6,8,9,11,13,14]. ReMASC includes various attack conditions with four types of recording devices and multiple recording environments. However, ReMASC has the following problems:

1. Recording devices have inconsistent composition ratios across recording conditions, making it difficult to disentangle device characteristics from environmental factors and to make fair comparisons.
2. The spatial relationship between microphones and sound sources varies across training and evaluation data, making it difficult to assess the impact of each condition on system performance.
3. The absence of validation data makes it difficult to suppress overfitting and adjust parameters.

Additionally, since fair evaluation across recording devices is not possible and the impact of each recording condition cannot be analyzed individually, the reliability of the evaluation framework is limited.

Therefore, in this study, we propose a new evaluation framework for spoofing attack detection using multi-channel information by redesigning ReMASC. Specifically, by providing data splits with unified conditions across recording devices through the redesign of ReMASC[1], fair and reproducible experimental design and model evaluation under various recording conditions become possible, contributing as a research foundation for related fields. By evaluating existing methods using the redesigned subsets, we revealed that the performance differences across recording devices that have been reported are attributable to characteristics inherent to the recording devices rather than condition bias.

The structure of this paper is as follows. First, Sect. 2 analyzes the composition of the ReMASC dataset, and Sect. 3 details the data cleaning and new subset splitting methods. Section 4 discusses the impact of recording devices and environmental conditions on detection performance based on evaluation experiment results using the redesigned dataset, and finally Sect. 5 summarizes this research.

2 Composition of ReMASC

This section analyzes the data composition of ReMASC and the label composition ratios across recording devices, and describes the problems with existing subset splits.

[1] https://github.com/shiotalab-tmu/remasc_curated_splits.

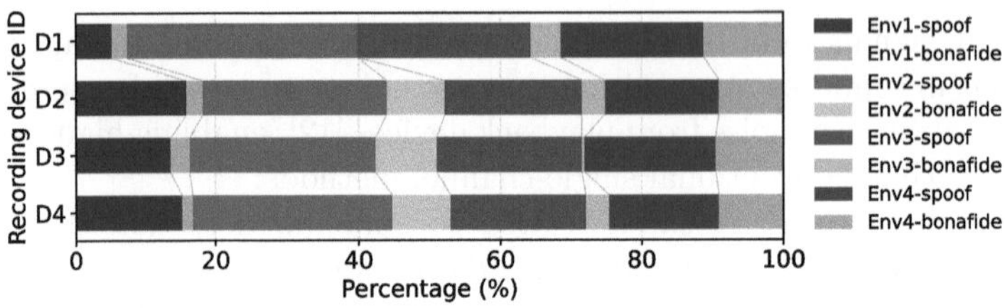

Fig. 1. Composition ratio of bonafide and spoofed speech by recording environment (Env) for recording devices D1–D4.

2.1 Recording Conditions of ReMASC

ReMASC is an audio corpus designed to improve the accuracy of spoofing detection for voice-controlled devices. To simulate the diverse environments in which voice-controlled devices operate, recordings were made under various conditions with different recording environments, playback devices, replay source recorders, speakers, position information, and recording devices for both bonafide and spoofed speech. The dataset contains 51 speakers: 50 humans and Text-to-speech (TTS). Four recording environments were employed: Env1 (outdoor), Env2 (quiet room), Env3 (room with background music), and Env4 (inside a car). Position information indicates the relative position between the recording device and the sound source, with labeling schemes varying by environment. In Env1, near and far distance labels are assigned only to spoofed speech. In Env2, labels indicating the absolute position of the recording device within the room and the relative position of the sound source with respect to that recording device are assigned to all audio. In Env3, where both the recording device and the sound source positions are fixed, no positional labels are assigned. In Env4, labels indicating vehicle motion and the speaker's position are assigned to bonafide speech, while sound source position labels are assigned to spoofed speech. Three types of replay source recorders, including TTS, were used. Four playback devices were used with labels assigned only to spoofed speech. Recording devices consist of four types of microphone arrays: D1 (2 channels), D2 (4 channels), D3 (6 channels), and D4 (7 channels).

2.2 Problems with ReMASC

Although ReMASC comprises audio recordings under diverse conditions, it has aspects that render it unsuitable as an evaluation framework for detecting replayed spoofing attacks. Although multiple synthesizers are used for TTS generation, containing elements such as multiple genders and dialects, the same speaker label is assigned, which may affect model performance analysis.

Next, there is the issue that the composition ratios of recording conditions differ across recording devices. Figure 1 shows the composition ratio of recording environments (Env) for each recording device, and the ratio of bonafide speech to spoofed speech (spoof) in each environment. As shown in Fig. 1, the composition

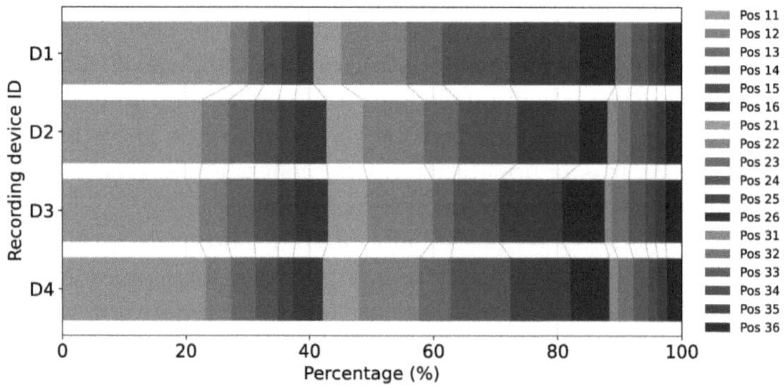

Fig. 2. Position information labels in Env2 for recording devices (D1–D4).

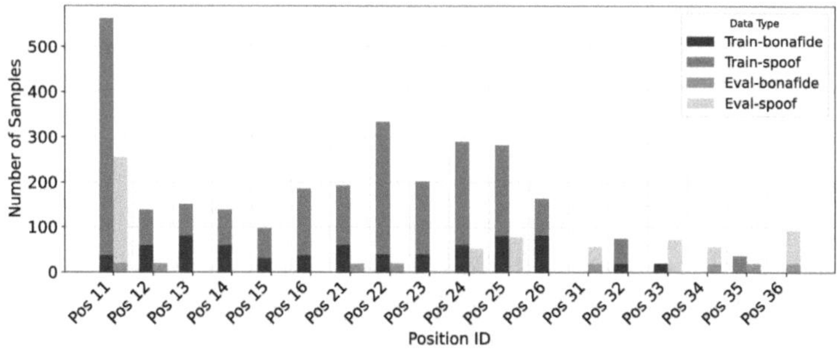

Fig. 3. Number of data items by relative position labels between recording device and playback device included in training and evaluation data for Env2 recorded with D2.

ratios of the recording environments differ across recording devices. Furthermore, even within the same recording environment, the ratio of bonafide to spoofed speech is inconsistent across recording devices. This causes problems in performance comparison across recording devices. The composition ratios of both recording environments and bonafide/spoofed speech differ across devices, making it impossible to separate device characteristics from differences in recording conditions. Furthermore, Fig. 2 shows the composition ratio of position information (Pos) in Env2 for each recording device. The figure shows that, even within the same environment, the composition of positional information varies across recording devices. This further prevents isolating device characteristics from differences in the composition of recording conditions.

Another problem is that the publicly available subsets do not allow independent analysis of the impact of various recording conditions on identification accuracy. The subsets are train and eval, with speaker labels mutually exclusive between them. However, conditions other than speakers—such as position information and recording environment—share values across both subsets. Figure 3 illustrates this issue using Env2 audio from recording device D2, showing the distribution of bonafide and spoofed (spoof) files by position label across train and eval. While Pos 11 contains both bonafide and spoof in both subsets (known), other positions exhibit inconsistent patterns: some appear in only one subset (unknown), while others show mixed patterns where only bonafide or spoof is known. Because known and unknown labels are mixed in recording conditions other than speakers, it is impossible to distinguish whether identification failure is due to unknown speakers or unknown conditions.

Finally, since the subsets consist only of train and eval, verification during training is difficult, hindering overfitting suppression and parameter optimization. Additionally, when using a subset of the training data for validation, the specific samples used are not documented, preventing reproducible and valid model evaluation.

3 Reconstruction of ReMASC

This section explains the reconstruction policy for ReMASC, which consists of two stages: data cleaning and splitting algorithms, designed to address the problems described in Sect. 2.2.

3.1 Data Cleaning

To standardize the composition ratios of recording conditions across recording devices, cleaning process is applied to the audio data in ReMASC. Each audio data is associated with six types of recording conditions: audio type (bonafide/spoof), recording environment, playback device, replay source recorder, speaker, and position information. Let the label sets for each recording condition be $\mathcal{L}_1, \ldots, \mathcal{L}_M$, then all condition combinations are represented by the Cartesian product $\mathcal{C} = \mathcal{L}_1 \times \cdots \times \mathcal{L}_M$ ($M = 6$). For fair comparison across recording devices, data must be consistent across all conditions. Therefore, TTS audio and D1 data were excluded, due to the issues in Sect. 2.2 and D1's lack of Env2 bonafide data (Fig. 1), respectively. Additionally, Pos0 data in Env4 were excluded, as its corresponding playback device (a built-in vehicular audio system) is unique to Env4 and contains only spoof audio.

After excluding TTS audio and D1 data, data cleaning was performed using the following procedure to further align the data volume for each condition combination. First, for each condition combination $c \in \mathcal{C}$, the number of data items $n_{c,d}$ for recording device d was aggregated, and the minimum number $k_c = \min(n_{c,d})$ was set as the adopted number of data items for that condition. Next, for all recording devices, k_c items of data belonging to combination c were randomly extracted. However, since condition combinations with extremely small amounts of data lack statistical reliability, combinations where $k_c < \tau$ were excluded from the analysis (in this work, $\tau = 10$). Finally, the cleaned dataset $\mathcal{D}'$ consists of recording devices D2, D3, and D4, and as shown in Table 1, the number of data items and bonafide/spoof ratio across recording devices are equalized.

This processing enables evaluation of performance differences originating from recording devices, independent of data volume bias.

Table 1. Number of utterances by recording device before and after data cleaning

Recording Device	Original		After Cleaning	
	Bona	Spoof	Bona	Spoof
D1	1,473	6,873	0	0
D2	2,452	8,212	2,017	4,651
D3	2,159	7,941	2,017	4,651
D4	2,365	8,311	2,017	4,651

3.2 Subset Splitting Policy

In this section, splitting data into train, dev, and eval to create one set ($\mathcal{D}_{\text{train}}$, $\mathcal{D}_{\text{dev}}, \mathcal{D}_{\text{eval}}$) is called a "data split." The data splits proposed are of two types: (1) fully-closed split where all conditions are known in training, development (validation), and evaluation data, and (2) partially-open split where only specific conditions are unknown. In both data splits, adjustments are made so that the data volume ratio is as close as possible to $|\mathcal{D}_{\text{train}}|:|\mathcal{D}_{\text{dev}}|:|\mathcal{D}_{\text{eval}}| = 3:1:1$ (target ratio) and the ratio of bonafide to spoof is equal across subsets. Additionally, since some recording conditions exist only in spoof, pseudo-labels following the spoof label distribution were randomly assigned to bonafide prior to data splitting. Without these labels, bonafide utterances cannot follow the same subset assignment as spoof in partially-open splits, breaking the control of known and unknown conditions.

Fully-Closed Split. In a fully-closed split, data is split so that the same conditions appear in all subsets of training, development, and evaluation. This allows model performance to be evaluated while excluding the impact of unknown conditions on identification performance, since the model does not encounter unknown conditions. Specifically, data sets matching condition combination $c \in \mathcal{C}$ from $\mathcal{D}'$ were randomly allocated to $\mathcal{D}_{\text{train}}, \mathcal{D}_{\text{dev}}, \mathcal{D}_{\text{eval}}$ according to the split ratio of 3:1:1. This enables fair comparison across recording devices and evaluation of baseline performance excluding the influence of unknown conditions while matching the recording conditions included in each subset.

Partially-Open Split: Splitting Algorithm. In a partially-open split, data is split so that only specific recording conditions are unknown. In this case, the utterance count ratio and bonafide/spoof ratio between each subset may deviate from the target ratio depending on how the condition labels are split. Therefore, an algorithm is needed that searches for data splits with only specific recording conditions unknown, while keeping the error from the target ratio as small as possible.

Let the set of labels for the recording condition to be made unknown be $\mathcal{L}$, and consider splitting this label set into three mutually exclusive subsets (L_{train},

L_{dev}, L_{eval}). At this time, when the number of label types $|\mathcal{L}|$ for the condition to be made unknown is large, the number of combination candidates becomes enormous, or when $|\mathcal{L}| = 2$, it becomes impossible to realize a mutually exclusive split into three subsets. Therefore, in this study, we decided to separate the data splitting algorithm depending on the number of label types for the condition to be made unknown as follows: (1) When the number of types is large: Heuristic search method, (2) When the number of types is small: Complete enumeration combination method, (3) When the number of types is 2: Binary split method. Below, we describe the details of each splitting algorithm.

When the Number of Label Types is Large. When the number of label types $|\mathcal{L}|$ is large, it is not practical to enumerate all label splits and select the optimal split. Therefore, we aim to obtain only a finite number of label splits by appropriately limiting the number of label combinations. We propose a heuristic search method that combines a label combination candidate generation algorithm to limit the number of combinations to be searched and a data split selection algorithm to retain appropriate data splits. The procedure for the candidate generation algorithm is shown in Algorithm 1, and the procedure for the data split selection algorithm is shown in Algorithm 2, respectively.

The label combination candidate generation algorithm (Algorithm 1) randomly splits the label set $\mathcal{L}$ for the recording condition to be made unknown into three parts to generate three label set subsets ($L_{\text{train}}, L_{\text{dev}}, L_{\text{eval}}$), and constructs the data subsets ($\mathcal{D}_{\text{train}}$, $\mathcal{D}_{\text{dev}}$, $\mathcal{D}_{\text{eval}}$) corresponding to those label subsets. At this time, constraint condition $\mathcal{K}$ is introduced to reject conditions where the data volume after label splitting is clearly insufficient, in order to prevent combinatorial explosion. For each obtained data split of the cleaned dataset $\mathcal{D}'$, the errors e_{utt}, e_{sratio} are calculated by the `CalculateErrors` function. Let $\mathcal{D}'^{\text{spoof}} = \{f \in \mathcal{D}' \mid f \text{ is spoof}\}$, and similarly $\mathcal{D}_s^{\text{spoof}} = \{f \in \mathcal{D}_s \mid f \text{ is spoof}\}$ for each subset. The utterance count error measures deviation from the target ratio 3:1:1:

$$e_{\text{utt}} = \left|\frac{|\mathcal{D}_{\text{train}}|}{|\mathcal{D}'|} - \frac{3}{5}\right| + \left|\frac{|\mathcal{D}_{\text{dev}}|}{|\mathcal{D}'|} - \frac{1}{5}\right| + \left|\frac{|\mathcal{D}_{\text{eval}}|}{|\mathcal{D}'|} - \frac{1}{5}\right|. \tag{1}$$

The spoof ratio error measures deviation from the overall spoof ratio:

$$e_{\text{sratio}} = \sum_{s \in \{\text{train, dev, eval}\}} \left|\frac{|\mathcal{D}_s^{\text{spoof}}|}{|\mathcal{D}_s|} - \frac{|\mathcal{D}'^{\text{spoof}}|}{|\mathcal{D}'|}\right|. \tag{2}$$

The label combination candidate combined with these errors becomes one element of the candidate set with error $\mathcal{P}_{\text{cand}}$. The search is repeated until the predetermined search time limit $P_{\max}$ is reached, yielding a set of label split candidates.

The subsequent data split selection algorithm (Algorithm 2) selects appropriate data split candidates from $\mathcal{P}_{\text{cand}}$ generated by Algorithm 1 according to the target. The procedure involves sequentially selecting appropriate candidates from $\mathcal{P}_{\text{cand}}$ and adding them to the selected data split set $\mathcal{S}_{\text{final}}$. For this purpose,

Algorithm 1. Heuristic Search Method Step 1: Label Combination Candidate Generation

Require: Cleaned data $\mathcal{D}'$, target label set $\mathcal{L}$
Require: Constraint conditions for splitting $\mathcal{K}$
Require: Maximum number of candidates $P_{\max}$
Ensure: Data split candidate set with error $\mathcal{P}_{\text{cand}}$
$\mathcal{P}_{\text{cand}} \leftarrow \emptyset$
while $|\mathcal{P}_{\text{cand}}| < P_{\max}$ **do**
  $(L_{\text{train}}, L_{\text{dev}}, L_{\text{eval}}) \leftarrow$ Randomly split label set $\mathcal{L}$ into 3 based on constraint $\mathcal{K}$
  $\forall s \in \{\text{train}, \text{dev}, \text{eval}\} : \mathcal{D}_s \leftarrow \{x \in \mathcal{D}' \mid x \text{ is labeled as } l,\ l \in L_s\}$
  $e_{\text{utt}}, e_{\text{sratio}} \leftarrow \text{CalculateErrors}(\mathcal{D}_{\text{train}}, \mathcal{D}_{\text{dev}}, \mathcal{D}_{\text{eval}})$
  $\mathcal{P}_{\text{cand}} \leftarrow \mathcal{P}_{\text{cand}} \cup \{((\mathcal{D}_{\text{train}}, \mathcal{D}_{\text{dev}}, \mathcal{D}_{\text{eval}}), e_{\text{utt}}, e_{\text{sratio}})\}$
end while
return $\mathcal{P}_{\text{cand}}$

Algorithm 2. Heuristic Search Method Step 2: Data Split Selection

Require: Candidate split set $\mathcal{P}_{\text{cand}}$ (output of Alg. 1), number of adopted data split sets N
Require: Diversity criterion $\mathcal{M}$
Ensure: Adopted data split set $\mathcal{S}_{\text{final}}$
$\mathcal{S}_{\text{final}} \leftarrow \emptyset$
while $|\mathcal{S}_{\text{final}}| < N$ **do**
  $\mathcal{P}_{\text{remain}} \leftarrow \mathcal{P}_{\text{cand}} - \mathcal{S}_{\text{final}}$
  $c_{\text{next}} \leftarrow \text{SelectCandidate}(\mathcal{P}_{\text{remain}}, \mathcal{S}_{\text{final}}, \mathcal{M})$
  if c_{next} is None **then**
    break
  end if
  $\mathcal{S}_{\text{final}} \leftarrow \mathcal{S}_{\text{final}} \cup \{c_{\text{next}}\}$
end while
return $\mathcal{S}_{\text{final}}$

there is a function SelectCandidate that selects appropriate candidates. SelectCandidate performs the process of selecting candidates that satisfy the diversity criterion $\mathcal{M}$ from the current unselected candidates $\mathcal{P}_{\text{remain}}$. Here, the diversity criterion $\mathcal{M}$ is a criterion that lowers the evaluation of candidates whose data volume ratio per subset or spoof ratio deviates from the target ratio, or whose label composition is too similar compared to already selected combination candidates. This series of processes is repeated until the number of selected data split sets reaches a target number N, as shown in Algorithm 2. This allows the construction of subset groups corresponding to label splits with small errors from the target ratio and low mutual correlation.

When the Number of Label Types is Small. When the number of label types $|\mathcal{L}|$ for the condition to be made unknown is small, it may not be possible to satisfy the target ratio of 3:1:1 for data volume in subsets train, dev, and eval. Therefore, when the number of label types is small, a target ratio is set individually, and

Algorithm 3. Data Splitting by Complete Enumeration Combination Method

Require: Cleaned data $\mathcal{D}'$, label set of recording condition to be made unknown $\mathcal{L}$
Require: Allocation ratio for each subset $r_{\text{train}}, r_{\text{dev}}, r_{\text{eval}}$
Ensure: Data split set $\mathcal{S}_{\text{total}}$

```
S_total ← ∅
P ← Set of all label splits that divide label set L into three mutually exclusive
    subsets (L_train, L_dev, L_eval) at ratio r_train : r_dev : r_eval
for each split (L_train, L_dev, L_eval) ∈ P do
    ∀s ∈ {train, dev, eval} : D_s ← {x ∈ D' | x is labeled as l, l ∈ L_s}
    S_total ← S_total ∪ {(D_train, D_dev, D_eval)}
end for
return S_total
```

all combinations satisfying that ratio are enumerated. This procedure is called the complete enumeration combination method. As shown in Algorithm 3, the procedure generates all label split candidates that split the label set $\mathcal{L}$ into three mutually exclusive subsets $(L_{\text{train}}, L_{\text{dev}}, L_{\text{eval}})$ to satisfy the target allocation ratio $r_{\text{train}} : r_{\text{dev}} : r_{\text{eval}}$ for each subset. Then, for each label split, data with the corresponding labels is extracted to construct subsets.

When Only Two Label Types Exist. When only two label types exist for the condition to be made unknown, it is not possible to construct a split that is mutually unknown to all three subsets. In that case, one label is assigned to eval, and the other label is assigned to train and dev. This policy is called the binary split method. For allocation to train and dev, random splitting is performed based on the predetermined ratio $|D_{\text{train}}|{:}|D_{\text{dev}}|$ while considering factors such as the ratio of utterance counts.

Partially-Open Split: Application to Each Condition. This section shows the specific settings and processing procedures for applying the splitting algorithms explained in the previous section to each recording condition included in ReMASC and actually constructing partially-open splits. Table 2 summarizes the number of labels $|\mathcal{L}|$, the adopted splitting policy algorithm, and constraint condition $\mathcal{K}$ for each recording condition set as an unknown condition.

Recording Environment. The label set $\mathcal{L}$ for recording environment consists of four types: Env1, Env2, Env3, and Env4 ($|\mathcal{L}| = 4$). Since the number of labels is small, the complete enumeration combination method was applied, and subsets were generated with constraint condition $\mathcal{K}$ set to $r_{\text{train}}{:}r_{\text{dev}}{:}r_{\text{eval}} = 2{:}1{:}1$. As a result, the final number of data split sets created was 12.

Playback Device. There are five types of playback device labels in total, but the fifth type, the built-in vehicular audio system, was excluded during data cleaning (Sect. 3.1). Therefore, data splitting was performed using four types of

Table 2. Applied algorithms and settings for each condition in partially-open split

Unknown Condition	$\lvert\mathcal{L}\rvert$	Split Method	Constraint $\mathcal{K}$ and Settings	#Splits
Recording Env.	4	Algo. 3	r_{train}:r_{dev}:r_{eval} = 2:1:1	12
Playback Device	4	Algo. 3	r_{train}:r_{dev}:r_{eval} = 2:1:1	12
Replay Source Rec.	2	Binary	$\lvert D_{\text{train}}\rvert$:$\lvert D_{\text{dev}}\rvert$ = 4:1	2
Speaker	49	Algo. 1,2	r_{train}:r_{dev}:r_{eval} = 3:1:1, $e_{\text{utt}}, e_{\text{sratio}} \leq 0.05$	15
Position (Env1)	2	Binary	$\lvert D_{\text{train}}\rvert$:$\lvert D_{\text{dev}}\rvert$ = 4:1	2
Position (Env2)	18	Algo. 1,2	$\lvert L_{\text{train}}\rvert \geq 6$, $e_{\text{utt}}, e_{\text{sratio}} \leq 0.05$	15
Position (Env4)	6	Algo. 1,2	$\lvert L_{\text{train}}\rvert \geq 3$, $e_{\text{utt}}, e_{\text{sratio}} \leq 0.2$	15

playback device labels. Under this setting, the complete enumeration combination method was applied as the splitting algorithm, and subsets were generated with constraint condition $\mathcal{K}$ set to r_{train}:r_{dev}:r_{eval} = 2:1:1. As a result, the final number of data split sets created was 12.

Replay source recorder. Since there are only two types of replay source recorder labels, the binary split method was applied. In this case, the number of data split sets is 2. The data allocation ratio for train and dev was set to $\lvert D_{\text{train}}\rvert$:$\lvert D_{\text{dev}}\rvert$ = 4:1.

Speaker. There are 49 types of speaker labels (Spk40 was excluded in data cleaning because of insufficient data amount). Complete enumeration of all combinations is not practical, so a heuristic search method was used. Constraint condition $\mathcal{K}$ was set to r_{train}:r_{dev}:r_{eval} = 3:1:1, and data split candidates were generated with $P_{\max} = 10^6$. The procedure for the diversity criterion $\mathcal{M}$ is as follows: (1) From the data split candidate set, keep only those where both e_{utt} and e_{sratio} are 0.05 or less. (2) If no data split has been selected yet, select the candidate with the lowest $e_{\text{utt}} + e_{\text{sratio}}$; otherwise, select the candidate that maximizes the mean Jaccard distance averaged over the three subsets and over all already-selected data splits. (3) Repeat step (2) until the number of selected data split sets reaches N (= 15).

Position Information. Position information labels have different meanings and numbers of label types for each recording environment, so the splitting policy needs to be changed for each environment. Below are the specific settings for each environment.

Env1: Position information labels consist of only two types, "near distance" and "far distance," so the binary split method was applied. In this case, the number of data split sets is 2. The data allocation ratio for train and dev was set to $\lvert D_{\text{train}}\rvert$:$\lvert D_{\text{dev}}\rvert$ = 4:1.

Env2: Position information labels are defined as 18 types in total by the product of 3 installation positions of the recording device and 6 combinations of distance and angle of the sound source relative to the device. Since the number of labels is large and exhaustive search is difficult, the heuristic search method was used. Constraint condition $\mathcal{K}$ was set to require that the train subset contains at least 6 types of labels ($|L_{\text{train}}| \geq 6$), and data split candidates were generated with $P_{\max} = 10^6$. The same diversity criterion $\mathcal{M}$ as in the Speaker condition was applied, resulting in 15 data splits.

Env3: Since position information is fixed to one pattern, this was excluded from partially-open splits regarding position.

Env4: In Env4, bonafide speech is assigned vehicle motion and speaker position labels, while spoofed speech is assigned only sound source position labels. Since bonafide position labels include vehicle motion while spoofed ones do not, data splitting was performed using only the sound-source position labels common to both. Constraint condition $\mathcal{K}$ was set to require that the train subset contains at least 3 positions ($|L_{\text{train}}| \geq 3$). Data split candidates were generated with $P_{\max} = 10^6$. The same diversity criterion $\mathcal{M}$ as in the Speaker condition was applied, with the threshold for both e_{utt} and e_{sratio} relaxed to 0.2 because no candidate satisfied the original threshold, resulting in 15 data splits.

4 Experiments

Using the re-designed, composition-matched subsets, we evaluate existing multi-channel spoofing detection methods to test whether reported device gaps are truly device-driven and to quantify condition effects via fully-closed vs. partially-open splits.

4.1 Experimental Conditions

In this experiment, we adopted mch-SSL-AASIST [13] as a spoofing-detection method that utilizes multi-channel input. This method inputs multi-channel acoustic features extracted by a pre-trained model based on self-supervised learning (SSL) into an AASIST backend [4] for identification, and high performance has been reported in prior studies.

The subsets used in this experiment were constructed using the method described in Sect. 3.2. The parameters involved in subset construction (τ, the thresholds for e_{utt} and e_{sratio}, and N) were determined based on preliminary experiments. Note that these parameters are specific to the present settings and are not universally fixed; in general, they can be set in various ways depending on the corpus and task, e.g., by setting the threshold for each error relative to the median error across candidates.

For training, the train subsets from each data split were used; for evaluation, the eval subsets were used. The dev set was used for early-stopping monitoring with a patience of 20 epochs; early stopping was disabled during the first 20 epochs of learning rate warmup. The final model adopted was the model from the epoch with the minimum EER on the dev subset.

For the SSL frontend, pre-trained wav2vec2.0 XLSR (0.3B) [1] was used, and the backend was trained from random initialization. Also, the parameters of the

SSL frontend were updated simultaneously with the backend. Since the recording devices in ReMASC (D2, D3, D4) have different numbers of channels, and the model structure changes accordingly, independent models were trained for each recording device. Other detailed training parameters were set to the same settings as in [13]. All random seeds for data cleaning, pseudo-label assignment, data splitting, and model training were fixed to 0. Data cleaning was performed once, and all splits were derived from the cleaned data.

As preprocessing, all audio data was downsampled to 16 kHz, and as in [3,6,9,13], the first 1 s of each utterance was extracted and used as input. EER was used as the evaluation metric. Training and evaluation were performed for both fully-closed split and partially-open split, and for the latter, the average EER across multiple subsets is reported.

4.2 Experimental Results

Table 3 shows the experimental results for each split condition. First, the conventional ReMASC subset (original, speaker-open setting) and the proposed partially-open split for the speaker are compared. In the original split, the EER across recording devices was relatively close at 7–11%, whereas in the new split, the performance gap widened significantly. The bias in recording conditions included in the conventional split likely obscured performance differences between recording devices, and unifying the composition ratios revealed differences attributable to inherent device characteristics. The tendency for D3 to achieve the lowest EER, followed by D2 and D4, was consistently observed across the fully-closed and most partially-open splits, reinforcing that the tendency reflects inherent device characteristics.

Next, we compare the impact of different unknown conditions on detection performance. The fully-closed split achieved a mean EER of 1.77%, while all partially-open splits showed degradation. The largest degradation occurred when the recording environment was unknown, with a mean EER of 26.13%. Analyzing the results for each data split, when the evaluation set consisted of Env4, the EER exceeded approximately 35%, indicating a severe impact of domain mismatch with in-vehicle noise sources, such as road noise and turn signals. The EER also approached 30% even without Env4 in the evaluation set, suggesting that differences in recording environments generally have a substantial adverse effect on detection performance. The second-largest degradation was for position in Env1 (mean EER of 20.88%). A closer look at individual splits revealed that the mean EER exceeded 27% when trained on near-field and evaluated on far-field data, but dropped to approximately 14% in the reverse case, indicating that performance degrades when evaluation data is noisier than training data. Note that position-based splits are conducted per environment, yielding fewer samples per subset, and that sensitivity to the random seed is also high. These findings suggest that environmental mismatch, especially noise types absent during training, most critically affects detection performance, and that robustness may be improved by incorporating Env4-like conditions via data augmentation and noise superimposition.

Table 3. EER (%) of mch-SSL-AASIST for each split condition. Average values calculated for all subset splits for each recording device and macro average values for all recording devices are shown.

Split Type	Unknown Condition	EER by Recording Device (%)			
		D2	D3	D4	Avg.
Fully-closed	–	3.66	0.47	1.17	1.77
Partially-open	Recording Env.	26.37	24.51	27.50	26.13
	Playback Device	11.96	2.33	15.77	10.02
	Position (Env1)	32.56	8.99	21.10	20.88
	Position (Env2)	6.04	0.39	16.11	7.51
	Position (Env4)	13.33	5.98	16.13	11.82
	Replay Source Rec.	7.98	2.03	8.22	6.07
	Speaker	10.39	1.41	10.74	7.52
Original [13]	Speaker	7.6	10.6	8.3	8.8

4.3 Discussion

From the results of this study, it became evident that the recording environment is the most dominant factor in multi-channel spoofing detection. In particular, in in-vehicle environments, reverberation, broadband noise, and road noise vary simultaneously, rendering features based on sound-source position unstable. This finding suggests that the spatial consistency exploited by existing methods, which assume a stable microphone array environment, can be severely degraded by environmental noise. Consequently, future model designs should explicitly consider environmental normalization and robustness to noise.

Furthermore, by unifying the composition ratios across recording conditions and introducing partially-open splits, this study enabled factor separation that was difficult to achieve with the conventional ReMASC setup. The result confirmed that the proposed framework functions as an evaluation methodology capable of independently analyzing the impact of individual recording conditions on system performance. This framework is applicable not only to spoofing detection but also to a wide range of audio-related tasks, such as far-field speaker recognition [7] and speech quality estimation [5,10], where multiple recording conditions are intricately intertwined.

On the other hand, this study has several limitations. First, since certain conditions were excluded during data cleaning, the overall coverage of the ReMASC dataset was reduced. In particular, the exclusion of recording device D1 resulted in incomplete preservation of device diversity. Second, although this study primarily focused on mch-SSL-AASIST, a more comprehensive comparison that includes beamforming-based methods [3,9] and spectrogram-based methods [6] remains an important direction for future work.

5 Conclusion

In this study, we redesigned the ReMASC corpus to enable fair and systematic evaluation of spoofing detection using multi-channel information. By unifying the composition ratios of recording conditions and introducing controlled evaluation splits, the proposed framework eliminates condition bias, enabling a precise analysis of device-specific performance characteristics. Experimental results confirm that the effects of individual recording conditions can be independently assessed, with unknown conditions causing notable performance degradation. The framework facilitates fair model comparison and factor analysis, and provides a solid foundation for spoofing detection and other audio-related tasks.

References

1. Babu, A.: XLS-R: self-supervised cross-lingual speech representation learning at scale. In: Proceedings of Interspeech, pp. 2278–2282 (2022)
2. Gong, Y., Yang, J., Huber, J., MacKnight, M., Poellabauer, C.: ReMASC: realistic replay attack corpus for voice controlled systems. In: Proceedings of Interspeech, pp. 2355–2359 (2019)
3. Gong, Y., Yang, J., Poellabauer, C.: Detecting replay attacks using multi-channel audio: a neural network-based method. IEEE Signal Process. Lett. **27**, 920–924 (2020)
4. Jung, J.W., et al.: AASIST: audio anti-spoofing using integrated spectro-temporal graph attention networks. In: Proceedings of ICASSP, pp. 6367–6371 (2022)
5. Li, C., et al.: ICASSP 2026 URGENT challenge. https://urgent-challenge.github.io/urgent2026/
6. Li, Z., et al.: Robust detection of machine-induced audio attacks in intelligent audio systems with microphone array. In: Proceedings of ACM SIGSAC, pp. 1884–1899 (2021)
7. Nandwana, M.K., van Hout, J., Richey, C., McLaren, M., Barrios, M.A., Lawson, A.: The VOiCES from a distance challenge 2019. In: Proceedings of Interspeech, pp. 2438–2442 (2019)
8. Neri, M., Virtanen, T.: Impact of microphone array mismatches to learning-based replay speech detection. In: Proceedings of EUSIPCO, pp. 1243–1247 (2025)
9. Neri, M., Virtanen, T.: Multi-channel replay speech detection using an adaptive learnable beamformer. IEEE Open J. Signal Process. **6**, 530–535 (2025)
10. Reddy, C.K., Gopal, V., Cutler, R.: DNSMOS: a non-intrusive perceptual objective speech quality metric to evaluate noise suppressors. In: Proceedings of ICASSP (2021)
11. Talukder, M., Xie, J.: Exploiting playback device's effect on multi-channel audio to secure voice assistants. In: Proceedings of GLOBECOM, pp. 6085–6090 (2022)
12. Yaguchi, R., Shiota, S., Ono, N., Kiya, H.: Replay attack detection based on spatial and spectral features of stereo signal. J. Inf. Process. **29**, 275–282 (2021)
13. Yamaguchi, T., Shiota, S., Tawara, N.: Investigating self-supervised learning-based front-end for multi-channel replay attack detection. In: Proceedings of APSIPA ASC, pp. 2098–2103 (2025)
14. Yang, Q., Cui, K., Zheng, Y.: Room-scale voice liveness detection for smart devices. IEEE Trans. Dependable Secure Comput. **21**(5), 4982–4996 (2024)

Network and Systems Security

Resource-Bounded Early Identification of Encrypted Video Traffic at Line Rate

Chong Chen[3], Lizhi Peng[1,3](✉), Liang Jiao[2], and Rui Li[2]

[1] Quancheng Laboratory, Jinan 250022, China
[2] National Computer Network Emergency Response Technical Team/Coordination Center of China Shandong Branch, Jining, China
{jiaol,lir}@cert.org.cn
[3] Shandong Key Laboratory of Ubiquitous Intelligent Computing, University of Jinan, Jinan 250022, China
plz@ujn.edu.cn

Abstract. End-to-end encryption and protocol-stack heterogeneity reduce path observability, yet operators still require early, payload-agnostic decisions at line rate under strict constraints: fixed memory, constant per-packet cost, and bounded latency. We propose an end-to-end framework in which the Network Interface Card (NIC) leverages symmetric Receive-Side Scaling (RSS) to provide multi-queue demultiplexing. On the fast path, a minimal observation updates a fixed-memory multi-tier sketch coarse filter and preserves compact short sequences for candidate flows; an arrival-driven scan further guarantees an upper bound on decision latency. On the slow path, we extract an 8-dimensional short-window feature set and apply a lightweight classifier. Experiments demonstrate strong early decidability and effectiveness in open scenarios, and a prototype achieves near line-rate throughput under saturated 10 GbE stress tests with zero drops and no backpressure.

Keywords: High-speed networks · Traffic identification · Machine learning

1 Introduction

End-to-end encryption has become the default practice for mainstream content delivery and video services [1]. Meanwhile, protocol-stack heterogeneity (e.g., Transport Layer Security (TLS) and Quick UDP Internet Connections (QUIC)) further weakens observability from the network path, rendering payload-dependent deep packet inspection and content features inapplicable in many scenarios. In this context, operators and large campus/data-center gateways still need to identify encrypted video flows as early as possible from mixed background traffic to support online tasks such as traffic engineering, congestion and bandwidth management, quality-of-service assurance, and security auditing. Such deployments are typically located at mirror ports or egress gateways; facing

© IFIP International Federation for Information Processing 2026
Published by Springer Nature Switzerland AG 2026
H. Janicke et al. (Eds.): SEC 2026, IFIP AICT 787, pp. 405–418, 2026.
https://doi.org/10.1007/978-3-032-27993-4_28

highly concurrent sessions and bursty traffic, the system must operate stably at line rate while satisfying three hard constraints: an approximately constant per-packet cost on the fast path, a strict fixed upper bound on state memory, and a provable upper bound on decision latency within a short observation window.

Related work falls into two lines: learning/representation-driven encrypted traffic classification (e.g., Deep Packet) [2], which is accurate but often requires longer observations or heavier inference, and line-rate measurement with resource-bounded data-plane structures (e.g., SketchVisor) [3], which is deployable but usually exposes only aggregated statistics. As a result, existing frameworks rarely retain, under a fixed memory budget, the short-window time–packet-length sequence evidence needed for early decisions, leaving a gap between line-rate deployability and usable evidence preservation.

Figure 1 illustrates the system architecture. To close this gap, we design a layered framework with three components: hardware demultiplexing, fixed-memory coarse filtering, and lightweight slow-path inference. The Network Interface Card uses symmetric Receive-Side Scaling (RSS) [4] to generate a direction-invariant flow identifier and steer packets to multiple queues. Fast-path workers reduce each arriving packet to a minimal observation tuple and update Multi-Tier Sketch (MTSketch) online. Under a fixed memory budget, MTSketch suppresses most background flows while preserving compact time–length evidence for a small set of candidates, and exports snapshots via an arrival-driven scanning mechanism once termination rules are met. The slow path computes DLTES-8(Directional Length–Time Early Statistics, DLTES-8) features from each snapshot and applies a lightweight classifier to output video/non-video decisions. Decoupling the fast and slow paths keeps the fast path constant-cost, while allowing the slow path to scale with available resources.

We summarize our contributions in this paper as follows:

- We propose MTSketch, a fixed-memory multi-tier coarse filtering structure. While keeping constant-cost fast-path processing at line rate, MTSketch preserves high-fidelity short "arrival-time–packet-length" sequence evidence for candidate flows. An arrival-driven scanning mechanism further provides a provable upper bound on termination-detection latency, enabling short-window early decisions under resource-bounded deployment constraints.
- We propose DLTES-8, an 8-dimensional short-window feature set for early encrypted video identification. Using only payload-agnostic signals (timestamps and packet lengths), it outperforms representative baselines under the same observation budget. We also release a public, labeled dataset (with aligned start-up windows) to enable reproducible and comparable research.
- We build an end-to-end prototype with multi-queue demultiplexing, a constant-cost fast path, and an asynchronous slow path. Real-link and high-load experiments achieve near line-rate throughput with zero drops and no backpressure, demonstrating practical deployability.

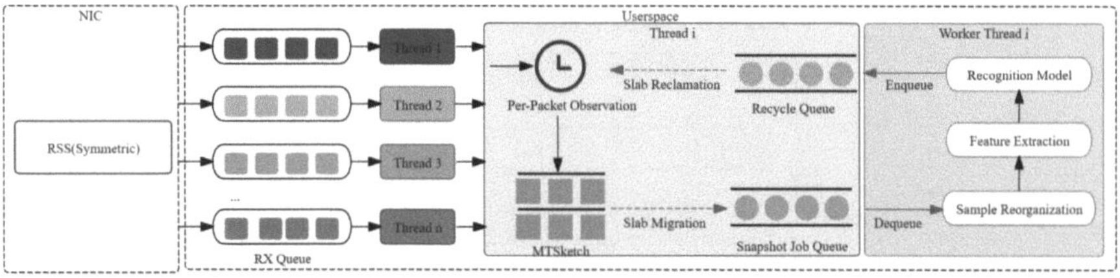

Fig. 1. System architecture of the proposed framework.

2 Related Work

Encrypted video traffic identification has mainly followed two directions. (i) Probe/endpoint fingerprinting with payload-agnostic signals (e.g., packet sizes and inter-arrival times/rates): Silhouette uses statistical features with thresholding for YouTube but needs extra tuning under low-bitrate/low-resolution settings (e.g., 240p), revealing robustness limits [5]; ITP-KNN leverages segmented-delivery ON/OFF intermittency for nearest-neighbor matching [6]; PPS-A applies CNNs to sliced packet patterns but depends on a longer window ($\approx 120\,\text{s}$) and higher overhead [7]; QoE-driven methods such as ReCLive emphasize online inference tied to application behavior while still trading observation length against inference cost [8]. Under open-world conditions, false positives remain non-trivial at realistic scale and under harsher settings (e.g., different vantage points, shorter flows), motivating evidence-efficient designs that generalize better [9]. In contrast to payload-agnostic schemes, HETC incorporates ciphertext payload features with lightweight learning to enable fast decisions under high traffic volume [10]. (ii) Line-rate/online deployment in switches/SDN: iTeleScope depends on mirroring and controller-assisted software processing, which can add overhead and create bottlenecks [11]; SETA++ scales via sampling and sketches, but sampling inevitably discards packet-level observations and weakens fine-grained timing evidence [12]; Le *et al.* propose sampling-based high-speed video identification without addressing flow preservation and evidence retention under high-speed constraints [13]. More recently, Akem *et al.* embed an ETC-aware Random Forest into P4 switches using packet-size and inter-arrival-time features, achieving line-rate throughput with sub-microsecond delay [14]. K-Flix further offloads clustering/nearest-centroid classification into programmable data planes, but it still primarily relies on accumulated/aggregated flow features, making precise short-window packet-level temporal evidence hard to preserve under a fixed resource budget [15]. Overall, a key gap remains: under fixed memory and constant per-packet cost, how to suppress massive background traffic and retain short-window evidence for a small candidate set with bounded termination delay, enabling engineering-grade early decisions.

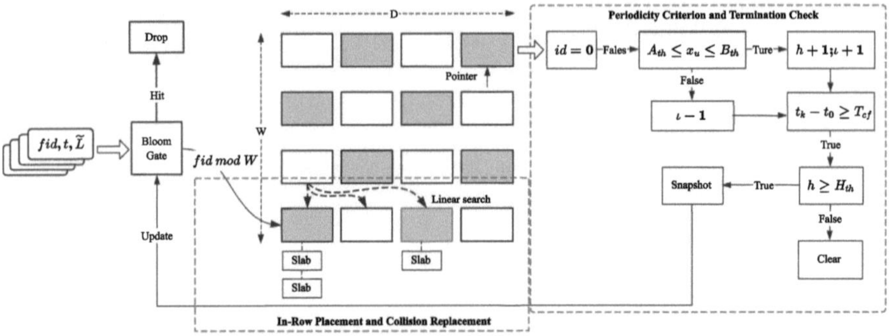

Fig. 2. Overview of the MTSketch structure.

3 Flow Identification and Per-Packet Observation

To unify data-plane observations while remaining payload-agnostic, for each arriving packet we retain only three types of information: a direction-invariant flow identifier fid, the arrival timestamp t, and the transport-layer payload length L_{pay} derived from header fields. We further encode direction consistently via a signed length $\tilde{L}$, so that each packet is abstracted into a minimal triplet $(fid, t, \tilde{L})$, which serves as the sole input to MTSketch.

The direction-invariant flow identifier (fid) is generated by the Network Interface Card (NIC) in hardware. A common practice is to parse packet headers and compute a flow hash in software to obtain the flow identifier; however, this procedure introduces additional per-packet processing overhead and limits scalability on high-throughput links. To reduce observation construction on the data plane to a stable constant cost, we leverage symmetric Receive-Side Scaling (RSS) on the NIC. For each TCP/UDP packet, the NIC computes a Toeplitz hash over the 4-tuple $(IP_s, port_s, IP_d, port_d)$ and outputs a 32-bit value, which we define as fid. Symmetric RSS is invariant under endpoint swapping, so both directions of the same bidirectional flow share the same fid, enabling stable flow attribution and queue mapping. Since 32-bit hashes may collide, their impact is absorbed by the subsequent bounded-memory placement and replacement mechanism in MTSketch.

The signed length $\tilde{L}$ is constructed as follows. For endpoints $(IP_s, port_s)$ and $(IP_d, port_d)$, we define a reference endpoint pair by lexicographic order, i.e., $A = \min_{\text{lex}}\{(IP_s, port_s), (IP_d, port_d)\}$ and $B = \max_{\text{lex}}\{(IP_s, port_s), (IP_d, port_d)\}$. If the packet direction is $(A \to B)$, we set $\tilde{L} = +L_{\text{pay}}$; if the direction is $(B \to A)$, we set $\tilde{L} = -L_{\text{pay}}$:

$$\tilde{L} = \begin{cases} +L_{\text{pay}}, & A \to B, \\ -L_{\text{pay}}, & B \to A. \end{cases} \tag{1}$$

We emphasize that the sign of $\tilde{L}$ indicates only a consistent direction with respect to (A, B) and is not equivalent to the semantic notions of uplink/downlink.

4 Multi-Tier Sketch Filtering

Multi-Tier Sketch (MTSketch) serves as the front-end coarse filter on the system data plane, targeting deployments that require line-rate processing, early decisions within short windows, and a fixed upper bound on resource consumption. Without inspecting payloads, it performs short-window modeling of flows using the per-packet minimal observation $(fid, t, \tilde{L})$: flows suspected to be video are promoted early as candidates and forwarded to the slow path for refined classification, while the vast majority of non-video flows are discarded directly at the front end. The fixed-resource constraint means that both state maintenance and the retention of sequential evidence operate strictly within a pre-configured memory budget, preventing resource usage from growing uncontrollably with the number of concurrent flows. To this end, MTSketch simultaneously guarantees: (i) constant per-packet cost on the fast path; (ii) a fixed memory upper bound; and (iii) a deterministic upper bound on the termination-detection delay after a window expires. Furthermore, to prevent long-lived, high-throughput "elephant" flows from monopolizing capacity, MTSketch places a Bloom filter in front of the sketch as an admission gate, thereby attenuating the interference of markedly non-target flows on sketch residency. The overall workflow of MTSketch is illustrated in Fig. 2.

4.1 Sketch Organization and Cell State

MTSketch maintains a two-dimensional table of size $W_{\text{rows}} \times D_{\text{cols}}$, with a total number of cells $N = W_{\text{rows}} \cdot D_{\text{cols}}$. The direction-invariant 32-bit flow identifier fid is mapped to a row as $r(fid) = fid \bmod W_{\text{rows}}$. Each row provides D_{cols} slots to absorb hash collisions while preserving flow-consistent local state. A cell (r, c) stores

$$C_{r,c} = (id, t_0, x, h, \iota, B), \tag{2}$$

where id is the resident flow identifier (with 0 denoting an empty slot), t_0 is the window start time, x is the arrival count in the current scanning period, h is the number of qualified-period hits, ι is an importance score, and B is a buffer that retains sequential evidence. For each arriving packet $(fid, t, \tilde{L})$, the written sample is $(\Delta t, \tilde{L})$, with $\Delta t = t - t_0$.

4.2 Arrival-Driven Scanning and Termination-Detection Bound

If cells were checked only upon hits, an expired window could be postponed indefinitely when a flow becomes temporarily silent. To provide a deterministic upper bound, MTSketch introduces a scanning period P and advances the checking progress in an arrival-driven manner: instead of relying on extra timer interrupts, the system updates the scan position on each packet arrival according to wall-clock time. Let t_k denote the arrival time of the k-th packet. We define the period index and the intra-period position as

$$u_k = \left\lfloor \frac{t_k}{P} \right\rfloor, \quad p_k = \left\lfloor \frac{N \cdot (t_k \bmod P)}{P} \right\rfloor \in \{0, \ldots, N-1\}. \tag{3}$$

The system keeps the previous arrival's (u_{k-1}, p_{k-1}) and, upon packet k, advances the scan from (u_{k-1}, p_{k-1}) to (u_k, p_k), performing one "period settlement and termination check" for each covered cell. This guarantees that every cell is checked at least once within any period P, thereby bounding the post-expiration snapshot/reset delay by $\leq P$.

4.3 Periodicity Criterion and Termination Check

MTSketch uses the stability of short-window periodicity as the basis for coarse filtering. For a resident flow, let x_u denote its arrival count in the u-th scanning period, and let $A_{\text{th}} < B_{\text{th}}$ be the activity-band thresholds: A_{th} specifies the minimum activity required within a period to filter out low-activity or sporadic bursty flows, while B_{th} specifies an upper bound to suppress excessively dense bursts from dominating the candidate set.

$$A_{\text{th}} \leq x_u \leq B_{\text{th}}. \tag{4}$$

If the above condition holds, the period is qualified; the cell updates $h \leftarrow h + 1$ and increases the importance score ι. Otherwise, ι is decayed, and the counter is reset as $x \leftarrow 0$ to start accumulation for the next period. With period-by-period settlement, the window-level activity pattern is compressed into the qualified-period count h, thereby capturing periodic stability with constant per-packet overhead.

Let T_{cf} denote the coarse-filtering window length. When $t_{\text{k}} - t_0 \geq T_{\text{cf}}$, MTSketch triggers termination and applies a hit threshold H_{th}: if $h \geq H_{\text{th}}$, it outputs a candidate snapshot (fid, t_0, B) to the slow path; otherwise, it resets the cell and releases the slot. Consequently, T_{cf} bounds the maximum observation duration, while $[A_{\text{th}}, B_{\text{th}}]$ and H_{th} control the per-period qualification strength and the number of qualified periods within a window, jointly determining the false-positive/false-negative trade-off.

4.4 In-Row Placement and Collision Replacement

For an arriving packet $(fid, t, \tilde{L})$, MTSketch accesses only its mapped row $r(fid)$ and operates within the D_{cols} slots of that row as follows. If a slot with $id = fid$ exists, the packet hits and the corresponding cell is updated. Otherwise, if an empty slot with $id = 0$ exists, the flow occupies the slot and the cell state is initialized. If neither condition holds, a collision occurs; MTSketch evicts the cell with the smallest importance score ι and takes over its slot. This policy increases the residency probability of flows that are more likely to become candidates and whose sequential evidence is more valuable under a tight capacity budget.

4.5 Multilayer Sequential Evidence and Memory Upper Bound

Unlike conventional sketches that maintain only counters, MTSketch retains compact sequential evidence in the form of $(\Delta t, \tilde{L})$ under a fixed memory budget, so that the slow path can infer without replaying raw packets. To accommodate long-tailed traffic distributions while ensuring that mice flows do not waste space and elephant flows can be sampled on demand, MTSketch adopts a two-tier design. Each cell embeds a fixed-capacity buffer $B^{(S)}$ that stores at most S sample pairs. Excess samples are appended in blocks to a slab list $B^{(\text{slab})}$, where each slab block holds b_{blk} sample pairs, and the total number of slab blocks is capped by L.

Let s_{pair} denote the number of bytes per sample pair, s_{unit} the per-cell metadata for sequential evidence, and s_{blk} the metadata per slab block. The memory consumption of the sequential-evidence subsystem is bounded by

$$M_{\text{seq}} \leq N \cdot S \cdot s_{\text{pair}} + L \cdot b_{\text{blk}} \cdot s_{\text{pair}} + N \cdot s_{\text{unit}} + L \cdot s_{\text{blk}}. \tag{5}$$

Since N, S, L, b_{blk}, s_{pair}, s_{unit}, and s_{blk} are deployment-time constants, M_{seq} has a strict fixed upper bound, thereby keeping resource usage predictable even as the number of concurrent flows varies.

5 Feature Extraction and Classification

The slow path performs inference solely from the payload-agnostic time–length sequence produced by coarse filtering, without replaying raw packets. All compute-intensive components (feature extraction and model inference) are placed on the slow path, thereby preserving the constant per-packet cost and fixed resource constraints on the fast path.

5.1 Input Snapshot and Sequence Notation

For a candidate flow f, the coarse filter outputs a snapshot $S(f) = (fid, t_0, B)$, where fid is the flow identifier and t_0 is the window start time. The evidence sequence is

$$B = \{(\Delta t_i, \tilde{L}_i)\}_{i=1}^{n}, \quad 0 \leq \Delta t_1 \leq \cdots \leq \Delta t_n \leq T_{\text{feat}}. \tag{6}$$

Here $\Delta t_i = t_i - t_0$ is the relative arrival time and $\tilde{L}_i$ is the signed payload length derived from the stable endpoint ordering. $T_{\text{feat}} \leq T_{\text{cf}}$ denotes the observation window used by the slow path for feature computation.

5.2 Directional Normalization

The sign of $\tilde{L}$ guarantees only endpoint consistency and is not equivalent to the semantic notions of uplink/downlink (UL/DL). To avoid semantic inversion, the slow path normalizes the two directions into a dominant direction and a minor direction, where the dominant direction is defined as the side that carries more bytes in an early prefix of the window. We take a prefix index set $W = \{i \mid \Delta t_i \leq \tau_{\text{reo}}, i \leq M\}$, i.e., endpoint normalization is performed using only the sample pairs within the first τ_{reo} seconds (default 2 s) or the first M packets (default 2000), whichever comes first, and compute

$$B^+ = \sum_{i\in W,\ \tilde{L}_i>0} \left|\tilde{L}_i\right|, \quad B^- = \sum_{i\in W,\ \tilde{L}_i<0} \left|\tilde{L}_i\right|. \tag{7}$$

Given a constant $\eta \in (0,1)$ and a minimum sample size $n_{\min}$, if

$$\left|B^+ - B^-\right| \geq \eta\left(B^+ + B^-\right), \quad |W| \geq n_{\min}, \tag{8}$$

we enforce that the dominant side corresponds to the negative sign by setting

$$s = \begin{cases} +1, & B^- \geq B^+, \\ -1, & B^- < B^+, \end{cases} \quad \hat{L}_i = s \cdot \tilde{L}_i. \tag{9}$$

Otherwise, the original sign is kept (equivalently, $s = +1$). We then define the observable abstraction

$$\hat{L}_i < 0 \Rightarrow \text{Dominant}, \quad \hat{L}_i > 0 \Rightarrow \text{Minor}. \tag{10}$$

Subsequent inference relies only on the dominant/minor abstraction and does not require it to coincide with the true UL/DL semantics.

5.3 DLTES-8: Short-Window Features

We construct an 8-dimensional short-window feature set, Directional Length–Temporal–Entropy–Spectral (DLTES-8), with feature vector $\phi(f) \in (\mathbb{R} \cup \{\perp\})^8$, where $\perp$ denotes an undefined or missing statistic (e.g., no samples in a direction). We define $D = \{|\hat{L}_i| : \hat{L}_i < 0\}$ and $M = \{|\hat{L}_i| : \hat{L}_i > 0\}$, and denote $n_D = |D|$, $n_M = |M|$, and $n = n_D + n_M$.

Size and direction asymmetry. Although payload content is hidden under encryption, the scale and share of traffic on the dominant direction within a short window can still indicate whether the service is distribution-oriented (one direction dominates with large volume) or interaction-oriented (more balanced in both directions), thereby providing a strong discriminative signal. We define the dominant mean length f_1 as mean(D) (with $f_1 = \perp$ if $n_D = 0$), the dominant median length f_2 as median(D) (with $f_2 = \perp$ if $n_D = 0$), the minor-direction 90th-percentile length f_3 as $P_{90}(M)$ (with $f_3 = \perp$ if $n_M = 0$), and the dominant packet ratio f_4 as n_D/n (with $f_4 = \perp$ if $n = 0$).

Temporal regularity. Segmented fetching and buffer control often induce burst–idle arrival patterns, so regularity differences can be observed using timestamp-only statistics. We define the mean inter-arrival gap

$$f_5 = \begin{cases} \frac{1}{n-1}\sum_{i=2}^{n}(\Delta t_i - \Delta t_{i-1}), & n > 1, \\ \perp, & n \leq 1, \end{cases} \tag{11}$$

and the packet-rate entropy by binning $[0, T_{\text{feat}}]$ with width δ to obtain counts $\{c_k\}$ and probabilities $p_k = c_k / \sum_k c_k$, then

$$f_6 = \begin{cases} -\sum_k p_k \log p_k, & \sum_k c_k > 0, \\ \perp, & \text{otherwise}. \end{cases} \tag{12}$$

Frequency-domain cues. If segment periodicity or buffer scheduling repeats approximately within a short window, the packet-count sequence exhibits concentrated spectral energy; frequency-domain peaks thus provide payload-agnostic evidence of quasi-periodicity. With bin width b, we form a packet-count sequence $\{r_j\}$ with $N = \lceil T_{\text{feat}}/b \rceil$ and compute its power spectrum $\{P_k\}$. Over a selected frequency set K (e.g., after DC removal), let $k^\star = \arg\max_{k \in K} P_k$. We then define the dominant frequency

$$f_7 = \begin{cases} \frac{k^\star}{Nb}, & \sum_{k \in K} P_k > 0, \\ \perp, & \text{otherwise}, \end{cases} \tag{13}$$

and the spectral peakiness

$$f_8 = \begin{cases} \frac{P_{k^\star}}{\frac{1}{|K|} \sum_{k \in K} P_k + \epsilon}, & \sum_{k \in K} P_k > 0, \\ \perp, & \text{otherwise}, \end{cases} \tag{14}$$

where $\epsilon > 0$ is a numerical stabilizer. The final feature vector is $\phi(f) = [f_1, \ldots, f_8]$.

5.4 LightGBM Classification and Decision

We adopt Light Gradient Boosting Machine (LightGBM) as the slow-path classifier $g(\cdot)$, which maps $\phi(f)$ to a video confidence score

$$\hat{p}(f) = g(\phi(f)) \approx \Pr\big(y = \text{video} \mid \phi(f)\big). \tag{15}$$

A final decision is made by thresholding with θ_{cls}:

$$\hat{y}(f) = \begin{cases} \text{video}, & \hat{p}(f) \geq \theta_{\text{cls}}, \\ \text{non-video}, & \text{otherwise}. \end{cases} \tag{16}$$

We choose LightGBM because it provides low and stable inference overhead, natively supports missing values ($\perp$) without imputation, and can model non-linear interactions among short-window statistical features.

6 Experiments

This section evaluates the proposed approach from three perspectives: early decidability, generalization, and line-rate deployability. We analyze the pass-through versus suppression trade-off of MTSketch under realistic background traffic to identify a deployable operating point; evaluate the performance limits of DLTES-8 under different short-window lengths and its advantage over baselines; and validate, under real-link deployment and high-load stress tests, that the prototype's processing overhead, packet-drop rate, and termination-detection delay satisfy line-rate and predictability requirements.

Table 1. Session Scale and Protocol Distribution Across Platforms

Video Platform	Sessions	Transport Protocol
YouTube	2947	QUIC
BiliBili	2890	QUIC; TCP+TLS1.3/TLS1.2
Twitch	1397	TCP+TLS1.3
Facebook	431	QUIC
Kick	819	TCP+TLS1.3
Other Platforms	1229	TCP+TLS1.3/TLS1.2

6.1 Dataset Construction

To evaluate early identification during the playback startup phase, we require short-window packet traces that (i) cover multiple platforms and protocols, (ii) can be aligned to the early playback stage, and (iii) provide session-level labels; however, existing public datasets rarely satisfy this combination. We therefore build two complementary datasets: Dataset 1 for controlled startup-phase evaluation and Dataset 2 for open-environment validation.

Dataset 1 (controlled replay) is collected under a controlled 100 Mbps access link. For each session, we extract a fixed 30 s window after playback starts (Table 1) and align the first-frame event to $t = 0$. Offline processing retains only L2–L4 header fields and timestamp/length metadata, with IP addresses and ports anonymized via salted hashing. Flows are aggregated by the direction-invariant 5-tuple, and the flow with the largest packet count within a session is labeled as the video main flow. The processed dataset is publicly available [16].

Dataset 2 (campus egress mirroring) is captured from a mirrored campus-gateway link to evaluate generalization and false-positive risks under real mixed-background traffic, containing 110,171 flows.

6.2 MTSketch Parameter Trade-Offs

To evaluate the filtering effectiveness of MTSketch under realistic mixed-service background traffic and to identify a deployable operating point, we scan

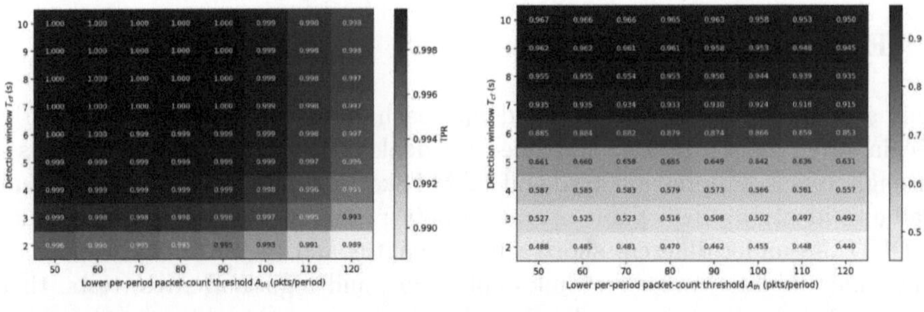

Fig. 3. Video coverage heatmaps for $H_{\text{th}} \in \{1, 2\}$. Period $P = 1$ s; A_{th} is in pkts/period; $T_{\text{cf}} \in [2, 10]$; $A_{\text{th}} \in \{50, \ldots, 120\}$; B_{th} is set to a high (non-binding) value.

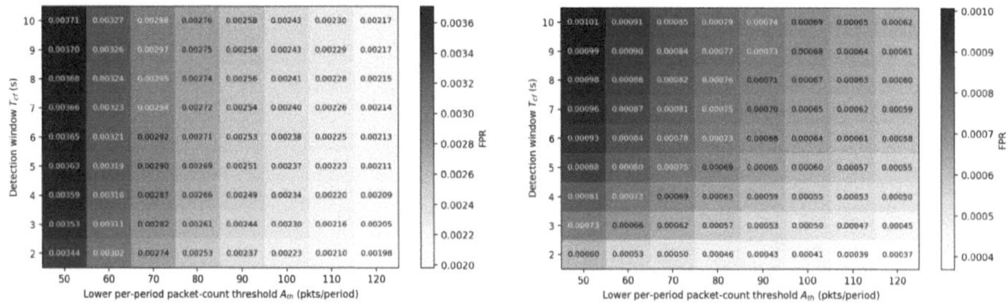

Fig. 4. Non-video FPR heatmaps for $H_{\text{th}} \in \{1, 2\}$. Settings are identical to the video coverage heatmaps.

$(A_{\text{th}}, H_{\text{th}}, T_{\text{cf}})$ on Dataset 2, using TPR to measure the completeness of video pass-through and FPR to measure the risk of non-video flows being admitted into the slow path. We fix $P = 1\,\text{s}$ because P determines the resolution of rhythm counting and, under arrival-driven scanning, provides an upper bound on the termination-detection tail, i.e., $\Delta_{\text{term}} \leq P$; setting it to $1\,\text{s}$ balances short-window resolution with a predictable tail. We further set B_{th} sufficiently large to weaken the effect of upper-bound gating: in open networks, most background flows are filtered out by failing to reach A_{th}, and the upper bound mainly affects a small fraction of bursty or extremely active flows. We therefore focus on the dominant trade-off introduced by lower-bound screening and the hit-based mechanism.

The results are shown in Fig. 3 and Fig. 4. The parameters exhibit mostly monotone effects and define a Pareto region: larger H_{th} and A_{th} reduce false admissions (with potential TPR loss), while T_{cf} trades observation time for risk (typically higher TPR but possibly higher FPR).

Accordingly, to prioritize video pass-through we use a permissive H_{th} (e.g., 1) and tune A_{th} to bound FPR; to prioritize background suppression we use a stricter H_{th} (e.g., 2) with moderate A_{th} and mid-range T_{cf}. We select operating points near the "elbow", where further tightening yields only marginal FPR gains but noticeably degrades TPR.

6.3 DLTES-8 Performance Evaluation

This section evaluates DLTES-8 from two aspects: early decidability and effectiveness in open scenarios. We first split Dataset 1 into training and testing sets with a 3:1 ratio, align the first video frame to $t = 0$, extract features from the first T_{feat} seconds after session startup, and sweep $T_{\text{feat}} \in [1, 10]\,\text{s}$. We use LightGBM as the classifier, tune hyperparameters via grid search, and report precision, recall, and F1 on the test set. As shown in Fig. 5, performance improves as T_{feat} increases while marginal gains diminish. We therefore set $T_{\text{feat}} = 6\,\text{s}$ as a default, since it lies near the "elbow" where DLTES-8 already attains stable discriminative power while keeping the observation horizon and runtime overhead small. In addition, using 6 s aligns the observation window with RSP-8, enabling a fair short-window comparison.

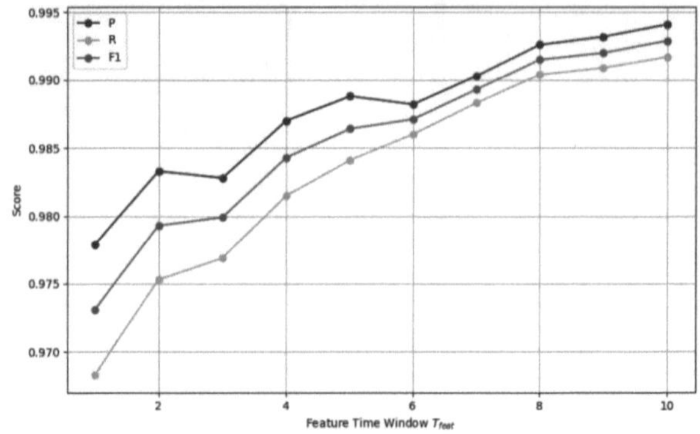

Fig. 5. Precision, Recall, and F1 score under different feature time windows T_{feat}.

We then compare against ITP–KNN [6] and RSP-8 [13] on Dataset 2 using precision/recall/F1, and also report the feature dimensionality and required observation horizon ("feature time" refers to the observation window length). Table 2 shows that, under the same short-window constraint, DLTES-8 outperforms the baselines; moreover, it maintains higher accuracy with substantially fewer features and a shorter observation horizon than ITP–KNN, validating its effectiveness for early identification under open mixed background traffic.

Table 2. Baseline Comparison

Method	Precision	Recall	F1	Features	Feature Time	Classifier
ITP–KNN	0.9089	0.9316	0.9201	70	15 s	KNN
RSP-8	0.9772	0.9769	0.9771	8	6 s	Random Forest
Ours (DLTES-8)	0.9866	0.9842	0.9854	8	6 s	LightGBM

6.4 System Evaluation and Line-Rate Stress Test

We evaluate deployability using a prototype running on a desktop host equipped with an Intel Core i7-12700K CPU, 32 GB RAM, and Ubuntu 20.04. The system is built on the Data Plane Development Kit (DPDK 20.11 with the `mlx5` driver) and uses an NVIDIA BlueField-2 NIC (25 Gbps). The data plane is implemented in C++/DPDK: the fast path performs only minimal header-field extraction and MTSketch updates, while the slow path executes feature extraction and inference via the LightGBM C-API. We pin one worker thread to each RX queue and decouple the fast and slow paths using a single-producer/single-consumer lock-free ring. We set the scan period to $P = 1$ s and configure MTSketch with $N = 65{,}536$ cells ($W_{\text{rows}} = 16{,}384$, $D_{\text{cols}} = 4$), $H_{\text{th}} = 1$, $T_{\text{cf}} = 6$, and $A_{\text{th}} = 100$, and set the feature window to $T_{\text{feat}} = 6$ s. Each cell maintains a fixed in-cell buffer of 128 sample pairs, and overflow evidence is managed by slab blocks, each holding 4,096 sample pairs. Unless otherwise stated, we enable a single RX queue.

Under a 1 Gbps campus mirrored trace, the system sustains 107,772 pps with an average fast-path cost of 742.7 cycles/packet. Snapshot enqueue incurs zero drops, the ring high-water mark remains at 1 (no backpressure), and the slab peak usage is 637/2047 blocks. On the slow path, the end-to-end latency per job averages 126.95 μs (dominated by feature extraction and inference), and each job processes 3,828 samples on average. Termination detection satisfies the bound $\Delta_{\mathrm{term}} \leq P$, with an average of 0.5088 s and a maximum of 1.0 s, and we observe no missed seconds.

Under a 10 GbE saturated synthetic-traffic stress test, four RX queues achieve an aggregate throughput of 14,874,785 pps ($\approx$ 99.96% line rate), with a fast-path cost of 599.6 cycles/packet and zero drops/backpressure throughout. Per-queue throughput ranges from 3.47–4.13 Mpps, while the per-packet cost remains stable (557.9–634.4 cycles/packet), indicating good load balancing and near-linear multi-queue scaling. Termination detection is tightly bounded: the average delay is 0.969–0.991 s and the maximum delay is 1.000 s on every queue, again satisfying $\Delta_{\mathrm{term}} \leq P$, with no missed-second events (`miss_sec` = 0). These results confirm that the system sustains line-rate processing with predictable termination latency under high load.

7 Conclusion

We propose an end-to-end, payload-agnostic line-rate framework for early identification, combining symmetric Receive-Side Scaling (RSS) multi-queue steering on the Network Interface Card (NIC), a fixed-memory coarse filter (MTSketch), and lightweight slow-path inference. The fast path updates with constant per-packet cost, and employs arrival-driven scanning to provide upper bounds on both memory usage and termination-detection latency, enabling provable early decisions within short windows. Experiments show that the method achieves strong early discriminability on both controlled startup traces and open campus egress mirroring traffic; in particular, DLTES-8 outperforms representative baselines using only eight features. A prototype reaches approximately 99.96% line-rate throughput under saturated 10 GbE stress tests, with zero packet loss and no backpressure, validating deployability.

Future work will incorporate slow-path label/confidence feedback to adaptively tune thresholds such as A_{th}, B_{th}, and H_{th} online, and extend evaluation to more platforms/protocols and harsher network conditions at higher link rates in realistic online environments.

Acknowledgement. This research was partially supported by Shandong Provincial Natural Science Foundation, China under Grant No. ZR2021LZH002, Jinan Scientific Research Leader Studio, China under Grant No. 202228114, Shandong Provincial Key Projects of Basic Research, China under Grant No. ZR2022ZD01, TaiShan Scholars Program under Grants No. tstp20240828.

References

1. Mazhar, M.H., Shafiq, Z.: Real-time video quality of experience monitoring for HTTPS and QUIC. In: Proceedings of IEEE INFOCOM, pp. 1331–1339 (2018). https://doi.org/10.1109/INFOCOM.2018.8486321
2. Lotfollahi, M., Jafari Siavoshani, M., Shirali Hossein Zade, R., Saberian, M.: Deep packet: a novel approach for encrypted traffic classification using deep learning. Soft. Comput. **24**(3), 1999–2012 (2019). https://doi.org/10.1007/s00500-019-04030-2
3. Huang, Q., et al.: SketchVisor: robust network measurement for software packet processing. In: Proceedings of the ACM SIGCOMM Conference, pp. 113–126 (2017). https://doi.org/10.1145/3098822.3098831
4. DPDK Project: Toeplitz Hash Library (RSS hash). DPDK Programmer's Guide
5. Li, F., Chung, J.W., Claypool, M.: Silhouette: identifying YouTube video flows from encrypted traffic. In: Proceedings of ACM SIGMM NOSSDAV, pp. 19–24 (2018). https://doi.org/10.1145/3210445.3210448
6. Liu, Y., Li, S., Zhang, C., Zheng, C., Sun, Y., Liu, Q.: ITP-KNN: encrypted video flow identification based on the intermittent traffic pattern of video and K-nearest neighbors classification. In: Krzhizhanovskaya, V.V., et al. (eds.) ICCS 2020. LNCS, vol. 12138, pp. 279–293. Springer, Cham (2020). https://doi.org/10.1007/978-3-030-50417-5_21
7. Bukhari, S.M.A.H., Afaq, M., Song, W.-C.: PPS: a packets pattern-based video identification in encrypted network traffic. In: UCC 2023, pp. 1–6 (2023)
8. Madanapalli, S.C., Mathai, A., Gharakheili, H.H., Sivaraman, V.: ReCLive: real-time classification and QoE inference of live video streaming services. In: Proceedings of IEEE/ACM International Symposium on Quality of Service (IWQOS), pp. 1–7 (2021). https://doi.org/10.1109/IWQOS52092.2021.9521288
9. Walsh, T., Barton, A., Kölsch, M.: Improved open-world fingerprinting increases threat to streaming video privacy but realistic scenarios remain difficult. Proc. Priv. Enhancing Technol. **4**, 130–145 (2025)
10. Yan, X., He, L., Xu, Y., Cao, J., Wang, L., Xie, G.: High-speed encrypted traffic classification by using payload features. Digit. Commun. Netw. **11**(2), 412–423 (2025)
11. Gharakheili, H.H., Lyu, M., Wang, Y., Kumar, H., Sivaraman, V.: iTeleScope: softwarized network middle-box for real-time video telemetry and classification. IEEE Trans. Netw. Serv. Manag. (2019). https://doi.org/10.1109/TNSM.2019.2929511
12. Kattadige, C., et al.: SETA++: real-time scalable encrypted traffic analytics in multi-Gbps networks. IEEE Trans. Netw. Serv. Manag. **18**(3), 3244–3259 (2021). https://doi.org/10.1109/TNSM.2021.3085097
13. Le, X., Wu, H., Yang, J., Cheng, G., Hu, X.: A method for identifying high-speed network video traffic based on composite features. J. Integr. Technol. **13**(5), 19–29 (2024)
14. Akem, A.T.-J., Fraysse, G., Fiore, M.: Encrypted traffic classification at line rate in programmable switches with machine learning. In: Proceedings of IEEE/IFIP NOMS, pp. 1–9 (2024). https://doi.org/10.1109/NOMS59830.2024.10575394
15. Cassola, A., Schaeffer-Filho, A.: K-Flix: clustering-based video streaming traffic identification in programmable data planes. In: Proceedings of SBRC, pp. 140–153 (2025). https://doi.org/10.5753/sbrc.2025.5862
16. UUuUUuUUo: Video-traffic-dataset (GitHub repository). https://github.com/UUuUUuUUo/Video-traffic-dataset. Accessed 18 Dec 2025

AlertSAGE: Semantic-Aware Alert Graph Embedding for Cybersecurity Incident Discovery

Shuang Jiang[1,2], Zhicheng Liu[3], Yijing Wang[1,2(✉)], Zhihao Zhang[1], Han Wang[1], and Yueyue Hu[1,2]

[1] Institute of Information Engineering, CAS, Beijing, China
{jiangshuang,wangyijing,zhangzhihao,wanghan,huyueyue}@iie.ac.cn
[2] School of Cyber Security, University of Chinese Academy of Sciences, Beijing, China
[3] National Computer Network Emergency Response Technical Team/Coordination Center of China, Beijing, China
liuzhicheng@cert.org.cn

Abstract. Addressing the "alert fatigue" challenge faced by Security Operations Centers (SOCs) and the limitations of existing methods, this paper proposes AlertSAGE, a Semantic-Aware Alert Graph Embedding framework for automated incident discovery. The framework first combines deep semantic encoding with sliding time windows to efficiently compress discrete alerts into context-rich "meta-alerts". Second, modeling these meta-alerts as graph nodes, it introduces a self-supervised Top-K Graph Transformer model that captures attack correlations and filters noise through dynamic graph learning and attention sparsification mechanisms. Finally, it utilizes an improved density clustering algorithm to identify attack incidents and supports human-in-the-loop verification. Experiments on the corrected CIC-IDS-2017 dataset demonstrate that AlertSAGE exhibits strong robustness in high false positive (43.8%) scenarios, achieving an overall noise reduction rate of 96.28% with recall of 99.97%, effectively supporting efficient noise reduction and attack tracing for NIDS alerts.

Keywords: Alert Fatigue · Semantic Analysis · Graph Transformer · Alert Aggregation · Network Intrusion Detection · Incident Discovery

1 Introduction

As cyber attacks evolve from simple malicious scans to Advanced Persistent Threats (APTs), Network Intrusion Detection Systems (NIDS) have become core defense components. However, in practice, to avoid missing critical threats, NIDS policies are often configured with high sensitivity, which leads to massive false positives and "benign triggers" caused by legitimate activities [22]. Research indicates that the false positive rates in real-world Security Operations Center

© IFIP International Federation for Information Processing 2026
Published by Springer Nature Switzerland AG 2026
H. Janicke et al. (Eds.): SEC 2026, IFIP AICT 787, pp. 419–433, 2026.
https://doi.org/10.1007/978-3-032-27993-4_29

(SOC) environments can reach as high as 99% [1]. The flood of ineffective alerts, combined with the shortage of analysts and difficulties in tool integration commonly faced by SOCs, results in a severe condition known as "alert fatigue" [15]. Massive information overload causes cognitive desensitization among analysts, making genuine attack signals easily overwhelmed. The 2013 Target data breach serves as a typical warning: critical alerts were not effectively processed, leading to catastrophic consequences [6]. This is not an isolated historical issue. Industry surveys show that alert fatigue remains a persistent and critical challenge that directly threatens the integrity of organizational and national cybersecurity defenses [15].

To mitigate alert fatigue, academia and industry primarily pursue two directions: 1) enhancing NIDS capabilities to improve alert quality at the source; 2) post-processing alerts generated by NIDS to reduce noise and perform correlation analysis. Compared to the first approach, alert post-processing methods offer stronger universality and applicability. They do not require modifying the internal mechanisms of existing NIDS, can adapt to various types of NIDS systems, and provide better flexibility and deployment convenience. Although existing post-processing methods (such as aggregation based on attribute similarity and community detection based on static graphs) have alleviated the problem to some extent, they still face several significant limitations: Insufficient utilization of payload semantics: existing methods often ignore payloads [3,10,11] or rely solely on simple matching [17], making it difficult to extract deep attack intent; Limitations of static graph structures: predefined static edge weights (e.g., based on fixed time windows) cannot dynamically capture complex topological relationships during attack evolution; Separation of semantic understanding and structural analysis: there is a lack of effective frameworks that can uniformly model both the semantic content of alerts and network topological structures.

To address these challenges, this paper proposes AlertSAGE (Semantic-aware Alert Graph Embedding), a semantic-aware alert graph embedding framework designed for automated incident discovery in SOCs. First, we design a hybrid aggregation strategy driven by semantics and rules, introducing sentence embedding models for deep semantic encoding to efficiently compress discrete alerts into context-rich "meta-alerts". Second, we construct temporal correlation graphs and propose a self-supervised Top-K Graph Transformer that dynamically learns node correlations and filters noise through attention sparsification mechanisms, generating high-quality attack representations. Finally, we utilize improved density clustering to automatically identify attack incidents and provide semi-supervised sampling suggestions to support efficient human-in-the-loop verification. Experiments on the corrected CIC-IDS-2017 dataset demonstrate that AlertSAGE exhibits strong robustness in high false positive (43.8%) scenarios, achieving a recall close to 100% and significantly outperforming existing mainstream methods.

The remainder of this paper is organized as follows: Sect. 2 reviews related work; Sect. 3 details our proposed attack incident discovery framework; Sect. 4 validates the effectiveness of the method through experiments; finally, Sect. 5 concludes the paper and outlines future work.

2 Related Work

Existing research on mitigating alert fatigue is mainly divided into two categories: enhancing NIDS capabilities and post-processing generated alerts.

Enhancing NIDS Capabilities: This category of research focuses on improving NIDS internal mechanisms to directly reduce false positive generation. To cope with dynamic changes in network traffic distribution (i.e., "concept drift"), systems such as A-NIDS [23] and ENIDrift [18] adopt adaptive machine learning frameworks. To improve detection accuracy, researchers have introduced generative models to construct signatures for zero-day attacks [14], point cloud analysis techniques [4], and deep graph learning models such as graph autoencoders and Graph Transformers [5,12]. To reduce dependence on large-scale labeled datasets, federated learning and contrastive learning techniques are used to improve performance in few-shot scenarios [7]. Additionally, research focuses on improving model interpretability (e.g., xNIDS [20]) and achieving continuous improvement through Human-in-the-Loop active learning [3] or differentiable rule optimization frameworks (e.g., CAPTAIN [16]). Although optimizing NIDS at the source is an ideal solution, this approach faces significant deployment challenges due to high device heterogeneity and expensive implementation costs in large networks or enterprise SOCs.

Alert Post-processing and Correlation Analysis: A more common and practical approach is to treat NIDS as an alert generator and focus on intelligent post-processing of its output. This approach decouples alert analysis from generation, offering better flexibility and compatibility. Alert prioritization strategies rank alerts by risk level. For example, AlertPro [19] uses reinforcement learning to dynamically guide analysts to focus on critical threats. Alert aggregation, correlation, and scenario reconstruction are core to noise reduction, including contextual analysis of alert sequences by systems such as DEEPCASE [3] and BiCAM [11], as well as aggregation based on attribute similarity (particularly payload content) [17]. Graph-based analysis methods have gained attention for their ability to naturally model relationships between entities. For instance, [2] uses Graph Convolutional Networks (GCN) for community detection to correlate alerts, DeepDRAC [9] focuses on recommending dispositions for identified alert clusters, and research has addressed attack detection under distributed and in-network data collection systems [13]. However, most existing graph methods rely on static graph structures, where edge connections are determined by fixed predefined rules (such as shared IPs within a time window), making it difficult to adapt to constantly changing attack patterns.

In summary, existing alert post-processing methods have made progress in noise reduction and correlation analysis, but still face challenges including insufficient payload semantic mining, limitations of static graph structures, and the separation of semantic and structural analysis. These limitations make it difficult to effectively capture semantic correlations and topological evolution of complex attacks in dynamic environments.

3 Methodology

3.1 Motivation and Problem Analysis

This section elucidates our motivation for designing hybrid aggregation strategies and graph correlation learning through real-world scenarios.

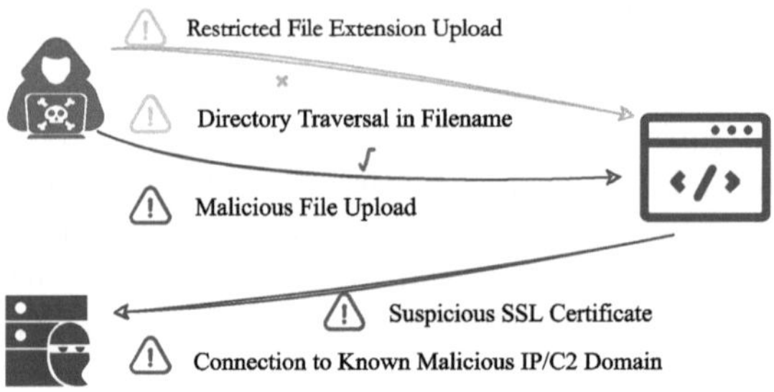

Fig. 1. Example of an Attack Scenario.

Alert Redundancy and Multi-view Detection. In real-world NIDS deployments, alert rules are often collaboratively authored by multiple security experts, inevitably leading to redundancy in the rule base. Furthermore, different rules may detect the same malicious traffic from varying perspectives. As shown in Fig. 1, an attacker's probing of a web upload page and subsequent successful upload may sequentially trigger multiple alerts such as "Restricted File Extension Upload," "Directory Traversal in Filename," and "Malicious File Upload".

Cross-Host Attacks and Contextual Correlation. Basic aggregation typically handles alerts only between single IP pairs (One-to-One). However, modern cyber attacks are often large-scale and distributed.

- **One-to-Many Scenarios:** A single attacker IP initiates port scans against numerous hosts within a subnet in a short period. This generates massive discrete alerts, which, if aggregated solely by single IP pairs, would be fragmented into hundreds of isolated clusters, making it difficult to identify the systematic scanning campaign.
- **Many-to-One Scenarios:** Multiple botnet IPs simultaneously attack a single victim host. Although alert clusters from each source IP are independent, they share the same target IP and exhibit highly similar behavioral patterns.
- **Chained Attack Scenarios:** As shown in Fig. 1, after compromising a web server via a file upload vulnerability, an attacker may implant a C2 trojan and communicate with a remote C2 server, triggering alerts like "Connection to Known Malicious IP/C2 Domain" and "Suspicious SSL Certificate".

The issues of alert redundancy, multi-view detection, and complex correlations in cross-host attacks highlight the deficiencies of existing methods in semantic understanding and dynamic topological analysis. This serves as the core motivation for proposing the AlertSAGE framework.

3.2 Framework Overview

To address massive and high-noise alert streams, we propose a systematic attack incident discovery framework. As shown in Fig. 2, the framework consists of three core modules: 1) Hybrid Alert Aggregation based on semantics and rules; 2) Dynamic Graph Representation Learning based on Top-K Graph Transformer; and 3) Automated Incident Clustering and Human-in-the-Loop Annotation.

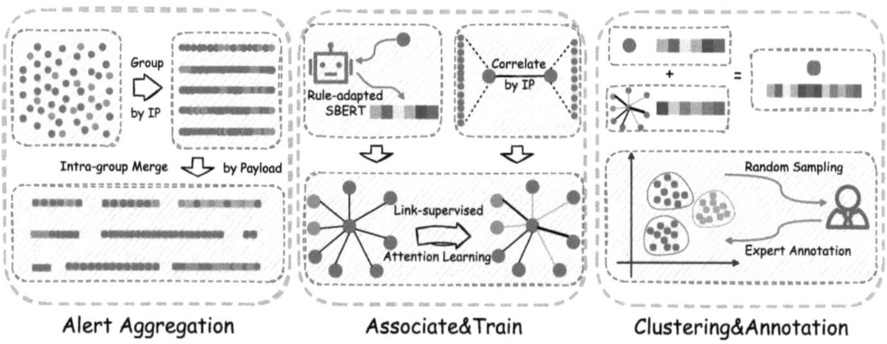

Fig. 2. Overview of the AlertSAGE Framework.

3.3 Hybrid Alert Aggregation

Raw alert streams often contain significant redundancy. To compress data while preserving key information, we design a two-stage hybrid aggregation mechanism:

1. **Semantic Aggregation (for alerts with payloads):** For alerts containing payload information, we first group them by bidirectional IP pairs (Source IP $\leftrightarrow$ Dest IP). Within each group, we introduce a strict sliding time window mechanism for aggregation: the system maintains a dynamic time window T_w, and new alerts are considered for merging only if the time difference from the current cluster falls within this window. To ensure timeliness, aggregation is performed in hourly time slices. A cluster capacity limit is also set to prevent overly large clusters. Under these constraints, we use a pre-trained Sentence-BERT model to map payloads into semantic vectors and calculate cosine similarity between the new alert and the current cluster. If similarity exceeds a threshold τ, the alert is assigned to that cluster.

2. **Rule Aggregation (for payload-less or scanning alerts):** For alerts without payloads, we adopt a rule aggregation strategy. Additionally, although some scanning alerts carry payloads, the content varies significantly due to different target ports, and semantic aggregation would incorrectly fragment the same scanning behavior. Therefore, for such alerts, we maintain the bidirectional IP grouping and employ strict rule matching: alerts are aggregated if they share the same signature ID within the time window.

Through hybrid aggregation, massive raw alerts are transformed into high-density "meta-alerts". Compared to raw alerts, these aggregated nodes encapsulate compressed events while adding key feature dimensions: traceability information (raw alert IDs); aggregated semantic profile (weighted distribution of attack rules/categories); temporal statistics (time span, alert count, frequency); and comprehensive severity distribution (count and proportion of alerts by severity level). These augmented features enrich the information carried by nodes and edges in subsequent dynamic graph learning.

3.4 Dynamic Graph Learning

To capture the temporal evolution of attack activities (e.g., Scanning → Exploitation → Privilege Escalation), we construct a dynamic attribute graph $G = (V, E)$. Here, the node set V consists of meta-alerts generated in the previous stage, with each node representing aggregated attack behavior between a pair of hosts within a specific time window. On this basis, we further define node feature representations and edge connection rules.

Node Feature Embedding. Each meta-alert (node) contains semantic and statistical information. We construct a multi-modal feature encoder fusing deep semantic features (mapping attack rule descriptions to vectors v_{text} via Sentence-BERT) and statistical features (alert count, frequency, ports, severity distribution, etc., standardized to vector v_{stat}). The final node feature is the weighted concatenation of both.

Temporal Correlation Graph Construction. We construct the edge set E based on spatiotemporal correlation. An edge $(u, v) \in E$ exists between two nodes u, v if and only if: 1) IP Correlation: their IP sets intersect (sharing at least one IP); 2) Temporal Constraint: their time periods overlap or the interval is less than a threshold $T_{\max}$.

Top-K Graph Transformer. Unlike traditional GCNs using fixed adjacency matrices, we propose a Top-K Graph Transformer model to optimize graph structure by learning dynamic edge weights. First, we calculate an initial physical weight $w_{uv}^{(0)}$ for each edge, comprehensively reflecting temporal tightness, alert severity, and entity association strength:

$$w_{uv}^{(0)} = (\alpha \cdot e^{-\lambda \Delta t} + \beta \cdot S_{sev}(u, v)) \cdot S_{IP}(u, v) \tag{1}$$

where Δt is the time difference, and $S_{sev}(u, v)$ and $S_{IP}(u, v)$ represent the severity score and IP correlation adjustment factor, respectively.

During forward propagation, multi-head self-attention is used to calculate attention scores between nodes, fusing feature similarity with physical edge weights. To filter noise connections, a Top-K sparsification mechanism is introduced: for each node, the K neighbors with the highest attention weights are selected for aggregation. The final node embedding is obtained by concatenating the node's own features with the aggregated context information and projecting to a specified dimension.

Model Training and Self-supervised Learning. We train the model using a self-supervised strategy based on edge weight reconstruction. A decoder is designed to reconstruct the association strength using node embeddings h_u, h_v:

$$\hat{w}_{uv} = \text{Sigmoid}\left(\text{MLP}([h_u \parallel h_v])\right) \tag{2}$$

The training objective is to minimize reconstruction error, making predicted weights for positive edges approach true physical weights, and those for negative edges approach 0:

$$\mathcal{L} = \frac{1}{|E|} \sum_{(u,v)\in E} (\hat{w}_{uv} - w_{uv})^2 + \frac{1}{|E_{\text{neg}}|} \sum_{(u,v)\in E_{\text{neg}}} (\hat{w}_{uv} - 0)^2 \tag{3}$$

After convergence, model parameters are frozen, and the node embedding matrix H is generated for subsequent attack incident identification.

3.5 Incident Discovery and Human-in-the-Loop

Based on the high-quality node embeddings generated by the Top-K Graph Transformer, we designed a complete incident discovery process including unsupervised clustering, human-in-the-loop verification, and incremental management.

Unsupervised Density Clustering and Noise Optimization: We employ an improved DBSCAN algorithm for clustering node embeddings. To address outlier noise, we propose a dual optimization strategy: a K-Nearest Neighbors(KNN) Soft Assignment Mechanism that recalls noise nodes to corresponding clusters via distance-inverse weighted voting; and a "Large Noise" Promotion Strategy that forcibly promotes outlier nodes containing massive raw alerts to independent candidate incidents.

Semi-supervised Sampling and Knowledge Base Construction: In the cold-start phase, we utilize the geometric properties of the embedding space to sample N representative samples closest to the cluster centroid, generating a "Review List". Analysts review core samples and assign labels, and the system automatically propagates attributes to the entire cluster and historical alerts via label propagation, rapidly building a labeled knowledge base.

Incremental Clustering and Automated Operations: In the online phase, new alerts generate node embeddings via aggregation and graph model inference. If a new node is close to a known cluster centroid, it is automatically assigned and inherits the label; otherwise, it is marked as unknown and cached in a noise pool. The system periodically re-clusters the noise pool, and once a new high-density cluster forms, it triggers the sampling push mechanism for expert confirmation, ensuring continuous learning and self-evolution.

4 Experimental Evaluation

To validate the effectiveness of the AlertSAGE framework, we conducted comprehensive experiments on a public network intrusion detection dataset. This section first introduces the dataset construction and preprocessing workflow, followed by the definition of evaluation metrics, and finally presents a detailed analysis of model performance based on experimental results.

4.1 Dataset Construction

Publicly available NIDS alert datasets generally lack complete payload information, making them unsuitable for deep semantic analysis. To address this, we constructed a high-quality alert dataset rich in payload semantics. We selected the corrected version of CIC-IDS-2017 (Fixed CIC-IDS-2017) proposed by Liu et al. [8] as the baseline. We used Snort 3.9.3 to detect replayed traffic, employing the Snort official registered user rule set and creating custom rules specifically for detecting DDoS attacks. The configured Snort system successfully detected 13 types of attacks (only DoS GoldenEye failed to trigger correct alerts). Using a matching algorithm, Snort alerts were matched with original traffic logs, and matched alerts inherited the labels of the original traffic. The final dataset contains 200,195 alert records, with DoS-related alerts (including DDoS) accounting for 72.55%, and Benign alerts 12.01% (indicating a false positive rate of 12.01%).

Snort Log Format and Field Selection: In this experiment, we extracted the following core fields for feature construction and correlation analysis: Spatiotemporal dimension: timestamp (temporal correlation), src_addr/dst_addr (IP correlation), src_port/dst_port (service port features), dir (determining service port direction); Semantic dimension: msg (rule description, used for text semantic encoding), b64_data (payload content, used for semantic similarity matching); Statistical dimension: priority (severity level, used for feature construction and edge weight calculation).

4.2 Experimental Setup

Experimental Environment and Hyperparameters: All experiments were conducted on a Linux server equipped with an Intel Xeon Gold 5218R CPU (2.10GHz, 40 cores), 692GB RAM, and two NVIDIA A100-PCIE-40GB GPUs.

The software environment included Python 3.12 and the PyTorch deep learning framework.

AlertSAGE employs a Graph Transformer (4 heads, 128 hidden dim, 64 output dim) with Top-K sparsification ($K = 10$), optimized via AdamW (lr=0.005, weight decay 10^{-5}). Key parameters include: aggregation $\tau = 0.75, T_w = 5$ min; graph construction $T_{\max} = 300s, \alpha = 0.7, \beta = 0.3, \lambda \approx 0.0033$; and clustering DBSCAN ($\varepsilon = 10, MinPts = 3$) with KNN ($K = 10$). Payload embedding uses all-MiniLM-L12-v2, while msg embedding uses a version fine-tuned on Snort rules via ESIMCSE [21].

To adapt to the processing requirements of streaming data in actual operations and ensure system real-time performance, the AlertSAGE model adopts an hourly slicing aggregation strategy. We partitioned the CIC-IDS-2017 dataset by hour, performing alert aggregation, dynamic graph construction, and model training independently for each time slice. Ultimately, the dataset formed a total of 48 temporal correlation graphs. After generating node embeddings for all time slices, we mapped these embedding vectors to a global feature space for merged clustering. The total runtime for the entire dataset is within 30 min.

4.3 Evaluation Metrics

To rigorously evaluate the model's ability to mitigate alert fatigue (noise reduction performance) and discover attack incidents (detection performance), we categorized evaluation metrics into two groups: Workload Reduction and Performance over Covered Events.

Workload Reduction. This set of metrics measures the system's compression efficiency and coverage capability. For clarity, we denote the final number of reported alerts as A (Alerts), the total number of original events as E_{total} (Total Events), the number of successfully aggregated events as E_{cov} (Covered Events), and the number of uncovered noise points as E_{uncov} (Uncovered Events). Specific metrics include: **Alerts:** The number of alert units presented after noise reduction (for AlertSAGE, this is the number of clusters; for baseline models, it is the number of clusters $\times$ 10 (sequence length)). **Coverage:** The proportion of original alerts successfully aggregated by the model, calculated as E_{cov}/E_{total}. **Reduction:** The compression efficiency within the scope of covered events, i.e., $1 - A/E_{cov}$. **Overall:** Reflects the overall alert reduction relative to the original data volume, calculated as $1 - (A + E_{uncov})/E_{total}$.

Performance over Covered Events: This set of metrics measures the classification accuracy of the model in identified attack incidents, using **Precision**, **Recall**, **F1-score**, and **Accuracy**. Where Precision is defined as the proportion of true attacks in clusters predicted as attack incidents.

4.4 Results and Analysis

To comprehensively validate the effectiveness of the AlertSAGE framework, we conducted comparative experiments with a state-of-the-art alert correlation method, DeepCASE [3]. DeepCASE is a deep learning framework based on attention mechanisms that treats alerts as time series and automatically reconstructs attack scenarios through contextual analysis. Considering that DoS/DDoS attacks constitute the vast majority (approximately 72.5%) of the CIC-IDS-2017 dataset, with relatively simple features and huge volume that can easily mask detection shortcomings for other complex, low-frequency attacks, we designed two experimental scenarios:

1. **Full Dataset:** Contains all 200,195 alerts.
2. **No-DoS Subset:** Excludes DoS/DDoS-related alerts, resulting in a significant increase in the proportion of Benign (false positive) alerts to 43.8%. This distribution with a high false positive rate more closely resembles a real SOC network environment.

The experimental results are shown in Table 1.

Table 1. Performance Comparison on Full and No-DoS Datasets

Scenario	Method	Workload Reduction				Performance over Covered Events			
		Alerts	Reduc.	Cov.	Overall	Prec.	Rec.	F1	Acc.
Full Dataset	DeepCASE	1150	99.41%	97.90%	97.33%	94.15%	99.51%	93.09%	91.82%
	AlertSAGE	**950**	**99.52%**	**99.55%**	**99.20%**	**97.67%**	**100.0%**	**98.82%**	**97.89%**
No-DoS Subset	DeepCASE	1290	97.46%	92.45%	90.10%	74.39%	97.23%	84.29%	70.79%
	AlertSAGE	**1158**	**97.85%**	**97.86%**	**96.28%**	**91.47%**	**99.97%**	**95.53%**	**94.72%**

As shown in Table 1, AlertSAGE demonstrates superior performance and robustness under a fair comparison where DeepCASE parameters were fine-tuned from the original code to optimal settings, ensuring similar noise reduction levels (Reduction) and consistent attack determination criteria. In the Full Dataset, AlertSAGE improved Precision to 97.67% and achieved 100% Recall. Even in the high-false-positive No-DoS scenario, while DeepCASE's Precision dropped significantly to 74.39%, AlertSAGE maintained a high Precision of 91.47% and a Recall of 99.97%. This performance discrepancy confirms that, compared to methods relying solely on sequence context, the introduction of the dynamic graph Transformer and semantic enhancement mechanisms can more effectively capture cross-host correlation features, thereby maintaining extremely high detection accuracy and recall in complex attack scenarios with scarce samples and severe noise interference.

4.5 Effect of Semantic Aggregation

Before graph learning, we statistically analyzed the effect of the semantic aggregation stage. The total number of nodes in the graph after aggregation is 12,971, of which 2,786 nodes utilize the payload-based semantic aggregation strategy and contain at least two original alerts. We further categorized these nodes by the number of aggregated rule types and label types (Benign/Attack/Mixed), as shown in Table 2.

Table 2. Rule Diversity Statistics of Semantic Aggregation Nodes

Rule Types	Nodes	Benign	Attack	Mixed
1	1976	1757	218	1
2	391	156	215	20
3	1	1	0	0

As can be seen from Table 2, nodes aggregating "1 rule type" are predominantly Benign, indicating that payload-based semantic aggregation effectively compresses benign redundant alerts repeatedly triggered by the same rule into a few clusters in practice. Among nodes aggregating "2 rule types," the proportion of Attack is higher, suggesting that for alerts triggered by multiple related rules in the same attack scenario, semantic aggregation can merge them into the same alert node. Meanwhile, the overall number of Mixed nodes is small, indicating that the semantic aggregation process largely avoids mixing a large number of attack alerts with benign alerts in the same cluster.

4.6 Effect of Graph-Based Learning

To evaluate the contribution of the graph structure and Top-K Graph Transformer, we designed an ablation variant, AlertSAGE-NoGraph. This variant retains the identical aggregation and feature encoding process—specifically, text semantic and numerical features reduced to 64 dimensions. However, instead of constructing an alert graph, we directly apply DBSCAN clustering in the embedding space to assess the embeddings' intrinsic quality. By adjusting the DBSCAN neighborhood radius parameter ε, we examined the impact of different clustering intensities on noise reduction and detection performance. The experimental results are shown in Table 3.

As shown in Table 3, with a smaller ε (e.g., 0.1), AlertSAGE-NoGraph exhibits lower Coverage and Recall, indicating that a significant number of true attacks remain within noise points. As ε increases, although Coverage improves, Precision drops rapidly; at $\varepsilon = 1.0$, both metrics are significantly lower than those of AlertSAGE. In contrast, AlertSAGE maintains 94.38% Coverage and 99.85% Recall at $\varepsilon = 10$. This demonstrates that the graph structure and

Table 3. Performance Comparison Before and After Removing Graph Structure on No-DoS Dataset

Method	ε	Alerts	Reduc.	Cov.	Overall	Prec.	Rec.	F1	Acc.
AlertSAGE	10.00	1123	97.83%	**94.38%**	94.77%	**92.06%**	**99.85%**	95.80%	95.06%
AlertSAGE-NoGraph	0.01	511	98.96%	**89.60%**	97.47%	**99.74%**	**94.11%**	96.84%	96.54%
AlertSAGE-NoGraph	0.10	429	99.17%	**93.59%**	98.43%	**97.76%**	**96.62%**	97.19%	96.85%
AlertSAGE-NoGraph	0.30	399	99.23%	**94.90%**	98.72%	**94.98%**	**97.58%**	96.26%	95.72%
AlertSAGE-NoGraph	0.50	364	99.31%	**96.64%**	98.91%	**87.08%**	**98.43%**	92.41%	90.87%
AlertSAGE-NoGraph	1.00	295	99.46%	**98.65%**	99.22%	**83.91%**	**99.22%**	90.92%	88.82%

Top-K Graph Transformer effectively utilize contextual information to aggregate semantically similar and closely related attack alerts into stable clusters, while noise points are more concentrated in scattered Benign traffic. This significantly improves the coverage of true attacks without sacrificing noise reduction capabilities. Figure 3 further illustrates the UMAP visualization comparison of node embeddings before and after introducing the graph structure (AlertSAGE-NoGraph with $\varepsilon = 0.1$).

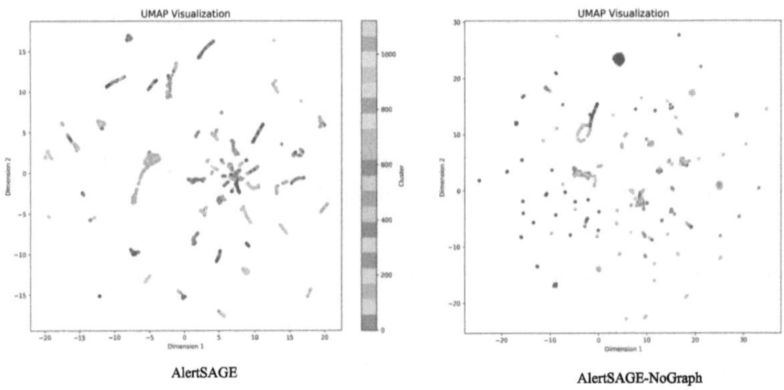

Fig. 3. UMAP Visualization Comparison of Node Embeddings.

5 Conclusion and Future Work

To address alert fatigue in SOCs, we propose AlertSAGE, an automated incident discovery framework. By integrating hybrid alert aggregation, Top-K Graph Transformer, and improved density clustering, AlertSAGE achieves efficient noise reduction and incident discovery. Experiments on a modified CIC-IDS-2017 dataset demonstrate that AlertSAGE significantly outperforms state-of-the-art methods. In high-false-positive (43.8%) scenarios, it maintains 97.85% reduction, 91.47% precision, and 99.97% recall. Ablation studies confirm the dynamic graph learning mechanism's critical role in capturing cross-host correlations and enhancing robustness in complex attack scenarios.

Future work will focus on: 1) Validating AlertSAGE on real-world SOC data to address the limitation of using a single synthetic dataset; 2) Collaborating with SOC personnel to integrate high-confidence detection rules with AlertSAGE. This includes using high-confidence alerts as "anchors" for graph learning, optimizing edge weights with rule-based priors, and fusing confidence scores to enable synergistic rule- and data-driven analysis.

Acknowledgements. This work was supported by the Key R&D Program of Shandong Province, China (Grant No. 2023CXGC010102).

References

1. Alahmadi, B.A., Axon, L., Martinovic, I.: 99% false positives: a qualitative study of SOC analysts' perspectives on security alarms. In: 31st USENIX Security Symposium (USENIX Security 2022), pp. 2783–2800 (2022)
2. Cheng, Q., Wu, C., Zhou, S.: Discovering attack scenarios via intrusion alert correlation using graph convolutional networks. IEEE Commun. Lett. **25**(5), 1564–1567 (2021). https://doi.org/10.1109/LCOMM.2020.3048995
3. van Ede, T., et al.: DEEPCASE: semi-supervised contextual analysis of security events. In: 2022 IEEE Symposium on Security and Privacy (SP), pp. 522–539 (2022). https://doi.org/10.1109/SP46214.2022.9833671
4. Fu, C., Li, Q., Xu, K., Wu, J.: Point cloud analysis for ML-based malicious traffic detection: reducing majorities of false positive alarms. In: Proceedings of the 2023 ACM SIGSAC Conference on Computer and Communications Security, pp. 1005–1019. ACM, Copenhagen Denmark (2023). https://doi.org/10.1145/3576915.3616631
5. Ghadermazi, J., Hore, S., Shah, A., Bastian, N.D.: GTAE-IDS: graph transformer-based autoencoder framework for real-time network intrusion detection. IEEE Trans. Inf. Forensics Secur. **20**, 4026–4041 (2025). https://doi.org/10.1109/TIFS.2025.3557741
6. Hartzog, W., Solove, D.: We still haven't learned the major lesson of the 2013 target hack. Fortune (2022)
7. Kim, Y., Dán, G., Zhu, Q.: Human-in-the-loop cyber intrusion detection using active learning. IEEE Trans. Inf. Forensics Secur. **19**, 8658–8672 (2024). https://doi.org/10.1109/TIFS.2024.3434647
8. Liu, L., Engelen, G., Lynar, T., Essam, D., Joosen, W.: Error prevalence in NIDS datasets: a case study on CIC-IDS-2017 and CSE-CIC-IDS-2018. In: 2022 IEEE Conference on Communications and Network Security (CNS), pp. 254–262 (2022). https://doi.org/10.1109/CNS56114.2022.9947235

9. Liu, Y., et al.: DeepDRAC: disposition recommendation for alert clusters based on security event patterns. IEEE Trans. Inf. Forensics Secur. **20**, 6443–6458 (2025). https://doi.org/10.1109/TIFS.2025.3580337
10. Liu, Y., et al.: A context-aware clustering approach for assisting operators in classifying security alerts. IEEE Trans. Software Eng. **51**(1), 153–171 (2025). https://doi.org/10.1109/TSE.2024.3497588
11. Luo, X., et al.: BiCAM: a bidirectional contextualized attentive model for analyzing the correlation of heterogeneous security events. IEEE Trans. Reliab. **74**(2), 2640–2654 (2025). https://doi.org/10.1109/TR.2024.3491894
12. Mao, Q., et al.: FeCoGraph: label-aware federated graph contrastive learning for few-shot network intrusion detection. IEEE Trans. Inf. Forensics Secur. **20**, 2266–2280 (2025). https://doi.org/10.1109/TIFS.2025.3541890
13. Mirnajafizadeh, S.M.M., Sethuram, A.R., Mohaisen, D., Nyang, D., Jang, R.: Enhancing network attack detection with distributed and in-network data collection system. In: 33rd USENIX Security Symposium (USENIX Security 2024), pp. 5161–5178 (2024)
14. Seo, H., Yoon, M.: Generative intrusion detection and prevention on data stream. In: 32nd USENIX Security Symposium (USENIX Security 2023), pp. 4319–4335 (2023)
15. Tariq, S., Baruwal Chhetri, M., Nepal, S., Paris, C.: Alert fatigue in security operations centres: research challenges and opportunities. ACM Comput. Surv. **57**(9), 1–38 (2025). https://doi.org/10.1145/3723158
16. Wang, L., et al.: Incorporating gradients to rules: towards lightweight, adaptive provenance-based intrusion detection. In: Network and Distributed System Security Symposium. Internet Society, San Diego, CA, USA (2025). https://doi.org/10.14722/ndss.2025.230822
17. Wang, W., Yi, P., Jiang, J., Zhang, P., Chen, X.: Transformer-based framework for alert aggregation and attack prediction in a multi-stage attack. Comput. Secur. **136**, 103533 (2024). https://doi.org/10.1016/j.cose.2023.103533
18. Wang, X.: ENIDrift: a fast and adaptive ensemble system for network intrusion detection under real-world drift. In: Proceedings of the 38th Annual Computer Security Applications Conference, pp. 785–798. ACM, Austin TX USA (2022). https://doi.org/10.1145/3564625.3567992
19. Wang, X., Yang, X., Liang, X., Zhang, X., Zhang, W., Gong, X.: Combating alert fatigue with AlertPro: context-aware alert prioritization using reinforcement learning for multi-step attack detection. Comput. Secur. **137**, 103583 (2024). https://doi.org/10.1016/j.cose.2023.103583
20. Wei, F., Li, H., Zhao, Z., Hu, H.: xNIDS: explaining deep learning-based network intrusion detection systems for active intrusion responses. In: 32nd USENIX Security Symposium (USENIX Security 2023), pp. 4337–4354 (2023)
21. Wu, X., Gao, C., Zang, L., Han, J., Wang, Z., Hu, S.: ESimCSE: enhanced sample building method for contrastive learning of unsupervised sentence embedding. In: Calzolari, N., et al. (eds.) Proceedings of the 29th International Conference on Computational Linguistics, pp. 3898–3907. International Committee on Computational Linguistics, Gyeongju, Republic of Korea (2022)

22. Yang, L., et al.: True attacks, attack attempts, or benign triggers? An empirical measurement of network alerts in a security operations center. In: 33rd USENIX Security Symposium (USENIX Security 2024), pp. 1525–1542 (2024)
23. Zha, M., Zhang, J., Yang, G., et al.: A-NIDS: adaptive network intrusion detection system based on clustering and stacked CTGAN. In: 2022 International Conference on Networking and Network Applications (NaNA), pp. 344–351. IEEE (2022). https://doi.org/10.1109/NaNA56854.2022.00062

BRIDG-Q: Barren-Plateau-Resilient Initialisation with Data-Aware LLM-Generated Quantum Circuits

Ngoc Nhi Nguyen[1(✉)], Thai T. Vu[1], John Le[1], Hoa Khanh Dam[1], Dung Hoang Duong[1], and Dinh Thai Hoang[2]

[1] University of Wollongong, Wollongong, NSW, Australia
nnn469@uowmail.edu.au, {tienv,johnle,hoa,hduong}@uow.edu.au
[2] University of Technology Sydney, Sydney, NSW, Australia
Hoang.Dinh@uts.edu.au

Abstract. Quantum circuit initialisation is a key bottleneck in variational quantum algorithms (VQAs), strongly impacting optimisation stability and convergence. Recent work shows that large language models (LLMs) can synthesise high-quality variational circuit architectures, but their continuous parameter predictions are unreliable. Conversely, data-driven initialisation methods such as BEINIT improve trainability via problem-adaptive priors, yet assume fixed ansatz templates and ignore generative circuit structure. We propose **BRIDG-Q** (**B**arren-Plateau-**R**esilient **I**nitialisation with **D**ata-Aware LLM-**G**enerated **Q**uantum Circuits), a neuro-symbolic pipeline that bridges this gap by coupling LLM-generated circuit architectures with empirical-Bayes parameter initialisation. BRIDG-Q uses AgentQ to generate problem-conditioned circuit topologies, removes generated parameters, and injects data-informed parameter initialisations to mitigate barren plateau effects. Evaluations on graph optimisation benchmarks using residual energy gap and convergence metrics show improved optimisation robustness, indicating that data-driven initialisation remains effective even for LLM-generated circuits, with oracle per-instance selection achieving approximately a 10% reduction in final residual energy.

*Reproducibility.*All source code and data used in this study are publicly available at: https://github.com/nellyy2505/BRIDG-Q

Keywords: Variational quantum algorithms · barren plateaus · parameter initialisation · empirical Bayes · Beta distribution · large language models · quantum circuit generation · neuro-symbolic optimisation

1 Introduction

Variational Quantum Algorithms (VQAs) are a leading approach for near-term quantum computation, enabling hybrid quantum–classical optimisation on noisy

© IFIP International Federation for Information Processing 2026
Published by Springer Nature Switzerland AG 2026
H. Janicke et al. (Eds.): SEC 2026, IFIP AICT 787, pp. 434–448, 2026.
https://doi.org/10.1007/978-3-032-27993-4_30

intermediate-scale quantum (NISQ) devices [17,21]. In a typical VQA, a parameterised quantum circuit (PQC) prepares a quantum state whose parameters are iteratively updated by a classical optimiser to minimise a problem-dependent cost function, such as the expectation value of a Hamiltonian [3,16]. Despite their expressive power, VQAs are highly sensitive to circuit design choices, optimisation dynamics, and, critically, the initialisation of variational parameters [22].

A central obstacle to scalable VQA training is the *barren plateau* phenomenon, in which the variance of cost-function gradients decays exponentially with system size, rendering gradient-based optimisation ineffective [15]. Subsequent studies have shown that barren plateaus are not only determined by circuit depth, but also strongly influenced by entanglement structure and the locality of the cost function [4,14]. As a result, uninformed parameter initialisation can cause optimisation to stagnate early, even when the circuit itself is sufficiently expressive.

Two largely independent research directions have recently emerged to address complementary aspects of this challenge. On the one hand, data-driven initialisation strategies construct problem-adaptive priors over circuit parameters, significantly improving gradient behaviour during training [13,23]. On the other hand, large language models (LLMs) have been shown to generate expressive variational circuit architectures directly from problem descriptions [6,10]. However, existing pipelines typically combine LLM-generated circuit structures with generic or heuristic parameter initialisation, while data-driven initialisation methods assume fixed ansatz templates and do not exploit generative circuit synthesis. As a result, circuit architecture generation and parameter initialisation remain largely decoupled in end-to-end VQA workflows.

In this work, we bridge these two lines of research through a *neuro-symbolic* approach [9]. In our setting, "neuro-symbolic" denotes the combination of **neural reasoning**, embodied by an LLM that synthesises variational circuit topologies from data and examples, and **symbolic inductive bias**, encoded through human-interpretable rules for parameter initialisation grounded in empirical Bayes principles. This design complements the flexibility of learned structure generation with principled control over optimisation dynamics.

Our framework provides the following contributions:

1. We introduce **BRIDG-Q**, a unified pipeline that couples LLM-generated variational circuit architectures with empirical-Bayes parameter initialisation. This approach explicitly addresses the disconnect between circuit synthesis and parameter optimisation in end-to-end VQA workflows.
2. Extending BEINIT [13], we propose a *gate-aware stratified Beta* initialisation scheme that applies role-specific parameter scaling to control early entanglement growth, hence mitigating barren plateau effects in deep circuits.
3. We conduct a paired empirical evaluation on approximately 580 graph-based optimisation instances from the AgentQ benchmark suite [10], using energy-gap and convergence-efficiency metrics to characterise both solution quality and optimisation dynamics.

The structure of this paper is as follows. First, we review background on barren plateaus in variational quantum algorithms, data-driven parameter initialisation, and recent progress in LLM-based circuit generation. We then introduce the BRIDG-Q framework, describing how LLM-generated circuit structures are combined with empirical-Bayes parameter initialisation, including the gate-aware stratified variant. Next, we define the evaluation metrics and experimental protocol used to assess both solution quality and convergence behaviour. We subsequently present paired empirical results on graph-based optimisation instances from the AgentQ benchmark, comparing BRIDG-Q variants against standard baselines. Finally, we discuss the implications of these findings, outline current limitations, and highlight directions for future work.

2 Related Work

Barren Plateaus and Parameter Initialisation. The scalability of variational quantum algorithms (VQAs) is fundamentally limited by optimisation pathologies such as barren plateaus, first formally identified by McClean *et al.*, who showed that gradient variance can decay exponentially with the number of qubits under random parameter initialisation [15]. Subsequent analyses by Cerezo *et al.* demonstrated that barren plateau behaviour depends on the locality of the cost function and the circuit structure [4], while Marrero *et al.* linked plateau formation directly to entanglement growth and the emergence of unitary 2-designs [2,14]. These results motivated a line of work aimed at controlling circuit expressivity, particularly during the early stages of training. A number of heuristic and geometric initialisation strategies have been proposed to mitigate these effects [7]. Grant *et al.* introduced *identity initialisation*, in which parameters are chosen so that the circuit evaluates close to the identity operator, thereby preserving gradient magnitudes at initialisation [8]. More recently, Zhang *et al.* proposed *Gaussian initialisation* schemes with depth-dependent variance, providing theoretical guarantees that gradients vanish at most polynomially with circuit depth [24]. While these methods offer important insights into trainability, they do not exploit problem-specific structure encoded in the input instance.

Empirical-Bayes Initialisation. BEINIT [13] proposes an empirical-Bayes approach to parameter initialisation, in which circuit parameters are sampled from a Beta distribution whose hyperparameters are estimated from problem data via maximum likelihood. This strategy demonstrably increases gradient variance and reduces the likelihood of barren plateaus in deep variational circuits. However, BEINIT assumes a fixed ansatz structure and treats circuit parameters homogeneously, without accounting for gate semantics or circuit topology generated dynamically. As a result, its applicability is limited to scenarios in which the circuit architecture is predefined.

LLM-based Circuit Generation. Recent work has shown that LLMs can generate expressive variational circuit topologies directly from problem descriptions, reducing the need for manual ansatz design [16,18]. AgentQ [10] exemplifies this direction by synthesising problem-conditioned circuits that achieve competitive performance across a range of graph-based optimisation tasks. Nevertheless, existing pipelines generate circuit structure and continuous parameters jointly, without explicitly modelling parameter initialisation as a separate problem-adaptive design stage. As a result, the generated parameters do not incorporate fitted problem-aware priors or trainability-driven initialisation principles.

3 Methodology: The BRIDG-Q Framework

We propose **BRIDG-Q**, a neuro-symbolic framework that unifies generative topology design with data-driven parameter initialisation. The architecture addresses the "compatibility gap" between the discrete, symbolic reasoning of LLMs and the continuous, geometric optimisation required for VQAs.

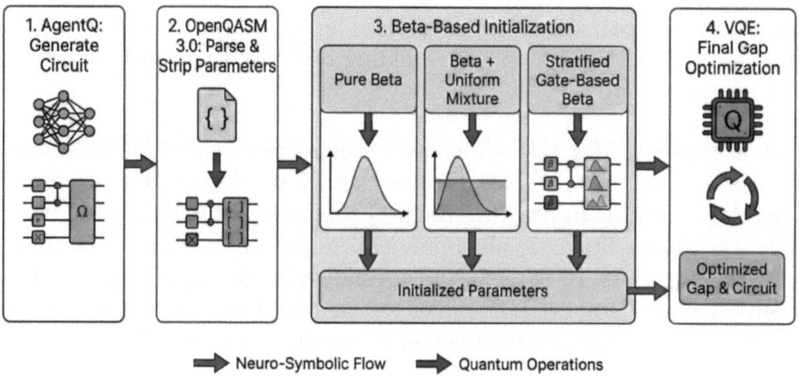

Fig. 1. Overview of the BRIDG-Q neuro-symbolic pipeline for variational quantum optimisation. Figure created with assistance from Gemini 3 and edited by the authors.

3.1 Architectural Overview

Figure 1 illustrates the BRIDG-Q pipeline as a directed acyclic workflow that transforms a graph-based combinatorial optimisation problem into an optimised variational quantum circuit. The design explicitly separates *circuit structure generation*, *parameter initialisation*, and *variational optimisation*. The workflow proceeds through four stages:

1. **LLM-Based Circuit Generation (AgentQ).** In the first stage, an LLM, AgentQ, is used to generate the *structure* of the variational ansatz. Conditioned on the input problem description, AgentQ produces an OpenQASM 3.0

[5] circuit specifying the gate sequence, qubit connectivity, and overall circuit layout. This stage is purely structural: although AgentQ emits numerical parameters, these are not retained, as they are not optimised with respect to the variational objective.
2. **OpenQASM Parsing and Parameter Stripping.** The generated OpenQASM 3.0 [5] code is then parsed to recover the circuit topology and identify all parameterised gates. Any numerical parameter values produced by the LLM are removed at this stage. The output of this step is a parameter-free circuit template that preserves the LLM-generated structure while deferring all continuous parameter choices to a dedicated initialisation module.
3. **Beta-Based Parameter Initialisation.** In the third stage, BRIDG-Q injects parameters into the stripped circuit using data-driven Beta priors. Problem-specific features, such as graph edge weights and Hamiltonian coefficients, are extracted from the input instance and normalised. These features are used to fit a Beta distribution via maximum likelihood estimation, following the BEINIT principle. From this learned prior, parameters are sampled using one of three variants: *pure Beta sampling*, a *Beta–uniform mixture*, or a *gate-aware stratified Beta scheme.*
4. **Variational Optimisation (VQE).** The initialised circuit is optimised using a standard VQE loop [20], yielding optimised parameters and a final residual energy gap.

Illustrative example: Max-Cut. Consider a four-node weighted Max-Cut instance with edges $\{(0,1,0.7),(1,2,0.3),(2,3,0.9),(0,3,0.5)\}$ and Hamiltonian $H = \sum_{(i,j)} w_{ij}\frac{1}{2}(I - Z_iZ_j)$. In Stage 1, AgentQ produces a circuit with four `ry` and three `crz` gates. In Stage 2, all numerical angles are stripped, leaving seven empty parameter slots. In Stage 3, the normalised edge weights $[0.7, 0.3, 0.9, 0.5]$ yield a fitted prior Beta$(1.8, 1.4)$; under the stratified variant, `ry` parameters are mapped to $[-\pi, \pi]$ while `crz` parameters are confined to $[-0.2, 0.2]$. Stage 4 then optimises via a standard VQE loop.

3.2 Data-Driven Priors: The BEINIT Formulation

As outlined in the architectural overview, BRIDG-Q explicitly removes all LLM-generated numerical parameters, leaving a symbolic circuit template. Section 3.2 describes how this template is populated with data-driven initial parameters using an empirical-Bayes formulation based on BEINIT [13].

Feature Extraction. The key idea behind this empirical Bayes formulation is to encode structural information about the optimisation problem into the parameter prior. Concretely, we construct a feature vector $\mathbf{x}_{\text{feat}}$ by aggregating information from two complementary sources:

- the **graph structure** of the problem instance, such as edge weights or capacities in the combinatorial graph, and
- the **Hamiltonian coefficients** extracted from the problem's cost function, provided by AgentQ as a `cost_hamiltonian` string.

All extracted values are parsed, normalised to the interval [0, 1], and concatenated into a single empirical data vector. Although BEINIT originally estimates its prior from labelled classical datasets, we show that graph- and Hamiltonian-derived features serve as an effective surrogate, enabling instance-specific prior construction without supervised labels.

Beta Distribution via MLE. Given the normalised feature vector $\{x_i\}_{i=1}^N$, we fit a Beta distribution using maximum likelihood estimation (MLE), where each $x_i \in [0, 1]$ denotes a scalar feature extracted from the input instance. The Beta density is defined as

$$f(x;\alpha,\beta) \;=\; \frac{x^{\alpha-1}(1-x)^{\beta-1}}{B(\alpha,\beta)}, \tag{1}$$

where α and β are shape parameters and $B(\alpha, \beta)$ denotes the Beta function. The optimal parameters are obtained by solving

$$(\hat{\alpha},\hat{\beta}) \;=\; \arg\max_{\alpha,\beta} \sum_{i=1}^{N} \log f(x_i;\alpha,\beta). \tag{2}$$

In practice, we perform a constrained Beta fit with fixed location and scale, and introduce a small numerical floor to avoid degenerate solutions. If the fitting procedure fails or the extracted features are constant, the method falls back to $\hat{\alpha} = \hat{\beta} = 1$, which corresponds to a uniform distribution.

Initialisation Variants. Building on the learned Beta prior, we implement the following *initialisation-only* variants within BRIDG-Q:

- **BRIDG-Q$^{\beta\text{–pure}}$.** All parameters θ_k are sampled directly from $\text{Beta}(\hat{\alpha}, \hat{\beta})$, then mapped to gate-specific angular ranges. This injects a strong inductive bias derived from the problem instance while retaining full expressive capacity.
- **BRIDG-Q$^{\beta\text{–mixture}}$.** To guard against overconfident or collapsed priors, we mix the learned Beta distribution with a uniform component:

  $$\theta_k \sim (1-\lambda)\,\text{Beta}(\hat{\alpha},\hat{\beta}) \;+\; \lambda\,\mathcal{U}[0,1], \tag{3}$$

  where $\lambda = 0.2$. This introduces controlled stochasticity at initialisation. While BEINIT injects Gaussian noise during training to escape saddle points [13], our use of a uniform mixture is restricted strictly to initialisation and serves to preserve exploration without modifying the optimisation dynamics.

3.3 BRIDG-Q$^{\beta\text{–stratified}}$: Gate-Aware Initialisation

While standard Beta-based initialisation already improves trainability by shaping the initial parameter distribution according to the problem instance, it still

Algorithm 1. BRIDG-Q Initialisation

Require: Circuit description Q; problem instance (G, H)
Ensure: Initial parameter vector $\boldsymbol{\theta}_{\text{init}}$
1: $C \leftarrow$ ParseOpenQASM(Q) {Recover gate list, wires, and param slots}
2: $C^{\emptyset} \leftarrow$ StripParameters(C) {Discard all LLM-emitted numeric values}
3: $\mathbf{x}_{\text{feat}} \leftarrow$ ExtractFeatures(G, H)
4: Normalise $\mathbf{x}_{\text{feat}}$ to $[0, 1]$
5: $(\hat{\alpha}, \hat{\beta}) \leftarrow$ MLE_BetaFit($\mathbf{x}_{\text{feat}}$)
6: $\boldsymbol{v} \leftarrow$ SampleBeta($\hat{\alpha}, \hat{\beta}, |\mathcal{P}|$) {$|\mathcal{P}| = \#$ parameterised gates}
7: **if** variant $= \beta$–mixture **then**
8: Replace a fraction λ of entries in $\boldsymbol{v}$ with $\mathcal{U}[0, 1]$
9: **end if**
10: $\boldsymbol{\theta}_{\text{init}} \leftarrow [\,]$; $p \leftarrow 1$
11: **for** each gate $g \in C^{\emptyset}$ in program order **do**
12: **if** g is parameterised **then**
13: $v \leftarrow \boldsymbol{v}[p]$; $p \leftarrow p + 1$
14: **if** variant $= \beta$–stratified **then**
15: **if** g.type $\in \{\texttt{rx}, \texttt{ry}, \texttt{u3}\}$ **then**
16: $\theta \leftarrow 2\pi v - \pi$
17: **else**
18: $\theta \leftarrow (v - 0.5) \cdot \epsilon$
19: **end if**
20: **end if**
21: Append θ to $\boldsymbol{\theta}_{\text{init}}$
22: **end if**
23: **end for**
24: **return** $\boldsymbol{\theta}_{\text{init}}$

applies a uniform scaling rule across all parameterised gates. In deep circuits, this can lead to excessive entanglement at initialisation, accelerating the formation of unitary 2-designs and inducing barren plateaus [19]. To address this limitation, we introduce **BRIDG-Q**$^{\boldsymbol{\beta\text{-stratified}}}$ which follows this principle: it restricts the initial strength of entangling gates while allowing single-qubit *driver* gates to fully explore the parameter space.

Core Idea. The key idea is to decouple where parameters come from (the Beta distribution learned via BEINIT) from how they are applied (gate-specific scaling rules). All parameters are sampled from the same Beta prior, then mapped to gate-dependent angle ranges based on functional role.

Algorithmic Procedure. Algorithm 1 summarises the BRIDG-Q initialisation process. Problem-specific features are extracted from the graph G and Hamiltonian H, normalised to $[0, 1]$, and used to fit a Beta distribution via maximum likelihood estimation, yielding shape parameters $(\hat{\alpha}, \hat{\beta})$ (lines 3–5). The circuit is then traversed in program order (lines 11–23). For each parameterised gate, a latent value is sampled from the fitted Beta prior (line 6), the functional role of the gate is identified, and a role-specific scaling transformation is applied to obtain the initial parameter value θ_k (lines 12–19). The resulting parameters are assembled into the initial vector $\boldsymbol{\theta}_{\text{init}}$ returned for optimisation (lines 21–24).

Gate-specific Scaling Rules. In practice, the stratification is implemented as follows:

- **Driver gates** (e.g., `rx`, `ry`, `u3`) receive parameters mapped to the full angular range,
$$\theta_k = 2\pi v_k - \pi, \tag{4}$$
corresponding to $[-\pi, \pi]$. This allows these gates to immediately explore the full Bloch sphere and drive meaningful state evolution.
- **Entangling gates** (e.g., `crz`, `crx`, `cry`) are initialised near the identity,
$$\theta_k = (v_k - 0.5)\,\epsilon, \tag{5}$$
where $\epsilon = 0.4$ by default, yielding a narrow range of $[-0.2, 0.2]$. This ensures that early entanglement is weak and gradually increases.

Rationale. By initialising entangling operations near the identity, BRIDG-Q$^{\beta\text{–stratified}}$ induces a weakly entangled starting regime even for deep circuits. This delays early randomisation and mitigates gradient collapse associated with approximate unitary 2-designs [19]. As optimisation proceeds, entanglement increases only where supported by gradient descent, enabling a smooth transition from a highly trainable regime to a more expressive circuit.

Remarks. Some single-qubit gates (e.g., `rz`) are conservatively scaled to prioritise stability at initialisation. This choice slightly restricts expressivity at $t = 0$ but does not limit the reachable parameter space during training.

4 Evaluation Metrics

We evaluate (i) solution quality via the residual energy gap and (ii) optimisation efficiency via iterations- and time-to-convergence. In practice, we report the evolution of the energy gap across optimisation steps and define it as

$$\Delta E(\boldsymbol{\theta}_t) \;=\; \left|E(\boldsymbol{\theta}_t) - E_{\text{exact}}\right|, \tag{6}$$

where $E(\boldsymbol{\theta}_t)$ denotes the variational objective value at optimisation step t. E_{exact} is the ground-truth optimal energy for the corresponding problem instance [1].

4.1 Primary metric: Energy gap

Here the variational objective is defined as

$$E(\boldsymbol{\theta}) \;=\; \langle\psi(\boldsymbol{\theta})|H|\psi(\boldsymbol{\theta})\rangle, \tag{7}$$

where H denotes the problem Hamiltonian. Throughout this work, we use the absolute difference in Eq. (6), which directly corresponds to the curves reported in our experimental results.

The energy gap provides a direct and task-aligned measure of performance. Rather than focusing on optimiser-specific signals, it evaluates whether the learned parameters actually produce a low-energy state for the target Hamiltonian [20]. This distinction is particularly important in the presence of barren plateaus: an optimiser may appear to converge or stabilise while remaining far from the true optimum [4,14]. By tracking $\Delta E(\boldsymbol{\theta}_t)$ over time, we capture both (i) *final solution quality*, where a smaller terminal gap indicates a better approximation to the optimal solution, and (ii) *convergence behavior*, reflected in how rapidly the energy gap decreases during optimisation.

The reference value E_{exact} is taken from the AgentQ benchmark suite, which provides a classically computed optimum objective value for each instance [10]. This fixed reference enables paired, instance-wise comparisons across initialisation strategies under identical problem instances.

4.2 Secondary metrics: Optimisation efficiency

Energy-gap curves convey both quality and dynamics, but two additional metrics are useful for quantifying efficiency in a single scalar per run.

Iteration Steps. We record the number of optimisation iterations executed, and in particular the *iterations-to-converge*:

$$T_{\text{conv}} = \min\{t : \Delta E(\boldsymbol{\theta}_t) \leq \varepsilon\}, \tag{8}$$

for a chosen tolerance ε. If the run never satisfies the criterion within a maximum budget $T_{\max}$, we set $T_{\text{conv}} = T_{\max}$ and treat it as non-convergent under the given budget. Since each iteration entails multiple circuit evaluations, T_{conv} serves as a proxy for total quantum-resource usage.

Time to converge. We measure wall-clock *time-to-converge* as

$$t_{\text{conv}} = \text{elapsed wall-clock time until Eq. (8) is first satisfied}, \tag{9}$$

including all forward evaluations (expectation estimation), gradient evaluations (if applicable), and classical optimiser overhead. This captures implementation-dependent costs not reflected by iteration counts.

5 Experimental Results

We evaluate BRIDG-Q using a paired comparison protocol in which all methods are tested on identical problem instances and circuit topologies, differing only in parameter initialisation.

5.1 Experimental Setup

Benchmark. Experiments are conducted on approximately 580 graph-based optimisation instances from the AgentQ benchmark [10], each consisting of a fixed problem Hamiltonian and an AgentQ-generated variational circuit expressed in OpenQASM 3.0. Following the AgentQ evaluation protocol, instances with missing baseline results or final baseline energy gap exceeding 5.0 are excluded, leaving 551 paired instances for analysis.

Initialisation Strategies. We compare the following methods, all evaluated on identical circuit topologies:

- **AgentQ (baseline):** LLM-generated parameters used directly.
- **Random:** Independent uniform sampling.
- **Uniform:** Deterministic uniform grid initialisation.
- **BRIDG-Q**$^{\beta\text{-pure}}$: Sampling from a fitted Beta prior.
- **BRIDG-Q**$^{\beta\text{-mixture}}$: Beta–uniform mixture ($\lambda = 0.2$).
- **BRIDG-Q**$^{\beta\text{-stratified}}$: Gate-aware Beta initialisation.
- **BRIDG-Q**$^{\beta\text{-best}}$: Oracle per-instance selection among Beta variants. This variant is reported solely to estimate the upper bound of Beta-based initialisation performance, and is not a deployable method.

Optimisation Settings. All methods share identical optimisation hyperparameters, summarised in Table 1.

Table 1. Experimental configuration shared across all evaluated initialisation strategies.

Parameter	Value
Optimiser	Adam [11]
Maximum iterations (T_{max})	400
Convergence threshold (ε)	0.05 (energy gap)
Baseline initialisation	AgentQ-generated
Beta mixture coefficient (λ)	0.2
Entangler scaling (ϵ)	0.4
Beta fitting method	MLE (fixed support)
Evaluation protocol	Paired, per-instance

Implementation and Compute Environment. All experiments are implemented in Python and executed on a Google Cloud Platform VM (`n1-standard-8`: 8 vCPUs, 30 GB RAM) equipped with a single NVIDIA T4 GPU, using Python 3.10 and CUDA 12.4.

5.2 Evaluation Results

Table 2 reports the paired performance of all initialisation strategies across 551 problem instances after baseline filtering. Results are summarised using mean residual energy, median paired improvement relative to the AgentQ baseline, success probability, and convergence latency, and wall-clock time.

Table 2. Paired comparison of initialisation strategies under identical problem instances.

Initialisation Method	Mean Residual	Median Improv.	Success Prob.	Conv. Latency	Time (s)
AgentQ (baseline)	0.440 ± 0.853	—	65.0%	236.3	1.99
Random	1.453 ± 4.079	−43.14%	42.6%	296.2	2.70
Uniform	1.447 ± 3.787	−37.86%	44.6%	314.5	2.67
BRIDG-Q$^{\beta\text{--pure}}$	1.203 ± 2.967	−18.23%	45.9%	331.7	2.66
BRIDG-Q$^{\beta\text{--mixture}}$	1.147 ± 3.265	−20.61%	44.8%	323.6	2.72
BRIDG-Q$^{\beta\text{--stratified}}$	1.373 ± 4.150	−7.39%	49.9%	342.9	2.73
BRIDG-Q$^{\beta\text{--best}}$	$\mathbf{0.368 \pm 1.522}$	**+10.39%**	**69.7%**	338.6	2.79

Paired Evaluation Protocol and Filtering. A run is considered successful if the final residual energy gap satisfies $\text{gap}_{\text{final}} \leq 0.05$. Instances for which the baseline initialisation produces a final gap greater than 5.0 (or no valid result) are excluded. All reported statistics are computed using strict per-instance pairing: a method contributes only when both it and the baseline produce valid energy gap and runtime measurements. We additionally report an oracle-selected variant, **BRIDG-Q**$^{\beta\text{-best}}$, which retrospectively chooses the best-performing BRIDG-Q variant per instance based on final gap (ties broken by runtime).

Baseline and Uninformed Strategies. AgentQ-generated initialisation provides a strong baseline, achieving a mean residual energy of 0.440 with a 65.0% success probability. In contrast, uninformed strategies such as random and uniform initialisation perform substantially worse across all metrics. Both exhibit large residual energies, negative median paired improvements (below −35%), and markedly lower success rates, confirming that naive initialisation is insufficient. We note that the large standard deviations in Table 2 reflect high instance-level variability inherent to the diverse graph structures in the benchmark; however, the consistent directionality of median paired improvements across all 551 instances, combined with the substantial gaps in success probability, suggest that the observed differences are unlikely to be attributable to noise alone.

Individual Beta-based Strategies. When evaluated individually, Beta-based initialisations (`BRIDG-Q`$^{\beta\texttt{-pure}}$, `BRIDG-Q`$^{\beta\texttt{-mixture}}$, and `BRIDG-Q`$^{\beta\texttt{-stratified}}$) improve upon random and uniform baselines but do not consistently outperform AgentQ. As shown in Table 2, their median paired improvements remain negative, indicating that no single fixed Beta prior is optimal across the full dataset.

Oracle-selected Beta Initialisation. To assess the upper bound of Beta-based initialisation performance, we report an oracle-selected variant, **BRIDG-Q**$^{\beta\text{-best}}$. For each instance, the oracle retrospectively selects the best-performing Beta-based strategy based on the final energy gap (with runtime as a tie-breaker). While not deployable, this analysis reveals that for a substantial fraction of instances, at least one Beta-based initialisation outperforms the AgentQ baseline.

Quantitatively, the oracle-selected Beta strategy achieves the highest success probability (69.7%) and a positive median paired improvement of +10.39%, representing an approximate 10% reduction in residual energy relative to AgentQ (Table 2). These results indicate that the limitation of Beta-based initialisation lies not in the expressiveness of the priors themselves, but in the absence of an instance-aware mechanism for selecting the most suitable prior (Fig. 2).

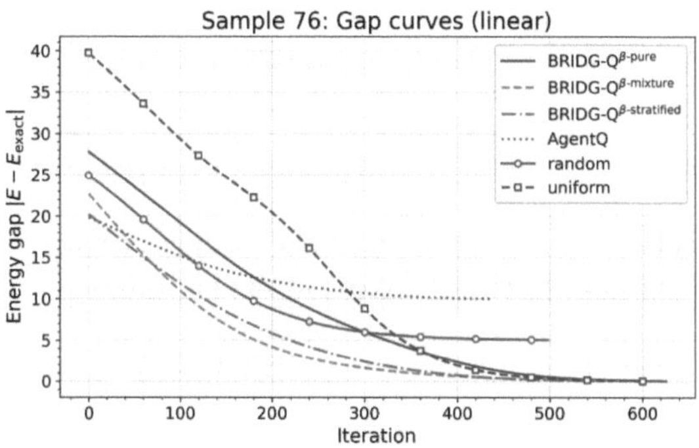

Fig. 2. Energy-gap trajectories for a representative problem instance (Sample 76). The plot shows the evolution of the absolute energy gap over optimisation iterations for different initialisation strategies. Beta-based methods (BRIDG-Q$^{\beta\text{-pure}}$, BRIDG-Q$^{\beta\text{-mixture}}$, and BRIDG-Q$^{\beta\text{-stratified}}$) exhibit slower initial convergence but continue to reduce the energy gap beyond the point where standard baselines (AgentQ, random, uniform) stagnate. In particular, BRIDG-Q$^{\beta\text{-stratified}}$ achieves the lowest final gap for this instance.

5.3 Discussion

Why Beta-based Methods Lose Individually. The inconsistent performance can be attributed to instance heterogeneity. Different graph structures and Hamiltonian distributions induce distinct optimisation landscapes [12], for which a single prior shape may be mismatched. As a result, fixed Beta priors may either under-regularise or over-constrain certain instances, leading to suboptimal convergence despite improvements over uninformed initialisation.

What the Oracle Result Reveals. The strong performance of the oracle-selected Beta variant demonstrates that data-driven priors are frequently beneficial, but their effectiveness is instance-dependent. The oracle exposes latent performance potential by showing that, for many instances, a suitable Beta-based initialisation exists that surpasses the LLM-generated baseline. This suggests that future gains depend less on inventing new priors and more on learning how to select or adapt priors based on instance-level signals.

Convergence Behaviour. Beta-based methods typically require more optimisation steps than the AgentQ baseline, reflecting prolonged exploration rather than inefficiency. By delaying early entanglement and gradient collapse, these methods maintain informative gradients for longer, which increases the likelihood of reaching lower-energy solutions.

Practical Considerations. Despite longer optimisation trajectories, wall-clock runtimes remain comparable across methods, indicating that improved robustness does not incur substantial computational overhead.

6 Conclusion

We presented **BRIDG-Q**, a neuro-symbolic framework that decouples LLM-based variational circuit synthesis from parameter initialisation in end-to-end VQA workflows. By injecting empirical-Bayes, gate-aware parameter priors into automatically generated circuit structures, BRIDG-Q addresses the mismatch between discrete circuit generation and continuous optimisation. Paired evaluation on a large AgentQ benchmark shows that while no single Beta-based strategy consistently outperforms the AgentQ baseline, oracle per-instance selection achieves an approximately 10% reduction in final residual energy with comparable runtime, indicating improved robustness in deep VQAs. These results highlight both the effectiveness and limitations of fixed, hand-designed priors, as performance remains instance-dependent and oracle selection is not deployable. Future work will therefore focus on practical, instance-aware or adaptive initialisation strategies, as well as extending this framework to broader problem classes, circuit families, and hardware-aware settings.

Funding Information. This research is partially supported by the ASQN BTQ Meso-Grants 2025.

References

1. Anschuetz, E.R., Kiani, B.T.: Quantum variational algorithms are swamped with traps. Nat. Commun. **13**(1), 7760 (2022). https://doi.org/10.1038/s41467-022-35364-5
2. Bañuls, M.C., Huse, D.A., Cirac, J.I.: Entanglement and its relation to energy variance for local one-dimensional hamiltonians. Phys. Rev. B **101**, 144305 (2020). https://doi.org/10.1103/PhysRevB.101.144305

3. Cerezo, M., et al.: Variational quantum algorithms. Nature Rev. Phys. **3**, 625–644 (2021). https://doi.org/10.1038/s42254-021-00348-9
4. Cerezo, M., Sone, A., Volkoff, T., Cincio, L., Coles, P.J.: Cost-function-dependent barren plateaus in shallow parametrized quantum circuits. Nat. Commun. **12**(1), 1791 (2021). https://doi.org/10.1038/s41467-021-21728-w
5. Cross, A., et al.: Openqasm 3: a broader and deeper quantum assembly language. ACM Trans. Quantum Comput. **3**(3) (2022). https://doi.org/10.1145/3505636
6. Dupuis, N., et al.: Qiskit code assistant: training LLMs for generating quantum computing code. In: 2024 IEEE LLM Aided Design Workshop (LAD), pp. 1–4. (2024). https://doi.org/10.1109/LAD62341.2024.10691762
7. Garcia-Saez, A., Latorre, J.I.: Addressing hard classical problems with adiabatically assisted variational quantum eigensolvers (2018). https://arxiv.org/abs/1806.02287
8. Grant, E., Wossnig, L., Ostaszewski, M., Benedetti, M.: An initialization strategy for addressing barren plateaus in parametrized quantum circuits. Quantum **3**,214 (2019). https://doi.org/10.22331/q-2019-12-09-214
9. Hitzler, P., Eberhart, A., Ebrahimi, M., Sarker, M.K., Zhou, L.: Neuro-symbolic approaches in artificial intelligence. National Sci. Rev, **9**(6), nwac035 (2022). https://doi.org/10.1093/nsr/nwac035, https://doi.org/10.1093/nsr/nwac035
10. Jern, L., Uotila, V., Yu, C., Zhao, B.: AGENT-Q: fine-tuning large language models for quantum circuit generation and optimization (2025). arXiv preprint
11. Kingma, D.P., Ba, J.: Adam: a method for stochastic optimization (2014). arXiv preprint
12. Krentel, M.W.: The complexity of optimization problems. In: Selman, A.L. (ed.) Structure in Complexity Theory. LNCS, vol. 223, pp. 218–218. Springer, Heidelberg (1986). https://doi.org/10.1007/3-540-16486-3_100
13. Kulshrestha, A., Safro, I.: BEINIT: avoiding barren plateaus in variational quantum algorithms. In: 2022 IEEE International Conference on Quantum Computing and Engineering (QCE), pp. 197–203. IEEE (2022). https://doi.org/10.1109/QCE53715.2022.00039
14. Marrero, C.O., Kieferová, M., Wiebe, N.: Entanglement-induced barren plateaus. PRX Quantum **2**(4), 040316 (2021). https://doi.org/10.1103/PRXQuantum.2.040316
15. McClean, J.R., Boixo, S., Smelyanskiy, V.N., Babbush, R., Neven, H.: Barren plateaus in quantum neural network training landscapes. Nat. Commun. **9**(1), 4812 (2018). https://doi.org/10.1038/s41467-018-07090-4
16. Mitarai, K., Negoro, M., Kitagawa, M., Fujii, K.: Quantum circuit learning. Phys. Rev. A **98**, 032309 (2018). https://doi.org/10.1103/PhysRevA.98.032309
17. Moll, N., et al.: Quantum optimization using variational algorithms on near-term quantum devices. Quantum Sci. Technol, 3(3), 030503 (2018). https://doi.org/10.1088/2058-9565/aab822
18. Ostaszewski, M., Grant, E., Benedetti, M.: Structure optimization for parameterized quantum circuits. Quantum **5**, 391 (2021). https://doi.org/10.22331/q-2021-01-28-391
19. Patti, T.L., Najafi, K., Gao, X., Yelin, S.F.: Entanglement devised barren plateau mitigation. Phys. Rev. Res. **3**(3), 033090 (2021). https://doi.org/10.1103/PhysRevResearch.3.033090
20. Peruzzo, A., et al.: A variational eigenvalue solver on a photonic quantum processor. Nat. Commun. **5**, 4213 (2014). https://doi.org/10.1038/ncomms5213
21. Preskill, J.: Quantum computing in the NISQ era and beyond. Quantum **2**, 79 (2018). https://doi.org/10.22331/q-2018-08-06-79

22. Qi, H., Xiao, S., Liu, Z., Gong, C., Gani, A.: Variational quantum algorithms: fundamental concepts, applications and challenges. Quantum Inf. Process. **23**(6), 1–32 (2024). https://doi.org/10.1007/s11128-024-04438-2
23. Rad, A., Seif, A., Linke, N.M.: Surviving the barren plateau in variational quantum circuits with bayesian learning initialization (2022). arXiv preprint
24. Zhang, K., Liu, L., Hsieh, M.H., Tao, D.: Escaping from the barren plateau via gaussian initialisations in deep variational quantum circuits. In: Advances in Neural Information Processing Systems, vol. 35, pp. 18612–18627. Curran Associates, Inc (2022)

Reinforcement Learning-Based Optimal Firewall Placement and Configuration (RL_OFPC)

Zahra S. Torabi(✉), David Eyers, and Veronica Liesaputra

School of Computing, University of Otago, Dunedin, New Zealand
torza566@student.otago.ac.nz

Abstract. Firewalls remain foundational to cybersecurity, yet their traditional perimeter-based role is challenged by the dynamic nature of modern zero-trust and virtualised networks. In these environments, virtual firewalls—software-defined security functions deployed within service graphs—provide flexible, fine-grained control over traffic flows. However, their scalability and performance are often constrained by sub-optimal placement and rule configuration, especially in large or rapidly evolving topologies. This research introduces the Reinforcement Learning–based Optimised Firewall Placement and Configuration (RL_OFPC) model, which addresses these challenges through two cooperating reinforcement learning agents. The FRC-Agent manages path computation and rule enforcement to satisfy hard security constraints, while the FPO-Agent determines optimal firewall locations that minimise the number of deployed firewalls and rule instances while maintaining proximity to critical network components. The model is evaluated against the state-of-the-art VEREFOO framework using both the Maximum Flow (MF) and Atomic Predicate (AP) algorithms across 120 synthetic topologies. Results demonstrate that RL_OFPC achieves up to 97.6% accuracy in Network Security Requirement (NSR) satisfaction, improves runtime efficiency by up to 27% in high-NSR environments compared with VEREFOO. However, as the number of Allocation Points (APs) increases, the model's exploration overhead grows, occasionally surpassing VEREFOO's scalability performance. Despite this, RL_OFPC consistently adapts better to topology modifications through localised Q-learning updates rather than full recomputation, confirming its suitability for dynamic, high-assurance network environments.

Keywords: reinforcement learning · virtual firewalls · firewall placement · network security requirement · scalability · adaptability

1 Introduction

Modern networks are increasingly defined by large-scale virtualisation, cloud-native deployments, and distributed service topologies [1]. While these advances

© IFIP International Federation for Information Processing 2026
Published by Springer Nature Switzerland AG 2026
H. Janicke et al. (Eds.): SEC 2026, IFIP AICT 787, pp. 449–462, 2026.
https://doi.org/10.1007/978-3-032-27993-4_31

deliver unprecedented flexibility and scalability, they also amplify the complexity of enforcing Network Security Requirements (NSRs) across rapidly evolving infrastructures [2]. Firewalls remain central to securing these environments, serving as critical control points for regulating access, isolating traffic, and protecting sensitive assets [3]. However, the effectiveness of firewall-based protection depends fundamentally on two interrelated decisions: *where* firewalls should be placed and *which* NSR should be configured on them as firewall rule set. Misplacement or inconsistent configuration can leave critical assets exposed, introduce rule conflicts, or create policy violations that adversaries may exploit [4]. As networks grow in scale and heterogeneity, manual and static approaches to managing firewalls become increasingly infeasible due to configuration errors [2], policy inconsistencies [5], and the rising frequency of rule anomalies in virtualised environments [6]. These challenges are further exacerbated by the dynamic nature of modern infrastructures. Virtual machines, microservices, and service chains are continuously instantiated, migrated, or removed, causing frequent changes in network topology that must remain aligned with security policies [7]. In such environments, administrators struggle to maintain accurate and up-to-date firewall configurations, as topology modifications can instantly invalidate previously correct placements or rule sets. Without adaptive support tools, administrators are forced to repeatedly reconstruct firewall policies, which is both time-consuming and error-prone [2]. Existing model-based systems [4,7–9] provide formal correctness guarantees but exhibit limited scalability as the number of Allocation Points (APs) and NSRs increases [8]. More critically, they rely on static optimisation mechanisms that require full recomputation whenever the network evolves, making them impractical for highly dynamic environments.

Reinforcement learning (RL) offers a compelling alternative for supporting administrators in such settings. RL enables agents to learn optimal sequential decisions through continuous interaction with the environment, making it particularly suitable for networks in which placement and configuration decisions must adapt to changes in topology, policy, and security constraints [2]. Unlike static optimisation, RL supports incremental updates, allowing the system to rapidly adjust without retraining or recomputing the entire decision space. This capability is essential for administrators who must maintain security correctness while coping with frequent network modifications [10,11]. Motivated by these challenges, this work introduces *RL_OFPC*, a reinforcement-learning framework that unifies firewall placement and rule configuration within a single autonomic architecture. RL_OFPC employs two cooperating agents: a Firewall Rule Configuration (FRC) agent that ensures conflict-free enforcement of NSRs, and a Firewall Placement and Optimisation (FPO) agent that learns optimal and topology-aware firewall deployments. By integrating correctness, optimisation, and adaptability, RL_OFPC addresses key limitations in existing approaches and provides administrators with a scalable and resilient mechanism for maintaining secure configurations in dynamic virtualised networks. The contributions of this work are as follows: (1) a unified reinforcement-learning framework that jointly automates firewall placement and rule configuration in virtualised networks; (2) an inherently adaptive optimisation process that handles topology changes through localised Q-learning without full recomputation; (3) a correctness-preserving FRC-Agent that installs conflict-free firewall rules to ensure complete NSR enforcement prior to optimisation; (4) an FPO-Agent that learns minimal, topology-aware firewall placements to reduce rule cardinality and deployment overhead while adapting to structural changes; (5) a comprehensive evaluation against the state-of-the-art VEREFOO framework over 120 synthetic topologies using both AP and MF configurations; and (6) empirical evidence that RL_OFPC achieves higher NSR satisfaction accuracy, improved scalability in policy-dense environments, and substantially better adaptability than VEREFOO under dynamic conditions.

The remainder of this paper is organised as follows. Section 2 reviews related work, while Sect. 3 presents the RL_OFPC framework. Section 4 describes the experimental setup and benchmarks used to compare RL_OFPC with VEREFOO on synthesised topologies. Section 5 reports scalability and adaptability results under increasing NSRs, APs, and topology changes. Section 6 analyses the findings, and Sect. 7 concludes the paper and outlines future directions.

2 Literature Review

A wide range of approaches has been proposed for firewall configuration, placement, verification, and optimisation. Table 1 compares representative tools across key dimensions. "Net." specifies whether a method targets traditional, virtualised, or hybrid networks. "FW-Pl." indicates support for firewall placement within Service Graphs (SGs), which model the logical network topology and relationships between services and required security functions, or Service Function Chains (SFCs), which represent ordered sequences of network functions that traffic must traverse to satisfy policy requirements. "Cfg." denotes the capability to generate, analyse, or manage firewall rule sets, while "Verif." captures whether correctness is ensured through formal or algorithmic validation. Soft-constraint optimisation is reflected by "OptR." for rule minimisation and "OptFW." for reducing the number of deployed firewalls. "Scal." reports the maximum problem size supported (e.g., number of rules or firewalls), and "Adapt." indicates whether the approach accommodates dynamic environments requiring re-evaluation under topology or policy changes.

The comparison reveals clear distinctions among existing approaches. Several well-established tools—including Firmato [12], FACE [14], STRONGMAN [23], FaVe [25], FireMason [19], NetPlumber [13], Formal Logic Analysis [17], Filtering Postures [15], and Rule Mining [21]—primarily address firewall rule analysis and configuration. Although some provide verification or rule-level optimisation, none support firewall placement, which limits their applicability in virtualised and distributed networks; among them, only STRONGMAN [23] and NetPlumber [13] offer limited adaptability to dynamic conditions. A smaller set of approaches—such as OpenMANO Policy Enforcement [18] and SFC Synthesis [22]—integrates firewall placement with configuration, but these methods either lack formal verification, exhibit limited scalability, or do not optimise firewall or rule counts.

Table 1. Comparison of state-of-the-art tools for firewall placement and configuration.

Approach	Net.	FW-Pl.	Cfg.	Verif.	OptR.	OptFW.	Scal.	Adapt.
Firmato [12]	Trad.	×	✓	✓	×	×	No Info	×
NetPlumber [13]	Virt.	×	✓	✓	×	×	52 Dev.	✓
FACE [14]	Trad.	×	✓	×	×	×	No Info	×
Filtering Postures [15]	Trad.	×	✓	×	×	×	10 Dev.	×
ConfigSynth [16]	Both	SG	×	✓	×	✓	20 FW	×
OpenMANO Policy Enforcement [18]	Virt.	SFC	✓	×	×	×	20 Dev.	✓
Formal Logic Analysis [17]	Trad.	×	✓	✓	×	×	No Info	×
FireMason [19]	Virt.	×	✓	✓	✓	×	500 Rules	×
Policy Mapping [20]	Both	×	✓	✓	×	×	5 FW	×
Rule Mining [21]	Virt.	×	✓	✓	✓	×	16 Rules	×
SFC Synthesis [22]	Both	SFC	✓	✓	×	×	No Info	×
STRONGMAN [23]	Trad.	×	✓	×	×	×	No Info	✓
Rule Set Minimization [24]	Both	SG	✓	×	✓	×	60 FW	×
FaVe [25]	Virt.	×	✓	✓	×	×	77,841 Rules	×
VEREFOO [4,7,8]	Both	SG	✓	✓	✓	✓	100 FW, 100 Rules	×

ConfigSynth [16] and Rule Set Minimization [24] consider placement optimisation but do not provide adaptability mechanisms for dynamic topologies. In contrast, VEREFOO [4,7,8] provides the most comprehensive functionality by jointly supporting placement, configuration, formal verification, and optimisation, scaling to 100 firewalls and 100 NSRs. Its main limitation is the lack of adaptability, as any topology change requires full re-execution. For this reason, VEREFOO serves as the primary benchmark against which RL_OFPC is evaluated, as the latter aims to retain correctness, optimisation, and scalability while explicitly addressing adaptability in dynamic network environments.

3 RL_OFPC Architecture

This section presents the architecture of RL_OFPC, a reinforcement learning–based framework for joint firewall placement and firewall rule configuration based on NSRs. As illustrated in Fig. 1 provides a high-level overview, illustrating how the RL_OFPC processes the Service/Allocation Graph (SG/AG) and Network Security Requirements (NSRs) through two coordinated reinforcement learning phases. In the first phase, the Firewall Rule Configuration Agent (FRC-Agent) computes valid flows, verifies rule correctness, resolves anomalies, and ensures that all *hard constraints*—particularly NSR compliance—are satisfied. In the second phase, the Firewall Placement Optimisation Agent (FPO-Agent) explores the topology to identify minimal, topology-aware firewall placements, reducing rule count and the number of deployed firewalls to meet *soft constraints* related to efficiency. The framework receives three main inputs: (1) the SG/AG graph, (2) the set of NSRs, and (3) initial topology information. The framework outputs an optimised, correctness-preserving firewall deployment that adapts when the network topology changes. The remainder of this section details the environment model, state representation, reward design, and the specific roles of the FRC-Agent and FPO-Agent.

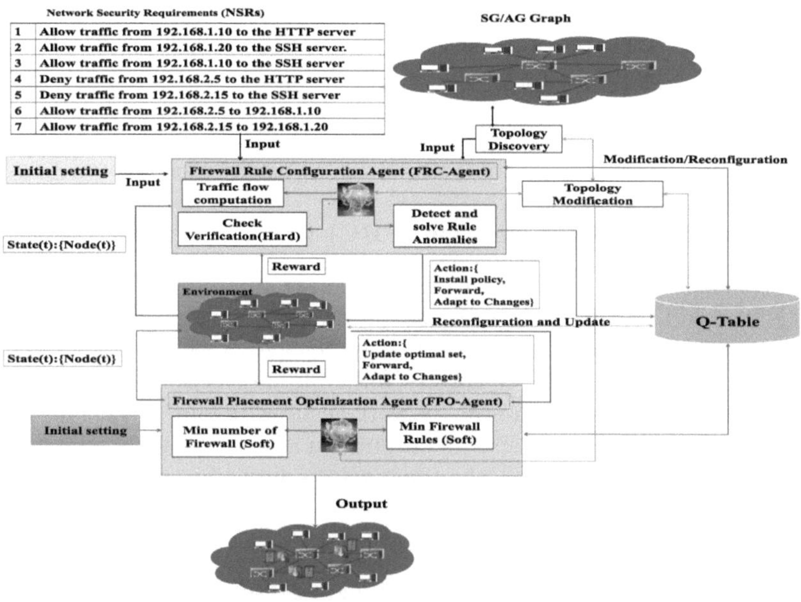

Fig. 1. High-level architecture of the RL_OFPC framework and its core components.

3.1 Topology Model and Learning Environment

RL_OFPC starts with topology discovery, representing the network's logical topology in the learning environment using a Service Graph (SG) and its extension, the Allocation Graph (AG). The SG is a directed graph $G_S = (N_S, L_S)$, where nodes denote endpoints and services, and edges represent admissible traffic flows. To enable firewall deployment, the SG is transformed into an AG, which extends the SG by adding Allocation Points (APs) as candidate firewall locations, yielding $G_A = (N_A, L_A)$ with $N_A = E_A \cup S_A \cup AP_A$ [4].

A Boolean allocation predicate

$$\text{allocated} : N_A \rightarrow \{\mathit{true}, \mathit{false}\} \tag{1}$$

indicates whether a node is included in the final deployment. Endpoints and services are always allocated, whereas an AP is allocated if and only if a firewall is placed at that location. Policy constraints further enforce that whenever a logical link is subject to a policy, a firewall must be deployed at the corresponding AP [8].

The learning environment is defined by the AG combined with the active NSRs, capturing topology, candidate firewall locations, and policy constraints. In RL_OFPC, the state representation encodes a comprehensive snapshot of the network derived from the Allocation Graph (AG). It encompasses endpoint nodes (E_A), service nodes (S_A)—including NATs, load balancers, gateways, and other intermediate network functions—and allocation points (AP_A). At each time step t, the system state is formally defined as

$$S_t = \{\text{State}(n_k, t) \mid n_k \in N_A\}, \tag{2}$$

where $N_A = E_A \cup S_A \cup AP_A$ represents the full set of nodes in the AG, and $\text{State}(n_k, t)$ captures the current attributes and conditions associated with node n_k at time t.

3.2 Firewall Rule Configuration (FRC) Phase

The FRC phase enforces all hard security constraints. The FRC-Agent computes NSR-compliant paths, installs and verifies firewall rules at candidate APs, resolves anomalies, and adapts to topology changes. Operating over the AG using reinforcement learning, it ensures full NSR satisfaction with correct forwarding behavior. Its inputs are the Network Security Requirements (NSRs) and the service/allocation graph, and its output is a set of APs with validated rule installations. At each time step, the agent selects actions from

$$A_t = \{a_1, a_2, a_3\}, \tag{3}$$

where a_1 installs or updates firewall rules, a_2 forwards traffic to a neighboring node, and a_3 updates policies in response to topology modifications. Each action induces a state transition

$$S_{t+1} = f(S_t, A_t), \tag{4}$$

allowing the agent to learn a policy that maintains rule correctness, policy compliance, and responsiveness to network dynamics.

Action selection follows an ε-greedy strategy due to its simplicity and low overhead in discrete state–action spaces. The agent balances exploration and exploitation by selecting the action with the highest Q-value with probability $1 - \epsilon$, and a random action with probability ϵ [11], as formalised in:

$$A_t = \begin{cases} \arg\max_a Q(S_t, a), & \text{with probability } 1 - \varepsilon, \\ \text{random action}, & \text{with probability } \varepsilon. \end{cases} \tag{5}$$

Although both FRC and FPO employ exploration, all candidate actions are validated against hard NSR constraints prior to deployment, ensuring that unsafe configurations are never applied to the operational network.

Reward Design and Learning. The reward function guides the agent toward correct, efficient, and adaptive rule deployment [10]. The node validity reward evaluates whether a selected node n, under a given policy π, is a suitable candidate for firewall rule deployment. It is formally defined as:

$$R_{\text{validity}} = \text{type\_compatible}(n, \pi) \wedge \text{in\_path}(n, \pi) \wedge \neg\text{redundant}(n, \pi) \tag{6}$$

where $\text{type\_compatible}(n, \pi)$ ensures that node n is a valid allocation point (i.e., not a server, host, NAT, or load balancer); $\text{in\_path}(n, \pi)$ verifies that the node lies on the NSR-determined forwarding path associated with policy π; and $\text{redundant}(n, \pi)$ checks whether π has already been applied at n. A positive reward R^+ is granted only when all validity conditions are satisfied, while violations result in a negative reward R^-, penalizing unsafe, redundant, or off-path actions. To prioritise adaptability, RL_OFPC assigns the highest reward R^c to topology changes detected by the Topology Modification Module, enforcing the priority relation $R^c > (R^+, R^-)$. Upon such changes, the agent triggers localized updates by modifying only the affected regions of the Q-table rather than recomputing global policies, enabling rapid and scalable adaptation to evolving network conditions.

At each time step t, the agent observes the current state S_t, selects an action A_t using an ϵ-greedy policy, receives an immediate reward R_t, and transitions to the next state S_{t+1}. The action–value function is updated using the Bellman equation [11]:

$$Q(S_t, A_t) \leftarrow Q(S_t, A_t) + \alpha\big[R_t + \gamma \max_{A'} Q(S_{t+1}, A') - Q(S_t, A_t)\big], \quad (7)$$

where $\alpha \in [0, 1]$ is the learning rate controlling adaptation speed, and $\gamma \in [0, 1]$ is the discount factor balancing immediate and future rewards [10]. Learning continues until Q-values converge and all Network Security Requirements (NSRs) are satisfied, after which the final Q-table is used for decision-making. Because decisions are derived from explicit Q-values and interpretable reward components (e.g., NSR coverage, performance metrics, and placement cost), firewall placements remain auditable and traceable for administrative verification.

Path Computation with AP and MF. Path computation in RL_OFPC is handled by the FRC-Agent using two complementary techniques: Atomic Predicate (AP) and Maximal Flow (MF) [9]. The AP-based approach decomposes traffic into minimal, non-overlapping packet classes, enabling fine-grained symbolic reasoning and preventing rule overlap and policy anomalies. This mode is particularly effective in dynamic environments requiring rapid reconfiguration.

In contrast, the MF-based approach aggregates traffic classes with identical end-to-end behavior, reducing computational complexity by reasoning at a coarser granularity. Before rule installation, anomaly detection is applied to preserve correctness. By supporting both AP and MF, RL_OFPC adaptively trades precision for scalability based on network size, policy density, and runtime constraints.

3.3 Firewall Placement and Optimization (FPO) Phase

The Firewall Placement and Optimization (FPO) phase constitutes the second stage of RL_OFPC and aims to minimize the number of deployed firewalls and rule complexity while preserving full NSR satisfaction. Leveraging the candidate Allocation Points (APs) and verified rule sets identified in the FRC phase, the FPO-Agent selects a minimal, topology-aware subset of APs—prioritizing proximity to security-critical components such as DMZs and gateways—to enable cost-efficient deployment and reduce redundancy. The agent adapts to topology changes and produces an optimized firewall placement with minimal overhead, operating under objectives, action spaces, and reward functions distinct from those of the FRC phase, as illustrated in Fig. 1.

The FPO phase defines an action set tailored to selecting optimal firewall nodes. It consists of three actions: *Update Optimal Set* (a_1), which conditionally adds or removes the current node based on its reward; *Forward* (a_2), which advances the agent to the next candidate node; and *Update Changes* (a_3), which instructs the agent to react to modifications in network topology or traffic conditions.

Its reward function combines policy coverage and structural criticality. The total reward R_{FPO} assigned to each candidate node is a weighted combination of two normalised sub-reward components:

$$R_{\text{FPO}} = w_1 \cdot f_{\text{coverage}} + w_2 \cdot f_{\text{critical}} \tag{8}$$

The weights w_1, w_2 reflect the relative priority of coverage and critical-node proximity and are tuned based on network requirements. The coverage-based component f_{coverage} evaluates whether the candidate node n_i contributes new policy coverage or subsumes existing rule sets in the current optimal set, and f_{critical} incentivizes placement near critical or high-connectivity nodes. A positive reward prompts the agent to add the node to the optimal set; otherwise, the agent skips the node and continues its exploration.

The Firewall Rule Minimization module reduces the rule footprint for each selected firewall by assigning a default action (either *ALLOW* or *DENY*) based on the dominant behaviour required by the flows traversing that node. Only deviations from this default behaviour are encoded as explicit rules. The process involves identifying flow types, selecting an appropriate default policy, marking exceptional flows, and pruning redundant or overlapping rules.

4 Experimental Setup

RL_OFPC is evaluated using synthetic network topologies from the publicly available VEREFOO dataset [4,7,8], ensuring a fair and consistent comparison with the state of the art. The datasets, available on GitHub[1], include complete network graph descriptions and Network Security Requirements (NSRs) encoded in XML format. In total, 120 synthetic topologies are used to assess scalability, with network sizes ranging from 10 to over 100 nodes and NSR counts varying between 10 and 100. To validate VEREFOO's reported scalability, its experiments were reproduced using the original configurations and open-source implementation [4]. Runtime performance was analysed under increasing numbers of NSRs and Allocation Points (APs) using one-way ANOVA tests at a 95% confidence level. No statistically significant differences were observed when varying NSRs with fixed APs (p-value = 0.734) or when increasing APs with a fixed NSR

[1] https://github.com/netgroup-polito/verefoo.

Table 2. Performance metrics for different learning rates (α) under varying NSR sets.

NSRs	$\alpha = 0.2$			$\alpha = 0.4$			$\alpha = 0.6$			$\alpha = 0.8$		
	Epochs	Runtime	Acc.	Epochs	Runtime	Acc.	Epochs	Runtime	Acc.	Epochs	Runtime	Acc.
20	380	5878	91.26	493	7248	92.37	593	9049	94.21	679	11571	**97.64**
40	508	14065	84.17	629	16065	87.27	730	18765	90.32	815	21287	**93.42**
60	874	24207	73.64	935	27707	81.58	1035	31308	82.76	1121	33830	**89.67**
80	997	37950	63.25	1137	41899	75.16	1237	48350	78.13	1323	50872	**85.87**
100	1295	62962	51.49	1442	70212	59.87	1543	81763	66.57	1628	84285	**81.95**

set (p-value = 0.339). Although minor overhead variations occurred, they were not statistically significant, confirming that the reproduced results closely match VEREFOO's original findings and provide a reliable baseline for comparison.

4.1 Parameter Settings for RL_OFPC

As introduced in Sect. 3.2, RL_OFPC is based on Q-learning and is governed by three key parameters: the learning rate (α), discount factor (γ), and exploration rate (ε). This subsection summarizes their empirical tuning and their impact on convergence behavior, runtime, and policy accuracy. Accuracy is used as the primary evaluation metric and is defined as the proportion of satisfied NSRs [4]:

$$\text{Accuracy (\%)} = \left(\frac{\text{Satisfied NSRs}}{\text{Total NSRs}} \right) \times 100. \tag{9}$$

A grid search was performed over $\alpha \in \{0.2, 0.4, 0.6, 0.8\}$, with γ and ε varied within $[0, 1]$. Each configuration was evaluated for NSR sets $\{20, 40, 60, 80, 100\}$ using three metrics: convergence (training epochs), runtime (ms), and accuracy. Table 2 reports the aggregated results. A clear trade-off emerges: higher α values yield consistently higher accuracy at the cost of longer convergence and increased runtime. For instance, $\alpha = 0.8$ achieves the highest accuracy of **81.95%** at NSR=100 but requires 1628 epochs, whereas $\alpha = 0.2$ converges faster but underfits, with accuracy decreasing to 51.49%.

Further tuning indicates that $\gamma = 0.6$ effectively balances short- and long-term rewards, while $\varepsilon = 0.2$ provides sufficient exploration without destabilizing convergence. Consequently, the configuration $\alpha = 0.8$, $\gamma = 0.6$, and $\varepsilon = 0.2$ was selected for RL_OFPC, offering a robust balance between accuracy, convergence stability, and computational overhead. Despite extensive evaluation, several limitations remain. First, synthetic topologies may not capture all characteristics of specialised real-world networks. Second, RL parameters were empirically tuned and may not be globally optimal across all scenarios. Third, the evaluation focuses on correctness and runtime, while fault tolerance and adversarial robustness are not explicitly addressed. Finally, RL training introduces computational overhead, which may challenge resource-constrained environments, although this cost is amortised over time.

5 Results and Analysis

A comparative evaluation of RL_OFPC and VEREFOO is presented, examining scalability, runtime efficiency, and adaptability under increasing security constraints and topology modifications.

5.1 Scalability and Performance Analysis of RL-OFPC and VEREFOO

This subsection evaluates the runtime scalability of RL_OFPC and VEREFOO under increasing Network Security Requirements (NSRs) and Allocation Points (APs), using both Maximum Flow (MF) and Atomic Predicate (AP) algorithms. Each configuration was executed 30 times, and mean runtimes are reported to ensure statistical robustness. Figure 2 presents six plots comparing the FRC phase, the FPO phase, and the complete framework for both algorithms.

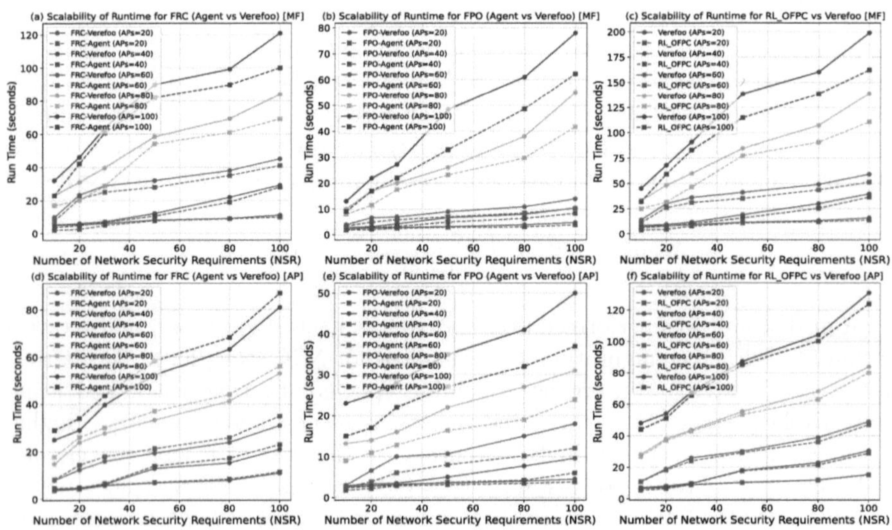

Fig. 2. Runtime comparison under increasing NSRs for Maximum Flow (MF) and Atomic Predicate (AP) algorithms, comparing RL_OFPC and VEREFOO and their respective FRC and FPO components.

Results Based on the Maximum Flow (MF) Algorithm. Under the MF algorithm, RL_OFPC demonstrates improved scalability as NSRs increase. As shown in Fig. 2(a), the FRC-Agent outperforms FRC-VEREFOO, with runtime reductions reaching approximately 17–20% at NSR = 100 for large AP configurations, due to learned rule reuse rather than repeated symbolic constraint solving. Similarly, Fig. 2(b) shows that the FPO-Agent outperforms FPO-VEREFOO across all AP and NSR settings, achieving up to 27% runtime reduction at high NSRs by avoiding exhaustive placement recomputation. At the system level (Fig. 2(c)), RL_OFPC matches VEREFOO at low NSRs but becomes 15–22% faster as policy density increases, confirming the scalability advantage of learning-based reuse over repeated MaxSMT recomputation.

Results Based on the Atomic Predicate (AP) Algorithm. The AP-based results highlight a trade-off between learning overhead and static efficiency. As shown in Fig. 2(d), FRC-VEREFOO outperforms the FRC-Agent at high AP and NSR values due to atomic predicate decomposition, which expands the FRC-Agent's state–action space and increases learning cost, while FRC-VEREFOO processes atomic flows statically without exploration overhead. In contrast, Fig. 2(e) shows that the FPO-Agent consistently outperforms FPO-VEREFOO under AP, achieving up to 25% runtime reduction at high NSR and AP values by leveraging learned placement heuristics and avoiding redundant firewall deployments. At the system level (Fig. 2(f)), RL_OFPC achieves average runtime reductions of 9–20% as NSRs increase. When APs become large, additional Q-learning overhead reduces scalability relative to VEREFOO in static AP-heavy scenarios, while RL_OFPC remains more efficient in policy-intensive and adaptive environments.

5.2 Runtime Evaluation Under Topology Modifications

This subsection evaluates runtime performance under dynamic topology changes, considering incremental node and link additions or removals and their impact on firewall configuration and placement in RL_OFPC compared to VEREFOO. Figure 3 illustrates runtime trends under increasing topology modifications for three network sizes. In subplot (a) (NSR=20, APs=20), both frameworks show similar runtime up to 20–30 modifications; beyond this point, RL_OFPC scales more efficiently. At 50 modifications, RL_OFPC requires approximately 1320 ms, while VEREFOO reaches about 1800 ms, reflecting a 36% increase, highlighting the benefit of localized updates over full recomputation. The advantage strengthens in larger configurations. In subplot (b) (NSR=60, APs=50), RL_OFPC achieves nearly 49% lower runtime at 40 modifications by incrementally updating Q-values instead of solving global constraints. Subplot (c) (NSR=100, APs=100) confirms this trend: at 50 modifications, VEREFOO exceeds 6100 ms, whereas RL_OFPC remains below 4400 ms, yielding a 27.9% reduction. Across all scenarios, the FRC-Agent and FPO-Agent outperform VEREFOO, demonstrating that RL_OFPC's decentralized learning-based adaptation improves runtime scalability in dynamic, large-scale networks.

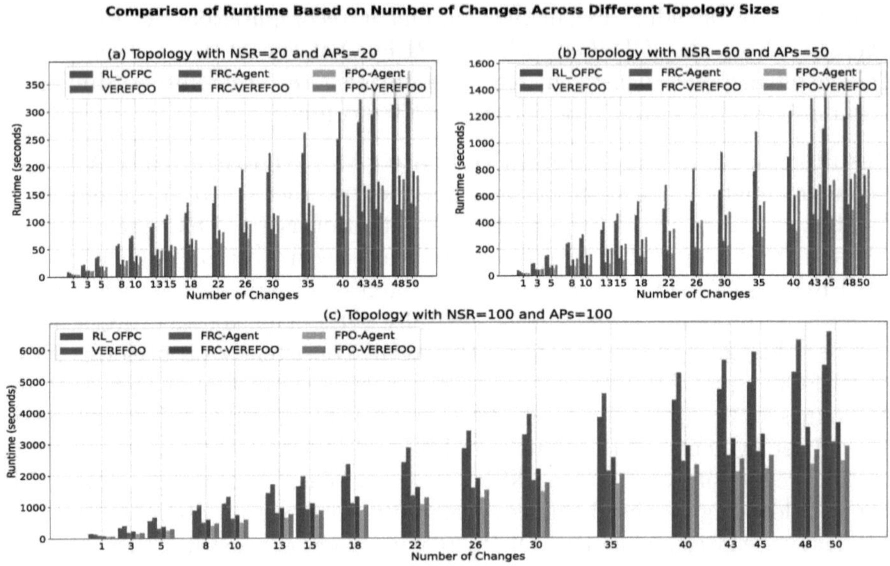

Fig. 3. Runtime comparison under incremental topology changes for RL_OFPC and VEREFOO: (a) NSR=20, APs=20; (b) NSR=60, APs=50; (c) NSR=100, APs=100.

6 Discussion

The comparative analysis reveals a clear crossover behaviour between VEREFOO and RL_OFPC as the balance between Allocation Points (APs) and Network Security Requirements (NSRs) changes. VEREFOO outperforms RL_OFPC when APs are high (≥ 80) and NSRs are low to moderate (≤ 30), where the NSR-to-AP fraction is small and the exploration overhead of Q-learning outweighs its benefits. In such sparse-policy environments with many candidate deployment locations, VEREFOO's static optimisation provides lower runtime and is therefore more suitable for administrators managing largely static networks. Conversely, as the NSR-to-AP fraction increases, RL_OFPC consistently outperforms VEREFOO by reusing learned policy patterns and avoiding redundant recomputation; for example, in dense-policy settings (NSRs ≥ 60, APs ≤ 60), RL_OFPC achieves up to 25–28% runtime reduction. From an operational perspective, this provides clear guidance: (1) when the NSR-to-AP fraction is below 1, VEREFOO is preferable; (2) when it reaches or exceeds 1.25, RL_OFPC becomes superior in scalability and efficiency. Accordingly, RL_OFPC is best suited for enterprise and cloud environments with policy-heavy configurations and strict compliance requirements, such as healthcare and financial networks.

7 Conclusion and Future Works

This work presented RL_OFPC, a reinforcement learning–based framework for automated firewall configuration and placement, consisting of an FRC phase for NSR-compliant path computation under hard constraints and an FPO phase for performance-aware placement optimisation. Evaluation using Atomic Predicate (AP) and Maximum Flow (MF) over 120 synthetic topologies demonstrates full NSR satisfaction and improved performance over VEREFOO in policy-dense and dynamic settings, with runtime reductions of 25–28% (MF), up to 28% (AP, NSR $\geq$ 60), and up to 60% under topology modifications (NSR=100, APs=100). VEREFOO remains more efficient in static scenarios with many Allocation Points (APs $\geq$ 80) and sparse policies (NSRs $\leq$ 30). RL_OFPC relies on tabular Q-learning, limiting scalability in large state spaces; future work will investigate (1) Deep Q-Networks (DQN) to address large-scale state-space limitations and (2) integration with a network digital twin to validate placement and configuration updates in a near real-time replica prior to deployment, reducing reconfiguration exposure and enabling safer adaptive operation.

Acknowledgments. The authors thank the School of Computing at the University of Otago for providing the computational resources and research environment required for this study.

Disclosure of Interests. The authors have no competing interests to declare.

References

1. Network functions virtualisation (NFV); architectural framework. ETSI ISG NFV: ETSI GS NFV, **2** (2015)
2. Bringhenti, D., Marchetto, G., Sisto, R., Valenza, F.: Automation for network security configuration: state of the art and research trends. ACM Comput. Surv. **56**(3), 1–37 (2023)
3. Liang, J., Kim, Y.: Evolution of firewalls: toward securer networks using next-generation firewall. In: IEEE CCWC, pp. 752–759. IEEE (2022)
4. Bringhenti, D., Marchetto, G., Sisto, R., Valenza, F., Yusupov, J.: Automated firewall configuration in virtual networks. IEEE Trans. Dependable Secure Comput. **20**(2), 1559–1576 (2022)
5. Al-Shaer, E.S., Hamed, H.H.: Discovery of policy anomalies in distributed firewalls. In: IEEE INFOCOM, vol. 4, pp. 2605–2616. IEEE (2004)
6. Hakani, D., Mann, P.S.: Intra firewall anomaly policies detection in cloud environment using firewall tree. Trans. Indian Natl. Acad. Eng , 1–10 (2024)
7. Bringhenti, D., Marchetto, G., Sisto, R., Valenza, F., Yusupov, J.: Automated optimal firewall orchestration and configuration in virtualized networks, pp. 1–7. (2020)
8. Bringhenti, D., Marchetto, G., Sisto, R., Valenza, F., Yusupov, J.: Towards a fully automated and optimized network security functions orchestration. In: ICCCS, pp. 1–7. IEEE (2019)
9. Bringhenti, D., Bussa, S., Sisto, R., Valenza, F.: A two-fold traffic flow model for network security management. IEEE Trans. Netw. Serv, Manag (2024)

10. Chen, C., Xue, F., Lu, Z., Tang, Z., Li, C.: RLMR: reinforcement learning based multipath routing for SDN. Wirel. Commun. Mob. Comput. **2022**(1), 5124960 (2022)
11. Casas-Velasco, D.M., Rendon, O.M.C., da Fonseca, N.L.S.: Intelligent routing based on reinforcement learning for software-defined networking. IEEE Trans. Netw. Serv. Manage. **18**(1), 870–881 (2020)
12. Bartal, Y., Mayer, A., Nissim, K., Wool, A.: Firmato: a novel firewall management toolkit. ACM Trans. Comput. Syst. **22**(4), 381–420 (2004)
13. Kazemian, P., Chang, M., Zeng, H., Varghese, G., McKeown, N., Whyte, S.: Real-Time network policy checking using header space analysis. In: NSDI, pp. 99–111 (2013)
14. Verma, P., Prakash, A.: FACE: a firewall analysis and configuration engine, pp. 74–81. IEEE (2005)
15. Guttman, J.D.: Filtering postures: local enforcement for global policies. In: IEEE Symposium on Security and Privacy, pp. 120–129. IEEE (1997)
16. Rahman, M.A., Al-Shaer, E.: Automated synthesis of distributed network access controls: a formal framework with refinement. IEEE Trans. Parallel Distrib. Syst. **28**(2), 416–430 (2016)
17. Govaerts, J., Bandara, A., Curran, K.: A formal logic approach to firewall packet filtering analysis and generation. Artif. Intell. Rev. **29**, 223–248 (2008)
18. Basile, C., Valenza, F., Lioy, A., Lopez, D.R., Perales, A.P.: Adding support for automatic enforcement of security policies in NFV networks. IEEE/ACM Trans. Netw. **27**(2), 707–720 (2019)
19. Hallahan, W.T., Zhai, E., Piskac, R.: Automated repair by example for firewalls. In: FMCAD, pp. 220–229. IEEE (2017)
20. Ranathunga, D., Roughan, M., Kernick, P., Falkner, N.: Mathematical foundations for mapping policies to network devices. In: SECRYPT, vol. 2, pp. 197–206. SCITEPRESS (2016)
21. Golnabi, K., Min, R.K., Khan, L., Al-Shaer, E.: Analysis of Firewall Policy Rules Using Data Mining Techniques. In: NOMS, pp. 305–315. IEEE (2006)
22. Schnepf, N., Badonnel, R., Lahmadi, A., Merz, S.: Rule-Based Synthesis of Chains of Security Functions for Software-Defined Networks. Electron. Commun. EASST **76**, (2019)
23. Keromytis, A.D., Anagnostakis, K.G., Ioannidis, S., Greenwald, M., Smith, J.M.: Managing access control in large scale heterogeneous networks. Wireless Pers, Commun (2003)
24. Yoon, M., Chen, S., Zhang, Z.: Minimizing the maximum firewall rule set in a network with multiple firewalls. IEEE Trans. Comput. **59**(2), 218–230 (2009)
25. Lorenz, C., Clemens, V., Schrötter, M., Schnor, B.: Continuous verification of network security compliance. IEEE Trans. Netw. Serv. Manag. **19**(2), 1729–1745 (2021)

AMPhitryon: Efficient Small Data Compression for Low-Bandwidth Covert Channels

Steffen Wendzel[1(✉)], Sebastian Zillien[1], and Sebastian Zander[2]

[1] Ulm University, Ulm, Germany
{steffen.wendzel,sebastian.zillien}@uni-ulm.de
[2] Murdoch University, Perth, Australia
s.zander@murdoch.edu.au
https://www.uni-ulm.de/en/in/omi/

Abstract. A plethora of known methods describe how policy-breaking transmissions can be conducted, e.g., through network censorship circumvention channels or through local covert channels. While some of these channels have very low capacities, only a few studies have been published on improving the content-compressibility for such channels. However, existing methods are either not useful for compressing *small* data, require to crawl third-party content (e.g., websites), or can only transfer data with small bitrates. Nevertheless, in reality typical payloads are often small (e.g., user credentials, status updates, or chat messages) and usually remain uncompressed, leaving more traces for an adversary to analyze.

We introduce AMPhitryon, a novel approach to compress *small* payloads <100 B (especially 4–20 B). It can be used with existing tools to compress small payloads, while larger payloads can be compressed with arbitrary compressors. AMPhitryon employs a local dictionary that is compiled incrementally in a context-specific setting (e.g., the context could be a network flow or a chat). Our evaluation shows that AMPhitryon achieves higher compression ratios for short messages than existing techniques. It reaches the lowest (best) compressibility ratios (down to 0.30) with the smallest payloads (<20 B).

Keywords: Data Compression · Internet Censorship · Network Security · Covert Channels · Network Traffic · Information Hiding

1 Introduction

Covert channels are policy-breaking, stealthy communication channels [22]. Although covert channels are often used for illegitimate purposes, they also have legitimate applications, such as hidden remote system administration, hidden sensor data collection, or censorship circumvention. The latter case of censorship circumvention becomes increasingly important as censorship is now present in several countries around the world [3,19].

© IFIP International Federation for Information Processing 2026
Published by Springer Nature Switzerland AG 2026
H. Janicke et al. (Eds.): SEC 2026, IFIP AICT 787, pp. 463–477, 2026.
https://doi.org/10.1007/978-3-032-27993-4_32

Typically, the core goal of censors is to block unwanted flows to sites serving undesired content, such as websites featuring critical opinions or chat platforms where undesired opinions are exchanged. Censorship can be circumvented using tools such as Tor, Psiphone, VPN setups, network steganography tools, obfuscation tools, or a combination of these (e.g., Tor obfuscation extensions). However, a censor can easily detect the use of some of these tools, such as Tor or VPNs. Hence, in this paper, we focus on tools that establish different forms of policy-breaking communication channels, referred to as *covert channels*, which are challenging to detect.

Successful detection of covert channels often depends on the amount of traffic that can be observed. In general, the less traffic is transmitted, the harder it is to detect covert channels, since they are designed to blend in as "noise in legitimate traffic [5,16]. For low data volumes, many statistical tests typically used to detect covert channels lack the power to distinguish between covert channels and legitimate traffic. In addition, more stealthy covert channels often have very low bandwidths, such as covert channels in games that provide up to 13 bit/s [21] or temperature-based covert channels that provide up to 12.5 bit/s [10]. Consequently, users will aim to compress the data before transmitting.

However, most existing compressors, such as GZip or BZip2, are not optimized for small messages that are typically exchanged on covert channels. In many scenarios, covert channels transfer many small payloads (i.e., <100 B), such as chat messages, username/password strings, or small fractions of website content (small images, scripts, or .css files). Existing compression algorithms have difficulties effectively compressing small data chunks, as these may contain only a few redundancies or the overhead of the internal dictionary is large.

In this paper, we address this compression problem by introducing a novel compression approach tailored to small payloads <100 B, with a focus on 4–20 B. Our approach is loosely based on the concept of *covert channel amplification* [18], i.e., transferring only small "pointers" to larger chunks of existing data accessible to the communicating peers (Alice and Bob). In our scenario, Alice and Bob iteratively build a dictionary that they both use to replace parts of messages with smaller pointers to the dictionary. For instance, Alice might send chat messages or part of a website to Bob. Every new byte string can be added to the dictionary used by Alice and Bob. Once a part of the string occurs again, Alice (and Bob) can simply refer to the particular byte string in the dictionary and decrease the size of even small payloads. Rather than building a dictionary on-the-fly, a pre-built dictionary optimized for certain types of messages could be used by Alice and Bob.

In particular, our key contributions are the following:

1. A novel lossless method to compress small messages dubbed AMPHITRYON[1], which can be used to minimize the "footprint" of censorship circumvention.

[1] We use "AMP" to refer to *amplification*. Moreover, reflected by the prefix *amphi-*, which can be translated as *on both sides*, our amplification relies on the combination of *both* components: the transferred (compressed) data channel and the dictionary component being pointed to by the compressed data. *Amphitryon* itself can be translated as *harassing both sides* [20].

It can be used with arbitrary circumvention tools and covert channels to compress the data prior to encryption or embedding.
2. An in-depth evaluation of AMPhitryon's compression performance, including a comparison with traditional compression approaches.

The key results of our evaluation show that AMPhitryon provides better compression performance than all state-of-the-art compressors when it comes to small messages. To aid replication studies, the AMPhitryon implementation is available at https://github.com/cdpxe/AMPhitryon.

The remainder of this paper is structured as follows. Section 2 discusses related work. Section 3 defines the censorship circumvention scenario and describes the design and implementation of AMPhitryon. Section 4 evaluates the proposed approach and compares it with traditional compression techniques. Section 5 concludes and outlines future work.

2 Related Work

Dictionary-based compression techniques emerged early, including those used by the GIF file format and the UNIX `compress` command [15]. These techniques rely on the presence of regularly occurring patterns that are used to form *dictionaries*. The core idea of these methods is to refer to dictionary elements in compressed data with references smaller than the data they refer to, leading to a reduction in size compared to uncompressed data [15].

Most common compression schemes, such as ZIP, GZip, LZMA/7z, utilize internal dictionaries stored in the data (i.e. file), which makes them less effective for applications focused on short messages. Two recently proposed compression schemes, *Brotli* [1] and zstd [11] are dictionary-based too and provide support for external dictionaries. We compare AMPhitryon with both.

Recently, Wendzel *et al.* introduced the idea of *covert channel amplification* in [18]. The amplification is achieved by transferring small pointers that refer to data chunks that are larger than the pointer itself. In that sense, fewer data must be sent than is actually transmitted. Such an amplification can be achieved in multiple ways. In case of DYST (*Did You See That?*) [18], a sender points to previously seen broadcast packets which hash values match the secret messages to be transferred. While DYST was the first attempt towards realizing covert channel amplification, its typical transmission rate is < 1 bit/s (< 59 bit/s when multiple pointers are used in parallel while reducing stealthiness). The transmission rate of DYST was increased through improved coding and reference strategies of SHP (*Silent History Protocol*) by Weißenborn and Wendzel [17], which improved DYST's bitrate by a factor of over 136 [17].

Another attempt to improve DYST was made by Zillien *et al.* with OPPRESSION (*Open Knowledge Compression*) [23]. OPPRESSION is an addition to censorship circumvention tools and requires the sender and receiver to crawl websites, such as Wikipedia or ProjectGutenberg to build dictionaries in the form of Patricia Tries (a variant of tree). To transfer a secret message, the sender must transfer a pointer to a tree node.

Keller and Litzinger [7] published a method to compress a packet's content and embed a secret message in the gained space. In comparison to earlier works, they focus on short packets (30 – 250 bytes) and apply a Huffman-inspired and run length-inspired coding on non-equidistributed payloads.

A related field is steganography by *cover selection*, where an image database is created and the values of the images are hashed. If the secret message matches a hash, the image is transferred instead. Several methods have been proposed to conduct or optimize the cover selection process, e.g., [2,4,8].

Recently, specialized compression techniques have also been proposed in other research domains. For example, Roy et al. proposed a novel lossless compression algorithm for Deoxyribonucleic acid (DNA) or ribonucleic acid (RNA) sequences that outperforms standard techniques, such as zstd or LZMA/7z [13].

In contrast to the vast majority of traditional compression schemes, AMPHITRYON separates the dictionary from the data to be transmitted. The only similar compression techniques are Brotli and zstd, which also use external dictionaries and have shown good compression performance on small data chunks. Furthermore, AMPHITRYON is not limited to (rather) low transmission rates, such as SHP and DYST, nor does it depend on downloading public websites (OPPRESSION) or image databases (cover selection steganography), which introduces synchronization issues and due to the size and public nature of these datasets might cause the attention of adversaries. Moreover, unlike OPPRESSION, AMPHITRYON does not focus solely on textual messages, but can also handle binary data. Compared to the work by Keller and Litzinger, AMPHITRYON can compress even smaller payloads (below 30 bytes). Finally, AMPHITRYON is the only method that has been designed to be part of covert channel tools in practical settings, as it can be incorporated by such tools before secret data is embedded or encrypted.

3 Scenario, Design and Implementation

In this section, we first define the threat scenario and then describe the design and implementation of AMPHITRYON.

3.1 Threat Scenario

We consider a scenario in which Alice and Bob want to remain stealthy in order to prevent being detected by an observer, for example, the case of censorship circumvention. We assume that in a scenario like censorship circumvention, often only small messages are exchanged, such as chat messages. To evade detection, Alice and Bob aim to use stealthy covert channels that typically have low bandwidths. In addition, they aim to minimize the amount of data exchanged, since the more data is being exchanged, the higher the likelihood that their communication will be detected. Hence, Alice and Bob employ AMPHITRYON to compress all their messages.

For instance, Alice may use an online chat tool that allows her to interact with other dissidents or remote human rights activists, including Bob. Alice is free to select any censorship circumvention tool in this setting as AMPHITRYON can serve as an extension for arbitrary tools. Rather than a censorship circumvention tool, Alice may use a stealthy, low-bandwidth covert channel to communicate with Bob and others. For example, covert channels in game traffic [21] or temperature-based covert channels [10] have very low bandwidths and would benefit from using AMPHITRYON to compress the data *before* encryption.

3.2 Design and Implementation

As AMPHITRYON is a compression system, it is independent of the particular censorship circumvention tool. A typical circumvention tool is provided with payload chunks, e.g., content of a chat or website. However, as any dictionary-based compression scheme [15], AMPHITRYON relies on the redundancy of patterns in the data to be compressed. AMPHITRYON cannot handle randomized content where byte values follow a discrete uniform distribution, i.e., a succeeding bit is set with approx. $p = 0.5$. Hence, the compression must be done on non-encrypted payload chunks *before* they are being encrypted or steganographically embedded. AMPHITRYON supports payload chunks with text or binary encoding.

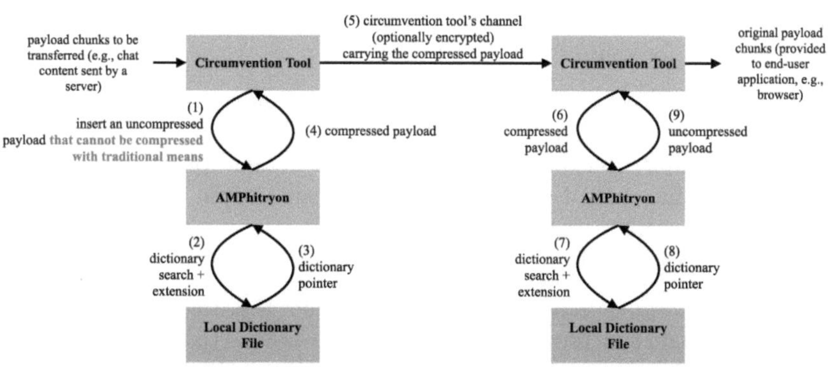

Fig. 1. Functionality and interaction of AMPHITRYON with censorship circumvention tool.

High-level Functionality Fig. 1 provides an overview of AMPHITRYON's functionality. Initially, payload data chunks are provided to the circumvention tool. In step 1, the circumvention tool provides small payload chunks to AMPHITRYON.[2] AMPHITRYON then compresses the data. AMPHITRYON scans the payload chunks for content that matches bit strings in the local dictionary (step 2). If a chunk is found in the directory, the original payload chunk is replaced with

[2] In case of large data, traditional compressors could be used instead of AMPHITRYON.

a pointer/reference to the dictionary (step 3). Otherwise, the chunk is encoded in its original form and added to the local dictionary so that it can be referenced in the future.

In other words, AMPhitryon's dictionary is *incremental*, i.e., every original message chunk that was not found in the dictionary will be added to it so that it can be used for compression should the message appear again.

Once all possible pointers have been set, the compressed data is fed back to the circumvention tool (step 4). The tool can then transfer the payload to a peer (step 5) and optionally encrypt it.

In step 6, the receiving end forwards the decompressed data to its local AMPhitryon. The data is decompressed using the local dictionary (steps 7 and 8). Note that original chunks are added to the local dictionary of the receiver so that they can be referenced by future pointers in the same way as during compression at the sender. Finally, the de-compressed payload is fed back to the circumvention tool (step 9), which provides it to the end-user's application.

Flow-dependency of Dictionaries AMPhitryon generates a novel dictionary for every communication so that the content of the dictionary is optimized for the specific use-case. For example, a chat in Italian builds a different dictionary than a chat in German, French, or English or a transfer of HTML content. However, by simply not deleting (but keeping) the dictionary of a previous communication, higher compression rates can be achieved from the start and the dictionary can be further enhanced leading to improved performance due to a higher chance of finding matches for chunks in the dictionary.

Bootstrapping in Practice AMPhitryon relies on sender and receiver both possessing the same dictionary. Since both observe the same packets (either before encryption or after decryption), they observe the same plaintext content. By following the same rule of adding every previously unseen byte string to their local dictionary, sender and receiver generate dictionaries with equal content. Compression becomes effective once a chunk is transferred more than once.

Dictionary Synchronisation AMPhitryon assumes that the sender and receiver dictionaries remain synchronized at all times. We assume that desynchronisation due to errors, data reordering, or loss is highly unlikely as either the covert channel is reliable or mechanisms for reliable data transfer are implemented on top of the covert channel but below the compression, encryption, and application layers. Attacks against the dictionary (dictionary poisoning) are possible, but since the access to the dictionary is protected, these could only be executed if the sender and/or receiver are compromised, which would also make them vulnerable to many other attacks.

Implementation We implemented AMPhitryon in C and evaluated it under Ubuntu Linux 22.04 and macOS 15.7. The code does not rely on additional libraries. We evaluated our implementation by compressing and subsequently decompressing millions of data chunks (we evaluated cryptographic checksums of all decompressed results to detect errors, which did not occur). Including compressor and decompressor, our implementation contains around 500 lines of code, sample data, and documentation: https://github.com/cdpxe/AMPhitryon.

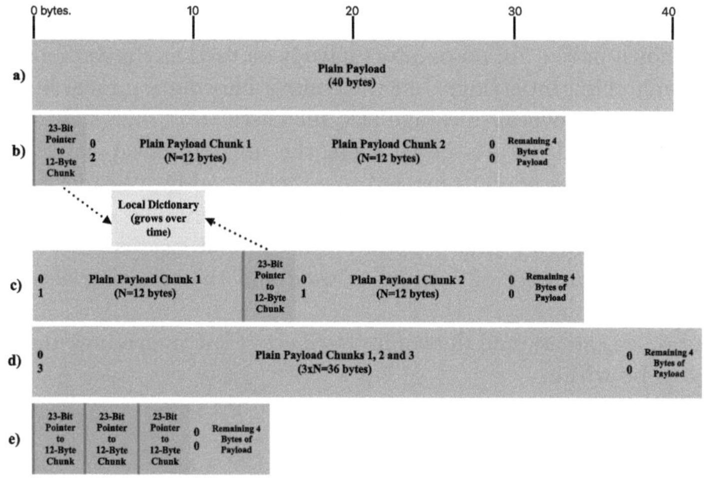

Fig. 2. AMPHITRYON's message format illustrated using a chunk size of $N = 12$. (a) plain payload, (b) likely scenario in which one pointer was found (red colored: MSB indicating that a 23-bit pointer follows), (c) scenario in which one pointer was found but more metadata is needed than in case b, (d) scenario in which no pointer was found and the message size *increases*, and (e) optimal case.

Compression Format AMPHITRYON compresses the input message using the data format as illustrated in Fig. 2 with a chunk size of $N = 12$ bytes. A magic bit shown as a red block indicates whether a pointer value (bit=1) or a number of original plaintext blocks follow (bit=0). To distinguish original plaintext chunks (including binary data) from pointers, plaintext blocks are preceded by length bytes in which the magic bit is not set. The following describes the control data added during the compression:

[0×80–0xff] The first bit is set. The following seven bits of this byte and the next 16 bits jointly represent a 23-bit pointer to a dictionary entry (the data being pointed to has the size N, called *chunk size*).

[0×01–0×7f] The first bit is not set. The following seven bits indicate how many original chunks follow.

[0×00] The first bit is not set and no full message chunk follows. The following bytes are original plaintext bytes that are the remaining bytes of size $\leq N$.

AMPHITRYON's compression relies solely on pointers being smaller than the data they refer to in the dictionary. The larger the chunk being pointed to, the higher the compression of the chunk, but the more challenging it is to find a matching dictionary entry. Since the magic bit requires one bit and the pointer size is 23 bits (3 bytes combined), chunk sizes of $N \geq 4$ bytes are a reasonable choice for our evaluation.

In our example of Fig. 2b, the original payload size of 40 bytes was reduced to a size of 33 bytes using only one pointer. Figure 2c shows a scenario where more fragmentation leads to a slightly smaller compression (34 bytes). A worst-case example is shown in Fig. 2d: no pointers have been used as the dictionary did not contain any matching bit strings, but the control information must be embedded nonetheless, i.e., the overall message size increases to 42 bytes. In such a case where the compressed data is larger than the uncompressed data, one should transfer the uncompressed data instead (e.g., indicated by a header bit that tells the receiver if the data is compressed, or alternatively, one could sacrifice the magic byte value 0xfe for this purpose). An optimal case is shown in Fig. 2e, where a maximum number of pointers is used and the resulting message size is only 14 bytes.

In general, we can assume the compressed size C of an original uncompressed message O to be within

$$3P \leq C \leq 3P + (O - NP) \cdot ((N + 1)/N),$$

with P being the number of 3-byte pointers that are set and N being the chunk size. In the ideal case, the original payload is completely replaced by pointers ($C = 3P$). In the typical case, the pointers replace NP bytes of uncompressed data with $3P$ bytes. For the remaining uncompressed $O - NP$ bytes, in the worst case the number of bytes increases by a factor of $(N+1)/N$ per chunk due to the necessary magic bytes. However, C will be smaller in many cases as multiple uncompressed chunks (up to 127) can be chained together with a single magic byte.

4 Evaluation

In this section, we evaluate the performance of AMPhitryon by comparing the compression with well-known off-the-shelf compression algorithms. We also investigate the dictionary sizes and computation times of AMPhitryon in different settings.

4.1 Dataset

We evaluated AMPhitryon using plausible and publicly available data. In particular, we have chosen IRC chat log files from the *irc-disentanglement* dataset provided by [6,9] and the *Chromium Conversations Corpus* [12] provided via the ConvoKit Python package[3]. Table 1 shows more information about the datasets.

The Ubuntu dataset contains chat messages from the `#ubuntu` IRC channel[4]. The Chromium dataset contains messages from developers commenting

[3] https://convokit.cornell.edu.

[4] https://irclogs.ubuntu.com.

Table 1. Chat message datasets

Dataset	Time-Frame	Messages	Log Files
Ubuntu	2005–2018	220,210	153
Chromium	2008–2016	2,853,885	1,357

on changes to the Chromium project. For the chromium dataset, we combined multiple days of messages, so each log file has at least 1,500 lines. We did not cut days; therefore, all messages from a single day are found in a single log file. We chose these datasets since chats would be one of the likely use cases of AMPHITRYON. A chat server sends and receives many small messages, which can be challenging to compress for regular compression algorithms. With the incremental dictionary of AMPHITRYON, the algorithm learns often-used words or phrases, which increases compression performance over time.

We filtered the datasets for outliers and cut all messages to a maximum length of 50 bytes, as longer messages are not the target for AMPHITRYON and could be effectively compressed with off-the-shelf algorithms. We identified lines as outliers that contained more than 15 consecutive instances of the same symbol. This removes extreme examples, but still leaves messages with repeated words in the dataset.

4.2 Compression Performance

We compared AMPHITRYON against four off-the-shelf compression algorithms: Gzip, Zstandard (zstd), LZMA2 and Brotli. For the four reference algorithms, we used the strongest compression settings available and compressed the log files line by line, simulating a message-by-message compression. To measure compression performance, we chose the compression ratio (R) between the message size before (M) and after compressing (C) [14]: $R = \frac{C}{M}$. We started with an empty dictionary for each log file and also compressed the files line by line, i.e., per chat message. We evaluated chunk sizes from 4 bytes up to 20 bytes to find the optimal chunk size.

Given that Brotli can utilize custom dictionaries, we also conducted Brotli tests with a custom dictionary. We first used AMPHITRYON once on the Chromium dataset and once on the Ubuntu dataset while saving a dictionary resulting from each run. Using these dictionaries, we then ran Brotli on the Ubuntu dataset with the Chromium dictionary and vice versa. We believe this is a reasonable approach, as both datasets share the same message structure but generally different content. This prohibits an "overfitted" and therefore unrealistic dictionary.

For all compression tests, we ran the algorithms on both datasets individually and combined the results for statistical analysis.

Figure 3 shows the compression performance of AMPHITRYON by chunk size. For this plot, we averaged the compression ratio over all lines for each file. Each line in the plot represents a single input file of the two datasets. We can see a generally optimal compression performance for AMPHITRYON with a chunk size between 7 and 12 bytes. Depending on the dataset, the optimal chunk size varies between 9 and 10 bytes.

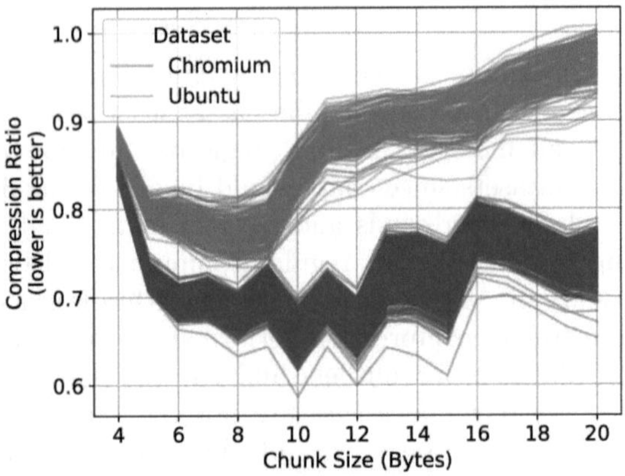

Fig. 3. AMPHITRYON compression performance by chunk size.

Figure 4 shows a ridge-line plot of the compression performance of the four selected algorithms. For AMPHITRYON we used a chunk size of 10. The plot shows the distribution of compression ratios for each algorithm. We can see that AMPHITRYON generally performed better than the other compression algorithms, with most of the ratios below 1.0. The off-the-shelf algorithms all perform significantly worse, with a majority of compression ratios above 1.0, which means sizes actually increased in the majority of cases.

We can see some outliers in both directions. The low outliers for the reference algorithms stem from repetitive lines that were not removed by our filters. Those lines include repeated short words, but not consecutive repeated characters. The high outliers can be explained by very short messages, as the reference algorithms always add a minimum overhead.

Table 2 shows the minimum, maximum, mean, and median compression ratios for each algorithm. We can see that AMPHITRYON performs very consistently without strong outliers. The mean compression ratio of AMPHITRYON is even better than the best performance of most other algorithms. Brotli's performance with the custom dictionary is nearly identical to the performance using the default dictionary (difference in mean compression ratio of 0.002).

4.3 Dictionary Size

For AMPHITRYON we also investigated the growth of the dictionary size after each chat line. Figure 5a shows a plot of this with minimum, maximum, median,

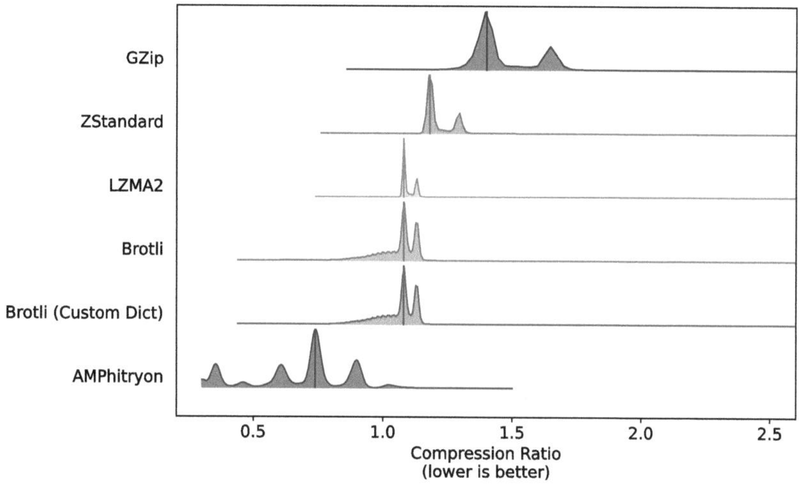

Fig. 4. Comparison of compression ratios of AMPHITRYON (chunk size 10) with existing compression standards.

Table 2. Minimum, maximum, mean and median compression ratios for different compression techniques (AMPHITRYON chunk sizes 4–20)

Algorithm	Min	Max	Mean	Median
AMPHITRYON	0.30	1.50	0.67	0.70
Gzip	0.86	11.0	1.47	1.40
LZMA2	0.74	3.0	1.10	1.08
Brotli	0.44	3.0	1.06	1.08
Brotli (Custom Dictionary)	0.44	3.0	1.06	1.08
ZStandard	0.76	5.5	1.22	1.18

and quartiles. The ridges in the plot stem from files in the dataset with less than 2,000 lines (mostly the Ubuntu dataset).

We can see that the dictionary size was still growing almost linearly for all files, which shows that the dictionary was not "saturated", and there would still be potential to gain by learning new chunks.

There is an inbuilt limit on the dictionary size at 8 MB (due to the 23-bit pointer). In our tests, as shown in Fig. 5a we did not encounter this limit, but it would be easy to implement a rotation where the oldest chunks are replaced in favor of newer ones.

We also tested the dictionary size with a single large file by combining all logs of the Ubuntu dataset into a single file. From Fig. 5b we can see that the dictionary size is growing roughly linearly for larger chunk sizes. Smaller chunk sizes do show a clear "saturation" effect as the dictionaries grow slower and slower. This is highlighted in the zoomed-in section of the plot.

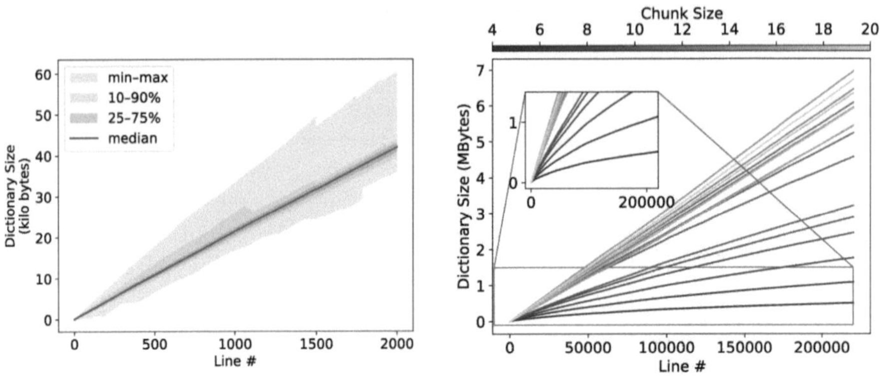

(a) *Average* AMPHITRYON dictionary size by line number (chunk size 10)

(b) AMPHITRYON dictionary sizes by line number for a large file

Fig. 5. Dictionary Sizes.

4.4 Computation Time

We also evaluated the computation times of AMPHITRYON when performing compressions with various configurations. We compressed messages with lengths from 4 to 50 bytes, chunk sizes ranging from 4 to 50 bytes, and predefined dictionaries of different sizes, from 10,000 B to 4,000,000 B. The results presented in Fig. 6 show the actual computation times, including file system access (writing the compressed output to file) and other overhead.[5] The experiments were conducted on a MacBook Pro laptop (M3 chip) running macOS 15.7. The plots show the best- and worst-case scenarios, one where a match is always found at the beginning of the dictionary and one where no match is found and the entire dictionary is searched. The data points for the plots are the averages over multiple runs with the same configuration. For the chunk size plot, the time is averaged over the message sizes, and for the message size plot, the time is averaged over the chunk sizes.

Figure 6a shows that the computation time decreases rapidly with increasing chunk size. This is expected, as with larger chunks, AMPHITRYON has to perform fewer dictionary searches. Figure 6b reveals that the computation time increases linearly with the message size. This shows the computational efficiency of AMPHITRYON. The results also show that the dictionary size does not have a significant impact on computation times.

4.5 Limitations

A limitation of AMPHITRYON is its dependence on redundancy in the payload. If payload is encrypted *before* being provided to AMPHITRYON, such redundancies cannot be found efficiently and the approach becomes ineffective. As mentioned,

[5] If compression outputs were written to memory, performance would improve further.

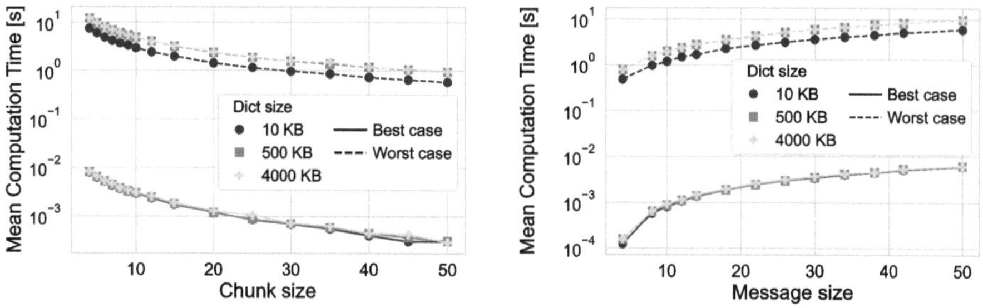

(a) Computation time vs. chunk size (log scale)

(b) Computation time vs. message size (log scale)

Fig. 6. Computation times for AMPHITRYON compression.

AMPHITRYON is tailored to process data *before* encryption at the sender and *after* decryption at the receiver.

Since compression occurs before encryption, as for any such approach, compression side channels could potentially reveal secret information. However, such attacks could only be carried out if the sender includes information in the messages that can be controlled by the attacker. If such attacks are relevant for the application in use, mitigation includes randomisation of any secrets or disabling the compression.

We did not conduct an analysis of highly resource constrained environments. Currently, our maximum dictionary size is limited to a few MBytes and many systems would be able to handle such a limit. However, one could easily limit the maximum number of pointers in a dictionary so that only a few kBytes are used, and older entries would be replaced more quickly with newer entries.

The pointer size is currently fixed to 23 bits, but using variable pointer sizes might provide improved compression ratios. Finally, we did not analyze the impact of pre-filled or recycled dictionaries, which could lead to higher compression gains at early stages of a communication.

5 Conclusions

Limiting the footprints of censorship circumvention channels and other types of covert channels is crucial to prevent these channels from being detected and protect the users from possible ramifications, such as legal action risks. In this paper, we introduced AMPHITRYON, a novel compression approach for small data chunks typically transferred through covert channels in censorship circumvention scenarios. The core idea of our method is to refer to data of a given context (e.g. chat messages) while building a compression dictionary on the fly.

Using datasets of real chat messages, our evaluation shows that AMPHITRYON significantly outperforms the existing compression methods GZip, zstd, LZMA2, and Brotli with small chat messages. AMPHITRYON achieves a respectable mean compression ratio of 0.67, while the mean compression ratios of all other techniques exceed 1.0 (which means on average message sizes *increased*).

Our approach does not rely on specific channel types, i.e., it does not matter whether the circumvention channel is a cryptographic or steganographic channel as long as the provided payload features some form of redundancy *before* being processed by AMPHITRYON and encrypted afterwards.

While we focus on censorship/covert circumvention as a scenario, one could apply AMPHITRYON to other scenarios as well. Potentially AMPHITRYON could even be applied outside of the security context. For example, it may be used for the compression of sensor data in low-bandwidth environments before data transmission.

In future work, we plan to integrate and evaluate our approach with popular censorship circumvention tools. We also aim to investigate whether a stronger compression can be achieved with a flexible pointer size, pre-filled dictionaries, and hybrid compression schemes.

Acknowledgments. Steffen Wendzel would like to thank Jörg Keller for the vivid discussions on DYST-like compression algorithms.

Disclosure of Interests. The authors have no competing interests to declare that are relevant to the content of this article.

References

1. Alakuijala, J., et al.: Brotli: a general-purpose data compressor. ACM Trans. Inf. Syst. (TOIS) **37**(1), 1–30 (2018)
2. Evsutin, O., Kokurina, A., Meshcheryakov, R.V.: Approach to the selection of the best cover image for information embedding in JPEG images based on the principles of the optimality. J. Decis. Syst. **27**, 256–264 (2018). Supp
3. Freedom house: freedom of the net report (2025). https://freedomhouse.org/sites/default/files/2025-11/Freedom_on_the_Net_2025_Digital.pdf
4. Fridrich, J.: Steganography in digital media: principles, algorithms, and applications, Cambridge University Press (2009)
5. Giani, A., Berk, V.H., Cybenko, G.V.: Data exfiltration and covert channels. In: Carapezza, E.M. (ed.) Sensors, and Command, Control, Communications, and Intelligence (C3I) Technologies for Homeland Security and Homeland Defense V. vol. 6201, p. 620103. SPIE (2006). https://doi.org/10.1117/12.670123
6. Gouravajhala, S.R., Vernier, A.M., Shi, Y., Li, Z., Ackerman, M., Kummerfeld, J.K.: Chat disentanglement: data for new domains and methods for more accurate annotation. In: Proc. 21st Annual Workshop of the Australasian Language Technology Association, (2023)
7. Keller, J., Litzinger, S.: Hiding information in short network packets. In: Proc. 9th European Interdisciplinary Cybersecurity Conference (EICC 2025), pp. 133–150 (2025). https://doi.org/10.1007/978-3-031-94855-8_9
8. Kharrazi, M., Sencar, H.T., Memon, N.D.: Cover selection for steganographic embedding. In: Proc. ICIP, pp. 117–120. IEEE (2006)

9. Kummerfeld, J.K., et al.: A large-scale corpus for conversation disentanglement. In: Proc. 57th Annual Meeting of the Assoc. for Comput. Ling, pp. 3846–3856. (2019). https://doi.org/10.18653/v1/P19-1374
10. Masti, R.J., Rai, D., Ranganathan, A., Müller, C., Thiele, L., Capkun, S.: Thermal covert channels on multi-core platforms. In: 24th USENIX Security Symposium, pp. 865–880. USENIX Association, Washington, D.C. (2015)
11. Meta platforms, Inc.: Zstandard. https://facebook.github.io/zstd/
12. Meyers, B.S., et al.: Chromium conversations (2018). https://doi.org/10.5281/zenodo.2590548
13. Roy, S., Maity, D.K., Mukhopadhyay, A.: A lossless reference-free sequence compression algorithm leveraging grammatical, statistical, and substitution rules. Briefings Funct. Genomics **24** (2025). https://doi.org/10.1093/bfgp/elae050
14. Salomon, D.: Data compression: the complete reference. Springer, 4 edn. (2007)
15. Sayood, K.: Introduction to data compression. Morgan Kaufmann Publishers, 2 edn. (2000)
16. Wails, R., Sullivan, G.A., Sherr, M., Jansen, R.: On precisely detecting censorship circumvention in real-world networks. In: Annual Network and Distributed System Security Symposium, NDSS 2024. The Internet Society, (2024). https://doi.org/10.14722/ndss.2024.23394
17. Weißenborn, C., Wendzel, S.: History covert channels with relative timing pointers: design, error resilience, and detectability. J. Inf. Secur. Appl. (2026). in press
18. Wendzel, S., Schmidbauer, T., Zillien, S., Keller, J.: DYST (Did you see that?): an amplified covert channel that points to previously seen data. IEEE Trans. Dependable Secure Comput. (TDSC) (2024). https://doi.org/10.1109/TDSC.2024.3410679
19. Wendzel, S., et al.: A survey of internet censorship and its measurement: methodology, trends, and challenges. Comput. Secur. **164** (2025). https://doi.org/10.1016/j.cose.2025.104732
20. Wikipedia: Amphitryon (2025). https://en.wikipedia.org/wiki/Amphitryon
21. Zander, S., Armitage, G., Branch, P.: Reliable transmission over covert channels in first person shooter multiplayer games. In: Proceedings of 34th Annual IEEE Conference on Local Computer Networks (LCN) (2009)
22. Zander, S., Armitage, G., Branch, P.: A survey of covert channels and countermeasures in computer network protocols. IEEE Commun. Surv. Tutorials **9**(3) (2007)
23. Zillien, S., Schmidbauer, T., Kubek, M., Keller, J., Wendzel, S.: Look what's there! utilizing the internet's existing data for censorship circumvention with OPPRESSION. In: Proc. 19th ACM ASIA Conf. Computer and Communications Security (AsiaCCS), ACM (2024). https://doi.org/10.1145/3634737.3637676

AutoSecGPU: Lightweight GPU-TEE Made Practical with Automatic Evidence Generation

Fengyuan Yu[1(✉)], Chenlin Huang[1(✉)], Renyu Yang[2], Hua Cheng[3], Yan Ding[1], Yuncong Ma[1], Keming Wang[1], and Zhihang Zhang[1]

[1] College of Computer Science and Technology, National University of Defense Technology, Changsha, China
{yufengyuan,clhuang,yanding,mayuncong,wkmyds,zhangzhihang25}@nudt.edu.cn
[2] School of Software, Beihang University, Beijing, China
renyuyang@buaa.edu.cn
[3] Beijing Big Data Advanced Technology Research Institute, Tsinghua University, Beijing, China
chenghua@ncic.ac.cn

Abstract. GPU Trusted Execution Environments (GPU-TEEs) enable AI users to deploy GPU-accelerated AI applications in the cloud while maintaining protection against untrusted system software and cloud operators. Some solutions accommodate the complex AI runtime within the TEE, resulting in significant TCB expansion. Lightweight GPU-TEEs address this issue by extracting evidence (e.g., kernel execution order and binaries) offline and enforcing their verification online.

Existing lightweight GPU-TEE designs delegate the responsibility of protecting application integrity to users. However, we observe that kernel parameters are highly complex, and users lack effective tools for evidence extraction. Attackers can exploit this gap to corrupt computation results, undermining the practicality of lightweight GPU-TEE solutions.

To address this problem, this paper presents AutoSecGPU, an automatic framework for offline evidence generation and online evidence verification that can be easily integrated into modern lightweight GPU-TEE systems. Users only need to run their AI application with the AutoSecGPU Extractor, which automatically generates complete evidence. The AutoSecGPU Verifier then checks program behaviors online against this evidence. We have implemented a prototype of AutoSecGPU on an ARM platform with an NVIDIA RTX 3090 GPU. We evaluate AutoSecGPU on representative AI models (DNNs and Transformers). Offline evidence generation averages 60.31 seconds for inference and 152.77 seconds for training, while online execution introduces only 10.8% and 7.1% overhead, respectively.

1 Introduction

The widespread adoption of AI has driven strong demand for organizations and individuals to develop and deploy customized AI applications. Modern AI work-

© IFIP International Federation for Information Processing 2026
Published by Springer Nature Switzerland AG 2026
H. Janicke et al. (Eds.): SEC 2026, IFIP AICT 787, pp. 478–492, 2026.
https://doi.org/10.1007/978-3-032-27993-4_33

loads can benefit from the elasticity and scalability provided by public cloud platforms, which offer large-scale GPU clusters and convenient execution environments. Consequently, users are increasingly migrating their AI applications to the cloud to take advantage of these benefits.

Public cloud platforms, however, expose multiple attack surfaces, and vulnerabilities in hypervisors and GPU drivers have been frequently reported in recent years [4,10,13]. In such environments, privileged attackers (e.g., cloud administrators and co-tenants) may attempt to steal sensitive data or tamper with the GPU computations of AI applications.

Trusted Execution Environments (TEEs) have emerged as a key mechanism for protecting sensitive applications and data in untrusted clouds. GPU-TEEs are specifically designed to protect GPU-accelerated AI applications, and have attracted growing attention from both academia [1–3,5–8,11,14,17,18] and industry [9].

Some designs [3,5–8,11,14,17,18] place large portions of the AI software stack into the TEE to achieve protection. However, incorporating a complex AI runtime into the TEE significantly increases the TCB (Trusted Computing Base) and expands the attack surface. To avoid this, other GPU-TEEs [1,2] adopt a lightweight approach. Only security-critical operations are implemented in a trusted domain, while the remainder of the AI runtime executes outside the TEE. These critical operations typically involve checks on important GPU runtime actions, such as data transfers and kernel launches. Specifically, evidence about AI applications is extracted offline. Evidence describes the expected behavior of the AI application, including rules governing kernel binaries, execution order, and parameters. Online verification then checks correctness against this evidence. This approach keeps the TCB minimal, avoids disrupting existing applications, and provides a reasonable balance between security and performance.

Existing lightweight GPU-TEEs shift the responsibility of evidence extraction to users. However, we observe that GPU kernel parameters are highly complex and often generated dynamically by the AI runtime, making them difficult to extract. Furthermore, users lack effective tools for evidence extraction. As a result, the extracted evidence is often incomplete, failing to cover all security-relevant information that requires protection. These gaps can be exploited by adversaries to compromise the integrity of AI applications protected by lightweight GPU-TEEs.

We present AutoSecGPU to address the above issues. AutoSecGPU consists of two main components. The first component is the AutoSecGPU Extractor, which collects the kernel binaries, kernel execution order, and kernel parameters required for integrity verification, and automatically generates the corresponding verification rules. The second component is the AutoSecGPU Verifier, which runs within the online GPU-TEE and verifies every kernel invocation and its parameters against the evidence extracted offline. We implement a prototype of AutoSecGPU on an ARM platform with an NVIDIA GPU. We evaluate the performance of AutoSecGPU using commonly used AI models, including DNNs and Transformers. Evidence generation takes, on average, 60.31 seconds for inference workloads and 152.77 seconds for training workloads. Online execution within AutoSecGPU incurs only 10.8% performance overhead for inference workloads and 7.1% for training workloads.

2 Background and Related Work

2.1 AI Runtime and GPU Execution

AI applications interact with the AI runtime (including the AI framework and GPU driver) through high-level abstractions such as operators, tensors, and computation graphs. These abstractions are ultimately lowered by the GPU runtime into low-level GPU hardware commands, which drive all critical operations. Commands related to kernel launches include the entry address of the kernel to be executed as well as the associated kernel parameters. DMA-related commands specify the source and destination of the data transfer as well as the length of the transmitted data. The source is always a DMA buffer created by the GPU runtime. All of these commands are written into command buffers by the GPU runtime before being issued to the hardware.

2.2 GPU-TEE

The increasing migration of AI applications to cloud GPUs has heightened the risk of security breaches [4,10,13]. Both buggy software stacks and potentially malicious insiders threaten the security of AI applications. Some GPU-TEEs embed the complex AI runtime within the TEE to safeguard AI applications.

Graviton [16], HIX [6], HETEE [19], ccAI [17], and Honeycomb [8] all require additional hardware assumptions beyond standard GPU platforms. Graviton [16] and HIX [6] rely on simulated extensions to the GPU or SGX to establish trusted CPU-GPU channels. HETEE [19] introduces an FPGA-based secure controller for bus-level protection, while ccAI [17] depends on a modified PCIe adapter card for secure CPU-GPU interaction. Honeycomb [8] runs AI applications within SEV-protected CVMs, but their interaction with the GPU relies on AMD-TIO protection, which is not supported in commercial products.

Cronus [7], ACAI [14], and GR-T [11] are GPU-TEEs based on the ARM architecture. Cronus [7] leverages the Secure EL2 extension to run AI applications in secure-world VMs, while ACAI [14] uses ARM CCA to run AI applications in Realm VMs. GR-T [11] places AI applications within remote VMs, which produce GPU commands to be executed by the client within TEEs. Cronus [7] and ACAI [14] protect interactions between the CPU and GPU through SMMU management.

SAGE [5] places the AI application inside an SGX enclave and adopts a time-optimal self-verifying function to establish a secure channel with the GPU without additional hardware security support. GEVisor [18] and XpuTEE [3] also protect AI applications using SGX, while a lightweight monitor running in VMX-root mode mediates and verifies critical I/O operations.

Implication 1: When using the above GPU-TEEs, AI applications must trust all components inside the TEE, which increases system complexity and expands the attack surface.

To keep the TCB minimal, other solutions adopt a lightweight approach. They keep the AI application outside the TEE and deploy a trusted verifier inside the TEE to supervise GPU execution. These systems rely on hardware-enforced memory isolation to ensure that GPU kernels and data cannot be tampered with during execution. Strongbox [2] leverages Stage-2 page tables to restrict CPU-GPU access to memory regions and uses the TZASC mechanism to constrain DMA operations from peripherals, thereby protecting both kernel integrity and data confidentiality. Cage [1] adopts a similar philosophy but builds isolation using GPC partitioning and the SMMU, effectively regulating both RAM access and DMA behaviors. Through these hardware mechanisms, lightweight approaches secure GPU execution without placing the complex AI runtime inside the TEE.

Implication 2: These lightweight solutions rely on the verifier to ensure the integrity of AI applications, with security depending on the user-provided evidence. However, obtaining such evidence is challenging, as discussed in Sect. 3.

3 Motivation

Existing GPU-TEE solutions have addressed the security issues of kernel binaries and kernel execution order. If these are compromised, an attacker may tamper with kernel logic or inject malicious kernels, potentially leading to incorrect computation results or data leakage. In practice, kernel-related information also includes kernel parameters, which have received little attention.

Impact of Kernel Parameters. To investigate the impact of kernel parameters on computation integrity, we conduct the following experiment. We randomly select 100,000 images from ImageNet and perform inference using the configuration described in Sect. 7.1. All workloads invoke the GEMM kernel (e.g., *ampere_sgemm_128x64_tn*), which includes a runtime scaling factor used in the GEMM operation. We modify this parameter of the first GEMM kernel by flipping its sign (e.g., from +1.0 to −1.0) at runtime to evaluate the impact of parameter attacks on computation results. The results are shown in Table 1. *Tampered* indicates that the parameter was maliciously modified at runtime. The accuracy decreases by a maximum of 32.55% and a minimum of 5.1%, with an average decrease of 16.36%. These results demonstrate that kernel parameters must be carefully protected, as unprotected parameters can be exploited by attackers to compromise computation results.

Complex Kernel Parameters. These parameters are complex and heterogeneous, encompassing multi-level nested structures with diverse fields such as tensor descriptors, shape metadata, stride configurations, and pointers to memory regions. They also include invalid padding regions introduced by complex

Table 1: Accuracy decrease (%) of end-to-end AI applications under tampered parameters.

Model	ResNet	VGG	DenseNet	ViT	EfficientNet	Swin
Baseline	90.39	87.81	92.78	76.85	89.34	85.77
Tampered	63.78	55.26	76.11	70.54	78.39	80.67

alignment requirements. This complexity stems from the software design principles of modern AI frameworks and high-performance kernel libraries. AI kernels (such as those for convolution, matrix multiplication, and normalization) may support multiple data types (e.g., float32, float16, int8) and various computation configurations (e.g., different kernel sizes or tensor layouts). The use of templates and generic structures allows the same algorithmic code to generate efficient variants for different types and configurations at compile time, avoiding the overhead of runtime type checks and branching. However, this approach has the side effect of increasing the complexity of parameter structures.

To quantify the complexity and variability of kernel parameters, we analyze the kernel parameters of representative AI workloads under the configurations described in Sect. 7.1. The results are shown in Table 2. We capture the kernels invoked during computation on a batch of data and analyze their parameters. The number of parameters per kernel ranges from 1 to 3. The average parameter sizes span a wide range, from a minimum of 75 bytes to over 100 bytes.

Table 2: Statistical analysis of kernel parameters in AI applications. Here, B, S, and T denote the number of basic data types, structs, and template classes involved in a single run, respectively. K denotes the number of kernels launched in a single run. P/K represents the average number of parameters per kernel, and L/P represents the average length (in bytes) of each parameter.

Model	Training						Inference					
	K	B	S	T	P/K	L/P	K	B	S	T	P/K	L/P
ResNet	67	11	38	16	2.09	98.06	20	9	10	3	1.65	190.59
Vgg	43	12	16	13	2.21	119.57	12	7	5	1	1.75	173.36
DenseNet	66	12	31	19	2.24	87.5	20	9	9	5	1.7	176.5
ViT	38	11	9	16	2.34	95.43	14	9	5	8	2.21	129.38
EfficientNet	80	11	31	26	2.02	75.25	24	8	10	9	1.75	110.19
Swin	85	15	20	28	2.07	91.6	32	10	8	18	2.34	101.25

Challenge. Users are typically concerned only with high-level semantics, such as the model structure at the Python level. However, a simple Python statement may be expanded at a lower level into a kernel with highly complex parameters.

Requiring users to manually parse the parameters of AI applications to generate evidence imposes a significant development burden and greatly reduces the practicality of lightweight GPU-TEE solutions.

More importantly, generating complete evidence that includes rules for verifying parameters is inherently challenging. First, the AI runtime is a multi-language complex, which makes static analysis difficult. Second, dynamic tracing captures only binary-level bytes. Potential pointers and padding regions within these bytes are unpredictable due to changes in the address space, making it difficult to analyze them and derive corresponding verification rules.

4 AutoSecGPU

To enhance both the security and practicality of lightweight GPU-TEE, we design an automatic framework for evidence extraction and verification, referred to as AutoSecGPU.

4.1 Threat Model and Assumptions

We assume that the offline environment is trusted, e.g., a local workstation. In this environment, users can safely run profiling and debugging tools to build their AI applications. The online environment resides in the cloud, which is considered untrusted and may be maliciously modified. We assume that the underlying platform provides a hardware root of trust and a trusted boot process that securely initializes the TEE. After initialization, however, any software outside the TEE (kernel, driver, GPU runtime, hypervisor) may be compromised. We do not consider DDoS attacks, physical attacks, or side-channel attacks, which is consistent with prior GPU-TEE solutions [1,2,6,16].

We assume that the offline and online environments use equivalent GPU models and runtimes, which is easily satisfied in cloud settings where users can rent the same GPU and CPU type as their local machine. We assume that privacy-sensitive preprocessing is already performed in the offline environment for security. The untrusted AI runtime can only launch GPU kernels and pass inputs or intermediate results between kernels.

4.2 Architecture and Workflow

The architecture of AutoSecGPU is shown in Fig. 1. It consists of two components: the Extractor and the Verifier. The Extractor generates evidence about the integrity of AI applications in the offline phase (details in Sect. 4.3) and can run as a portable dynamic library. The Verifier checks the dynamic behaviors of AI applications against the evidence (details in Sect. 4.4) to ensure the integrity of online AI applications, and can be directly integrated into the verifier of an existing lightweight GPU-TEE.

In the offline phase, users run their AI application on one batch of data with the Extractor. The Extractor mediates each kernel invocation and collects the

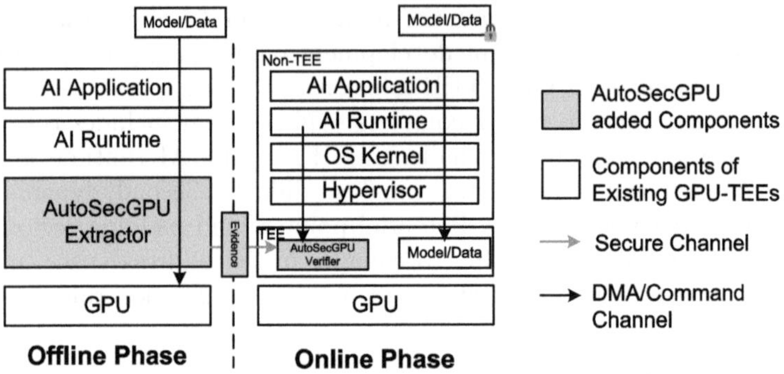

Fig. 1: The architecture and workflow of AutoSecGPU.

binaries, execution order, and parameters of kernels. It then produces verification rules from this information, which are packaged into evidence.

At the beginning of the online phase, users attest the GPU-TEE on the cloud via remote attestation and establish a secure channel. They then send the evidence, together with the keys for data and model weights, to the GPU-TEE via the secure channel. Next, they upload and start the AI application under the protection of the GPU-TEE. The GPU-TEE ensures the secure loading of data and model weights through access control or cryptographic mechanisms. The AutoSecGPU Verifier, which runs within the GPU-TEE, checks whether each launched kernel and its associated parameters conform to the evidence generated offline.

4.3 AutoSecGPU Extractor

The AutoSecGPU Extractor consists of three steps: Parameter Parsing, Rule Derivation, and Evidence Packaging.

Parameter Parsing. To parse kernel parameters, AutoSecGPU adopts a hybrid approach combining static and dynamic analysis. This approach is based on two key observations:

- Padding regions are never accessed by the kernel during execution.
- Pointer regions are used in memory accesses; non-pointers are not.

Based on the first observation, AutoSecGPU employs static analysis on the kernel binary. It identifies instructions that directly read from parameter regions and records the offsets and access sizes of these instructions. Bytes not accessed by any instruction are considered unused padding.

Based on the second observation, AutoSecGPU uses dynamic analysis. During runtime, each kernel is instrumented to record the target addresses of all memory access instructions. If an accessed memory region corresponds to a buffer used by the AI application, and the starting address of this buffer matches an

8-byte chunk of the kernel parameter, then this chunk is identified as a pointer. All remaining parameter regions are treated as non-pointer values.

Rule Derivation. AutoSecGPU assigns different verification rules to different types of parameters. For padding parameters, the **rule** is to skip them without any checks. For non-pointer parameters, the **rule** is that their values during online execution must match those recorded in the evidence. Accordingly, the AutoSecGPU Extractor records their values and associates them with the kernel execution order. For pointer parameters, the **rule** is that the relationships between pointers must remain consistent with those recorded in the evidence during online execution. To this end, the AutoSecGPU Extractor records the sources and targets of each pointer. If a pointer in the current kernel matches a pointer from the previous kernel, it indicates that the output of the previous kernel serves as input to the current kernel. If a pointer in the current kernel refers to a data buffer or a model weight buffer, it indicates that the kernel performs computation on that data. This information represents the data flow between kernels.

Evidence Packaging. In addition to evidence about parameters, the AutoSecGPU Generator also records other information, including the hashes of kernel binaries and the kernel execution order. These records are transformed into verification rules and packaged together to form the complete evidence, which is then transferred to the online GPU-TEE via the secure channel.

4.4 AutoSecGPUVerifier

The AutoSecGPU Verifier in the online GPU-TEE parses the rules recorded in the evidence and checks kernel behavior accordingly. For kernel binaries, which are transferred to the GPU via DMA, the Verifier computes a hash of the DMA buffer contents to confirm the identity of the kernel. Kernel execution order is then verified once the binary check passes. As for kernel parameters, since they are directly included in the kernel launch command, they can be extracted and verified directly against the evidence.

5 Implementation

To validate AutoSecGPU, we prototype it on Linux kernel with the ARMv8-A architecture. We select the Phytium 2000-Plus platform to evaluate the performance of AutoSecGPU. This board features a 64-core ARMv8 CPU running at 1.8 to 2.2 GHz. For GPU selection, we choose NVIDIA products due to their predominant use in datacenter services and excellent software compatibility. We select the NVIDIA RTX 3090 (24 GB) for online execution. The system runs Linux kernel v5.11.22, PyTorch v1.13.1, CUDA v11.2 (userspace driver), cuDNN v8.1.1, and the open-source NVIDIA GPU kernel-space driver v515.76.

The AutoSecGPU Extractor is built on NVBit [15], an NVIDIA-provided dynamic binary instrumentation framework, which allows precise tracing of kernel-level memory accesses and parameter usage. The Extractor comprises 536 LoC. To evaluate the overhead of online verification, we implement a prototype of a lightweight GPU-TEE. It uses AES-GCM-256 to encrypt and decrypt sensitive data, and SHA-256 to protect the integrity of kernel binaries. It leverages dynamic Stage-2 page tables to protect DMA buffers and command buffers during verification. To prevent attacks from other AI applications, it parses GPU page tables sent via DMA to ensure they do not overlap with those of other applications. To protect against malicious devices, the functionality of configuring IOMMU page tables is moved inside the GPU-TEE. Since the CPU vendor does not provide a mechanism to modify the EL3 firmware, we place the GPU-TEE at EL2 for performance measurement. The runtime TCB of AutoSecGPU is only $\sim 4k$ lines of code, of which 427 lines are dedicated to evidence verification.

6 Security Analysis

We analyze the security of AutoSecGPU by examining potential attack vectors and explaining how the system mitigates each threat.

Attack 1: Kernel Binary Tampering. An adversary may attempt to modify kernel binaries before execution, for example, by altering instructions or injecting malicious kernel segments. AutoSecGPU records hashes of the kernel binaries during the offline phase. At runtime, the AutoSecGPU Verifier checks the binaries in use, effectively preventing unauthorized modifications.

Attack 2: Kernel Parameter Forgery. An adversary may forge malicious kernel parameters to trigger out-of-bounds memory accesses, corrupt data, or alter kernel semantics. AutoSecGPU generates parameter-related rules during the offline phase and verifies critical fields during the online phase, ensuring that runtime parameters conform to the expected behavior and thereby mitigating parameter forgery attacks.

Attack 3: Kernel Execution Order Manipulation. An attacker may tamper with the AI runtime to distort the intended execution order or inject unauthorized kernels. AutoSecGPU enforces an authenticated execution order derived from the offline phase. Any deviation from the expected order or any unauthorized kernel invocation is detected and rejected.

Attack 4: Malicious Cross-Device DMA. An adversary controlling another DMA-capable device on the same node may attempt to corrupt GPU command buffers or data buffers via DMA. AutoSecGPU leverages the IOMMU to isolate GPU-accessible DMA regions from other peripherals, preventing malicious DMA modifications from affecting correctness.

By automatically generating evidence for AI application execution in the offline phase and enforcing verification in the online phase, AutoSecGPU effectively prevents the major attacks targeting GPU task execution, significantly enhancing the security and practicality of lightweight GPU-TEE designs.

7 Evaluation

We address the following questions in this section:
Q1: How much overhead is introduced by offline evidence generation?
Q2: How much overhead is introduced by online evidence verification?
Q3: What is the additional memory overhead introduced by evidence verification?

7.1 Experimental Setup

We select six AI applications, including DNNs and Transformers, to evaluate the end-to-end performance overhead introduced by AutoSecGPU verification. The benchmarks include ResNet, VGG, DenseNet, EfficientNet, ViT, and Swin (Swin Transformer), evaluated on the ImageNet dataset. The model weights are provided by the PyTorch community [12]. We evaluate our approach in both inference and training scenarios.

We use a fixed batch size in all experiments to ensure fair comparison. This choice is reasonable in practice: for training workloads, the batch size is typically kept constant throughout execution; for inference workloads, online AI applications tend to aggregate incoming requests into a fixed, large batch size to maximize throughput. When incoming requests do not fill a batch, the system can apply padding or introduce short delays before processing.

Powers-of-two batch sizes are commonly adopted in practice, as they improve GPU execution efficiency through better memory alignment and thread scheduling. Accordingly, we set the batch size to 64 for training and 512 for inference, corresponding to the largest power-of-two batch sizes that all evaluated applications can successfully run on the evaluated hardware platform.

In experiments for offline evidence generation, we evaluate two configurations: Baseline and AutoSecGPU. The Baseline refers to running AI applications without the AutoSecGPU Extractor, while AutoSecGPU denotes execution with the AutoSecGPU Extractor enabled. In experiments for online evidence verification, we evaluate three configurations: Baseline, AutoSecGPU, and AutoSecGPU$_i$. The Baseline refers to running online AI applications without the protection of a GPU-TEE. AutoSecGPU refers to running AI applications under the protection of a GPU-TEE, with verification against complete evidence, including kernel binaries, execution order, and parameters. AutoSecGPU$_i$ denotes a variant with incomplete evidence that excludes kernel parameters.

7.2 Overhead of Offline Evidence Generation

Overhead of Critical Operations During Offline Evidence Generation. We measure the overhead introduced by evidence generation on critical operations, including *cudaMalloc*, *cudaMemcpy*, and *cudaLaunchKernel*. For *cudaMalloc* and *cudaMemcpy*, the overhead is negligible because the Extractor only needs to record the relevant addresses. To evaluate the overhead on *cudaLaunchKernel*, we create a vectorAdd program as the experiment target. The program performs element-wise addition on two double-precision vectors with 10,000 elements and writes the results to a new vector, involving two load instructions and one store instruction. Under baseline execution, the kernel completes in 0.15 ms, whereas execution with the Extractor takes 621.7 ms. This is because data collection and transmission are inserted before each memory access instruction. When executed by thousands of concurrent GPU cores, these operations contend for the shared data collection channels, leading to high-frequency contention and significant overhead.

Overhead of End-to-End AI Applications During Offline Evidence Generation. We run different AI applications with the AutoSecGPU Extractor to generate evidence. The results are presented in Table 3. For training, the overhead ranges from 20.35×to 51.75×, with an average of 41.32×. For inference, the overhead ranges from 8.3×to 24.75×, with an average of 18.13×. As noted above, most of the overhead arises from multiple GPU cores contending for the same data collection channels. In training scenarios, computations involve both forward and backward propagation, resulting in a larger computation load and consequently higher overhead. Nevertheless, this overhead is acceptable in practice, as the user only needs to execute a single run to generate the corresponding evidence. Once generated, the evidence can be reused repeatedly during online execution.

Table 3: Overhead (s) of end-to-end AI applications.

Model (train)	ResNet	VGG	DenseNet	ViT	EfficientNet	Swin
Baseline	3.31	5.86	2.52	6.85	2.41	2.38
AutoSecGPU	124.8	327.21	87.93	139.43	101.24	136.04
Overhead	**37.7**×	**55.83**×	**34.89**×	**20.35**×	**42.01**×	**57.15**×
Model (infer)	ResNet	VGG	DenseNet	ViT	EfficientNet	Swin
Baseline	3.03	5.62	1.82	6.56	2.06	2.07
AutoSecGPU	50.44	139.1	31.86	54.5	38.84	47.14
Overhead	**16.64**×	**24.75**×	**17.5**×	**8.3**×	**18.85**×	**22.77**×

7.3 Overhead of Online Evidence Verification

Overhead of Critical Operations During Online Evidence Verification. We measure the overhead introduced by evidence verification on critical operations, including *cudaMalloc*, *cudaMemcpy*, and *cudaLaunchKernel*. We compare AI applications running on unmodified Linux with those running under AutoSecGPU, as shown in Table 4. The time of *cudaMalloc* increases by $\sim 0.58\%$. The *cudaMemcpy* H2D overhead increases by $\sim 0.51\%$, and *cudaMemcpy* D2H by $\sim 0.49\%$. *cudaMalloc* triggers the transmission of page tables to the GPU.

However, these page tables have a regular structure and relatively small size, so AutoSecGPU verification incurs negligible overhead. For *cudaMemcpy*, verification is straightforward and only requires ensuring that the source and destination addresses are correct, so AutoSecGPU verification introduces minimal overhead. To evaluate the performance of *cudaLaunchKernel*, we run the vectorAdd program and measure the kernel execution time. The kernel completes in approximately 0.15 ms in the baseline environment, and execution within the GPU-TEE also takes 0.15 ms, showing no observable increase due to efficient verification.

Table 4: Overhead (ms) of critical operations during online evidence verification.

cudaMalloc	4 MB	64 MB	256 MB	1 GB	4 GB
Baseline	0.1285	1.0502	1.7150	16.9651	87.9210
AutoSecGPU	0.1286	1.0510	1.7436	17.0878	88.2729
cudaMemcpy H2D	4 MB	64 MB	256 MB	1 GB	4 GB
Baseline	0.6411	10.0455	40.1359	160.4922	641.9087
AutoSecGPU	0.6420	10.1678	40.6310	160.5029	641.9202
cudaMemcpy D2H	4 MB	64 MB	256 MB	1 GB	4 GB
Baseline	0.6463	10.0464	40.1368	162.4865	649.8908
AutoSecGPU	0.6466	10.1677	40.6311	162.4892	649.8937

Overhead of End-to-End AI Applications During Online Evidence Verification. To evaluate the performance of online AI applications, we feed 100,000 inputs to the AI applications and compare their duration under different configurations. The results are presented in Fig. 2 (a) and (b). Online evidence verification incurs 6.1 to 8.8% overhead (7.1% on average) for training and 8.8 to 13.8% (10.8% on average) for inference. This overhead is comparable to that of existing lightweight GPU-TEE solutions such as StrongBox (10%) and Cage (3%). Within the total overhead, the overhead of parameter verification is negligible, at 0.01 to 1.37% for training (0.63% on average) and 0.23 to 0.88% for inference (0.49% on average). Compared to offline evidence generation, the overhead of online verification is substantially smaller, as it does not modify the kernel but only checks kernel launches. Since training typically takes much longer than inference, the relative overhead for training is smaller than that for inference. In summary, the verification performed by the AutoSecGPU Verifier is efficient.

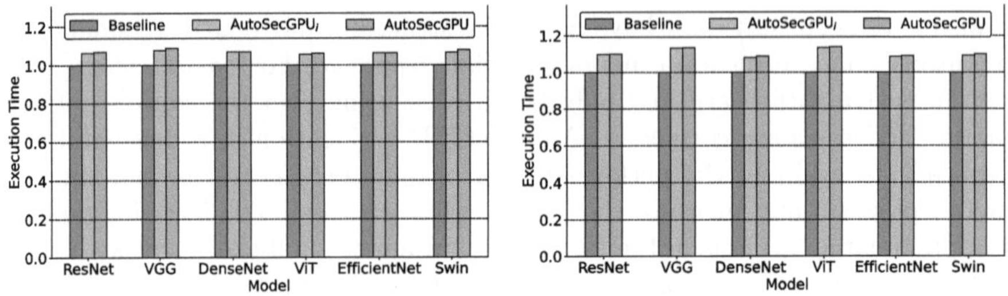

(a) AI Training Applications. (b) AI Inference Applications.

Fig. 2: Overhead of end-to-end AI applications during online evidence verification.

7.4 Evidence Memory Consumption

AutoSecGPU evidence introduces additional storage overhead, as it stores information about kernel binaries, execution order, and parameters. Among these, parameter-related evidence occupies the majority of the storage due to its complexity. We evaluate the storage requirements for different applications, as shown in Table 5. In the training scenario, evidence size ranges from 106.06 KB to 887.24 KB, with an average of 494.83 KB. In the inference scenario, it ranges from 30.33 KB to 490.85 KB, with an average of 180.34 KB. This additional storage consumption is modest and acceptable.

Table 5: Evidence Memory Consumption (KB) of AI applications.

Model (train)	ResNet	VGG	DenseNet	ViT	EfficientNet	Swin
Memory Consumption	427.48	106.06	887.24	321.92	597.74	628.54
Model (infer)	ResNet	VGG	DenseNet	ViT	EfficientNet	Swin
Memory Consumption	160.27	30.33	490.85	39.76	170.61	190.21

8 Conclusion

Existing lightweight solutions shift the responsibility of evidence extraction for execution integrity to users. However, kernel parameters are complex and difficult to extract, thereby undermining the effectiveness of lightweight GPU-TEE solutions. To address this problem, this paper presents AutoSecGPU, an automatic framework for offline evidence generation and online evidence verification that can be readily integrated into modern lightweight GPU-TEE systems. We have implemented a prototype of AutoSecGPU on an ARM platform with an NVIDIA RTX 3090 GPU. We evaluate the performance of AutoSecGPU using commonly used AI models, including DNNs and Transformers. Evidence generation takes, on average, 60.31 seconds for inference workloads and 152.77 seconds for training workloads. Online execution within AutoSecGPU incurs only 10.8% performance overhead for inference workloads and 7.1% for training workloads.

Acknowledgments. This work was supported by the National Natural Science Foundation of China (62472432).

References

1. Deng, Y., et al.: Cage: complementing arm CCA with GPU extensions. In: Proceedings of the 2022 ACM SIGSAC Conference on Computer and Communications Security, CCS 2022, Los Angeles, CA, USA, November 7–11, 2022, pp. 769–783. ACM (2022)
2. Deng, Y., et al.: Strongbox: a GPU TEE on arm endpoints. In: Proceedings of the 2022 ACM SIGSAC Conference on Computer and Communications Security, CCS 2022, Los Angeles, CA, USA, November 7–11, 2022, pp. 769–783. ACM (2022)
3. Fan, S., Hua, Z., Xia, Y., Chen, H.: XpuTEE: a high-performance and practical heterogeneous trusted execution environment for GPUs. ACM Trans. Comput. Syst. **43**(1–2), 1–27 (2025)
4. IBM: Cost of a data breach report 2023. https://www.ibm.com/security/data-breach (2023)
5. Ivanov, A., et al.: SAGE: software-based attestation for GPU execution. In: 2023 USENIX Annual Technical Conference, USENIX ATC 2023, Boston, MA, USA, July 10–12, 2023, pp. 485–499. USENIX Association (2023)
6. Jang, I., Tang, A., Kim, T., Sethumadhavan, S., Huh, J.: Heterogeneous isolated execution for commodity GPUs. In: Proceedings of the Twenty-Fourth International Conference on Architectural Support for Programming Languages and Operating Systems, ASPLOS 2019, Providence, RI, USA, April 13–17, 2019, pp. 455–468. ACM (2019)
7. Jiang, J., et al.: CRONUS: fault-isolated, secure and high-performance heterogeneous computing for trusted execution environment. In: 55th IEEE/ACM International Symposium on Microarchitecture, MICRO 2022, Chicago, IL, USA, October 1–5, 2022, pp. 124–143. IEEE (2022)
8. Mai, H., et al.: Honeycomb: Secure and efficient GPU executions via static validation. In: 17th USENIX Symposium on Operating Systems Design and Implementation, OSDI 2023, Boston, MA, USA, July 10–12, 2023, pp. 155–172. USENIX Association (2023)
9. NVIDIA: NVIDIA confidential computing. https://www.nvidia.com/en-us/data-center/solutions/confidential-computing/
10. Pan, G., Lin, X., Ying, X., Wang, J., Wu, C.: Scavenger: Misuse error handling leading to QEMU/KVM escape, Black Hat Asia (2021)
11. Park, H., Lin, F.X.: Safe and practical GPU computation in trustzone. In: Proceedings of the Eighteenth European Conference on Computer Systems, EuroSys 2023, Rome, Italy, May 8–12, 2023, pp. 505–520. ACM (2023)
12. PyTorch: Pytorch models and pre-trained weights (2023). https://docs.pytorch.org/vision/main/models.html

13. Singh, B., Kashyap, R.: Back to the future: a radical insecure design of KVM on ARM. Black Hat USA (2018)
14. Sridhara, S., et al.: ACAI: extending arm confidential computing architecture protection from CPUs to accelerators. CoRR abs/2305.15986 (2023)
15. Villa, O., Stephenson, M., Nellans, D.W., Keckler, S.W.: Nvbit: a dynamic binary instrumentation framework for NVIDIA GPUs. In: Proceedings of the 52nd Annual IEEE/ACM International Symposium on Microarchitecture, MICRO 2019, Columbus, OH, USA, October 12–16, 2019, pp. 372–383. ACM (2019)
16. Volos, S., Vaswani, K., Bruno, R.: Graviton: trusted execution environments on GPUs. In: 13th USENIX Symposium on Operating Systems Design and Implementation, OSDI 2018, Carlsbad, CA, USA, October 8–10, 2018, pp. 681–696. USENIX Association (2018)
17. Wang, C., et al.: CCAI: a compatible and confidential system for AI computing. In: Proceedings of the 58th IEEE/ACM International Symposium on Microarchitecture, pp. 340–353. Association for Computing Machinery (2025)
18. Wu, X., Tian, D.J., Kim, C.H.: Building GPU tees using CPU secure enclaves with Gevisor. In: Proceedings of the 2023 ACM Symposium on Cloud Computing, SoCC 2023, Santa Cruz, CA, USA, 30 October 2023–1 November 2023, pp. 249–264. ACM (2023)
19. Zhu, J., et al.: Enabling rack-scale confidential computing using heterogeneous trusted execution environment. In: 2020 IEEE Symposium on Security and Privacy, SP 2020, San Francisco, CA, USA, May 18–21, 2020, pp. 1450–1465. IEEE (2020)

Privacy, Identification, Authentication and Access Control

Privacy-Preserving Clinical Data De-Identification and Evaluation Framework Using Synthetic Data

Ebenezer Addo-Maclean, Hatem Ahriz(✉), and Muhammad Shadi Hajar

Robert Gordon University, Aberdeen, UK
{e.addo-maclean,h.ahriz,m.hajar}@rgu.ac.uk

Abstract. The growing availability of clinical notes presents a significant opportunity for medical AI and research, yet access remains constrained by the need to protect patient privacy. This work introduces a modular de-identification pipeline designed to balance strict privacy requirements with the preservation of clinical utility. The system begins with hybrid Protected Health Information (PHI) detection, combining rule-based filters, dictionary matching, and a fine-tuned BioClinicalBERT model. Its core innovation lies in configurable substitution logic and a multi-dimensional framework for adversarial risk evaluation. Unlike traditional approaches, the pipeline incorporates quantitative assessments of quasi-identifier uniqueness, semantic leakage, and masked language model predictability to simulate realistic privacy threats. A large synthetic corpus of 500,000 annotated clinical notes was used to enable both model training and adversarial testing, ensuring that the system could be stress-tested and evaluated under controlled conditions. The evaluation generated reproducible audit reports that document the effective redaction of sensitive information while quantifying the preservation of clinical meaning, thereby demonstrating the pipeline's potential to support privacy protection and data utility. This work offers a scalable and transparent mechanism for privacy-preserving data exchange, setting a new standard for de-identification by integrating threat simulation, utility evaluation, and principled risk modeling.

Keywords: Data Privacy · Protected Health Information (PHI) · Health Insurance Portability And Accountability Act (HIPAA) · General Data Protection Regulation (GDPR) · Named Entity Recognition (NER) · Natural Language Processing (NLP) · Quasi-Identifier (QID)

1 Introduction

Artificial intelligence (AI) is reshaping healthcare by powering tools that analyse patient data, suggest diagnoses, summarize doctorâĂŞpatient conversations, and uncover patterns across millions of records. At the centre of this transformation are unstructured clinical notes including discharge summaries, referrals and

© IFIP International Federation for Information Processing 2026
Published by Springer Nature Switzerland AG 2026
H. Janicke et al. (Eds.): SEC 2026, IFIP AICT 787, pp. 495–509, 2026.
https://doi.org/10.1007/978-3-032-27993-4_34

progress notes that capture rich medical detail. However, this richness comes at a cost. The notes are saturated with Protected Health Information (PHI), such as names, dates, and locations, which fall under strict regulations like Health Insurance Portability And Accountability Act (HIPAA) and the General Data Protection Regulation (GDPR). As a result, research access is tightly constrained [1], highlighting the importance of de-identification in facilitating data sharing.

De-identification has emerged as an essential approach, aiming to remove or obscure PHI while maintaining the utility of clinical data for research and analysis. HIPAA sets standards for this process, while GDPR requires PHI to be handled with fairness and transparency [2]. The difficulty lies in striking a balance between preserving the research utility of clinical data and ensuring patient privacy. Traditional approaches often struggle to achieve this balance, as they may overlook subtle indirect identifiers commonly referred to as quasi-identifiers such as dates, locations, or demographic attributes, which can still enable re-identification when combined with external data sources. Building on these limitations, it becomes clear that current de-identification approaches, whether manual or automated, remain fragile, slow, error-prone, and vulnerable to adversarial re-identification across varied datasets [3,4].

These vulnerabilities are not theoretical but have been reflected in real-world disputes. For example, in Dinerstein v. Google LLC, de-identified records were shared under HIPAA's Safe Harbor rules, yet concerns arose that Google's external datasets could enable re-identification. Although the case was ultimately dismissed, it underscored that legal compliance does not always guarantee protection against privacy risks [5]. Such examples underline the need for frameworks that go beyond superficial de-identification to ensure robust privacy and meaningful data utility [6]. The risks are amplified by advances in adversarial techniques. Re-identification no longer requires direct identifiers as attackers can exploit quasi-identifiers, semantic cues, or metadata. GDPR's Recital 26 therefore insists on anonymization that removes any "reasonable likelihood" of re-identification, not just obvious identifiers [7]. Even when direct PHI is removed, residual patterns may still reveal identities [4,8].

Despite these challenges, many de-identification systems are still benchmarked on outdated datasets such as MIMIC-III or i2b2, which lack the complexity of modern threats [9]. Evaluations often focus narrowly on precision and recall, neglecting adversarial resilience. In contrast, synthetic datasets offer a safer testing ground by avoiding exposure of real patient information, but they often fail to capture the intricate PHI structures and semantic subtleties of authentic clinical notes [9]. Without adversary-aware testing or multidimensional evaluation, systems risk being optimized for benchmarks rather than real robustness [10].

This paper addresses these gaps by proposing a modular framework for generating, modifying, and evaluating PHI-rich synthetic clinical notes from a privacy-first, adversary-aware perspective. Instead of only measuring what is removed, the framework also examines what might leak, combining concepts from privacy modelling (e.g., k-anonymity), NLP robustness, and adversarial machine learning. By exposing the trade-off between residual risk and substitution accuracy, it functions as more than a redaction tool but a defensive platform for measuring privacy, preserving utility, and strengthening trust. In this way, it lays the groundwork for clinical NLP systems that are technically effective, legally compliant, and ethically sound.

The remainder of this paper is structured as follows. Section 2 reviews existing de-identification methods and their limitations, with emphasis on privacy risks and adversarial vulnerabilities. Section 3 presents the design of the proposed ShieldPHI pipeline, detailing each of its five phases. Section 4 reports experimental results across detection accuracy, semantic fidelity, and privacy risk metrics. Finally, Sect. 5 concludes the study and outlines opportunities for further improvements.

2 Related Work

The de-identification of clinical free-text has emerged as a critical challenge in privacy-preserving healthcare NLP, driven by the increasing availability of electronic health records (EHRs) and the stringent requirements of regulations such as HIPAA and GDPR [1]. Early efforts focused on rule-based and statistical approaches, later giving way to neural and transformer-based systems, and more recently to scalable NLP pipelines designed for production. Each wave of methods reflects advances in accuracy and precision, but also exposes persistent gaps in utility, adversarial robustness, and risk evaluation.

2.1 Rule-Based and Statistical Systems

Systems such as Philter [11] and MIST [12] represent early attempts to automate PHI detection using rule-based heuristics and statistical models. Philter integrates curated blacklists, whitelists, and regular expressions with statistical filters to achieve high token-level precision and inter-rater reliability. MIST employs Conditional Random Fields (CRFs) trained on annotated corpora, achieving competitive F1 scores across varied document types. These systems are lightweight, interpretable, and easy to deploy, making them appealing for institutions with limited resources.

However, their reliance on surface-level heuristics and static dictionaries limits their adaptability to unseen data and adversarial contexts. Neither Philter nor MIST supports PHI substitution or post-redaction risk assessment, leaving residual information exposed and potentially vulnerable to semantic leakage and quasi-identifier re-identification. While effective in controlled settings, they fall short of modern, regulation-driven privacy-preserving NLP.

2.2 Neural NER Systems

With the rise of deep learning, NeuroNER [13] introduced a neural architecture for biomedical Named Entity Recognition (NER) built on a bidirectional

LSTM-CRF. It integrates with the BRAT annotation tool and provides real-time training visualization via TensorBoard, achieving strong performance on datasets such as CoNLL-2003 [14] and i2b2 [15]. Its modular design has helped democratize access to neural NER models in clinical NLP.

Yet, NeuroNER is not tailored for privacy-preserving deployment. It relies on gold-labeled data and lacks support for PHI substitution, adversarial evaluation, or risk tiering. Its emphasis on entity detection, rather than privacy modeling or utility preservation, makes it more suitable for annotation pipelines than for end-to-end de-identification frameworks.

2.3 Domain-Specific Language Models

The introduction of BioBERT [16] marked a major advance by pre-training BERT on PubMed [17] and Pune Municipal Corporation (PMC) corpora [18], significantly improving biomedical NER, relation extraction, and QA. BioBERT captures domain-specific semantics effectively, providing a strong backbone for downstream clinical NLP. However, it was not designed with de-identification in mind and lacks mechanisms for PHI substitution or risk assessment.

Building on this, ClinicalBERT [19] has been fine-tuned on clinical narratives and incorporated into DeIDClinic [3]. DeIDClinic combines rule-based filters, dictionaries, and transformer models, introducing multi-layered masking and document-level risk assessment via contextual embeddings and cosine similarity. It achieves an F1 of 0.9732 for PHI entities and flags semantically unique records as high risk, offering a more holistic privacy audit compared to earlier systems. This integration signals a shift from token-level detection toward adversary-aware privacy auditing.

However, DeIDClinic has notable limitations. Its risk assessment relies heavily on semantic uniqueness without incorporating probabilistic threat modeling or differential privacy techniques, which may lead to overestimation of re-identification risk. Additionally, its substitution logic is rule-driven and lacks contextual generation, which can result in semantic drift in narrative-heavy notes.

2.4 Scalable NLP Pipelines

SparkNLP [20] represents a scalable, production-ready framework for clinical NLP, optimized for distributed environments. Its clinical NER modules outperform alternatives like Stanza [21] and SciSpacy [22] across biomedical datasets, even without transformers. With features such as assertion detection, entity linking, and de-identification, SparkNLP is well-suited for enterprise use and large-scale processing of clinical corpora.

Nevertheless, SparkNLP's privacy capabilities remain limited. Its de-identification functions emphasize entity recognition without comprehensive substitution logic or adversarial evaluation. Issues such as semantic leakage, membership inference, and quasi-identifier uniqueness are not fully addressed, leaving gaps for deployment under regulations like GDPR's Recital 26. Compared to frameworks like DeIDClinic, it lacks adversary-aware evaluation and nuanced configurability, underscoring the need for integrated pipelines that balance scalability with privacy guarantees.

2.5 Evaluation Gaps and Benchmark Limitations

Despite notable advances, de-identification systems remain constrained by evaluation practices that fail to capture real-world risks. Most studies still rely on legacy datasets such as MIMIC-III and i2b2, which, while valuable for benchmarking, lack the diversity, complexity, and adversarial threat modeling characteristic of modern EHRs [9,10]. This reliance risks overfitting to curated corpora and underestimating vulnerabilities present in unstructured clinical notes.

Evaluation metrics also remain overly focused on precision and recall, with limited consideration of broader privacy risks such as semantic leakage, membership inference, and quasi-identifier uniqueness. For example, a system may achieve near-perfect F1 scores yet still expose sensitive patient information through residual context or rare attribute combinations, leaving it non-compliant with GDPR Recital 26 and HIPAA Safe Harbor provisions [5,8].

Recent attempts to address these limitations include the use of synthetic datasets such as Synthea, which provide safer environments for training and evaluation [3]. However, while synthetic corpora capture broad linguistic and clinical patterns, they often fail to reproduce the subtle, irregular PHI structures found in authentic EHRs [9]. Synthetic data enables scalable and privacy-safe experimentation, but future validation on real-world clinical corpora remains essential to assess generalizability and robustness under authentic documentation variability. Additionally, advanced frameworks such as DeIDClinic [3] emphasize entity masking and document-level risk scoring, but do not include adversarial resilience testing or ensuring utility preservation for downstream analytics.

Altogether, these gaps highlight the need for adversary-aware de-identification pipelines that go beyond surface-level masking. Our work addresses this challenge by integrating substitution strategies that preserve semantic utility while neutralizing identifiers, coupled with adversarial evaluation including membership inference attacks and semantic similarity checks to assess re-identification risk under realistic threat models. This dual focus bridges the gap between compliance-driven entity removal and holistic privacy assurance, providing a more robust framework for privacy-preserving clinical data sharing.

3 Methodology

This study introduces shieldPHI, a modular de-identification pipeline designed to redact PHI from clinical notes while preserving semantic fidelity and enabling adversarial risk evaluation. The methodology is organized into five key phases: synthetic clinical note generation, hybrid PHI detection, configurable substitution, adversarial risk assessment, and evaluation. The entire implementation was developed in Python, leveraging libraries such as `Transformers` (for BioClinicalBERT fine-tuning), `scikit-learn` (for evaluation metrics), `PyTorch` (for model training), `Faker` (for dummy value generation) and `sentence-transformers` (for semantic similarity analysis). To promote transparency and reproducibility, the full codebase, including configuration files and audit scripts, is publicly available on GitHub.

3.1 Synthetic Clinical Note Generation

This phase addresses the challenge of data scarcity by constructing a large corpus of accurately annotated synthetic data, with all annotations performed internally by the authors using predefined PHI labeling schemas.

- **Dataset Selection:** We utilize synthetic patient data from Synthea, an open-source framework developed by MITRE that generates realistic patient records in FHIR and CSV formats [23]. A custom parser extracts demographics (e.g., age, city), conditions (e.g., SNOMED codes), and encounter dates to populate note templates. Synthea simulates longitudinal patient journeys, producing records that mirror real-world healthcare. However, as raw Synthea lacks the stylistic complexity of free-text notes, we augment it with linguistic variety and PHI injections to better stress-test de-identification [24].
- **PHI Dictionaries:** A dedicated module loads external lexicons (e.g., forenames, surnames, hospital names) and generates a consistent set of synthetic identifiers (e.g., SSN, phone numbers, IDs). Public datasets such as the SSA Baby Names (1880–2024) and CORGIS Hospital Names are leveraged for realism and diversity [25,26].
- **Note Generation:** Jinja2 templates [27] are used to render realistic note structures (e.g., admission notes, referrals). PHI spans are systematically injected, and functions generate both character-level offsets and token-level BIO labels using the BioClinicalBERT tokenizer. Subword tokens are correctly masked to avoid training noise, enabling robust NER model training.
- **Scale of Data:** Our system produces 500,000 synthetic notes to ensure statistical significance for deep learning model training. A subset of 200 notes is reserved for adversarial testing and semantic fidelity evaluation.

Figure 1 shows an excerpt of a synthetic operative note generated by ShieldPHI. Each record contains the full clinical text (`raw_text`), character offsets and PHI categories (`phi_spans`). Tokens and BIO labels are also generated internally for NER model training.

3.2 Hybrid PHI Detection Pipeline

This phase constructs a layered detection system that integrates deterministic and contextual methods.

- **Regex Detector:** Curated regular expressions capture structured PHI (e.g., SSN, phone numbers, dates). Regex matches are aligned with token boundaries using spaCy to reduce false positives.

```
{
  "note_type": "operative_report",
  "raw_text": "Operative Report
  Patient: Bader Ray,
  surgery date: 2023-01-06
  Procedure performed by Dr. Wright at Memorial Medical Center...",
  "phi_spans": [
    {"start": 27, "end": 36, "type": "PATIENT_NAME"},
    {"start": 52, "end": 62, "type": "DATE_ISO"},
    {"start": 101, "end": 124, "type": "FACILITY"}
  ],
  "tokens": ["Patient", ":", "Bader", "Ray", ",",
             "surgery", "date", ":", "2023", "-", "01", "-", "06"],
  "bio_labels": ["O", "O", "B-PATIENT_NAME", "I-PATIENT_NAME",
                 "O", "O", "O", "O", "B-DATE_ISO", "I-DATE_ISO",
                 "I-DATE_ISO", "I-DATE_ISO"]
}
```


Fig. 1. Example of a generated synthetic operative report with annotated PHI spans.

- **Dictionary Detector:** This module detects entities such as patient names, providers, and facilities by matching tokens against curated external lexicons.
- **NER Model:** A BioClinicalBERT model fine-tuned on the synthetic corpus provides contextual detection for PHI types such as names, locations, and dates that are difficult to capture using rules or dictionaries.
- **Merging and Conflict Resolution:** Outputs from all three detectors are merged using a configurable priority map (e.g., Regex > Dictionary > NER). This ensures that overlaps or conflicts yield a single, most reliable contiguous segment of text identified as containing protected health information (PHI span).

```
INFO:__main__:Detecting PHI in note 4b69a672-a514-5d46-5335-7c3f1e6171ad...
INFO:__main__:Regex detector detected 4 spans:
INFO:__main__:  1. DATE_ISO [40:50]: '2023-01-03'
INFO:__main__:  2. MRN [274:284]: '1715033349'
INFO:__main__:  3. MRN [477:487]: '1715033349'
INFO:__main__:  4. ZIP_CODE_US [255:260]: '23049'

INFO:phi_detection.dictionary_detector:[DictionaryDetector.detect]
Detection complete: found 2 spans across 2 dictionaries.
INFO:__main__:Dictionary detector detected 2 spans:
INFO:__main__:  1. FACILITY [421:463]: 'Martin Luther King, Jr. Community Hospital'
INFO:__main__:  2. FACILITY [445:463]: 'Community Hospital'

INFO:__main__:NER detector detected 13 spans:
INFO:__main__:  1. PROVIDER [30:35]: 'Adams'
INFO:__main__:  2. DATE_ISO [39:49]: '2023-01-03'
INFO:__main__:  3. PATIENT_NAME [59:73]: 'Naseer Shankar'
INFO:__main__:  4. AGE [80:81]: '7'
INFO:__main__:  5. ADDRESS [231:246]: '080 Hale Lights'
INFO:__main__:  6. ZIP_CODE [252:256]: '2304'
INFO:__main__:  7. PHONE [267:280]: '+44-171503334'
```

Fig. 2. Log output from the PHI Detection Pipeline.

Figure 2 illustrates the structured log output from the hybrid PHI detection phase, capturing the spans identified by the Regex, Dictionary, and NER components.

3.3 Configurable PHI Substitution

Detected PHI is replaced with de-identified surrogates to minimize utility loss.

- **Configurable Strategies:** Substitution rules are defined in YAML. Strategies include:
  - *Dummy:* Replace PHI with synthetic values (e.g., Faker-generated names, hospitals).
  - *Shift:* Perturb values such as dates or ages by a fixed, patient-specific offset to preserve temporal consistency.
  - *Hash:* Replace identifiers (e.g., SSN) with consistent cryptographic hashes for cross-document linkage.
  - *None:* Preserve or fallback if no substitution is configured.
- **Substitution Engine:** This module applies the configured strategy to each PHI span. It produces both the substituted text and a mapping log linking original and replaced values, enabling transparency and reproducibility.

```
Original Note (excerpt):
----------------------------------------
Patient: Anas Adil, surgery date: 2023-01-05
Procedure performed by Dr. King at Bon Secours Hospital.
Follow-up appointment scheduled for 2023-01-23.

Substituted Note:
----------------------------------------
Patient: Rebecca Chambers, surgery date: 2023-04-05
Procedure performed by Dr. Karen Williams at Guerra-Jones Hospital.
Follow-up appointment scheduled for 2023-04-23.

Replacements:
----------------------------------------
Anas Adil              → Rebecca Chambers
Dr. King               → Dr. Karen Williams
Bon Secours Hospital   → Guerra-Jones Hospital
2023-01-05             → 2023-04-05
2023-01-23             → 2023-04-23
```

Fig. 3. An example output of a substituted note.

Figure 3 illustrates detected PHI spans such as names, dates, and facilities are replaced with synthetic but contextually coherent entities defined in the YAML substitution rules. This preserves narrative readability while ensuring irreversible de-identification.

3.4 Adversarial Risk Assessment

This phase quantifies residual privacy risks and is a key differentiator of the pipeline.

- **Quasi-Identifier (QID) Uniqueness (0-1):** Calculates how uniquely a tuple of quasi-identifiers (e.g., city, age, diagnosis) appears across the corpus. Higher uniqueness implies greater re-identification risk.
- **SBERT Leakage Probe (0-1):** Uses Sentence-BERT embeddings to measure semantic similarity between original and substituted text. High similarity may indicate semantic leakage of sensitive information.
- **Masked Language Model Audit (0-1):** A pre-trained BERT model predicts masked PHI tokens from surrounding context, estimating the ease of re-identification.
- **Membership Inference Simulator (0-1):** Estimates whether a de-identified note could still be linked to its source corpus based on persistent, unique non-PHI phrases.
- **Residual PHI:** Ensures that no PHI remains post-substitution.
- **Risk Scorecard:** The Risk Scorecard integrates all risk metrics and assigns each note a composite risk tier (low, medium, high) through threshold-based aggregation. Notes exhibiting any of the following characteristics of residual PHI, quasi-identifier uniqueness above 0.9, semantic leakage exceeding 0.65, masked language model (MLM) predictability greater than 0.05, or membership inference scores above 0.8 are labeled high risk, while notes meeting fewer criteria fall into medium or low tiers. The thresholds were selected empirically to provide conservative privacy protection and reflect well-established risk factors highlighted in the de-identification and re-identification literature. This tiering mechanism is fully configurable and enables interpretable, multidimensional privacy auditing suited to varied organizational or regulatory risk tolerances.

```
Audit Report (Note ID: 3e1a2cc2-f8cf-dd89-ce44-98463fa99d54)
------------------------------------------------------------
Residual PHI: AGE
QID Uniqueness Score:          1.0000
Semantic Leakage Score:        0.6743
Masked LM Predictability:      0.0000
Membership Inference Score:    1.0000
Risk Tier:                     HIGH

Audit Notes:
Residual PHI detected (AGE).
High QID uniqueness and membership inference risk.
------------------------------------------------------------
```

Fig. 4. An adversarial risk assessment

Figure 4 illustrates an adversarial risk assessment output. Each de-identified note undergoes multi-dimensional auditing to quantify re-identification risk.

Metrics include quasi-identifier (QID) uniqueness, semantic leakage, masked language model (MLM) predictability, and membership inference likelihood. High-tier scores indicate elevated re-identification risk, prompting further mitigation or review.

3.5 Evaluation Framework

The final phase provides a unified evaluation of privacy protection and utility preservation.

- **Privacy Metrics:** Detected PHI spans are compared against ground truth annotations to compute precision, recall, and F1 score. Alignment is ensured using BIO-tagging.
- **Semantic and Utility Metrics:** SBERT cosine similarity, token count delta, and concept retention are measured to assess semantic fidelity. Ontology-based mappings ensure that clinical meaning is preserved [9].
- **Reporting:** Results are aggregated into per-note and corpus-level reports, providing risk tier distributions and performance breakdowns by note template.

4 Experiments and Results

The proposed de-identification pipeline was evaluated across three dimensions: PHI detection accuracy, semantic fidelity preservation, and adversarial privacy risk. Model development followed a standard train–validation-test split to ensure unbiased evaluation. Of the 500,000 Synthea-generated clinical notes, 70% were used for training, 15% for validation and the remaining 15% were held for final testing. Additionally, a subset of 200 notes from the test partition was selected for detailed adversarial evaluation to assess susceptibility to linkage and re-identification attacks.

All experiments are conducted in a reproducible environment using Docker containers and version-controlled configurations. Dependencies are managed via Poetry in Python 3.10, ensuring portability and replicability.

4.1 PHI Detection Performance

The PHI detection module was trained using a fine-tuned BioClinicalBERT model on the training split of the synthetic corpus. Although the dataset is large, the number of training epochs was determined by empirical validation behaviour rather than dataset size. As shown in Table 1, the model's validation loss and the F1 score stabilised by Epoch 3, indicating convergence. However, Epoch 4 yielded a small but consistent improvement in validation loss (0.003950 $\rightarrow$ 0.003913) and the F1 score (0.992297 $\rightarrow$ 0.992300). Preliminary experiments beyond four epochs produced no further gains and showed early signs of overfitting. Thus, four epochs represented the optimal stopping point, capturing the final marginal performance improvement while preserving generalization.

The final evaluation yielded an overall PHI F1 score of 0.9786, with precision at 0.9963 and recall at 0.9633, as shown in Table 2. Template-specific F1 scores ranged from 0.9440 (discharge summaries) to 1.0000 (admission notes), as shown in Table 3, confirming strong entity-level reliability across clinical note types.

Table 1. PHI detection performance across training epochs.

Epoch	Train Loss	Val Loss	Precision	Recall	F1	Accuracy
1	0.004200	0.003993	0.998360	0.985924	0.992103	0.998258
2	0.003900	0.003977	0.998648	0.986003	0.992285	0.998268
3	0.003900	0.003950	0.998675	0.986000	0.992297	0.998269
4	0.004000	0.003913	0.998668	0.986013	0.992300	0.998269

Table 2. Overall evaluation metrics summarizing PHI detection performance, semantic fidelity, and privacy risk indicators

Metric	Value	Description
Overall PHI Precision	0.9963	Accuracy of PHI identification
Overall PHI Recall	0.9633	Sensitivity to PHI occurrences
Overall PHI F1-score	0.9786	Combined precisionâĂŞrecall balance
Average SBERT Similarity	0.6576	Semantic coherence after redaction
Average MLM Predictability	0.0362	Text predictability post-redaction
Average Concept Retention	0.7550	Clinical content preserved
Average Token Count	42.3	Mean token difference pre/post redaction
Average Membership Inference Score	1.0000	Memorization risk indicator
Notes with Residual PHI	50	Out of 200 total notes
Notes Above High QID Threshold	200	High-risk quasi-identifier notes
Dominant Risk Tier	High (100%)	All notes classified high-risk

4.2 Semantic Fidelity and Utility Preservation

Semantic preservation was measured using SBERT similarity and concept retention metrics. The average SBERT similarity across redacted notes was 0.6576, with variation from 0.6240 (operative reports) to 0.6804 (discharge summaries). Concept retention averaged 75.5%, while the mean token count delta was 42.3% tokens, reflecting structural changes introduced by substitution.

Although similarity scores indicate moderate semantic drift, especially in substitution-heavy templates such as consultation notes, manual inspection confirmed that grammatical and contextual coherence was largely preserved, maintaining clinical usability.

4.3 Template-Level Risk Distribution

Table 3 summarizes risk distributions across note templates. All notes were classified as high risk, reflecting the pipeline's conservative tiering and the intrinsic re-identification risk of structured demographic clinical patterns. This finding underscores the need for enhanced QID obfuscation and defense mechanisms against membership inference.

Table 3. Template-level PHI detection, semantic fidelity, and risk distribution.

Template	Avg PHI F1	Avg SBERT Sim.	High-Risk Notes	Total Notes
Admission Note	1.0000	0.6599	23	23
Consultation Note	0.9780	0.6450	42	42
Discharge Summary	0.9440	0.6804	27	27
History & Physical	0.9926	0.6649	27	27
Operative Report	0.9968	0.6240	21	21
Progress Note	0.9928	0.6399	22	22
Referral Note	0.9626	0.6777	38	38

All 200 adversarial test notes were classified as high risk, but this outcome reflects the design of the evaluation rather than a deficiency in the scoring method. The subset was intentionally constructed as a stress-test sample: notes were chosen for rare demographic and clinical event combinations and were generated from a limited set of templates, resulting in structurally similar narratives. This template uniformity amplified membership-inference scores, while the rare quasi-identifiers naturally pushed QID uniqueness to the upper range. Under these deliberately adversarial conditions, high-risk assignments are expected. In a more heterogeneous real-world corpus, the scorecard would produce a more varied risk distribution.

4.4 Comparison with Existing Systems

To contextualize performance, Table 4 compares ShieldPHI with existing de-identification systems, including rule-based approaches (Philter), neural sequence taggers (NeuroNER), and hybrid deep learning systems (SparkNLP, DeIDClinic).

ShieldPHI achieves comparable PHI detection F1 (≈ 0.98) to state-of-the-art systems, while offering additional strengths: *configurable substitution*, *semantic fidelity preservation*, and *multi-layered adversarial auditing*. These capabilities, absent in prior systems, directly target the evolving landscape of privacy threats beyond baseline PHI recognition.

Table 4 compares the proposed pipeline with widely cited de-identification systems. The reported F1 scores for existing systems are taken from their respective publications and therefore reflect performance on different datasets. As a

Table 4. Comparison of ShieldPHI with existing de-identification systems.

System	Detection Method	PHI Types	Semantic Fidelity	Stylometric Safeguards	Adv. Risk Simulation	F1 Score
Philter	Rule-based	30	Low (mask only)	None	None	~0.91
NeuroNER	BiLSTM+CRF	15	None	None	None	~0.90
BioBERT	Transformer	18	None	None	None	0.89–0.92
SparkNLP	DL+Regex	25	High (obfuscation)	Partial	Limited	~0.96
DeIDClinic	ClinicalBERT+Rules	27	High (surrogates)	Partial	Partial	0.97
ShieldPHI	**Hybrid**	**20**	**High (configurable surrogates)**	**Full**	**Yes (multi-layered)**	**0.98**

result, this comparison should not be interpreted as a direct performance benchmark, but rather as a qualitative contextualization of methodological capabilities (e.g., PHI coverage, semantic fidelity, and adversarial safeguards). The table highlights functional distinctions rather than claiming superiority across identical evaluation conditions.

5 Conclusion

This work presents a modular, privacy-preserving clinical text de-identification pipeline that integrates hybrid PHI detection, configurable substitution, and multidimensional risk auditing. Using a synthetic corpus of 500,000 Synthea-generated notes, the system achieved strong performance (F1 = 0.9786), consistent reliability across diverse note templates, and comprehensive auditing of privacy risks. Fine-tuning BioClinicalBERT enabled robust detection, while the YAML-driven substitution framework ensured semantic coherence and auditability. Most importantly, the pipeline extends beyond benchmark-driven evaluations by integrating and adapting metrics for semantic leakage, membership inference, and quasi-identifier uniqueness to the clinical de-identification setting. This multi-layered auditing approach provides a holistic assessment of privacy risks, aligning with regulatory frameworks such as HIPAA's Safe Harbor and GDPR's Recital 26. Several limitations remain. Synthetic data cannot fully represent the complexity of real clinical narratives, constraining generalizability and adversarial realism. High membership inference scores (1.0) reflect corpus homogeneity and the absence of differential privacy, complicating memorization assessment. Substitution, though semantically aligned, does not yet employ contextual embeddings or style transfer to enhance fluency. The conservative risk-tiering scheme may overestimate risks when semantic uniqueness does not imply practical re-identification. Multilingual and cross-lingual PHI detection also remain unsupported. Future work will evaluate the pipeline on real clinical corpora under IRB oversight, incorporate differential privacy and noise-based regularization to mitigate memorization, and enhance substitution with context-aware generation and style-preserving paraphrasing. Expanding to multilingual settings via cross-lingual transformers and integrating federated learning will further broaden applicability and compliance.

References

1. Altalla, B., et al.: Evaluating GPT models for clinical note de-identification. Sci. Rep. **15**(1), 3852 (2025)
2. Ciampi, M., Sicuranza, M., Silvestri, S.: A privacy-preserving and standard-based architecture for secondary use of clinical data. Information **13** (2022)
3. Paul, A., Shaji, D., Han, L., Del-Pinto, W., Nenadic, G.: DeIDClinic: a multi-layered framework for de-identification of clinical free-text data (2024). arXiv preprint
4. Sarkar, A.R., Chuang, Y.-S., Mohammed, N., Jiang. X.: De-identification is not enough: a comparison between de-identified and synthetic clinical notes. Sci. Rep. **14**(1), 29669 (2024)
5. Duffourc, M.N., Gerke, S.: Health care AI and patient privacy–dinerstein v google. JAMA **331**(11), 909–910 (2024)
6. Murtaza, H., et al.: Synthetic data generation: state of the art in health care domain. Comput. Sci. Rev. **48**, 100546 (2023)
7. The European Parliament and the Council of the European Union. Recital 26 – eu gdpr (2016). https://www.privacy-regulation.eu/en/r26.htm. Accessed 21 Nov 2025
8. Aguelal, H., Palmieri, P.: De-anonymization of health data: a survey of practical attacks, vulnerabilities and challenges (2025)
9. John, X., et al.: Cole: Diri: adversarial patient reidentification with large language models for evaluating clinical text anonymization. AMIA Summits Transl. Sci Proc. **355** (2025)
10. Kovačević, A., Bašaragin, B., Milošević, N., Nenadić, G.: De-identification of clinical free text using natural language processing: a systematic review of current approaches. Artif. Intell. Med. **151** (2024)
11. Norgeot, B., et al.: Protected health information filter (philter): accurately and securely de-identifying free-text clinical notes. NPJ Digit. Med. **3**(1), 57 (2020)
12. Aberdeen, J., et al.: The mitre identification scrubber toolkit: design, training, and assessment. Int. J. Med. Informatics **79**(12), 849–859 (2010)
13. Dernoncourt, F., Lee, J., Szolovits, P.: Neuroner: an easy-to-use program for named-entity recognition based on neural networks. In: Proceedings of the 2017 conference on empirical methods in natural language processing: system demonstrations, pp. 97–102 (2017)
14. juliangarratt. Conll 2003 Dataset. https://www.kaggle.com/datasets/juliangarratt/conll2003-dataset/data. Kaggle dataset; Accessed 21 Nov 2025
15. i2b2 tranSMART Foundation. Informatics for integrating biology & the bedside. https://www.i2b2.org/. Accessed 21 Nov 2025
16. Lee, J., et al.: BioBERT: a pre-trained biomedical language representation model for biomedical text mining. Bioinformatics **36**(4), 1234–1240 (2020)
17. National Library of Medicine. Pubmed data (2025). https://pubmed.ncbi.nlm.nih.gov/download/. Accessed 21 Nov 2025
18. Pune Municipal Corporation. PMC open data. https://hwww.pmc.gov.in/en/b/pmc-open-data. Accessed 21 Nov 2025
19. medicalai. Clinicalbert. https://huggingface.co/medicalai/ ClinicalBERT. Accessed 21 Nov 2025
20. Kocaman, V., Talby, D.: Spark NLP: natural language understanding at scale. Softw. Impacts **8**, 100058 (2021)

21. Stanford NLP Group. Biomedical & clinical model performance (2020). https://stanfordnlp.github.io/stanza/biomed_model_performance.html. Accessed 21 Nov 2025
22. Neumann, M., King, D., Beltagy, I., Ammar, W.: Scispacy: fast and robust models for biomedical natural language processing. arXiv preprint arXiv:1902.07669 (2019)
23. The MITRE Corporation. The MITRE corporation (2023) synthea synthetic data overview. https://mitre.github.io/fhir-for-research/modules/synthea-overview (2023). Accessed 21 Nov 2025
24. Hodges, R., Tokunaga, K., LeGrand, J.: A novel method to create realistic synthetic medication data. JAMIA Open **6**(3), ooad052 (2023)
25. rmiller415. SSA popular baby names (1880–2024). https://www.kaggle.com/datasets/rmiller415/ssa-popular-baby-names-1880-2024 (2025). Kaggle dataset. Accessed 21 Nov 2025
26. Kafura, D.: The corgis datasets project (2023). https://corgis-edu.github.io/corgis/csv/hospitals/. Accessed 21 Nov 2025
27. Pallets Projects. Jinja (2020). https://jinja.palletsprojects.com/en/stable/changes/#version-2-11-1

Revealing Power Imbalances in Data Privacy: A Privacy Privilege Model

May Alhajri[1,2](✉), Carsten Rudolph[1], and Gillian Oliver[1]

[1] Monash University, Melbourne, VIC 3800, Australia
{may.alhajri,carsten.rudolph,gillian.oliver}@monash.edu
[2] King Faisal University, Al-Ahsa 31982, Saudi Arabia
mnalhajri@kfu.edu.sa

Abstract. Privacy is often conceptualised in oversimplified and fragmented ways that overlook the structural power dynamics that governs personal data in digital ecosystems. Existing approaches focus on compliance or isolated technical safeguards and therefore fail to capture how data practices redistribute influence among users, service providers, and regulators. This paper introduces the Privacy Privilege Model (PPM), a formal and conceptual framework grounded in Category Theory. PPM models actors as `objects`, privacy-relevant relationships as `morphisms`, and Privacy-Enhancing Technologies (PETs) as `functorial` transformations that reshape these relationships. The PPM models privacy power along three dimensions CTA: control, transparency, and accountability. Through this structure, the model explains how PETs modify these dimensions by altering the direction and strength of the information flows. Examples such as encryption and consent mechanisms show how technical interventions not only affect risk reduction outcomes but also governance properties. The framework provides a portable and expressive way to reason about privacy as a system of evolving power relations. It supports scholars, practitioners, and policymakers in evaluating the broader governance implications of PET adoption and encourages more rigorous mental models of privacy beyond compliance driven views.

Keywords: Privacy · Privacy Privilege Model · Power imbalances in privacy · Privacy governance · Privacy Enhancing Technologies · Category Theory

1 Introduction

As digital ecosystems have recently shifted towards processing large amounts of personal information, privacy concerns have to extend beyond individual rights and technical protections. This imposes a growing concern around structural power imbalance and loss of agency among users, service providers, regulators, and other parties involved [32]. The United Nations Special Rapporteur on the right to privacy has noted that modern digital technologies process personal

© IFIP International Federation for Information Processing 2026
Published by Springer Nature Switzerland AG 2026
H. Janicke et al. (Eds.): SEC 2026, IFIP AICT 787, pp. 510–524, 2026.
https://doi.org/10.1007/978-3-032-27993-4_35

information in invasive and large-scale ways that often fail to respect individuals' reasonable expectations of privacy [29]. Zuboff's concept of "surveillance capitalism" further illustrates how service providers commodify personal data, reshaping power dynamics across digital platforms [32]. Legal and sociotechnical research highlights that privacy should be seen as a key part of digital governance, not just as a personal right [3,31]. PETs play a crucial role in mitigating specific privacy risks; however, existing evaluation frameworks primarily evaluate technical guarantees, compliance criteria, or utility trade-offs [5,30]. As a result, there is a need to understand the governance-level effects of PETs deployment, how PETs alter who controls data, who has visibility into its use, and who is accountable for its misuse [21]. Thus, addressing these structural questions requires a modelling language that represents how privacy relationships between actors change under different technological interventions. Such a language must capture both the entities in the system and the directional flows of governance relations among them. Category Theory (CT) provides this capability: it describes systems in terms of objects and relations and formally expresses how these relations transform under intervention [19].

Building on Cheng's categorical treatment of privilege and sociotechnical abstraction [7,8], we extend these ideas to privacy governance by proposing the *Privacy Privilege Model* (PPM). PPM is a category-theoretic framework for modelling how privacy-related power is distributed among actors and how it is transformed by PETs, enabling structured reasoning about system-level transformations. PPM models actors as `objects`, privacy-relevant actions as typed `morphisms`, and PETs as `functors` that transform these `morphisms` between system states. PPM captures these shifts along three *CTA* governance dimensions: *control* (C), *transparency* (T), and *accountability* (A). Rather than asking whether "privacy is protected," PPM asks who *gains* or *loses Control*, *Transparency*, or *Accountability* when information moves between actors, and how PETs may mitigate these effects. By providing a mathematically grounded, structurally expressive model of privacy power shifts, PPM offers a new lens through which to analyse and design PETs, not merely as technical tools but as interventions in privacy governance. The model also supports stakeholders in developing a more precise understanding of the complex power dynamics in data sharing and of the effects of using PETs.

This paper offers the following contributions: (1) It proposes a category-theoretic framework *Privacy Privilege Model* (PPM) for representing actors, privacy actions, and system changes caused by PETs; (2) It explains how PETs act as functorial interventions that change governance relations in a privacy system; and (3) It demonstrates PPM applicability with specific PET examples that highlight its effects at the governance level. To the best of our knowledge, no existing framework simultaneously (1) represents privacy as an explicit relational network among actors, (2) models PETs as transformations of that network, and (3) links those transformations to governance consequences expressed in terms of control, transparency, and accountability at the system level.

2 Background and Related Work

Digital platforms are gaining more control over personal data and decision-making, creating privacy power imbalances in which service providers hold greater authority and visibility than individuals [26]. These imbalances are worsened by black-box data practices such as opaque analytics [15], algorithmic profiling [25], and cross-context data linkage [3,21], which limit individuals' ability to understand or contest how their data is used. As a result, loss of agency emerges not primarily from poor individual choices, but from underlying structural asymmetries embedded in digital systems [9,16,17]. Privacy has therefore been conceptualised as a structural feature of socio-technical infrastructures, where data relations distribute social and institutional power rather than simply protecting individual rights [10,28,31]. These dynamics vary across horizontal (peer-to-peer) [27] and vertical (institution-to-individual) relations [4], motivating the need to understand privacy as a relational structure of power among actors and to analyse how that structure changes when interventions(e.g. PETs or privacy-reducing practices) are introduced.

Building on this perspective, privacy theories and governance models emphasise that addressing structural asymmetries requires attention to contextual, relational, and institutional factors beyond individual choice. Contextual Integrity [22], for example, frames privacy in terms of role-dependent information flow norms. Relational accounts such as networked privacy [6], group privacy [13], and relational data governance [31] highlight how privacy risks and protections emerge across interconnected actors and groups. Regulatory and standards frameworks [12,18,23] reflect these concerns by imposing obligations related to accountability, transparency, and responsible data handling. Together, these approaches establish privacy imbalance as a systemic governance problem, but they remain largely descriptive and do not offer formal methods for modelling how relational structures evolve when technologies intervene.

In parallel, PETs have been evaluated in terms of leakage guarantees, utility trade-offs, and robustness against adversarial behaviour [11,14,24]. In addition, some studies extend PET evaluation to contextual [2], compliance-oriented [20], and domain-specific settings [1]. These assessments provide a useful technical basis for understanding what PETs can do, how strong their protections are, and the trade-offs they entail. What remains less clear is how such results can be systematically used to support governance-level reasoning when PETs are applied within socio-technical systems. Our proposed PPM model builds on existing PET evaluations by providing a system-level framework that interprets established PET properties in terms of their effects on governance power and relationships among actors.

To support such governance-level reasoning, it is important to make explicit which dimensions of governance are affected by socio-technical interventions. Across regulatory, standards, and governance literature, recurring concerns centre on who can decide, who can see, and who must answer for data-intensive practices. This focus is reflected in the General Data Protection Regulation (GDPR) provisions on data-subject rights and controller obligations [12], ISO/IEC 29100 principles on openness and responsibility [18], OECD privacy guidelines, the NIST Privacy Framework [23], and reinforced by relational data-governance research [31]. In PPM, these recurring dimensions are grouped under the labels *Control*, *Transparency*, and *Accountability* (CTA), which serve as a cross-cutting abstraction for reasoning about the governance implications of socio-technical interventions, including PETs. While CTA captures a broad range of governance-relevant effects, PPM is not limited to these dimensions and can be extended to incorporate more specific, application-dependent properties (e.g., linkability) where appropriate.

Operationalising governance dimensions such as CTA at the system level requires a formal language capable of representing actors, relationships, and their transformation. Category Theory (CT) provides a mathematical framework for modelling systems in terms of `objects`, relations (`morphisms`), and structure-preserving transformations (`functors`). Beyond mathematics, CT has been adopted as a general modelling approach for scientific and socio-technical systems, emphasising relational structure and compositionality. Cheng's work [7,8], for example, demonstrates how categorical reasoning can illuminate privilege and social power, showing that abstract relational tools can be applied to questions of justice and responsibility. CT's focus on relational structure and transformation makes it well suited for modelling privacy as a network of actor-to-actor `objects` and PETs as `functorial` transformations of those `morphisms`, enabling analysis of how interventions reconfigure system structure rather than merely comparing static states.

Together, these related works highlight the importance of structural power asymmetries, relational privacy theories, governance principles, and technical PETs. However, existing approaches typically address these aspects in isolation. These gaps motivate the introduction of PPM, a category-theoretic framework that makes privacy power relations explicit and provides a structured way to analyse how PETs reconfigure governance dynamics within socio-technical systems.

3 Proposed Privacy Privilege Model (PPM)

This section introduces our proposed PPM, including an overview of the model and its formal categorical structure. It explains its role in analysing privacy-relevant relations among actors, and then shows how actions and PETs are modelled to capture changes between *pre*- and *post*-intervention system states.

3.1 PPM Overview

PPM provides a structural lens for understanding privacy governance in socio-technical systems. It offers a lean and accessible language for reasoning about how data sharing redistributes governance power. At its core, PPM captures the idea that loss of privacy is not merely a matter of data exposure, but a redistribution of decision power and oversight across entities. The most basic example is a person `sharing` personal information with a company, i.e., in order to use their services. Without any safeguards, this person will lose control over the data, there will be no transparency on what the company can and will do with that data, and accountability beyond service-level agreements will be minimal.

PPM captures these governance dynamics at two layers: (1) the asymmetries created by baseline privacy actions, and (2) the additional transformations introduced by PETs. First, actions such as `share`, `forward`, and `audit` already establish CTA relations, granting control to a service provider, extending that control downstream, or enabling regulatory oversight. Second, PETs then alter these relations: some links strengthen (greater user control or oversight), others weaken (reduced access or visibility), and some may be disrupted entirely. Taken together, these effects show how privacy power shifts as data flows evolve and as safeguards are introduced, which PPM uses to create systematic comparison of pre- and post-PET system states.

Formally, to capture these governance dynamics, PPM adopts standard category-theoretic constructs: `objects` for actors, `morphisms` for privacy relations, and `functors` for PETs transformations. A system before and after applying a PET is represented as `categories` $\mathcal{P}_0$ and $\mathcal{P}_1$ with identical objects. PPM also annotates morphisms with ordinal CTA labels, in which PET then shifts them as a functor $F_{\text{PET}} : \mathcal{P}_0 \to \mathcal{P}_1$ by strengthening, weakening, or eliminating CTA and/or `morphisms`. Figure 1 illustrates how such transformations alter the governance structure CTA of a simple data-sharing scenario with user U, a service provider SP, a secondary data user S, a mediator M and a regulator R.

Fig. 1. PPM as a PET functor $F_{\text{PET}} : \mathcal{P}_0 \to \mathcal{P}_1$ that transforms relations.

U shares data with SP, who in turn can then share it with the secondary data user S. The **left side** shows a scenario with limited privacy protection. We assume that SP confirms the data received with U, which provides some level of transparency. M and R contribute to accountability via observing activities or regulating data storage. The **right-hand** diagram shows the situation after applying a hypothetical PET. We assume the data is encrypted in a way that SP can only use it for a particular service, but cannot get access to the actual data itself. The thicker control arrow from U to SP shows that U now has more control over the data. Now, if we assume that with the encrypted data, SP cannot confirm to have received the data in the same way, transparency might be reduced, denoted by the dashed arrow. However, as SP can no longer share data with S, the relation to S is disrupted which is denoted by a dashed arrow.

Supported by the visualisation, PPM functions both as a precise analytical tool and as a portable mental model for understanding privacy-related power dynamics. By making the effects of privacy actions and PETs explicit, it helps evaluate governance trade-offs across CTA dimensions and clarifies how digital service designs redistribute power, visibility, and oversight.

3.2 PPM Definitions

This subsection introduces the formal elements of PPM used throughout the paper. It defines the core constructs required to represent actors, privacy-relevant relations, and their transformation under PETs.

(1) Categories: Privacy States. PPM analysis compares two snapshots (privacy states) of the same system mainly distinguished by the set of PETs applied:

$$\mathcal{P}_0 \quad \text{(before a PET)} \qquad \text{and} \qquad \mathcal{P}_1 \quad \text{(after a PET)}.$$

Each snapshot is a category with set of actors (`objects`); links (`morphisms`) between actors to shows relations and PETs (`functor`) that change these relations and its actors's privacy power governance. It should be noted that PETs can reduce what can be done with the data and improving overall power of some actors. Thus, to capture these changes, the underlying"system" as such might change in different states modelled as two or more categories after PETs applied but the `objects` remain mostly the same in both states $\mathcal{P}_0$ and $\mathcal{P}_1$:

$$\mathrm{Ob}(\mathcal{P}_0) = \mathrm{Ob}(\mathcal{P}_1) = \{a, b, c..\}.$$

(2) Objects: Actors/Entities. In both categories $\mathcal{P}_0$ and $\mathcal{P}_1$, the `objects` are the set key stakeholders who plays different roles in privacy ecosystem by initiating actions (e.g. `share, grant`).

Definition 1 (Object Set of $\mathcal{P}_0$). *Let $\mathcal{P}_0$ denote the baseline category of actors in the privacy ecosystem. The set of objects is* $\mathrm{Ob}(\mathcal{P}_0) = \{U, SP, M, S, R\}$ *where U, SP, M, S, and R denote, respectively, Users, Service Providers, Mediators, Secondary Consumers, and Regulators.*

(3) Morphisms represent privacy-relevant actions between objects, abstracted as discrete actions (e.g., `share`). Each morphism encodes a directed information relation from one `object` to another and may give rise to changes in the overall CTA privacy power configuration of the system.

Definition 2 (Morphism). *A morphism $f : A \to B$ is a directed action from a source actor A (e.g., a user) to a target actor B (e.g., a service provider).*

Definition 3 (Atomic Morphism Set). *We define a finite set of* atomic actions (morphisms) $\mathcal{A}$[1], *where each* $a \in \mathcal{A}$ *denotes a basic privacy-relevant action of the form* $a : A \to B$ *with* $A, B \in \mathrm{Ob}(\mathcal{P}_i)$ *and* $\mathrm{Ob}(\mathcal{P}_i) = \{U, SP, M, S, R\}$. *These morphisms represent direct interactions among the actors,* abstracting away *from contextual constraints.*[2]

$$\mathcal{A} = \left\{ \begin{array}{l} \texttt{share}\,,\ \texttt{store}\,,\ \texttt{access}\,,\ \texttt{delete}\,,\ \texttt{verify}\,, \\ \texttt{audit}\,,\ \texttt{observe}\,,\ \texttt{transform}\,,\ \texttt{forward}\,, \\ \texttt{request}\,,\ \texttt{notify}\,,\ \texttt{grant}\,,\ \texttt{report} \end{array} \right\}$$

While morphisms represent abstract actions, in PPM, each morphisms (arrow) also carries a governance CTA tag that identifies the privacy-relevant characteristics of the action. These tags, graphically represented by labels to the morphism arrows and are defined formally in Definition 4. This lets PETs transform not only which arrows exist but also their governance strength.

(4) CTA Governance Annotations: Each morphism (arrow) is paired with CTA triple that encodes how privacy power is distributed along three orthogonal dimensions: *Control* (C), *Transparency* (T), and *Accountability* (A). For a morphism (arrow) $f_{CTA} : A \to B$, it carries a CTA tags C_{AB}, T_{AB}, A_{AB}, we interpret its governance meaning as follows:

- *Control* (C): Measures how much *decision power* B *gains* from A.
- *Transparency* (T): Measures how much *visibility* A *provides to* B.
- *Accountability* (A): Measures how much *responsibility* B *bears to* A.

Definition 4 (CTA annotation). *We use a coarse ordinal scale*

$$\mathbb{O} = \{\text{NONE}, \text{LOW}, \text{MED}, \text{HIGH}\}, \ \textit{with}\ \text{NONE} \prec \text{LOW} \prec \text{MED} \prec \text{HIGH}$$

Each arrow $f : A \to B$ *carries a governance tag* $\alpha(f) = (C, T, A) \in \mathbb{O}^3$ *(see Table 1).*

In real-world systems, multiple `morphisms` (actions) may exist between a given pair of actors A and B, donated as $\mathrm{Hom}(A, B)$. Since each morphism $f : A \to B$ carries a CTA annotation (Definition 4), we then need to provide a summarised governance view for this Hom-set. Thus, we define the *CTA projection* (Definition 5) as the maximum, per dimension, across all morphisms between the same actor pair.

[1] The list $\mathcal{A}$ is illustrative rather than exhaustive; it can be refined to fit any scenario.
[2] Context-dependent constraints (e.g., consent validity, jurisdiction) can be modeled in future work via profunctors and 2-cells.

Table 1. Example of actions with CTA annotations

Action	Description	$\alpha(f) = (C, T, A)$
share $_{U \to SP}$	U shares data with SP	(MED, MED, NONE)
grant $_{SP \to S}$	SP grants S access	(HIGH, MED, NONE)
observe $_{M \to SP}$	M observes/forwards traffic	(LOW, MED, NONE)
report $_{R \to SP}$	R requires report trails from SP	(NONE, MED, MED)

Definition 5 (CTA Projection). *Let $A, B \in \mathrm{Ob}(\mathcal{P}_i)$, and let* $\mathrm{Hom}(A, B)$ *be the set of morphisms from A to B in the given privacy state $\mathcal{P}_i$. Then, the projected governance levels between A and B are defined as:*

$$C_{A,B} := \max_{f \in \mathrm{Hom}_{\mathcal{P}_i}(A,B)} C(\alpha(f)), \quad \textit{and similarly for } T_{A,B}, A_{A,B}.$$

This projection view $C_{A,B}, T_{A,B}, A_{A,B}$ are not new morphisms; they are *summary labels* for diagram edges, computed from the underlying `morphisms` $f_{CTA} = (a, \alpha(f))$ with $a \in \mathcal{A}$ (Definitions 2, 3, 4). For example, suppose there are two `morphisms` from A to B, contains:

$$Hom_{A,B} = \begin{cases} f_1 : \texttt{share}, & \text{with } \alpha(f_1) = (\text{MED}, \text{LOW}, \text{NONE}) \mid C(\alpha_1) = \text{MED} \\ f_2 : \texttt{grant}, & \text{with } \alpha(f_2) = (\text{HIGH}, \text{NONE}, \text{NONE}) \mid C(\alpha_2) = \text{HIGH} \end{cases}$$

Hence, the projection C value of $Hom_{A,B}$ is: $C_{A,B} := \max\{\text{MED}, \text{HIGH}\} = \text{HIGH}$. This means that even if some actions only provide MED or LOW power shifts, the *maximum observed shift* defines the governance projection value. In this case, B gains high Control over A due to at least one strong action (**grant**).

Definition 6 (CTA label set). *For $\mathcal{P}_i$, we define all diagram labels as*

$$\mathsf{Labels}(\mathcal{P}_i) := \{ C_{A,B},\ T_{A,B},\ A_{A,B} \mid A, B \in \mathrm{Ob}(\mathcal{P}_i) \}.$$

These are the quantities shown next to arrows are used in diagrams (see Table 2).

CTA Projection labels in $\mathcal{P}_1$ are recomputed with a prime (e.g. C'_{AB}) after PETs applied and defined as:

$$C'_{A,B} = \max_{f \in \mathrm{Hom}_{\mathcal{P}_0}(A,B)} C\big(\alpha(F(f))\big), \quad \text{and similarly for } T'_{A,B}, A'_{A,B}.$$

(5) Functors. In PPM, a PET is modelled as a `functor` maps one category to another (e.g. $\mathcal{P}_0$ to $\mathcal{P}_1$) while preserving structure. Meaning, `objects` and `morphisms` remain mostly the same across categories, but their privacy impact (CTA annotation) changes, shifting governance power along C, T, A. However,

Table 2. CTA label examples

Label	Interpretation
$C_{U,SP}$	Net control shift from U to SP.
$T_{SP,U}$	Net transparency from SP to U.
$A_{R,SP}$	Net enforceability from regulator R over SP.
$C_{SP,S}$	Net onward control from SP to S.

some PETs can introduce or remove some `objects` and `morphisms`. For example, some PETs might require additional actors, such as a Trusted Third Party or a Certification Authority. For this paper, these are not included in this view of the systems, as they are implicitly included in the PET. Thus, a thorough privacy investigation would then need to create a different category that also includes these objects.

Definition 7 (PET as functor). *A PET induces a functor* $F_{\text{PET}} : \mathcal{P}_0 \longrightarrow \mathcal{P}_1$ *satisfying:*

- *Object preservation:* $F_{\text{PET}}(O) = O$ *for all* $O \in \text{Ob}(\mathcal{P}_0)$.
- *Morphism mapping: For every action* $f : A \to B$ *in* $\mathcal{P}_0$, $F_{\text{PET}}(f) : A \to B$ *is an action of the* same type *in* $\mathcal{P}_1$, *with a possibly updated CTA label* $\alpha(F_{\text{PET}}(f))$.

Example 1 (PET Encryption as a Functor). Suppose we have these actions in $\mathcal{P}_0$: $U \xrightarrow{\texttt{share}} SP \xrightarrow{\texttt{forward}} S$. An encryption PET F_e might: *strengthen* $C_{U,SP}$ by restricting SP's ability to access raw data (user retains more control); and *disrupt* $C_{SP,S}$ by making onward sharing ineffective (e.g., encrypted raw data unreadable by S). This yields:

$$F_e(f_{\texttt{share}}) = f'_{\texttt{share}} \text{ with higher } C, \quad F_e(f_{\texttt{forward}}) = f'_{\texttt{forward}} \text{ with } C = \text{NONE}.$$

In Fig. 2, we compute the post-PET projection using the CTA projection function, comparing pre/post values such as $C_{A,B}$ and $C'_{A,B}$.

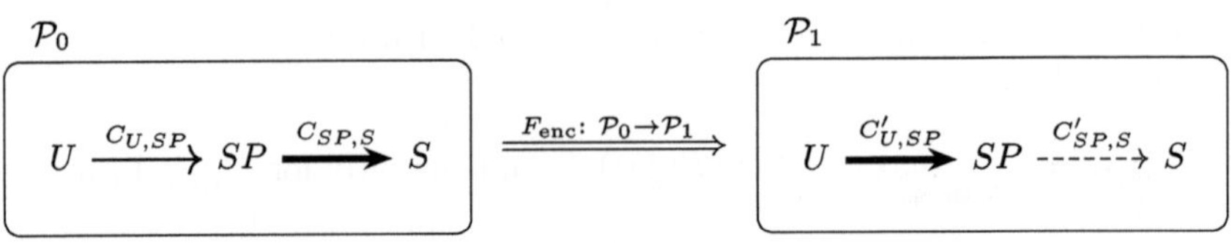

Fig. 2. Encryption affects on relations transforming the system states.

3.3 Functorial Properties

In category theory, a `functor` preserves identities and composition, i.e., $F(\mathrm{id}_O) = \mathrm{id}_{F(O)}$ and $F(g \circ f) = F(g) \circ F(f)$, thereby forming a *strict* `functor`. In the PPM, this corresponds to PETs (`functors`) that adjust the strength of individual actions while preserving the overall structure of data flows. However, many PETs can not be fully modeled as *strict* `functors` as they alter downstream behaviour in ways that break strict compositionality. For example, an encryption PET may strengthen an upstream `share` action while rendering a subsequent `forward` ineffective, so that transforming the whole path differs from composing the transformed steps. Such effects are more naturally modelled using *lax* or *oplax* `functors`, which relax composition preservation and allow PETs to weaken or disturb action chains. In this paper, we limit our treatment to `functors` in general for analytical clarity; a formal account of `functors` types *lax* and *oplax* PET transformations is left for future work.

4 Case Studies: PET-Induced Governance Shifts

We now demonstrate the use of the PPM through two cases: `data at rest` in a fitness tracking service and `data in transit` over a public network. In each case, we compare a baseline system to a PET-enhanced system and show how CTA projections shift across actors.

4.1 Case 1: Fitness Tracker

A user U wears a fitness tracker. The service provider SP ingests raw step and heart-rate readings and stores them. When U later asks for a weekly average, SP computes it over the raw data they already hold. In the baseline, U loses effective control after sharing; SP can retain and reuse raw readings and may forward them to a profiling company S. Transparency to U is minimal unless SP actively confirms what was received and when.

(a) Assumptions and Scope. For this scenario we focus on:

- **Three actors**: $\{U, SP, S\}$ (from $\mathrm{Ob}(\mathcal{P}_0)$, Definition 1);
- **Query type**: aggregates (totals/averages); baseline storage is raw; post-PET returns aggregates only;
- **Four actions**: `share` , `store` , `forward` , `report` (from $\mathcal{A}$, Definition 3);
- **CTA labels**: $C_{U,SP}$, $C_{SP,S}$, $T'_{SP,U}$, $C'_{U,SP}$, $C'_{SP,S}$ (from $\mathsf{Labels}(\mathcal{P}_i)$, Definition 5)
- **Two PETs**: signed receipts (F_{sig}) and homomorphic encryption (F_{he}) .

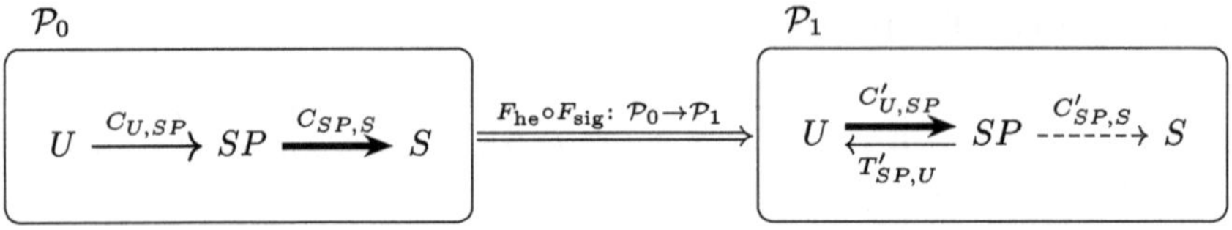

Fig. 3. Fitness tracker scenario view: PETs as a set of functors mapping $\mathcal{P}_0$ to $\mathcal{P}_1$.

(b) Diagrammatic Illustration: Figure 3 illustrates a pre→post shift produced by applying a set of PETs to a minimal system consisting of a user U, a service provider SP, and a secondary data user S. On the left, the baseline shows U sharing raw data with SP, who can in turn forward it to S. The thin control arrow $C_{U,SP}$ indicates that, after sharing, U retains only limited effective control over the data, while $C_{SP,S}$ captures the possibility of onward sharing. The composite morphism from U to S through SP exists but is not drawn, since its practical effect is a further loss of control for U. Transparency back to the user is minimal in this baseline state and therefore not shown. As in our notation elsewhere, the labels summarise, via the CTA projection, the strongest control effect across underlying actions (e.g., `share`, `store`, `forward`) between each pair of actors. The right-hand diagram shows the situation after applying a combined PET, $F_{\text{PET}} = F_{\text{he}} \circ F_{\text{sig}}$. First, signed receipts (F_{sig}) increase transparency from SP to U, represented by the added parallel arrow $T'_{SP,U}$. Then, homomorphic encryption (F_{he}) enables SP to compute aggregates without accessing cleartext, which thickens the control arrow $C'_{U,SP}$ (indicating more control retained by U) and disrupts onward sharing to S, shown as a dashed $C'_{SP,S}$. Actors remain the same across panels; what changes are the relations and their CTA strength, depicted by thin (weak), thick, and dashed arrows. Labels C_{AB}, T_{AB} summarise via the CTA projection over all relevant actions in $\mathcal{A}$.

4.2 Case 2: Data in-Transit

A user U submits personal data to a service provider SP over the public network. In the baseline, traffic can be observed and even modified by an intermediary (e.g., ISP or network operator) M. U has little visibility into what SP actually received. We consider two interventions: (i) channel encryption (TLS), which blocks M from reading or tampering with in-transit data, and (ii) a signed receipt from SP to U that attests to the data received and the time of receipt. Together, they reduce intermediary power while increasing transparency to U.

(a) Assumptions and Scope. For this scenario we focus on:

- **three actors**: $\{U, SP, M\}$ (from Ob($\mathcal{P}_0$), Definition 1);
- **query/flow**: point-to-point data transition from U to SP;
- **four actions**: `share`, `store`, `forward`, `report` (from $\mathcal{A}$, Definition 3);

- **CTA labels:** $C_{U,SP}$, $C_{M,SP}$, $T'_{SP,U}$, $C'_{M,SP}$, $C'_{U,SP}$ (from $\mathsf{Labels}(\mathcal{P}_i)$, Definition 5);
- **two PETs**: TLS[3] channel encryption (F_{TLS}) and signed receipt using digital signature (F_{sig}).

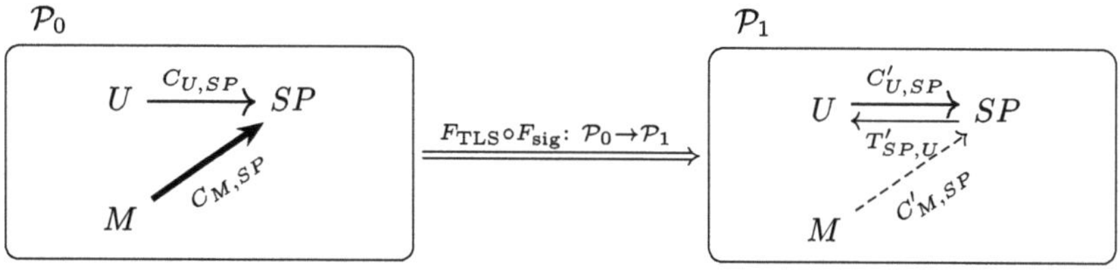

Fig. 4. Secure transport scenario: PETs as a set of functors mapping $\mathcal{P}_0$ to $\mathcal{P}_1$.

(b) Diagrammatic Illustration. Figure 4 shows a pre→post shift produced by applying TLS and a signed receipt to a minimal system consisting of a user U, a service provider SP, and a network intermediary M. On the left, the baseline category ($\mathcal{P}_0$) shows U sending data to SP while M sits on the path. The thin control arrow $C_{U,SP}$ indicates that, after sharing, U has limited influence over what happens at SP, and the diagonal $C_{M,SP}$ captures the intermediary's practical ability to read or modify traffic in transit (indicating high control). Transparency back to U is minimal and therefore not shown. As elsewhere, the diagram labels summarise, via the CTA projection, the strongest control effect across underlying actions (e.g., `share`, `store`, `forward`). The right-hand diagram shows post-category ($\mathcal{P}_1$) the situation after applying a combined PET, $F_{\text{PET}} = F_{\text{TLS}} \circ F_{\text{sig}}$. First, the signed receipt (F_{sig}) increases transparency from SP to U, represented by the added parallel arrow $T'_{SP,U}$. Second, TLS (F_{TLS}) encrypts the channel, disrupting the intermediary's ability to observe or tamper with the flow, shown as a dashed $C'_{M,SP}$. Note that the control arrow $C'_{U,SP}$ remains thin: neither TLS nor the receipt changes U's decision power over data once received by SP. Actors remain the same across panels; what changes are the relations and their CTA strength, depicted by thin (weak) and dashed (disrupted) arrows.

5 Conclusion

This paper introduced the Privacy Privilege Model (PPM), a structured, category-theoretic framework for analysing data privacy through evolving power relations. PPM enables scholars, practitioners, and policymakers to reason about privacy beyond individual rights or technical protections. By modelling actors

[3] TLS is Transport Layer Security, a cryptographic protocol that provides secure, encrypted communication between A and B.

as objects, privacy relationships as typed morphisms annotated with *Control*, *Transparency*, and *Accountability* (CTA) tags, and PETs as functorial transformations, PPM makes governance shifts explicit and reveals where power is lost, strengthened, or redirected. Through illustrative scenarios, we showed how PETs (e.g., homomorphic encryption, TLS, signed receipts) reshape governance relations by strengthening user control, constraining onward flows, and improving transparency, while still leaving certain decision powers with service providers. PPM thus provides *a portable conceptual/mental tool* for researchers, system designers, and regulators to reason about how PET configurations redistribute governance power in socio-technical systems, complementing protocol-level guarantees with a system-level perspective. The current model uses coarse ordinal CTA tags, assumes static pre/post snapshots, and abstracts away contextual constraints. We also restricted the analysis to strict functors, whereas real-world PETs often behave laxly. Our future work will extend PPM with richer categorical structures (e.g., profunctors, 2-cells) to capture contextual obligations and constraint regimes, formalise lax PET transformations, and validate the model through empirical case studies and applied tooling.

References

1. Alhajri, M., Rudolph, C., Shahraki, A.S.: A blockchain-based consent mechanism for access to fitness data in the healthcare context. IEEE Access **10**, 22960–22979 (2022). https://doi.org/10.1109/access.2022.3154106
2. Balsa, E., Shvartzshnaider, Y.: When pets misbehave: a contextual integrity analysis. preprint arXiv (2023). https://doi.org/10.48550/arXiv.2312.02509
3. Barocas, S., Nissenbaum, H.: Big data's end run around procedural privacy protections. Commun. ACM **57**(11), 31–33 (2014). https://doi.org/10.1145/2668897
4. Bazarova, N.N., Masur, P.K.: Towards an integration of individualistic, networked, and institutional approaches to online disclosure and privacy in a networked ecology. Curr. Opin. Psychol. **36**, 118–123 (2020). https://doi.org/10.1016/j.copsyc.2020.05.004
5. Binns, R.: Fairness in machine learning: lessons from political philosophy. In: Friedler, S.A., Wilson, C. (eds.) Proceedings of the 2018 conference on fairness, accountability, and transparency, vol. 81, pp. 149–159. PMLR (23–24 Feb 2018)
6. Boyd, D., Marwick, A.E.: Social privacy in networked publics: Teens' attitudes, practices, and strategies. In: A decade in internet time: Proceedings of the Symposium on the Dynamics of the Internet and Society (2011)
7. Cheng, E.: X+Y: A Mathematician's Manifesto for Rethinking Gender. Basic Books (2020)
8. Cheng, E.: The Joy of Abstraction: An Exploration of Math, Category Theory, and Life, Profile Books (2022)
9. Choi, H., Park, J., Jung, Y.: The role of privacy fatigue in online privacy behavior. Comput. Hum. Behav. **81**, 42–51 (2018). https://doi.org/10.1016/j.chb.2017.12.001
10. Dencik, L., Hintz, A., Redden, J., Treré, E.: Data Justice, SAGE Publications (2022). 1st edn
11. Dwork, C., McSherry, F., Nissim, K., Smith, A.: Calibrating noise to sensitivity in private data analysis. In: Halevi, S., Rabin, T. (eds.) TCC 2006. LNCS, vol. 3876, pp. 265–284. Springer, Heidelberg (2006). https://doi.org/10.1007/11681878_14

12. European Union: Regulation (EU) 2016/679 of the European parliament and of the council of 27 April 2016 on the protection of natural persons with regard to the processing of personal data and on the free movement of such data, and repealing directive 95/46/ec (general data protection regulation) (2016). http://data.europa.eu/eli/reg/2016/679/oj. Accessed 01 Nov 2022
13. Floridi, L.: Group Privacy: a defence and an interpretation. In: Taylor, L., Floridi, L., van der Sloot, B. (eds.) Group Privacy. PSS, vol. 126, pp. 83–100. Springer, Cham (2017). https://doi.org/10.1007/978-3-319-46608-8_5
14. Garg, S., Jain, A., Sahai, A.: Leakage-Resilient zero knowledge. In: Rogaway, P. (ed.) CRYPTO 2011. LNCS, vol. 6841, pp. 297–315. Springer, Heidelberg (2011). https://doi.org/10.1007/978-3-642-22792-9_17
15. Guidotti, R., et al.: A survey of methods for explaining black box models. ACM Comput. Surv. (CSUR) **51**(5), 1–42 (2018). https://doi.org/10.1145/3236009
16. Hargittai, E., Marwick, A.: "What can I really do?" Explaining the privacy paradox with online apathy. Int. J. Commun. **10**, 3737–3757 (2016)
17. Hoffmann, C.P., Lutz, C., Ranzini, G.: Privacy cynicism: a new approach to the privacy paradox. Cyberpsychology J. Psychosocial Res. Cyberspace **10**(4) (2016). https://doi.org/10.5817/CP2016-4-7
18. ISO/IEC 29100: Information technology – security techniques – privacy framework (2024). https://www.iso.org/standard/85938.html
19. Mac Lane, S.: Categories for the Working Mathematician. GTM, vol. 5. Springer, New York (1978). https://doi.org/10.1007/978-1-4757-4721-8
20. Near, J.P., et al.: Guidelines for evaluating differential privacy guarantees. US Department of Commerce, National Institute of Standards and Technology (2025). https://doi.org/10.6028/NIST.SP.800-226
21. Nissenbaum, H.: Privacy as contextual integrity. Washington Law Review **79**(1), 119–158 (2004)
22. Nissenbaum, H.: Privacy in context: technology, policy, and the integrity of social life. Stanford University Press (2010)
23. NIST: NIST privacy framework: a tool for improving privacy through enterprise risk management. Technical Report Version 1.0, National Institute of Standards and Technology (2020). https://www.nist.gov/privacy-framework
24. Oude Roelink, B., El-Hajj, M., Sarmah, D.: Systematic review: comparing ZK-snark, ZK-stark, and bulletproof protocols for privacy-preserving authentication. Secur. Priv. **7**(5), e401 (2024). https://doi.org/10.1002/spy2.401
25. Pasquale, F.: The black box society: the secret algorithms that control money and information. Harvard University Press (2015). https://doi.org/10.4159/harvard.9780674736061
26. Quinn, K., Epstein, D.: Dimensionalizing privacy to advance the study of digital disempowerment. Big Data Soc. **10**(2) (2023). https://doi.org/10.1177/20539517231221739
27. Raynes-Goldie, K.: Aliases, creeping, and wall cleaning: understanding privacy in the age of Facebook. First Monday (2010). https://doi.org/10.5210/fm.v15i1.2775
28. Taylor, L.: What is data justice? the case for connecting digital rights and freedoms globally. Big Data Soc. **4**(2) (2017). https://doi.org/10.1177/2053951717736335
29. UN Human Rights Office (OHCHR): Privacy and data protection: Increasingly precious asset in digital era says UN expert. Press release (2022). https://www.ohchr.org/en/press-releases/2022/10/privacy-and-data-protection-increasingly-precious-asset-digital-era-says-un. Accessed 20 Oct 2025

30. Veale, M., Binns, R.: Algorithms that remember: model inversion attacks and data protection law. Philos. Technol. **31**(2), 1–18 (2018). https://doi.org/10.1098/rsta.2018.0083
31. Viljoen, S.: A relational theory of data governance. Yale Law J. **131**(2), 573–654 (2021). http://www.jstor.org/stable/45400961
32. Zuboff, S.: The age of surveillance capitalism: the fight for a human future at the new frontier of power. PublicAffairs, New York, first trade paperback edition. edn (2019)

Adaptive Attribute Inference Attack: Exploiting Privacy Risks Under Adversarial Perturbations

Xinyu Liu[1], Yanrong Lu[1,2(✉)], Aohan Sun[2], Wencheng Yang[3], Yan Li[3], and Michael N. Johnstone[4]

[1] College of Safety Science and Engineering, Civil Aviation University of China, Tianjin 300300, China
yr_lu@cauc.edu.cn
[2] School of Computer and Artificial Intelligence, Civil Aviation University of China, Tianjin 300300, China
[3] School of Science, Engineering and Digital Technologies, University of Southern Queensland, Toowoomba, QLD 4350, Australia
[4] School of Science, Edith Cowan University, Joondalup, WA 6027, Australia

Abstract. Machine learning models deployed in sensitive applications face two commonly studied but rarely unified risks: adversarial vulnerability and attribute privacy leakage. A widely held intuition suggests that adversarial perturbations and adversarial training, by degrading utility or distorting confidence scores, may incidentally suppress attribute inference attacks. In this paper, we show that this assumption is misleading. We introduce an Adaptive Attribute Inference Attack (AAIA) framework tailored to adversarial environments, which quantifies privacy risk under distribution shifts induced by adversarial perturbations. AAIA has two stages: Adaptive Shadow Model Attack (ASMA), which learns the adversarial output distribution to estimate the worst-case privacy risk ceiling via non-linear score mappings, and Adaptive Thresholding Attack (ATA), which diagnoses leakage severity by optimizing the inference threshold based on calibration data. Using AAIA, we uncover a counter-intuitive phenomenon termed Inverted Leakage, where adversarial perturbations induce a deterministic probability inversion and the prediction outputs systematically flip relative to the true attribute labels. Experimental results demonstrate that adversarial robustness changes the form of attribute leakage rather than eliminating it, underscoring the need for defenses that explicitly decouple sensitive attributes from robust representations.

Keywords: Adversarial Attack · Attribute Inference Attack · Privacy Risk

1 Introduction

The pervasive deployment of machine learning models in sensitive domains, such as facial recognition and medical diagnosis, has precipitated two criti-

© IFIP International Federation for Information Processing 2026
Published by Springer Nature Switzerland AG 2026
H. Janicke et al. (Eds.): SEC 2026, IFIP AICT 787, pp. 525–539, 2026.
https://doi.org/10.1007/978-3-032-27993-4_36

cal yet often isolated concerns: model security and data privacy [1,2]. Security research primarily focuses on adversarial robustness, aiming to defend models against malicious perturbations designed to induce misclassification [3,4]. Conversely, privacy research examines risks such as attribute inference attacks, where adversaries attempt to deduce sensitive private information from model outputs [5,6]. Despite the parallel development of these two fields, their intersection remains underexplored. A prevailing intuitive assumption suggests that adversarial defenses, which typically degrade model utility and introduce stochasticity or gradient masking, might implicitly serve as a privacy shield by obfuscating the semantic features necessary for attribute inference [7,8].

However, this assumption overlooks the fundamental nature of adversarial perturbations. Rather than acting as random noise that simply erases information, adversarial perturbations induce systematic distributional shifts in the model's feature space [9]. Standard Attribute Inference Attacks (AIAs), which rely on rigid heuristics and the presumption of a positive monotonic correlation between confidence scores and attribute presence [10], are ill-equipped to handle the distributional distortions caused by adversarial attacks. Consequently, standard AIAs often fail when applied to adversarially robust models or models under adversarial attack, yielding AIA performance in the random guessing level. Crucially, the failure should not be misinterpreted as effective privacy protection; instead, it fosters a false sense of security, which means the private information is not actually under protection [11–13].

To exploit and analyze privacy risks in adversarial settings where probability distributions are fundamentally altered, we propose a two-stage framework that determines both the maximum potential risk and the structural nature of the leakage. First, we deploy ASMA to establish the worst-case risk ceiling by modeling non-linear output mappings. Second, we introduce ATA to diagnose the severity of leakage by identifying optimal decision thresholds via distribution analysis. This dual approach distinguishes whether sensitive information is merely inferable via complex extraction or explicitly exposed through deterministic shifts.

Applying the AAIA framework, we uncover a counter-intuitive phenomenon: Inverted Leakage. Our analysis reveals that adversarial perturbations do not eliminate sensitive attributes but instead induce a deterministic probability inversion, systematically flipping outputs relative to true labels. While the inversion successfully fools standard AIAs, our methods demonstrate that the sensitive signal is exposed with high precision, definitively refuting the hypothesis that adversarial perturbations provide collateral privacy benefits.

Our main contributions are summarized as follows:

- We propose an Adaptive Attribute Inference Attack (AAIA) framework to systematically exploit and analyze attribute privacy risks in adversarial environments (adversarially perturbed queries and adversarially trained models). AAIA separates risk exploitation from leakage diagnosis, enabling both worst-case evaluation and interpretable leakage characterization.

- As the exploitation stage of AAIA, we present Adaptive Shadow Model Attack (ASMA). By training a proxy classifier to fit the adversarial output distribution, ASMA establishes a privacy risk upper bound, revealing that sensitive attributes are not erased but are deterministically mapped to complex, recoverable non-linear distributions.
- As the diagnostic stage, we introduce Adaptive Thresholding Attack (ATA). ATA serves as a diagnostic tool to measure the severity of the leakage. By systematically sweeping the decision threshold to characterize the leakage profile, ATA quantifies the variation of the privacy leakage under different thresholds.
- Through a comprehensive comparative analysis using our proposed framework AAIA, we reveal a counter-intuitive phenomenon termed Inverted Leakage. We demonstrate that adversarial perturbations often induce a deterministic probability inversion, where prediction outputs systematically flip relative to true attribute labels. The finding challenges the assumption that adversarial noise acts as a privacy shield, showing instead that it exposes sensitive signals through systematic probability flips.

The remainder of this paper is organized as follows. Section 2 reviews the related work in adversarial attack and privacy domains. Section 3 details our proposed AAIA framework, introducing ASMA for the risk estimation and ATA for the leakage diagnosis. Section 4 presents our experiment setups. Section 5 presents the experimental evaluation across diverse architectures and analyzes the phenomenon of inverted leakage. Finally, Sect. 6 concludes the paper and outlines future research directions.

2 Related Work

2.1 Adversarial Training for Robustness

Adversarial training remains the most effective defense strategy against adversarial attacks, where models are trained on adversarial examples to learn robust feature representations [3,4,14]. Recent advancements have focused on improving the trade-off between accuracy and robustness. Zhang et al. proposed probabilistic robustness frameworks [15], while Liu et al. explored parameter interpolation techniques [16]. Other works have investigated the validity of perturbation generation in single-step adversarial training [17] and robustness-congruent updates [18]. In our work, we utilize these adversarial training methods to construct robust models as target models, aiming to evaluate whether the feature representations learned for robustness inadvertently suppress or preserve sensitive attributes.

2.2 Attribute Inference Attacks

AIAs aim to deduce sensitive properties of input data from model outputs, posing a significant privacy threat [5]. While early work demonstrated that confidence scores leak training data properties [6], recent studies have questioned the feasibility of such attacks under strict settings [19]. However, standard AIA methods typically assume clean input queries. Our research extends the AIA domain by investigating AIA in the adversarial setting, specifically examining how attackers can extract attributes from the distorted probability distributions output by both non-robust and robust models.

2.3 Adversarial Robustness and Privacy Risks

The intersection of adversarial robustness and data privacy is complex and often contradictory. Some early studies hypothesized that the robust features learned via adversarial training might align with privacy goals. Wu et al. and Ding et al. explored using adversarial training for privacy-preserving visual recognition and feature extraction, suggesting that robustness could help filter out non-robust sensitive features [7,8]. Conversely, Song et al. highlighted a fundamental tradeoff, arguing that robust models may be more susceptible to membership inference attacks due to their increased memorization of training data [11]. In the context of federated learning, Zhang et al. found that adversarial training could exacerbate privacy leakage [12]. Theoretically, Ilyas et al. argued that adversarial examples are features rather than bugs, implying that robust models rely on human-aligned features which might still carry sensitive semantic information [9,20]. Our work provides a definitive answer to the debate in the context of attribute inference: we demonstrate that robust models, despite their resistance to adversarial attacks, fail to protect against adaptive AIA (e.g., ASMA proposed in this paper) as the sensitive attributes are deterministically encoded into the robust feature space.

3 Methodology

To systematically exploit and analyze privacy risks in adversarial settings, we propose the Adaptive Attribute Inference Attack (AAIA) framework that operates in two sequential stages to determine both the maximum potential risk and the structural nature of the leakage. As shown in Fig. 1, we first deploy ASMA as the primary exploitation vector to establish the worst-case risk ceiling by leveraging its capacity to fit non-linear mappings and maximize sensitive information extraction. Given the black-box nature of the shadow model's training process, we subsequently introduce ATA. By employing an adjustable thresholding strategy, we quantitatively measure the degree of privacy leakage, providing an interpretable metric to assess how much the sensitive information is exposed. We assume an attacker with black-box access to the target model's output scores. The attacker possesses a calibration dataset $\mathcal{D}_{cal}$ that follows the same distribution as the training data, and knows the ground-truth sensitive attribute labels for the calibration set. The threat model reflects a realistic scenario where an adversary can collect a small set of labeled data similar to the target domain and interact with the target model.

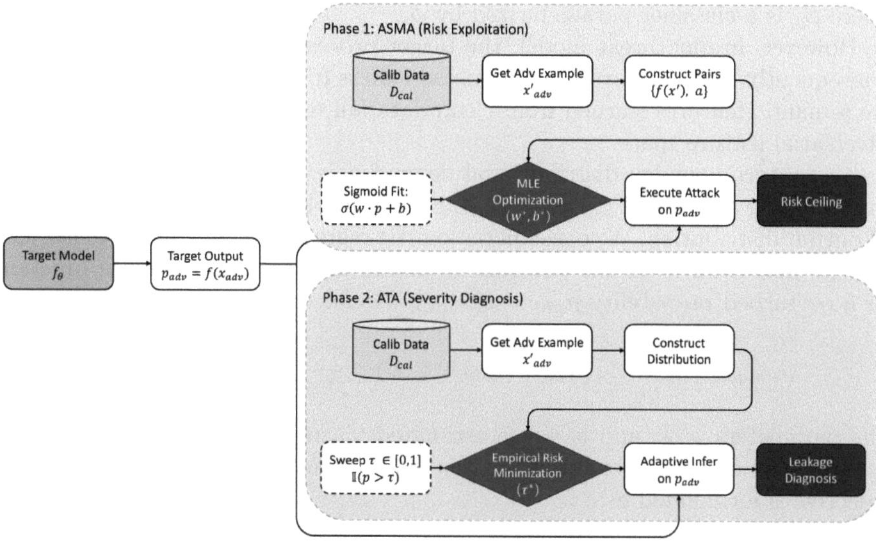

Fig. 1. Adaptive Attribute Inference Attack (AAIA) framework overview

3.1 Target Models and Training Objectives

We consider a classification model $f_\theta : \mathcal{X} \to [0,1]^K$ parameterized by θ. For a given input x and label y, the standard non-robust model is trained by minimizing the empirical risk over the clean data distribution $\mathcal{D}$:

$$\min_\theta \mathbb{E}_{(x,y)\sim\mathcal{D}}[\mathcal{L}_{BCE}(f_\theta(x), y)] \tag{1}$$

where $\mathcal{L}_{BCE}$ represents the binary cross-entropy loss.

In contrast, adversarially robust models are trained to resist adversarial perturbations. The objective is formulated as a min-max optimization problem, where the model minimizes the loss against the worst-case adversarial example generated within an ϵ-ball:

$$\min_\theta \mathbb{E}_{(x,y)\sim\mathcal{D}}\left[\max_{\|x'-x\|_p\leq\epsilon} \mathcal{L}_{BCE}(f_\theta(x'), y)\right] \tag{2}$$

Our attack methods evaluate the privacy leakage on both non-robust models (Eq. 1) and robust models (Eq. 2) under adversarial attack conditions.

3.2 Phase I: Adaptive Shadow Model Attack (Risk Exploitation)

In scenarios where the model is not subjected to adversarial attacks, the standard shadow model attack typically involves training a binary classifier $\mathcal{S}_{std}$ on clean calibration data to mimic the target model's behavior. The training objective is to minimize prediction error on the clean distribution $\mathcal{D}_{clean}$:

$$\min_\phi \sum_{(x,a)\in\mathcal{D}_{cal}^{clean}} \mathcal{L}_{BCE}(\mathcal{S}_\phi(f(x)), a) \tag{3}$$

where $\mathcal{S}_\phi$ is a classifier parameterized by ϕ.

However, in our threat model, the target processes adversarial inputs x_{adv}. Consequently, the standard shadow model suffers from the distribution shift, as the semantic features learned from clean data fail to generalize to the distorted adversarial feature space.

To capture complex distributional dependencies in adversarial settings, we formulate the attack as a parameter estimation problem directly on the adversarial output distribution. We construct a logistic regression-based shadow classifier $\mathcal{G}_{shadow}$ and train it on the adversarial calibration set. The inference function for a perturbed probability $p_{adv} = f(x_{adv})$ is defined as:

$$\mathcal{G}_{shadow}(p_{adv}) = \sigma(w_{adv} \cdot p_{adv} + b_{adv}) = \frac{1}{1 + e^{-(w_{adv} \cdot p_{adv} + b_{adv})}} \tag{4}$$

The parameters w_{adv} and b_{adv} are estimated via maximum likelihood estimation on the adversarial examples in the calibration dataset. The optimization objective is formulated as:

$$w_{adv}^*, b_{adv}^* = \underset{w_{adv}, b_{adv}}{\arg\min} \sum_{i=1}^{M} \mathcal{L}_{BCE}\left(\mathcal{G}_{shadow}(f(x_{adv}^{(i)})), a^{(i)}\right) \tag{5}$$

where $\mathcal{L}_{BCE}(\hat{y}, y) = -[y \log \hat{y} + (1-y)\log(1-\hat{y})]$ represents the standard log-loss, and M denotes the total number of adversarial examples in the calibration set.

By explicitly fitting the parameters to the adversarial feature space, ASMA captures complex dependencies and potential non-linear mappings, ensuring the inference capabilities that the standard non-robust model $\mathcal{S}_{std}$ cannot achieve. Furthermore, ASMA can exploit the outputs or calibration sets of both non-robust and robust models when they are subjected to adversarial attacks.

3.3 Phase II: Adaptive Thresholding Attack (Severity Diagnosis)

Since the shadow model operates as a black-box, we introduce ATA as an analytical tool to explicitly measure the degree of privacy leakage. A standard AIA operates on the rigid assumption of a direct, monotonic correlation between confidence scores and attribute presence. It employs a fixed heuristic threshold $\tau_{fixed} = 0.5$, blind to the actual data distribution. When applied to adversarial examples x_{adv}, the inference function becomes:

$$\hat{a} = \mathcal{G}_{std}(f(x_{adv})) = \mathbb{I}(f(x_{adv}) > \tau_{fixed}) \tag{6}$$

where $\mathbb{I}(\cdot)$ denotes the indicator function, which takes the value 1 if the condition inside is true and 0 otherwise. Standard methods fail to account for the distributional shift induced by x_{adv}, relying on rigid priors that are statistically invalid in adversarial settings.

To address distributional shifts in adversarially robust or adversarial-attacked models, we redefine the inference task as an empirical risk minimization problem.

Unlike standard methods, we do not presuppose a decision boundary. Instead, we utilize a calibration dataset $\mathcal{D}_{cal}$ containing adversarial examples to strictly quantify the distributional shift. The attacker identifies the optimal threshold τ^* by minimizing the classification error over the observed adversarial distribution:

$$\tau^* = \arg\max_{\tau \in [0,1]} \sum_{i=1}^{M} \mathbb{I}\left(\mathbb{I}(f(x_{adv}^{(i)}) > \tau) = a^{(i)}\right) \tag{7}$$

By formulating the attack as an optimization problem on $\mathcal{D}_{cal}$, ATA theoretically guarantees the optimal decision boundary for the specific adversarial distribution, surpassing heuristic baselines regardless of whether the leakage is direct, shifted, or inverted. Specifically, by systematically sweeping the threshold τ across the probability spectrum and observing the corresponding variations of privacy leakage, we can confirm whether the privacy risk stems from an explicit distributional shift or is primarily determined by the identification of the optimal threshold.

The final adaptive inference decision for a target input x_{target} is then given by:

$$\hat{a} = \mathcal{G}_{thr}(f(x_{target}); \tau^*) = \mathbb{I}(f(x_{target}) > \tau^*) \tag{8}$$

The optimization process ensures that the decision boundary is strictly derived from the observed statistical properties of the target model's output, enabling the inference mechanism to automatically generalize to the specific distribution of the target model.

4 Experimental Setup

Our experiments utilize the CelebFaces Attributes (CelebA) dataset [1], a large-scale repository containing 202,599 celebrity images. Each image is resized to 128×128 pixels, normalized to the range $[-1, 1]$, and annotated with 40 binary attributes. To facilitate our experimental evaluation, we uniformly adopt the 'Male' attribute as the primary inference target across all settings. To prevent information leakage during the training of shadow models or threshold tuning, we strictly partition the dataset into disjoint training, calibration, and testing sets.

We evaluate three distinct model architectures to ensure the generalizability of our findings: a standard convolutional neural network CNN, a deep residual network ResNet-18, and a vision transformer ViT to investigate potential differences in attention-based mechanisms under privacy attacks. Furthermore, to assess whether the adversarial training confers privacy benefits, we also train adversarially robust models with Fast Gradient Sign Method (FGSM) [3], Projected Gradient Descent (PGD) [4], and Momentum Iterative Method (MIM) [21].

We simulate a privacy-conscious scenario where adversarial attacks are applied to the target model. To this end, we employ three representative gradient-based adversarial training algorithms under the L_∞ norm constraint. Specifically, we utilize PGD with a maximum perturbation $\epsilon = 0.1$, step size $\alpha = 0.02$. For rapid generation, we employ the FGSM with $\epsilon = 0.03$. Additionally, we test the MIM with $\epsilon = 0.03$ and a decay factor of $\mu = 1.0$ to evaluate attacks that integrate momentum to escape local maxima.

To comprehensively assess the trade-off between model utility and privacy, we employ four metrics: (1) prediction accuracy, which represents the target model's performance on the primary attribute classification task; (2) precision, which measures the reliability of an attacker's positive inferences; (3) attack accuracy, to measure the ratio of the attacker's correct predictions, serving as a direct indicator of privacy violation severity under fixed or adaptive thresholding strategies; and (4) Area Under the Curve (AUC). Leveraging standard statistical theory [22], where AUC quantifies the degree of separability between class distributions, we treat the AUC as a bidirectional measure of leakage. Consequently, any significant deviation from 0.5, the random guessing value, indicates privacy failure: a value near 1.0 signifies direct leakage, while a value near 0.0 reveals inverted leakage. Both extremes represent highly deterministic signals that our AAIA framework can exploit.

5 Experiment Results

In this section, we present a comprehensive empirical evaluation of attribute privacy leakage, primarily investigating whether adversarial attacks mitigate privacy risks or merely alter leakage polarity. We further analyze the reliability and variations of these leaked signals and compare the performance of our ASMA and ATA methods across different model architectures. Finally, we assess the efficacy of post-processing defenses, specifically temperature scaling, to assess whether the confidence calibration can successfully obscure sensitive attributes.

5.1 Privacy Risks of Adversarial Training

To investigate whether adversarial training is an effective defense strategy against privacy leakage, we evaluated the performance of adversarially robust models against our ASMA and ATA methods across CNN, ViT, and ResNet-18 architectures. The empirical results largely refute the hypothesis that adversarial training enhances data privacy. As presented in Table 1, sensitive attributes remain highly distinguishable within the feature space of robust models, with AUC scores for our methods predominantly exceeding 90% across most configurations. Furthermore, ASMA consistently outperforms ATA. For instance, while ATA underperforms in degraded models, ASMA maintains an AUC of 98.17% even in the PGD-ResNet18 case. The high AUC is due to the shadow model's capacity to learn complex, non-linear mappings from confidence scores, extracting residual leakage that simpler linear methods miss.

A notable exception to the high leakage trend is the ResNet-18 model trained with PGD, where the ATA AUC drops to 63.36%. However, the apparent privacy improvement comes at a catastrophic cost to model utility, as the robust model accuracy falls to a mere 62.98%. It is because that the model has effectively lost its capability to perform the primary classification task. Consequently, the reduced leakage in this specific case is not the result of an effective privacy-preserving mechanism but rather a byproduct of severe performance degradation, where the model fails to encode both the primary task and sensitive attributes effectively.

Table 1. Model performances and privacy risks of robust models trained with different adversarial training methods

Adv-Training Method	Model Architecture	Non-robust Model Accuracy	Robust Model Accuracy	ASMA AUC	ATA AUC
FGSM	CNN	98.25%	89.79%	99.83%	96.62%
FGSM	ViT	98.4%	97.75%	99.84%	99.74%
FGSM	Resnet18	98.44%	94.95%	99.85%	98.93%
PGD	CNN	98.33%	91.82%	99.84%	97.79%
PGD	ViT	98.38%	96.45%	99.83%	99.46%
PGD	Resnet18	93.7%	62.98%	98.2%	63.36%
MIM	CNN	98.17%	92.6%	99.81%	98.17%
MIM	ViT	98.43%	97.36%	99.85%	99.53%
MIM	Resnet18	98.64%	90.06%	99.89%	96.72%

5.2 Analysis of Attribute Inference Risks

We prioritized precision as a critical metric to evaluate the reliability of leakage, as it isolates the trustworthiness of the attacker's positive assertions from random noise. Figure 2 illustrates the contrast in precision across different architectures. For non-robust models, the results are alarmingly consistent; across FGSM, PGD, and MIM attacks, the precision remains near-perfect, consistently exceeding 92% for CNN, ViT, and ResNet-18. The consistently high precision underscores a severe privacy risk, demonstrating that sensitive attributes in non-robust models are fully exposed to attribute inference attackers with near-certainty.

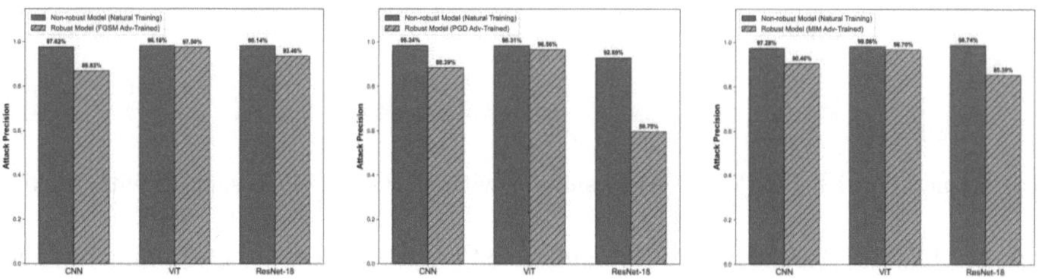

(a) FGSM (b) PGD (c) MIM

Fig. 2. ATA precisions of non-robust and robust models with different training methods and model architectures

Adversarial training creates only limited divergence under AIAs. While precision generally decreases compared to non-robust baselines, it remains dangerously high in most configurations. The robust ViT architecture exhibits high susceptibility, maintaining precision above 96%, likely due to the self-attention mechanism capturing global contextual dependencies that resist local perturbations. In contrast, robust CNN and ResNet models show slight degradation, yet precision typically stays between 85% and 90%. The only significant drop 59.75% occurs in the PGD-ResNet18 case, which aligns with the previously analyzed utility collapse in Sect. 5.1. Overall, adversarial training fails to disrupt the semantic link between input and sensitive attributes, leaving robust models vulnerable to adaptive AIAs (e.g., the proposed ASMA and ATA).

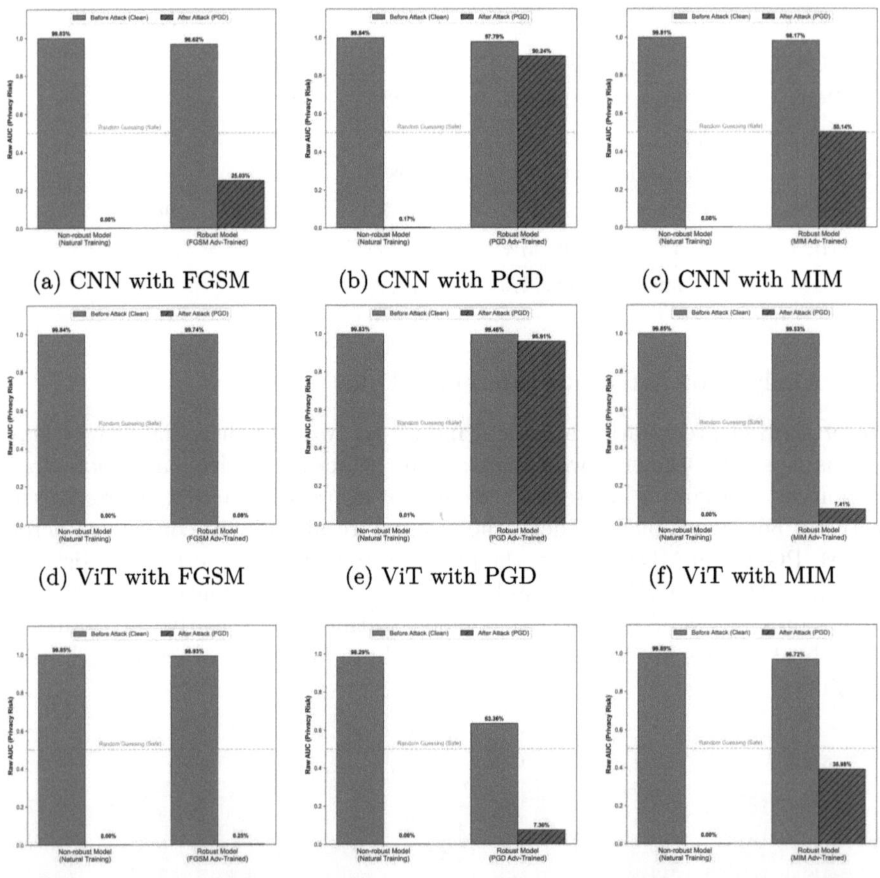

(a) CNN with FGSM (b) CNN with PGD (c) CNN with MIM

(d) ViT with FGSM (e) ViT with PGD (f) ViT with MIM

(g) Resnet-18 with FGSM (h) Resnet-18 with PGD (i) Resnet-18 with MIM

Fig. 3. AIA raw AUCs of non-robust and robust models with different training methods and model architectures before and after PGD attacks

5.3 Analysis of Inverted Leakage Patterns

To systematically investigate the universality of inverted leakage, we visualized the impact of adversarial attacks across nine experimental setups in Fig. 3, contrasting non-robust and robust models. For non-robust models, the results reveal a universal pattern of collapse where the raw AUC drops from a near-perfect positive correlation of approximately 100.00% on clean data to a near-perfect inversion of approximately 0.00% under PGD attacks. The uniformity confirms that without defensive training, the optimization landscape consistently favors a semantic flip to maximize loss, rendering adversarial attacks ineffective as a privacy defense strategy for non-robust models. The phenomenon of inverted leakage may also explain why adversarial attacks can enhance privacy in certain scenarios. Since some privacy attacks fail to recognize adversarial patterns, they mistakenly regard near-zero values as effective privacy protection, which is actually misleading.

The behavior of adversarially robust models exhibits significant architectural divergence. ResNet-18 fails to rectify the inversion, with raw AUC remaining suppressed near zero across all attacks. Robust ViT displays a mixed response, maintaining direct correlation under PGD but succumbing to inversion under FGSM and MIM. Although the robust CNN under MIM attack achieves 50.14%, near the random guess value, it is an isolated success. Overall, the results demonstrate that the adversarial attack alters the manifestation of the leakage, either exposing it as direct or locking it into a persistent inversion, rather than eliminating the underlying semantic dependency.

5.4 Privacy Leakage Dynamics Under Varying Thresholds

To empirically validate the diagnostic capability of our proposed ATA method and characterize the structural nature of privacy leakage, we conducted a threshold sweeping analysis on CNN models. The resulting leakage profiles reveal a fundamental divergence in distributional behavior between non-robust and robust models, exposing distinct leakage mechanisms. As illustrated in Fig. 4, non-robust models exhibit a distinct U-shaped inverted leakage profile under adversarial attacks. It indicates that non-robust models are highly susceptible to probability perturbations, where the adversarial attack successfully flips the prediction confidence to the opposite extreme, resulting in near-zero accuracy at the standard threshold but high recoverability at the probability extremes.

In contrast, robust models maintain a standard bell-shaped profile even under attack, peaking near the center. Instead of being flipped like the non-robust model, the robust model identifies the attack features and stabilizes the predictions consistent with the original semantics. Paradoxically, the resistance facilitates privacy leakage: by preventing the probability inversion, the robust model ensures that sensitive attributes are deterministically and correctly inferred with high confidence.

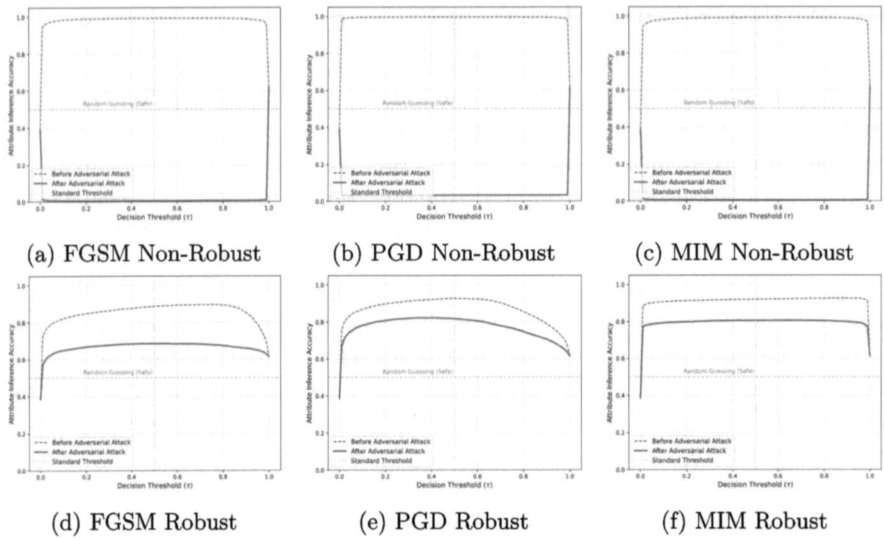

(a) FGSM Non-Robust (b) PGD Non-Robust (c) MIM Non-Robust

(d) FGSM Robust (e) PGD Robust (f) MIM Robust

Fig. 4. ATA accuracy of non-robust and robust models under different thresholds

5.5 ATA Against Temperature Scaling Defense

Finally, we evaluate the effectiveness of temperature scaling [23] as a privacy defense mechanism, with the results detailed in Table 2. The objective is to determine whether recalibrating the confidence scores could obscure the deterministic signals exploited by our ATA method. However, the results indicate that the temperature scaling fails to provide privacy protection. For all non-robust models across FGSM, PGD, and MIM attacks, the ATA AUC on robust models remains at approximately 0.00%. The near-zero value, which stands in contrast to the near-perfect above 99% AUC on clean data, confirms that the inverted leakage persists mostly unaffected with temperature scaling.

The temperature scaling results on robust models further confirm the failure in privacy defense. While the robust CNN under PGD adversarial training exhibits a direct leakage with an AUC of 81.23%, the robust ResNet-18 consistently maintains a severe inverted leakage pattern, with the AUC dropping as low as 0.25% under FGSM and 0.35% under PGD. Even in cases where the leakage is partially mitigated, e.g., Robust CNN under MIM at 50.32%, the overall trend demonstrates that temperature scaling cannot fundamentally alter the separability of the feature space. Since temperature scaling is a monotonic transformation, it preserves the relative ranking of the prediction probabilities. Consequently, the adaptive attacker can simply bypass the temperature scaling defense by relying on the rank-based separation, rendering the calibration effort futile against proposed ATA.

Table 2. Model accuracy and ATA AUCs with temperature scaling defense before and after adversarial attacks

Adv-Training Method	Model Architecture	Model Type	Model Accuracy	ATA AUC (Under Adversarial Attack?)	
				Yes	No
FGSM	CNN	Non-robust	98.25%	0.00%	99.83%
FGSM	CNN	Robust	89.79%	25.15%	96.62%
FGSM	Resnet18	Non-robust	98.44%	0.00%	99.85%
FGSM	Resnet18	Robust	94.95%	0.25%	98.93%
PGD	CNN	Non-robust	98.33%	0.02%	99.83%
PGD	CNN	Robust	91.82%	81.23%	97.79%
PGD	Resnet18	Non-robust	98.63%	0.00%	99.87%
PGD	Resnet18	Robust	84.4%	0.35%	92.66%
MIM	CNN	Non-robust	98.17%	0.00%	99.81%
MIM	CNN	Robust	92.6%	50.32%	98.17%
MIM	Resnet18	Non-robust	98.64%	0.00%	99.89%
MIM	Resnet18	Robust	90.06%	38.97%	96.72%

6 Conclusion

This work introduces the AAIA framework, which employs ASMA and ATA to evaluate attribute leakage risks under adversarial conditions. Experiments demonstrate that adversarial robustness yields inverted leakage, leading to exploitable prediction flips. Our future work will focus on developing defense methods that decouple sensitive attributes from robust features.

Acknowledgements. We would like to thank all the editors and anonymous reviewers for their helpful advice. This paper is supported by the National Key Research and Development Program of China (2023YFB4302901), National Natural Science Foundation of China (No. 61802276), Tianjin Natural Science Foundation Project (24JCZDJC 01000), and the Fundamental Research Funds for the Central Universities of China (No.3122025091).

References

1. Liu, Z., Luo, P., Wang, X., Tang, X.: Deep learning face attributes in the wild. In: Proceedings of the IEEE International Conference on Computer Vision, pp. 3730–3738 (2015)
2. Mo, K., et al.: Security and privacy issues in deep reinforcement learning: threats and countermeasures. ACM Comput. Surv. **56**(6), 1–39 (2024)
3. Goodfellow, I.J., Shlens, J., Szegedy, C.: Explaining and harnessing adversarial examples. In: International Conference on Learning Representations (2015). https://doi.org/10.48550/arXiv.1412.6572

4. Madry, A., Makelov, A., Schmidt, L., Tsipras, D., Vladu, A.: Towards deep learning models resistant to adversarial attacks. In: International Conference on Learning Representations (ICLR), vol. 6, pp. 4138–4160 (2018)
5. Gong, N.Z., Liu, B.: You are who you know and how you behave: attribute inference attacks via users' social friends and behaviors. In: 25th USENIX security symposium (USENIX Security 16), pp. 979–995 (2016)
6. Mehnaz, S., Dibbo, S.V., Kabir, E., Li, N., Bertino, E.: Are your sensitive attributes private? novel model inversion attribute inference attacks on classification models. In: 31st USENIX Security Symposium (USENIX Security 22), pp. 4579–4596 (2022)
7. Wu, Z., Wang, Z., Wang, Z., Jin, H.: Towards privacy-preserving visual recognition via adversarial training: a pilot study. In: Proceedings of the European conference on computer vision (ECCV). pp. 606–624 (2018)
8. Ding, X., Fang, H., Zhang, Z., Choo, K.K.R., Jin, H.: Privacy-preserving feature extraction via adversarial training. IEEE Trans. Knowl. Data Eng. **34**(4), 1967–1979 (2020)
9. Ilyas, A., Santurkar, S., Tsipras, D., Engstrom, L., Tran, B., Madry, A.: Adversarial examples are not bugs, they are features. In: Proceedings of the 33rd International Conference on Neural Information Processing Systems, vol. 32, pp. 125–136 (2019)
10. Jayaraman, B., Evans, D.: Are attribute inference attacks just imputation? In: Proceedings of the 2022 ACM SIGSAC Conference on Computer and Communications Security, pp. 1569–1582 (2022)
11. Song, L., Shokri, R., Mittal, P.: Privacy risks of securing machine learning models against adversarial examples. In: Proceedings of the 2019 ACM SIGSAC conference on computer and communications security, pp. 241–257 (2019)
12. Zhang, J., Chen, Y., Li, H.: Privacy leakage of adversarial training models in federated learning systems. In: Proceedings of the IEEE/CVF conference on computer vision and pattern recognition, pp. 108–114 (2022)
13. Sun, A., Lu, Y., Yang, W., Zhang, J.: Counterfactual adversarial examples for mitigating privacy risk in adversarially robust models. In: Asia-Pacific Web (APWeb) and Web-Age Information Management (WAIM) Joint International Conference on Web and Big Data, vol. 16114, pp. 333–351. Springer, Singapore (2026)
14. BenSaid, E., Neji, M., Jabberi, M., Alimi, A.M.: Deep keypoints adversarial attack on face recognition systems. Neurocomputing **621**, 129295 (2025)
15. Zhang, Y., et al.: Adversarial training for probabilistic robustness. In: Proceedings of the IEEE/CVF International Conference on Computer Vision. pp. 1675–1685 (2025)
16. Liu, X., Yang, Y., He, K., Hopcroft, J.E.: Parameter interpolation adversarial training for robust image classification. IEEE Trans. Inf. Forensics Secur. **20**, 1613–1623 (2025)
17. Ge, Y., Li, Y., Han, K.: Rethinking the validity of perturbation in single-step adversarial training. Pattern Recogn. **158**, 111007 (2025)
18. Angioni, D., et al.: Robustness-congruent adversarial training for secure machine learning model updates. IEEE Trans. Pattern Anal. Mach. Intell. **47**(9), 7457–7469 (2025)
19. Zhao, B.Z.H., et al.: On the (in) feasibility of attribute inference attacks on machine learning models. In: 2021 IEEE European Symposium on Security and Privacy (EuroS&P), pp. 232–251. IEEE (2021)
20. Rosberg, F., Englund, C., Aksoy, E.E., Alonso-Fernandez, F.: Adversarial attacks and identity leakage in de-identification systems: an empirical study. IEEE Trans. Biometrics Behavior Identity Sci. **8**(2), 169–178 (2026)

21. Dong, Y., et al.: Boosting adversarial attacks with momentum. In: Proceedings of the IEEE Conference on Computer Vision and Pattern Recognition, pp. 9185–9193 (2018)
22. Hanley, J.A., McNeil, B.J.: The meaning and use of the area under a receiver operating characteristic (roc) curve. Radiology **143**(1), 29–36 (1982)
23. Guo, C., Pleiss, G., Sun, Y., Weinberger, K.Q.: On calibration of modern neural networks. In: Proceedings of the 34th International Conference on Machine Learning. Proceedings of Machine Learning Research, vol. 70, pp. 1321–1330 (2017)

Homogeneous Control of Security Functions via Cross-Domain Delegation

Nicola Poidomani[1], Daniele Canavese[2(✉)], Daniele Bringhenti[1], Fulvio Valenza[1], and Matteo Repetto[2]

[1] Politecnico di Torino, Turin, Italy
nicola.poidomani@studenti.polito.it,
{daniele.bringhenti,fulvio.valenza}@polito.it
[2] CNR-IMATI, Genoa, Italy
{daniele.canavese,matteo.repetto}@cnr.it

Abstract. Open Command and Control (OpenC2) was designed to facilitate the orchestration of heterogeneous cyber-defense technologies through a vendor-agnostic language. However, while the standard integrates secure transfer protocols, it lacks a common prescriptive mechanism for (IAM). This choice leaves a significant architectural gap, jeopardizing the applicability of Managed Security Service (MSS), where cross-domain delegation is a critical issue. This paper addresses this gap by proposing a robust (IAM) framework based on the OAuth2 mechanism. Our work addresses the 'impedance mismatch' between the browser-centric approach of OAuth2 and automated, non-interactive OpenC2 controllers. To this end, we introduce a novel Headless User Agent component that manages user credentials without requiring human interaction via a browser or other tools. Additionally, we integrate fine-grained access control for the execution of OpenC2 commands, which implements the basic security principle of least privileges. The overall solution is implemented as a modular extension of the `otupy` OpenC2 library, and supports both HTTP and MQTT transfer bindings. Experimental validation demonstrates the functional correctness of the identity management and access control layers. At the same time, performance analysis quantifies the overhead introduced by per-request token introspection at approximately 14.5 ms, confirming the approach's viability for real-time operational environments.

Keywords: OpenC2 · OAuth 2.0 · Authentication · Security Automation · Managed Security Services

1 Introduction

The relentless evolution of digital applications and infrastructures into complex, heterogeneous, and multi-ownership service chains has created a fertile ground for cyberattacks. High-frequency, automated, and Artificial Intelligence (AI)-driven attacks have obsoleted static and perimeter-based defense models, and made traditional, reactive, and human-led defense mechanisms insufficient [18].

© IFIP International Federation for Information Processing 2026
Published by Springer Nature Switzerland AG 2026
H. Janicke et al. (Eds.): SEC 2026, IFIP AICT 787, pp. 540–554, 2026.
https://doi.org/10.1007/978-3-032-27993-4_37

To maintain operational resilience, organizations are increasingly shifting towards complex Security Orchestration and Automated Response (SOAR) solutions that require coordinating heterogeneous security technologies, such as firewalls, Intrusion Detection Systems (IDS), and endpoint protection platforms, into a cohesive defense fabric [8]. Additionally, the growing complexity of attacks and the ever-evolving threat landscape require skills and operational capacity that small businesses cannot afford, hence pushing them to externalize security services [11]. In these scenarios, the current heterogeneity of security tools and lack of interoperability between different vendors result in largely fragmented environments, which hinder orchestration and delay response times [5]. Indeed, the traditional reliance on proprietary Application Programming Interfaces (API) or inflexible adaptation layers, such as Cloud Access Security Brokers (CASB), has proven insufficient for scalable automation, creating a strong demand for open, standardized interfaces to discover and uniformly control cyber-defense functions.

To address this interoperability challenge, the Organization for the Advancement of Structured Information Standards (OASIS) consortium has proposed Open Command and Control (OpenC2), a vendor-agnostic language designed to command and control cyber-defense functions at machine speed. By abstracting specific actions (e.g., block an IP address, quarantine a file) from the underlying implementation, OpenC2 promises to unify the operational layer of cyber defense across diverse infrastructures. The specification defines in detail the overall language, extension mechanisms, and serialization requirements, and builds on the existing security layers of common transfer protocols, namely Hyper-Text Transfer Protocol (HTTP) and Message Queuing Telemetry Transport (MQTT). While this approach is perfectly acceptable for encryption and integrity of point-to-point message exchanges, it breaks the expected homogeneity across domains for authentication and authorization, which becomes a major issue in the context of Managed Security Services (MSS). As a matter of fact, in these scenarios organizations still deploy security appliances, but delegate monitoring, analysis, detection, and response operations to external Security Operation Centers (SOC) operated by third-party operators. The latter require therefore access to security tools to run commands in the customer's infrastructure (e.g., to change firewall rules, to isolate a compromised host), but this should happen without giving them unrestricted administrative access or sharing long-term credentials. An additional challenge is given by the participation in collaborative security operations encompassing entire service chains, where a long-lived mutual trust relationship is unlikely to be established between service owners and one or more security providers [18].

Despite of the broad range available for the HTTP protocol[1], MQTT only implements a few authentication mechanisms, namely username/password, X.509 certificates, and JSON Web Token (JWT). The only common option is limited to the transport of Open Authorization 2.0 (OAuth2) tokens, which is quite common today, but without defining the backing IAM framework, espe-

[1] https://www.iana.org/assignments/http-authschemes/http-authschemes.xhtml.

cially for access control. Moreover, three of the four authorization-granting flows defined by OAuth2 require human interaction, whereas the last one (Client Credential Flow) requires strong trust between the service owner and the security provider (often the same entity). In the managed security service deployments we target, the service owner often requires the enforcement actions to be attributable to a specific operator identity or role (enabling separation of duties), a feature that Client Credentials do not natively support. Our goal is therefore not to replace Client Credentials universally, but to enable deployments where user-bound authorization is required while OpenC2 controllers remain non-interactive.

Our work improves the OpenC2 design, coupling it with a comprehensive IAM framework based on OAuth2. We propose an architecture where OpenC2 Producers operate as OAuth2 Clients, obtaining time-limited, revocable access tokens to interact with Consumers. The main contributions of our work are: 1. a non-interactive *Authorization Code* flow where a Headless User Agent replaces the browser and removes the user-centric delegation; 2. fine-grained access control on the execution of OpenC2 commands, able to distinguish between monitoring and enforcement operations on different digital resources; 3. extension of an open-source OpenC2 library to support multiple token-based IAM frameworks with a concrete implementation for OAuth2—the source code which is freely available online[2].

The rest of the paper is organized as follows. Section 2 reviews the current state-of-the-art about homogeneous interfaces to security functions and IAM frameworks. Section 3 gives an overview of the OpenC2 language and framework. Section 4 illustrates the modified Authorization Code flow for non-interactive OpenC2 sessions, whose implementation is described in Sect. 5 and validated in Sect. 6. Finally, we give our conclusion and future work in Sect. 7.

2 Related Work

OpenC2 [10], standardized by OASIS [1,2], adopts an imperative command-response paradigm optimized for machine-to-machine communications. It defines a vendor-agnostic language to instruct cyber-defense technologies (the *Actuators*) to perform specific actions (e.g., `deny`, `query`) on specific targets (e.g., `ipv4_connection`, `file`).

To ensure secure access and delegation in such distributed architectures, several established identity management protocols are available, though typically decoupled from command standards:

- SAML [4] is an XML-based standard for exchanging authentication and authorization data between an Identity Provider and a Service Provider. While historically dominant in enterprise SSO, its verbose XML payloads make it less suitable for constrained M2M environments.

[2] https://github.com/matterepe/otupy.

- OAuth2 [6] is the industry standard for authorization, enabling third-party applications to obtain limited access to an HTTP service via access tokens. Its JSON-friendly format and clear separation of roles make it the de facto choice for modern API protection.
- OIDC [21] acts as a simple identity layer built on top of the OAuth2 protocol. It allows clients to verify the identity of the end-user based on the authentication performed by an Authorization Server, effectively bridging the gap between authorization and authentication.

Despite the availability of such protocols, early general-purpose OpenC2 implementations were limited to basic message serialization and lacked support for transport-layer protocols. More comprehensive implementations emerged only in subsequent years, typically incorporating HTTP as the primary transport mechanism (e.g., *OIC* [15,17], *Yuuki* [16]) and, less frequently, MQTT (e.g., *Otupy* [19]). However, none of these solutions provided native support for IAM integration. To the best of our knowledge, this work represents the first OpenC2 extension to fully integrate an IAM framework based on OAuth2.

3 OpenC2 Primer

OpenC2, developed by OASIS, provides a vendor-agnostic, machine-readable language to orchestrate cyber defense operations at machine speed. Its primary goal is to enable interoperability among heterogeneous security technologies, such as firewalls or IDS, by decoupling the command logic from the underlying implementation details.

The framework relies on a request-response architecture defined by two primary roles [2]: the Producer and the Consumer. The *Producer* is the orchestration entity responsible for decision-making and issuing commands. The *Consumer* is the managed entity that receives, parses, and executes the commands. The specific execution logic is handled by internal components known as *Actuators*, which translate the abstract instructions into device-specific actions.

The operational workflow begins with the Producer generating a *Command*. The syntax is structured around a semantic tuple [1]: an *Actuator* (the subject which will run the command, e.g., a specific firewall instance), an *Action* (a verb specifying the operation to perform, e.g., `deny`, `query`), a *Target* (the object of the action, e.g., `ipv4_connection`), and some optional *Arguments* (complements that specify how or when the action is performed, e.g., `start_time`). To ensure consistency across different devices, OpenC2 utilizes *Actuator Profiles*, which define the valid subset of actions and targets for specific security functions (e.g., SPF [12]).

Commands are serialized (typically in JSON format) and transmitted over agnostic transfer protocols such as HTTPS [13] or MQTT [14]. Upon receipt, the Consumer routes the message to the appropriate actuator for execution and returns a *Response* containing a status code (e.g., 200 OK).

4 OAuth2 Integration in OpenC2

The OAuth2 [6] framework enables users to access their own data and resources within a third-party application without sharing their credentials. The third party obtains limited access to digital resources on behalf of its owner. OAuth2 identifies the following roles:

- *Resource Owner (RO)*: the owner of a protected resource who has the right to grant access (usually a person using a web browser);
- *Resource Server (RS)*: the entity hosting the protected resource and enforcing access control (usually a web server or file storage service);
- *Client*: an application accessing a protected resource on behalf of ROs (e.g., a web application that accesses a user's files);
- *Authorization Server (AS)*: an application that issues cryptographic tokens for accessing a protected resource after successful authentication of its owner.

In the OAuth2 workflow, when the RO uses a Client of a third party, the latter asks a grant to the former to access one private resources of his/hers. Such a grant is then used to retrieve a token from the AS, which is then provided to the Resource Server to obtain the resource. After validating the token, the Resource Server will give access to the protected resource. There are four mechanisms for granting access to a Client: three require human intervention, and the last one implies that protected resources are owned by the client. The *authorization code* is the far most common user-initiated and browser-driven mechanism used by web applications that need access to a user's personal data. In this case, the Client (web application) redirects the browser of the user (RO) to the login page of the Authentication Server, where the user provides their credentials and an authorization code is released to the Client.

The entire OAuth2 workflow is designed for use with HTTP, since many operations rely on HTTP redirections. However, OAuth2 tokens use standard formats (e.g., JWT), which are used by many other protocols (including MQTT).

4.1 Security Delegation with OpenC2

Beyond plain authentication, the most challenging aspect of an IAM for OpenC2 is the possibility to support delegation models, including MSS. Here, the main purpose is to allow system administrators to grant security operators selective access to digital infrastructures and services for security monitoring and enforcement under access- and role-based access control policies, without the overhead of managing static trust relationships and credentials. This allows far more flexible, dynamic, and scalable authorization frameworks, once the attributes and roles of external entities are guaranteed by trusted identity providers. Typical application scenarios range from the management of different teams within the same organization (e.g., developers, devops, security staff) to externalization to one or more security service providers, including new forms of collaborative detection and response strategies across service and software supply chains [18].

Once the dichotomy between service owners and security operators is clear, OpenC2 entities can be mapped to OAuth2 roles in a quite straightforward way:

- Developers, system administration, service providers are ROs that deploy security functions (protected resources) in their own infrastructures and services;
- A Producer is a Client operated by a security provider that needs to access security functions;
- A Consumer is the Resource Server of the service/infrastructure owner that controls security functions;
- A *User Agent (UA)* replaces the user's browser, which is used for web applications.

The high-level integration of the OAuth2 flow into OpenC2 operation is illustrated in Fig. 1. This simplified workflow establishes a clear separation of duties by decoupling identity the life-cycle management from the command execution logic. Among the four grant types available for OAuth2, the authorization code best fits the target scenario we address (besides being the recommended option), because it leaves the RO the control to grant or deny the security operator. However, this flow is designed to be user-initiated and browser-driven, which turns into a critical "impedance mismatch" with the intended usage of OpenC2 agents, which are typically automated scripts, background daemons, or Command Line Interface (CLI) tools lacking a graphical interface.

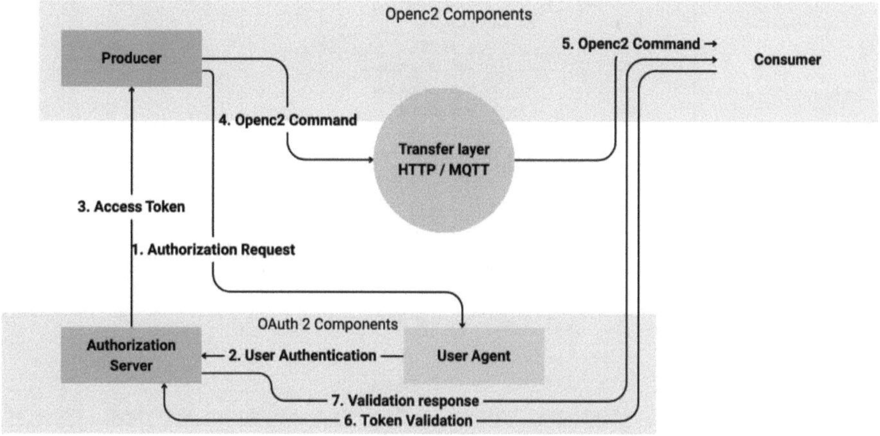

Fig. 1. High-level workflow of the OAuth 2.0 integration in OpenC2.

To address the above issue, we designed a headless Authorization Code flow that maintains compatibility with existing implementations (especially Authentication Servers). It includes a User Agent that automates the login process and verification of third-party attributes.

Specifically, the workflow proceeds as follows. First, the Producer submits an authorization request to the UA (step 1). The UA then contacts the AS to validate the request (step 2) and subsequently returns an access token to the Producer (step 3). Once the authorization phase is completed, the OpenC2 operational workflow can begin. Using a supported transfer protocol (typically HTTP or MQTT), the Producer sends a command to the Consumer, embedding the obtained access token (steps 4 and 5). Upon receipt, the Consumer contacts the AS to validate the access token (step 6), which, in turn, provides the corresponding validation response to the Consumer (step 7). If the authentication and authorization checks are successful, the Consumer proceeds with the execution of the requested command.

4.2 Headless Authorization Code Workflow

Figure 2 shows the Provider-initiated OAuth2 authorization sequence for OpenC2, giving a more detailed view of the workflow with respect to Fig. 1. The main steps are as follows:

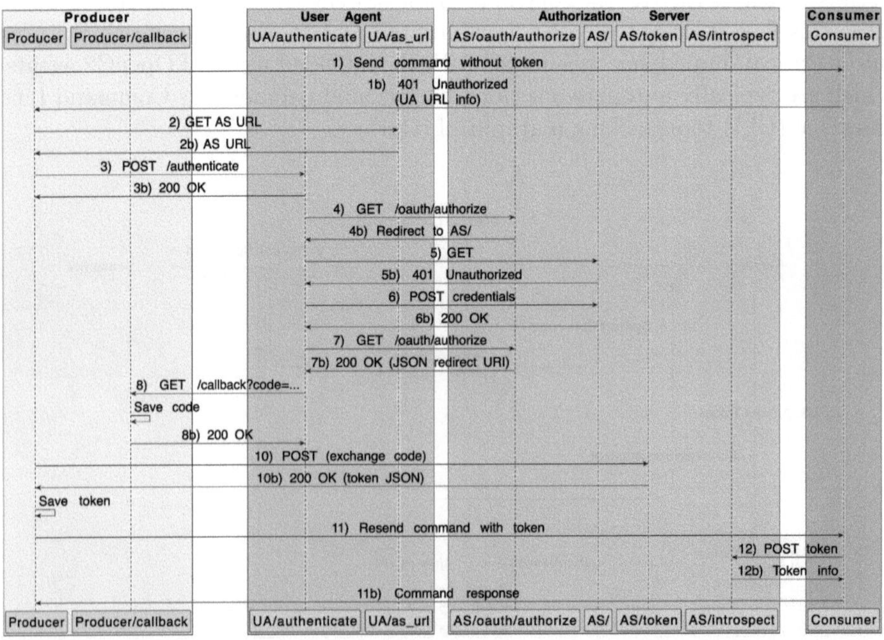

Fig. 2. Sequence diagram of the complete authentication and command execution flow.

a. *Discovery and Trigger* (steps 1 and 1b): The flow is triggered automatically when a Producer sends a command without a valid token ("lazy initiation"). If the Consumer rejects the request (e.g., via HTTP 401 Unauthorized), the response includes the endpoint (URL) of the User Agent.

b. *Authorization Grant* (from step 2 to step 7b): If authorization is requested in the response, the Producer extracts the UA endpoint and initiates an OAuth2 session. The UA determines whether to grant access (e.g., checking the claimed identity and perhaps a X.509 certificate), and, if needed, it retrieves an authorization grant from the AS. The decision may come from a human operator or (preferably) be fully automated according to access policies.
c. *Token Issuance* (from step 8 to step 10b): Upon successful authentication, the AS delivers a single-use authorization code to a callback endpoint previously registered by the Producer. This prevents spoofing attacks from malicious actors. The Producer then directly supplies this code to the AS via a secure back-channel to get an access token.
d. *Authenticated Execution* (from step 11 to step 11b): The Producer retransmits the command, including the authorization token (e.g., as a Bearer Token in HTTP). The Consumer validates it, typically via an introspection call to the AS, and enforce local fine-grained RBAC / ABAC policies.

4.3 Fine-Grained Authorization Model

While the OAuth2 framework efficiently handles identity verification and delegation (authentication), it does not inherently define *which* specific OpenC2 commands an authenticated Producer is allowed to execute. To address this, our proposed architecture includes a fine-grained authorization layer that acts as a Policy Enforcement Point (PEP) downstream of the identity check.

The authorization logic is designed around the RBAC model, enhanced with attribute-based constraints. We adopt a formal decision engine based on the PERM (Policy, Effect, Request, Matchers) metamodel [9], where every incoming OpenC2 command is mapped to a request triple consisting of:

- *Subject*: The identity of the Operator, extracted from the OAuth2 access token (e.g., the *client_id* or a specific role claim).
- *Target*: The specific security capability being targeted, corresponding to the *Actuator* profile (e.g., a particular firewall instance) or specific resources defined in the command target.
- *Action*: The operation attempted by the Producer, which corresponds directly to the OpenC2 command verb (e.g., `deny`, `query`, `update`).

The model enforces a strict *deny-by-default* strategy: a command is executed only if a matching policy rule explicitly allows the specific combination of subject, actuator, and action.

5 Implementation

The proposed authentication framework has been implemented as a modular extension of `otupy`,[3] a comprehensive open-source Python library designed to

[3] https://github.com/mattereppe/otupy/.

facilitate the development of OpenC2 entities (e.g., security controllers and actuator managers).

The library architecture is centered around two core classes, `Producer` and `Consumer`, which abstract the complexity of creating, serializing, and transmitting OpenC2 messages. `otupy` employs a flexible, pluggable, and extensible architecture where new serialization formats and transfer protocols can be incrementally added, in addition to profile definitions and actuator implementations. To this purpose, a few generic classes (`Encoder`, `Transfer`, `Actuator` provides a common interface that must be implemented by concrete components (e.g., `JSONEncoder`, `HTTPSTransfer`), which are then composed at run-time to create custom protocol stacks (see Fig. 3).

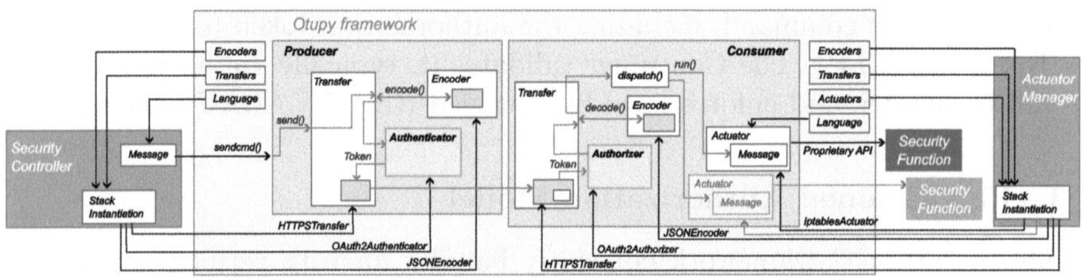

Fig. 3. Overview of the `otupy` architecture.

According to this approach, we provided two interface classes for token-based authentication (`Authentication`) and authorization (`Authorizer`) for the `Producer` and `Consumer`, respectively. The former is expected to retrieve a valid token using any IAM framework; the latter is expected to validate it. Both classes have been inserted as shim layers into the message processing pipeline (see Fig. 3), ensuring that the core business logic remains agnostic to the underlying authorization handshake.

While we currently only provide concrete instances for OAuth2, respectively via the `OAuth2Authenticator` and `OAuth2Authorizer` classes, this approach allows to further extend the framework with additional IAM frameworks without the need to modify the core library. The UA is instead an additional component of the framework that does not require strict integration with OpenC2 components. Our implementation leverages the Flask web framework[4] for HTTP-based components and the `Authlib` library for OAuth2 entities.

5.1 OAuth2 Authentication for Producers

A simple security controller was implemented as a CLI application that instantiates an OpenC2 stack using `OAuth2Authenticator` for authentication, implementing the lazy initiation strategy. The `Producer` initially attempts to dispatch

[4] https://flask.palletsprojects.com/.

the command without credentials. Upon receiving a `401 Unauthorized` response (which carries the User Agent discovery URL), the authenticator triggers the grant flow. Once a valid token is obtained, the authenticator provides it to the `Transfer` binding for inclusion in the outgoing message:

- *HTTP Binding*: The token is added to the standard `Authorization` header using the Bearer scheme [7].
- *MQTT Binding*: The token is embedded into the message properties or payload, ensuring the broker and subscriber can extract it for validation [3].

5.2 OAuth2 Token Validation at the Consumer

Access control at the `Consumer` is enforced by the `OAuth2Authorizer` class, which lies between the Transfer layer and the Actuator logic. This component intercepts every incoming request to perform real-time validation via *Token Introspection* [20], treating tokens as opaque strings to ensure immediate revocation capabilities.

The validation logic handles the protocol-specific rejection mechanisms defined by the architecture:

- In *HTTP*, unauthorized requests are rejected with a `401 Unauthorized` status code.
- In *MQTT*, where synchronous error codes are not native to the publish-subscribe model, the Consumer publishes a specific OpenC2 response message with a `401` status to the Producer's response topic.

Crucially, in both cases the rejection payload includes the URL of the UA, providing the Producer with the entry point to initiate the authentication flow.

5.3 Headless User Agent

The UA is the central entity that verifies the identity of security operators before granting them access to security functions. This component is designed to solve the architectural "impedance mismatch" between the M2M OpenC2 approach and the user-initiated, browser-driven OAuth2 Authorization Code flow.

Although our headless grant flow would also allow to implement the UA as an interactive dashboard for human operators, we prefer a fully-automated approach. Our UA is implemented as a lightweight web service that exposes two endpoints:

- `/as_url`: A discovery endpoint that allows the Producer to dynamically retrieve the base URL of the AS for retrieving the token, hence removing the need for static configuration.
- `/authenticate`: The endpoint used by the Producer to request the access grant.

Internally, the complex logic is encapsulated in a dedicated `AuthAgent` class, which manages the authorization phase. This component uses the Python `requests` library to create a persistent `Session` object, which preserves cookies across HTTP redirects. The `AuthAgent` automates the authorization grant process: it accesses the AS authorization endpoint, programmatically handles the login form submission, and approves the consent screen if necessary. Finally, it intercepts the resulting authorization code and delivers it to the Producer's callback URL. This mechanism effectively translates the interactive OAuth2 authorization ceremony into a fully automated machine-to-machine exchange, while preserving backward compatibility with existing OAuth2 ASs (e.g., Keycloack) replicas can run behind a load (e.g., Google, Facebook, Apple).

Note also that, although we describe the UA as a distinct component, it can be implemented as a replicated service rather than a single instance. In a production deployment, multiple UAs replicas can run behind a load balancer, thus eliminating a single point of failure scenario and increasing the system's responsiveness.

5.4 Policy Enforcement with Casbin

To implement the authorization model described in Sect. 4.3, the Consumer integrates *Casbin*[5], a lightweight and efficient open-source access control library. This integration follows the modular design pattern of `otupy`: the enforcement logic is injected into the message processing pipeline as a middleware, positioned immediately after the token introspection step.

We extended the `OAuth2Authorizer` component to function as the Policy Enforcement Point. The workflow proceeds as follows:

1. *Context Extraction*: Upon successful token validation, the middleware extracts the user's role from the token payload.
2. *Mapping*: The incoming OpenC2 message is parsed to map the Target to the policy Object and the command Action to the policy Action.
3. *Enforcement*: The middleware invokes the Casbin enforcer with the tuple $\langle role, target, action \rangle$. The enforcer then evaluates this request against a CSV-based policy file loaded at startup.
4. *Decision*: If the enforcer returns `False`, the Consumer halts the execution and returns a `403 Forbidden` response, preventing any interaction with the underlying security function.

6 Validation and Performance Analysis

The experimental validation of the proposed framework was conducted to verify two key aspects: the functional correctness of the identity management implementation and the performance overhead introduced by the OAuth2 authentication layer.

[5] https://casbin.org/.

The test environment was hosted on a single machine to eliminate network latency and jitter and improve the reproducibility of numerical results. The setup included an OpenC2 Producer, a User Agent, and a Consumer running as local processes, while a Keycloak[6] instance was deployed in a Docker container as AS.

6.1 Functional Validation

The primary objective of the functional testing was to verify that the Consumer correctly enforces access control via Token Introspection, hence distinguishing between authorized and unauthorized requests.

A simple test suite was created to verify the following scenarios:

- *Missing Token*: Commands sent without credentials were consistently rejected by the Consumer with a `401 Unauthorized` status.
- *Invalid/Expired Token*: Requests carrying revoked or expired tokens were denied. In these cases, the introspection call to Keycloak returned "`active: false`," and the Consumer dropped the request after returning an unauthorized error.
- *Valid Token*: Requests carrying a valid, active access token (issued by Keycloak) successfully passed the introspection check and were forwarded to the command processing logic, returning a `200 OK` status.

6.2 Performance Analysis

To measure the latency introduced by the whole OAuth2 IAM framework, we compared two scenarios while sending the same set of OpenC2 commands:

- *Baseline*: A standard command/response exchange with no authorization.
- *Secure*: Full framework enabled, including token generation and introspection with Keycloak.

Table 1 reports the latency measured at the Producer side. We distinguish between the overall latency, which covers the entire operation lifecycle (including local serialization and deserialization of OpenC2 commands/responses), and the transfer latency, which strictly isolates the network round-trip time and the remote processing at the Consumer side.

Table 2 breaks down the internal processing time at the Consumer. As shown, the overhead is almost entirely concentrated in the authorization logic stage ($\approx$ 11.5 ms), which handles the token introspection call to the external Authorization Server. All performance tests were conducted using the HTTP transfer binding, and the reported values represent the average of 100 distinct iterations. We do not account for command execution because, in our simple setup, we used a dummy actuator that performed no concrete operation.

[6] https://www.keycloak.org/.

Table 1. Producer-side performance comparison (Mean RTT).

METRIC	BASELINE [MS]	SECURE [MS]	OVERHEAD [MS]
overall latency	4.88	19.35	14.47
transfer latency	3.67	17.40	13.73

Table 2. Consumer-side Processing Time Breakdown.

PROCESSING STAGE	BASELINE [MS]	SECURE [MS]	OVERHEAD [MS]
total processing	1.01	13.20	12.19
decoding	0.43	0.71	0.28
authorization logic	*0.37*	*11.86*	*11.49*
encoding	0.21	0.63	0.42

As shown in Table 1, the secure implementation incurs approximately 14.5 ms of overhead per transaction. The breakdown in Table 2 clarifies that the majority of this latency ($\approx$ 11.5 ms) is concentrated in the authorization logic stage. Packet-level analysis confirmed that this overhead is primarily driven by the HTTP round-trip required for the token introspection call to Keycloak. While this represents a significant relative increase compared to the baseline, it is the expected cost of performing a real-time validity check against a centralized authority, a trade-off that ensures immediate token revocation capabilities. A practical optimization to decrease the overhead is to cache positive introspection responses until token expiry to avoid repeated introspection for bursty command sequences, although this approach might introduce a small delay in detecting token revocation.

7 Conclusion

The lack of uniform authentication and authorization mechanisms breaks the claimed generality and portability of the OpenC2 language. This paper addressed this issue by proposing and validating a modular authentication framework based on OAuth2, tailored explicitly for M2M communication.

The primary contribution is the development of a headless authorization code flow, which resolves the impedance mismatch between automated tools and the OAuth2 user-initiated, browser-driven scheme. By bridging this gap, our solution implements a uniform delegation model essential for MSS environments. It allows operators to undertake security workflows that control security functions on behalf of service and infrastructure owners using time-limited, revocable access tokens, without the need for static, overwhelming credential management.

Future enhancements to the framework will focus on optimizing performance and hardening the security posture. To mitigate the latency overhead observed during validation, possible strategies include introducing *token caching* on the

Consumer side and supporting self-contained JWT tokens, enabling local validation without per-request remote introspection. Furthermore, the exchange's security could be strengthened by adopting PKCE (Proof Key for Code Exchange), providing robust protection against authorization-code interception attacks in distributed deployments.

Acknowledgments. This project has received funding from the European Union's Horizon Europe Research and Innovation Programme under GA No. 101168144. The views and opinions expressed are those of the authors only and do not necessarily reflect those of the European Union or the European Cybersecurity Competence Centre.

Disclosure of Interests. The authors have no competing interests to declare that are relevant to the content of this article.

References

1. Open command and control (OpenC2). OASIS standard (November 2019), language Specification Version 1.0, Committee Specification 02
2. Open command and control (OpenC2) architecture. OASIS standard, (2022). version 1.0, Committee Specification 01
3. Banks, A., Briggs, E., Borgendale, K., Gupta, R.: Mqtt version 5.0. OASIS Standard (March 2019). https://www.rfc-editor.org/rfc/rfc6750.txt
4. Cantor, S., Kemp, J., Philpott, R., Maler, E.: Assertions and protocols for the oasis security assertion markup language (saml) v2.0. Oasis standard. OASIS (2005)
5. Gaehtgens, F., Hoover, J.: Top strategic technology trends for 2022: cybersecurity mesh. Gartner Report (2021)
6. Hardt, D.: The oauth 2.0 authorization framework. RFC 6749 (2012). https://www.rfc-editor.org/info/rfc6749
7. Jones, M., Hardt, D.: The oauth 2.0 authorization framework: bearer token usage. RFC 6750 (2012). https://www.rfc-editor.org/rfc/rfc6750.txt
8. Lawson, C., Shoard, P.: Market guide for security orchestration, automation and response solutions. Gartner Report (2023), ID G00774602
9. Luo, Y.: Casbin: an authorization library that supports access control models like ACL, RBAC, ABAC. https://casbin.org/docs/how-it-works (2018). Accessed 30 May 2025
10. Mavroeidis, V., Brule, J.: A nonproprietary language for the command and control of cyber defenses - OpenC2. Comput. Secur. **97**, 101999 (2020)
11. Norton, K.: How many security tools do organizations have, and what are their consolidation plans? IDC, Document number: #US51973524 (2024)
12. Open command and control (OpenC2) profile for stateless packet filtering (2019). version 1.0, Committee Specification 01
13. Specification for transfer of OpenC2 messages via https (2019). version 1.0, Committee Specification 01
14. Specification for transfer of openc2 messages via mqtt (2021). version 1.0, Committee Specification Draft 03
15. OASIS OpenC2 TC: Openc2 integration framework (oif) orchestrator (2022). https://github.com/oasis-open/openc2-oif-orchestrator
16. OASIS OpenC2 TC: Yuuki: Openc2 consumer framework (2022). https://github.com/oasis-open/openc2-yuuki

17. OASIS OpenC2 TC: Openc2 integration framework (oif) device (2024). https://github.com/oasis-open/openc2-oif-device
18. Repetto, M.: Chaining digital services: challenges to investigate cyber-attacks at run-time. IEEE Commun. Mag. **62**(5), 88–94 (2024)
19. Repetto, M.: Otupy: a flexible, portable, and extensible framework for remote control of security functions. Comput. Secur. **158**, 104597 (2025). https://doi.org/10.1016/j.cose.2025.104597
20. Richer, J.: Oauth 2.0 token introspection. RFC 7662 (2015). https://www.rfc-editor.org/rfc/rfc7662.txt
21. Sakimura, N., Bradley, J., Jones, M., de Medeiros, B., Mortimore, C.: Openid connect core 1.0 (2014). https://openid.net/specs/openid-connect-core-1_0.html

PatMine: Advancing Cloud Security Through Graph-Based Context-Aware Access Pattern Mining

Vakkalagadda Satya Sai Prakash(✉), Srinivas Reddy Gopu, and Rajidi Satish Reddy

TCS Research, Tata Consultancy Services Ltd., Pune, India
vakkalagaddasaiprakash@gmail.com, {srinivas.greddy,rajidis.reddy}@tcs.com

Abstract. The dynamic nature of cloud environments introduces significant challenges to enforcing the Principle of Least Privilege (PoLP). Unlike traditional on-premises systems with relatively static roles, cloud Identity and Access Management (IAM) involves highly granular, and ephemeral and cross-service permissions that evolve with workload and context. This complexity often leads to **privilege sprawl** - accumulation of excessive or stale permissions—which increases the attack surface, security risks and undermines compliance.

Existing privilege refinement techniques rely on homogeneous similarity measures that fail to capture contextual and semantic relationships inherent to cloud environments. To address this gap, a novel context-aware pattern-mining framework, **PatMine** is introduced for refining access privileges through discovery of semantically rich usage patterns. PatMine introduces context-aware distance modeling using graph-based Feature-Specific Distance Measure (FSDM), and Uniform Distance Measure (UDM) that preserve semantic dependencies across IAM attributes. These distance measures enable the clustering of semantically similar access events, from which PatMine derives fine-grained, context-aware IAM policies that enforce PoLP without disrupting legitimate workflows.

Unlike traditional recommenders, PatMine does not introduce new permissions; it refines existing privileges by adding contextual constraints or reducing permission scopes. Experiments on Google Cloud Platform (GCP) logs demonstrate that PatMine achieves up to 0.92 cluster cohesion and reduces excessive privileges by 35–40%, while maintaining operational continuity. By embedding contextual semantics into distance computation, PatMine operationalizes least-privilege enforcement for dynamic, multi-tenant cloud environments, providing a foundation for adaptive, context-aware access governance.

Keywords: Cloud Identity and Access Management (IAM) · Principle of Least Privilege · Pattern Mining · User Behavior Monitoring · Privilege Sprawl

© IFIP International Federation for Information Processing 2026

Published by Springer Nature Switzerland AG 2026
H. Janicke et al. (Eds.): SEC 2026, IFIP AICT 787, pp. 555–569, 2026.
https://doi.org/10.1007/978-3-032-27993-4_38

1 Introduction

Cloud computing has emerged as a foundational paradigm in contemporary information technology, underpinning a wide spectrum of industry verticals and heterogeneous technology platforms. Its architectural attributes—such as scalability, elasticity, and distributed multi-tenant infrastructure—offer substantial operational and economic advantages. However, these benefits also introduce complex security challenges arising from inherent system complexity, rapid technological evolution, and increasingly sophisticated threat vectors. Key concerns include the management of diverse identity types (both human and machine), the protection of devices and applications accessing geographically distributed cloud resources at scale, and the mitigation of risks associated with Artificial Intelligence (AI) and Machine Learning (ML) workloads.

Recent analyses of cloud security incidents and audit findings [1,2] indicate that while misconfigurations and credential misuse are frequently observed, their root cause often identified as **privilege sprawl**—commonly referred to as privilege creep—the accumulation of excessive, stale, or overly broad permissions that persist beyond operational necessity. Privileges initially provisioned to support development velocity, automation, or cross-service workflows often remain active long after their intended purpose, expanding the attack surface and increasing the risk of lateral movement and privilege escalation [3,10,24].

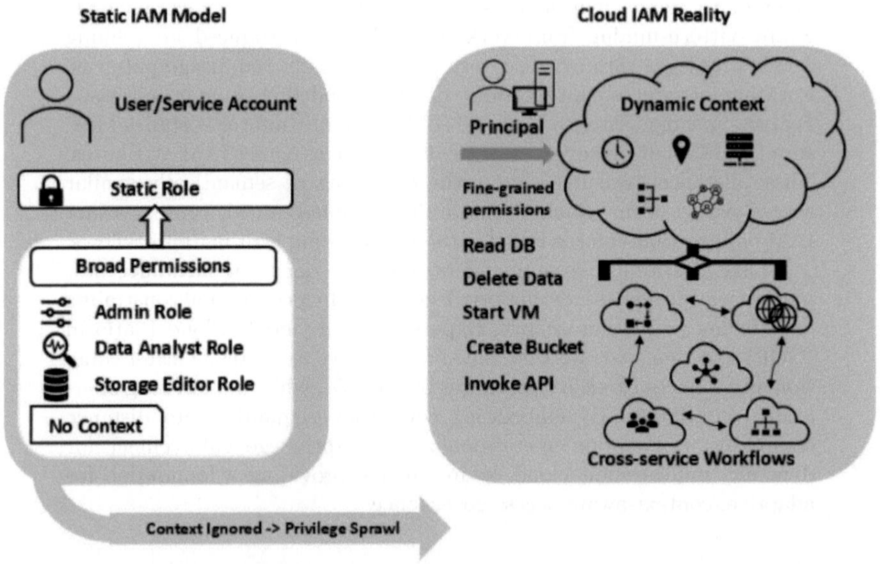

Fig. 1. Limitations of static access control models in cloud IAM environments. Dynamic execution contexts cause coarse-grained roles to accumulate excessive permissions, leading to privilege sprawl.

Cloud IAM environments differ fundamentally from traditional on-premises systems (Refer Fig. 1) due to ephemeral identities, hierarchical resource structures, fine-grained API-level permissions, cross-service dependencies, and dynamically varying behavioral contexts such as execution time, location, and workload state.

The excessive accumulation of privileges frequently originates from transient resources, federated identity frameworks, service accounts, and dynamically invoked Application Programming Interfaces (APIs) that operate across multiple administrative domains [4,22]. Given that cloud services often span heterogeneous projects and geographically distributed regions, privileges initially provisioned for temporary workflows or automated processes frequently remain active beyond their intended duration.

A viable strategy for mitigating privilege creep involves the application of the Principle of Least Privilege (PoLP), which mandates that users and services operate with only the minimal permissions required to perform their designated functions [17]. Enforcing PoLP in cloud environments is particularly challenging due to dynamic resource allocation, provider-controlled IAM mechanisms, and complex interdependencies among distributed resources. Enforcing PoLP in cloud environments requires understanding not only which permissions are granted, but how, when, and under what contextual conditions they are exercised. Existing privilege refinement techniques - including role mining, static policy analysis, and frequency-based usage models - treat access events as homogeneous or context-dependent, limiting their ability to distinguish legitimate operational behavior from excessive privilege accumulation. Their lack of ability to capture behavioral dimension motivates context-aware privilege analysis.

1.1 Motivation

Cloud IAM environments embody a fundamental operational paradox: permissions must remain sufficiently flexible to support automation and cross-service workflows, yet restrictive enough to prevent misuse. In practice, organizations accumulate privileges faster than they can reassess or revoke them. Empirical analysis indicate that more than 80% of cloud security breaches stem from the misuse or misconfiguration of IAM roles and service accounts [10,12].

Consider an enterprise scenario involving a data-engineering workflow on Google Cloud Platform (GCP). A service account, **etl-service@projecta.com**, is configured to read data from BigQuery in Project A and write transformed results to Cloud Storage in Project B. During initial deployment, engineers assign broad administrative roles - roles/bigquery.admin and roles/storage.admin - to prevent pipeline failures. As the workflow stabilizes, these roles remain unchanged, granting privileges far beyond what is operationally required. Conventional role-mining or frequency-based clustering techniques analyzing audit logs would observe consistent BigQuery and Storage API invocations and infer that the existing roles are necessary, thereby reinforcing over-privileged configurations. However, such approaches fail to recognize that the same functionality could be achieved using narrowly scoped, context-specific permissions -

such as bigquery.jobs.create and storage.objects.create - restricted to the service account's VPC network.

This examples highlights a key limitation of existing privilege optimization techniques: statistically frequent access does not imply contextual necessity. A privilege analysis model must therefore capture how permissions are exercised under specific operational contexts, rather than merely identifying which permissions are used. These observations motivate **PatMine**, designed to address this gap by learning contextually coherent access patterns that can be translated into least-privilege policy constraints, enabling continuous privilege refinement without disrupting legitimate workflows.

The contributions of this paper are threefold:

1. Contextual distance modeling for IAM access pattern mining. We introduce FSDM and UDM—two novel distance modeling paradigms that integrate contextual and semantic understanding of cloud IAM data into pattern mining.
2. PatMine system design and implementation. We present a complete, implementable framework that integrates FSDM/UDM with DBSCAN to discover behavioral clusters and convert them into context-aware IAM policies.
3. Evaluation on GCP IAM logs. Using realistic datasets, we demonstrate that PatMine achieves better cluster cohesion and up to 40% privilege reduction, outperforming conventional models while maintaining workflow integrity.

The remainder of this paper is structured as follows: Sect. 2 reviews relevant work on privilege-usage mining, access control models, and graph-based security analytics. Section 3 defines and describes the privilege sprawl problem. Section 4 presents the PatMine architecture, detailing graph construction, similarity measure definition, similarity computation, and privilege optimization recommendations. Section 5 presents the evaluation setup. Section 6 presents PatMine's experimental results on IAM logs, discusses implications, and limitations. Finally, Sect. 7 concludes the paper.

2 Background and Related Work

Prior work addressing privilege sprawl and access optimization in cloud and enterprise systems can be broadly classified into three categories: preventive access control models, post-deployment validation and pruning mechanisms, and behavior-driven privilege mining approaches. While these techniques address complementary aspects of access governance, none adequately capture the contextual and semantic dimensions of cloud IAM behavior required for fine-grained least-privilege enforcement.

2.1 Preventive Access Control Models

Preventive access control models, including RBAC [23], ABAC [19,25], PBAC [14], and JIT/JEA [21] mechanisms, aim to constrain privilege assignment at provisioning time. While effective in structured or static environments, these approaches rely on administrators to anticipate permissible behaviors and do not adapt to evolving access patterns in highly dynamic cloud environments, particularly in environments where service accounts, ephemeral workloads, or federated identities interact dynamically across hundreds of cloud projects [27].

The Just-in-Time Administration (JIT) & Just-Enough-Administration (JEA) provisioning models [21] grant ephemeral permissions tailored to specific tasks or sessions, thereby reducing runtime risk. However, these mechanisms lack the capability to automatically evaluate long-term privilege utilization or retroactively refine existing role assignments, allowing privilege sprawl to persist in the background.

2.2 Post-Deployment Validation and Pruning

Post-deployment validation techniques, including cloud-native IAM analyzers [5,6], audit privileges after deployment to identify exposure or unused access. However, these approaches primarily rely on static policy analysis and lack behavioral or semantic interpretation of access events.

Adaptive IAM Validation [16] and Dynamic Policy Refinement [8,20] frameworks advance incorporates real-time feedback loops that monitor access decisions and adjust policies upon detecting deviations. Although these mechanisms enhance policy consistency, they remain dependent on predefined rules or risk models and lack the capability to learn from actual long-term access behaviors.

Privilege pruning through usage analytics is another approach where unused permissions are identified and automatically revoked [13]. These heuristic models typically operate under binary assumptions - classifying permissions as either used or unused - without accounting for any behavioral context. Consequently, this oversimplification can lead to the inadvertent removal of permissions required under rare yet legitimate conditions, thereby introducing operational disruptions (Table 1).

2.3 Behavior-Driven Privilege Mining

Behavior-driven privilege mining techniques analyze audit logs to infer access patterns and optimize privilege assignments. Role mining [15,23] and log-based sequence modeling have demonstrated effectiveness in identifying structural or temporal patterns. Frameworks such as DeepLog [12] and LogMine [26] model event sequences to detect anomalies and recurring patterns. However, these approaches were primarily designed for operational anomaly detection rather than privilege inference. When applied to IAM datasets, they inadequately capture the heterogeneous semantics of features (e.g., principal email, resourceName, IP Address, and permission), leading to overly generalized or misclassified clusters.

Pattern-mining-based privilege analysis endeavors to address this limitation. Approaches such as High-Utility Temporal Pattern Mining (HUTPMiner) [7] and sequence clustering have demonstrated potential for behavioral modeling, but

Table 1. Limitations of existing privilege management approaches in cloud IAM

Approach Type	Representative Works / Systems	Key Mechanism	Limitations in Cloud Context
Preventive Access Design	RBAC [23], ABAC [19,25], JIT/JEA [21]	Predefined roles or temporary privilege grants	Cannot adapt to real-time context; rely on manual policy definition
Continuous Validation and Pruning	Adaptive IAM [16], AWS Access Analyzer [6], Privilege Pruning [13]	Static analysis and binary usage detection	Lack semantic understanding of behavior; high false positive/negative rates
Behavioral Pattern Mining	LogMine [26], DeepLog [12], HUTPMiner [7]	Clustering or Sequencing based on generic metrics	Cannot interpret feature semantics; poor differentiation of contextual behaviors

they typically assume homogeneous feature spaces and employ generic distance metrics that ignore semantic relationships among IAM entities.

By learning not only when permissions are exercised but also why and how, PatMine facilitates for the formulation of context-aware least-privilege policies that align with operational practices and security objectives. Consequently, PatMine is positioned as a complementary and extensible framework that augments, rather than replaces, existing IAM enforcement mechanisms.

3 Problem Definition

This section defines the problem definition and its operational assumptions. The problem addressed by PatMine can be formally stated as follows:

Given: A set of cloud access events E $= e_1, e_2, ..., e_n$, where each event e_i is defined by a tuple of features ⟨principal, resource, permission, method, service, $caller_ip$, $user_{agent}$, time, date, day, month⟩, obtained from audit logs.

Goal: Identify clusters of events representing semantically coherent user or service-account behaviors such that: (1) Each cluster corresponds to a legitimate, contextually bounded operational behavior. (2) The clusters collectively form a baseline behavioral profile for each principal.

Formally: Let D be a distance function over the feature space F $= f_1, f_2, ..., f_k$. PatMine defines:

$$D_{patmine}(x, y) = \sum_{i=1}^{k} w_i \cdot d_i(x_i, y_i)$$

where d_i are feature-specific distance functions derived from contextual and semantic properties (e.g., graph distance for permissions, hierarchical distance for resources, circular distance for time) and w_i are uniform or manually tuned weights.

The objective is to find clusters C $= C_1, C_2, ..., C_m$ such that: Intra-cluster distances are minimized (high behavioral cohesion); Inter-cluster distances are maximized (distinct behavioral roles); Each cluster can be mapped to a policy condition satisfying least-privilege constraints.

3.1 System Assumptions

PatMine relies on the following assumptions that reflect realistic operational conditions and are consistent with existing cloud IAM security guarantees:

1. The underlying cloud IAM, audit logs, permission usage data, resource identifiers, attribute metadata and resource hierarchy metadata are assumed correct, reflect true access events, and unaltered by adversaries.
2. The Contextual Knowledge Graph (CKG) is assumed to reflect IAM entity relationships at the time of computation. PatMine does not override the underlying organizational metadata.

4 System Architecture and Methodology

The PatMine system is designed to infer context-aware privilege usage patterns from heterogeneous cloud logs. PatMine leverages contextual and semantic knowledge from cloud environments to redefine how similarity between access events is computed and interpreted.

The system operates in five modular phases, shown in Fig. 2: (1) Log Ingestion and Preprocessing, (2) Contextual Feature Engineering, (3) Distance Measure Construction, (4) Pattern Discovery via Clustering, and (5) Policy Synthesis and Validation (Fig. 3).

4.1 Log Ingestion and Preprocessing

The input to PatMine comprises cloud access logs, typically obtained from GCP's Cloud Audit Logs, Data Access Logs, or Admin Activity Logs. Each log record is represented as: L = (principalEmail, IP Address, callerUserAgent, permission, resourceName, serviceName, timestamp, location, projectID, labels).

Irrelevant events (e.g., system-internal or health check calls) are filtered out using static filters, and categorical features are encoded with hierarchical identifiers derived from cloud metadata (e.g., projects/finance-dash/instances/sql-server-01).

Temporal decomposition produces contextual features such as hour of access, day of week, month, and session duration. These derived features capture temporal regularity, enabling identification of recurring behavioral intervals.

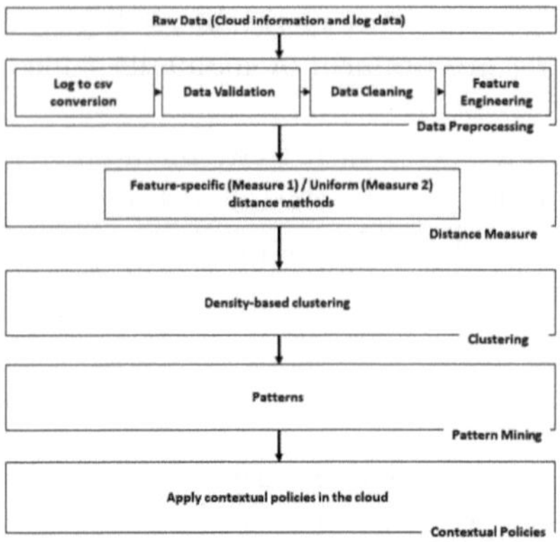

Fig. 2. PatMine: System Flow

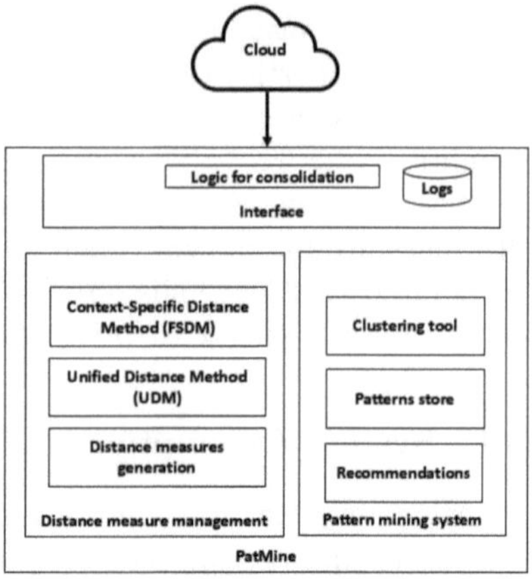

Fig. 3. PatMine: Components

4.2 Contextual Feature Engineering

Cloud IAM entities exhibit hierarchical and relational semantics. For example, *roles/editor* subsumes *roles/viewer*. *compute.instances.start* implies dependency on *compute.instances.get*. A principal may inherit privileges via groups or service accounts. To encode these relationships, PatMine maintains a Cloud Knowledge Graph (CKG) comprising nodes for principals, roles, resources, permissions, and services. The CKG captures principles, roles, permissions, resources, and their semantic relationships.

The CKG is dynamically updated from IAM configuration snapshots and metadata APIs. This contextual graph becomes the semantic backbone for the distance computation in the next phase.

4.3 Distance Measure Construction

PatMine's novelty lies in its context-aware distance computation, where each feature is evaluated with a function sensitive to its meaning and context. PatMine defines two complementary measures:

Feature-Specific Distance Measure (FSDM). FSDM tailors distance calculations to individual feature characteristics, ensuring high precision in clustering access logs. FSDM specifies templates to be used for different features types as presented in Fig. 4. A Graph-based feature may be specified a distance method template that focuses on relationships, hierarchies and specific attributes of the feature. Similarly, a temporal feature may be specified a distance method template that focuses on circular differences between the temporal values. Thus, each feature type is specified a different distance method template. While the template majorly includes a relationship difference function, and a hierarchical difference function along with attributes that can primarily be secrecy level or privacy level attribute of the value/node, administrators or the operations team can specify additional attributes of the nodes to be included in the distance calculation process.

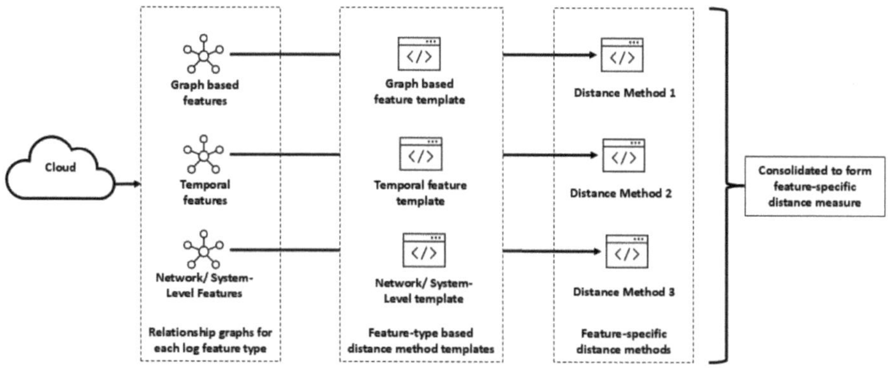

Fig. 4. Feature-Specific Distance Measure

Each feature f in log records L has a corresponding feature-specific function. The total distance is the weighted aggregation:

$$D_{FSDM}(L_i, L_j) = \sum_{f \in F} w_f \times d_f(L_i[f], L_j[f])$$

Where:

- w_f is the optional adaptive weight selected based on considered feature specific importance,
- d_f differs based on feature type (string, hierarchical, temporal, relational). Where feature specific distance methods d_f, as defined in Table 3, are based on the following:
  - Graph-Based Distance: For hierarchical or categorical features (e.g., permissions, resources). For example, Permissions Distance is defined as follows:

$$d_{\text{permissions}}(x, y) = \text{shortest\_path}(x, y) \times \text{secrecy\_level}(x, y)$$

  - Euclidean Distance: For numerical features (e.g., frequency, timestamp differences).
  - Circular Distance: For temporal features where the number difference is considered in a circular representation (e.g., time of the day, month, day of the week).

Uniform Distance Measure (UDM). For scalability, PatMine also supports a Uniform Distance Measure (UDM), which provides a generalizable distance computation using graph-derived semantic relations. Mathematical Representation:

$$D(L_i, L_j) = \frac{\sum_{i=1}^{n} w_i \cdot d_i(L_i, L_j)}{\sum_{i=1}^{n} w_i}$$

where,

$$d_i(L_i, L_j) = \begin{cases} \text{MinHops}(x, y) + \text{Relation}(x, y) + \text{AttrDiff}(x, y), & \text{if graph-representable} \\ \text{StringDiff}(x, y), & \text{otherwise} \end{cases}$$

Here, MinHops(x, y): Minimum traversal distance between two nodes in CKG.

Relation(x, y): Semantic closeness (e.g., permissionâĂŞroleâĂŞresource coupling).

AttrDiff(x, y): Number of differing attributes across entities.

StringDiff(x, y): Normalized textual similarity for non-graph features.

This Uniform structure allows PatMine to compute context-aware distances without per-feature customization. While less precise than FSDM, UDM scales linearly and supports real-time policy evaluation.

4.4 Pattern Discovery via Clustering

PatMine integrates the distance measures into a clustering model. Each access event is represented in a multidimensional feature space, and clustering is performed utilizing the modified clustering models. The resulting clusters correspond to consistent privilege usage behaviors—recurring patterns in how a user or service account accesses resources under specific contexts.

4.5 Policy Synthesis and Validation

Each discovered cluster C represents a privilege usage pattern. Context-aware IAM policy templates, defined by conditional statements, can be defined from the generated cluster attributes. For example:

If ((principalEmail == "*devuser@gcp.com*") and
(serviceName == “compute.googleapis.com”) and
(methodName in [“instances.start”, “instances.stop”]) and
(hour between 9 and 17) and (location == “us-central1”)): **allow Else: deny**

5 Evaluation Setup

This section evaluates the effectiveness of PatMine in discovering context-aware privilege usage patterns and refining access policies under the Principle of Least Privilege (PoLP). We analyze PatMine along two dimensions: (1) clustering performance and interpretability, and (2) privilege reduction and policy accuracy.

5.1 Experiment Setup

Dataset & Environment. We collected audit logs from a Google Cloud Platform (GCP) enterprise deployment hosting multiple projects (finance-core, data-ops, ml-research) spanning a six-month operational period. Dataset Characteristics are presented in Table 2.

Each user is associated with multiple projects and roles, representing an enterprise with multiple teams. The logs contain a mixture of user-initiated and automated service-account events recorded through Cloud Audit Logs. To maintain privacy, all logs were anonymized and stripped of PII. Feature extraction is focused on roles, resources, access times and user behaviors. Experiments were conducted on a GCP VM (n2-standard-8, 64GB RAM) using Python 3.10, Neo4j for the Knowledge Graph, and PostgreSQL (pg8000).

Baseline Models. We compared PatMine's clustering-based pattern discovery with four baseline approaches: K-Means (with Euclidean Distance Measure), Hierarchical Clustering (with Cosine Similarity), DBSCAN (with Jaccard Distance), Decision Tree, PatMine - FSDM, PatMine - UDM.

5.2 Clustering Algorithm

PatMine uses a well-established clustering algorithm, DBSCAN (Density-Based Spatial Clustering of Applications with Noise) [9,11], for its ability to identify clusters of arbitrary shapes and handle noise effectively. It distinguishes noise from meaningful clusters, providing a robust approach to uncovering access patterns within dynamic and diverse cloud environments.

The DBSCAN algorithm requires proper configuration of **Epsilon** (ϵ) and **Minimum Points (MinPts)** for optimal performance, and to balance the sensitivity and specificity of the algorithm. Parameters are tuned empirically where, ϵ is the radius within which to search for neighboring access log entries, and $MinPts$ is the minimum number of log entries required within the ϵ-radius to form a dense cluster (computed as $MinPts = 2{*}dim$, where dim is the dimension of the dataset [18]).

Table 2. Dataset Characteristics

Parameter	value
Users	90
Roles	320 custom roles
Permissions	9800 unique
Log Events	2.4 million
Resource-object graph nodes	12,000
Environment	16-core CPU, 64 GB RAM

Table 3. List of features.

Feature	Example Value	Distance calculation method
User Email	user.email@mail.com	Hierarchy of user, relation(and number of hops) between the user node parents
Caller Ip	192.168.23.32	Difference in each octet with increased weightage from fourth to first octet
Caller Supplied User Agent	google-api-go-client/0.5	Difference in the agents in the string
Permission	compute.rules.create	Hierarchy, number of hops between the permissions
Access granted	true/false	Generic string comparison
Service	compute.gapis.com	Hierarchy, number of hops between the services
Resource Name	projects/ops/ruleAB	Hierarchy of the resources, number of hops between the resource parents
Location	us-central	Generic string comparison
Project_id	internal	Hierarchy, number of hops between the project folders
Timestamp	2023-02-02T06:18:18.66Z	Circular differences for day of the week, date, month, hour sub-features

5.3 Evaluation Metrics

We evaluate PatMine using standard **clustering quality metrics (Silhouette Score, Davies-Bouldin Index (DBI))** and **policy effectiveness metrics** (**Precision** - fraction of retained permissions actually used, **Recall** - fraction of used permissions correctly retained, **Privilege Reduction Rate (PRR)** - percentage of unused permissions removed). These metrics jointly capture behavioral cohesion, policy correctness, and the extent of excessive privilege elimination.

6 Results and Discussion

As shown in Table 4, PatMine (FSDM, UDM) achieves higher clustering cohesion and lower DBI values than baseline models, indicating more behaviorally consistent access patterns. PatMine also achieves higher precision and recall while removing a substantially larger fraction of unused permissions (PRR), demonstrating effective privilege reduction without sacrificing operational correctness.

These findings affirm that incorporating cloud-contextual knowledge in distance computation directly enhances IAM privilege refinement—a critical step toward adaptive, context-aware access control in enterprise cloud environments.

Computational and Storage Overheads. The primary trade-off in PatMine lies between semantic precision and computational overhead. FSDM provides

Table 4. Results

Metric/Model	K-Means	Hierarchical Clustering	DBSCAN	Decision Tree	PatMine (FSDM)	PatMine (UDM)
a. Clustering Performance Results						
Clusters Formed	110	577	32	2463 Rules	512	619
Silhouette Score	0.83	0.82	0.48	0.75	0.18	0.12
DBI	1.21	1.35	1.12	1.62	0.88	0.94
b. Policy Accuracy Results						
Precision (P)	0.79	0.74	0.84	0.68	0.92	0.95
Recall (R)	0.84	0.81	0.46	0.85	0.91	0.93
PRR	43%	41%	55%	34%	80%	85%

finer contextual discrimination at the cost of increased computation of approximately 2.0x standard DBSCAN, whereas UDM offers scalable approximation with modest precision loss with 1.2x computational overhead over standard DBSCAN. This design enables deployment flexibility based on organizational scale and latency constraints.

Maintaining a Contextual Knowledge Graph (CKG) introduces storage and update overhead; however, this cost is amortized by improved policy accuracy and reduced risk of false privilege removal. In practice, graph partitioning and incremental updates can mitigate scalability concerns.

Limitations. Although PatMine demonstrates significant strengths, it also exhibits certain limitations that warrant further exploration:

- Accurate, current contextual metadata (roles, resources, relationships) is critical; outdated data can cause clustering errors, requiring regular synchronization.
- Large graphs increase latency in distance computations; graph partitioning and incremental methods can alleviate this challenge.
- Incorporating temporal, hierarchical, and network attributes raises preprocessing time; selective sampling and distributed pipelines can reduce this burden.

7 Conclusion and Future Work

This paper presented PatMine, a context-aware privilege refinement framework for cloud IAM that integrates semantic, contextual, and hierarchical information into access pattern mining. Through evaluation on real-world GCP audit logs, PatMine demonstrated improved clustering cohesion and significant reduction of excessive privileges while preserving legitimate workflows.

Future work includes extending PatMine to cross-cloud environments and supporting incremental clustering for continuous adaptation. Further quantitative comparison and analysis with state of the art models is also in the pipeline, which did not happen with this paper considering the lack of standard IAM datasets and requiring state of the art models to be re-implemented to work on the dataset used for PatMine.

References

1. cisa.gov. https://www.cisa.gov/sites/default/files/publications/Cloud%20Security%20Technical%20Reference%20Architecture.pdf. Accessed 28 Oct 2025
2. ENISA Threat Landscape 2023| ENISA – enisa.europa.eu. https://www.enisa.europa.eu/publications/enisa-threat-landscape-2023. Accessed 28 Oct 2025
3. Hidden Dangers of Privileged Access: Privilege Sprawl | Beyond Trust – beyondtrust.com. www.beyondtrust.com/blog/entry/pitfalls-of-privilege-privilege-sprawl#:~:text=Projects%20to%20secure%20privileged%20access%20often%20leave%20out,privileged%20accounts%2C%20such%20as%20logins%20to%20social%20media. Accessed 28 Oct 2025
4. Identity and Access Management |CSA – cloudsecurityalliance.org. https://cloudsecurityalliance.org/research/topics/identity-and-access-management. Accessed 28 Oct 2025
5. Policy Intelligence overview | Google Cloud Documentation – docs.cloud.google.com. https://docs.cloud.google.com/policy-intelligence/docs/overview. Accessed 28 Oct 2025
6. Using AWS Identity and Access Management Access Analyzer - AWS Identity and Access Management – docs.aws.amazon.com. https://docs.aws.amazon.com/IAM/latest/UserGuide/what-is-access-analyzer.html. Accessed 28 Oct 2025
7. Afriyie, M.K., Nofong, V.M., Wondoh, J., Abdel-Fatao, H.: Efficient mining of non-redundant periodic frequent patterns. Vietnam J. Comput. Sci. **8**(04), 455–469 (2021)
8. Athanere, S., Thakur, R.: Adaptive access control model using risk-based technique in dynamic environment. In: Artificial Intelligence and Sustainable Computing: Proceedings of ICSISCET 2021, pp. 253–267. Springer (2022)
9. Bi, F., Wang, W., Chen, L.: Dbscan: density-based spatial clustering of applications with noise. J. Nanjing Univ **48**(4), 491–498 (2012)
10. Bistolfi, N., Georgescu, A., Hodson, D.: The data enclave advantage: a new paradigm for least-privileged data access in a zero-trust world. arXiv:2510.09494 (2025)
11. Deng, D.: Dbscan clustering algorithm based on density. In: 2020 7th international forum on electrical engineering and automation (IFEEA), pp. 949–953. IEEE (2020)
12. Du, M., Li, F., Zheng, G., Srikumar, V.: Deeplog: anomaly detection and diagnosis from system logs through deep learning. In: Proceedings of the 2017 ACM SIGSAC Conference on Computer and Communications Security, pp. 1285–1298 (2017)
13. D'Antoni, L., et al.: Automatically reducing privilege for access control policies. Proc. ACM Program. Lang. **8**(OOPSLA2), 763–790 (2024)
14. El Sibai, R., Gemayel, N., Bou Abdo, J., Demerjian, J.: A survey on access control mechanisms for cloud computing. Trans. Emerg. Telecommun. Technol. **31**(2), e3720 (2020)
15. Frank, M., Buhmann, J.M., Basin, D.: On the definition of role mining. In: Proceedings of the 15th ACM symposium on Access Control Models and Technologies, pp. 35–44 (2010)

16. Sakong, W., Kim, W.: An adaptive policy-based anomaly object control system for enhanced cybersecurity. IEEE Access **12**, 55281–55291 (2024)
17. Saltzer, J.H., Schroeder, M.D.: The protection of information in computer systems. Proc. IEEE **63**(9), 1278–1308 (1975)
18. Sander, J., Ester, M., Kriegel, H.P., Xu, X.: Density-based clustering in spatial databases: the algorithm GDBSCAN and its applications. Data Min. Knowl. Disc. **2**, 169–194 (1998)
19. Sanders, M.W., Yue, C.: Mining least privilege attribute based access control policies. In: Proceedings of the 35th Annual Computer Security Applications Conference, pp. 404–416 (2019)
20. Saqib, M., Mehta, D., Yashu, F., Malhotra, S.: Adaptive security policy management in cloud environments using reinforcement learning arXiv:2505.08837 (2025)
21. sdwheeler: Overview of Just Enough Administration (JEA) - PowerShell – learn.microsoft.com. https://learn.microsoft.com/en-us/powershell/scripting/security/remoting/jea/overview?view=powershell-7.5. Accessed 28 Oct 2025
22. Singh, A.P., Kuzminykh, I., Ghita, B.: Industry perception of security challenges with identity access management solutions. In: 2024 IEEE International Black Sea Conference on Communications and Networking (BlackSeaCom), pp. 312–315. IEEE (2024)
23. Vaidya, J., Atluri, V., Guo, Q.: The role mining problem: finding a minimal descriptive set of roles. In: Proceedings of the 12th ACM symposium on Access control models and technologies, pp. 175–184 (2007)
24. Van Tilborg, H.C., Jajodia, S.: Encyclopedia of cryptography and security. Springer Science & Business Media, vol. 1 (2011)
25. Xu, Z., Stoller, S.D.: Mining attribute-based access control policies. IEEE Trans. Dependable Secure Comput. **12**(5), 533–545 (2014)
26. Zhang, H., et al.: Logminer: a system audit log reduction strategy based on behavior pattern mining. In: MILCOM 2022–2022 IEEE Military Communications Conference (MILCOM), pp. 292–297. IEEE (2022)
27. Zhou, Z., et al.: Context-aware access control model for cloud computing. Int. J. Grid Distrib. Comput. **6**(6), 1–12 (2013)

Convolutional Auto-Encoder-Based Finger Vein Spoof Generation and Detection

Kashif Shaheed[1(✉)] and Umair Ul Hassan[1,2(✉)]

[1] Insight Research Ireland Centre for Data Analytics, Data Science Institute, University of Galway, Galway, Ireland
kashif.shaheed@universityofgalway.ie

[2] J.E. Cairnes School of Business and Economics, University of Galway, Galway, Ireland
umair.ulhassan@universityofgalway.ie

Abstract. Finger vein (FV) recognition is considered a secure biometric trait compared to other biometric modalities, such as fingerprint, face, etc., because it is less affected by external factors such as physiological changes with age and environmental conditions like temperature and humidity. However, with the advancement of deep learning, some spoofing techniques have been developed using advanced generative models, which are an emerging threat to finger vein recognition. Therefore, to improve the reliability of FV falsification detection systems. We have proposed a model that utilizes a Convolutional Auto-Encoder (CAE) to produce realistic counterfeit finger vein images. Our proposed method uses a three-stage approach: (i) a CAE that generates counterfeit FV images; (ii) a second Auto-Encoder (AE) used as a denoising or enhancement model that works as a post-processor to improve the quality of generated images; (iii) and, for the spoof detection task, we utilize multiple machine learning classifiers, namely, CatBoost, LightGBM, Random Forest, and XGBoost, to assess its effectiveness in identifying presentation attacks. The Structural Similarity Index (SSIM) is used to evaluate the quality of generated images, and statistical analysis shows that the image quality obtained with the proposed models (CAE+AE) was significantly better (p-value < 0.05 with a high Cohen effect size) than that obtained with the CAE model alone for image generation. The CatBoost classifier showed superior performance, achieving remarkably low Attack Presentation Classification Error Rate (APCER), Bona-fide Classification Error Rate (BPCER), and Average Classification Error Rate (ACER) values of 0.8%. These results demonstrate that our proposed method improves the security of the biometric finger vein system.

Keywords: Biometrics · Presentation Attack Detection · Convolutional Auto-Encoder · Spoof Detection

1 Introduction

The primary stages of the evolution of identity verification in security technology are: Key-based, Password-based, and Biometric-based approaches [1]. The

© IFIP International Federation for Information Processing 2026
Published by Springer Nature Switzerland AG 2026
H. Janicke et al. (Eds.): SEC 2026, IFIP AICT 787, pp. 570–584, 2026.
https://doi.org/10.1007/978-3-032-27993-4_39

key-based method of identity authentication has a high chance of getting lost because they require physical possession of items such as an identification card (ID) or an employee card. Password-based identity verification solutions require memorization and are susceptible to external exposure. For example, remembering credentials such as a strong password is easy to forget; and if written down, then it could be stolen. In this regard, biometric technologies offer a better approach to identification by eliminating the need for possession or memory, and they are less vulnerable to external threats. Biometrics have been thoroughly researched and employed in various security domains due to their precision and user-friendliness.

Biometric identification systems based on pattern recognition are known to be susceptible to spoofing attacks through image tampering or compromised information [1]. Therefore, exploration of biometric anti-spoofing protection methods has been a crucial area of research. It includes investigation of safeguards against the recognition of fictitious samples for bogus claims in palm-print and finger vein [2], face [3], fingerprint [4], ear [5], and voice [6]. Unlike surface biometrics, such as the face or fingerprint, finger vein patterns are internal traits captured using near-infrared imaging. However, synthetic spoofing in this context refers to digitally generated or reconstructed vein images that can be injected into recognition systems at the sensor or system level. With advances in generative modeling, such synthetic samples pose emerging risks to biometric authentication systems. Although recent developments in deep learning have witnessed progress in protection techniques against these spoofing attacks, Generative Adversarial Networks (GANs) are considered to enhance the generation of synthetic samples. The GAN based generators and discriminators, if trained competitively, are promising for generating images with distinct features distributed similarly to real images. Studies have shown that Convolutional Neural Networks (CNNs) can distinguish images created by GANs, but of those, applications of high pass filters to processed images were more prominent, changing the frequency domain nature and preserving them in low-frequency components [7]. These results increase the challenges faced when detecting spoofing attacks in biometric recognition systems. Previous works have used Cycle-consistent Adversarial Networks (CycleGAN) to synthesize FV images to train spoof detectors [8]. However, these methods are limited in producing intricate and sufficiently detailed counterfeit FV image samples.

To address issues listed above, we propose a new technique to produce counterfeit FV images and a corresponding system to detect fake finger-veins. In contrast to prior research, our study offers the following contributions:

- We introduce a CAE-based generative model to address the limitations of existing methods in generating elaborate fake FV images. This innovative approach effectively produces high-quality fake images that can successfully challenge conventional FV recognition systems and help to improve the reliability of spoof detection systems.

- A deep learning-based AE is incorporated into our method to decrease noise and improve image quality efficiently. This methodology is statistically verified using the SSIM, showcasing a significant enhancement.
- A comparative study of various machine learning models(namely, Random Forest, XGBoost, LightGBM, and CatBoost) is presented for synthetic spoof attack detection tasks. The CatBoost classifier shows outstanding performance, attaining exceptionally low values of 0.80% for the ACER, BPCER, and APCER metrics. These findings emphasize the strength and effectiveness of our method in improving biometric security.

The remainder of the paper is structured as follows: Sect. 2 discusses relevant work, Sect. 3 describes the proposed technique, and Sects. 4, 5, and 6 offer the experimental results, discussion, and conclusion, respectively.

2 Related Work

The study of FV spoofing can be categorized into two main areas: examination of spoof attack methods and improvement of detection methods. Therefore, to present a current state-of-the-art, we examine research on spoof attacks, including synthetic objects and images. In addition, we classify and evaluate research on spoofing detection using machine learning.

2.1 Using Fake-Generated Images

Advanced GANs model produce data through competitive training of generator and discriminator networks. This has resulted in several beneficial outcomes: (1) They serve as a data augmentation technique in limited datasets where data collection poses challenges [9]. (2) GANs enable the creation of labeled data in segmentation domains where manual annotation would require significant resources [10]. (3) They reduce the negative impact on image quality caused by changes in lighting conditions, blurring, and noise [11]. However, the ability of GANs models are to accurately reproduce legitimate images presents a risk of deception in biometric authentication, particularly deepfakes. Although several studies have been conducted on detecting fake images in the face, iris, and fingerprint recognition, there is still a lack of studies specifically focused on detecting fake FV images. Prior research utilizing CycleGAN to generate counterfeit FV images for spoofing can still be improved, especially in creating detailed false images [8].

2.2 Spoof Detection Using Machine Learning

Several conventional approaches have been developed for spoof detection based on machine learning. Raghavendra and Busch [12] utilized a steerable pyramid to extract data on different image sizes and orientations. They employed a support vector machine (SVM) to detect spoofing and perform binary classification, distinguishing between actual and fraudulent images. Tirunagari et al. [13] utilized dynamic mode decomposition (DMD), a method for examining the dynamic properties of data. They mainly applied a windowed dynamic mode decomposition (W-DMD) technique, which involved sliding a window across the entire temporal range of the data. Subsequently, features were isolated and categorized utilizing SVM. Using a linear SVM, Kocher et al. [14] applied LBP (Localized Binary Patterns) to extract features and classify between genuine and counterfeit examples. Also, Nguyen et al. [15] suggested using the Fourier transform (FT) to convert the images into the frequency domain. This allowed them to infer the spectral frequencies represented in the image. Additionally, they employed Haar and Daubechies wavelet transforms to probe further into the low- and high-frequency components. It eventually used SVM for spoof detection. In addition, Bok et al. [16] FV films were used to acquire the characteristics of heart rate and blood flow signals using a Discrete Fourier Transform. These characteristics were then used to train a support vector machine for the purpose of spoof detection. Nevertheless, a limitation of the previously described studies is the decline in the effectiveness of identifying spoof attempts caused by implementing different techniques for generating spoof data. Here, we refrain from presenting detailed results because these methods involved different datasets and different methods, making the comparison of detection results and error rates unfeasible.

3 Proposed Method

This section details the proposed methodology. Figure 1 presents the flowchart of our methodology, which consists of two main procedures: performing the spoof attack and the spoof detection. The first step in the spoof attack protocol is to preprocess the input image, which includes scaling the original image, followed by synthetic FV image generation using a first CAE model (Sect. 3.1). Finally, we apply post-processing, deep enhancement technique, involving second model with an AE architecture for noise removal and quality increase (Sect. 3.2). In the anti-spoofing phase, both the real image and the one produced by the CAE model are used as inputs. A CatBoost classifier is then used to classify images as either real or fake.

3.1 Proposed Convolutional Auto-Encoder Model

This section, which relates to producing synthetic FV images by the CAE model, is a step-by-step guide. The AE is trained to reproduce the original FV images, after which the decoder part of the model generates new synthetic images. An AE is a network type designed to obtain meaningful data structures, usually by creating images [17]. Our proposed model has two primary elements: the encoder and the decoder.

Encoder: The encoder compresses the input image content and generates a latent representation of lower order. This is done through a series of convolutional layers followed by a series of combinations of pooling layers.

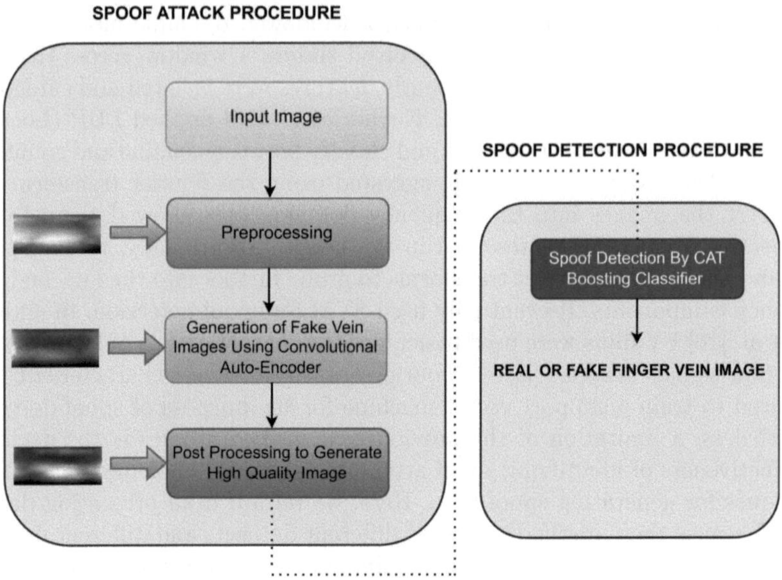

Fig. 1. Flow Diagram of the Proposed Method.

- **Convolution layer:** A convolution operation is formally defined as Eq. (1):

$$Y[i,j] = \sum_{m=0}^{M-1} \sum_{n=0}^{N-1} X[i+m, j+n] \cdot K[m,n] \tag{1}$$

  where Y is the output features map, X is the input image, and K is the convolution kernel. This layer performs feature extraction from the input image, which makes it possible to learn important features [18].

- **Max Pooling:**It is employed for the reduction of the spatial dimension of the feature map hence forth referred to as Eq. (2):

$$Y[i,j] = \max\big(X[i:i+S,\ j:j+S]\big) \tag{2}$$

  The pool size, referred to as S, enables the encoder to concentrate on the most essential characteristics. The encoder in this work consists of three consecutive convolutional layers followed by max-pooling layers to obtain a 10-dimensional latent vector that captures the important features of the input images.

Decoder: The decoder employs transposed convolution layers to rebuild the image from the latent representation. This technique may be considered as the reverse of the convolution operation, expressed mathematically as Eq. (3):

$$X[i,j] = \sum_{m=0}^{M-1} \sum_{n=0}^{N-1} Y[i+m, j+n] \cdot K[m,n] \tag{3}$$

where Y represents the latent representation, and K represents the transposed convolutional kernel. In this architectural design, the model can acquire the ability to expand the representation into higher level of characteristics of an image and finally into the pixel values, therefore producing novel images from the latent space.

The output of the encoder precisely defines the latent space, which yields a compressed version of the crucial information from the input image. An optimal latent dimension of 10 is selected to balance preserving important characteristics and achieving effective compression. This decision is consequential, as a reduced dimension may result in significant information loss, while an increased dimension may not adequately compress the data.

Loss Function: This AE employs Mean Squared Error (MSE) as its loss function, which is defined as Eq. (4)

$$\text{MSE} = \frac{1}{N} \sum_{i=1}^{N} \left(X_i - \hat{X}_i \right)^2 \tag{4}$$

where X_i represents the initial image, $\hat{X}_i$ denotes the reconstructed image, and N signifies the number of pixels in the image. This loss function estimates the discrepancy that may exist between the input and output images, directing the training procedure [19]. Table 1 illustrates the configuration of the proposed model i.e., the number of layers, activation function details, and parameters at each layer.

3.2 Image Enhancement Using Auto-Encoder Model

The image generated by the encoder was further refined and enhanced using the AE model. The AE is to improve the quality of images by reducing noise and artifacts. This model aims to train and rebuild images with reduced noise from inputs that may contain noise. The CAE generation model operates on input images of size 128×300. However, the enhancement autoencoder includes three successive 2×2 pooling operations, requiring the spatial dimensions to be divisible by 8 for consistent downsampling and upsampling. Since 300 is not divisible by 8, the width was adjusted to 304 to ensure integer feature map dimensions during the encoding–decoding process. Table 2 represents the architecture configuration of the proposed AE model used for image enhancement.

3.3 Proposed Detection Model

We have used the feature descriptor used in [22] to extract the features from generated images and then used CatBoost [20], a novel gradient-boosting method that effectively utilizes categorical features while minimizing information loss. Among other gradient-boosting algorithms, CatBoost stands out as it tackles the problem of target leakage by employing ordered boosting, a highly efficient version of gradient-boosting techniques [20]. Moreover, this method is effective in

Table 1. Configuration of the proposed model: number of layers, output shape, parameters, and activation functions.

Layer Type	Output Shape	Parameters	Activation Function
Input Layer	(128, 300, 1)	-	-
Conv2D	(128, 300, 32)	320	ReLU
MaxPooling2D	(64, 150, 32)	-	-
Conv2D	(64, 150, 64)	18,496	ReLU
MaxPooling2D	(32, 75, 64)	-	-
Conv2D	(32, 75, 128)	73,856	ReLU
Flatten	(307200)	-	-
Dense	(10)	3,072,010	ReLU
Dense	(307200)	832	ReLU
Reshape	(32, 75, 128)	-	-
UpSampling2D	(64, 150, 128)	-	-
Conv2DTranspose	(64, 150, 64)	73,792	ReLU
UpSampling2D	(128, 300, 64)	-	-
Conv2DTranspose	(128, 300, 1)	577	Sigmoid

dealing with small datasets. CatBoost is capable of handling categorical features as well. Mainly, this treatment is carried out in the preprocessing phase and involves converting the initial category variables into one or more numerical values. CatBoost mainly utilizes binary decision trees as its predictor. Equation (5) below shows the explanation of the estimated output.

$$\hat{y}_i = \sum_{k=1}^{K} J_k(x_i) \cdot \mathbf{1}(x_i \in D_k) \tag{5}$$

where, $\hat{y}_i$ represents the prediction for the i-th sample. $J_k(x_i)$ denotes the decision tree function for the k-th tree. D_k is the disjoint region that corresponds to the leaf nodes of the k-th tree. $\mathbf{1}(x_i \in D_k)$ is defined as the indicator function that takes the value 1 if x_i belongs to D_k, and 0 otherwise. K is the number of trees in the ensemble.

4 Experimental Results

4.1 Experimental Settings and Database

We have used one publicly available database: the SCUTFVD database [21] to assess the performance of proposed model. The SCUTFVD dataset consists of 3,600 real images captured from three fingers (ring, index, and middle) of 100 individuals. We have used 2,160 images in our experiment. The SCUTFVD dataset was split into mutually exclusive training and testing sets at the sample

Table 2. Configuration of the proposed model: number of layers, output shape, parameters, and activation functions.

Layer Type	Output Shape	Parameters	Activation Function
Input Layer	(128, 304, 1)	-	-
Conv2D	(128, 304, 32)	320	ReLU
MaxPooling2D	(64, 152, 32)	-	-
Conv2D	(64, 152, 64)	18,496	ReLU
MaxPooling2D	(32, 76, 64)	-	-
Conv2D	(32, 76, 128)	73,856	ReLU
MaxPooling2D	(16, 38, 128)	-	-
Conv2D	(16, 38, 128)	147,584	ReLU
UpSampling2D	(32, 76, 128)	-	-
Conv2D	(32, 76, 64)	73,792	ReLU
UpSampling2D	(64, 152, 64)	-	-
Conv2D	(64, 152, 32)	18,464	ReLU
UpSampling2D	(128, 304, 32)	-	-
Conv2D	(128, 304, 1)	289	Sigmoid

level, such that no identical images appear in both sets. A series of three experiments was primarily conducted to assess the efficacy of the proposed technique. The initial experiment examines the ability of the proposed CAE model for image generation. The second experiment is performed to assess the quality of the generated images using the statistical metric of structural similarity - SSIM. The third experiment evaluates the efficacy of the finger vein spoof detection process and compares the results with other methods.

4.2 Training and Testing Loss of Proposed Cascaded AE Network

Our current study involved the development of an AE deep learning architecture designed explicitly for image generation. We utilized a dataset consisting of 2,160 images. The dataset was divided into two parts: 80% reserved for training (1,728 images) and 20% for validation (432 images). Through 10 epochs of training, we tracked the training and validation loss to evaluate the model's effectiveness. The training and validation loss plots, presented in Fig. 2, show a clear decreasing trend during the training. This indicates that the model is properly converging to an optimal performance. The results show how the model has developed abilities to reconstruct the images offered in the training images. The result reaffirms that the AE generalizes well to reconstruct the training images. Both the training and the validation loss, along with their corresponding variations over an epoch, reflect positively on the performance of the AE model in terms of capturing the information from the dataset. This has some relevance to future research for image generation techniques to prevent presentation attack problems in a biometric system.

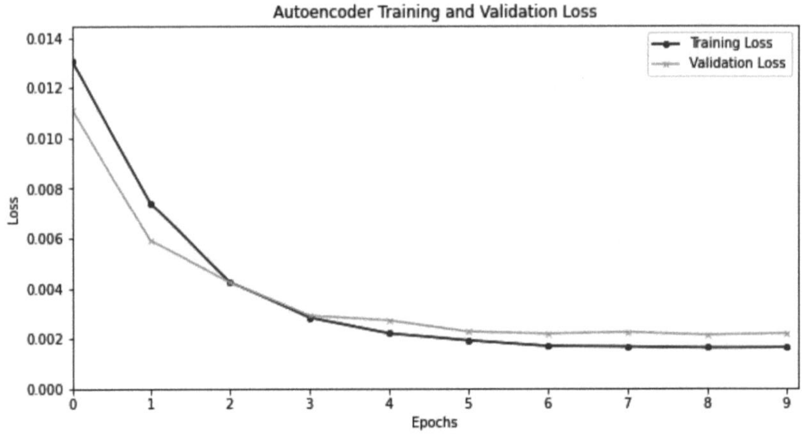

Fig. 2. The loss function of the convolutional AE model.

Next, we use an AE model to enhance images that have already been generated using an AE. For this, we trained our model on 500 generated images, using a train-test split ratio of 4:1. We kept the number of epochs to 10. The validation and training loss of the model clearly shows downward trends, as illustrated in Fig. 3. Therefore, the results confirm that our proposed model can enhance the quality of images. We further applied our model to improve the quality of the generated images.

4.3 Quality Assessment of Generated Images

In our second experiment, our primary objective was to statistically assess the extent of similarity between the generated and a realistic image. To do this, we conducted statistical significance tests based on the computed SSIM values for randomly selected 30 images, as presented in Table 3. We evaluated two approaches on the images: one involving the generation of the image using a CAE and another including the generation and enhancement of the image using the CAE model and AE model for enhancement.

First, we tested for the normality of the two distributions using the Shapiro-Wilk test for paired samples. The results showed W-statistic values of 0.973 ($p = 0.633$) for image generation and 0.966 ($p = 0.437$) for image generation + enhancement, indicating the normality of both sets. Since we are dealing with quality score values dependent on the same image source, we applied the paired T-test method to check for the statistical difference in results before and after enhancement. The test gave a T-statistic value of 3.909 with a p-value of 0.0005,

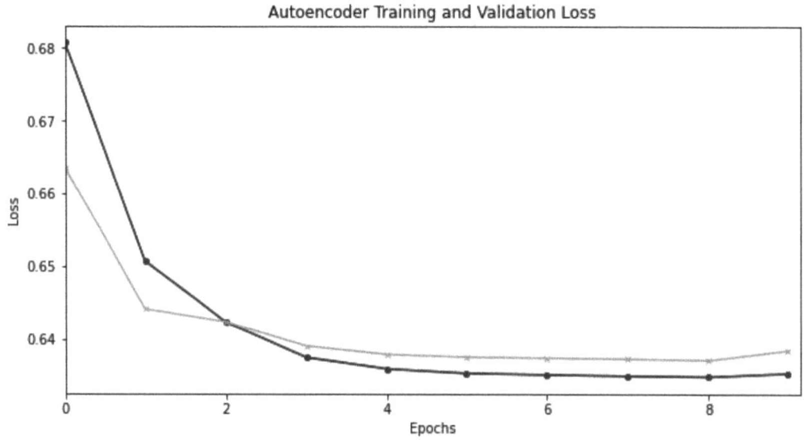

Fig. 3. The loss function of the AE model.

showing a significant difference between the SSIM values of the images before and after enhancement and confirming that the observed effect is far from random chance. It is also evident from the results of the T-test that the statistical mean of the SSIM values after the enhancement is higher than those for image generation, indicating a substantial improvement in image quality. Furthermore, it is inadequate to merely show statistical significance; we also need to know whether the effect size is worthy of interest. Thus, we employed Cohen's d statistical measure to quantify the effect size of the statistically observed difference. A high Cohen effect size of 0.714 was obtained from the analysis. This confirms that image quality enhancement has a substantial effect on the results, and it is highly impactful in real-world applications. Consequently, the image quality obtained with the CAE model + AE model for enhancement is significantly better than that obtained with the CAE model for generation alone.

4.4 Synthetic Spoof Attack Detection

The efficacy of presentation attack detection was assessed using the generated and acquired images. Our study employed four distinct machine learning classifiers, specifically LightGBM, XGBoost, CatBoost, and Random Forest, to evaluate their efficacy. The lower values of APCER, BPCER, and ACER represent the better performance of the spoof detection system. It can be observed (Table 4) that the APCER, BPCER, and ACER values were the lowest when employing the CatBoost classifier. All the scores achieved in the experiment for ACER, BPCER, and APCER are equal on all used metrics and were at 0.80%. Conversely, the LightGBM model recorded ACER, BPCER, and APCER as 1.20%, 0.80%, and 1.60%, respectively. The XGBoost and Random Forest models obtained ACER, BPCER, and APCER of 1.20%, 1.60%, and 0.80%, respectively. Consequently, while assessing machine learning classifiers for the presen-

Table 3. SSIM quality score of different images before and after enhancement.

Images	CAE for Image Generation	CAE for Image Generation + CAE for Image Enhancement
IMG_1	0.76	0.82
IMG_2	0.68	0.72
IMG_3	0.54	0.65
IMG_4	0.57	0.66
IMG_5	0.59	0.71
IMG_6	0.64	0.62
IMG_7	0.56	0.80
IMG_8	0.53	0.70
IMG_9	0.63	0.59
IMG_10	0.67	0.74
IMG_11	0.71	0.71
IMG_12	0.73	0.71
IMG_13	0.64	0.73
IMG_14	0.64	0.61
IMG_15	0.71	0.65
IMG_16	0.73	0.78
IMG_17	0.72	0.69
IMG_18	0.57	0.57
IMG_19	0.45	0.62
IMG_20	0.57	0.71
IMG_21	0.59	0.55
IMG_22	0.53	0.58
IMG_23	0.61	0.81
IMG_24	0.64	0.65
IMG_25	0.72	0.71
IMG_26	0.66	0.70
IMG_27	0.53	0.56
IMG_28	0.65	0.73
IMG_29	0.62	0.68
IMG_30	0.61	0.68

Table 4. FV spoof detection performance of various models.

Model	APCER (%)	BPCER (%)	ACER (%)	Accuracy (%)
CAE with LightGBM	1.60	0.80	1.20	99.0
CAE with XGBoost	0.80	1.60	1.20	98.8
CAE with Random Forest	0.80	1.60	1.20	98.8
CAE with CatBoost	0.80	0.80	0.80	99.2

* *To the best of our knowledge, the SCUTFVD dataset has not been previously used for joint spoof image generation and detection.*

tation attack problem, it is evident that CatBoost exhibits greater performance. Also, it can be noticed while measuring the effectiveness of the model solution in terms of accuracy that the proposed CatBoost classifier has achieved 99.2% accuracy, which is better than the 99.0% accuracy of LightGBM. The accuracy of the two classifiers, Random Forest and XGBoost classifier, was documented as 98.8%. Consequently, it can be inferred that our proposed method achieved satisfactory performance and may serve as a crucial part of finger vein verification presentation attack systems.

To clearly illustrate the comparison of the mentioned machine learning classifiers' performance, we present the Detection Error Tradeoff (DET) curve. From Fig. 4, we observe that the performance of Random Forest is reasonably good compared to other classifiers such as LightGBM and XGBoost. However, it is evident that the performance of our proposed CatBoost classifier surpasses all other machine learning classifiers, indicating that the proposed approach is the most effective choice for synthetic presentation attack detection in finger vein recognition technology.

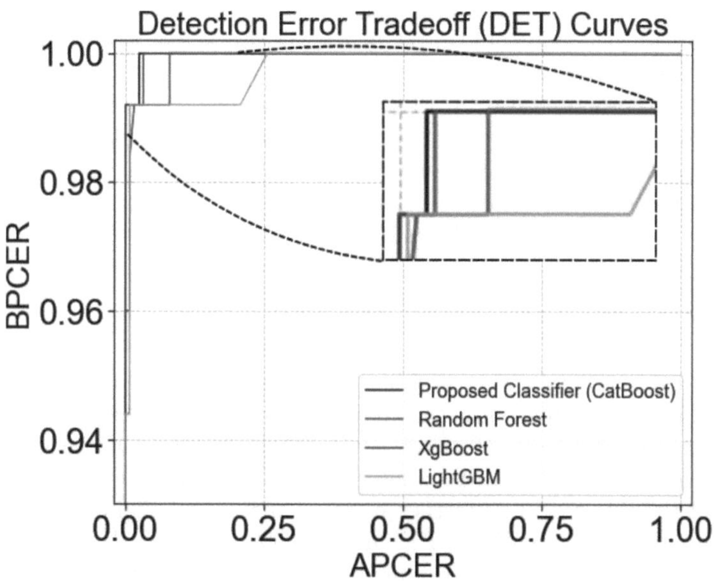

Fig. 4. DET curves comparing the performance of the proposed CatBoost-based classifier with Random Forest, XGBoost, and LightGBM for finger vein spoof detection in terms of APCER and BPCER.

5 Discussion

In this work, we proposed CAE+AE framework that achieved low APCER, BPCER and ACER values,indicating strong spoof generation and detection performance on the SCUTFVD dataset. Although the performance is evaluated using single dataset using sample-level split protocol. However, identical images were not shared between training and testing sets, a subject-disjoint and cross-dataset evaluation would provide stronger evidence of robustness and generalization. Future work will extend the evaluation to cross-sensor, cross-dataset, and subject-disjoint settings.

In this study, spoof detection is evaluated using synthetic attacks generated by the proposed CAE-based model. While this controlled setup allows systematic analysis of the generation–detection pipeline, it may not fully reflect the diversity of spoofing strategies encountered in practical deployments. Future work will include cross-generator evaluation using alternative generative architectures to assess robustness against unseen attack distributions.

With respect to GAN-based approaches reported in prior work, direct quantitative comparison is challenging due to differences in datasets, protocols, and evaluation strategies. Unlike adversarial training methods, the proposed CAE-based framework focuses on structured latent representation learning with stable training and reduced architectural complexity. The addition of a secondary AE for enhancement significantly improves structural similarity, as supported by statistical testing and effect size analysis. Nevertheless, direct benchmarking under a unified protocol would provide a more comprehensive comparison and is planned for future investigation.

Overall, the proposed framework provides a controlled approach for studying synthetic finger vein spoof generation and presentation attack detection. While the reported results indicate strong performance within the tested configuration, further evaluation under subject-disjoint, cross-dataset, and cross-attack scenarios is necessary to fully characterize real-world robustness.

6 Conclusion

To address the synthetic attack problem in the finger vein recognition system. In this paper, we proposed a synthesis model utilizing a CAE+AE to produce high-quality, challenging FV spoof images. Initially, we have applied a simple CAE model to generate high-quality counterfeit FV synthetic spoof images. Then, we applied the AE model to further improve the image quality and produce a noise-free high-quality synthetic FV spoof images. Afterwards, to evaluate the performance of the detection system, we applied the CatBoost classifier and compare with other Machine learning models such as Random Forest, XGBoost, and LightGBM. The CatBoost showed exceptional performance by achieving low ACER, BPCER, and APCER levels, all below 0.80%. These results showed that the proposed work reduces the spoof threat and advances the security for biometric finger vein recognition systems. Our proposed CAE+AE method effectively tackles the issues related to producing high-quality fake FV images to better evaluate the system against a synthetic attack. The CatBoost classifier shows impressive performance and would be interesting to see the potential directions for future anti-spoofing studies. The only limitation of the proposed work is to evaluate the proposed method on another available public dataset, which will be the basis for future research. And, we will extend this work to evaluate extensively the performance of the proposed work for generalization across datasets, sensors and subject-disjoint which is an important aspect to see for the presentation attack problem. In addition, we will introduce a more sophisticated spoof detection system based on an advanced deep learning model such as diffusion model, advanced generative models to detect the more challenging synthetic attacks problem on large scale.

Acknowledgements. This work was supported in part by Interreg Atlantic Area co-funded by the European Union under grant EAPA 0016/2022 (ENEPORTS) and Taighde Éireann – Research Ireland under grant 12/RC/2289 P2 (Insight). For the purpose of Open Access, the author has applied a CC BY public copyright licence to any Author Accepted Manuscript version arising from this submission.

References

1. Nguyen, D.T., Yoon, H.S., Pham, T.D., Park, K.R.: Spoof detection for FV recognition system using NIR camera. Sensors **17**(10), 1–34 (2017). https://doi.org/10.3390/s17102261
2. Wang, H., Su, L., Zeng, H., Chen, P., Liang, R., Zhang, Y.: Anti-spoofing study on palm biometric features. Expert Syst. Appl. **218**, 119546 (2023). https://doi.org/10.1016/j.eswa.2023.119546
3. Shu, X., Li, X., Zuo, X., Xu, D., Shi, J.: Face spoofing detection based on multiscale color inversion dual-stream convolutional neural network. Expert Syst. Appl. **224**, 119988 (2023). https://doi.org/10.1016/j.eswa.2023.119988
4. Kho, J.B., Lee, W., Choi, H., Kim, J.: An incremental learning method for spoof fingerprint detection. Expert Syst. Appl. **116**, 52–64 (2019). https://doi.org/10.1016/j.eswa.2018.08.055
5. Toprak, I., Toygar, Ö.: Detection of spoofing attacks for ear biometrics through image quality assessment and deep learning. Expert Syst. Appl. **172**, 114600 (2021). https://doi.org/10.1016/j.eswa.2021.114600
6. Javed, A., Malik, K.M., Malik, H., Irtaza, A.: Voice spoofing detector: a unified anti-spoofing framework. Expert Syst. Appl. **198**, 116770 (2022). https://doi.org/10.1016/j.eswa.2022.116770
7. Neves, J.C., Tolosana, R., Vera-Rodriguez, R., Lopes, V., Proença, H., Fierrez, J.: GANprintR: improved fakes and evaluation of the state of the art in face manipulation detection. IEEE J. Sel. Top. Signal Process. **14**(5), 1038–1048 (2020). https://doi.org/10.1109/JSTSP.2020.3007250
8. Kim, S.G., Choi, J., Hong, J.S., Park, K.R.: Spoof detection based on score fusion using ensemble networks robust against adversarial attacks of fake FV images. J. King Saud Univ. Comput. Inf. Sci. **34**(10), 9343–9362 (2022). https://doi.org/10.1016/j.jksuci.2022.09.012
9. Yang, H., Fang, P., Hao, Z.: A GAN-based method for generating FV dataset. In: ACM International Conference Proceedings Series (2020). https://doi.org/10.1145/3446132.3446150
10. Ciano, G., Andreini, P., Mazzierli, T., Bianchini, M., Scarselli, F.: A multi-stage GAN for multi-organ chest X-ray image generation and segmentation. Mathematics **9**(22), 1–16 (2021). https://doi.org/10.3390/math9222896

11. Choi, J., Hong, J.S., Kim, S.G., Park, C., Nam, S.H., Park, K.R.: RMOBF-Net: network for the restoration of motion and optical blurred FV images for improving recognition accuracy. Mathematics **10**(21) (2022). https://doi.org/10.3390/math10213948
12. Raghavendra, R., Busch, C.: Presentation attack detection algorithms for FV biometrics: a comprehensive study. In: Proceedings of the 11th International Conference on Signal-Image Technology and Internet-Based Systems (SITIS), pp. 628–632 (2016). https://doi.org/10.1109/SITIS.2015.74
13. Tirunagari, S., Poh, N., Bober, M., Windridge, D.: Windowed DMD as a microtexture descriptor for FV counter-spoofing in biometrics. In: 2015 IEEE International Workshop on Information Forensics and Security (WIFS) (2015). https://doi.org/10.1109/WIFS.2015.7368599
14. Kocher, D., Schwarz, S., Uhl, A.: Empirical evaluation of LBP-extension features for FV spoofing detection. Lecture Notes in Informatics (LNI), Proceedings Series of the Gesellschaft fur Informatik, vol. P-260 (2016). https://doi.org/10.1109/BIOSIG.2016.7736921
15. Nguyen, D.T., Park, Y.H., Shin, K.Y., Kwon, S.Y., Lee, H.C., Park, K.R.: Fake FV image detection based on Fourier and wavelet transforms. Digital Signal Process. **23**(5), 1401–1413 (2013). https://doi.org/10.1016/j.dsp.2013.04.001
16. Bok, J.Y., Suh, K.H., Lee, E.C.: Detecting fake FV data using remote photoplethysmography. Electronics **8**(9), 1–10 (2019). https://doi.org/10.3390/electronics8091016
17. Hinton, G.E.: Reducing the dimensionality of data with neural networks. Nature **313**, 504–507 (2006)
18. Nair, V., Hinton, G.E.: Rectified linear units improve Restricted Boltzmann machines. In: ICML 2010 - Proceedings of 27th International Conference on Machine Learning, pp. 807–814 (2010)
19. Chen, S., Guo, W.: Auto-encoders in deep learning–a review with new perspectives. Mathematics **11**(8), 1–54 (2023). https://doi.org/10.3390/math11081777
20. Prokhorenkova, L., Gusev, G., Vorobev, A., Dorogush, A.V., Gulin, A.: CatBoost: unbiased boosting with categorical features (2019). arXiv:1810.11363
21. BIP-Lab: SCUT-SFVD: A Finger Vein Spoofing/Presentation Attack Database. https://github.com/BIP-Lab/SCUT-SFVD. Accessed 20 Sept 2024
22. Shaheed, K., Szczuko, P., Ullah, I., Mojeed, H., Balogun, A.O., Capretz, L.F.: Finger vein presentation attack detection method using a hybridized gray-level co-occurrence matrix feature with light-gradient boosting machine model. In: Proceedings of IEEE International Symposium Digital Forensics and Security (ISDFS) (2024). https://doi.org/10.62036/isd.2024.54

Author Index

© IFIP International Federation for Information Processing 2026

Published by Springer Nature Switzerland AG 2026
H. Janicke et al. (Eds.): SEC 2026, IFIP AICT 787, pp. 585–587, 2026.
https://doi.org/10.1007/978-3-032-27993-4

MIX
Papier aus verantwortungsvollen Quellen
Paper from responsible sources
FSC® C105338

If you have any concerns about our products,
you can contact us on
ProductSafety@springernature.com

In case Publisher is established outside the EU,
the EU authorized representative is:
Springer Nature Customer Service Center GmbH
Europaplatz 3, 69115 Heidelberg, Germany

Printed by Libri Plureos GmbH
in Hamburg, Germany